Almighty God moved upon the hearts of Johnnie Moore and Jerry Pattengale to tell the horrific stories of modern-day martyrdom, and how the church triumphant advances because of it. The persecuted show us the path to truly live as disciples of the one true God.

> MICHELE BACHMANN, dean of Regent University and former member of US Congress

The stories in this book are difficult to read and tragic, but so very important. And they are beautiful, as is any life abandoned to Christ. *The New Book of Christian Martyrs* is a profound gift, updating what others have started and confronting a culture in which we are constantly told to live for self. I'm profoundly grateful.

> JOHN STONESTREET, president of the Colson Center for Christian Worldview

The passion Johnnie Moore holds for the Word of God and the suffering Church has been evident in my years of friendship with him. This work glorifies God through telling the stories of the martyrs of our faith, while inspiring a new generation to fulfill the Great Commission.

> DOUG CLAY, general superintendent of the Assemblies of God

Scripture compels us to *remember well* when great sacrifices have been made. *The New Book of Christian Martyrs* helps us do just that. Through these true accounts, we are inspired to *remember well* the loving sacrifices that have been made by friends of Jesus, and to take up our own cross and follow Jesus wherever that may lead . . . just as they did.

> SANTIAGO "JIMMY" MELLADO, president and CEO of Compassion International

A classic powerful resource for this generation and beyond. Nothing like it. . . . Stories of faithful and courageous followers of Jesus for the past two thousand years, right up to the present day. The organization and writing is so compelling I could not stop reading these accounts—many through tears. My faith and understanding of God increased with each page. A must for every household.

> JO ANNE LYON, general superintendent emerita of The Wesleyan Church

Few people have been as impressed with the witness of those who in fact did give their lives as martyrs as Johnnie Moore and Jerry Pattengale. Their stories inspire every one of us in these days that so fiercely and dangerously threaten not only our families and freedom, but our very lives. In our present day, it appears no one is more hated than Christians who are serious about God's Word and doing his will. God wants every one of us to be challenged and inspired by those who were martyred to live every moment of our lives sold out to pleasing God, fulfilling the Great Commission. Wow—what a book! God bless you, Johnnie and Jerry. Christians will be motivated as they read the testimonies you've shared so clearly and effectively.

> **JAMES ROBISON**, founder and president of LIFE Outreach International, Fort Worth, Texas

As a new believer during my freshman year at university, I discovered *Foxe's Book of Martyrs*. It was one of the first Christian books I ever read. I can still feel the fire that came into my heart with every passing page, and to this day, decades later, it continues to impact my life in incredible ways. Gratefully, and out of the burning heart of Johnnie Moore, this classic has been resurrected and brought up to date for today's new generations and those who are coming. Even as I type these words, I am praying that its reading will become a defining moment of everyone who opens it. Get it . . . keep it close . . . read it . . . and reap!

> **O. S. HAWKINS**, former pastor of First Baptist Church in Dallas and author of *The Joshua Code* and the Code series of devotionals

In Acts 1:8, Jesus tells the disciples, "But you shall receive power when the Holy Spirit has come upon you; and you shall be witnesses to Me in Jerusalem, and in all Judea and Samaria, and to the end of the earth" (Acts 1:8, NKJV). The Greek word for witnesses is *martys*. Among its meanings is one who certifies the truth by a willingness to die. The strength, spread, and sustainability of our faith is due to men and women whose lives and deaths certified the truth of the gospel. Johnnie Moore and Jerry Pattengale chronicle such a cloud of witnesses. May we in our reading be inspired to do the same.

> **BISHOP CLAUDE ALEXANDER**, senior pastor of The Park Church in Charlotte, NC

The New Book of Christian Martyrs reminds us that martyrs are not distant, historical figures but real people willing to sacrifice everything for Christ. Readers will find the weight of suffering experienced by these individuals lifted by the inspiring impact of how God continues to use their legacy. Johnnie Moore and Jerry Pattengale have created a labor of love that's sure to be a timeless resource for generations to come.

CHRIS HODGES, senior pastor of Church of the Highlands and author of *Out of the Cave* and *Pray First*

When we choose to follow Jesus, we are choosing to share in his sufferings, as Paul writes in Romans 8. Through this, we also share in his glory. Johnnie Moore and Jerry Pattengale remind us of this as they recount the compelling stories, both across history and in our own time, of remarkable heroes of the faith who have gone before us and, in their death and suffering, have come into life and glory in Jesus.

D. MICHAEL LINDSAY, president of Taylor University

From the early centuries of the church, Christians have written martyrologies—catalogues of the martyrs to inform and inspire the saints. Johnnie Moore and Jerry Pattengale's *The New Book of Christian Martyrs*, an up-to-date twenty-first-century martyrology, continues this important tradition. These sacred records remind us that persecution is present, not past; it is to be expected; it is not abnormal; and it wears many different faces in our world today. The authors point out that we are now living in one of the greatest ages of Christian persecution, and that, as Paul said to Timothy, "all who desire to live a godly in life in Christ Jesus will be persecuted" (2 Timothy 3:12). American Christians must be informed of this sobering reality, so we can pray regularly for the persecuted church, speak up for human rights/religious liberty, and be ready to stand faithfully for Christ when persecution comes our way.

DONALD SWEETING, president of Colorado Christian University

The epic battle between darkness and light will only intensify as we approach the climactic Day of the Lord. Johnnie Moore and Jerry Pattengale have reminded us all to be strong in the Lord and in the power of his might during these times of great spiritual warfare. *The New Book of Christian Martyrs* chronicles the power of a heart fully surrendered to the love of God and tempered with the zero victim mentality of Christ, in overcoming the forces of darkness.

Just as the testimonies of these martyrs have influenced my life, let them touch you when you see that they have given all to Jesus. Then after your life is touched by them, I want you to reach out and touch others—to share your faith with them. In one sense, we who are believers are all martyrs. Did not Paul tell us, "I am crucified with Christ; when He died I died, but now I am living but I am not living my life, I am living for Jesus Christ" (Galatians 2:20, paraphrased)? Because we are all martyrs having died with Christ, let us read the stories of these heroes of faith and live for Christ.

Moore and Pattengale have brought back to life one of history's most important texts, and a copy should be in every single Christian home. This is an instant classic which honors those whose faith cost them everything and reminds the rest of us of the blessing it is to be Christian.

a modern update to *Foxe's Book of Martyrs*

The New Book ⊕F Christian Martyrs

JOHNNIE MOORE ✦ JERRY PATTENGALE

**The Heroes of Our Faith from the
1st Century to the 21st Century**

TYNDALE
MOMENTUM®

A Tyndale nonfiction imprint

Contents

Introduction

From Nero's Rome to Nairobi's Islamist extremists, Christians in every century have been slaughtered at the hands of enemies of Christ. Once set ablaze as human torches in Roman gardens, now believers are plucked from Kenyan buses and beheaded by al-Shabaab militants.

Eusebius, who wrote during the third and fourth centuries, says Christians died under Roman leaders in "great numbers"—many poor and forgotten by history, along with many "who were distinguished by family and career."[1] The atrocities under Nero, Domitian, Trajan, and Diocletian have filled volumes.

The stories of some of these early martyrdoms have become legendary, including those of Jesus' disciples. The upper panel of the famous title page of the first King James Bible (1611) depicts the apostles holding the implements their persecutors allegedly used to put them to death. For instance, Bartholomew holds the knife with which he was flayed; Andrew holds the X-shaped cross on which he was crucified; and Simon the Zealot holds a saw.[2] These heroes of our faith suffered horrific deaths, and their testimonies have impacted countless millions over many centuries. They loved Jesus with their lives and with their self-sacrificial deaths.

Countless numbers have been slain since the fall of Rome, but many believers today do not realize that Christians are still dying cruel deaths throughout much of the world. Thousands die annually for their faith in Jesus. Most of these modern stories are not legendary; in fact, most of them are unknown.

By even the most conservative estimates, we are currently witnessing a wave of martyrs.[3] George Weigel, a distinguished senior fellow of the Ethics and Public Policy Center, states, "More Christians died for the faith in the twentieth century than in the previous nineteen centuries of Christian history combined." Weigel states that Christians are obligated to be in solidarity with the persecuted church during this, "the greatest era of persecution in Christian history. . . . The assault on the Christian faithful today is ongoing, extensive, and heart-rending."[4]

The authors of this book have interviewed many surviving family members and friends of modern martyrs, and one of those who reviewed the manuscript is even a descendant of a sixteenth-century martyr whose story was included in the original edition of *Foxe's Book of Martyrs*. His name was William Sweeting, and he was burned alive, alongside James Brewster, on October 18, 1511. Sweeting's descendant Dr. Donald S. Sweeting is now a scholar and the distinguished Chancellor of Colorado Christian University.

We have pored over pages of historic Christian texts. Every retelling of these deaths evokes emotion, usually pride, and often questions about how to tell the world what is happening.[5]

This work is especially inspired by—and at points drawn directly from—*Foxe's Book of Martyrs*, but it also includes accounts from other works and traditions, and a recounting of some of the most impactful modern martyrdoms. John Foxe wrote not only about martyrs in ancient history but also about those in his day, as we have done. He believed the world needed to know about these heroes of the faith and to venerate their stories. The perpetrators needed to have their names recorded in infamy and the victims their sacrifice inscribed with glory for future generations to remember them. Foxe devoted his career to this objective so that his world and all who followed might know. Our world needs a fresh reminder as we endure this global phenomenon of Christian persecution.

John Foxe has been indispensable in awakening the conscience of countless generations of Christians. He took up this challenge in the sixteenth century, and it was his life's work (d. 1587). Foxe's readers understood the terminology, passion, and purpose of his intense prose—simmering with righteous anger; we have followed suit in this volume. His no-nonsense style with a flair for graphic descriptions propelled his controversial work to ubiquity, becoming one of the most-read books in the English language, often chained alongside Bibles in chapels and cathedrals, the books being both expensive and extremely popular. His tome was also on the short list of books carried by a litany of characters—famous and infamous. Early American households with any books at all had the Holy Bible and often *Foxe's Book of Martyrs*. It's our ambition to resurrect this tradition in the homes of Christians worldwide—introducing new generations to the stories and lessons of Christians who have suffered and continue to suffer for Jesus in every corner of the globe.

The abbreviated title *Foxe's Book of Martyrs* had soon supplanted in public discourse the long original title (*Actes and Monuments of these Latter and Perillous Days, Touching Matters of the Church*). The complete title of his second edition in 1570—the best-edited and most careful edition—included the full longer title (given here in modern English, adding to the above):

> . . . *wherein are comprehended and described the great persecutions and horrible troubles that have been wrought and practiced by the Romish Prelates, specially in this Realm of England and Scotland from the year of our Lord a thousand, unto the time present.*

With each new edition came new stories, and one volume became two. Four editions were eventually published during Foxe's lifetime alone (1563, 1570, 1576, and 1583). All four editions are now electronically accessible online. The University of Sheffield, in partnership with the University of Bangor, compiled and maintains the best resource site on Foxe.[6]

Several organizations carry on the task of chronicling and researching the plight of modern martyrs. Under Caesar's Sword, a robust effort at the University of Notre Dame, is shedding considerable light on the scope and scale of global persecution, and especially the responses of Christians under persecution. Organizations like Barnabas Fund and The Voice of the Martyrs provide valuable information and inroads to help those serving Christ and desiring "to fulfill His Great Commission—no matter the cost."[7] The Open Doors organization even has a site that includes a world watch-list ranking.[8] Reminiscent of John Foxe, but from a very different place among faith traditions, the organizers of Under Caesar's Sword write on their website's homepage:

> Christians around the world are being brutally persecuted, facing imprisonment, torture, and even death. We shed light on their responses so that the world may know their stories and that others facing persecution may forge similar paths of witness and resistance.[9]

In many ways, the worldwide church can empathize with the essence of Foxe's stories. Two-thirds of the world's estimated 2.3 billion Christians live in danger. They are often oppressed, poor, and suffering as ethnic or religious minorities. Conservative estimates record around ten thousand Christians have died in each of the last ten years because of their faith.[10]

Sometimes these massacres take place in countries that have real religious freedom. On the day we were editing this very page, a gunman slayed twenty-six people during their Sunday worship service in Sutherland Springs, Texas. Such needless loss not only saddens us but also makes us angry.

In many countries, brothers and sisters in Christ lie warm in their graves or in ashes—lost for now, but not forever. May this update to John Foxe's seminal work help keep them in our thoughts and frame their testimonies for future generations.

While this volume carries on with Foxe's original candor and intention, we will differ from Foxe in one key commitment: to commemorate Christians across a wide spectrum of faith traditions. We selected accounts strategically, knowing we can but represent the wider collection of stories.

At the center of each believer's life and death is the cross of Christ—a symbol we also find etched in some of their early hideouts, clutched in the hands of Chinese martyrs, mounted atop cathedrals, and today displayed in retrofitted worship spaces in strip malls.

Something transpires in the lives of many of Christ's followers—a brazen fortitude—from Stephen in Acts 7 to ISIS casualties. Something we have become too familiar with in the beginning of this digital century through boastful images posted by the tormentors and murderers. This courage inspires Christians to follow Christ to the ends of the earth, even if it means their own ends.

Not all Christians are called to make the ultimate sacrifice, but all are called to be ready. Christ's outstretched arms reflect not only his death on the cross but his embrace of all who seek him. Christianity is steeped in historicity, as evidence abounds for its narrative—a nearly unfathomable message of mercy and grace, often demonstrated in the face of oppression.

Nearly all accounts that follow use the term *martyr* in its traditional sense, referring to those who died for their faith. In the New Testament's original Greek, the word *martus* (from which we get the word "martyr") refers to a witness, and what a special cloud of witnesses we have in our tradition—literally too many to recount, and millions unknown. In a few instances we include accounts, as did John Foxe, of "martyrs" who endured severe persecution or oppression for their faith but may not have died through direct confrontation.[11] We also tell the stories of others whose devotion to the gospel of Jesus led them into danger and death, though they were not targeted specifically for their faith.

From oppression and persecution to torture and death, we thank and salute all of those on this sacrificial continuum. Unfortunately, it continues today and in parts of the world in even greater numbers than ever before.

Justin Martyr, before his beheading in AD 165, declared, "The more we are persecuted, the more do others in ever increasing numbers embrace the faith and become worshippers of God through the name of Jesus."[12] Tertullian claimed, "The blood of the martyr is the seed of the church" (an adapted version).[13] If so, the harvest ahead will be significant. At the very least, it's safe to say "The blood of the martyrs is the inspiration for the church."

This volume represents a trail of martyrs that should be included in even a cursory look at human history. A trail worn with a faith in and of eternal consequence. A path through history that finds countless martyrs of different ethnicities and languages championing the same biblical teachings. A trail that finds martyrs' recognition that divine, transcendent standards will judge human actions pure and putrid. To read the histories and sacrifices of this sea of witnesses otherwise is problematic.

When one person or group takes the life of another because of religious belief, we call it a murder. When this person or group martyrs several people for such a cause, it is still homicide—even if now we consider it a social crisis. When thirty million people die because of religious differences, it is still murder, but now it is also a humanitarian catastrophe.

It is evil writ large.

We live in such a day. It appears that a growing number of uneducated people are casting biblical standards aside, often for inhumane leanings of whatever brand. Illogic written boldly in bestsellers. Graphic violence on the big screen and horrendous videos on iPhones. Many educated people are doing the same, often complicit as leaders, and as a result, our sensitivities to such atrocities are in danger of becoming numb.

Stanley Fish, a controversial public intellectual, argues that public classrooms are no place to give moral answers, as the title of his book suggests: *Save the World on Your Own Time*.[14] The British education system took the opposite approach, and now requires its high schools to help students understand the evils of ISIS—in their required Religion Education (RE) curriculum.[15] We agree—the persecuted, including those facing martyrdom, need a voice.

The authors of this current volume took a break from studying both ancient and recent accounts of individuals and groups who suffered and died for their faith to watch the film *Silence* (2016).[16] Imagine examining the original editions of John Foxe (1563) in the reading room in Cambridge University Library, then thirty minutes later slipping into a matinee showing of *Silence* in the Light Cinema in Leisure Park. From woodcut images of William Tyndale and Jan Hus burning at the stake, to a theater replete with cafés, a wall of candy machines, and games.

Calling it surreal would be an understatement—this tension between the worlds of the crucified and the comfortable. The smell of popcorn wafting through an almost empty theater while Christians on screen hang on crosses amid smoldering tar pits. Hearing in one ear kids persuading parents for more soda while in the other ear Martin Scorsese's film characters face complex decisions of the will—the ramifications of dying for their faith (especially for others).

Connecting history to current audiences is challenging. Foxe's bulky book and woodcut pictures helped his readers realize that the thirteen-year-old mutilated Christian was just as precious as their own daughter. That Polycarp was no less important than their father or grandfather. That the Jews killed in Spain were as real as their own classmates. That the hymns the fourteen nuns sang while the guillotine beheaded them during the French Revolution are melodies that connect to their own songs of faith.

Living in God's sovereign providence, we try to understand the remarkable stories of heroism of martyrs, and the complexities of decisions they confronted. Under severe persecution, some believers lapsed, at times to save others' lives (as in Japan), yet the church continued to grow worldwide. As many believers did during Christ's time on earth, some today opt to walk away from his challenge unto salvation, echoing the words of Jesus' followers along the Sea of Galilee: "This is a hard teaching. Who can accept it?" (John 6:60, NIV). For various reasons, many choose to prioritize ephemeral gains over eternal glory. But one's rejection of the truth can never nullify that truth. Conversely, a person's sacrifice for it accents and encourages the faith of others. John Foxe believed that the stories of those who died for their beliefs needed to be told, and telling them was an encouragement to stand faithful against evil.

In this light, we are typing at times through tears, trying to capture new stories of slaughtered Christians occurring all too often. Inasmuch as we are able, this is our first response. It is our best effort, one whose publication took almost two years longer than we anticipated, the majority of a decade. It is only because of our publisher, Tyndale House Publishers, whose namesake is one of history's great martyrs, that we were able to continue with this labor of love. The sobering yet compelling truth is that we could have kept writing this book the rest of our lives, with so many stories still unfolding. Perhaps we will for new editions. Like the Gospels, the apostolic letters, and early church martyrologies, what is written here is but a glimpse of the pain and suffering Jesus and his followers endured.

So please read, and read often and to others. Let us learn from and honor our dear, broad Christian family. Let us have communion with the saints.

The New Testament through the Battle of Tours (AD 732)

From the Stoning of Stephen to the Religious Clashes of Europe

POLYCARP, BISHOP OF SMYRNA

Polycarp was eighty-six years old when the Romans executed him. The thought of anyone burning alive is horrific, of a man near ninety is unconscionable, of a pillar of the community is senseless, and of a revered humanitarian accents the human capacity for evil.

As word reached Smyrna that Roman officials were executing those not paying allegiance to the Imperial Cult, the Christians persuaded Polycarp to hide at a farm. He was evading the captain of the police (who had the fitting name Herod). Though Polycarp moved to another farm, his pursuers captured two slave boys from the household who revealed his location—and in turn, Polycarp refused to keep running. He also fed his captors a large meal before leaving.

After Polycarp had a candid exchange with Herod and his father, and rough treatment, they skipped usual protocol and took him straight to the stadium. There, according to the chronicler, amid the mayhem a voice from heaven rang out: "Be strong, Polycarp, and play the man." And he did.

As the crowds clamored to get to the stadium, he remained firm. After additional pleas for their elderly bishop to save himself, Polycarp replied, "Eighty-six years have I been his servant, and he has done me no harm. How then can I blaspheme my King who has saved me?"[1] After many called for the beasts, the magistrate determined to burn him (since Roman law forbade the use of beasts after the festival ended). When the soldiers moved to nail Polycarp to the stake, he convinced them he would go freely. And told them that they were focusing only on the temporal flames but should be worried about the eternal ones.

According to the account, the fires formed a vault and didn't touch him, so the guards killed him with a dagger—and reportedly, a fragrant smell filled the arena.[2] His death inspired churches throughout the Roman Empire after the church of Smyrna circulated his testimony.

Various writers connect Polycarp's life to those of the apostles—with some crediting the apostle John himself as appointing Polycarp bishop of Smyrna. Polycarp was certainly friends with the legendary Ignatius, the bishop of Antioch martyred ca. AD 110. This familiarity is evident in Ignatius's personal comments in his letter to Polycarp.[3] Irenaeus, himself martyred in Lyon, France, ca. AD 202, also links Polycarp to the apostles. He was born in Smyrna, and had heard Polycarp preach (and refer to a "John"). He seems to campaign for his former pastor's relationship with the apostles.[4] Polycarp's statement became legendary, and appears in other martyr accounts in various versions, like the following—"All my life have I served thee, and never have ye forsaken me, so how can I forsake you now?"[5] Polycarp's execution is the earliest recorded martyrology in Christian history beyond the New Testament.

CHAPTER ONE
New Testament Martyrs

By this we know love, that he laid down his life for us, and we ought to lay down our lives for the brothers. 1 JOHN 3:16

Now when they heard these things they were enraged, and they ground their teeth at him [Stephen]. But he, full of the Holy Spirit, gazed into heaven and saw the glory of God, and Jesus standing at the right hand of God. And he said, "Behold, I see the heavens opened, and the Son of Man standing at the right hand of God." . . . And as they were stoning Stephen, he called out, "Lord Jesus, receive my spirit." And falling to his knees he cried out with a loud voice, "Lord, do not hold this sin against them." And when he had said this, he fell asleep. ACTS 7:54-56, 59-60

The torments of martyrdom are probably most keenly felt by the bystanders.[1] RALPH WALDO EMERSON

Horrid images of Christians enduring torture, and even vivid executions broadcast live by terrorists, are available at our fingertips—Christian heroes who sacrificed all for the sake of Christ. Each one stands in the lineage of Stephen—the first recorded martyr of the church (though John the Baptist had already been beheaded while Christ walked the earth).

Stephen was the first of the seven great men the apostles selected to help care for the poor in Jerusalem. These men, with clear evidence of God's Spirit on them, helped ensure that no widows, orphans, or needy were overlooked in the church's generosity. Stephen became known for his powerful preaching, a threat to established leaders. They considered his teachings blasphemy and stoned him.

The thud of rocks crushing Stephen's body and the inhumane jeering of his accusers remained seared in the consciousness of at least one bystander: the future apostle Paul (Acts 7:57-58). He would not soon forget God's glory redounding from Stephen's eyes as he gazed into heaven. Only after the Damascus Road experience and Paul's conversion would he fully appreciate what he'd witnessed that day. Paul went from carrying letters from the Jewish high priest to capture Christians for trial and possible death—official orders—to writing letters on behalf of Christ, the highest of priests—spiritual orders. Paul determined, "Christ will be honored in my body, whether by life or by death" (Philippians 1:20), but the memory of persecuting Christians haunted him: "I am the least of the apostles, unworthy to be called an apostle, because I persecuted the church of God" (1 Corinthians 15:9).

We don't have the names of most individuals persecuted under Paul and his fellow tormentors during the New Testament era, but the accounts in Scripture and in tradition herald their sacrifice. Of the New Testament leaders, we have compelling accounts of around twenty-five who paid the ultimate price,[2] many of whom are outlined in the following timeline. While many of the first-century martyrdoms are recorded in different manners (sometimes conflicting) by different writers, we have enough early information to be reasonably sure they died cruel deaths for Christ. In addition to the first-century text of the New Testament, early Christian accounts, and the wealth of sources in subsequent centuries, Roman sources like Josephus and Pliny corroborate the common thread of persecution.[3]

Early Persecutions: A Timeline

While scholars often vary on dates, the following represents a common timeline with approximate dates.[4]

A.D.	EVENT
35	Stephen martyred; Paul converted
42	Apostle James beheaded by Herod Agrippa I
64	Nero launches persecution
65	Peter and Paul executed
80s	Domitian develops emperor worship
107	Simeon, cousin of Jesus and bishop of Jerusalem, killed for political (anti-Semitic) reasons
approx. 110	Ignatius, bishop of Antioch, martyred in Rome
155 (166?)	Polycarp martyred
155, 160	Justin Martyr writes *First* and *Second Apology*
165	Justin beheaded
177	Forty-eight Christians massacred in Lyons and Vienne
197	Tertullian writes his *Apology*
202	Emperor Septimius Severus forbids conversions to Christianity; Leonidas, Origen's father, is beheaded
203	Perpetua and Felicitas martyred, along with several others
235-36	Theologian Hippolytus and other church leaders persecuted by Emperor Maximin Thrax
248	Persecutions in Alexandria
250	Emperor Decius orders sacrifice to Roman gods; Origen jailed and tortured; Pope Fabian, along with bishops of Antioch and Jerusalem, is martyred; Cyprian, bishop of Carthage, and Dionysius, bishop of Alexandria, flee their cities
251	Decius dies; Cyprian returns to his city, where he deals with Christians who've denied faith during persecution; theologian Novation asserts that lapsed Christians cannot be readmitted to the church, creating schism

A.D.	EVENT
252-53	Emperor Gallus revives persecutions instituted by Decius
254	Origen dies
257-60	Cyprian and Pope Sixtus II martyred
270-75	Emperor Aurelian establishes state cult of the Roman sun god, whose birthday is said to be December 25; renews persecution of Christians
275	The Neoplatonist philosopher Porphyry writes *Against the Christians*
298-302	Civil service and army purged of Christians
303	Great Persecution begins February 23. Edicts order church buildings to be destroyed, Scripture confiscated and burned, Christians to lose civil rights, and clergy to be imprisoned and forced to offer sacrifices; in 304, all people are ordered to sacrifice or be executed
305	Roman emperors Diocletian and Maximian abdicate, leading to a pause in persecution
306	Constantine named Augustus by troops; Maximinus II resumes persecution in the east; Council of Elvira, held in Spain, approves severe penalties for various sins
311	Emperor Galerius issues edict of toleration shortly before his death; Maximinus II continues persecution in Egypt and Palestine
312	Constantine defeats Maxentius, expanding his rule to the western part of the Roman Empire
313	Constantine and Licinius, emperor of the east, issue Edict of Milan, which grants toleration of Christianity
324	Constantine defeats Licinius to become emperor of the entire Roman Empire; sanctions Christianity across empire, which helps end persecutions in most territories

✠ John the Baptist

Crowds of people flocked to the Jordan River to hear the Baptizer's message of repentance and the coming of God's Kingdom. John was the last of a long line of prophets proclaiming the coming of the Messiah. His greatest legacy was his role as a forerunner of Jesus, announcing him as the coming Messiah and baptizing him.

From before John's birth, he was consecrated for God's purposes. His birth was announced to his elderly parents by none other than the angel Gabriel, who stands "in the presence of God" (Luke 1:19). As a child, John leapt in his mother's womb during the visit of Mary, who was pregnant with our Lord. Around thirty years later, Jesus met John at the Jordan River, and after John baptized him, the heavens opened and the Holy Spirit descended like a dove on Christ (Matthew 3:16).

But John also had to navigate the king's anger and fear. Imagine a president intimidated by Billy Graham's or Mother Teresa's message. King Herod feared John indeed, but considered him "a righteous and holy man." The Bible says, "When he heard [John], he was greatly perplexed, and yet he heard him gladly" (Mark 6:20). Nonetheless, Herod imprisoned John for repeatedly condemning his marriage to his half brother's wife, Herodias. When her daughter, Salome, pleased the king with her dancing, Herod promised her before his guests, "Ask me for whatever you wish. . . . Whatever you ask me, I will give you, up to half of my kingdom" (Mark 6:22-23). And after consulting her scandalous mother, Salome rushed back in and said, "I want you to give me at once the head of John the Baptist on a platter" (Mark 6:25). With this, Mark's Gospel records the cost of following our Lord—everything.

> The king was exceedingly sorry, but because of his oaths and his guests he did not want to break his word to her. And immediately the king sent an executioner with orders to bring John's head. He went and beheaded him in the prison and brought his head on a platter and gave it to the girl, and the girl gave it to her mother.

When his disciples heard of it, they came and took his body and laid it in a tomb.

MARK 6:26-29

In the eyes of their assailants, many Christian martyrs, like John the Baptist, died not so much for following Christ but for challenging their status quo. Those in power felt questioned or criticized. Men and women like John, whose godly teaching exposed the moral and ethical depravity around him, often challenge the lives and actions of those in control of both their societies and their personal fates.

CULTURAL CONNECTION

John the Baptist's Death in Media

The tension between John the Baptist and Herodias, Salome's seductive dancing, King Herod's predicament, and the gruesome image of John's head on a platter—all have elicited considerable attention from artists throughout the centuries. Numerous famous painters and sculptors, including Caravaggio and Jan Rombouts, have vividly imagined John's beheading. English officials found one depiction repulsive, banning Oscar Wilde's play *Salome* (1891) for forty years. Albert Camus cast his novel *The Fall* (1956) around the character Jean-Baptiste Clamence, based on John. In similar fashion, Joseph Conrad's main character in *Nostromo* (1904) is Gian Battista. Henry Wadsworth Longfellow presented the Pharisees and Sadducees encountering John the Baptist, who refuses to identify himself. Instead of giving his name, John eventually recites the words of Isaiah as in John 1:23 (lines 66–70). The poem's title, "Vox Clamantis," means "A Voice That Cries Out."[5]

STEPHEN Stephen is the first martyr recorded in the New Testament after our Lord's crucifixion and resurrection. Acts 6 informs us that Stephen was "of good repute, full of the Spirit and of wisdom" (verse 3). He was so strong in representing Christ's message that the religious authorities who challenged him "could not withstand the wisdom and the Spirit with which he was speaking" (verse 10). After seizing Stephen in Jerusalem and "gazing at him, all who sat in the council saw that his face was like the face of an angel" (Acts 6:15). His powerful recitation of God's work from Abraham through "the Righteous One" (Christ, Acts 7:52) infuriated them. They dragged him out of the city, gnashed their teeth at him, and stoned him to death.

JAMES THE APOSTLE Around a decade after Stephen's martyrdom, Herod Agrippa launched more severe attacks against Christians, laying "violent hands" on them, and he killed James "with the sword" (Acts 12:1-2, ca. AD 41–42). James and John were the "Sons of Thunder," who exhibited a bold and convincing presence. Their parents were Zebedee and (a different) Salome—possibly a first cousin of Mary, mother of Christ. According to Clement of Alexandria (ca. AD 150–215), James's boldness convicted his accuser—who asked for forgiveness, became a Christian, and was beheaded alongside James.

PHILIP Philip had been with Jesus during remarkable conversations, conversions, and miracles that would change the world, from the baptism with John to the feeding of the five thousand. He was certain of his Savior. Many commentaries note his penchant for practicality (e.g., asking Jesus how to feed the crowds and helping the Greeks to meet Jesus [John 6 and 12]). His time with Jesus gave him courage to stand for his faith—and Philip has become a model for many present-day ministries. He came from Bethsaida, the hometown of Andrew and Peter, and saw extraordinary events in places that before Christ's intervention had been ordinary. Early church sources report his death by crucifixion in Hierapolis in Phrygia (modern Turkey), after being imprisoned and scourged. In 2011, Francesco D'Andria claimed to have found St. Philip's tomb at Hierapolis inside an early church built over the site. He assumed the relics were exhumed, and then taken to Constantinople and eventually Rome to the church named in his honor.[6]

MATTHEW Originally called Levi (mentioned in Mark 2:14 and Luke 5:27), Matthew composed the first book of the New Testament. He had been a tax collector for the Romans, but at Jesus' call, he left his booth to follow Jesus and invited all his friends and associates to meet the Messiah as well. Different accounts of his martyrdom present varying stories, including burning, beheading, and stoning. John Foxe chooses the account of Matthew dying in Nadabah (Ethiopia) by the halberd, a slicing axe blade mounted on a long pole. The Ante-Nicene Fathers collection of writings by the church fathers (to AD 325) includes an apocryphal account with details of Matthew's heroic survival of the king's death threats. The king was prompted by a demon disguised as a soldier—but Matthew was saved each time by God. He survived an attack of ten cannibalistic soldiers sent by the king to tear apart him and the local bishop, and eat them.

In this account, Jesus appears in the form of a beautiful boy with a torch, rushes at the "man-eaters," and burns out their eyes. Next the evil king has Matthew pinned to the beach with nails piercing his hands, paper covering him and smothered with dolphin oil. Local idols (some in gold) were placed around him—but God sent fire to devour the pagan gods and soldiers, and Matthew, angelic in appearance, remained unharmed. The king then put Matthew's body in a lead box and secretly threw it into the sea—but onlookers had seen Matthew leave his body beforehand and then reappear later.[7] The famous Baroque artist Caravaggio depicts Matthew's death at the altar by sword in "The Martyrdom of Saint Matthew" (1600).[8]

DID YOU KNOW? *Ossuaries*

Burial boxes called ossuaries tie first-century Jerusalem to first-century martyrs. Some dead bodies were initially placed in sarcophagi (literally, "flesh eaters") until the flesh decayed, after which the bones were removed into ossuaries, much smaller stone chests, around 2.5 feet long. While we know of ossuaries from outside the last century of the Second Temple period, their popularity from the middle of Herod the Great's reign (ca. 20 BC) to the destruction of the Temple in AD 70 helps place remains easily within this period (and often connected to families of the

Pharisees).[9] At least two of these artifacts very likely relate to the stories of Christian martyrs. One ossuary discovered in southeast Jerusalem (1990) clearly belonged to Joseph Caiaphas, based on the name etched on its side. Caiaphas is the high priest in the story of Jesus' trial. Though some debate its definite link to the high priest, the authenticity of this burial box is generally accepted and is usually on display at the Israel Museum. Another ossuary box, though much more controversial, is the James Ossuary. First announced to the world in 2002, it had been in a controversial collector's possession for decades. Its inscription reads, "James, son of Joseph, brother of Jesus." While the ossuary's first-century date is not in question, various factions of researchers have come to competing conclusions about the last part of the inscription "Brother of Jesus." However, there continues to be strong support among some for the full inscription's authenticity. Often overlooked is that the ossuary's owner, collector Oded Golan, produced for his trial a 1976 photo of the bone box in his home, thirty years before he offered it for sale. This helped in securing his acquittal on the forgery charge.[10]

JAMES THE BROTHER OF JESUS As might be expected, the treatment of Jesus' family members draws special attention from the writers and chroniclers of Christian martyrs. The great church historian Eusebius (fourth century) gives three accounts of James's death, based on available sources, all adding considerable detail and variations.[11]

Josephus, the first-century Jewish historian, mentions the death of "the brother of Jesus, who was called Christ, whose name was James." He claims that the high priest Ananus despised James's boldness and quickly tried him and others, and then stoned them before the new procurator, Albinus, arrived. Albinus relieved Ananus because many Jews were upset about illegal executions; they had met him en route to his new post in Jerusalem. In the account by Hegesippus (AD 170), the Pharisees pushed James from the top of the Temple after his speech motivated more to follow Christ. When he didn't die from the fall, they stoned him. The *Roman Martyrology* states, "James, who is called the Brother of the Lord and the first bishop of Jerusalem, was thrown from the pinnacle of the Temple whereby his legs were broken. Then he was beaten on the head with a fuller's club and died. He was buried [near that spot] not far from the Temple." Before they crushed his head with the club used for pounding cloth, he knelt on his knees that were calloused like those of camels from his daily prayers, and prayed for them. He was ninety-four years old.

Voices from the Past

Hegesippus records that James, before being shoved from the "summit of the Temple," proclaimed: "Why ask ye me concerning Jesus the Son of man? He Himself sitteth in heaven, at the right hand of the Great Power, and shall come on the clouds of heaven."

HEGESIPPUS, *Commentaries on the Acts of the Church,* **Book V, ca. AD 170**

MATTHIAS Chosen to replace Judas Iscariot, Matthias was the only apostle not personally called by Jesus. Accounts of his ministry and death vary. Some traditions and early sources record him working among cannibals ("meat-eaters") in Ethiopia, where he was stoned to death. Other traditions place him near the Black Sea, where he was stoned. And other sources, which John Foxe relies on, have him dying in Jerusalem, where he was stoned and then beheaded.

ANDREW According to later sources, Andrew, the older brother of Peter, died as valiantly as his younger brother had served the church. He challenged Roman officials in Patras near the Ionian Sea, where allegedly his bones remain in the Cathedral of St. Andrew. Instead of cowering in the presence of the cross upon which he would die, he welcomed it. He died on an X-shaped cross, a saltire, bound instead of nailed. In one account, Regulus (a monk from Patras) took some of Andrew's bones to Scotland and built a shrine there. St. Andrew's Cross became part of Scotland's flag, and Andrew became Scotland's patron saint. In other accounts, the bones end up in Scotland at modern St. Andrews, and the alleged presence of these relics brought about a military victory for King Angus and the Picts.[12]

MARK While the New Testament references a "Mark" eight times, though never in the Gospels, later traditions generally consider them all to be the same person—the writer of the second Gospel. He is also closely associated with Peter, serving as his interpreter in Rome. Others, especially those influenced by the work of Thomas Oden, claim that he was the first to preach in Egypt and became the founder of Alexandrian Christianity.[13] After the first-century biblical accounts of Mark's missionary service, sources are silent until the fourth century. Eusebius, relying on sources he had gathered, chronicles Mark's brutal martyrdom. After serving as the bishop of Alexandria (a role Eusebius tells us he passed to Anianus in AD 62–63[14]), he was attacked by the pagan citizens. They dragged him through the streets, pulling him with ropes through fire and tearing his body to pieces.[15]

SIMON PETER Peter seems the most celebrated or discussed of the apostles. He walked on water with Jesus. He made bold outbursts in defense of Christ, yet denied Christ three times. And he's pictured in many great paintings—including those in the Sistine Chapel—receiving the keys to the Kingdom. Simon's nickname, Cephas (also known later as Peter, from the Latin *petrus*, meaning *rock*), given him by our Lord, represents well his boldness in life and death (Matthew 10:2). According to early church writers Hegesippus and Jerome, he displayed amazing resolve in Rome when he was martyred by Nero.[16] Christ had chosen Peter for a special place among the apostles and the church (John 21). He also foretold Peter's death: "'When you are old, you will stretch out your hands, and another will dress you and carry you where you do not want to go.' (This he said to show by what kind of death he was to glorify God)" (John 21:18-19). The church fathers' accounts of his death in Rome indeed reflect this prophecy. He had fought the magician Simon after battling an assortment of witchcraft, from vicious dogs to demons carrying Simon. The local Christians had warned Peter to flee because of Nero's wrath for killing Simon the Sorcerer by spoiling his trick. As Peter approached the gate, however, he saw Jesus face-to-face.

"Lord, whither goest Thou?"

And Our Lord responded: "I go to Rome, to be crucified anew!"

"To be crucified anew?" asked Peter.

"Yes!" said Our Lord.

And Peter said: "Then, Lord, I too return to Rome, to be crucified with Thee!"

Whereupon Our Lord ascended to Heaven, leaving Peter all in tears.[17]

When pressed again, Peter answered that he cared only for the message of the cross, and thus was sentenced to crucifixion.

And when Peter came in sight of the cross, he said: "My Master came down from Heaven to earth, and so was lifted up on the Cross. But I, whom He has deigned to call from earth to Heaven, wish to be crucified with my head toward the earth and my feet pointing to Heaven. Crucify me head downwards, for I am not worthy to die as my Master died." And so it was done: the cross was turned, so that he was fixed to it head downwards.[18]

A later letter attributed to Dionysius the Areopagite (Acts 17:34) claims he was a witness to the martyrdoms of Peter and Paul in Rome. In his alleged seventh letter to the Romans, after reflecting on these apostles' planting of the Corinthian church, Dionysius notes they continued their teaching ministry in Rome, where they were martyred "at the same time."[19]

PAUL The apostle Paul contributed the most books to our New Testament, and though the exact number is debated, God used him to record and pass on a significant part of his revelation "in verbal propositional form."[20] To appreciate the ultimate sacrifice of the martyrs in this study, we especially need to pause and cite the words Paul wrote by divine leading. From his very hands came the words that likely returned to him during his own imminent death:

I tell you this, brothers: flesh and blood cannot inherit the kingdom of God, nor does the perishable inherit the imperishable. . . . For this perishable body must put on the imperishable, and this mortal body must put on immortality. When the perishable puts on the imperishable, and the mortal puts on immortality, then shall come to pass the saying that is written:

"Death is swallowed up in victory."
"O death, where is your victory?
   O death, where is your sting?"

The sting of death is sin, and the power of sin is the law. But thanks be to God, who gives us the victory through our Lord Jesus Christ.

Therefore, my beloved brothers, be steadfast, immovable, always abounding in the work of the Lord, knowing that in the Lord your labor is not in vain.

1 CORINTHIANS 15:50, 53-58

Paul went to his death with God's promises emblazoned on his mind and heart. Like Peter, Paul also suffered martyrdom in Rome under Nero—and in some traditions on the same day. In the account of Abdias (of whom Foxe asks "if his book be of any substantial authority"), Paul led Nero's two esquires to faith in his sepulcher before they led Paul out to "the place of execution."[21] Before he "gave his neck" he made the sign of the cross on his forehead.[22] In Dionysius's letter to Timothy, he states he was present as Paul's assistant, recording the moving account of the last words between the two apostles after the crowd pummeled them and spat on them. "Paul said to Peter: 'Peace be with thee, cornerstone of the Church, shepherd of the lambs of Christ!' And Peter said to Paul: 'Go in peace, preacher of truth and good, mediator of salvation to the just!' Thereafter Dionysius followed his master Paul, for the two apostles were put to death in different places."[23]

JUDE Jude, also called Thaddeus, was the brother of James (and many take this to mean he was also Jesus' brother, noted in Mark 6:3 and Matthew

13:55). He is identified as the author of the book of Jude. It's one of the clearest authorship statements of the New Testament—"Jude, a servant of Jesus Christ and brother of James" (Jude 1:1). However, his relationship to Jesus is not clear, as some interpret the Greek word for *brother* as its alternative designation for *cousin*. In the Catholic Douay-Rheims Bible, commentators identify him as "Judas Jacobi" or "Judas the brother of James" (Luke 6:16 and Acts 1:16). Like our Lord, he was crucified, purportedly ca. AD 72 in Edessa (modern Turkey).[24] The area of his ultimate sacrifice became the first of the Crusader States of the twelfth century. He is recognized as a patron saint of the Armenian Orthodox Church, and the saint of "lost causes," an attribute memorialized in the robust charity St. Jude Children's Research Hospital (opened in 1962).

BARTHOLOMEW Scripture tells us very little about Bartholomew. Two key fourth-century Christian writers, Eusebius and Jerome, discuss his missionary work in India—so successful that 12,000 converts came to retrieve his body after King Astreges had him beaten with rods and then the idolaters crucified or beheaded him. Astreges charged him as a magician, saying Bartholomew tricked the king's brother Polymius (or Polemius), also a king, into converting. In one account, Bartholomew challenged Astreges's god Baldad (or Baldach) to a fight with God, and soon all the pagan idols crumbled—infuriating Astreges. After Bartholomew's death, according to one account, demons that had been cast from King Astreges's priests turned and killed the king and his priests. Polymius was made bishop.

In *The Golden Legend* account, citing writer Theodorus, the executioners (in Alban, Armenia) flayed Bartholomew, ". . . that some say that he was crucified and was taken down ere he died, and for to have greater torment he was flayed and at the last beheaded."[25] This is vividly depicted in Jusepe de Ribera's *Martyrdom of Saint Bartholomew* (1644). Though a later tradition, the flaying of St. Bartholomew is a common motif in representing his passion: "Among the many excellent statues that adorn the cathedral of Milan, none is more justly admired than one of St. Bartholomew flayed alive, representing the muscles, veins and other parts with inimitable softness and justice."[26]

THOMAS Later tradition asserts that Thomas, like Bartholomew, ministered in India. History has hung the moniker "Doubting Thomas" on him for being skeptical of Jesus' resurrection until seeing the actual scars (John 20:24-29). However, John 11 shows his boldness, challenging his fellow apostles to join Jesus in Judah even if it meant death (verse 16). According to the second-century Acts of Thomas, his martyrdom came at the end of four soldiers' spears. In this apocryphal account, Thomas has an extended interaction with King Gondophares about the building of a palace. While it's difficult to ascertain the authority of these written accounts,[27] archaeologists have found several coins in the Kabul Valley in Afghanistan attesting to this first-century king.

LUKE Luke served as a physician, an author of one of the Gospels, and a faithful companion of Paul, even accompanying him to Rome. According to later sources, Greek pagan priests in Boeotia (central Greece) hanged Luke on a green olive tree at age eighty-four. His relics are now in Padua, Thebes, and Prague.[28] We know much more of his life than his death, but nonetheless such a great man died not touching this earth, closer to heaven than his accusers.[29]

SIMON To help distinguish him from Simon Peter, this Simon was also called "Zelotes" or "the Zealous" (Luke 6:15; Acts 1:13). Early accounts place him in ministry in nearly all of the known world.[30] Writers record his death in various places, including Persia, Iberia, and Britain—but agree on his death by crucifixion. And in a heralded version, his tormentors sawed his body into pieces. This is why he is commonly depicted with a saw (as in the King James cover page illustration, 1611).[31]

JOHN Though he suffered persecution, John was the only apostle not to die a horrific but celebrated martyrdom. The "beloved disciple" wrote the last of the four Gospels, and three of his letters to the churches are included in the New Testament. He composed the book of Revelation from the island of Patmos—banished there by emperor Domitian. Foxe notes that various miracles are attributed to John, "reported in sundrye chronicles."[32] He made a miraculous escape from a cauldron of boiling oil. Isidorus relates several miracles during John's times of persecution—including surviving poison, and then healing two others who also drank it. He died at age ninety-nine.[33]

BARNABAS Barnabas spent considerable time with the apostle Paul assisting in ministries and became a church leader himself. Although he and Paul eventually had a dispute and parted ways for a bit, Barnabas was clearly passionate about Christ and his teachings.

> The report of this came to the ears of the church in Jerusalem, and they sent Barnabas to Antioch. When he came and saw the grace of God, he was glad, and he exhorted them all to remain faithful to the Lord with steadfast purpose, for he was a good man, full of the Holy Spirit and of faith. And a great many people were added to the Lord.
>
> ACTS 11:22-24

We also know of Barnabas's zeal for the gospel. He traveled from his place of ministry in Antioch to Paul's hometown, Tarsus, and brought him to Antioch to minister. "For a whole year they met with the church and taught a great many people. And in Antioch the disciples were first called Christians" (Acts 11:26).

He was a Cypriot Jew whose name means "son of encouragement" (Acts 4:36-37), and a cousin of John Mark who was also from Cyprus. Sources record tradition stating Barnabas was stoned to death in Salamis, Cyprus, due to his very effective preaching.[34]

Vintage Foxe

Wherein marvellous it is to see and read the numbers incredible of Christian innocents that were slain and tormented, some one way, some another, [as] Rabanus[35] saith, and saith truly, Some slain with sword; some burnt with fire; some with whips scourged; some stabbed with forks of iron; some fastened to the cross or gibbet; some drowned in the sea; some their skins plucked off; some their tongues cut off; some stoned to death; some killed with cold; some starved with hunger; some their hands cut off, or otherwise dismembered, have been so left naked to the open shame of the world, etc. Their kinds of punishments, although they were divers, yet the manner of constancy in all these martyrs was one.[36]

The Roman prefect who tried washing his hands of our Christ was almost lost to history among critics of the Bible's historicity. Then in 1961, archaeologists had good fortune while excavating the theater at Caesarea Maritima. They discovered the "Pilate Stone," a piece of limestone that builders had reused in a stairway. What is left of the broken text on it clearly identifies Pontius Pilate from the New Testament narrative. It's also contemporary to his lifetime—he was the Roman prefect from AD 26 to 36. It can be seen at the Israel Museum and states, "*Tiberieum . . . Pontius Pilate . . . prefect of Judea.*"

+ Historic Sources
An excerpt from *Martyrs Mirror*, 1660[37]

SUMMARY OF THE MARTYRS OF THE FIRST CENTURY
This first century did not pass without the shedding of much blood of the saints; for, since Jesus Christ Himself, the leader of all true believers, was subject to it, it was just, that His members should follow in the same path. . . . After the death of Christ, the fire of persecution raged exceedingly, consuming nearly all of the beloved apostles and friends of Christ, according to the flesh. We have described those who followed Christ, their Captain, into suffering and death, according to the order of time; they are the following persons: Stephen the deacon; the apostles, James, Philip, Barnabas, Mark the evangelist, Peter, Paul; some companions and friends of Paul—as Aristarchus, Epaphras, Silas, Onesiphorus, Prochorus, Nicanor, Parmenas, Olympas, Carpus, Trophimus, Materus, Egyetus, Hermagoras, Onesimus, Dionysius of Athens, and Timothy; but the latter was slain a few years after the others. In the meantime the preceding ones are followed by Andrew, Bartholomew, Thomas, Matthew, Simon Zelotes, Matthias,

Luke the evangelist, Antipas, the faithful martyr of Jesus, John, whom Jesus loved, Urticinus, Vitalis, etc., all of whom obtained the martyr's crown, as may be seen from the following account.

To Jesus Christ, the Son of God, we have accorded the first place among the martyrs of the new covenant; not in the order of time, for herein John was before, and preceded with his death; but on account of the worthiness of the person, because He is the head of all the holy martyrs, through whom they all must be saved.

Voices from the Past

So, when many even of the ruling class believed, there was a commotion among the Jews, and scribes, and Pharisees, who said: "A little more, and we shall have all the people looking for Jesus as the Christ."

HEGESIPPUS, *Commentaries on the Acts of the Church*, Book V, ca. AD 170

CHAPTER TWO
The Great Persecutions

When he opened the fifth seal, I saw under the altar the souls of
those who had been slain for the word of God and for the witness
they had borne. They cried out with a loud voice, "O Sovereign Lord,
holy and true, how long before you will judge and avenge our blood
on those who dwell on the earth?" Then they were each given a white
robe and told to rest a little longer, until the number of their fellow
servants and their brothers should be complete, who were to be
killed as they themselves had been. REVELATION 6:9-11

Now I am beginning to be a disciple. May naught of things visible
or invisible seek to allure me, that I may attain unto Jesus Christ.
Let there come on me fire and cross and conflicts with wild
beasts, wrenching of bones, mangling of limbs, crushing of the
whole body, grievous torments of the devil may I but attain to
Jesus Christ. IGNATIUS OF ANTIOCH, LETTER TO THE ROMANS

The wave of large-scale persecutions, sometimes empire-wide, hit communities large and small. No cities escaped the threat of persecution, though the intensity varied depending on the ire of local authorities. At times, they publicly humiliated Christians or hammered their bodies as well as their souls. Far-flung territories like Palestine had their own dynamics that resulted in an additional layer of attacks. The stoning of Stephen and beheading of John the Baptist by religious and civic leaders, along with the mad throng of common citizens, was a taste of the forthcoming oppression that would blanket much of the region.

Some persecutors devised sordid tortures for the Christians—a dizzying reality to imagine. There was no limit to their brutality, and history grants examples from Carthage to Rome to Lyon.

The overall popularity of violent entertainment also undergirded these public martyrdoms. For example, in AD 107 Emperor Trajan used five thousand pairs of gladiators for the celebration of a military victory. For perspective, the attendance at many of these events was larger than at the average college football game in North America today.[1] Across the Roman Empire, in scores of stone-hewn amphitheaters, tens of thousands of spectators would yell in unison from their seats calling for the graphic demise of captives, often including Christians. The environment was one of anticipation, filled with maniacal chanting for inhumane acts.

In Rome, midday was especially full of carnage. This was "the time when criminals were executed. Public execution was done in order to warn the spectators against committing any of these acts. Murderers, arsonists and Christians were thrown to wild beasts (*damnatio ad bestias*) or made to fight each other as impromptu gladiators. Often they were beheaded or crucified, or sometimes even burned alive by dipping a tunic, called a *tunica molesta*, in a naphtha-soaked substance and setting it on fire."[2] Society began to wallow in a new low. The word *fornication* comes from the Latin *fornix*, for the "arch," under which prostitutes often greeted customers at the games.

We cannot be certain from the early sources how many Christians suffered, and in which specific public spaces. "It is, of course, probable enough that some of the Christians condemned *ad bestias* suffered in the Colosseum, but there is just as much reason to suppose that they met their death in one of the other places dedicated to the cruel amusements of imperial Rome; for instance, in the Circus Flaminius, the Gaianum, the Circus of Hadrian, the *Amphitheatrum Castrense*, and the Stadium of Domitian."[3]

Christians throughout the centuries have gathered sand from these places as relics—stained with the martyrs' blood. But the protection or recognition of these sites as martyria is varied, including the Roman Colosseum. It alone seated at least 50,000 spectators, and the Codex-Calendar of 354 boasts 87,000.[4] For historical perspective, Vespasian commissioned the building of the Colosseum in AD 70, overlapping with the Jewish Temple's destruction and displacement of both Jews and Christians from the Holy Land. While adherents of two religions were fleeing for their lives, the Romans were preparing for one mammoth party—or more correctly, parties in perpetuity.

Vespasian's son Titus, who led the campaigns in Palestine commemorated in the Arch of Titus in Rome, opened the Colosseum a decade later (AD 80). Ironically, in this massive stone gift to the Roman populace, many martyred Christians' lives are now a gift to billions who follow in their legacy. The Colosseum is the largest shrine officially commemorated to Christian martyrs. Pope Benedict XIV's plaque from the 1749 ceremony is visible at the entrance. (See "The Arenas" in chapter 4.)

Persecutors' capacity for evil treatment seemed ever expanding. Maniacal pleasure eclipsed mercy. Imperial decrees sanctioned depravity. In AD 156, the amphitheater in Smyrna (modern Turkey) saw the grisly death of Polycarp, an eighty-six-year-old leader who had also been a humanitarian among them most of his life. (One martyr is recorded as being 120 years old.) In Carthage, Perpetua and Felicitas were both new mothers, Felicitas having delivered only a few days before entering the arena. Eulalia of Spain was only thirteen. Each story gives testament to new depths of atrocity.[5]

During the first four centuries, several "great" persecutions of Christians ensued. From the fourth through the seventh centuries, these subsided as Christianity continued to expand, but not without conflict. Christians also killed many among their own in order to protect against heresy.

Then came the carnage between the Christians and Muslims—followers of the newer Abrahamic religion, with beliefs similar to Christianity—Judaism, and Zoroastrianism. Similarities? Yes. But core differences would lead to regional conflicts, and eventually international religious war. The sociopolitical differences persist to the present, though serious efforts are underway in some parts of the world for peaceful coexistence between the Abrahamic traditions (Judaism, Christianity, and Islam). We could fill volumes with accounts from this era alone as the Great Persecutions took countless lives.

Voices from the Past

Justin [Martyr] . . . was honoured with a divine martyrdom, owing to the philosopher Crescens, a man who strove to make his life and conduct conform to his title of Cynic. It was he who devised the plot against Justin; for Justin had repeatedly refuted him in debate with an audience present, and now at the last by his martyrdom bound on his brow the trophies of victory of the truth he ever proclaimed. That martyrdom he himself, truly the most philosophical of men, clearly foretold . . . exactly as it was so soon to happen to him. This is what he wrote: I to expect to be plotted against and clapped in the stocks by one of those I have named, or maybe by Crescens, who calls himself a philosopher yet is a lover not of wisdom but of showing off. He does not deserve the name of philosopher, seeing that he publicly criticizes what he does not understand, alleging that Christians are godless and impious, his object being to win the favor and applause of the deluded masses. For if he lashes out at us without studying Christ's teaching he is most unscrupulous and much worse than simple people, who as a rule refrain from arguing and making false statements on subjects they know nothing about: if he has studied it and failed to understand its greatness, or has understood it but for fear of being suspected behaves in this shameful way, there is all the more reason to call him ignoble and unscrupulous, yielding as he does to the ignorant and senseless prejudice and suspicion. I would like you to know that by putting certain questions of this kind for him to answer I found out—in fact, proved—that he really is totally ignorant.

EUSEBIUS, HE, IV. 16

✠ Justin Martyr

Many who were martyred during Emperor Marcus Aurelius's reign remain unnamed, from the slaughters at Vienna and Lyon, to community purges largely lost to history.[6] But some of these martyrs are known to us through martyrologies and through their literary works. Justin Martyr's *Second Apology* was written just four years before he and his colleagues were led to their executions.[7]

As Justin had predicted, Crescens, the self-promoting philosopher, entrapped him. The second-century writer Tatian reports:

> That wonderful man, Justin, rightly declared that these people were no better than bandits. Crescens, for instance, who made his lair in the great city, went beyond everyone in his offenses against boys, and was passionately devoted to money-making. He urged others to despise death, but was so afraid of it himself that he did his best to compass the death of Justin as a calamity, simply because by preaching the truth Justin convicted the philosophers of gluttony and fraud.
>
> *AGAINST THE GREEKS,* 18–19

CULTURAL CONNECTION

Valentine's Day and the Martyrs

Every February 14 when we see hearts posted on windows and Valentine cards exchanged, we witness a holiday linked to both Geoffrey Chaucer and the persecution of the saints. Chaucer wrote in *Parlement of Foules*, "For this was on seynt Valentyns day, / Whan every foul cometh there to chese his mate."[8] He is talking about the Garden of Love, and later writers would liken the birds' mating calls and singing to men and women falling in love.[9] Valentine's Day initially commemorated the saint's burial near Rome. His third-century journey ca. AD 269 purportedly included caring for the persecuted. This physician-priest was seized along the Via

Flaminia (the road from Rome to the Adriatic Sea) near the cemetery later named for him and visited by the Christian Crusader knights.[10] After the soldiers bludgeoned Valentine and his deacon, they beheaded him. The best early source has Emperor Claudius II (known as "the Cruel") failing to convert Valentine to paganism and then beheading him.

Legends attaching Valentine to romantic notions are numerous and without convincing historic corroboration. One legend has him refusing to stop officiating marriages after Emperor Claudius II prohibited his soldiers to wed.[11] In the classic *Butler's Lives of Saints*, we find the supposed origin of valentine cards: "To abolish the heathen's lewd superstitious custom of boys drawing the names of girls in honor of their goddess Februta Juno, on the 15th of this month, several zealous pastors substituted the names of saints in billets given on this day."[12] Another legend claims he left a note for the jailer's daughter, whom he had befriended and shared the gospel with, and signed it "From your Valentine." The holiday practices in America today come from somewhat disconnected and late notions.

Although at least three Valentines surface in martyrologies, the existence of one Valentine (the physician) is well supported by very early cultic actions and remains. Inscriptions beginning in 318 date the early association of the Via Flaminia cemetery with Valentine, and a basilica in his honor was erected around 350.[13] In his article "Valentine's Dynamic Love," Chuck Colson combines comments by John Wesley and Richard Neuhaus on the sacrifice of heroic Christians: "Like Valentine, Athanasius, and Wilberforce—and like God himself—true love must sometimes take a stance of opposition for the objective good of the beloved. True love will dismantle false worldviews. True love will reveal where lesser loves have become gods. True love will be against the world for the world, because true love knows what the world needs most."[14]

DID YOU KNOW? *The Acts of the Martyrs*

Many accounts of the earliest martyrs come from Eusebius of Caesarea (d. 340), in part because after the book of Acts, his is the first surviving church history. Many earlier writers are preserved only through his inclusion of their quotes or extended citations. In the fourth century, Eusebius wrote his *History of the Church* (often abbreviated *HE* from its Latin title, *Historia Ecclesiastica*). Like the destruction of full libraries and museums under ISIS in the modern era, the Romans ordered Christian books destroyed on various occasions. Fortunately, Eusebius managed to travel and collect stories in numerous countries, and had access to surviving texts, including in his hometown of Caesarea. Origen had studied there for twenty years and Pamphilus, Eusebius's mentor, built on his library. One of these earlier collections was his own *Martyrs of Palestine*, included in *History of the Church*. Many of the ancient sources Eusebius cites have been lost, except for his excerpts.

The Islamic wave of conquests destroyed many of the libraries and personal collections Eusebius had used. The first English translation of *History of the Church* wasn't produced until ca. 1550, and along with it, chroniclers gathered a trove of other martyr accounts into what became known as *Acts of the Martyrs* (Latin, *Acta Martyrum*). These accounts have varying levels of reliability, with some considered strong sources, like that of Perpetua (probably edited and finished by Tertullian) and *The Life and Passion of St. Cyprian* by Pontius. Pontius (identified by Jerome), was a deacon under Cyprian in Carthage (mid-third century).

The *Acts of the Martyrs* presented the early church with a list of heroes of the faith, a resource used against pagans long after the persecutions ended. Theodoret of Cyrrhus (ca. 420–430) paraded the martyrologies before pagan critics: "No one grave conceals the bodies of each of them [martyrs], but they are shared out among towns and villages, which call them saviours of souls and bodies, and doctors, and honor them as founders and protectors."[15] As with much of history, the confluence of eyewitness accounts and tradition melded into the stories retold through the generations.[16] Before Gutenberg's press (1454), manuscripts were often stitched into a codex[17] and carried by priests, monks, and evangelists. Though we often talk about "The Book of Martyrs," especially *Foxe's Book of Martyrs* from the sixteenth century, most of these sources rely on hundreds of documents from the last two thousand years.

✠ Insights from Roman Martyrology

What It Means to Die Like a Christian

The *Roman Martyrology* serves two purposes—liturgical and devotional—and has become a regular part of Catholic life, assigning at least one saint per calendar day. This resource is a helpful reminder of what a mélange of writers through the centuries have recorded about those who have given their lives for our Lord. The following was adapted from the *Martyrology* for the *National Catholic Register*.[18] It summarizes the varied fates of the saints from each month, including these samples:

January: St. Concordius, priest and martyr, who in the time of the Emperor Antoninus, was first beaten with rods, then stretched on the rack, and afterward afflicted in prison. There he was consoled by an angel and at length ended his life by the sword.

May: James, who is called the Lord's brother and the first bishop of Jerusalem, was cast headlong from a pinnacle of the Temple, and his legs being broken, and his brains scattered by a blow from a fuller's club, he died, and was buried not far from the Temple.

September: The holy martyrs Andochius, priest; Thyrsus, deacon; and Felix, who were sent by blessed Polycarp, bishop of Smyrna, from the East to evangelize France, and were there cruelly scourged and hung up by their hands all day long and cast into the fire; but since they were not burnt, at length their necks were broken with heavy bars and thus they were gloriously crowned.

This grisly calendar of events from the *Roman Martyrology* serves to remind us of the faithfulness of saints who, for their love of Christ, suffered unspeakable torment and torture. Their example of faithful devotion to Christ inspires us to deeper commitment, and to remember our persecuted brothers and sisters all over the world who continue to suffer for Christ.

Voices from the Past

There is no day in the whole year unto which the number of five thousand martyrs cannot be ascribed, except only the first day of January.

ST. JEROME (d. AD 420), *Epistle to Chromatius and Heliodorus*

+ Historic Sources

Excerpt from Eusebius, *Histories,* about the survivors of the persecutions at Lyons in AD 177.

They were also so zealous in their imitation of Christ . . . that, though they had attained honor, and had borne witness, not once or twice, but many times— having been brought back to prison from the wild beasts, covered with burns and scars and wounds—yet they did not proclaim themselves martyrs, nor did they suffer us to address them by this name. If any one of us, in letter or conversation, spoke of them as martyrs, they rebuked him sharply. . . . And they reminded us of the martyrs who had already departed, and said, "They are already martyrs whom Christ has deemed worthy to be taken up in their confession, having sealed their testimony by their departure; but we are lowly and humble confessors."

Vintage Foxe

Likewise under Julianus the wicked Apostata [Julian the Apostate], certain there were which constantly suffered martyrdom by the Heathen idolators, as Emylianus, who was burned in Thracia, and Domitius, which was slain. Theodorus also for singing of a Psalm at the removing of the body of Babylas . . . being apprehended, was so examined with exquisite torments, and so cruelly excruciate from morning almost to noon, that hardly he scaped with life. Who being asked afterward of his friends, how he could abide so sharp torments, said that at the first beginning he felt some pain, but afterward there stood by him a young man, who as he was sweating, wiped of his sweat, and refreshed him with cold water oft times: wherewith he was so delighted, that when he was let down from the engine, it grieved him, more than before.[19]

THE GREAT PERSECUTIONS A history of the early church is in large part an attempt to understand how it managed to spread and survive amid numerous persecutions, both regional and empire-wide and subsequently, to describe the rise of the hermitages and monasteries after the persecutions stopped.

The Persecution of New Testament Martyrs

Although this time of persecution is not usually listed among the main persecutions, or the numbered persecutions of Eusebius and others in history, it is undoubtedly important in the formation of the church. We don't have the names of most of those persecuted under Paul (before his conversion) and other tormenters during the New Testament era. However, we have enough accounts in Scripture (like Stephen, the apostle James, and John the Baptist) and in tradition (like the martyrdoms of Peter and Paul) to herald their sacrifice. Chapter 1 has already detailed some of the New Testament era leaders whose compelling accounts of ultimate sacrifice have passed down through the centuries.[20]

The First Persecution—Under Nero (AD 54–68)

When a fire burned much of Rome in AD 64, many blamed Nero, who was not actually present. After relentless pressure, he allowed the blame to go on the Christians—since many lived in areas that the fire missed. Suetonius, the Roman biographer, wrote, "Punishment was inflicted on the Christians, a class of men given to a new mischievous superstition." Tacitus, the Roman historian (d. 120) and friend of Emperor Trajan (98–117), gives us the most condemning account of Nero's actions in an effort to nullify the wave of criticism for the fire:

Nero fastened the guilt and inflicted the most exquisite tortures on a class hated for their abominations, called Christians by the populace. . . . Accordingly, an arrest was first made of all who confessed; then, upon their information, an immense multitude was convicted, not so much of the crime of arson, as of hatred of the human race. Mockery of every sort was added to their deaths. Covered with the skins of beasts, they were torn by dogs and perished, or were nailed to crosses, or were doomed to the flames. These served to illuminate the night when daylight failed. Nero had thrown open his gardens for the spectacle, and was exhibiting a show in the circus, while he mingled with the people in the dress of a charioteer or drove about in a chariot. Hence, even for criminals there arose a compassion; for it was not, as it seemed, for the public good, but to glut one man's cruelty, that they were being destroyed.[21]

Some modern accounts cast Nero's persecution as widespread, but the ancient sources seem to show it was contained mainly in the area of Rome. What Tacitus means by "an immense multitude" is unknown, but we must conclude it was a horrific scene. His description "cannot simply be dismissed as an overstatement, because Tacitus, a pagan, had no love for Christians and hence no reason to exaggerate their numbers. An exaggeration would only have reflected positively on Christianity, for it would have implied that the population of Christians was so large that it was possible to persecute an "immense multitude." Moreover, a large Christian population would also have implied that the pagan gods did not meet people's spiritual needs."[22]

The Second Persecution—Under Domitian (AD 81–96)

We know few names among those Christians martyred under Emperor Domitian. It appears that at first he became frustrated and banished them from Rome around AD 95. He also executed his niece and her husband— Flavia Domitilla and Flavius Clemens—for being "atheists" (as many Romans called the Christians, referring to their repudiation of the Roman gods). According to Scottish New Testament scholar William Ramsay, Domitian's persecution was horrific:

> The persecution of Domitian burned itself ineradicably into the memory of history; . . . so strong and early a tradition as that which constitutes Domitian the second great persecutor cannot be discredited without wrecking the foundations of ancient history. Those who discredit it must, to be consistent, resolve to dismiss nine-tenths of what appears in books as ancient history, including most that is interesting and valuable.[23]

Indirect evidence for this persecution is perhaps found in Revelation 1:9, the reference to "tribulation" and "patient endurance."[24] Many think this and the tenor of the book reflects persecutions in Asia Minor and John's banishment to the island of Patmos, especially chapters 13 and 17. Some claim the same type of evidence exists in *First Clement*, a letter written from the church in Rome to the church in Corinth.[25] Around seventy-five years after Domitian's reign, Melito (bishop of Sardis) and Hegisippus (a Christian chronicler) record this. Both writers died in AD 180. Their works are the basis for Eusebius's account.

Though Origen (d. 254) reported that few Christians had died up until Domitian's time,[26] it seems in tension with either the groups in Rome put to death under Nero, or the various types of persecutions that likely overlapped this era, which Pliny the Younger reported a few years later to Trajan. And numerous accounts during the persecutions simply fail to name many of the victims. The Roman historian Dio Cassius also mentions Domitian's persecution of those espousing Jewish beliefs and "atheism." Though Christians are not expressly mentioned, this reference would logically include them since many were from Jewish backgrounds and the same charge was often lodged against them.

Eusebius is rather certain about Domitian's cruelty. "Many were the victims of Domitian's appalling cruelty. . . . Finally, he showed himself the successor of Nero in enmity and hostility to God. He was, in fact, the second to organize persecution against us." Eusebius also reports that Domitian "ordered the execution of all who were in David's line."[27] However, Eusebius includes an account of his change of mind late in his reign. Considerable debate continues about Domitian's actual treatment of Christians.

Voices from the Past

After his midlife conversion to Christianity, Tertullian was disgusted by the games, gods, and events represented in Roman arts and arenas. As a young man he had loved to go to the amphitheaters and watch people die. But one of the things that impressed him over the years and led finally to his conversion was the WAY Christians died, with dignity and with prayer and with their hands raised to God. One of his classic arguments against Rome's persecution of Christians and their God was the Romans' obvious contempt for their own gods:[28]

"Other of your (Roman) writers, in their wantonness, even minister to your pleasures by vilifying (your) gods. Examine those charming farces of your Lentuli and Hostilii where in the jokes and the tricks it is your . . . deities which afford you Romans merriment. . . . Your dramatic literature, too, depicts all the vileness of your gods. The Sun (Apollo) mourns his offspring (Phaeton) cast down from heaven and you (Romans) are full of glee; Cybele (a mother goddess) sighs after the scornful swain (her son/paramour Attis who castrated himself), and you do not blush. . . . When the likeness of a god is put on the head of an infamous wretch, when one impure and trained up for the art in all effeminacy represents a Minerva or a Hercules, is not the majesty of your gods insulted and their deity dishonored? Yet you not merely look on, but applaud. You are, I suppose, more devout in the (Colosseum), where after the same fashion your deities dance on human blood, on the pollutions caused by inflicted punishments, as they act their themes and stories, doing their turn for the wretched criminals, except that these too often put on divinity and actually play the very gods. . . . We must explain all these things by the contempt in which (your) gods are held by those who actually do these things and by those for whose enjoyment they are done."

The Third Persecution—Under Trajan (AD 98–117)

One of the most frequently cited of early sources on Christianity is that of Pliny the Younger to Emperor Trajan around AD 111. Likewise, at least one legendary martyrdom is associated with Trajan—his execution of Bishop Ignatius of Antioch. Both the letter and response involve copied letters that give details of these encounters, and simultaneously corroborate the emperor's execution orders. Pliny writes to Trajan:

> Meanwhile, in the case of those who were denounced to me as Christians, I have followed the following procedure: I interrogated them as to whether they were Christians; those who confessed I interrogated a second and a third time, threatening them with punishment; those who persisted I ordered executed. For I had no doubt that, whatever the nature of their creed, stubbornness and inflexible obstinacy surely deserve to be punished. . . . An anonymous document was published containing the names of many persons. Those who denied that they were or had been Christians, when they invoked the gods in words dictated by me, offered prayer with incense and wine to your image, which I had ordered to be brought for this purpose together with statues of the gods, and also cursed Christ—none of which those who are really Christians can, it is said, be forced to do—these I thought should be discharged. Others named by the informer declared that they were Christians, but then denied it, asserting that they had been but had ceased to be, some three years before, others many years, some as much as twenty-five years. . . . For the contagion of this superstition has spread not only to the cities but also to the villages and farms. But it seems possible to check and cure it. . . . Hence it is easy to imagine what a multitude of people can be reformed if an opportunity for repentance is afforded.[29]
> **PLINY THE YOUNGER,** *Letter to Trajan,* **ca. AD 111**

In Pliny's full letter, we find that not only did he torture two deaconesses, but that the women were slaves. Both their gender and their social status were evidence of the inclusive nature of the church of that era. These deaconesses would have been put to death based on Pliny's own account of treating those confessing Christ.

> Pliny's torturers, known as *tortures* and *carnifices*, began their
> gruesome work, probably using some mixture of the typical
> methods of their trade, namely scourging, laceration with hooks,
> and burning. The women had two options. They could either
> remain silent, enduring progressively more brutal tortures, or they
> could answer the questions put to them, thus revealing a similar
> description of Christian worship as was outlined before by those
> who apostatized from the faith. If they took the second of these
> two paths—which, based on Pliny's own account, seems to be the
> case—it would not have spared them further tortures.[30]

For the millions of people who have marveled at the great remains of classical Roman edifices, accounts like this reveal a morbid aspect of the city's foundation. Tourists often walk from the Arch of Titus, depicting his destruction of the Second Jewish Temple (and slaughter of many of Israel's inhabitants), through the Forum remains, and gaze at the modern salute to Roman greatness in Italy's stunning "Unification of Italy" building (the Vittoriano on Capitoline Hill). What may escape many of them is that the empire, with its countless ruins of marble and concrete, was built on the backs of the oppressed and conquered—including the backs of Christ-followers like those Pliny systematically tortured and killed.

The Fourth Persecution—Under Marcus Aurelius (AD 161–180)

The Stoic emperor Marcus Aurelius, author of *Meditations*, is often represented as a wise and noteworthy ruler, but his reputation needs to be weighed against evidence of ruthless treatment toward Christians, whom he reportedly considered obstinate fools for dying for such a cause.[31] The modern Netflix docudrama series *Roman Empire* represents his astute leadership and celebrated status in season one, but it fails to mention the brutality of his reign.[32] Eusebius, however, describes in detail the forty-eight martyrs in Vienne and Lyons in southeastern Gaul (modern France). These serve as an exclamation mark on inhumane actions, regardless of the emperor's treatment of Christians otherwise.[33] Esteemed Bible scholar Larry Hurtado concludes, "But, however you slice it, in the reign of this oft-regarded noble Emperor (not simply in times of more dubious characters such as Nero), Christians were objects of official ire as well as popular hostility."[34] The empire was suffering a horrendous plague and local communities likely used Christians as scapegoats, especially with an edict requiring people to show loyalty to the Roman gods.

Evidence in the writings of Abercius, Orosius, Justin, and the martyrs of Pergamum supports the existence of a general edict by the joint emperors, sometime during AD 161–168, ordering sacrifices to placate the angry gods. This same evidence, when put within the context of Roman tradition and the events of the last few years of joint rule by Marcus Aurelius and Lucius Verus, further suggests that this empire-wide edict was issued sometime during AD 166–168. This general edict, taken by itself, was not specifically aimed at the Christians, but it clearly could have resulted in their persecution.[35]

The persecutions under Aurelius's orders produced some of the most remarkable and heroic martyrdom accounts in the Christian tradition, including Blandina at Lyons, and prominent leaders like Justin Martyr. The twelve Scillitan martyrs in Numidia (North Africa) suffered around the end of his reign. *Acts of the Scillitan Martyrs*, which chronicles their deaths, is the earliest surviving document of the Christians in North Africa.

+ ## Historic Sources

The persecution of Christians in France is among the worst on record. The records relate horrific measures taken to persuade Christians to honor the Imperial cult, or to punish them for not doing so. Soon after the events, members of the churches involved widely circulated summaries of these events (martyrologies).

Sanctus [at Lyons, AD 177] also nobly endured all the excessive and super-human tortures which man could possibly devise. For the wicked hoped, because of the continuance and greatness of the tortures, to hear him confess some of the alleged unlawful practices. But he opposed them with such firmness that he did not tell them even his own name, nor that of his nation or city, nor if he were slave or free. In answer to all these questions, he said in Latin, "I am a Christian." . . . But his body bore witness to what had happened. It was all wounds and welts, shrunk and torn up. It had externally lost the human shape. In him Christ suffering worked great wonders, destroying the enemy. He was an example to the others that there is nothing fearful where there is the Father's love, and nothing painful where there is Christ's glory.[36]

The Fifth Persecution—Under Severus (AD 193–211)

Tertullian notes about his period, "Christians were made not born."[37] Although Severus seems appreciative of Christians, scattered regional confrontations in cities led to various martyrdoms. Pope Victor of Rome and Origen's father, Leonidas, were among the casualties. But the account of Perpetua, Felicitas, and their colleagues in Carthage would become one of the most celebrated and well-documented of all martyrdoms. The account likely is from Perpetua's own diary, finished posthumously by eyewitnesses and edited by Tertullian. We will look at it more closely when we discuss the martyrdoms of Perpetua and Felicitas.

The Sixth Persecution—Under Maximinus (AD 235–238)

Many Christians died during the reign of Maximinus, especially in Cappadocia (modern Turkey), where the local leader tried to exterminate all of them. Two Roman bishops were among the martyrs, as were a few senators. The Christian prelate Hippolitus was also a victim. "During this persecution, raised by Maximinus, numberless Christians were slain without trial, and buried indiscriminately in heaps, sometimes fifty or sixty being cast into a pit together, without the least decency."[38]

The Seventh Persecution—Under Decius (AD 249–251)

Many of the previous persecutions reached throughout much of the empire in varying degrees, depending on local magistrates' interests. But Decius ordered an empire-wide persecution—an aggressive attempt to obliterate Christianity. All major centers of Christianity felt the emperor's wrath, including key cities like Ephesus and Jerusalem. Decius had systematized an approach to ensuring loyalty. He required a receipt (*libellus*) proving an individual had offered a sacrifice in a civil-religious service. Decius executed bishop Fabian of Rome, in part for the kind treatment the former emperor, Philip, had shown Fabian. Various other bishops fell victim, either martyred or imprisoned like Dionysius of Alexandria. Origen was among the hundreds of casualties, dying after his release from the injuries he had sustained. Many gory accounts from Crete and Antioch also survive.

The Eighth Persecution—Under Valerian (AD 253–260)

A few years after Decius's passing, Valerian drafted a series of edicts aimed at the leaders of the church. These edicts exiled bishops, forbade all Christian assemblies, and provided for the dismissal of Christian servants from the imperial household and their banishment to work on the imperial estates. The martyrs under Valerian number in the thousands, with huge casualties in Carthage and the rest of North Africa. The prolific bishop Cyprian and many of his students and parishioners died during these attacks. In nearby Utica, the proconsul placed three hundred Christians around a boiling limekiln and ordered them to sacrifice to Jupiter or jump in—they all took the leap. Some accounts from Valerian's persecution have become quite well known—especially that of Rufina and Secunda, two noblewomen from Rome. Their fiancés denied Christ to avoid the emperor's wrath, but these two women stood firm. Another among the many others was Stephen, bishop of Rome, who died with his feet tied to the tail of a bull.[39]

Vintage Foxe

[The eighth persecution] began under Valerian, in the month of April, 257, and continued for three years and six months. The martyrs that fell in this persecution were innumerable, and their tortures and deaths as various and painful. The most eminent martyrs were the following, though neither rank, sex, nor age were regarded.

Rufina and Secunda were two beautiful and accomplished ladies, daughters of Asterius, a gentleman of eminence in Rome. Rufina, the elder, was designed in marriage for Armentarius, a young nobleman; Secunda, the younger, for Verinus, a person of rank and opulence. The suitors, at the time of the persecution's commencing, were both Christians; but when danger appeared, to save their fortunes, they renounced their faith. They took great pains to persuade the ladies to do the same, but, disappointed in their purpose, the lovers were base enough to inform against the ladies, who, being apprehended as Christians, were brought before Junius Donatus, governor of Rome, where, AD 257, they sealed their martyrdom with their blood. . . .

Let us draw near to the fire of martyred Lawrence, that our cold hearts may be warmed thereby. The merciless tyrant, understanding him to be not only a minister of the sacraments, but a distributor also of the Church riches, promised to himself a double prey, by the apprehension of one soul. First, with the rake of avarice to scrape to himself the treasure of poor Christians; then with the fiery fork of tyranny, so to toss and turmoil them, that they should wax weary of their profession. With furious face and cruel countenance, the greedy wolf demanded where this Lawrence had bestowed the substance of the Church: who, craving three days' respite, promised to declare where the treasure might be had. In the meantime, he caused a good number of poor Christians to be congregated. So, when the day of his answer was come, the persecutor strictly charged him to stand to his promise. Then valiant Lawrence, stretching out his arms over the poor, said: "These are the precious treasure of the Church; these are the treasure indeed, in whom the faith of Christ reigneth, in whom Jesus Christ hath His mansion-place. What more precious jewels can Christ have, than those in whom He hath promised to dwell? For so it is written, 'I was an hungered, and ye gave me meat: I was thirsty, and ye gave me drink: I was a stranger, and ye took me in.' And again, 'Inasmuch as ye have done it unto one of the least of these my brethren, ye have done it unto me.' What greater riches can Christ our Master possess, than the poor people in whom He loveth to be seen?"

O, what tongue is able to express the fury and madness of the tyrant's heart! Now he stamped, he stared, he ramped, he fared as one out of his wits: his eyes like fire glowed, his mouth like a boar formed, his teeth like a hellhound grinned. Now, not a reasonable man, but a roaring lion, he might be called.

"Kindle the fire (he cried)—of wood make no spare. Hath this villain deluded the emperor? Away with him, away with him: whip him with scourges, jerk him with rods, buffet him with fists, brain him with clubs. Jesteth the traitor with the emperor? Pinch him with fiery tongs, gird him with burning plates, bring out the strongest chains, and the fire-forks, and the grated bed of iron: on the fire with it; bind the rebel hand and foot; and when the bed is fire-hot, on with him: roast him, broil him, toss him, turn him: on pain of our high displeasure do every man his office, O ye tormentors."

The word was no sooner spoken, but all was done. After many cruel handlings, this meek lamb was laid, I will not say on his fiery bed of iron, but on his soft bed of down. So mightily God wrought with his martyr Lawrence, so miraculously God tempered His element the fire; that it became not a bed of consuming pain, but a pallet of nourishing rest.[40]

The Ninth Persecution—Under Aurelian (AD 270–275)

The persecutions under Aurelian included Alban, possibly the first recorded martyr in Britain. Various martyrs in Rome, France, and other locations appear on the martyrs' lists under Aurelian. However, the death of 6,666 Christian soldiers in the Theban Legion is one of the boldest manifestations of an emperor's hatred of Christians (though the exact number is curious). Eucherius, bishop of Lyon, reported in the early fifth century that at first a tenth of the Christian soldiers were put to death, then a tenth of the remainder who also refused to sacrifice to the Roman gods (which was all of this tenth), and then all of the remainder were put to the sword. The emperor had his own troops slaughter nearly 7,000 of his own men who had served him well.

The Tenth Persecution—Under Diocletian (AD 284-305)

Constantine rose to the sole leadership of the empire a decade too late to save thousands of Christians. Diocletian issued at least four edicts, increasingly severe. In Nicomedia, the eastern capital in the empire (in modern Turkey), his edicts caused the death of 268 Christians. His edicts also called for the destruction of churches and the burning of Scriptures. All the inhabitants in one Phrygian city (western Turkey) were deemed Christians, and imperial soldiers razed the entire town and massacred its inhabitants. Diocletian also ordered the destruction of Christian documents, making the survival of thousands of ancient biblical texts remarkable.

Not lost in the records of Diocletian persecutions is the connection of diverse Christian communities through these events. Summaries of the martyrologies were recorded and shared with other communities. Also, Christians from one area bore witness in another, such as the Egyptians who withstood horrendous torment in Tyre before their deaths.[41]

Vintage Foxe

The Tenth Persecution, under Diocletian . . . was occasioned partly by the increasing number and luxury of the Christians, and the hatred of Galerius, the adopted son of Diocletian, who, being stimulated by his mother, a bigoted pagan, never ceased persuading the emperor to enter upon the persecution, until he had accomplished his purpose. The fatal day fixed upon to commence the bloody work, was the twenty-third of February, AD 303, that being the day in which the Terminalia were cele-brated, and on which, as the cruel pagans boasted, they hoped to put a termination to Christianity. On the appointed day, the persecution began in Nicomedia, on the morning of which the prefect of that city repaired, with a great number of officers and assistants, to the church of the Christians, where, having forced open the doors, they seized upon all the sacred books, and committed them to the flames. The whole of this transaction was in the presence of Diocletian and Galerius, who, not contented with burning the books, had the church levelled with the ground. This was followed by a severe edict, commanding the destruction of all other Christian churches and books; and an order soon succeeded, to render Christians of all denomination outlaws. The publication of this edict occasioned an immediate martyrdom, for a bold Christian not only tore it down from the place to which it was affixed, but execrated the name of the emperor for his injustice. A provocation like this was sufficient to call down pagan vengeance upon his head; he was accordingly seized, severely tortured, and then burned alive. All the Christians were apprehended and imprisoned; and Galerius privately ordered the imperial palace to be set on fire, that the Christians might be charged as the incendiaries, and a plausible pretence given for carrying on the persecution with the greater severities. A general sacrifice was commenced, which occasioned various martyrdoms. No distinction was made of age or sex; the name of Christian was so obnoxious to the pagans that all indiscriminately fell sacrifices to their opinions. Many houses were set on fire, and whole Christian families perished in the flames; and others had stones fastened about their necks, and being tied together were driven into the sea. The persecution became general in all the Roman provinces, but more particularly in the east; and as it lasted ten years, it is impossible to ascertain the numbers martyred, or to enumerate the various modes of martyrdom. Racks, scourges, swords, daggers, crosses, poison, and famine, were made use of in various parts to dispatch the Christians; and invention was exhausted to devise tortures against such as had no crime, but thinking differently from the votaries of superstition. A city of Phrygia, consisting entirely of Christians, was burnt, and all the inhabitants perished in the flames. Tired with slaughter, at length, several governors of provinces represented to the imperial court, the impropriety of such conduct. Hence many were respited from execution, but, though they were not put to death, as much as possible was done to render their lives miserable, many of them having their ears cut off, their noses slit, their right eyes put out, their limbs rendered useless by dreadful dislocations, and their flesh seared in conspicuous places with red-hot irons. It is necessary now to particularize the most conspicious persons who laid down their lives in martyrdom in this bloody persecution.[42]

Julian the Apostate (AD 361–363)

Just when the Christians thought Constantine's reign had put an end to the persecutions, Julian came to the throne. Accenting this surprise, he was Emperor Constantine's nephew. He passed edicts forbidding Christians to serve in various posts, and restoring the pagan temples. But he allowed deposed Christian clerics to return home, including Athanasius to Alexandria (the twentieth bishop of Alexandria, who would be exiled five times during his forty-five-year bishopric). It was a cunning move made not out of kindness, but to sow dissension between various sects.[43]

After stripping the Christian leaders of tax benefits and incomes, and making them repay past benefits, many pagan communities applauded Julian and some turned on the Christians, as seen by the lynching of Bishop George in Alexandria. And in many places riotous fights broke out between the different Christian factions—as Julian had hoped. But Julian failed to realize that he could not force the masses to love paganism. It was dying.

This is what Julian misunderstood. Christianity had taken far too firm a root to be dislodged, and as Gregory pointed out (*Oration*, IV.74), to try to oust them would do nothing less than to destroy the Roman Empire and endanger the commonweal worse than the efforts of the enemy.[44]

One of the best third-party observations of Christianity's spread can be found in Julian's reaction to what he saw in Antioch, written to his high priest:

> The Hellenic religion does not prosper as I desire. Why do we not observe that it is their [Christians'] benevolence to strangers, their care for the graves of the dead and the pretended holiness of their lives that have done most to increase atheism [Christianity]?[45]

Whatever good deeds the Christians were doing out of their beliefs and their own funds, Julian ordered measures to try to replicate them. That is, conscripting public funds to promote pagan charities to upstage the Christians. It didn't work, nor could it—the imperial coffers could not have sustained it. He tried to break the spirit of the Christians, to turn them on each other, and to support their enemies. His last effort was to rebuild the Temple in Jerusalem, which ended when some type of natural disaster occurred (possibly an explosion of trapped gasses).

Julian's disdain for Athanasius prompted him to order the priest persecuted after wealthy citizens in Alexandria began converting to Christianity. The feisty Athanasius, archenemy of the Arians, spent his last few years back in Alexandria, where he died peacefully in AD 366, three years after Julian died by the spear trying to conquer the rest of Mesopotamia.

Voices from the Past

Then [during the Alexandrian persecutions] one really was a believer. . . . Then, too, the faithful were few in numbers but were really faithful, advancing along the straight and narrow path leading to life.[46]

ORIGEN, *Homilies on Jeremiah*, IV.3

DID YOU KNOW? *Reliquary*

The bones of martyrs were so important to the surviving church members that they would often divide the bones and artifacts (anything directly associated with them), taking them to churches across the world. Some saints and their immediate friends, like St. Francis of Assisi, were afraid that their bodies might be divided before they were actually dead. A martyr's remains are "relics" and held in a "reliquary." These were often in the shape of coffins, some of which were glass so pilgrims could see their remains. Countless stories of miracles (involving pilgrims) are associated with these reliquaries—a key criterion for holy sites. Sometimes pilgrims would travel to the site and place their head on the remains, directly if the tomb's contents were accessible. St. Jerome admitted to shuddering in the presence of relics.[47] However, he was not alone, as throngs of citizens ignored pagan shrines and poured out of Rome to visit the local martyria where reliquaries were held.[48] Many of these sites were marked with "*hic*" or "here marks the place."[49]

+
Historic Sources

The following are two quotes from the great theologian Theodoret of Cyrrhus (ca. 420-430), who indefatigably debated pagans and championed the saints' and martyrs' replacement of the impotent pagan gods. His apologetic work, *The Cure of Pagan Maladies or the Truth of the Gospels Proved from Greek Philosophy*,[50] published before AD 423, devotes five of its twelve discourses to defending the veneration of Christian martyrs— whom pagans labelled as "absurd" and "the utmost folly."

THE IMPORTANCE OF MARTYRS TO THE CHURCH

The sun by the action of heat makes wax moist and mud dry, hardening the one while it softens the other, by the same operation producing exactly opposite results; thus, from the long-suffering of God, some derive benefit, and others harm; some are softened, while others are hardened.[51]

No one grave conceals the bodies of each of them [martyrs], but they are shared out among towns and villages, which call them saviours of souls and bodies, and doctors, and honor them as founders and protectors.[52]

Vintage Foxe

Of Benjamin the Deacon thus writeth the said in his fifth book, that after 4 years of his imprisonment, at the request of the Roman Legate he was delivered, who afterward because contrary to the king's commandment he preached and taught the Gospel of Christ, was most miserably excarnificated [flesh removed], having 20 sharp pricks of reeds thrust under his nails, but when he did but laugh at that, then in his priuye yarde had a sharp reed thrust in with horrible pain. After that a certain long stalk ragged and thorny being thrust into his body by the nether part, was forced into him, with the horribleness of the pain whereof, the valiant and invincible soldier of the Lord, gave over his life.[53]

CHAPTER THREE

Martyred Leaders of the Growing Church

Do not fear those who kill the body but cannot kill the soul. Rather fear him who can destroy both soul and body in hell. **MATTHEW 10:28**

Jesus told his disciples, "If anyone would come after me, let him deny himself and take up his cross and follow me. For whoever would save his life will lose it, but whoever loses his life for my sake will find it." **MATTHEW 16:24-25**

The cross is laid on every Christian. The first Christ-suffering which every man must experience is the call to abandon the attachments of this world. It is that dying of the old man which is the result of his encounter with Christ. As we embark upon discipleship, we surrender ourselves to Christ in union with his death—we give over our lives to death. Thus it begins; the cross is not the terrible end to an otherwise God-fearing and happy life, but it meets us at the beginning of our communion with Christ. When Christ calls a man, he bids him come and die. It may be a death like that of the first disciples who had to leave home and work to follow him, or it may be a death like Luther's, who had to leave the monastery and go out into the world. But it is the same death every time—death in Jesus Christ, the death of the old man at his call.[1] DIETRICH BONHOEFFER, *THE COST OF DISCIPLESHIP*

The number of courageous Christians who lost their heads, hearts, or entire bodies to the devil's designees from the apostolic age until the end of the Great Persecutions is dizzying. Of course, such persecution has continued somewhere in the world intermittently until the present age. This chapter looks more closely at heroic stories from the apostolic age through the next few centuries. It's one of five chapters in this section, which ends with the resurgence of persecution during the rise and spread of Islam.

When Christ hung on the cross for us, it was more than an act of love for onlookers (including his enemies), or for the billions of followers who have looked to the cross ever since. His silhouette against the darkening sky was also a reminder of evil's disdain for good. It foreshadowed the evil one's relentless pursuit of Christians until all of Revelation's prophecies come to pass.

We saw in chapter 1 the treatment of Christ's first disciples, an oppression that began in the first century. Tacitus (AD 55–120), a historian and magistrate during Trajan's rule (98–117), reports that Nero had persecuted an "immense multitude" (*multitude ingens*).[2]

As we will also see in chapter 4 with the account of our sisters in Carthage and Lyon, persecutors acquired a taste for Christian blood—and they were overall no respecter of persons, regardless of age, gender, or status. Most of our heroes represented in this section were directly or indirectly tied to the several "great" persecutions of Christians, which we discussed in sequence in chapter 2 to help grasp the overall flow of history. After looking at some Christian heroines in our next chapter, we close this section with the plight of Christ followers under the Persians, and then under the rise of Islam.

One of the issues of the early editions of Foxe's *Actes and Monuments* was the sheer size of the volumes. What began as one short, hefty book would expand into two weighty folio-size volumes with an increasing number of stories. New editions have been developed over five centuries, and unfortunately new martyr stories are as plentiful now as they were during the first few centuries. We will leave space at this book's end to cover the latter, and throughout this work we aim to give but a representation of the great sacrifice of our Christian family throughout the last two thousand years.

Many modern scholars still debate the extent of the early persecutions. Nonetheless, it is clear that Christians were persecuted with varying levels of intensity during the first four centuries. Alvin J. Schmidt highlights these realities in *How Christianity Changed the World*, contrasting the estimates of the eminent Rodney Stark, "who is reportedly a non-Christian," with those of the Christian accounts of Eusebius. "He [Stark] rejects the multiple thousands figure of Eusebius first cited in the fourth century, apparently because Eusebius was a Christian historian." Schmidt then asks if Stark's own religious orientation is a question following this rationale. He concludes, "Many modern scholars lend support to the reports of Eusebius and Tacitus. Even W. H. C. Frend, although hesitant to receive Eusebius's figures without some reservation, says that 'the martyrdoms in Egypt [alone] could easily have run into four figures.'"[3]

Schmidt is in good company, as he is citing two highly respected modern scholars, which shows a bit of the difficulty in covering these early persecutions. But he makes the following astute observation, citing important German scholars Ludwig Hertling and Engelbert Kirschbaum:

> It would be false to judge the terror of the persecutions only by
> the number of those who were executed. When a person escaped
> with his [or her] life, it did not mean that he [or she] suffered
> nothing at all from persecution. Exile, painful tortures, flight,
> confiscation of property or at least business losses, the separation
> of families—something or other of this sort was experienced by
> very many Christians, if not by the majority.[4]

COLLUTHUS One of the more reliable accounts of a martyrdom in Egypt is that of the revered physician Colluthus of Antinoe—a city along the Nile in central Egypt. An amazing Sahidic Coptic text of Luke's Gospel resides in the Robert Van Kampen Collection in Orlando, Florida. Besides being a passage from the "beloved physician" (St. Luke), it has a written reference to Father Colluthus, in the Coptic vernacular, written atop the page. Though faded, it is fully legible using multispectral imaging; it reminds the Coptic community to read this page during the feast day of this physician-saint.

Jennifer Hevelone-Harper, a professor at Gordon College, embraces this martyrology's historical accuracy. "The narrative has several internal ingredients which seem to indicate that the text is an eyewitness account."[5]

This tale of family intrigue and community disarray showcases the bold stand by Father Colluthus, or "Aba Colta" (martyred ca. AD 304). After Colluthus spent three years in prison, a new magistrate brought him before his family. It was a last resort to get the popular physician and leader to offer the token sacrifice to the emperor. Colluthus was asked if he wanted his wife to become a widow and his children fatherless over this seemingly small gesture. But it was not a small gesture for a committed Christian. Two other apostate bishops, Apollonius and Plutarch, had already recanted, earning them the dubious label *lapsi*. But not Colluthus. Much like Polycarp, bishop of Smyrna, Colluthus stated that God had never forsaken him, so how could he forsake God?

Complicating this situation for Colluthus, he had relatives involved in the judiciary process. His brother-in-law, Governor Arianus, considered Colluthus stubborn and inconsiderate of his sister. Against the backdrop of the apostate bishops who did lapse, the ancient text captures Arianus's frustration:

> It is the governor who is pleading with you and advising you! The
> governorship has humbled itself for you. . . . There was a man
> here on a charge of murder. This man wants to live; but as for
> you, Colluthus, something evil possesses you, to make you destroy
> yourself with murderers.[6]

The scene must have been horrific. The governor burnt his sister's husband at the stake while friends and family watched. This further supports the historicity of the account—since many later versions have him beheaded, which leaves bones for relics.

The Fashionable Coptic Cross

Historic ties to Egyptian Christianity; legendary theories about its design concealing a map to the Ark of the Covenant; even a purported mystical link to eternity—the Coptic cross appears in diverse settings in modern culture, whether as jewelry, printed media, or body art. Former US President Barack Obama often carries a Coptic cross among his keepsakes to remind him of certain people he has met.[7] Guitarist Stevie Ray Vaughn, one of the best guitarists of all time, wore one often during the late 1980s until his accidental death in 1990. Keith Richards, founding member of the Rolling Stones, allegedly wears one as well.

By contrast, in Egypt and other Muslim-majority places, wearing a Coptic cross shows one's deep religious commitment. For Copts (Egyptian Christians or those who identify with the Coptic Church headquartered there), the Coptic cross tattooed on their wrist represents their unmistakable commitment to Christ. During various times of radical uprisings in Muslim-controlled regions, the cross's very presence has led to many martyrdoms.[8]

This cross design is almost an overstatement on the liturgical vestments of Coptic priests and monks. Besides the consecrated one they can hold or wear, the bishops' caps ("worn under the hood of the *burnus* [cape]") have crosses embroidered with gold or silver thread. During services, Coptic deacons wear caps with four crosses around the sides and one upright on top. And many of their remaining vestments are replete with crosses, e.g., the epitrachelion (a 6' by 6" rectangular cloth worn mainly down the front), which is worn over the sticharion (a long robe with sleeves, also with crosses). The same may be worn with a separate vestment of additional sleeves, along with the omophorion and orarion, akin to a shawl and a sash. The Coptic priest is the epitome today, as in antiquity, of a cross bearer.[9]

DID YOU KNOW? *Anargyroi–Physicians*

During the era of the Great Persecutions, the Romans executed Christian physicians known for refusin payment—practicing "without silver" (in Greek—*anargyros*, singular). Colluthus was among this number, which had in common three things: They were physicians who (1) practiced gratis, (2) demonstrated Christian beliefs, and (3) were canonized by the church for martrydom.[10] The cult of the anargyroi (plural) developed around these martyrs, with Colluthus's Egyptian shrine serving as the locus of a healing cult for centuries. Some of the earliest martyrdoms among Christian physicians include Ursicinus in Ravenna (ca. AD 67), the Sardinian doctor Antiochus (AD 110), and Alexander of Lyon (AD 177).[11] The two most famous of the anargyroi are Cosmas and Damian of the third century. The martyrdoms of early physicians like Luke and Alexander reverberated throughout the church. Owsei Temkin of Johns Hopkins University, a prominent authority on Christian physicians, concludes that the executions of Alexander and Luke (who are mentioned in Colossians 4:14), "and sundry others after [them] confirms the existence of physicians among the early Christians as well as the acceptance of physicians by the Christian communities."[12]

While all martyrdoms had a sense of both the majestic faith and macabre treatment by tormentors, the torture of Christians at Canopus in Egypt represent some of the cruelest. It's fitting that we know of Canopus today mainly through the Canopus jars found in funeral sites. Cyrus and John were two anargyroi martyred there in AD 303 after the beheading of four women to whom they were ministering.

> In the presence of Athanasia and her daughters [the eldest being fifteen] their sides were burnt with torches and salt and vinegar were poured into their wounds.[13]

Cyril of Alexandria (ca. 438) reflects the popularity of this pair in one of his sermons.[14] He also combated the cult of Isis in Menuthi (Menouthis), Egypt, by moving the relics of Cyrus and John there. The Church renamed the new location Abukir—a derivation of the Greek "Abba Cyrus."[15]

In Antioch in AD 304, Zenobius, a pastor and respected physician, had his sides ripped out with hooks on the dreaded rack. Zenobius "died with great fortitude under the tortures applied to his sides," a method explained in detail in the *Acta Sanctorum*.

Blaise, Diomedes, and Domninus were all physicians executed in the fourth century. We know the most about Blaise, the young bishop from Sebaste, Armenia, from a wealthy family. He suffered in AD 316 under Licinius, and died from flagellation with iron combs. Hagiographic sources note he was then beheaded.[16] Diomedes was arrested and martyred in Nicaea in Bithynia around AD 300. A decade later, officials sentenced Domninus to labor in the mines, and then Maximinus burned him at the stake in Palestine.[17]

The last martyrdom of an anargyros in late antiquity occurred toward the end of the fifth century, considerably after Christianity's legal dominance. Hunneric, king of the Vandal kingdom in North Africa, flayed alive Aemilian in AD 484 during his attacks against the Arians.[18]

ALEXANDER Vivid accounts tell of the especially cruel executions of Christians in the area near Lyon. (See Blandina's story in the next chapter for another such martyrdom.) One to suffer there in AD 177 was the physician Alexander. The connection of this site in the Rhone valley with communities in Asia Minor was strong, and his martyrdom would have been told throughout the churches in Asia Minor.[19] "Between 130 and 180 a succession of teachers, working mainly in Alexandria, dominated Christian intellectual life and spread their influence to Italy and Rome, to Asia Minor, and even among the Christians in the Rhone valley [including Basilides (flourished 130–150), Valentinus (flourished 140–160) and Heracleon (flourished 170–180)]."[20]

Eusebius preserves the story of Alexander the physician's martyrdom, which represents his zealousness during life and his ultimate "glorification" during death.

> While these were being examined, a certain Alexander, a Phrygian
> by birth but a doctor by profession, who had lived in the Gauls
> for many years and was known almost to all for his love of God
> and for his boldness in preaching the Word (for he was not
> without a share of the divine grace of the Apostles), was standing
> by the tribunal and by his expression of face encouraged them to

confession. To those who were standing around the tribunal he appeared as one giving birth. But the mobs were annoyed that those who had earlier denied the faith were now confessing it again, and they cried out against Alexander as the one who was, and when he said that he was a Christian, he [the governor] flew into a rage and condemned him to the wild beasts again. They passed through all the instruments devised for torture in the amphitheatre and endured a heroic contest. Finally they too were offered as sacrifice. Alexander neither groaned nor even uttered the slightest cry, but conversed with God in his heart.[21]

Voices from the Past

As Polycarp was being taken into the arena, a voice came to him from heaven: "Be strong, Polycarp, and play the man!"[22]

The Martyrdom of Polycarp, Second Century AD

MARTYRS IN ANAZARBUS, ASIA MINOR Anazarbus, at the base of the Sis Pass in Cilicia (northeast coastal area of modern Turkey, above Cyprus), played critical roles in the region's military and political history since its founding by the Assyrians. Though it became a Christian stronghold in the fourth century, martyrdoms colored its path.

Emperor Numerian's agents beheaded Thalalaeus in AD 284 in Cilicia. He was the son of a Roman general and a native of Lebanon, and had tried avoiding confrontation in Anazarbus, where he practiced medicine. One Greek account adds that they bound him with rope and tossed him into the sea, but he struggled back to the shore. The exact details of his execution remain unclear. As with Valentine, an early cult developed around cities associated with his last days. Procopius (sixth century) informs us that Justinian restored the monastery of Thalalaeus in Jerusalem during the early sixth century.[23]

In AD 286, two years after the beginning of Diocletian's reign, Domnina died in Anazarbus's prison after numerous beatings ordered by the Roman prefect Lysias. The same fate under Lysias befell Marinus, an elder at Anazarbus. Theodula died in Anazarbus around AD 303, during the first year of the Diocletian persecutions. She was accompanied by three companions we know by name: Boethus, Evagrius, and Makarios (Macarius). Her execution spurred numerous legends, usually beginning with her converting Helladius, who had petitioned the evil prefect, Pelagius, to attempt to convert the "prisoner." After subjecting Theodula to various tortures, Helladius is the one who ended up converted, and then "received the crown of martyrdom when they cut off his head with a sword and threw his body into the sea."[24] Theodula's martyrology also includes an account of her blowing on the statue of Hadrian (serving as an idol), causing it to crumble. The martyrology of the Antiochian Orthodox Christian Archdiocese of North America includes the following account for February 5:

> St. Theodula was thrown into a blazing oven, but remained
> unharmed. After this, she was stretched out on a metal plate
> where boiling tar, wax and oil were poured on her, but the red-hot
> plate shattered into pieces, and the fire scorched many people,
> including Pelagius, who died of fright. However, St. Theodula
> remained unharmed.
>
> Seeing this miracle, many people came to believe in Christ,
> among whom were Macarius and Evagrius. The pagans continued
> to torture the Christians through the heating of an oven. They
> threw Sts. Theodula, Macarius, Evagrius and many others who
> believed in Christ into it. They all suffered martyrdom, and were
> translated into life immortal.[25]

John Chrysostom preached a sermon on Julian of Anazarbus (also known as Julian of Antioch), who suffered a horrendous martyrdom around AD 305 during the Diocletian persecutions. He was of senatorial rank at only eighteen years of age, when they imprisoned him. His tormentors marched him through various cities for around a year before subjecting him to a terror-ridden drowning. After sewing him into a sack with scorpions, vipers, and sand, they threw him into the sea. His mother had followed him from a distance, but was eventually also captured and tortured—after encouraging Julian in his faith. Various accounts emerged about where his body washed ashore, with the common one being in faraway Alexandria.

PANTELEIMON The richly endowed Russian monastery of St. Panteleimon on the iconic Mt. Athos is a testament to one of the most popular of the anargyroi (Christian physicians). Panteleimon (Greek for "the all-compassionate [one]"[26]) served as physician to co-emperor Galerius Maximian at Nicomedia. Jealous court physicians turned on Panteleimon, eventually compelling the emperor to have him tortured and martyred. However, Panteleimon had anticipated this turn of events when the Diocletian persecutions entered Nicomedia. He donated his wealth to poor Christians, which only aggravated his less beneficent medical colleagues.

Multiple attempts were made to kill Panteleimon, Emperor Maximian's physician, after he converted to Christianity. During the Diocletian persecution, Panteleimon's enemies reported him to the emperor, who urged him to renounce his faith. When Panteleimon refused, he was brutally persecuted. He was hung from a tree and scraped with iron hooks, burned, and stretched on a rack. When those tactics failed, his enemies tried to kill him by throwing him into boiling tar and then drowning him. Each time he remained unhurt.

> By order of the emperor they brought the Great Martyr
> Panteleimon to the circus to be devoured by wild beasts.
> The animals, however, came up to him and licked his feet.
> The spectators began to shout, "Great is the God of the
> Christians!"[27]

Next, Panteleimon prayed as he was tied to an olive tree. A soldier attacked him with a sword, which became as soft and harmless as wax. As Panteleimon finished his prayer, bystanders heard a voice from heaven, calling the saint to Christ's heavenly Kingdom.

Hearing the Voice, the soldiers fell down on their knees before the holy martyr and begged forgiveness. They refused to continue with the execution, but St. Panteleimon told them to fulfill the emperor's command, because otherwise they would have no share with him in the future life. The soldiers tearfully took their leave of the saint with a kiss.

When the saint was beheaded, the olive tree to which the saint was tied became covered with fruit. Many who were present at the execution believed in Christ. The saint's body was thrown into a fire, but remained unharmed, and was buried by Christians. St. Panteleimon's servants Laurence, Bassos and Probus witnessed his execution and heard the Voice from Heaven.[28]

IGNATIUS OF ANTIOCH Followers of the Way were first called Christians at Antioch, and Ignatius, one of the city's earliest bishops, introduced a number of other significant firsts. He was the first to use the word "catholic" meaning "universal" church. And he was the first outside the New Testament (on record) to refer to the virgin birth of Christ. Among his lasting contributions to the Church is his support of monepiscopacy (one bishop or leader over a local church—a system that would expand to regions in the fourth century), and he was adamant about the presence of bishops at key church events. We find strong evidence of this in Ignatius's letters, recognizing the role of bishops for various functions. He left seven letters that scholars the ilk of J. B. Lightfoot deem authentic. More than any of the other early Christians, he gives us the "martyr complex"—or what others call the "persecution ethic"—that somehow we should "attain to Christ" this way. In Ignatius's letter to the Romans we find him almost running to martyrdom—seeking it and making it clear he wants them to help him in the process.

I die for Christ of my own choice, unless you hinder me. I beseech you not to show "inopportune kindness" to me. Let me be given to the wild beast, for by their means I can attain to God. I am God's wheat, and I am being ground by the teeth of the beast so that I may appear as pure bread. Rather coax the beasts, that they may become my tomb, and leave no part of my body behind, that I may not be a nuisance to anyone when I have fallen asleep. Then shall I be truly a disciple of Jesus Christ, when the world shall not even see my body.[29]

Scholars like the eminent Edwin Yamauchi note that "for some unknown reason" Ignatius went to Rome during Trajan's reign and was martyred. And he was eager to do so.[30] His life and his death in the early second century (assumed to be caused by wild beasts in the Colosseum) became one of the most heralded martyrdoms in the early church, and Ignatius became one of the first martyrs mentioned by name outside the New Testament. "He was certainly one of the most prominent Christians of the time immediately succeeding the apostles. But Antioch was also home to some religious debates, and while Ignatius denounced division as 'the beginning of evil,' the bishop engaged in debate with tenacity."[31] We find that energy in his letters. Ignatius writes:

From Syria unto Rome I am fighting with wild beasts by land and sea, by night and day, bound to ten leopards, that is, a bunch of soldiers, whose usage grows still harsher when they are liberally treated. Yet through their unjust doings I am more truly learning discipleship. Yet am I not hereby justified. May I have Joy of the beasts that are prepared for me. I pray too that they may prove prompt with me. I will even entice them to devour me promptly, and not to refrain, as they have refrained from some, through fear. And even though they are not willing without constraint, I will force them. Pardon me. I know what is expedient for me. Now I am beginning to be a disciple. May naught of things visible or invisible seek to allure me, that I may attain unto Jesus Christ. Let there come on me fire and cross and conflicts with wild beasts, wrenching of bones, mangling of limbs, crushing of the whole body, grievous torments of the devil may I but attain to Jesus Christ.[32]

Christians throughout the ages have been fascinated with the legacy of the saints, and nothing was more precious to millions of pilgrims than martyrs' bones, or any physical remains. We saw this in our discussion of reliquaries—coffins or special containers sometimes discovered and/or moved centuries after the saints' actual deaths. Many small churches, or martyria (plural for *martyrium*), were built over the sites of the saints' remains, sometimes with sunken floors to allow pilgrims a place to worship closer to the actual relics. Many of the earlier martyria had a *fenestella,* a passageway from the altar to the actual tomb.

A comparable contemporary expression of this longing to be close to sacred history occurs in Jerusalem's Temple Mount tunnels. Near Warren's Gate, about 150 feet in, a Plexiglas window allows a limited view of Herodian stones where crowds of women gather to pray. For non-Muslims, this is the closest accessible spot to the traditional site of the original Holy of Holies beneath the Dome of the Rock.

As with the crowded site in the Jerusalem tunnels, one of the difficulties with the early martyria was their inaccessibility. Many relics were eventually *translated* or officially transported from remote locations, often to a church in a larger city, and reinterred. The first such translation occurred in AD 354, involving the remains of Babylas, who was Patriarch of Antioch until his death in AD 253. He died imprisoned during the Decian persecutions, heralded by his followers for refusing a pagan emperor special entrance into his cathedral.

A martyrium became not only a place built over relics, but a term for a recognizable church architectural style, with or without a saint's remains. It involves a central plan, often in the shape of a cruciform and/or an octagonal room supporting a dome. The pronounced martyrium style is perhaps most closely associated with Constantine's original structure of the Church of the Holy Sepulchre in Jerusalem (what the Orthodox Church calls the Church of the Anastasis—Greek for *resurrection*). Constantine consecrated it in AD 335, and eventually an edicule (a word derived from the Latin for *small temple*) was built over the alleged site of Christ's burial.

Among the more entrancing of the martyria is that of the Catacomb of Callixtus (named for Pope Callixtus, AD 217–222) on the Appian Way near Rome. This burial ground, known simply as the Cemetery, is likely the first church-owned land. At one point, it contained the remains of several popes from the second to the fourth centuries. All of the relics were translated to churches by the ninth century, and the martyrium faded into obscurity, only rediscovered in the nineteenth century.

ORIGEN Origen, like many great Christian leaders, had an amazingly long life of service. Before his long stay in Caesarea and eventual death from the tortures enacted during the reign of Maximinus, he avoided constant threats of persecution in Alexandria. He became popular as a teacher of basic education, both because he was brilliant and because the other teachers had fled from fear of persecution.[33] Barely escaping lynching, like Polycarp, he moved from house to house. In his case, however, groups of students kept following him. At one point soldiers were posted around his house trying to catch him.

He became ascetic, taking literally biblical passages about not having two coats or wearing shoes (Matthew 6:34 and 10:10). He fasted and often refused food. During this time, several of his students were caught and martyred, six men by the axe or sword: Plutarch, Heraclides, Hero, two named Severus, and Basilides (the guard who led Potamiana to execution). Also "of the women" (implying others) was Herais who received "the baptism of fire" (recorded by Origen, reflecting on her status of still being under instruction and yet to receive Christian baptism with water). In this context, Origen continued his asceticism, limiting his sleep and not using a bed. "He displayed an enthusiasm beyond his years (around seventeen), and patiently enduring cold and nakedness, went to the furthest limit of poverty. . . ." His friends couldn't persuade him otherwise, "so that he ran the risk of upsetting and even ruining his own constitution."[34] In one account (which some consider a fabrication by a jealous bishop), he even took literally Matthew 19:12 and castrated himself to keep from lusting.[35]

Origen would move to another early center of church influence, Caesarea Maritima. Among his many writings was the first systematic

Christian theology, *On First Principles*. He also wrote the important *Hexapla*, an edition of the Bible in one Hebrew column and five Greek columns which compared these versions of Scriptures. With the help of seven secretaries, he became a writing machine, which prompted Jerome a century later to ask, "Has anyone read everything that Origen wrote?" Origen would thrive until AD 250, when Emperor Decius had him imprisoned and tortured. Though he outlived the evil emperor, he died from this treatment in 254.

Voices from the Past

Sometimes ten or more, sometimes over twenty were put to death, at other times at least thirty, and at yet others not far short of sixty; and there were occasions when on a single day a hundred men as well as women and little children were killed.

EUSEBIUS, *HE* II

Vintage Foxe

In Egypt and Lybia, thirty bishops were martyred, and many other Christians cruelly tormented; and, AD 386, George, the Arian bishop of Alexandria, under the authority of the emperor, began a persecution in that city and its environs, and carried it on with the most infernal severity. He was assisted in his diabolical malice by Catophonius, governor of Egypt; Sebastian, general of the Egyptian forces; Faustinus the treasurer; and Herachus, a Roman officer.

The persecution now raged in such a manner, that the clergy were driven from Alexandria, their churches were shut, and the severities practiced by the Arian heretics were as great as those that had been practiced by the pagan idolaters. If a man, accused of being a Christian, made his escape, then his whole family were massacred, and his effects confiscated.[36]

Voices from the Past

*I fell in love with the prophets and these men who had loved Christ;
I reflected on all their words and found that this philosophy alone was
true and profitable.*[37]

JUSTIN MARTYR, second century

No one who is rightly minded turns from true belief to false.[38]

JUSTIN MARTYR, response to the prefect before his execution, AD 165

DID YOU KNOW? *Beheading over Burning*

There is a reason many of the edited accounts of martyrs include
beheading. A burned martyr leaves few if any relics for the cult of the
saints. First, many martyrs did die by the sword or axe. Eusebius reports
of a gory massacre in Thebais, that they massacred so many Christians
that they dulled their "murderous axe" and "the executioners themselves
grew utterly weary and took turns to succeed one another." In other
cases, especially with high-profile Christians, the temptation to endorse
stories of discovered relics was immense. The common ending of the
story became beheading even though earlier versions included burning (though as we shall see with Polycarp, not all burning destroyed
the bones).

The veneration of relics prompted the building of thousands of
shrines throughout Christendom. Since the presence of the saints
(Latin, *praesentia*) was thought to exist with any official relic, the "joy
of proximity" could be claimed simultaneously by hundreds of communities for the same martyr. Millions of pilgrims from the early Church
to the present have believed such holy bones have power. "The fullness
of the invisible person could be present at a mere fragment of his physical remains and even at objects. . . . As a result, the Christian world
came to be covered with tiny fragments of original relics and with
'contact relics.'"[39]

This "contact relic" phenomenon turned the spatial world of the saints into a network of holy places. For example, in Egypt at Menouthis, Antinoe, and Cyrrhus, the bones of the martyrs were present. For the Christians who knew well the local history, the proximity to their saints was close. Soon, hundreds of shrines with mere relics of contact claimed a *praesentia* of a saint. The mid-second-century eyewitness account of Polycarp's martyrdom implies the early emphasis on relics and the desire to enjoy immediate proximity to the saint:

> When therefore the centurion saw the contentiousness . . . , he put the body in the midst, as was their custom, and burnt it. Thus we, at last, took up his bones, more precious than stones, and finer than gold, and put them where it was meet. There the Lord will permit us to come together according to our power in gladness and joy, and celebrate the birthday of his martyrdom, both in memory of those who have already contested, and for the practice and training of those whose fate it shall be.[40]

✚ Historic Sources

Following is an excerpt from the early fifth-century sermon of Bishop Maximus of Turin. Over time, the veneration of saints gained spiritual, historical, and financial significance. What began as a genuine admiration for those who paid the ultimate sacrifice eventually became not only the pride of a church or a city, but part of a large and prosperous pilgrimage network.

Though we should celebrate, brothers, the anniversaries of all the martyrs with great devotion, yet we are to put our whole veneration into observing the festivals especially of those who poured out their blood in our own hometown. Though all the saints are everywhere present and aid everyone, those who suffered for us intervene for us especially, for when a martyr suffers, he suffers not only for himself, but for the fellow citizens. . . . So all the martyrs should be most devoutly honored, yet especially those whose relics we possess here. For the former assist us with their prayer, but the latter also with their suffering. With these we have a sort of familiarity: they are always with us, they live among us.[41]

Vintage Foxe

This section from the 1570 version of *Actes and Monuments* shows the determinations of the Christians who survived the horrendous torture of the Lyon persecutions not to be called martyrs—but to relegate that title only to those who died.

Thus have ye heard the whole discourse of Justinus, and of the blessed saints of France, Vetius, Zacharias, Sanctus, Maturus, Attalus, Blandina, Alexander, Alcibiades, with other, recorded and set forth by the writing of certain Christian brethren of the same church and place of France. In the which aforesaid writing of theirs moreover appeareth the great meekness & modest constancy of the said Martyrs described in these words: such followers were they of Christ, who when he was in the form of God, thought it no robbery, to be equal with God, being in the same glory with him, that they not once nor twice, but oft times suffering Martyrdom, and taken again from the beasts, and bearing wounds, tearings and scars in their bodies, yet neither would count themselves Martyrs, neither would suffer us so to call them: but if any of us either by word or letter, would call them Martyrdom, they did vehemently rebuke them: saying that the name of Martyrdom was to be given to Christ, the faithful and true Martyr, the firstborn of the dead, and the captaine of life, testifying moreover that Martyrdom belongeth to such, who by their martyrdom were already passed out of this life, and whom as Christ by their worthy confession hath received unto himself, and hath sealed up their martyrdom by their end finished: As for them, which were not yet consummated, they (said they) were not worthy the names of martyrs, but only were humble and worthy confessors, desiring also their brethren with tears, to pray without ceasing for their confirmation. Thus they performing in deed that which belonged to true martyrs, in resisting the heathen with much liberty, and great patience, without all fear of man, being replenished with the fear of God, refused to be named of their brethren for martyrs.[42]

CHAPTER FOUR

Women Martyrs in the Early Church

Who knows whether you have not come to the kingdom for such
a time as this? ESTHER 4:14

There is neither Jew nor Greek, there is neither slave nor free,
there is no male and female, for you are all one in Christ Jesus.
GALATIANS 3:28

Is the distinction between living for Christ and dying for Him, after
all, so great? Is not the second the logical conclusion of the first?
ELISABETH ELLIOT, *SHADOW OF THE ALMIGHTY*

Christianity brought an explosive message of hope and eternal salvation,
and while it might surprise some, it also brought a positive new reality for
women's roles and their treatment in Christian societies. This consequence
of Christ's powerful, countercultural message underpinned an amazing and
passionate commitment to him by women in the early church. Their historic testimonies have motivated millions, spawned legendary tales, and
still influence the naming of Christian children.

Christ modeled a heightened appreciation for women and care for the disenfranchised.[1] "The world Jesus entered largely discriminated against women" (John 4:27), which he challenged directly by his teaching and actions.[2] The Gospels record many cases of Jesus addressing them in public, like the woman at the well in Sychar, the widow of Nain, the woman with the bleeding disorder, the woman crippled for eighteen years, and the group of women following him en route to Golgotha. It is here we find the backdrop of the courage of women martyrs and his foreknowledge of their trials. Jesus observed that his current and future oppressors, indicative of all who reject his message, "will begin to say to the mountains, 'Fall on us,' and to the hills, 'Cover us.' For if they do these things when the wood is green, what will happen when it is dry?" (Luke 23:30-31). In contrast to his critics (who were unaware of the Temple's coming destruction in AD 70), history records a host of heroic women in the worst times of persecutions who not only proclaimed his name, but carried his cross—many unto death.[3]

Christ also treated women with respect, which included holding them accountable for sins just as he did all people.[4] "He rejected the false criteria upon which the double standard was built. He measured men and women by the same standards, the inner qualities of character and not by such accidents of birth as ethnic or sexual differences. He affirmed women by His manner, example, and teaching."[5] Women were the first to Jesus' tomb, and often the first and most aggressive in serving throughout history.

The very testimony and veneration of women in the New Testament enhances its believability and historical veracity—a forger would never have cast such a countercultural dynamic. "Deaconesses (female deacons) such as Phoebe (Rom. 16:1; 1 Tim. 3:11) played a vital role in the early church. They assisted at baptism of women and ministered to women who were sick. . . . Origen stated that in his day the 'order of widows' was considered an ecclesiastical rank. They nursed the sick and evangelized pagan women."[6]

As we saw in chapter 2 in the letter from Pliny the Younger to Emperor Trajan (ca. AD 111), the ranks of Christians had grown to the point where the church could no longer be ignored. Its countercultural approach even made it difficult for Pliny to interpret its activities through his explicitly Roman lens. For instance, his passing reference in that letter to "two female slaves who were called deaconesses" speaks volumes into our understanding of the implementation of Christ's teachings as they related to the disenfranchised of all types. It also tells us that many unidentified women of various ranks claimed Christ—a commitment which cost some of them their lives.

We will look at both the unnamed and named among the women martyrs, worthy subjects of any book of saints.

CATHERINE OF ALEXANDRIA The shield at St. Catherine's College in Oxford, England, sports four "breaking wheels" associated with the fourth-century torture of Catherine of Alexandria. This macabre wheel became known as Catherine's wheel and is perhaps a precursor to a gymnast's "cartwheel" (lateral somersault) because of the turning motion of its victims. Strangely, one of the world's top academic institutions is named for one of the most famous of all martyrs, a woman no less in a male-dominated world, and an elusive figure among ancient sources.[7]

Some Christian heroes' courage generated volumes of books and stories and left a string of monuments and dedicated buildings in their wake. Martyrs like Catherine of Alexandria grew so popular that it is now difficult to separate history from what scholars call hagiographic license (that is, embellishment). However, Catherine's heroism has common threads that point back to true historical events: her exceptional intelligence, rare physical beauty, brazen courage, and impenetrable faith. After surviving torture and scourging, outwitting scholars and philosophers, and the miraculous destruction of her torture contraption, her memory lives on. She is most literally an icon. Although none of her contemporaries recorded her life, plenty of others kept her testimony alive. Everything we know of her comes through tradition, or *traditio*, the passing down of the best things from the past.[8]

After considerable torture, trials, and tests, she was martyred in Alexandria (AD 305), around the beginning of Maxentius's rule as emperor. As a native of Alexandria born into a wealthy family around 287, she received a stellar education and demonstrated a remarkable intellect. Various later accounts note that she was stunningly beautiful and simply brilliant—finishing school as a teenager.

Two episodes in her life bring to mind the biblical Esther, as well as Monica, Augustine's mother (d. 387). Like Monica, who was also from North Africa in an era with high emphasis on dreams,[9] Catherine had a life-changing vision of Mary and infant Jesus. She was fourteen and became a Christian through this event. Like Esther, at around age eighteen she sought an audience with her monarch, personally confronting Maxentius about his treatment of Christians.

Her intelligence intrigued Maxentius, and he called fifty orators, whom she out debated—and some of the pagans even converted. Maxentius tried to marry her, but she informed him of her marriage to Christ and consecration to him as a virgin. Those she converted were tortured and executed, and she was imprisoned and scourged—but would not recant. After a couple of hundred visitors, many of whom were converted and then executed, Maxentius ordered her to be tortured on the infamous spiked wheel. Like crucifixion, it was reserved for the worst of criminals; people's limbs were strung through the spokes and smashed with large tools. It is a brutal testimony to human depravity and reprobate minds. However, through a miracle it crumbled in her presence (and thus became known as the Catherine wheel). Afterward, the befuddled emperor simply had her beheaded.

She remains one of the most popular Christian martyrs, especially among "the Fourteen Holy Helpers" (a group of Roman Catholic saints venerated for their power of intercession). She is the patron of philosophers and scholars and is believed to help protect against sudden death.[10] She "inspired generations of philosophers, consecrated women, and martyrs."[11] In 1911, the Archbishop of Baltimore commented on these saints and the Roman Martyrology: "The Saints are not merely heroes; they are models."[12] What we know and celebrate about Catherine, historical or otherwise, certainly manifests both roles.

The Popularity of the Name Catherine

Many leaders and celebrities carry the name Catherine or Katherine, from the Greek cognate *katharos*, meaning "pure." For starters, Henry VIII had three wives named Catherine, and Princess Catherine (Kate) Middleton, married to Prince William, continues this royal trend. The name's most popular year for new babies in America was 1917.[13] Perhaps a sign of the times in American culture is that in 2019, Catherine and Katherine ranked as the 243rd and 120th most popular names among girls, but Delilah (the Philistine who betrayed Samson) came in at 88th.[14] In the Christian tradition, the name Catherine traces to Catherine of Alexandria and other early saints.

DID YOU KNOW? *St. Catherine's Monastery*

Tradition holds that upon Catherine's martyrdom, angels took her body to the holy mountain of Sinai. At 8,500 feet above sea level, this tallest mountain in the Sinai Peninsula—later renamed Mount Catherine—is commonly associated with the site of Moses receiving the Ten Commandments, though the other leading contender is the adjacent Jebul Musa. Round stone structures in the area, *nuwamis*, are traditionally associated by local Bedouins with the children of Israel, attested by an entry by the pilgrim Etheria in her diary (fourth or fifth century AD). Hermits had frequented the area during second- and third-century persecutions. Constantine's mother, Helena, visited the mountain in AD 327 and dedicated the Church of the Burning Bush (later named St. Catherine's Chapel) to commemorate Moses' meeting with God. Emperor Justinian built the monastery around this chapel in the sixth century.

Around AD 800, monks claimed to find Catherine's bones and interred them in the basilica. The sensational report of holding St. Catherine's remains forever changed the site's name. The Cathedral of Transfiguration's name changed to St. Catherine, along with that of the monastery itself. Since then her name has been inextricably linked to the area—the town, mountain, and one of the oldest serving monasteries in the world.

Legendary accounts of scholar and Bible treasure hunter Constantin von Tischendorf (d. 1874) romanticized the field of biblical antiquities and the mysterious hidden treasures at St. Catherine's. One of the world's oldest libraries, found at Sinai, bears Catherine's name as well, as that is where Tischendorf brought to the world's attention the oldest most complete copy of the Christian Bible, dating to the early fourth century. The "Sisters of Sinai" (identical Scottish twins, both widowed after three years and both polyglots) rediscovered the Syriac Sinaiticus,[15] a palimpsest (reused vellum) with the top text "a racy collection of the lives of female saints," but the under text (the original text) a fourth-century Syriac copy of the Gospels (preserving a late second-century tradition).[16] The sisters also helped discover Codex Climaci Rescriptus, one of the best early copies of the New Testament in Palestinian Christian Aramaic.[17] It now resides in the Museum of the Bible in Washington, DC, though a few of its leaves were recently discovered at St. Catherine's Monastery.[18] The Library of Congress has a list of 3,300 of the monastery's manuscripts and photographed copies of 1,687 of them.[19]

THE WIFE OF PETER Clement of Alexandria (d. AD 215) informs us of the martyrdom of Peter's wife, a person indicated in Scripture only by the mention of Peter's mother-in-law in Mark 1:29-31. Clement comments: "They say, accordingly, that the blessed Peter, on seeing his wife led to death, rejoiced on account of her call and conveyance home, and called very encouragingly and comfortingly, addressing her by name, 'Remember thou the Lord.' Such was the marriage of the blessed, and their perfect disposition toward those dearest to them."[20]

Like millions of Christian martyrs through the centuries, many of the early women are known only by their context or association, but their names are written in the Book of Life.

THE ANONYMOUS DEACONESSES Various extrabiblical sources corroborate the effect of Christ's message to women. One of the most cited of early sources is that of Pliny the Younger to Emperor Trajan around AD 111. In a passage from this letter (in the "Voices from the Past" feature on pages 86–87), we find that not only did Pliny torture two deaconesses, but that the women were slaves—both evidence of the inclusive nature of Jesus' message.

We can assume these deaconesses were put to death based on Pliny's own account of treating those confessing Christ. Some of the earliest known women martyrs, like Peter's wife, remain unnamed, but their testimonies speak to us two thousand years later. In this case, it is not difficult to read between the lines to know the fate of these deaconesses and many others under Pliny's watch.

EUPHEMIA The great Council of Chalcedon of AD 451, in modern Turkey, was the largest of the early church councils, and it took place in the basilica built on the traditional site of Euphemia's martyrdom. The 520 bishops (or their designees) met at the very location where the Romans burnt her alive "after her teeth were knocked out with a hammer."[21] It allegedly took place in the first year of the Great Persecution that Emperor Diocletian ordered in AD 303. The persecutions lasted for a decade in some parts of the empire, ravaging Christian communities, especially in the East.

Diocletian's talons struck hard in Chalcedon, just across the Bosporus from Byzantium—ironically, the future center of Christianity in Constantinople (modern Istanbul). Whereas Marcus Aurelius considered the Christians worthless fools, Diocletian saw them as legitimate threats to the empire. After all, he had already been oppressing the Christians. He also had endured the arduous task of visiting the oracle (priestess) of Apollo on the remote cliffs at Delphi near the Gulf of Corinth on Mt. Parnassus. The Pythia, or priestess, confirmed his suspicions about Christians.

Euphemia was one of fifty Christians rounded up at the beginning of these attacks. Though no contemporary accounts remain, eighty years later the travelogue of Egeria references a visit to the site of Euphemia's martyrdom. The *Martyrologium Hieronymianum* (*Martyrology of Jerome*) from the early fifth century also includes it, and numerous accounts centuries later recount the discovery of her relics, later discarded by Muslim invaders into the bay in a stone sarcophagus, their eventual recovery, and then their dissemination to various holy sites around the world.

FIVE SCILLITAN MARTYRS In AD 180, there were five women among the twelve martyrs in Scillium, Numidia, a region that included parts of modern Libya, Tunisia, and Algeria, where, sadly, the execution of Christians extends to recent history. As in so many cases of injustice, the Roman officials considered Christians deranged. "Saturninus the governor said: 'You can have mercy from our lord the emperor, if you return to your senses.'"[22] Two references in the account (officially called *The Acts of the Scillitan Martyrs*, the oldest Christian document in North African history[23]) reveal familiarity with New Testament books. One is a comment that reflects 1 Timothy 6:16. The other refers to the presence of other New Testament texts. "Saturninus the governor said: 'What sort of things do you have in that case of yours?' Speratus said: 'Books and letters of Paul, a righteous man.'" After heated exchanges with the Christians, Saturninus said, "Stop being part of this madness!" He offered them thirty days to think through their initial refusal to sacrifice to the imperial cult. They responded with certainty of their faith. Finally, he threw up his hands.

> Saturninus the governor read aloud the sentence from a tablet [referring to a wax tablet, a detail that further corroborates the story]: "Concerning Speratus, Nartzalus, Cittinus, Donata, Vestia, Secunda and the others who have confessed that they live according to the Christian religion: because in spite of the opportunity given to them to return to the Roman way of life, they have stubbornly persisted in maintaining theirs, I have decided that they be put to the sword."
> Speratus said: "We offer thanks to God."
> Nartzalus said: "Today we are martyrs in heaven. Thanks to God."

After the record of their sentence to be executed, the text ends: "All [Christians] said: 'Thanks to God.' And immediately they were decapitated for the name of Christ."[24]

PERPETUA AND FELICITAS The world's ear leaned toward Carthage after countless references to Perpetua's martyrdom. Even the esteemed Augustine of Hippo in North Africa cites her. Carthage was the place of her birth and heroic death in its arena (AD 203). Perpetua's diary was likely preserved through Tertullian, her Carthaginian contemporary. It is a detailed firsthand account from her imprisonment and torture until shortly before her death—then finished by a contemporary editor. It is one of the earliest surviving texts from a Christian woman—and of a Christian martyrdom.

She was joined by Felicitas, her slave and co-martyr, and their companions.[25] All were catechumens, or new Christians taking classes and likely yet to be baptized. There were three men and two women in all, and Perpetua had a newborn son still nursing. Felicitas was well along in her pregnancy. It was indeed a pitiful yet somehow glorious sight. Felicitas rejoiced at delivering her daughter shortly before the day of her execution, which allowed her to go to "her victory" with her Christian friends. Otherwise, she would have gone later with strangers and violent criminals.

Perhaps Perpetua's wealthy upbringing and special treatment during the early part of her ordeal afforded her the chance to record her last days up to her final summons, with another writer adding her eulogy. Saturus adds to her words with his firsthand account, and of his own visions (before his death). It ends with an edited finale.[26] The account shows the logistics and human emotions of dealing with a newborn under duress, the darkness of a dungeon, Felicitas's travails of childbirth while remaining fully aware of her imminent death, the roughness of soldiers, and the efforts of people to prevent a noblewoman like Perpetua (and her friends) from what they believed was a senseless death. After all, they reasoned, she could save her life and her son's, and the anguish of her husband and family—let alone the embarrassment—merely by offering incense to the emperor or the imperial cult.

William Shakespeare's "A rose by any other name . . ." is but a romantic echo of Perpetua's statement to her father, after he begged her to renounce Christ for her freedom from prison.

"Father do you see this vase here? Could it be called by any other name than what it is?"

"No," he replied.

"Well, neither can I be called anything other than what I am, a Christian."[27]

Her detailed account captures not only her own journey, but also a rare look into a martyr's family. Her father endured a beating with a rod for interrupting her trial—bringing her son to the judge while pleading for her to recant. Near her final day, he plucked out part of his beard and continued to wail. We see in this vivid account both the determination of one deeply in love with Christ, and the depths of brokenhearted sadness.

Before she turns over the account to Saturus, she ends with the conclusion of a vision about her upcoming fight against the beasts in the arena—at an event, of all things, to celebrate the emperor's birthday. She concludes: "And I awoke; and I understood that I should fight, not with beasts but against the devil; but I knew that mine was the victory."[28] She shared her last meal (granted as a Roman custom before execution) with her Christian colleagues as an *agape* (love) feast, their form of communion.

The editor gives us a poetic account of Felicitas's death, her translation from this world to the next (Tertullian is a leading candidate for the editor, built upon an eyewitness account). She was elated to have delivered a child in safety and gave the newborn to her sister to rear. She entered the arena with joy "that she might fight with the beasts, came now from blood to blood, from the midwife to the gladiator, to wash after her travail in a second baptism."[29]

During Perpetua's final hour, she refused further insult and did not wear the robe of a pagan priestess of Ceres. She also began singing praises to God, to inspire her colleagues as the gladiators began to scourge and mutilate them. The Christians gave themselves to as many beasts as possible, enduring leopard, bear, and boar. The account describes a raised bridge in the arena to which they tied martyrs like bait. One of the boars actually turned on the gladiator.

A crazed bull, which the writer says was raised by the devil himself for just this occasion, then attacked Perpetua and Felicitas. At first, the soldiers had forced the women to strip and then to wear nets, but the sight of new mothers was so indecent that it was even off-putting to this bloodthirsty crowd. After the women switched to robes, the raging bull attacked and gored them. We catch another glimpse of Perpetua's fortitude, pinning up her hair in the midst of the frenzy. To leave her hair down would indicate mourning, whereas this was her moment of triumph and victory.

Tertullian cites her diary elsewhere, "She was tossed, and fell on her loins; and when she saw her tunic torn from her side, she drew it over her as a veil for her middle, rather mindful of her modesty than her suffering. Then she was called for again, and bound up her disheveled hair; for it was not becoming for a martyr to suffer with disheveled hair, lest she should appear to be mourning in her glory."[30] She then tended to Felicitas, raising her to her feet to face the bull anew with dignity—and covering her own hip exposed through her ripped robe. Her decency trumped her torment.

In the end, the gladiators ensured their deaths with the sword. Perpetua's executioner was a novice, and his first thrust between her bones wrought pain but not death. She exposed her neck to assist in her final moment in the flesh. The noblewoman died nobly at age twenty-two, but her story, detailed by eyewitnesses, lives with us till today.

BLANDINA The image is horrifying. A frenzied crowd in a massive arena in Lyon cheered as a woman was fried in a heated iron chair. As if that was not enough, exhausted from trying to torture her to death, the soldiers dropped her into a basket and then threw her to a wild bull to gore and trample her. Such was the bloody yet glorious fate of Blandina, the slave girl who died one of the most vividly recorded martyrdoms in history. She died along with the host of venerated martyrs of Lyon in AD 177. Today, visitors to the remains of the expansive *Amphithéâtre des Trois Gaules* (the historic arena) see a pole erected in her honor.

Blandina was initially affixed to a pole as food for wild beasts. However, according to tradition, none touched her—to the disappointment of onlookers.[31] Her presence, appearing with her outstretched arms as if being crucified, inspired the others being tortured in front of her. Some were mangled beyond recognition. Others were swollen. Most were scourged. Christians with Roman citizenship were spared these tortures and simply beheaded.

Attempting to persuade Blandina to renounce her faith after she survived the pole, her persecutors brought her into the arena to watch the carnage for successive days, then like Samson at the Philistine temple, brought her out as the highlight of the ceremonies—to conclude their grisly festivities. They ushered her into the arena with a fifteen-year-old Christian, Ponticus. She encouraged him in his bravery as he endured his torture before the deranged crowd. After they both again rejected the idols and stood firm in their faith, the ancient source informs us "the mob was infuriated with them, so that the boy's tender age called forth no pity and the woman no respect."[32]

The emperor Marcus Aurelius (emperor AD 161–180) was especially bent on making spectacles of the Christians. Ironically, writers from Machiavelli to Edward Gibbon call him one of the "Five Good Emperors," all adopted sons and all less tyrannical than other emperors. This puts the intense persecution of the Lyon Christians even more in perspective; it is among the worst on record for the early church. Like so many others, it was timed with special festivities, and drawn out over several days. We know of these events through a letter sent from the church of Lyon to the churches of Asia Minor, and fortunately recorded by Eusebius in his *Ecclesiastical History*, written early in the fourth century.

Eusebius records in the letter, "After the whips, after the beasts, after the griddle, she was finally dropped in a basket and thrown to a bull. Time after time the animal tossed her, but she was indifferent now to all that happened to her, because of her hope and sure hold on all that her faith meant, and of her communing with Christ. Then she, too, was sacrificed, while the heathen themselves admitted that never yet had they known a woman suffer so much or so long."

She entered that special place of veneration for saints, much like Perpetua and Felicitas. Today, western Christians may find it difficult to imagine the singular treatment of any one of these glorious martyrs. Perhaps the closest we come in modern society are images of the twenty-one Egyptian Copts in their orange suits whom ISIS beheaded on the Libyan beach in 2015. We also hear regular news of horrors, gruesome murders and torture, and the seemingly insatiable desire for blood sports and violent movies. Any and all of these remind us that humankind is still capable of exacting the worst offenses on the pure and innocent.

Tertullian, a contemporary in Carthage of many of these martyrs, addresses this very subject. Though he writes from Northern Africa instead of France, his words describe well Blandina's hope in her final hours.

> The world has the greater darkness, blinding men's hearts. The world imposes the more grievous fetters, binding men's very souls. The world breathes out the worst impurities—human lusts. The world contains the larger number of criminals, even the whole human race. Then, last of all, it awaits the judgment, not of the proconsul, but of God. Wherefore, O blessed, you may regard yourselves as having been translated from a prison to, we may say, a place of safety. It is full of darkness, but ye yourselves are light; it has bonds, but God has made you free. Unpleasant exhalations are there, but ye are an odour of sweetness.[33]

By the power of the written word—both through the anonymous editor, inclusion in Tertullian's writings, and Eusebius's choice of sources from among many—we have the following description of the context of the Lyon martyrdom after Blandina's ultimate sacrifice:

> Not even this was enough to satisfy their insane cruelty to God's people. Goaded by a wild beast, wild and barbarian tribes were incapable of stopping, and the dead bodies became the next object of their vindictiveness. Their defeat did not humble them, because they were without human understanding; rather it inflamed their bestial fury, and governor and people vented on us the same inexcusable hatred, so fulfilling the Scripture: "Let the wicked man be wicked still, the righteous man righteous still." Those who had been suffocated in gaol [dungeon] they threw to the dogs, watching carefully night and day to see that no one received the last offices at our hands. Then they threw out the remains left by the beast in the fire, some torn to ribbons, some burnt to

cinders, and set a military guard to watch for days on end of the trunks and severed heads of the rest, denying burial to them also. Some raged and ground their teeth at them, longing to take some further revenge on them; others laughed and jeered, magnifying their idols and giving them credit for the punishment of their enemies; while some who are more reasonable, and seemed to have a little human feeling, exclaimed with the utmost scorn: "Where is there a God? And what did they get for their religion, which they preferred to their own lives?"[34]

After exposing their bodies for six more days they burnt them to ashes. Then, in their attempt to prevent any resurrection, "swept them" into the nearby Rhone River. Today, we know little if anything about some of their tormentors' carved idols—other than happenstance discoveries through archaeology. Conversely, according to reports from the Pew Research Center and the scholarship at Gordon-Conwell Theological Seminary, Christianity is the only religion with a major presence on every continent. It appears the martyrs' ashes flowed far from Lyon and past Orange, Avignon, Arles, and even beyond the Mediterranean.

EULALIA The killers of Christians cast such a wide net that during the Great Persecutions many with similar names often have conflated stories. Such is the case with Eulias and Julias in Spain during the Diocletian persecution. But here we recount Eulalia of Merida, the capital of Lusitania. Though the city was wealthy with many fine appointments, "it was adorned, famous, and renowned for the martyrdom, blood, and tomb of the blessed virgin Eulalia" in AD 304.[35]

When Eulalia was thirteen, her parents knew her bold commitment to Christ was dangerous, so they tried to hide her. However, Eulalia snuck out at night and entered the city. The next day she burst through the doors of the officials and confronted them on their treatment of Christians. She yelled at them, "I pray you what a shame is it for you thus rashly and without advisement to destroy and kill men's souls, and to throw their bodies alive against the rocks, and cause them to deny the omnipotent

God. Would you know, O you unfortunate, who I am? Behold, I am one of the Christians: an enemy to your devilish sacrifices, I spurn your idols under my feet. I confess God omnipotent with my heart and mouth. Isis, Apollo, and Venus, what are they? Maximian himself, what is he? The one a thing of nothing, for that they be the work of men's hands, the other but a castaway, because he worships the same work."[36] Her insult of Maximian, the adopted, ruthless son of Diocletian and co-emperor, was especially infuriating to the judge. Though a "Lord of substance," she notes about the co-emperor, also dubbed Hercules by Diocletian, he prostrated himself before an idol.

Eulalia was persistent, "Go dear hangman and burn, cut, and mangle my body. It is an easy matter to break a brittle substance, but you can try all you want and fail to hurt my inward mind." The judge's response was predictable: "Hangman, take her and pull her out by her hair, and torment her to the uttermost. Let her feel the power of our country gods, and let her know what the imperial government of a prince is."

However, he then tried to woo her with flattery, reminding her that her youth and beauty might bring her great dowries and romance. He reminded her of her fate by looking at the nearby tools ("furniture") of torture. "Either you will be beheaded with this sword, or these wild beasts will pull you to pieces, or while your friends and family wail you'll be thrown into these flames." And reminding her of the ease of escape, as judges and executioners often did with these Christians on trial, he said, "I ask again, what great matter is it for you to avoid an easy escape? If you will simply take and put with your fingers a little salt and incense into the burners [recognizing the emperor's deity], you will be delivered from all of these punishments."[37]

Her death was horrific yet honorable. The hangmen pulled her joints apart—a less than remarkable human feat for her tormenters considering she was only thirteen. It was a pitiful asterisk on man's fallen nature. While the beasts tore her sides "to the hard bone," she continued to sing praises. But in one of the most macabre accounts, like that of the new mothers Perpetua and Felicitas in Carthage, they mutilated this young saint.

A warm fountain her mangled members with fresh blood bathed her white and fair skin. Then proceed they to the last & final torment, which was, not only the goring & wounding of her mangled body with the iron grate, and hurdle, & terrible harrowing of her flesh: but burned, on every side with flaming torches her tormented breasts and sides. Her hair hanging about her shoulders in two parts divided (wherewith her chastity and virginity were covered) reached down to the ground: but when the crackling flame flew about her face, kindled by her hair, and reached the crown of her head: then she desiring swift death, opened her mouth and swallowed the flame, and so rested she in peace.[38]

AGNES OF ROME The very threat of taking a thirteen-year-old girl's innocence moves most of us to incensed fury, but not the Prefect of Rome, who championed the call of Maximian Herculeus to remove the Christians. Caught in his crosshairs was Agnes of Rome; she was from a wealthy family but gave up earthly pleasures for eternal bliss. This "constant damsel and martyr of God" fought off numerous attempts to compromise her commitment and died (ca. AD 301) with "undefiled and unspotted virginity." The judge's tactics had failed to persuade her to offer incense to Minerva, and to ask this goddess for forgiveness for her perceived arrogance. Upon realizing her bold defense of Christ and her vow of chastity, the judge had her stripped and placed in public—with the intention of having her violated and abandoned in the brothels. Agnes confronted the judge, her words given here in Foxe's sixteenth-century language:

> Christ is not so forgetful of those that be his, that he will suffer violently to be taken from them their golden and pure chastity, neither will he leave them so destitute of help. He is always at hand and ready to fight for such as are shamefast and chaste virgins, neither suffreth he his gifts of holy integrity or chastity to be polluted. Thou shalt saith she, willingly bathe thy sword in my

blood if thou wilt, but thou shalt not defile my body with filthy lust, for any thing thou canst do.[39]

Most onlookers took pity on her and looked away. Eventually a man with "uncircumcised eyes" lusted for her. According to the fifth-century *Acts of Agnes*, suddenly "a flame of fire like a flash of lightning" burst from the skies, "striking his eyes out of his head." As his companions carried away his fried body wailing, Agnes sang praises to God for her delivery. The judge was livid and immediately called for the executioner, who was a stout man. After Agnes praised him for his size, and was thankful that he would not bring shame in a faulty attempt to kill her, she gave the following speech:

> I will make haste to meet him, and will no longer protract my
> longing desire: I will willingly receive into my person the length
> of thy sword, and into my breast will draw the force thereof,
> even unto the hilts: That thus I being married unto Christ
> my spouse, may surmount and escape all the darkness of this
> world, that reacheth even unto the skies. O eternal governor,
> vouchsafe to open the gates of heaven once shut up against all
> the inhabitants of the earth, and receive (O Christ) my soul that
> seeketh thee.[40]

(In other words, she was dramatically challenging the soldier to thrust the sword into her all the way to its handle and she would go willingly to her Lord, the final judge.)

She then knelt with the sword behind her neck and asked Christ to prepare it, and her. The 1570 version of Foxe's *Actes and Monuments* (*Book of Martyrs*) records her final moments with these words: "The executioner then with his bloody hand, finished her hope, and at one stroke cut off her head, and by such short and swift death did he prevent her of the pain thereof."[41]

OTHER WOMEN AMONG THE MEDITERRANEAN MARTYRS

Tradition and later accounts hold that a believer named Lucy met martyrdom (AD 304) in Syracuse, Sicily, after rejecting a suitor. Accounts differ on whether they beheaded her or burnt her alive. She allegedly gave much of her wealth to the poor, infuriating her betrothed. Later accounts note that a team of oxen were unable to pull her away to the brothel as part of her sentence. This prompted a pile of wood to be placed on her head, but the fire didn't consume her (a common hagiographic convention). Eventually she was beheaded. A fifteenth-century account notes that her eyes were first gouged out before her beheading, which led to her designation as patroness of the blind.

According to the eighth-century account *The Acts of St. Afra*, a venerated saint of Augsburg was a converted prostitute from Cyprus, St. Afra. Like the biblical story of Rahab assisting the spies in Jericho, she and her mother, Hilaria, helped hide Bishop Narcissus of Spain during the Diocletian persecutions. During his prolonged concealment in Augsburg, his teachings led to her conversion and to her execution in AD 304.[43]

CAECILIA Caecilia became the patroness of music and among the most famous martyrs of Rome beyond the great apostles. She also is the progenitor of a nineteenth-century play, *The Martyrdom of St. Cicily*, and of St. Caecilia in Rome. The various versions of her story are all remarkable. The governor, after two days attempting to boil her alive in a tub, resorted to having her beheaded. Even this went awry and after several hacks to her neck, lying in bloody bathwater, she lived another three days. The core account also includes her marriage to Valerian, but she would not consummate. On her wedding night, she told her husband of her vow of perpetual virginity in consecration to Christ, which he, according to the account, honored. In turn, he was baptized and (in later accounts)[44] saw an angel next to her. Not only did he convert, but also his brother and around four hundred others. In time, some of the soldiers and guards who were charged with their executions also converted. The main officer in charge, Maximus, was scourged to death with leaded balls for his newfound faith.

The exact date of her martyrdom varies widely—from the third century under Alexander Severus to the early fourth century under Diocletian. At the latest, it would have transpired years before the church's dedication ca. AD 430, and long before Pope Symmachus held a council there in AD 490. While no authentic early account remains, all the ancient Latin missals and breviaries include her story. A pilgrim left a rough drawing of St. Caecilia in the cemetery of San Lorenzo around the sixth or seventh century.[45]

This story has a theme similar to that of the totally legendary account of Pelagia of Rome, who allegedly refused to marry Diocletian's son because of her vow to Christ. The jilted suitor in turn killed himself, her pagan mother sent her to Diocletian, and she refused him as well—so he had her burnt alive inside a bull made of brass. Her body gave off such a strong, sweet aroma that it blanketed Rome. The soldiers sent four lions to devour the body, but instead they protected it. But we know this account to be false because Diocletian didn't have a son.

APOLLONIA OF ALEXANDRIA The treatment of elderly Christians at the hands of Roman oppressors is dizzying, especially the case of Apollonia (AD 249, shortly before the Decian persecution). John Foxe includes an account of a virgin "well stricken in years."[46] In most civilized societies we look for special treatment and security for children and those on the fringes of health and self-care. However, the opposite was afforded Apollonia. The Roman officials first knocked all her teeth "out of her jaws." The image of such horrific treatment brings tears, yet her resilience is a reminder of one's capacity in Christ. While they stoked the huge fire for her execution, she grew silent and seemed to have that time of "pause" for reflection before they grabbed her. Instead, she leapt into the fire. She is aptly named the patroness of dental issues and dentists, and the subject of the famous painting by Jean Fouquet, *The Martyrdom of Apollonia*, ca. 1452–1460.

THE MARTYRS NAMED BY DIONYSIUS, BISHOP OF ALEXANDRIA, AD 247-248, 264-265

In Dionysius's letter to Fabius of Antioch, which also records the story of Apollonia, he recounts the brutal response to many other Christians during a riot in Alexandria. Oftentimes unrest or ill turns of events were blamed on the Christians. They dragged Quinta by her feet through the streets, dashed her body against millstones, and eventually stoned her to death. The fate for Christians grew worse after Decius instigated his persecution in AD 250. Four women were burnt along with Epimachus and Alexander. "The virgin Ammomarion also was long tortured. The aged Mercuria and Dionysia, a mother of many children, suffered by the sword."[47] Large groups were martyred, certainly including women as well, along with the throngs carried off by the Saracens.

WOMEN MARTYRS MENTIONED IN EUSEBIUS'S HISTORIES

Many of our earliest sources come through Eusebius, such as those mentioned in his various quotations from Dionysius. Among his accounts of martyrdom, we catch yet another glimpse of the breadth and cruelty of these assaults on the faithful. Citing Origen, he notes that Herais, a catechumen (a new Christian studying for water baptism), was baptized by fire. Potamiana received repeated horrific treatment; her endurance—like that of other women such as Perpetua in Carthage—persuaded others to convert. In Potamiana's case, her Roman guard, Basilides, was moved by her witness and placed his faith in Christ. They executed him as well. (Read the entire account in the third "Voices from the Past" section in this chapter.)

Voices from the Past

The bearing of many of the martyrs has been singularly heroic. You will be struck, in reading Foxe's Acts and Monuments, *to find how many of the humblest men and women acted as if they were of noblest blood. In every age the line of martyrs has been a line of true nobility.*[48]

C. H. SPURGEON

DID YOU KNOW? *The Arenas*

The word *arena* comes from the Latin *harena,* meaning a place of combat, referring to a sandy field in the midst of crowds. It likely derives from a word for *sand* used by the Etruscans, early settlers in Italy. The organizers of the massive amphitheater events needed tons of sand to soak up the blood from the carnage. With advanced engineering for the raised floor in the largest ancient amphitheater ever built, the Roman Colosseum (seating over fifty thousand), would have been for naught if the gladiators slipped on the bloody floor.

The Colosseum remains the most famous stadium in history, partly because of its size, but also because of its iconic walls that afford a rare glimpse of ancient grand structures. But another part of its fame is due to the throngs of Christian pilgrims visiting it as the world's largest martyrs' shrine, dedicated by Pope Benedict XIV. Even its name is a reminder of the oppression the early church faced. The name *Colosseum* refers to the audacious 100-foot bronze statue of Nero that stood nearby. The megalomaniac emperor built it atop razed houses after the infamous fire (AD 64) of Rome. Nero blamed the fire on the Christians, whom legend says he used as human torches in his nearby gardens.

The amphitheaters were once the center of the Roman populace's world. Most of these are visible only through tremendous archaeological efforts. These huge arenas housing cheering crowds during Christian martyrdoms eventually went silent. It would have been unfathomable for twenty thousand or so witnesses of Blandina's gruesome treatment to imagine the closure and neglect of the Amphitheater of the Three Gauls.

Today, unlike the Colosseum in Rome, only half of that theater's walls remain—and the most prominent feature that draws the crowds is the singular pole erected in the arena in remembrance of Blandina.

In Caesarea Maritima in modern Israel, the site of the former capital of Rome's province, the amphitheater is once again visible, but only after more than $40 million in restoration. Christian pilgrims flock to the site not for its former imperial grandeur but for its church history. The same is true in Tunis at the remains of its ancient amphitheater (which at its height of use had fifty arches), which these authors have visited. It is likely the site of Perpetua's and Felicitas's martyrdom, and today not much more than its foundation remains—except for a memorial cross from 1887 celebrating the lives of these Christian martyrs and their companions.[49]

Voices from the Past

Basilides . . . led to martyrdom the celebrated Potamiœna, who is still famous among the people of the country for the many things which she endured for the preservation of her chastity and virginity. For she was blooming in the perfection of her mind and her physical graces. Having suffered much for the faith of Christ, finally after tortures dreadful and terrible to speak of, she with her mother, Marcella, was put to death by fire.

They say that the judge, Aquila by name, having inflicted severe tortures upon her entire body, at last threatened to hand her over to the gladiators for bodily abuse. After a little consideration, being asked for her decision, she made a reply which was regarded as impious.

Thereupon she received sentence immediately, and Basilides, one of the officers of the army, led her to death. But as the people attempted to annoy and insult her with abusive words, he drove back her insulters, showing her much pity and kindness. And perceiving the man's sympathy for her, she exhorted him to be of good courage, for she would supplicate her Lord for him after her departure, and he would soon receive a reward for the kindness he had shown her.

Having said this, she nobly sustained the issue, burning pitch being poured little by little, over various parts of her body, from the sole of her feet to the crown of her head. Such was the conflict endured by this famous maiden.

Not long after this Basilides, being asked by his fellow-soldiers to swear for a certain reason, declared that it was not lawful for him to swear at all, for he was a Christian, and he confessed this openly. At first they thought that he was jesting, but when he continued to affirm it, he was led to the judge, and, acknowledging his conviction before him, he was imprisoned. But the brethren in God coming to him and inquiring the reason of this sudden and remarkable resolution, he is reported to have said that Potamiœna, for three days after her martyrdom, stood beside him by night and placed a crown on his head and said that she had besought the Lord for him and had obtained what she asked, and that soon she would take him with her.

Thereupon the brethren gave him the seal of the Lord; and on the next day, after giving glorious testimony for the Lord, he was beheaded. And many others in Alexandria are recorded to have accepted speedily the word of Christ in those times. For Potamiœna appeared to them in their dreams and exhorted them.[50]

EUSEBIUS, *The Histories*, bk. 6, ch. 5

Vintage Foxe

John Foxe fills many pages of his volumes with letters from or about martyrs, like the following from John Huss. Huss references the noble stance of Catherine of Alexandria and his desire to have the same effect, but at this point admits failing to convert the fifty scholars examining him. He became one of the heralded Protestant martyrs after being burned at the stake July 6, 1415 (now a national holiday in the Czech Republic), and was counted among Martin Luther's heroes.[51]

And when I said, that I was desirous to be instructed, if I did in any thing err, then they heard the chief Cardinal [Cambiensis] answer again: because thou wouldest be informed, there is no remedy, but thou must first revoke thy doctrine, according to the determination of 50 bachelors of divinity appointed. O high instruction. After like manner, St. Catherine also should have denied and revoked the verity of God and faith in Christ, because the 50 masters likewise did withstand her: which notwithstanding, that good virgin would never do, standing in her faith unto death: But she did win those her masters unto Christ, whereas I cannot win these my masters by any means. These things I thought good to write unto you, that you might know how they have overcome me, with no grounded Scripture nor with any reason: but only did assay with terrors and disceites to persuade me to revoke and to abjure. But our merciful God, whose law I have magnified, was and is with me, and I trust, so will continue, and will keep me in his grace unto death. Written at Constance after the feast of John Baptist, in prison and in bands, daily looking for death, although for the secret judgments of God, I dare not say whether this be my last epistle: for now also almighty God is able to deliver me.[52]

CHAPTER FIVE

The Rise of Islam

Beloved, do not be surprised at the fiery trial when it comes upon you to test you, as though something strange were happening to you. But rejoice insofar as you share Christ's sufferings, that you may also rejoice and be glad when his glory is revealed. If you are insulted for the name of Christ, you are blessed, because the Spirit of glory and of God rests upon you. **1 PETER 4:12-14**

You can kill, but not hurt us. **JUSTIN MARTYR**

God is swifter to us than we are to God. **'ABD AL-MASĪH**

After the legalization of Christianity by the leaders of the Roman Empire, the public profile of the church changed dramatically. Christians worshiped openly from Portugal to the Middle East, as far north as Britain and all along the northern coast of Africa. The Mediterranean world was Christianized to the point that this faith became the official religion, and all of this was happening where the faith had once been ruthlessly persecuted.

That church was now palpitating with its love for Jesus in every corner of the modern world. It was a truly living church.

After Constantine came to power, the martyrdom of the early years of Christianity was soon replaced with a type of imperial patronage throughout the Roman Empire. This once largely underground movement had emerged as a dominant cultural force and was now able to express itself on its own terms and in all aspects of public life.

Its cultural ascendancy would present a new set of challenges once unfamiliar during its cultural obscurity. Yet the faith would persist despite it all.

Soon enough, its cultural prominence was challenged and the state of Christianity began to change yet again for millions of believers. These changes were especially prominent throughout North Africa and in the cradle of Christianity, the Middle East.

In much of the Middle East, many were under Sassanid rule until that empire's collapse in AD 651, or—to be more precise—until Muslim forces arrived. The Sassanids, named after Sasan from an area of modern Iran, were the chief rival to the Roman Empire for four centuries and represented the last of Persian dominance in the pre-Islamic world. Christians in that region, along with a whole culture, were about to go through major changes.

There was a time of transition during Islam's early medieval conquests throughout the Middle East, along the coast of Africa and into Spain and Portugal.[1] In this caliphate expansion, John Foxe saw likenesses to the prophecies of the Antichrist, so much so that sometimes it seems as if he's forcing the dates into his apocalyptic calculations. Violence marked the early campaigns of the Muslims (initially called Saracens, or Muslim Arabs). Foxe sees this area, especially the campaigns after Muhammad's death (AD 632), as a hinge of history. These campaigns paint the backdrop for his representation of events overlapping with the "mark of the beast" in the book of Revelation (demonstrating Christianity's age-old tendency to consider its present challenges as signs of the end times).

> Another mystery there is in the Revelations, Apoc. 3, where the number of the beast is counted 666. Whereby may seem by all evidences, to be signified the first origin and springing of these beastly Saracens, as by sequel hereof may appear by the first rising up of this devilish sect of Mahumete [Muhammad]. . . .

As Munsterus counteth, it was in the year of our Lord 622. Martin Luther and John Carion referreth it to the 18th year of the reign of Heraclius, which is the year of our Lord 630. Unto the which number the computation of the Beast signified in the Apocal. doth not far disagree, which numbreth the name of the Beast, with three Greek letters: χ, ξ, σ [chi, xi, sigma] which Greek letters after the supputation of the Grecians, make the number of 666.[2]

In these same passages he also thought the strength of Islam in his day (ca. 1516 to 1587) would quickly be severed by the strength of the Christian church, but that didn't happen. On the contrary, the Ottomans had swept most of the Christian East, perhaps most visible in the historic walls of Old Jerusalem, and the occupation of Constantinople—now Istanbul—which they had conquered in 1453. This was a generation before Foxe emerged on the scene. Regardless of his prophetic calculations and personal views, during these seventh- to ninth-century Islamic campaigns beginning with Muhammad's era, and the thirteenth to twentieth centuries of the Ottomans, countless Christians paid the ultimate sacrifice in their wake.

In the prevailing Islamic culture of Christianity's conquerors, adherents called this military acquisition of new territories *futūḥ*, a word akin to "liberate" or "opening." That is, liberating what they perceive as illegitimate hierarchies or governments (non-Islamic) "to the new revelation and dispensation," or simply put, to convert them to Islam.[3] They were immensely successful. "Within two decades, the forces of the first three caliphs overran Palestine, Syria, Mesopotamia, Persia, Egypt, and much of North Africa. . . . They continued the process of expansion, and their empire soon reached from India to Morocco. In 711, the Moors (Islamicized Berbers) crossed the Strait of Gibraltar and conquered Visigothic Spain. They swept north into France, but the Muslim tide finally was halted by Charles Martel at the Battle of Tours in 733."[4] It is likely impossible for a modern audience to understand how astonishing this conquest was, and how the conquerors—and in some cases the conquered—perceived Islam's growth as proof of its theological legitimacy. Some Christians did convert because they were convinced; others agreed to live under the patrimony of their conquerors, paying taxes in exchange for the right to remain; and others yet faced incomprehensible deaths because they refused to live in submission to Islamic culture or to convert.

Christians nearly always found themselves marginalized to some degree even in the best-case scenarios. Therefore, they were always vulnerable to state persecution, and myriad Christians lost their lives for their faith.

Many recent scholars have made strong cases that the earliest decades of Christian-Muslim relations were not as horrific as later church historians record, especially non-Syriac sources. These arguments seem to have merit; after all, Syrian Christians represented those most directly involved.[5] That said, however accommodating the Muslim victors were, thousands of Christians were massacred in battle or shortly after battles, countless were oppressed or enslaved, and historical sources have identified at least 270 individual noteworthy martyrs from this era. They are often distinguished in history, as they were at the time, as the so-called "new martyrs" or "neo-martyrs."[6] That is, new after the age of the Great Persecutions.

> Unlike the classical [early church] martyrs—many of whom were
> killed for shirking what hagiographers portrayed as a timeless
> paganism—the new martyrs were executed for reneging on a faith
> and culture that truly surrounded them and which some had
> even embraced. . . . These martyrs were a varied group, including
> monks, soldiers, shopkeepers, village priests, craftsmen, princes,
> and bishops. They were women and men, young and old, peasants
> and nobles. Although capital punishment disproportionately
> affected certain groups, especially the clergy, martyrs hailed from
> across the social spectrum of the early medieval Middle East.[7]

Most of the time, life under Muslim rule did not involve the immediate threat of violent persecution. In the aftermath of Islamic conquest and initial persecution, Jews, Christians, and Muslims came to live together in these territories in relatively integrated societies. But the centuries seemed to have changed the level of tolerance, and the decentralized polity and theology of Islam meant that there were vast variations of practices across the Islamic world. This resulted in different types of experiences for non-Muslims.

Rather than ending persecution of non-Muslims in these regions, new variations of martyrdom emerged as some Islamic states struggled to reassert Islamic identity in pluralistic communities. In this way the casual familiarity, and in many cases friendliness, between the Abrahamic faiths under Muslim rule resulted in official state actions. These were manifest in marginalization at best, interspersed with periodic bouts of extreme suppression, or worse.

The ease with which Jewish, Christian, and Muslim scholars, professionals, and laity were at times able to live and work alongside one another seemed to threaten the distinctiveness of Islam and its supremacy in conquered territories.[8] Contributing to this anxiety was the fact—as hard as it is to comprehend for modern Turkey, Egypt, and Iraq—that the Christians in the general population often vastly outnumbered the ruling class of conquerors throughout regions belonging to the former Roman and Byzantine empires. These tensions of Islamic supremacy and distinctiveness were at the root of most Christian persecution.

The "new martyrs" were victims of a still-young faith with a lingering ethos of conquest itself. Islam was also in many ways underdeveloped and therefore still finding its footing as a cultural and theological institution. These internal uncertainties were manifest in their own infighting between Sunni and Shiite factions, with their own share of inter-Islamic assassinations. Some of these victims became such a part of the Islamic story that their martyrs are the subject of annual commemorations in Shia Islam in particular. This infighting, combined with the uncertainties of ruling and intermingling with Christian and Jewish subjects, at times had especially tragic outcomes for these marginalized communities. In this religious and political climate, crimes like blasphemy (against teachings of the Quran) and de-conversion among Jews and Christians could result in capital punishment. The reasoning behind these acts of violence did not mitigate their brutality, as we will see. As in the Spanish Inquisition, one of the worst offenses was to leave the faith, even after the convert (in Spain, often a Jew) had been strongly pressured to convert. Both the Muslims and Catholic inquisitors shared in these inhumane, relentless efforts to exact religious conformity.

The references in Foxe to the Prophet Muhammad are barbed assessments that reflect the tenor of his sixteenth-century disdain for all "heretics and oppressors." His treatment of the time period also stretches far beyond the neomartyrs to the countless lives lost in later clashes. Whether addressing the general decay of the church in his discussion of William the Conqueror (1066), or his current generation's international military campaigns against the Sunni Ottomans, Foxe is anything but kind. In his discussion of the latter, he notes: "But in process of time, began from better to worse, to decrease and decline into much superstition and inconvenience: partly through the coming in of [Muhammad]."[9] In the latter, closer to his European sensitivities and the Ottoman conquests, he calls them a "detestable" or "wicked" sect. (See "Vintage Foxe" near the end of this chapter.)

In the modern era, we often hear Islam referenced as a "religion of peace" or something similar. While there are absolutely elements of Islamic theology one might call upon to construct a hermeneutic of peace, it is also true that the religion has been easily weaponized for war too often throughout its history. This is the fate of most religions in the world, including Christianity, yet Robert Wilken, an eminent historian from the University of Virginia, summarizes this tendency with intensity toward Islam:

> In recent years, there has been much moralistic posturing over the brutality of the Crusaders and thoughtless pontificating about their historical import. Out of ignorance, many conveniently ignore that the Crusades were part of a Christian counteroffensive against the occupation of lands that had been Christian for centuries before the arrival of Islam.[10]

After the horrific attacks on New York City's twin towers on 9/11/2001, President George W. Bush gave his heralded "Peace Speech" (September 17, 2001). He shared with Americans and the world audience, "The face of terror is not the true faith of Islam. That's not what Islam is all about. Islam is peace. These terrorists don't represent peace. They represent evil and war."[11] Perhaps this is not out of step with Wilken's essay on the matter—the need to respect another world religion. However, just as the Muslim citizens facing the Christian Crusaders in the twelfth century would not have seen Christianity as peace, vast populations among the conquered would have called the violent Muslim troops anything but peaceful. In his book chronicling the long coexistence of many Christian and Muslim populations, Philip Jenkins shares the following about the Ottomans, attributing their tactics as much to their Turkish heritage as to their religion:

> Ottoman forces carried out notorious massacres against Christian populations, and particularly targeted Christian clergy and leaders. In 1480, the Turks destroyed the Italian city of Otranto, killing twelve thousand and executing leading clergymen by sawing them. The destruction of Nicosia in Cyprus in 1570 may have inflicted still more casualties. Accounts of Ottoman warfare and punishment include such gruesome techniques as impaling, crucifixion, and flaying [skinning alive].[12]

While crucifixion clearly preceded Christianity, it became—and often remains—a preferred way of murdering Christians who are forced to die like their Savior. Yet, despite it all, Jenkins also reminds us of the resilience of Christianity, even amid these atrocities. "Turks termed Balkan Christians *rayah*, 'the herd,' as animals to be sheared and exploited as necessary. As a Bosnian Muslim song declared: The *rayah* is like the grass, Mow it as much as you will till it springs up anew."[13]

Contemporary scholars throughout the Islamic world, but especially in the Arabian Gulf and in Southeast Asia, are undertaking remarkable theological work to find the elusive common ground between Islam and Christianity. Islamic scholars meeting in Morocco drafted the Marrakesh Declaration in 2016, and over one thousand scholars from the Muslim World League convened in Mecca to sign the Charter of Mecca in 2019. Pope Francis and the Grand Sheikh of Al-Azhar issued the Document on

Human Fraternity in 2019 on the occasion of the first visit of a pontiff to the Arabian Peninsula. And then there was the groundbreaking Bahrain Declaration for Peaceful Coexistence issued in 2017 under the patronage of Bahrain's King Hamad bin Isa Al Khalifa. The Bahraini king's name is interesting for Christians as "bin Isa" literally translates to "son of Jesus." King Hamad's father and predecessor was named after Jesus, whom all Muslims consider a prophet second only to Muhammad himself. All of these documents recognize the shared humanity of adherents to the Abrahamic faiths and call for religious freedom in various forms. The Bahrain Declaration goes so far as to endorse the rights of individuals to change religion (convert). The documents all draw from key moments of Islamic history, especially during the era of the Prophet Muhammad and also of the Abbasid Caliphate, when Muslims, Jews, and Christians coexisted in relative peace and prosperity.

In his provocative essay "Christianity Face to Face with Islam," Robert Wilken presents an overview of Islam's rise and explores possibilities for collaboration between these two religions, in spite of their histories—but not forgetting them. Though his characterization carries more than a hint of hyperbole, it is worth duly noting his argument that "the divide between Christianity and Islam is great and the search for a usable past looks unpromising." While making strong points on finding common ground today, he also places into historic context the world of millions of Christians losing freedoms and oftentimes their lives.

> Over its long history, Islam has been very bad for Christianity. In North Africa and Asia Minor, the arrival of Muslim armies led in a short period of time to the destruction of Christian communities. In the Middle East, *dhimmitude* was a suffocating institution that eventually sucked the oxygen out of communities, turning them in on themselves as they bent their energies to the sole end of survival. Although during the early centuries of Muslim rule there was fruitful intellectual and cultural intercourse, it did not last and has largely been forgotten. To this day a great part of the world remains effectively closed off to Christians.

Violence has been a persistent strain in Muslim history. . . . So there is much to ponder and, for Christians living in the Muslim world, much to fear.[14]

The martyrs that follow faced such fear with supernatural magnanimity. That's why many branches of Christianity honor several of them as saints. Perhaps the biggest irony is the conspicuous silence of accounts of these neomartyrs by the East Syrians or Nestorians, who had the distinction of being the leading Christian communities in Iraq and Iran. This contrasts sharply with their aggressive efforts to record earlier martyrs, including those by the Sassanid Empire—the Zoroastrians of Persia.

After representing the life of the first neomartyr, Peter of Capitolias, we will pause to look at the fall of Jerusalem to the Persians (simultaneous with the rise of Islam elsewhere). A few decades later, Jerusalem fell to the Muslims. To represent these important events we include St. Sophronius, who lived through both of these, and died in Jerusalem the first year of Islamic rule.

These neomartyrs found themselves in the eastern part of Christendom, experiencing an organized threat that Western Christianity seemed to dismiss or ignore. Islam arose while Christianity was fractured over the Monophysite controversy (claiming Jesus had only a divine nature, not human) and lesser squabbles. Philip Jenkins's *God's Continent* (2007) begins with the recounting of Muslim protests over the publication of Salman Rushdie's *Satanic Verses* (1989). Some demonstrators sported the placard "Islam—Our Religion Today, Your Religion Tomorrow." Jenkins comments: "Over the past few years, serious scholars have debated whether there might be some truth to this piece of bumper sticker futurology."[15] A few years later, an imam in Spain said, "Before, Muslims were guests who would leave. Today Islam is among us."[16] During Islam's early expansion, such observations and debates among Western leaders were not forthcoming or forceful enough before the Caucasus and Fertile Crescent were covered with the crescent of a new religion and sprinkled with the relics and ashes of martyrs.

PETER OF CAPITOLIAS One of the most gruesome and prolonged public executions of a Christian took place in Damascus in AD 715.

When Peter of Capitolias took ill at age sixty, thirty years after committing to the monastic life, he summoned the leading Muslims for a meeting. Though they expected to hear his wishes for his last will and testimony, what followed shocked them. Peter had desired to be martyred and wanted all to be clear of his ardent faith in Christ—so he began extolling the virtues of Christianity while blasting the teachings of Islam. Like Ignatius of Antioch, he was indeed prompting martyrdom. But an unexpected turn of events ensued—he recovered!

Desiring to join in the triumph of the early Christian martyrs, he began preaching against both Islam and Muhammad in the streets of Capitolias, with the expected result of arrest and transport to Caliph Wanni in Damascus. Peter's impassioned exchanges with the caliph brought his predictable end as the Umayyad officials applied "an array of punishments lifted directly from the Qu'ran"[17] (the *hiraba*, or unlawful violence or warfare):

> Indeed, the penalty for those who wage war against Allah and His
> Messenger and strive upon earth [to cause] corruption is none but
> that they be killed or crucified or that their hands and feet be cut
> off from opposite sides or that they be exiled from the land. That
> is for them a disgrace in this world; and for them in the Hereafter
> is a great punishment. QURAN 5:33, SAHIH INTERNATIONAL[18]

In Islamic sources, this appears to be traced to the punishment Muhammad imposed on camel thieves among his ranks outside of Medina.

In the medieval world, the punishment of "heretics" often became public spectacles. Peter's inhumane treatment at the hands of his Muslim captors was no exception. Various accounts of Peter's martyrdom exist, but the original account of John of Damascus appears lost. The Mystagogy Resource Center records the following:

On 10 January 715, the Holy Martyr was taken back to Capitolias, and there he was made a spectacle of the people, especially to his children, who are taken out of their monastic cells that they had lived in since childhood, and they were placed in the first row of spectators. The executioner first tore out the Saint's tongue at its root; the next day he cut off a hand and a foot; and on Sunday, in the presence of yet a greater crowd, the remaining hand and foot of the Martyr were cut off. After this he was blinded and crucified, where he was pierced three times with a spear and subsequently died by being beheaded.

Soldiers kept watch over his body for five days and then burnt it, throwing his ashes into a nearby river, and even took care to wash everything that may have touched his holy relics so as to prevent the faithful from venerating it.[19]

MARTYRS OF *HIRABA* The distinct maiming and torture sequence noted in *hiraba* (Quran 5:33) befell many Christians, especially during the initial conquest period of Islam (*futūḥ*), and certainly beyond it. In AD 852 in Córdoba, Spain, long after the *futūḥ*, Rogelius and Servusdei ended up on racks on the banks of the Guadalquivir River. Eulogius (who was himself subsequently beheaded in 857 for hiding Christians) recorded the particulars of the Cordoba persecutions in a detailed account of the martyrdoms of this decade. He notes that Rogelius and Servusdei appeared in racks on the riverbank only after their hands and feet were chopped off, and they were beheaded. The pattern distinctly follows the guidelines in Quran 5:33. Maka'tl in Armenia suffered a similar fate for converting from Islam to Christianity. By order of the ninth-century Turkish general Bugha al-Kabir (Bugha the Great), his tongue was cut out and his hands and feet hacked off.[20] Abbot Samson mentions an early case "around 860, when a Christian man was executed. Ibn Sahl mentions the case of a woman named Dhabba who affirmed that Jesus was God and who was either burned or decapitated. In 850, a man from Córdoba who claimed to be a prophet gave his exegesis of the Qu'rān. When he refused to retract, he was crucified."[21]

SOPHRONIUS AND THE FALL OF JERUSALEM (UNDER THE PERSIANS AND MUSLIMS) Unlike most martyrs in this collection, Sophronius is said to have died not by sword or saw, but from a devastated heart over the desecration of the Christian holy sites in Jerusalem. During his lifetime, Jerusalem fell first to the Zoroastrians in AD 614—during the last macabre hurrah of Persia's Sassanid Empire. Then in AD 637, the year before Sophronius's death, it fell to the Muslims under Umar the Great.

Sophronius (AD 560–638) was born in Damascus and around age twenty became an ascetic in Egypt before entering the monastery of St. Theodosius, five miles east of Bethlehem. He traveled often with the prolific church chronicler and Byzantine monk John Moschus, and would intersect with the lives of many leaders, including Patriarch John the Almsgiver of Alexandria.

His role in recording Patriarch John's life would foster many legends. John helped thousands of those displaced from Jerusalem before fleeing for his own life. Sophronius's biography of John, though not extant, was the key source later chroniclers used to preserve John's story.

Sophronius was in Alexandria when the attacks began, and he fled with Patriarch John and John Moschus.[22] The patriarch had given much of his church's funds to aid besieged Christians in and around Jerusalem, and refugees in his own city, and he had secured the release of thousands of Christian hostages, including a thousand nuns. But eventually he realized the need to avoid a plot against his own life.[23] The patriarch died on the journey, but not before he enjoyed time in his native country of Cyprus (ca. 620). Afterward, Sophronius, Moschus, and eighteen other monks continued to Rome, where Moschus also died. Sophronius escorted his body back to Palestine for burial in the monastery of St. Theodosius.

He returned during tough times for Christians in their holy lands. Having fallen to the Persians early in the tenure of Patriarch Zacharias (609–632), they were soon also besieged by Muslims. Zacharias had helped to preserve the holy relics at the Hagia Sophia in Constantinople, which became good training for his post in Jerusalem. In AD 614, after an initial nonviolent overthrow, the Persians massacred around 17,000

Christians and took many others hostage, including Zacharias, whom they held captive 614–628. Around 4,500 hostages didn't fare as well and were executed. It's fitting that after his long captivity, which Emperor Heraclitus ended by defeating the Persians, Zacharias reentered Jerusalem alongside Heraclitus, who carried on his shoulder a relic of relics, the "True Cross."[24]

This was the world Sophronius was trying to serve and protect, eventually becoming Patriarch of Jerusalem in 635.[25] The Orthodox Church in America posts this about St. Sophronius's last days:

> Toward the end of his life, Saint Sophronius and his flock lived through a two year siege of Jerusalem by the Moslems. Worn down by hunger, the Christians finally agreed to open the city gates, on the condition that the enemy spare the holy places. But this condition was not fulfilled, and Saint Sophronius died in grief over the desecration of the Christian holy places.[26]

GEORGE THE BLACK One of the earliest known neomartyrs, George the Black, suffered the miserable fate of being sawed in half. This act seems to us almost unthinkable, but it's only one of many gruesome martyrdoms, including the many due to *hiraba*. George the Black was born into a Christian home in or near Syria. Muslim invaders captured him at age eight, according to Anastasius of Sinai's *Narrationes*. George lived in the second generation after Muhammad's death in 632, himself dying sometime in the 650s or 660s. Anastasius (631–ca. 700) was abbot of St. Catherine's Monastery at Mount Sinai, and a contemporary of George. Apparently, George had confessed Islam, then retracted as an adult. A fellow slave who had renounced his Christianity and endorsed Islam reported him. George called him a Christ-hating apostate. When George's master asked him to join him in his Muslim prayers, George refused, and that alone mandated an order to have him sawed in half. Fellow Christians in Damascus buried him in a memorial chapel.

PETER, ANTHONY, AND JOHN OF SYRACUSE As horrific as all martyrdom is, there are scenes that are especially jarring, not just for their brutality but also for their ingenuity. Peter and Anthony were brothers raised in a Christian family in Syracuse on the island of Sicily. When it was raided by Arab armies, the boys were captured and subsequently forced into service in an Arab court. While publicly observing the liturgies and practices of Islam, they continued their Christian faith in secret. When this was discovered, the boys resolutely stood by their faith and refused to recant. The presiding emir, Abū Ishāq Ibrāhīm II, responded with profound ruthlessness.[27]

Peter and Anthony were whipped and beaten all over their bodies with iron rods and wooden clubs until their "bare bones were as tender as flesh, and their flesh became as clay. And they became so bloodied that it was as if they were of one mixture."[28] A pair of copper tongs was used to castrate the boys and their testicles were placed in their mouths. The emir brought out their father, John, before them and slit his throat before throwing his body on them and setting all three on fire.

ANDREW OF SYRACUSE Andrew was another believer taken into custody once Sicily fell under Muslim rule. But rather than being enlisted in the court of the emir, this much older man was imprisoned. After many years of refusing to renounce his faith, Ibrāhīm II ran a spear through his chest. Because Andrew did not immediately die, a second spear was placed in his back. "Because the two spears passed through his innards, the brave struggler fell to the ground. Then he was beheaded," and demonstrating the ever-present power of faith in virtually all of these accounts, the author concludes that his torturers "delivered his holy soul into the hands of God, and [he] ascended victoriously to the heavens."[29]

DID YOU KNOW? *Jizyah*

Under Muslim rule, Christians often converted to the religion of the ruling class. One of the many reasons for these conversions was a heavy tax, known as *jizyah*, which applied only to non-Muslims living under

Islamic rule. Jews and Christians were classed together in Islamic societies, along with other non-Muslim populations, as *dhimmis* (protected ones).[30] They were declared ineligible to serve in the military, and besides, most Christian communities throughout the Middle East and North Africa were then, as they are now, pacifist. So the *jizyah* was technically a tax to account for professional military protection of those who could not officially join in the defense of their communities.

DID YOU KNOW? *Apostasy*

Christians are accustomed to seeing this term only in the context of those defecting from Christianity, but Muslims leveled the same charge when converts to Islam later converted back to Christianity or for any native-born Muslims who converted. This defection of Muslims (or those born into Muslim families) to Christian faith was the cause of many martyrdoms discussed in this chapter.

CULTURAL CONNECTION

Museums and Golden Reminders of Persecution

We can often walk through museums mesmerized by our ancestors' rich artifacts, like the hoards of coins found in Israel. Some of these articles corroborate the historicity of Roman rulers mentioned in the New Testament. Other images confirm buildings and events from church history. Others still, including one of the most spectacular discoveries in the last few decades, are linked to rampant atrocities against Christians. Around 2,000 gold coins were found in an eleventh-century shipwreck in Caesarea's bay in 2015.[31] Most of these coins are 24-karat dinars minted by two of the fourteen Fatimid caliphs from Cairo and North Africa, Al-Hakim bi-Amr Allah ("Ruler by God's command") and his son al-Zahir (AD 996–1036). Al-Hakim infamously ordered the destruction of the Church of the Holy Sepulchre and many other churches in the area (October 1009).[32] His conscripted cohorts would have succeeded in obliterating the site, as they even hammered the bedrock in places, but the materials from the collapsed dome saved it from complete destruction. This bold attack not only reached the ears of leaders throughout Christendom, but it would also help fuel the Crusades a century later, coupled with the Seljuk Turks' treatment of pilgrims after their conquest (in 1077).[33] Al-Hakim forced Christians at times to wear iron crosses and ride horses using wooden saddles. He killed various Christians, but also numerous Sunnis and court employees. It is little wonder after such exploits—and killing all the dogs in Egypt (because barking annoyed him)—that contemporaries called him the "Mad Caliph."

DID YOU KNOW? *Hagiographies or Martyrologies?*

While adherents of many religions have been persecuted throughout history, only Christianity has commemorated its martyrs so openly and frequently. Ancient Christian *hagiographies* (biographies of saints) and *martyrologies* (biographies of martyrs) accounted for most of the popular literature of the early church. These works kept the prospect of martyrdom at the forefront of Christian minds and emphasized faithfulness and self-sacrifice with deep roots in Scripture.

Veneration of martyrs was so pivotal in the life of ancient Christianity that it has been referred to as "the only form of popular devotion in the early church."[34] It was so central to Christian worship and identity that the original name for churches as we know them today was *"martyries."*[35] These chapels were built to honor the faithful dead, and their burial sites became focal points for Christian gatherings and liturgies.

Since that time, stories of martyrdom and the practice of cataloguing them as defining moments of Christian identity have been an important part of Christian literature and culture. This volume is a continuation of that ancient tradition, celebrating great Christians of the past and reminding ourselves of what and who we are—members of the crucified body of Jesus, who was among other things a victim of violence in our long tradition.

We hope this book inspires new generations of Christians whose discipleship is too often devoid of persecution to honor the stories of those whose faith demanded life and death.

VAHAN OF GOGHTN Vahan is a popular name in Armenia today, and little wonder with the courageous story of Vahan, who was trafficked to Damascus as a slave in chains at age four in the eighth century.

He would have inherited a wealthy estate in Goghtn but the Muslims burned his father and other noblemen in their churches in Goghtn in 701. While some see this horrific act as "a singularly violent moment in the early Muslim-Christian encounter in the Caucasus,"[36] these were frightful times for Christians. "A Moslem was fined only 5,000 souzehs for killing a Christian. Any attempt to revolt was cruelly suppressed; an example is the burning of 1,775 Armenian hostages in the churches of Nakhjavan and Khram."[37]

In Damascus, Vahan's princely status likely landed him in service in the Umayyad court, where he converted to Islam, as most slaves did out of self-preservation. There he excelled. A new leader came to power in 717 and released the Armenian slaves, though the ruler asked Vahan to return after visiting his homeland. However, Vahan had converted to Christianity (and was thus considered an apostate from Islam), and after his conversion he even entered a monastery. He experienced a sort of second baptism due to the tears he shed over his time as a Muslim.

This haunting memory prompted Vahan to return to eastern Syria and confront his captors in Rusafa.[38] While he boldly proclaimed his faith and publicly denounced Islam, in so doing he signed his death warrant. They summarily tortured and then beheaded him.[39] Christian Sahner, a professor at Oxford, states, "The company of Arab princes in Damascus could make a Muslim of a Christian hostage, but the company of Christian clergy and nobles in Armenia could also make a Christian martyr of a Muslim courtier."[40]

'ABD AL-MASĪḤ The abbot of Mt. Sinai 'Abd al-Masīḥ ("Servant of Christ") died around AD 860 during the reign of the Umayyads. His native city was Najran in what is today Saudi Arabia, a known Christian community with legendary martyrs from the 520s. However, from around age twenty to thirty-three he traveled with Muslim friends from his native city. Though he intended to go to Jerusalem, his friends "continually beguiled him and sought his stumbling, with the result that he went raiding with them. . . . He surpassed them in the severity of his rage and in the hardness of his heart against the Byzantines." And raid he did, practicing jihad for thirteen years, trampling "every sacred thing" and joining in their Muslim prayers.[42]

While spending the winter in the Valley of Lebanon (in Greek, Helioupolis), he became interested in the public readings of a Christian priest and converted. The verse that especially convicted him was Matthew 10:37: "Whoever loves father or mother more than me is not worthy of me, and whoever loves son or daughter more than me is not worthy of me." This prompted an emotional repentance.

As a new Christian, 'Abd al-Masīḥ parted from his friends, sold all of his possessions (weapons and his horse), and gave the funds to the poor before journeying to Jerusalem at last. He became a monk, and Patriarch John sent him to the Mar Saba Monastery, where he remained for five years before making his way to Sinai—becoming its abbot. After around seven years, he decided to announce to the Muslim authorities his past and his Christian conversion, but when they came for him, they could not see him. His time had not yet arrived for martyrdom, but it eventually would.

While traveling into the city to protest taxes, including one for being Christian, he encountered his old friends among a group of Muslim pilgrims. One began shouting his name and told of his exploits, and they began to look for a scar on his right shoulder, which they indeed found.

> They [Muslim pilgrims] stripped him of his cloak and robe, and
> found the scar as he had said to them. So they bound him with
> the cords of the beasts, and joined him to his companion monks,
> who were three in number. They undid his bonds and at night
> pleaded with him to flee, saying to him, "We will remain with
> them, to do with us what they will, and offer ourselves in your
> stead." He answered them saying, "It is more fitting that I be your
> ransom, by myself."[43]

The whole affair became as extravagant as 'Abd al-Masīḥ had been in his early days, as his companions herded him to authorities and eventually to the governor.

> The governor said to him, "Be ashamed of yourself! For you are
> a man of high birth and dignity!" 'Abd al-Masīḥ replied, "Shame
> from Christ my God is more compelling than shame from you!
> Do what you like."[44]

So they did exactly that. In what appears to be a mock trial, people "bore witness to what they did not know," and he was found guilty. The ancient source is a bit curious here, because he was obviously guilty of becoming a Christian (apostasy from Islam), so the other charges seemed unnecessary.

He brought him out [of the jail] and offered him Islam, but ['Abd al-Masīh] did not accept it from him, and [his] response offended [the governor's] hearing. At that [the governor] went into a rage, and ordered that he be beheaded. And indeed they carried it out. Then [the governor] ordered that [his body] be concealed from the Christians and burned. So they carried it until they reached a well at Balighah, which had been laid waste. They threw his body into it, cast upon it great quantities of wood, and kindled a fire in it so that the wood was consumed. They set a guard over it so that the Christians would not steal [his remains]."[45]

Nine months later, monks from St. Catherine's sought help from people in Ramla to recover his body. However, they "were extremely anxious about this, fearing both the sultan and the depth of the well" (180 feet deep), but ten "strong young men" risked the descent at night with candles and a basket on a rope, with one monk lowered down into the depths of the well.

The first thing that appeared of ['Abd al-Masīh] was his skull, which shone like snow. Then he brought out the rest of his body: the fire had not burned it, and had not caused it any damage at all. [The monk] rejoiced exceedingly at that, and great was his wonder. He took one of his arms and hid it, and likewise took some of his bones, then put the rest into the basket and called to them to pull it up.[46]

The rest of the story is included below because as much as any martyrology it shows the veneration of a saint's relics. As the editor of the modern translation notes, "There is the final comedy of the human wrangling over the relics, . . . an opportunity to examine the history of the cult of the saints—and to think about the various ways in which all Christians seek down-to-earth assurance of the presence and power of God."[47] The account continues,

When they had pulled it up, all those who were above snatched at [his remains] and fled to the lower church. Three of them remained behind, and brought up the monk. When they had brought him up, they went to St. Kyriakos and found [their companions] wrangling over [the remains]. The monk who had been below continually resisted them until he was able to take his head, and they left him the arm that he had taken in the well. Then they buried ['Abd al-Masīh] in the diakonikon, except for the forearm and thigh, which they held back in order to bring [the martyr] out to the people that they might receive a blessing through him. And the monks departed for the Mount with his head, and there they celebrated his feast.[48]

CYRUS OF HARRAN Many Christians faced martyrdom as a result of jealousy over their giftedness, or the martyr's own misunderstanding of the complex rules of their new Muslim overlords. For some, like Cyrus of Harran, it was both. Cyrus found himself caught between the collapse of the Umayyads, for whom he may have led a group of Christian cavalrymen, and the victorious Abbasids.[49]

According to an ancient document written a few years after Cyrus's death, *Chronicle of Zuqnin*, and later versions like that of Michael the Syrian, we learn that he was executed not for helping the Umayyads, but for apostasy.[50] That is, his accusers claimed he had registered as a Muslim, and now was a practicing Christian. Since one's religious claim was both private and public, but the public listing overruled the private, the judge tried to determine if Cyrus had registered as both. It's unclear if he inadvertently registered on the wrong list—the *diwan* instead of the *jizya*. The former was for taxes and a share of Islamic spoils of war. The latter is the poll tax on non-Muslims.

When the judge pressed him on being registered as one or the other, he tried to press him to convert to Islam like the throngs of other Christians, including some of the priests. Cyrus was clear in his Christian convictions, and after rejecting the judge's offers of position and wealth, he also called these Christian converts to Islam lapsed, weak, and foolish. After being imprisoned he managed to escape, fleeing to Edessa. After four years, as we saw with Vahan, he felt convicted to return to Syria for trial in 770 and boldly proclaimed the gospel—an invitation to martyrdom that led to his death.[51]

Jihad appears often in the Quran, and its meaning (or main emphasis) appears to change among interpreters, depending on their century and division of Islam. It is one of the more nuanced terms in Muslim theology and history. Ultimately, it means *striving* or *struggling*, but the context of this struggle in Islam has varied dramatically. Many have interpreted the imperative to *jihad* in strictly spiritual terms, as in striving for righteousness against the evils of society or our own inclinations. More commonly, *jihad* has been associated with war and acts of violence.[52] During the first 150 years of Islamic conquests, especially in what the Sunni branch calls the Rashidun (the great caliphate following Muhammad's death, AD 632–661), it was associated with violent conquest. But as expansion stopped, it took on a more spiritual meaning. However, the militant aspect surfaced anew in the eighteenth century with Wahhabism (named after an Islamic leader in Saudi Arabia).

In our own time, this concept has gained widespread attention through the prominence of Islamic terrorism and extremism in global news. Just as Christian scholars attempt to stem the flow of deviant teaching, Muslim exegetes point to the long and varied history of the term *jihad*, separating this important theological concept from radicalism within their ranks.

> The term "jihad" however means to struggle or strive in order to promote what is good and prevent what is wrong—a fundamental moral imperative within Islam. Such striving can be accomplished through personal spiritual purification, social reform, and, when applicable, through military defense of those who have been persecuted. Militants and Islamophobes alike focus on the notion of jihad as armed combat.
>
> The most frequently cited verse to make this point is Quran 9:5, which states: "And when the sacred months have passed, then kill the polytheists wherever you find them and capture them and besiege them and sit in wait for them at every place of ambush."[53]

But as we're seeing in this chapter, violent acts in the name of Islam against unbelievers, or "infidels," are not a postmodern development, but date to an early era of Islamic religion and expansion.[54] "It's clear that ISIS and other militant groups today are not carrying out a military jihad as understood by mainstream scholars. . . . Those who describe the actions of these militant groups as jihad are part of the problem, not the solution."[55]

IBN RAJĀ The story of Ibn Rajā of Egypt largely mirrors that of the apostle Paul with one major exception—Ibn Rajā was not martyred for his faith. He was tortured and humiliated but in the last moment, and against all odds, he was not killed. As a young man, Ibn Rajā openly persecuted Christians. But whereas Paul held the coats of the men who murdered Stephen, this committed young scholar, zealous for Islamic law, personally beat a Christian apostate with his shoe before that person was beheaded and burned.

Years later, on a pilgrimage to Mecca, Ibn Rajā experienced mystical visions that led him to convert. Because of his background and the circumstances of this conversion, he was christened at his baptism with the new name "Paul."

On learning of his conversion, his family immediately wanted to kill him themselves, but after being "touched by pity" they decided in their beneficence that it might be enough just to make him watch his own brother rape the mother of his son. They imprisoned and starved him and planned to drown him in the Nile, but their request to the highest judge in Cairo for a harsh sentence backfired and ended, somehow, in a sudden release. Islamic authorities essentially sided with Ibn Rajā against his family, and he spent the rest of his life as a Christian monk, actively writing against Islam, and was somehow allowed the freedom to do so. Some of his writing survives to this day.[56]

PERFECTUS THE MONK The possibility of generous rulings in Islamic courts could at times provide a periodic sense of security among Christians living in Muslim lands. The story of Perfectus is in this sense an opposite to that of Ibn Rajā in that he expected leniency and was given death by Muslim authorities.

One day while walking down the road, he was promised immunity regarding his religious views by a group of Muslims who approached him. He reluctantly shared his view of Muhammad as a false prophet who had "corrupted the malleable hearts of the masses with his deadly venom."[57] He openly criticized Muhammad for allegedly forcing Zayd (his adopted son) to divorce his wife Zaynab so that she could marry Muhammad instead.[58] Perfectus appears to have shocked this group by presenting Muhammad as a "patron of lust and a slave to the pleasures of iniquity."[59]

Perfectus was subsequently led to a judge and thrown in prison. When given a chance to recant, he instead argued even more forcefully, "I have reviled and still do revile your prophet as the man of demons, a sorcerer, an adulterer, and a liar."[60] They decapitated him so viciously that his blood is said to have "smeared the feet of his executioners."[61]

ISAAC AND ARGIMIRUS Isaac and Argimirus weren't martyred together, but they were martyred in the same city (Cordoba), and on similar charges—Isaac in 851 and Argimirus in 856. They were both government officials who were privileged in society, and they died for denouncing doctrines sacred to Islam.

While every martyrdom is a tragedy, these two stand out, given their location and civic status. They surprised their Muslim peers by bucking the cultural expectations of the Cordoban elite, and invited death instead, in an obvious protest of state violence against the Christian community. The government's retribution in these cases showed in one case a degree of sadistic ingenuity, while the other, no less sadistic, lacked imagination. Argimirus was "placed on a small horse and impaled," and Isaac was crucified by the side of the Guadalquivir River.[62]

DAVID OF DWIN Sometime in 703 or 704, an Arab soldier of noble birth was executed for leaving his Muslim faith and becoming a Christian. During his soldier days he encountered Christians, became mesmerized by their teachings, and was baptized with the new name David. He seems to have lived out his life among other Christians with considerable freedom until a new Islamic governor began to assert more direct control over the Christian community. Like other martyr accounts dealing with apostasy during this era, David revealed his beliefs thinking it "not right that the truth be hidden."[63] After an argument with the judge, he was crucified—but they insisted that he be crucified facing west, toward Mecca. His martyrology records that the cross miraculously turned east so that in his final triumph he further rejected Islam with a victorious Christianity.

+ Historic Sources

Many church historians nod to the Etchmiadzin Cathedral in Armenia as the oldest in Christendom, with archaeological remains dating to around AD 303. Its patron was the Armenian king Tiridates the Great (reigned AD 298-330). Gregory the Illuminator factored heavily in this king's conversion and the Christianization of Armenia.[64] Etchmiadzin is located near the Khor Virap monastery, built on the site where Gregory languished in a deep dungeon for thirteen years.

AN EXCERPT FROM HISTORY OF ST. GREGORY AND THE CONVERSION OF ARMENIA, MID-FIFTH CENTURY

When the Muslims conquered the Christian territories in and around ancient Armenia, they were conquering spiritual descendants of the remarkable Saint Gregory, or Gregory the Illuminator. They were also conquering the first country that had adopted Christianity as its official religion (AD 301) due in large part to the life, diligence, and persistence of this unique leader—the Armenian Apostolic Church's first head and its patron saint.[65] Though not the first Christian minister in Armenia, he initiated mass conversion and according to his biographer, Agathangelos, baptized 190,000 converts. . . . The story below picks up after Gregory expounded on the gospel message, but also likened the king's rejection of it to that of a mule's intelligence.

AGATHANGELOS, BOOKS 1 AND 2

With that he ordered Gregory to be bound and strung up, with a muzzle over his mouth and a heavy block of salt hung on his back. After a week of this torture, Gregory was brought before the king, who said: "Now like a mule you have carried a load. But worse things can happen to you if you further insult our deities."

Gregory, however, had not been subdued by his suffering. He told the king that he did not mind tortures, and that only those who worship idols need fear the Lord's wrath.

So Tiridates tortured him further, hanging him by one foot for seven days. But Gregory passed the time in prayer. He recalled in his prayer how God had prepared mankind for eternal life, a gift which we threw away with our disobedience. Yet God did not abandon us. Rather He sent the prophets, and finally His own Son, to show us His will. Christ became the image of God so that we, who love to worship images, might finally worship the Truth. He gave us a wooden cross rather than wooden idols. He called us to sacrifice as Christ had sacrificed, and to partake of His body and blood as we had once eaten sacrificial animals. . . .

Even this terrible torture, which broke his body, did not sway Gregory. After a week of it, he was again brought before Tiridates, who asked him once more to pay homage to the idols. Gregory again refused, and Tiridates submitted him to many more hideous tortures. But Gregory withstood them all and told the king: "I can endure all this not through my own power but by the Lord's grace. Now you will see that nothing can separate us from His love."

It was about this time that a prince of the court told Tiridates that Gregory was the murderer of Anak's son. [Anak had killed Tiridates's father.] Upon hearing this, Tiridates ordered Gregory to be put in a deep pit until he died. As it turned out, Gregory would be there for thirteen years.

The following picks up after the story of Tiridates's murder of the beautiful nun, Hripsime, and many of her assistants. Emperor Diocletian had informed Tiridates that his scouts had spotted her—to paint for his selection—but she fled. Both Diocletian and Tiridates were furious with the Christians due to her flights and rejections.

[The soldiers] tortured Hripsime to death [and then] dragged their bodies out and threw them as food for the prowling dogs.

Tiridates was unashamed of what he had done. Indeed his heart was more inflamed against the Christians and especially against Gayane, who had counseled his wonderful Hripsime not to yield to him. He commanded that the abbess should be killed, and so she was taken to the place used for criminals' executions. But like her companions, Gayane was unafraid, and expressed her wish to join her sisters speedily. She died as they had, with a prayer on her lips.

King Tiridates was not an introspective man, . . . [and went hunting]. . . .

Suddenly, Tiridates fell from the chariot, as if struck down by a demon. He began to rave and grunt, like an animal. As their king was crazed, so all the people suddenly seemed to be, and there was chaos and ruin throughout the city and from the highest to the lowest of the king's household.

But one person had a solution. The king's sister, Chosroesidokht, had a heavenly vision which told her that only the prisoner in the pit, Gregory, could end the terrible nightmare. At first people said she too was mad; Gregory must be dead after so many years in the awful place. But the vision came to her again and again, and each time it disturbed her more. So it was finally decided to send one of the young princes to Artaxata. When he arrived, the prince convinced some people there to lower long ropes into the pit, and he called out: "Gregory, if you are down there, let us know!" They felt a tug on the rope, and pulled it up out of the pit. There was Gregory, his body blackened by dirt to the color of coal. The people helped him get clean, and brought clean clothing for him, and he was taken to Vagharshapat with joy and high hopes that he could remedy the situation there.

A pitiful sight greeted him in the great city: the people, raving and foaming at the mouth, rushed toward him like wild dogs. He knelt and prayed, and at once the people regained at least enough of their senses to listen to him. The king knelt before him and begged forgiveness. But Gregory pulled Tiridates to his feet and said: "I am just a man like you. The One who has had mercy on you is your creator, the Lord and Creator of all things."

Gregory gathered up the remains of those who had been martyred—no dog had touched the bodies, and they were not decomposed—and he enshrouded them and took them to the nuns' former dwelling place. He spent that night praying for the salvation and repentance of the Armenian populace.[66]

Vintage Foxe

The following is from the 1576 Foxe edition, and shows the open and unabashed assessment of Islam by Christian writers (and leaders)—a sentiment expressed commonly into the twentieth century.[68] By the sixteenth century, the Christian-Muslim divide had become more complex than religious differences. On Pentecost Sunday in 1453, the Ottomans conquered Constantinople, the jewel of Eastern Christianity that had been a Christian symbol of strength since AD 330, and for a time was one of the Crusader States (the Latin Empire, 1204–1261). Then in 1517 (the same year Martin Luther's Ninety-Five Theses ushered in the Protestant Reformation), the Ottomans conquered the Mamluks of Egypt, and claimed the caliphate—the designation of overseeing the Islamic world. And in 1571— only a few years before this edition of Foxe—the Catholic Coalition led by Spain's Phillip II dealt immense casualties to the Muslim Ottomans at the Battle of Lepanto—killing 30,000. The conflict between the religions was raging, which shows the context for Foxe's candid use of the adjective *detestable* (sometimes rendered as *wicked*). Foxe writes:

Near about this time, in the year of our Lord, 666, the detestable sect of [Muhammad], began to take strength & place: Although Polychronicon differing a little in years, accounteth the beginning of this sect somewhat before. But the most diligent searchers of them which write now, referreth it to this year, which well agreeth with the number of the beast, signed in the Apocalypse. That is 666. Of this [Muhammad] came the kingdom of Agarenes (whom he after named Saracens) to whom he gave sundry laws, patched of many sects and religions together, he taught them to pray ever to the South: And as we keep the Sunday, so they keep the Friday: which they call the day of Venus. He permitted them to have as many wives as they were able to maintain: to have as many concubines as they list: to abstain from use of wine, except upon certain solemn days in the year: to have & worship only one God omnipotent: saying, that Moses & the Prophets were great men, but Christ was greater, and greatest of all the Prophets: as being born of the virgin Mary by the power of God, without man's seed: and at last was taken up to heaven, but was not slain: but an other in his likeness for him, with many other wicked blasphemies in his law contained. At length this kingdom of the Saracens began to be conquered of the Turks, and so in process of time wholly subdued to them.[69]

The Late Middle Ages through the King James Bible (1611)

From the Khans' Swords to Burning Saints

WILLIAM TYNDALE

William Tyndale's life and martyrdom speak volumes into the lives of millions of people—literally. He produced the first printed New Testament in English and paid for it with his life. His translation of the New Testament (1526) and half of the Old Testament (translated during his year and a half in prison) would change the course of history for English-speaking Christians.

After leaving England and publishing his New Testament in Germany, Tyndale lived in Antwerp, taking refuge from Henry VIII, Cardinal Wolsey, Sir Thomas More, and Bishop Tunstall. Printed copies were smuggled into England in bags of flour and bolts of cloth, and Tyndale's opponents bought up and destroyed every copy they could find. However, their plan backfired. The funds helped Tyndale and his allies to produce exponentially more English Bibles. A spy (Henry Phillips) helped authorities capture Tyndale and eventually brought about his execution in 1536.

In 1535, during Tyndale's long incarceration near Brussels, he wrote asking for supplies to help him finish his English translation of the Bible's Hebrew text, clothes to keep him warm, and a lamp to combat the prolonged darkness. English authorities condemned him as a heretic the next year, beginning with a "degradation ceremony" that ritually removed him from the priesthood and stripped his priestly attire piece by piece, along with the symbolic scraping of his hands. They showed him the communion elements (bread and wine), then removed them. After marching him to a public square, they made him "stand atop a pile of logs and kindling that had been dusted with gunpowder. Guards lashed him to an upright post. They placed a rope and chain noose around his neck. Given an opportunity to say some final words, Tyndale prayed simply, 'Lord, open the king of England's eyes.' Following that, he was strangled to death and his body burned."[1]

He had been "singularly addicted" to Scripture since his youth, fueled by seeing Martin Luther's Bible for the German people.[2] Tyndale wanted his own relatives and neighbors to have the Scriptures—their own personal Bible, much in line with Erasmus's exhortation: "Let all the conversations of every Christian be drawn from this source. . . . Only a very few can be learned, but all can be Christian, all can be devout, and—I shall boldly add—all can be theologians."[3]

In his twenties, Tyndale pursued studies at Oxford and then Cambridge, mastering many languages in the process. While tutoring the children of his patrons the Walshes, his interaction with priests reinforced his desire for a vernacular translation, in part due to the growing biblical illiteracy prompted by the waning use of Latin.[4]

The Church had good reason to be worried about common language translations. "Their fear was not without precedent, as the dissemination of misunderstood or radical biblical teachings had played out various times in history."[5] A similar concern led colleges to teach theology as "the queen of the sciences," which students studied only after showing competency in the basic subjects—akin to general education courses today.

Within three years after Tyndale's martyrdom, Henry VIII's eyes were opened. He ordered Tyndale's assistant, Myles Coverdale, to produce *The Great Bible* in the English vernacular, and in 1539 required it placed in all English churches.

CHAPTER SIX

Christians Martyred at Diverse Hands

Have I not commanded you? Be strong and courageous. Do not be frightened, and do not be dismayed, for the LORD your God is with you wherever you go. JOSHUA 1:9

Be strong and courageous. Do not fear or be in dread of them, for it is the LORD your God who goes with you. He will not leave you or forsake you. DEUTERONOMY 31:6

Christ was not a powerless victim but a powerful sacrifice.
LUMEN RESEARCH INSTITUTE SYMPOSIUM, SEPTEMBER 27, 2019

Don't you see that the more of them [Christians] that are punished, the greater the number of the rest becomes? This does not seem to be the work of man. This is the power of God. These are the evidences of his appearance.[1] LETTER TO DIOGNETUS, SECOND CENTURY

Charles Martel stopped the Muslim advances at the Battle of Tours (AD 732), but Christians had been fighting other forces leading up to this key event in France—and unfortunately one of these forces consisted of other Christians. These battles between factions of Christianity would continue for centuries. While some of these Christian confrontations took place in the renegade exploits of certain Crusades, especially the infamous Fourth (sacking Zara and Constantinople), this chapter addresses the sweeping theological conflicts that manifested themselves in armies and regions. And in the lives of countless Christians from the various factions.

Long before the seventh century when Muhammad and his forces began attacking Christian-controlled regions, Christians had been attacking one another. With four different centers of the Church—Antioch, Rome, Alexandria, and Constantinople—different views and alliances developed. The West (especially Rome) did not want to recognize any patriarchal centers lacking a direct historic connection to one of the apostles, a power play to exclude Constantinople. Conversely, the Eastern Orthodox Church not only endorsed its Byzantine center, but recognized the Pentarchy, adding Jerusalem as one of five patriarchal centers.

Geographic alliances and doctrinal differences both created divisions. At least a dozen multi-church gatherings (or councils) dealt with foundational questions before the familiar Council of Nicaea in AD 325. The latter was the first of the seven ecumenical (or churchwide) councils from the fourth to eighth centuries. Strong personalities surfaced throughout these centuries, many with unwavering support from either the East or the West, but rarely both.

While these councils helped unify the Church in doctrine—including the Nicene Creed—some serious rifts occurred. Perhaps none of the councils' rejected theological movements loomed larger in Christianity's early history than Arianism, which came from the teachings of Arius, a Libyan presbyter.

Arius rejected the Trinity doctrine, claiming God the Father existed before Jesus and that Jesus was not equal to God. Both the First Council of Nicaea (325) and the First Council at Constantinople (381) found Arianism problematic, and ultimately heretical. However, it spread through significant regions and among key military leaders. Some of the conquerors of Orthodox Christian lands were Arian Christians. At times they were as relentless in persecuting the Nicene (or orthodox) Christians as were pagans.

Similarly, the third ecumenical council in Chalcedon (AD 451), the highest attended with around 520 church leaders present, evaluated many bishops for orthodoxy. For example, the council officially rejected Bishop Dioscorus of Alexandria, which angered the Coptic Church in Egypt and created a lasting split between three of the Oriental Orthodox Churches (Coptic, Armenian, and Syriac) and the Eastern Orthodox Church. Although both sides remained clearly within the Christian fold, they retained stark differences over polity and some liturgical matters.

The Second and Third Councils of Constantinople also dealt with heresy questions (Nestorianism and Monophysitism in 553, and Monothelitism in 680).[2] The last of these major councils, the Second Council of Nicaea (AD 787) dealt with Iconoclasm ("breaking of icons"). This became yet another cause of disagreement between the Eastern and Western churches (Greek Orthodox and Roman Catholic).

The original work of John Foxe is rather tough on Catholicism, and throughout his work he targets the popes and Catholic leaders, but the fuller story includes countless martyrs within the Roman Catholic tradition— enough to fill several volumes.

However, during a few eras the Catholic Church, like most long-standing religious institutions, had its low points.

> Unity was the keynote of medieval society; and this unity was achieved by the universal institutions of the Holy Roman Empire, by the hierarchal Roman Church and allegiance to it, and the spiritual standardization of the sacraments and the creeds; but underneath this unity were always rumblings of dissent. These rumblings were to become at the time of the Reformation a volcanic explosion that would tear asunder the fabric of medieval religion.[3]

These institutions were concerned about any variant affiliations that threatened the status quo. Some groups blasted as heretics, like the followers of Peter Waldo (Waldensians), were mainly a threat to order, not orthodoxy. Instead of classifying them as victims of the "papal persecutions" as Foxe does, we have chosen the phrase "universal institutions" to help us explain the various motives involved in killing so many Christians.

Foxe was a Protestant. He had an affinity for the Waldensians and Albigensians who were providing Bibles in the people's vernacular language—much the same issue for which John Wycliffe, William Tyndale, and their followers were persecuted. The Roman Catholic Church found it problematic for uneducated preachers among the Waldensians and Albigensians to offer comparisons between the New Testament church and that centered in Rome. Foxe compiled his book only a few years after many of his Protestant friends lost their lives in the Marian persecutions (1553–1558).

Queen Mary I could not have been more Catholic. Her mother's parents were the Catholic monarchs of Spain who colonized the New World for the Church, King Ferdinand II (of Aragon) and Queen Isabella I (of Castile). Henry VIII jilted Catherine of Aragon (Mary's mother), and then Catholics in general through his roller-coaster marriages and religious pursuits, all of which understandably frustrated Mary. She attempted to roll back the English (Protestant) Reformation, putting to death around three hundred Protestants, mainly through burning them at the stake.

Against this horrific backdrop of the Marian era from his Protestant English perspective, Foxe wrote:

> Thus far our history of persecution has been confined principally
> to the pagan world. We come now to a period when persecution,
> under the guise of Christianity, committed more enormities
> than ever disgraced the annals of paganism. Disregarding the
> maxims and the spirit of the Gospel, the papal Church, arming
> herself with the power of the sword, vexed the Church of God
> and wasted it for several centuries, a period most appropriately
> termed in history, the "dark ages." The kings of the earth, gave

their power to the "Beast," and submitted to be trodden on by the miserable vermin that often filled the papal chair.[4]

Reading any one source on these persecuted groups, we must keep in mind the author's lens toward the groups and individuals discussed.

Unlike the monks and friars, who sought to bring about internal reform, the Cathari or Albigenses, the Waldenses and other sects, such as the Petrobrusians, arose as an external revolt to purify religion in the late twelfth century. The frequency of corruption in the life and practice of the papal hierarchy and the secular activities of the papacy made many react against the lack of spiritual power that they often saw in their parish churches. More information concerning these medieval sects has been preserved by their enemies than by their friends, and therefore accurate information about them is scarce.[5]

As with all martyrs throughout history, it matters less who swung the sword or who lit the fires that consumed these faithful witnesses; the crucial matter, rather, is what consumed them as their heads were severed or their bodies burned. They spilled blood because they believed in a Savior who had spilled his innocent blood for them.

OPPRESSION FROM ALL SIDES
Proterius

The Council of Chalcedon evaluated the orthodoxy of a number of bishops. Among them was Dioscorus, whom they deposed, selecting Proterius to succeed him. The Coptic Church hotly contested the new bishop, even to the point of bloodshed.

This occasioned a dangerous insurrection, for the city of Alexandria was divided into two factions; the one to espouse the cause of the old, and the other of the new prelate. In one of the commotions,

the Eutychians [whom the councils deemed heretical] determined
to wreak their vengeance on Proterius, who fled to the church for
sanctuary: but on Good Friday, AD 457, a large body of them
rushed into the church, and barbarously murdered the prelate; after
which they dragged the body through the streets, insulted it, cut it
to pieces, burnt it, and scattered the ashes in the air.[6]

Keep in mind, this is a Christian patriarch killed in his line of duty. To
this day, while the Eastern Orthodox Church considers Proterius a saint,
Copts do not even recognize him as a legitimate patriarch.

Evagrius Scholasticus, a Syrian scholar from Antioch, gives further details
of Proterius's death and notes he had "discharged the functions of his office."
As with many records from these centuries of the great councils, the author's
allegiances significantly color the account. Scholasticus wrote during the late
sixth century from Syria and was clearly pro-Chalcedonian.

Some of the Alexandrians, at the instigation of Timotheus,
according to the written report made to Leo, despatch[ed]
Proterius when he appeared, by thrusting a sword through
his bowels, after he had fled for refuge to the holy baptistery.
Suspending the body by a cord, they displayed it to the public in
the quarter called Tetrapylum, jeering and vociferating that the
victim was Proterius; and, after dragging it through the whole city,
committed it to the flames; not even refraining themselves from
tasting his intestines, like beasts of prey, according to the account
of the entire transaction contained in the petition addressed by
the Egyptian bishops and the whole clergy of Alexandria to Leo,
who, as has been said, was invested with the imperial power on
the death of Marcian.[7]

These types of events challenge our understanding of *martyr*, as
Proterius didn't die at the hands of "the enemy" of Christ, but was tor-
tured and killed by a group that diverged because of their Christology.
Both groups professed the truth of Christ—so much so that deviation from

their interpretations of his message was considered heresy. Details such as "tasting his intestines" are likely embellishments to disparage the attackers, whom the author considered heretics. However, Proterius did die for his faith, likely at the violent hands of people who thought they were defending the same gospel.

Hermenigildus

Hermenigildus was a Gothic prince of Spain whose wife, Ingonda, had led him out of his Arian beliefs and fostered his conversion to orthodoxy.

> When the king heard that his son had changed his religious sentiments, he stripped him of the command at Seville, where he was governor, and threatened to put him to death unless he renounced the faith he had newly embraced. The prince . . . began to put himself into a posture of defence; and many of the orthodox persuasion in Spain declared for him. The king, exasperated at this act of rebellion, began to punish all the orthodox Christians who could be seized by his troops, and thus a very severe persecution commenced: he likewise marched against his son at the head of a very powerful army. The prince . . . was at length besieged and taken at Asieta. Loaded with chains, he was sent to Seville, and at the feast of Easter refusing to receive the Eucharist from an Arian bishop, the enraged king ordered his guards to cut the prince to pieces, which they punctually performed, April 13, A.D. 586.[8]

Not only did this involve an Arian Christian (deemed heretical) killing an orthodox Christian (like those of us who endorse the Nicene Creed), but also an Arian father killing his orthodox son. All this on the high holy day of Christianity—Easter. The bizarre and troubling backdrop does not diminish in the least Hermenigildus's commitment to Christ as he stood in chains making the ultimate sacrifice, while rejecting the tainted sacraments.

Martin of Rome

The fate of Martin, bishop of Rome, seems about as dumbfounding as any of these attacks on Christian leaders. Martin lost his life fighting heresy, though his death seemed more attached to accusations of collaborating with the Muslims, accusations later withdrawn. In the end, both the Orthodox and Roman churches tried saving him, and later would canonize him.

> Martin, bishop of Rome, was born at Todi, in Italy. He was
> naturally inclined to virtue, and his parents bestowed on
> him an admirable education. He opposed the heretics called
> Monothelites, who were patronized by the emperor Heraclius
> [AD 610–641]. Martin was condemned at Constantinople, where
> he was exposed in the most public places to the ridicule of the
> people, divested of all episcopal marks of distinction, and treated
> with the greatest scorn and severity. After lying some months in
> prison, Martin was sent to an island at some distance, and there
> cut to pieces, A.D. 655.[9]

In 1800, Pope Pius VII wrote about St. Martin's plight in his *Diu Satis* (*On a Return to Gospel Principles*):

> Indeed, the famous Martin who long ago won great praise for
> this See, commends faithfulness and fortitude to Us by his
> strengthening and defense of the truth and by the endurance of
> labors and pains. He was driven from his See and from the City,
> stripped of his rule, his rank, and his entire fortune. As soon as
> he arrived in any peaceful place, he was forced to move. Despite
> his advanced age and an illness which prevented his walking, he
> was banished to a remote land and repeatedly threatened with
> an even more painful exile. Without the assistance offered by the
> pious generosity of individuals, he would not have had food for
> himself and his few attendants. Although he was tempted daily in

his weakened and lonely state, he never surrendered his integrity. No deceit could trick, no fear perturb, no promises conquer, no difficulties or dangers break him.[10]

Killian

In the case of the Irish preacher Killian (or Killien), we are also reminded of the importance of standing up for biblical principles. The apostle Paul did so when he called out the sin of illicit sexual relations among believers in 1 Corinthians 5. Killian also did so with the very duke he had helped to convert.

> Killien was born in Ireland, and received from his parents a pious and Christian education. He obtained the Roman pontiff's license to preach to the pagans in Franconia, in Germany. At Wurtzburg he converted Gozbert, the governor, whose example was followed by the greater part of the people in two years after. Persuading Gozbert that his marriage with his brother's widow was sinful, the latter had him beheaded, A.D. 689.[11]

In other accounts, it is actually Gozbert's wife, Gellian (a non-convert), who had him killed in her new husband's absence. She sent men to behead Killian and his two colleagues, Colman and Totnan, while they were preaching in the city square of Würzburg.[12] In this rendition, Gellian goes insane. The relics of the three martyrs, including their skulls, are annually processed through the city in a glass coffin on their feast day.

PERSECUTIONS FROM THE EIGHTH THROUGH THE TENTH CENTURY

Boniface

Boniface (680–754) has been called the "father of the German church." He established numerous Benedictine monasteries in German territories, which he divided into dioceses. Prominent among them was Fulda (in central Germany), now the site of the saint's tomb, where the German

Catholic bishops hold their ecclesiastical conference each year to venerate Boniface's life and death.

Throughout his lifetime, Boniface exhausted himself fighting corruption within the remnants of the Merovingian church, holding various high positions for leaders wanting reform. The Merovingians, under the first king of France, Clovis I, had factored prominently in the Catholic conversion of France and surrounding regions in Belgium and Germany and provided the religious context for Charlemagne's Catholic allegiance and that of subsequent Holy Roman emperors. Clovis was baptized Catholic on Christmas Day, AD 496. However, as we see among succeeding generations of various Christian groups, reform was needed. Meanwhile, the Merovingians dominated the territories north of Italy (the kingdom of the Lombards, AD 568–774). However, the Merovingians were waning, though still officially in power until the pope deposed their last king in 751, then turned to the Carolingian family.

Boniface constantly challenged or tried to balance the close tie between the Carolingian rulers and the Catholic Church. His spiritual leadership became legendary after the incident of the pagan oak of Thor at Geismar (the Donar Oak, or Jupiter's Oak).[13] He allegedly chopped down the sacred tree, and much like Elijah's episode with the Canaanites' god, dared Thor to strike him down. Afterward he built a church from the Oak of Thor. In one account, he stopped the pagan's axe from sacrificing a child, and then, after chopping down the great oak with one stroke, pointed out a small fir tree representing the child; being Christmas Eve, it became associated with the Christmas season (i.e., the Christmas tree).

After retiring as archbishop of Mainz, Boniface returned to his original mission field—Friesland, a northern province in what is now the Netherlands. But local tribes were enraged at his relentless destruction of pagan shrines. In 754, a raiding party of pagan Frisians slaughtered Boniface and over fifty others. He was seventy-three years old.

Boniface and his recruits, including many Saxon priests from his homeland in England, had been in the midst of tremendous success, realizing the conversion of thousands of pagans. One of the treasures with him was the *Ragyndrudis Codex*. It is now on display in Fulda (with a nail hole and marks likely from the robbers' attack).

> The day before Pentecost Sunday that year, Boniface had arranged for a huge confirmation ceremony for his new converts in the open fields on the plain of Dokkum on the banks of the Borne River. . . . He and his companions had set up a tent and altar there to await the arrival of the neophytes . . . when suddenly a raiding party from one of the unconverted bands of barbarians descended on the camp. Boniface told his companions calmly to trust in God and not to fear dying for the Catholic Faith. Crying out for vengeance for their false pagan gods, whose existence the missionaries were denying, the heathens killed Boniface and his companions with battle axes, spears, and clubs. Boniface, it was later learned, was the first to fall.
>
> When his new converts arrived for their confirmation, they found the bodies of Boniface and the others. Weeping, they took the body of Boniface back to Fulda.[14]

DID YOU KNOW? *Ragyndrudis Codex—The Shield of a Saint*

Thousands of relics are associated with martyrs, but rarely do they evidence the actual moment of torment and death of the saint. In 754, Boniface was carrying this collection of religious essays, possibly written by a laywoman. When the pagan tribe of Frisians attacked and began hacking to death the Anglo-Saxon Boniface and around fifty of his companions, Boniface held up the codex (a manuscript book bound at the spine). The five deep cuts in the original binding and cover, and into the pages, corroborate the early tenth-century account of his martyrdom. The common assumption is that the damage represents sword and axe blows. The nail hole through the book is in keeping with the anti-Christian practice of nailing such texts to a tree. It is one of three of his personal books that survive, all kept in Fulda, Germany, where the saint is buried.

The Armorian Martyrs

In the ninth century AD, Christians began using the term "Saracen" for Arabs in general who converted to Islam (the Greeks had earlier used it for the Arabs in the Sinai Peninsula). They had stormed through the eastern empire, including Armorian, a city in Upper Phrygia, where the Saracens killed forty-two Christians in 845. For instance,

> Flora and Mary, two ladies of distinction, suffered martyrdom at the same time. Perfectus was born at Corduba, in Spain, and brought up in the Christian faith. Having a quick genius, he made himself master of all the useful and polite literature of that age; and at the same time was not more celebrated for his abilities than admired for his piety. At length he took priest's orders, and performed the duties of his office with great assiduity and punctuality. Publicly declaring Mahomet an impostor, he was sentenced to be beheaded, and was accordingly executed, A.D. 850; after which his body was honorably interred by the Christians.[15]

Adalbert

This bishop of Prague died by darts (feathered spears)! Apparently, death by various violent means was a strong possibility if you enraged pagan priests in the late tenth century in that region. Adalbert had a storied journey before arriving in Dantzic on the Baltic coast (Gdańsk today in northern Poland). His ability to lead many of "the infidels" (Baltic Prussians) to Christ directly led to the holes pounded into his chest on April 23, 997.[16]

He began as a Bohemian missionary from a wealthy family, was often in trouble for his conservative views in foreign lands, and was even pulled from duties and lived as a hermit for several years. He was relentless in his evangelism, constantly offending people with less overt goals while trying to convert pagans.

Regardless of the controversies around his life, the Prussians sold his body back to Christians for its weight in gold. Today he posthumously holds many honorary titles, including the patron saint of the Czech—called by his birth name, Vojtěch.

PERSECUTIONS IN THE ELEVENTH CENTURY
Alphage of Canterbury

Martyrs can be found among those from rich and poor backgrounds, and everywhere in between. No tax records were affixed to martyrs as they hung in the gallows or marched to the pyres. The tormentors of Alphage—archbishop of Canterbury—couldn't seem to separate his wealthy birth and relatives from his core beliefs. His eyes were fixed on Christ upon the cross, not the cross he bore for Christ.

The Danes had sacked Canterbury and slaughtered thousands of Christians, but Alphage refused to recant and give in to their ransom scheme or disclose the location of the church's treasury. Instead, he endured horrendous torture before being beheaded (April 19, AD 1012). There are two accounts of his death, the first from the early *Anglo Saxon Chronicle*:

> The raiding-army became much stirred up against the bishop, because he did not want to offer them any money, and forbade that anything might be granted in return for him. Also they were very drunk, because there was wine brought from the south. Then they seized the bishop, led him to their "hustings" on the Saturday in *the octave of Easter*, and then pelted him there with bones and the heads of cattle; and one of them struck him on the head with the butt of an axe, so that with the blow he sank down and his holy blood fell on the earth, and sent forth his holy soul to God's kingdom.[17]

The details of his heroic stance as found in Foxe:

> While he was employed in assisting and encouraging the people, Canterbury was taken by storm; the enemy poured into the town, and destroyed all that came in their way by fire and sword. He

had the courage to address the enemy, and offer himself to their swords, as more worthy of their rage than the people: he begged they might be saved, and that they would discharge their whole fury upon him. They accordingly seized him, tied his hands, insulted and abused him in a rude and barbarous manner, and obliged him to remain on the spot until his church was burnt, and the monks massacred. They then decimated all the inhabitants, both ecclesiastics and laymen, leaving only every tenth person alive; so that they put 7236 persons to death, and left only four monks and 800 laymen alive, after which they confined the archbishop in a dungeon, where they kept him close prisoner for several months.

During his confinement they proposed to him to redeem his liberty with the sum of 3000 pounds, and to persuade the king to purchase their departure out of the kingdom, with a further sum of 10,000 pounds. As Alphage's circumstances would not allow him to satisfy the exorbitant demand, they bound him, and put him to severe torments, to oblige him to discover the treasure of the church; upon which they assured him of his life and liberty, but the prelate piously persisted in refusing to give the pagans any account of it . . . but exhorted them to forsake their idolatry, and embrace Christianity. This so greatly incensed the Danes, that the soldiers dragged him out of the camp and beat him unmercifully. One of the soldiers, who had been converted by him, knowing that his pains would be lingering, as his death was determined on, actuated by a kind of barbarous compassion, cut off his head, and thus put the finishing stroke to his martyrdom.[18]

Gerard of Venice

The Venetian monk Gerard had served God in a religious house since age five. Like many Christians, he wanted to visit the Holy Land and celebrate Christ at the sites closely associated with his earthly journey. However, while he was passing through Hungary, its king, Stephen I, persuaded him to stay in his country to assist with the rampant "infidelity." He convinced Gerard that his desire to visit the Holy Sepulchre had been God's method of delivering him to the lost people in Hungary.

While Gerard accepted this call, he refused to live in the luxury of the court and moved to a hermitage for seven years at Beel—regularly fasting and praying with one other ascetic named Maur. Then the king appointed him bishop of Chonad.

> Gerard considered nothing in this dignity but labours, crosses, and the hopes of martyrdom. Two-thirds of the inhabitants of the city of Chonad were idolaters; yet the saint, in less than a year, made them all Christians. His labours were crowned with almost equal success in all other parts of the dioceses. The fatigues which he underwent were excessive, and the patience with which he bore all kinds of affronts was invincible. He commonly traveled on foot but sometimes in a wagon: he always read or meditated on the road.[19]

During Gerard's tenure, numerous hermitages sprung up. With much of the appeal of Francis of Assisi, and the compassion of Pope Francis (2013–) that has endeared him to millions, bishop Gerard had won the hearts of the masses.

> All distressed persons he took under his particular care, and treated the sick with uncommon tenderness. He embraced lepers, and persons afflicted with other loathsome diseases with the greatest joy and affection; often laid them in his own bed, and had their sores dressed in his own chamber.[20]

When his Christian patron, King Stephen, died in 1038, things changed drastically for Gerard. Stephen's nephew Peter began persecuting Gerard. In 1042, Peter's own subjects forced this "debauched and cruel prince" to leave, but the Holy Roman Emperor restored him and he continued his persecution. Subsequently, King Stephen's cousin, Andrew, struck a bargain to be crowned—to eradicate Christianity from Hungary and restore idolatry (though he would later return to supporting Christianity once installed). Gerard's martyrdom along with three other bishops occurred in 1045 at the hands of Duke Vatha, who hated the very memory of King Stephen.

> The ambitious prince came into the proposal, but Gerard being informed of his impious bargain, thought it his duty to remonstrate against the enormity of Andrew's crime, and persuade him to withdraw his promise. In this view he undertook to go to that prince, attended by three prelates, full of like zeal for religion. The new king was at Alba Regalis, but, as the four bishops were going to cross the Danube, they were stopped by a party of soldiers posted there. They bore an attack of a shower of stones patiently, when the soldiers beat them unmercifully, and at length despatched them with lances.[21]

One account declares that they first put him in a wagon and rolled it down a hill, pierced him with a lance, and then crushed his head. Another notes that he was put in a barrel with knives or spikes and rolled down a hill into a battle among pagan forces. One has the new king ("prince") Andrew saving the fourth bishop from martyrdom, which proved the turning point of the kingdom back to Christianity. That same account shares that before being run through with a lance, Gerard prayed, "Lord, lay not this to their charge; for they know not what they do."[22] Gerard never reached the Holy Land, but came by another route to an even holier kingdom.

Stanislaus of Poland

Stanislaus became bishop of Cracow in 1071 after his life among secular clergy. He learned benevolence from his wealthy Polish family. Stanislaus found himself alone as he challenged the cruel Bolislaus (Boleslaw), the second king of Poland. He finally gave up and excommunicated the king, and instructed the cathedral canons to avoid serving him by canceling the Divine Offices (prayers scheduled at fixed times day and night). In the end, when the king couldn't partake of Christ's body and blood, he chose to take the bishop's instead.[23] In one account, in addition to the king stabbing Stanislaus at the altar, he also dismembered him.[24]

> The king, greatly exasperated at his repeated freedoms, at length determined, at any rate, to get the better of a prelate [Stanislaus] who was so extremely faithful. Hearing one day that the bishop was by himself, in the chapel of St. Michael, at a small distance from the town, he despatched some soldiers to murder him. The soldiers readily undertook the bloody task; but, when they came into the presence of Stanislaus, the venerable aspect of the prelate struck them with such awe that they could not perform what they had promised. On their return, the king, finding that they had not obeyed his orders, stormed at them violently, snatched a dagger from one of them, and ran furiously to the chapel, where, finding Stanislaus at the altar, he plunged the weapon into his heart. The prelate immediately expired on May 8, A.D. 1079.[25]

Pope John Paul II, formerly archbishop of the see of St. Stanislaus, gave a special tribute to the saint from his homeland. In 2003, he wrote to the Polish Church that Stanislaus "proclaimed faith in God to our ancestors and started in them . . . the saving power of the Passion and Resurrection of Jesus Christ. . . . He taught the moral order in the family based on sacramental marriage. He taught the moral order within the State, reminding even the king that in his actions he should keep in mind the unchanging Law of God."[26]

THE WALDENSIAN CRUSADE "Some men's personal lives are eclipsed by the movements they start. Peter Waldo was such a man."[27] Waldo (Valdes) was a radical ascetic—denying earthly pleasures in the most extreme fashion. It's perhaps hard to fathom in many parts of Western culture today, but he attracted quite a following. He was a Lyon merchant who chose a life of apostolic poverty in 1173. Waldo was moved by Jesus' words, such as the story of the rich man who came to Jesus. However, Waldo's response was radically different. He left all of his possessions (including fields, ponds, and the like) with his wife, gave his funds to a nunnery for his girls, and the rest to feed the poor during the famine.

Like many religious groups, his followers, the Waldensians, split over differences, and one key sect received Church protection. From Lyon, Waldo's influence spread throughout Europe, all the way to Bohemia. Many of the Waldensians were either oppressed or attacked during intermittent crusades from the Church, including the Inquisition.

On the surface, it appears that Waldo and his followers should be applauded for their piety and for preaching Christ where no clerics were available. But when groups of Waldensians rejected ecclesiastical authority and some of the Church's doctrines, such as infant baptism and purgatory, the Church called them heretics and considered them a threat. The movement survived when some of the French Waldensians fled to the Alps of Savoy and Piedmont, and others to central Europe.

In an unfortunate turn of events, a wave of Waldensians were slaughtered in the fourteenth century in Calabria, the southwest section of Italy. They had settled on wastelands after emigrating, and through their concerted efforts they transformed the area. Though the magistrates were pleased, the bishops and local priests constantly complained about this group's divergent practices (not honoring Church rituals and customs), particularly that they failed to give a tithe to the Roman Church.

Pope Pius IV sent Cardinal Alexandrino, whom Foxe decried as "a man of very violent temper and a furious bigot, together with two monks, to Calabria, where they were to act as inquisitors."[28] He used the Eucharist as a litmus test in the Waldensian towns of St. Xist and La Garde. At the first town the Waldensians ran into the woods and hid. Frustrated, Cardinal Alexandrino went to the second city, locked the gates and used the same litmus test, but lied to them. He told them that the Waldensian Christians in St. Xist had participated, so the people of La Garde committed to do the same. Satisfied, he then returned with a vengeance to the poor Christians in the woods. The cardinal ordered his soldiers to kill as many of them as they could find, whereupon the Waldensians began to fight back, with the result that many on both sides were killed. The cardinal, enraged, obtained reinforcements from the viceroy of Naples.

The viceroy launched a reprehensible plan, pardoning all kinds of people of their crimes and offenses, "on condition of making a campaign against the inhabitants of St. Xist, and continuing under arms until those people were exterminated." When we step back and try to envision what was transpiring, it would be like the government in our home area sending convicted felons—not just police or military—to hunt us down and kill us on sight. It's like what the Rwandan government did with the hate radio broadcasts leading up to its country's 1994 genocide.

The viceroy brought troops to join the cardinal and his regular forces to hunt down the Waldensians in the woods.

> Some they caught and hanged up upon trees, cut down boughs and burnt them, or ripped them open and left their bodies to be devoured by wild beasts, or birds of prey. Many they shot at a distance, but the greatest number they hunted down by way of sport. A few hid themselves in caves, but famine destroyed them in their retreat; and thus all these poor people perished, by various means, to glut the bigoted malice of their merciless persecutors.[29]

The centuries have not eased the sadness in the extermination of the St. Xist Christians, nor the desire to salute them. The forces then returned to La Garde and tried to persuade the Waldensian Christians to accept full restoration of properties and freedoms if they embraced Roman Catholicism. If they refused, the armed forces threatened them with torture and death. The account is extremely graphic, but note that even Foxe—almost foaming with hatred for the papacy—includes a strong hint that many of the Catholics tried to help the victims (or were "more compassionate than the rest"), and were treated as heretics as well. The Waldensian Christians and the compassionate Catholics who aided them were being killed by those in power, political leaders in religious garb, not primarily for any heresy.

Despite promises and threats, the Waldensians refused to renounce their convictions, with the result that thirty of them were tortured on the rack, to send a message to the rest. Those put on the rack were tortured severely—"one Charlin, in particular, was so cruelly used that his belly burst, his bowels came out, and he expired in the greatest agonies." Those who survived the racks, as well as the rest of the Christians, "boldly declared that no tortures of body, or terrors of mind, should ever induce them to renounce their God, or worship images." In response, the cardinal had some stripped naked and beaten to death with iron rods, some dismembered with knives, some thrown to their deaths from towers, and many coated with pitch and burned alive.

One particularly sadistic monk, receiving the cardinal's permission, cut the throats of eight men, women, and children as if butchering animals. He then quartered the corpses and displayed the body pieces on stakes driven into the ground throughout the countryside in a thirty-mile area. Other atrocities abounded:

> The four principal men of La Garde were hanged, and the
> clergyman was thrown from the top of his church steeple. He
> was terribly mangled, but not quite killed by the fall; at which
> time the viceroy passing by, said, "Is the dog yet living? Take him
> up, and give him to the hogs," when, brutal as this sentence may
> appear, it was executed accordingly.
>
> Sixty women were racked so violently, that the cords pierced
> their arms and legs close to the bone; when, being remanded
> to prison, their wounds mortified, and they died in the most
> miserable manner. Many others were put to death by various cruel
> means; and if any Roman Catholic, more compassionate than
> the rest, interceded for any of the reformed, he was immediately
> apprehended, and shared the same fate as a favorer of heretics.[30]

When official duties required the viceroy to return to Naples and the cardinal to Rome, the marquis of Butane was comissioned to finish the destruction they had begun. And that he did, "acting with such barbarous rigor, that there was not a single person of the reformed religion left living in all Calabria."[31]

+ Historic Sources

JOHN MILTON'S SONNET 18, "ON THE LATE MASSACRE IN PIEDMONT"
The following is about the arduous journey of the Waldensians, who
found favor with many of the Protestant reformers. The basis of this
poem is the horrendous treatment of the Waldensians in northwest Italy–
Catholic troops massacred around two thousand citizens and forcibly
converted about the same number in 1655. Unlike the Albigensians, also
deemed heretics by the Roman Catholic Church, the Waldensians persisted through horrible trials, but faced another onslaught.[32] John Milton
(1608-1674) was prolific and rather open about his religious views, made
evident in what many consider his key works–*Paradise Lost, Paradise
Regained*, and *Samson Agonistes*.[33]

ON THE LATE MASSACRE IN PIEDMONT

Avenge, O Lord, thy slaughter'd saints, whose bones
*   Lie scatter'd on the Alpine mountains cold,*
*   Ev'n them who kept thy truth so pure of old,*
*   When all our fathers worshipp'd stocks and stones;*
Forget not: in thy book record their groans
*   Who were thy sheep and in their ancient fold*
*   Slain by the bloody Piemontese that roll'd*
*   Mother with infant down the rocks. Their moans*
The vales redoubl'd to the hills, and they
*   To Heav'n. Their martyr'd blood and ashes sow*
*   O'er all th' Italian fields where still doth sway*
The triple tyrant [the pope]: that from these may grow
*   A hundred-fold, who having learnt thy way*
*   Early may fly the Babylonian woe.*

THE ALBIGENSIAN CRUSADE In 1209, the papacy launched a concerted attack against divergent teachings. A group in southern France known as the *Cathari* (the "pure" ones, the *Cathars*) were more commonly known as the *Albigensians* because many lived in the French town of Albi in Languedoc. They were attacked for heresy, though accounts of their views differ. They were charged with embracing Manichean dualism: the belief in one god of light (Truth, of the New Testament), and one of dark (Error, of the Old Testament). Ironically, they did not believe in heaven or hell.[35] This view is clearly heretical. Other historical accounts call them "evangelized Christians" (though any holding the above dualism could not be considered orthodox).[36] Their initiation into Christianity involved repentance, dietary restrictions and avoidance of marriage/sex, and a ceremony of the laying on of hands and the placing of the Gospel of John on their forehead.

In an era when heresy was taken extremely seriously, there was plenty here for Christian (Catholic) authorities to worry about. Since the Albigensians believed there was an ongoing struggle between spirit and matter, their resolve was a constant purification from matter. They condemned procreation, marriage, material items in worship, and the eating of food. The latter was obviously problematic and therefore being vegetarian was an acceptable compromise. The strictest sects believed they could preserve the souls of weaker ascetics through self-starvation (*endura*). In addition to their unorthodox and heretical teachings, the Albigensians refused to take oaths, which caused serious problems in a feudal society. And their belief that human governments were evil put them in an untenable position with authorities.

Pope Alexander III commissioned his legate Peter of Castelnau not to kill the Albigensians, but to convert them back to Catholicism. Fate flipped in 1208, when a group of Albigensians killed Peter near St. Gilles Abbey. This murder gave land-hungry French monarchs a pretense to launch the Crusade, and they slaughtered the alleged heretics at Muret in 1213.[37]

The forces claiming Rome's support took few prisoners in Béziers—an Albigensian stronghold city nine miles from the Mediterranean. When asked how to differentiate the heretics from the orthodox Christians, a papal legate allegedly answered, "Kill them all. God will know his own."[38] An "appalling massacre" followed here and elsewhere in southern France where "it was difficult to discover leading Cathars and their sympathizers."[39]

One prominent monastic order grew out of this fight against the heretics. Dominic (1170–1221) went to the region to debate the leading Cathars and founded a house (school) for preachers to help with the defense. This became the Order of Friars Preacher, or Order of Preachers (O.P.), or more commonly the Dominicans—which helped change the face of European history.

In England, about thirty Cathars, men and women, were tried for heresy ca. 1165.

> They [the Cathars, or Albigensians who immigrated from southern France] laughed at threats uttered in all piety against them in the hope that through fear they might be brought to their senses, and misapplied the word of the Lord "Blessed are they that suffer persecution for justice's sake, for theirs is the kingdom of heaven." Thereupon, the bishops, taking precautions lest the heretical poison should spread more widely, publicly denounced them as heretics and handed them over to His Catholic Highness for corporal punishment. He commanded that the brand of heretical infamy be burned on their brows, that they be flogged in the presence of the people, and that they be driven out of the city.

And he strictly enjoined anyone from presuming to give them shelter or offer them any comfort. When the sentence had been declared, they were led away, rejoicing in their just punishment, their master leading them jauntily and chanting "Blessed are ye when men shall revile you". . . . Then the detestable group were branded on the brows, and suffered a just severity—as a mark of his primacy he who was their leader receiving a double brand on brow and chin. Stripped of their clothing to the waist and publicly flogged with resounding blows, they were driven out of the city, and perished miserably in the bitter cold, for it was winter and no one offered them the slightest pity.[40]

Many hagiographies or histories lump the Waldensians and Albigensians together. However, the latter were clearly considered heretical—both during that era and by current standards of orthodoxy. This is not the case with Peter Waldo and his followers (who were more of a nuisance to the official Church). In both cases, countless people died due to their radical beliefs. These persecutions would last for centuries in other regions. John Foxe, though listing the Cathars (Albigensians) as heretics, seems to represent their plight as Christians with radical teachings.

In the year 1620 also, the persecution against the Albigenses was very severe. In 1648 a heavy persecution raged throughout Lithuania and Poland. The cruelty of the Cossacks was so excessive that the Tartars themselves were ashamed of their barbarities. Among others who suffered was the Rev. Adrian Chalinski, who was roasted alive by a slow fire, and whose sufferings and mode of death may depict the horrors which the professors of Christianity have endured from the enemies of the Redeemer.[41]

The term *see* refers to an area of jurisdiction under a bishop or another leader. It derives from the Latin *sedes*, meaning seat—a seat of authority. A similar usage from the Latin for chair—*cathedra*—came to mean their chair of authority, or "cathedral."

In the case of Holy See, "Holy" denotes the superlative or top see, that is, the Roman pontificate (at least as recognized by the Western Church). Other sees are generally called "ecclesiastical" sees, or "church-wide," a term derived from the Latin transliteration of Greek *ekklesia*, a gathering, tied to the Greek for "calling out" or "to summon," which implies that an ecclesiastical meeting is a summoned gathering of the church.[42]

Historic Sources

AN EXCERPT FROM *MARTYRS MIRROR*, 1660

This Dutch collection of martyrdoms goes by various names, from the common one above, to the slightly longer one highlighted on the original cover: "The Bloody Theatre or Martyrs Mirror," to the full one that also includes, ". . . of the Defenseless Christians Who Baptized Only upon Confession of Faith, and Who Suffered and Died for the Testimony of Jesus, Their Saviour, From the Time of Christ to the Year A. D. 1660." The following is the "Author's Invocation" for that first edition. It affords a glimpse of the responsibility felt in translating these heroic actions for Christ, helping to preserve them for future generations.

Pardon me, O my Lord and my God! that I, who am but dust and ashes, approach Thee. Gen. 18:27. I fear to come to Thee, because Thou art a consuming fire, while I am wood, hay and stubble, subject to be burned; yet I must not remain away from Thee, because I have that which is Thine, yea, which is Thy most precious treasure, even the blood and offering of the saints; I must needs come and offer it to Thee.

May it be well pleasing to Thee, my dear Savior, that I offer that which long since has been offered up to Thee. But I have full confidence that Thou wilt not reject me. I believe I have the assurance that this will be acceptable to Thee, for

Thy servant David, a man after Thine own heart, sang, "Precious in the sight of the Lord is the death of his saints." Ps. 116:15.

Moreover Thou knowest, O my Saviour and Redeemer, the steadfast faith, the unquenchable love, and faithfulness unto death, of those of whom I have written, and who gave their precious lives and bodies as a sacrifice to Thee.

Besides, Thou hast spared my life, that I unworthy and weak as I am for such a task, might yet perform it; for snares of death had compassed me, keeping me bound nearly six months during last fall, winter and spring, so that I often thought I could not survive; nevertheless Thy power strengthened life, Thy hand rescued me and by Thy grace was I led safely through, so that in the midst of my difficulties and contrary to the advice and opinion of the physicians (for the zeal and love of Thy saints had taken complete possession of me), I wrote and finished the greater part of this work.

The sacrifices which are acceptable unto Thee are a broken spirit, etc. Ps. 51:17. But this offering, O God, was accompanied with many tears, caused partly by my distress, as I, on account of the weakness of my nature, called upon Thee for help, partly through joy, as I found and experienced Thy comfort and help.

Yet that which more than all else caused my tears to flow was the remembrance of the sufferings and the death of Thy martyrs, who altogether innocent, as defenceless lambs, were led to the water, the fire, the sword, or to the wild beasts in the arena, there to suffer and to die for Thy name's sake. However, I experienced no small degree of joy as I contemplated the living confidence they had in Thy grace, and how valiantly they fought their way through the strait gate.

Ah! how often did I wish to have been a partaker with them; my soul went with them, so to speak, into prison; I encouraged them in the tribunal, to bear patiently, without gainsaying or flinching, their sentence of death. It seemed to me as though I accompanied them to the place of execution, scaffold or stake, saying to them in their extremity, Fight valiantly dear brethren and sisters; the crown of life awaits you. I almost fancied that I had died with them; so inseparably was my love bound up with them; for Thy holy name's sake.

I therefore entreat Thee once more, O my God, to let this sacrifice be well pleasing in Thy sight, and to accept it from me, Thy most humble servant, as a token of love towards Thee as well as toward Thy blessed martyrs.

But before I leave this, strengthen me with Thy good Spirit, and arm me with the consolation of Thy grace, that I may not only confess Thee here with my mouth, but also honor Thee by a virtuous and pious conversation (Ps. 119:5), in the most holy faith, not refusing, if necessity require it and Thy honor be promoted thereby, to give my life and body into suffering and death, so that I may become like unto Thy dearest friends, my slain fellow brethren and sisters, and receive with them the same reward in the great day of Thy recompense.

This is the desire and petition of him, whose name is known to Thee, and who entreats Thee for grace now and in the hour of his death, and in the ages of eternity. O Lord, so let it be I For Thine, O God, is the kingdom, and the power, and the glory, forever and ever. Amen.

T. J. VAN BRAGHT
DORT, JULY THE 23RD, 1659[43]

Vintage Foxe

A good Christian is bound to relinquish not only goods and children, but life itself, for the glory of his Redeemer: therefore I am resolved to sacrifice everything in this transitory world, for the sake of salvation in a world that will last to eternity.[44]

CHAPTER SEVEN

The Christian Crusades— A New Type of Martyr

All authority in heaven and on earth has been given to me. Go therefore and make disciples of all nations, baptizing them in the name of the Father and of the Son and of the Holy Spirit, teaching them to observe all that I have commanded you. And behold, I am with you always, to the end of the age. MATTHEW 28:18-20

I will make you into a great nation, and I will bless you; I will make your name great, and you will be a blessing. I will bless those who bless you, and whoever curses you I will curse; and all peoples on earth will be blessed through you. GENESIS 12:2-3, NIV

God arranges for himself to be in need, or he pretends to be, so that he can award to those fighting for him wages: the remission of their sins. . . . Take the sign of the cross. . . . If the cloth itself is sold it does not fetch much; if it is worn on a faithful shoulder, it is certain to be worth the kingdom of God.[1] BERNARD OF CLAIRVAUX (1090–1153)

If you are an Arabic-speaking, Greek-Orthodox going to a French school it makes you deeply skeptical if you have to listen to three different accounts of the Crusades—one from the Muslim side, one from the Greek side and one from the Catholic side.

NASSIM NICHOLAS TALEB, LEBANESE-AMERICAN ENTREPRENEUR, AUTHOR OF *THE BLACK SWAN*

Muslim advances stretched for centuries after Muhammad's death in AD 632. Many Christians died protecting their homes, culture, and religious sites. Others died centuries later during the ill-fated and theologically suspect Crusades.

The Voice of the Martyrs' abridgement of John Foxe's work calls the Crusades "perhaps Christendom's greatest historical embarrassment."[2] Yes, the atrocities many of the Crusaders committed are inexcusable and certainly out of step with biblical teaching—and in most cases they were clearly in defiance of orders from Christian leaders. But the revisionist narrative that the Islamic growth was a time of peaceful expansion is simply mistaken.

It is absolutely the case that in certain times and places, perhaps best demonstrated by the Constitution of Medina, Islam coexisted peacefully with its Jewish, Christian, and pagan neighbors. The Prophet Muhammad had a particular appreciation for and fascination with Christian monks, as illustrated in the letter held in St. Catherine's Monastery in Egypt's Sinai desert, addressed to the monks there in AD 628.

> This is a message from Muhammad . . . as a covenant to those
> who adopt Christianity, near and far, we are with them. Verily
> I . . . and my followers defend them, because Christians are my
> citizens; and by God/Allah! I hold out against anything that
> displeases them. . . . Neither are their judges to be removed
> from their jobs nor their monks from their monasteries. No one
> is to destroy a house of their religion, to damage it, or to carry
> anything from it to the Muslims' houses. . . . Verily, they are my

allies and have my secure charter against all that they hate. No one is to force them to travel or to oblige them to fight. The Muslims are to fight for them. If a female Christian is married to a Muslim, it is not to take place without her approval. She is not to be prevented from visiting her church to pray. Their churches are to be respected. They are neither to be prevented from repairing them nor the sacredness of their covenants.[3]

Yet, it is also true that from very early throughout most of Islam's expansion, there were accounts of slaughters, not to mention the practice of forcing slave children to become professional fighters—the *mamluks*. They captured many of these Christian boys in Christian regions of Egypt, then groomed and forced them to kill others—often Christians.

Amr ibn al-As, one of Muhammad's companions, brutally swept through Northern Egypt in AD 640, just eight years after Muhammad's death. John of Nikiu, a bishop of the Nile delta, records one such conquest: "[W]hen with great toil and exertion they had cast down the walls of the city, they forthwith made themselves masters of it, and put to the sword thousands of its inhabitants and soldiers, and they gained an enormous booty, and took the women and children captive and divided them amongst themselves, and they made that city a desolation."[4]

Though sources clash on the motives and actual blame for the atrocities of the Crusades, many pilgrims and Christian servants died in the process—fully trusting in biblical teachings and papal instructions. What should not be lost in this discussion is what Pope Urban II shared at the Council of Clermont in AD 1095. Keep in mind that in addition to numerous gory accounts like the ones above, by the time of Urban's speech, the Muslims had conquered two-thirds of the Christian world!

Baldric of Dol, an abbot in central France, recorded Pope Urban's speech around six years after the First Crusade and had it proofed by an eyewitness who accompanied the Crusaders:

We have heard, most beloved brethren, and you have heard what
we cannot recount without deep sorrow how, with great hurt
and dire sufferings our Christian brothers, members in Christ,
are scourged, oppressed, and injured in Jerusalem, in Antioch,
and the other cities of the East. Your own blood brothers, your
companions, your associates (for you are sons of the same
Christ and the same Church) are either subjected in their
inherited homes to other masters, or are driven from them, or
they come as beggars among us; or, which is far worse, they are
flogged and exiled as slaves for sale in their own land. Christian
blood, redeemed by the blood of Christ, has been shed, and
Christian flesh, akin to the flesh of Christ, has been subjected to
unspeakable degradation and servitude.[5]

It is easy in an age of pluralism and political correctness to highlight the
gross missteps that followed as the Westerners abused many of the populations they conquered or passed through, sometimes even fellow Christians.
However, Urban gave this speech due to the pleas of the Byzantine emperor
because the Seljuk Turks were slaughtering Christians.

The account of Ani is one of many, but enough to sear horrific images
of a religious rival's wrath into the mind of a people. Ani was one of the
most advanced and largest cities of its day, with perhaps as many as 100,000
people. It was also known as the "City of 1001 Churches." Its stark remains
are now a key heritage site for Christians in Armenia.

The city fell before the ruthless Turks led by Alp Arslan (Muhammad
bin Dawud Chaghri). An Arab historian recorded the following eyewitness
account from Aristakes (an Armenian Christian). It paints the grimmest of
pictures and provides further context for Pope Urban's words:

Now the [Seljuk] king came with many myriads of armed troops
and entered our land, spreading dread and terror among those far
and near. The armed [Seljuk] troops poured into the city like the
foaming billows of the sea. Putting the Persian sword to work,
they spared no one.

One could see there the grief and calamity of every age of humankind. For children were ravished from the embraces of their mothers and mercilessly hurled against rocks, while the mothers drenched them with tears and blood. Father and son were slain by the same sword. The elderly, the young, priests and deacons also died by the same sword. The city became filled from one end to the other with bodies of the slain, and [the bodies] became a road. From the countless multitude of the slain, and from the corpses, that great stream which passed by the city became dyed with blood. Wild and domesticated beasts became the cemeteries of those corpses, for there was no one to cover over the bodies of the slain with the needed earth, no one to bury them. The lofty and beautiful palace was burned because of the injustices committed within it.[6]

This remains a politically sensitive subject, and both authors of this book work regularly across these religious lines. Though Christian-Islamic conflict endures in several regions, it is also true that the relationship between Muslims and Christians in our world is, in some places, better than it has been in centuries.

While most civilized countries have moved toward peaceful coexistence between religious groups, some of the same heroic sacrifices that prompted John Foxe to write are unfortunately still occurring. Many Christians remain victims, oppressed or persecuted by Islamist groups—still paying the ultimate sacrifice for their faith in Christ as radicalized causes claim inspiration from the Quran. The last chapter of this book represents modern Christians' battle against these radicalized groups, including numerous interviews with family survivors of these Christian martyrs.

THE ROAD TO JERUSALEM AND BACK The Umayyad Caliphate, or the Arab Kingdom, was immense and divided between two branches of this family, the Sufyanids who ruled 661-684, and the Marwanids (684-750). Without getting into the complexities of these factions, its capitals were Damascus in modern Syria (661–744) and Harran in modern

Turkey (744–750) until the Umayyads fell to the Abbasids (the third caliphate after Muhammad).

The Umayyads believed that the road to sack Constantinople went through Cordoba and Spain, and a much different Islamic caliphate would eventually get there (the Ottomans). However, the sack would take another seven centuries and a different route.

Umayyad forces succeeded in taking Byzantine Carthage in 698, converting the local Berber people, and then invaded Spain in 711 before their major advance in Europe. Charles Martel, appropriately nicknamed "the Hammer," led his forces against the Muslim troops in 732 at the Battle of Tours in France, one hundred years after Muhammad's death. Martel's victory in this battle likely prevented the Muslims from conquering all of Europe.

The Christians continued their intermittent challenges against Islamic groups elsewhere, marshalling a massive resistance commonly called the Crusades—*in the name of the cross.* From the eleventh to the thirteenth centuries, large forces marched to the Holy Lands to fight the Seljuk Turks (Sunni Muslims who had conquered Persia), and the Abbasid Caliphate (based in Baghdad).[7] Regardless of whether the papal orders were inspired or ill-advised, or the end results abysmal, many Christians marched for what they thought were meaningful commitments to Christ and their fellow believers.[8] The majority of early crusading pilgrims were ill-equipped to fight the Seljuk Turks, who had

> captured Baghdad in 1055, defeated a large Byzantine army in 1071, seized Jerusalem in 1076, and neared Constantinople, capturing Nicaea in 1092. The general peace that had allowed pilgrims to access holy sites, since the first Muslim conquest in the seventh century, came to an end. It was against this new, aggressive expression of Muslim faith that the first crusade was formed, not so much to establish a kingdom but to negotiate access to Christian pilgrimage sites. Later the crusaders faced the [mamluks], a slave class brought from the Caucasus to serve in the Seljuk armies.[9]

The military conflict didn't end with the Crusades. While the Battle of Tours had stopped the Muslim advance through Europe, it didn't rid Iberia of these intruders from North Africa. The term "Moor" became the catch-all term for the Muslims of African descent who were conquering southwestern Europe—beginning with Visigoth Spain in 711.[10] Fast-forward another three hundred years, and the Catholic monarchs Ferdinand and Isabella conquered the last of the Moors in Granada in 1492.

Christian-Muslim conflict would continue through the early twentieth century as the Ottoman Empire dominated the region for six hundred years (1299–1923), controlling most of the territory around the Mediterranean, Adriatic, and Black Seas. At one time, their empire encompassed much of Southeastern Europe and the Middle East—with plenty of traces of their successes enduring today, even the pronounced crenelated top of Jerusalem's Old City walls.

CULTURAL CONNECTION

Architectural Reminders of the Christian-Muslim Conflict

One need look no further than the major historic buildings in Istanbul (formerly Constantinople) and Córdoba for reminders of the Christian-Islamic duel. Both cities have architectural wonders that began as early churches before changing hands.[11] These are the Hagia Sophia, once the greatest church in Christendom, and the Mosque-Cathedral of Córdoba, officially named the Cathedral of Our Lady of the Assumption.

The Hagia Sophia—the greatest domed building in the world until St. Peter's Basilica—served as the seat of the Greek Orthodox Church and was the cathedral of Constantinople from 537 until the city fell to the Ottomans in 1453. The victors repurposed the Hagia Sophia as a mosque, stripping or covering its many Christian images and symbols. It remains a stunning silhouette against the sunset landscape—an iconic Christian cathedral surrounded by Islamic minarets. Since 1935 it has served as a secular museum for Turkey, one of its most popular historical sites, visited by over three million annually.

The Mosque-Cathedral of Córdoba was repurposed as a cathedral after the Reconquista of the city in 1236. The striking Moorish architecture leaves little doubt of the main purpose of its design. Its hypostyle hall and priceless array of red marble columns still dazzle visitors. Moorish governors from around Iberia donated precious stones, materials, and other adornments during the mosque's construction.

In both cases, there is positive cooperation between the religions—celebrating the shared history of the spaces (though, under the leadership of Turkish President Recep Tayyip Erdoğan, there have been frequent rumors that the Hagia Sofia could be converted back into a mosque as Erdoğan's increasingly Islamist administration threatens modern Turkey's historic secularism).

DID YOU KNOW? *Knights of the Crusades*

The Crusades gave rise to three religious orders. These include the Knights Hospitaller and the Knights Templar, both founded in the First Crusade, and later came the Teutonic Knights during the Third Crusade.

The Knights Hospitaller were also called the Order of St. John, charged around 1099 with caring for the sick among the pilgrims, but they soon became a powerful military order protecting the Latin Kingdom of Jerusalem. Over the centuries, they relocated to Rhodes as Byzantium fell, then to Malta, renamed as the Knights of Malta (sporting the Maltese cross).

The Knights Templar wore large red crosses on their chests and were charged with protecting the pilgrims en route to the Holy Land. However, the majority among their early ranks were builders and other workers. They were also known as the Poor Knights of Christ and of the Temple of Solomon because they stayed at the site of Solomon's Temple. Bernard of Clairvaux applauded them in his *In Praise of the New Knighthood*: "A new sort of chivalry has appeared on earth . . . that tirelessly wages . . . war both against flesh and blood and against the spiritual forces of evil. . . . Go forward in safety, knights, with undaunted souls drive off the enemies of the cross of Christ."[12] However, their very military and banking successes proved their undoing as regional leaders became jealous of their wealth and power. Ruling authorities burned fifty-four Knights Templar at the stake in Paris in 1310, and dissolved the order in 1312, giving their possessions to the Hospitallers.

The Teutonic Knights (Order of the Cross) were the last of these orders established (1192), and initially helped the wounded after the siege of Acre. Like the other orders, they grew in military proficiency and soon conquered many of the borderlands, then took over Prussia (1280) and retained some power until Napoleon. Today, a vestige remains in Austria—and the order has returned to its original mission of caring for the sick and operating charities.

THE CHRISTIAN THEOLOGY OF THE CRUSADES–THE INDULGENCE ROAD TO MARTYRDOM

The Battle of Tours was a Christian response to a Muslim attack on home soil, but the Christian Crusades were overt forays into Muslim-controlled territories. It is difficult to separate the theological underpinnings from the battles themselves. After all, another battle would ensue as Protestants ("protesters") rejected these same teachings a few centuries later—especially the Catholic doctrine of penance.

There are strong links between penance, the correlating practice of granting indulgences, and papal leverage in recruiting Crusaders. "These were essentially promises of forgiveness and eternal life, given in exchange for monetary contributions and/or dying for the cause of Christ."[13]

Pope Alexander II first exercised the use of indulgences in 1063, promising eternal salvation to Iberian Christians if they died fighting Muslims. The practice became the official position of the Roman Catholic Church in 1075.

This issue is not only key to understanding the Crusades—hordes of Christians, often without weapons or inadequately trained, marching against the Islamic military forces—but to understanding the original *Foxe's Book of Martyrs*. We have not taken Foxe's approach here, as he was so incensed with the use of what he believed were erroneous doctrines and the leveraging of them for institutional and personal gain. Most of his tome bashes Catholics. However, in the process he missed the pious lives of the majority of priests and nuns, and many martyrs who merit our respect and admiration. Foxe only nods to the whole crusading enterprise.

Many of the Crusaders (certainly not all) were protecting religious pilgrimages to their holy sites—but on lands long occupied by those of other religions. And they were doing so thinking they were being obedient to God and the teachings of Jesus, all while protecting his heritage as instructed by his vicar on earth—the Pope.

After Pope Alexander II established indulgences, Pope Urban offered a special indulgence in 1095 "to those who go" (First Crusade). In 1144, Bernard of Clairvaux (d. 1153) connected crusading to the eternal spiritual benefit. Reacting to the Muslim conquest of Edessa, Bernard called for a new crusade, saying, "The knight of Christ, I say, is safe in slaying, safer if he is slain. He is accountable to himself when he is slain, to Christ when he slays."[14]

THE CRUSADES IN HISTORICAL CONTEXT Most historians number four to five large Crusades, with smaller campaigns bringing the total to nine or ten. There are a few contenders for starting points to these Crusades, including the attacks on heretics in southern France noted above. But historians usually start with Byzantine emperor Alexius I Comnenus. He appealed to Pope Urban II for help in opposing Muslim attacks, a welcome plea for many factions of Christianized Europe. Alexius particularly wanted help in removing "unbelievers" from Anatolia (modern Turkey). The stage was set for a major show of piety and patriotism.

Christian-Muslim tensions were heightened when al-Hakim bi-Amr Allah, the Fatimid caliph of Cairo, destroyed the Church of the Holy Sepulcher—built over the traditional site of Jesus' crucifixion and resurrection. His forces beat parts of the structure down to bedrock, and the rest was saved only by the collapsed roof. Christians would later be permitted to rebuild and resume pilgrimages, but this only increased allegations of Muslim atrocities. Intense Christian piety and lay interest in religious affairs resulted in overwhelming popular support for the First Crusade.

The Crusades pitted Christians against Muslims, but others fell victim, including both European and Middle Eastern Jews during various campaigns. One Count Emicho slaughtered thousands of Jews in the Rhineland in 1096, confiscating their wealth—against the direct order of the pope.

The Crusaders made ephemeral military gains and temporarily freed holy sites for Christian pilgrimages. They formed short-lived Crusader States with fortresses dotting foreign landscapes. However, during these Crusades Christians sometimes not only killed civilian Jews, but also other Christians. Crusaders in the Fourth Crusade sacked one of their own stalwart centers, Constantinople, along with the nearby Catholic stronghold of Zara.[15]

For the sake of our study here of martyrs, we are left to deal with the victims of these misguided Crusaders. Christians in cities targeted by greedy merchants suffered from a double jeopardy. Those in Zara and Constantinople died as Christians in a Christian city—being within the wrong walls at the wrong time. However, their suffering was at the hands of other Christians, operatives of privateers. Martyrs or witnesses—all the same.

Unfortunately, even with Christian flags hanging from their city walls and houses, the last thing these believers saw were the crosses on the shields of misguided Christian invaders—conscripted Christian crusaders serving Venetian overlords (who had provided their ships for passage to the Holy Land and were demanding these attacks to pay their bills).

Ironically, while many of these Crusaders had joined up for the papal promise of remission of sins, the pope immediately excommunicated the Christian combatants for their atrocities, a punishment akin in their minds to an eternal death sentence.

This Fourth Crusade was a debacle so tragic that one of the most popular popes of the post-Reformation era, Pope John Paul II, apologized for this Crusade's massacre of Eastern Christians at Constantinople. In 2004, he apologized to three hundred million Eastern Orthodox Christians through their leader, Bartholomew I, "In particular, we cannot forget what happened in the month of April 1204. . . . How can we not share, at a distance of eight centuries, the pain and disgust?"[16]

So we find ourselves in tricky waters as we want to venerate the faithful.

Glory and gold seemed to eclipse God's message. Nonetheless, Christians died for their faith. Some by the hands of other Christians, but most under Arab *saifs* (swords).

CULTURAL CONNECTION

The Use of *Crusaders* as a Nickname

Many schools have heralded the nickname *Crusaders*, assigning a heroic status to those medieval zealots who participated in one of the nine major Christian Crusades (1095–1291) with large crosses on their shields, signifying their Christian faith. Indeed, many faithful believers died out of such devotion, fully believing they were serving Christ and his people. However, most of these escapades were grim forays attached to misguided missions. In the First Crusade, overzealous Crusaders massacred the population of Jerusalem—including many Jews. "This event and the very name of the 'crusade' or 'crusaders' are still disdained by many Semitic peoples, and rightly so. In light of the carnage and inhumane acts, many schools have shed their nickname of 'Crusaders,' like Wheaton College (IL). Campus Crusade for Christ, which originally referred more to evangelistic crusades rather than historic battles, also reevaluated its name. Even though the organization was well received among American Christians, it changed its name to Cru."[17] As modern historians of all faith traditions represent the Crusades' broader context, the moniker "crusader" continues to wane in popularity.

THE FIRST CRUSADE When Byzantine Emperor Alexius requested assistance with the Seljuk Turks, Pope Urban II responded with a much grander commitment that nearly eclipsed the Eastern Church's priorities.[18] At the Council of Clermont (1095), he challenged all Christians not only to join a war against the Turks, but further claimed that "Christ commands it." He pressured listeners into participating: "O, how many evils will be imputed to you by the Lord Himself, if you do not help those who, like you, profess Christianity!"[19]

Urban made it clear that to die on crusade in a state of repentance and confession would guarantee immediate entry to Heaven, doing away with any necessity of penance after death: papal grants associated with this promise [such as those earlier by Pope Alexander II against the Muslims] were the origins of the system of indulgences, later to cause such problems for the Western Church.[20]

The prime target shifted from Anatolia and Byzantine concerns to Jerusalem. Urban's call for the "war of the Cross" or "crusade" inspired chants that became the motto of the Crusades—"God wills it!"[21]

+ Historic Sources

EXCERPTS FROM DIFFERENT ACCOUNTS
OF POPE URBAN II'S SPEECH AT CLERMONT (1095)

Few speeches in recorded history have had the effect of Pope Urban II's charge to rescue Christians in Byzantium and the Holy Lands. On one hand, it may have appeared as if the speech was rather successful. Crusaders took Jerusalem and established Crusader States. But these were short lived, and countless lives lost among many faith traditions. He gave the speech in the southwestern corner of France (Aquitaine) at the Council of Clermont to around 300 clerics. The original records were lost, but five accounts have survived, including the following two, and a short reflection on the event by Urban himself.[22]

For your brethren who live in the east are in urgent need of your help, and you must hasten to give them the aid which has often been promised them. For, as the most of you have heard, the Turks and Arabs have attacked them and have conquered the territory. . . . They have killed and captured many, and have destroyed the churches and devastated the empire. . . . Carry aid promptly to those Christians and . . . destroy that vile race from the lands of our friends. . . . All who die by the way, whether by land or by sea, or in battle against the pagans, shall have immediate remission of sins. This I grant them through the power of God with which I am invested. O what a disgrace if such a despised and base race, which worships demons, should conquer a people which has the faith of omnipotent God and is made glorious with the name of Christ! **FULCHER OF CHARTRES (PRESENT AT THE COUNCIL),** *in Gesta Francorum Jerusalem Expugnantium*, **CA. 1100**

From the confines of Jerusalem and the city of Constantinople a horrible tale has gone forth and very frequently has been brought to our ears, namely, that a race from the kingdom of the Persians, an accursed race, a race utterly alienated from God, a generation forsooth which has not directed its heart and has not entrusted its spirit to God, has invaded the lands of those Christians and has depopulated them by the sword, pillage and fire; it has led away a part of the captives into its own country, and a part it has destroyed by cruel tortures; it has either entirely destroyed the churches of God or appropriated them for the rites of its own religion. They destroy the altars, after having defiled them with their uncleanness. They circumcise the Christians, and the blood of the circumcision they either spread upon the altars or pour into the vases of the baptismal font. When they wish to torture people by a base death, they perforate their navels, and dragging forth the extremity of the intestines, bind it to a stake; then with flogging they lead the victim around until the viscera having gushed forth the victim falls prostrate upon the ground. Others they bind to a post and pierce with arrows. Others they compel to extend their necks and then, attacking them with naked swords, attempt to cut through the neck with a single blow. What shall I say of the abominable rape of the women? To speak of it is worse than to be silent. The kingdom of the Greeks is now dismembered by them and deprived of territory so vast in extent that it can not be traversed in a march of two months. On whom therefore is the labor of avenging these wrongs and of recovering this territory incumbent, if not upon you? You, upon whom above other nations God has conferred remarkable glory in arms, great courage, bodily activity, and strength to humble the hairy scalp of those who resist you. **ROBERT THE MONK (PROBABLY PRESENT AT THE COUNCIL),** *recorded in Historia Hierosolymitana*, **1107**

Peter the Hermit's First Crusaders

Throughout history we learn of passionate leadership which often coincided with historic events. However, in the story of Peter the Hermit we learn of uninformed and misguided passion and its disastrous consequences.

Urban's speech inspired Peter the Hermit, an ascetic from around Amiens (approximately seventy-five miles north of Paris). "A former soldier, Peter was a short, elderly man [around age fifty] whose face was almost as long and sad as that of the donkey he always rode. His garments were filthy. His bare feet had not been washed in years. He ate no meat or fruit, living almost entirely on wine and fish."[23] He recruited a mélange of zealots— around 20,000 women and men, from poor knights to enthusiastic peasants. As they journeyed to Jerusalem, eight of Peter's crusaders, far behind the mass of others, were robbed and killed. Peter didn't believe it until they went to the town of Semlin and found their corpses hanging on the walls.[24]

His ragtag group of untrained and ill-equipped "peasant idealists and zealots" preceded the more organized and professional campaign, and met with horrendous defeat and a massacre at Civetot, where they were slaughtered or enslaved at the hands of the Turks and few succeeded in retreating beyond Anatolia (modern Tukey).[25] Peter was not present (fetching supplies in Constantinople) and Walter the Penniless led them to their slaughter near Nicaea.

Peter survived, though he had unsuccessfully tried to leave. After the Crusade he founded the monastery at Neufmoutier.[26]

The more formal campaign reached Jerusalem in 1099 after sacking many cities en route. They represented an "international military force—with a large nucleus of knights from central and southern France, Normandy, and Norman Sicily."[27] They massacred the population— including many Jews.

"During the First Crusade, the persecution of the Jews began during the European trek of the campaign, attacking communities in Metz, Cologne, Trier, Mainz, Speyer, and Worms. One of the sad ironies of these events is that European Jews had helped to finance many of the participants. Perhaps the debtor relationship only fueled racism."[28] Many Christian leaders tried to protect them against the rapacious renegade actions, like the bishops of Worms and Speyer and the archbishop of Mainz. "The crusaders who were killing Jews were defying their Christian leaders and brothers, and their actions ought not be imputed to all of Christendom."[29]

In addition to reclaiming the holy sites, the conquerors established four small Crusader States ("kingdoms") at Edessa, Tripoli, Antioch, and the most prominent at Jerusalem (covering modern Israel and the West Bank). Its center shifted to Acre during times of attack and was the last of the Crusader kingdoms to fall in 1291. In the long view of history, these enclaves of zealous Christians had little lasting effect as they soon fell to an aggressive and angry Muslim empire after the Crusades ended.[30]

Though their mixed motives were undoubtedly problematic, thousands of men and women heard Pope Urban's exhortation and faithfully followed, accepting the pontiff's words as a call from Christ to succor their Eastern brothers and sisters.

THE SECOND CRUSADE Although the numbering of the Crusades is somewhat difficult due to various independent and lesser waves following on the heels of the First Crusade, the Second Crusade is traditionally associated with the popular Bernard of Clairvaux (1090–1153). He was "a contributor to the writing of the Rule of the Knights Templars—an order of crusaders who took monastic vows."[31] In 1101, he reacted to the Muslim conquest of the Crusader State city of Edessa—and preached a new crusade.

Conrad II of Germany and Louis of France led armies into Asia Minor in 1147. These efforts proved impotent, and even endangered the Crusader States' survival in 1149 with an ill-advised and unsuccessful attack on Damascus. Bernard, as we quoted earlier, wrote the following for the new knighthood of warrior-monks: "The knight of Christ, I say, is safe in slaying, safer if he is slain. He is accountable to himself when he is slain, to Christ when he slays."[32]

Two Hundred Beheadings at Hattin

The Battle of Hattin (1187) was an abysmal loss for the twenty thousand Crusaders, as few escaped the brilliant maneuvering of the famous Saladin—who also enjoyed the comfort of twice the number of troops. This battle was the fulcrum of Muslim dominance throughout the region as Saladin would go on to take over fifty cities.

Twice he was able to block the Crusaders at Hattin (near Tiberias) from the water sources as they were stranded in arid hills of Galilee. All the while, he paraded camels in front of them, laden with water and milk for his own troops. They burned grass fields around them and provoked the Crusaders to desperate and fatal actions.

Saladin's son was among the chroniclers of the event, along with Arab historian Ibn al-Athīr. After the battle, Saladin brought around two hundred prisoners, all Hospitallers or Templars, and had them executed before his men. The account is macabre, especially with the large red crosses on the fronts of most victims:

> [Saladin] ordered that they should be beheaded, choosing to have them dead rather than in prison. With him was a whole band of scholars and sufis [practitioners of Sufism] and a certain number of devout men and ascetics; each begged to be allowed to kill one of them, and drew his sword and rolled back his sleeve. Saladin, his face joyful, was sitting on his dais, the unbelievers [knights] showed black despair.[33]

Saladin specifically targeted these knights, who had all taken monastic vows. These men stood, and fell, for their beliefs.

THE THIRD CRUSADE The Third Crusade boasted some of Europe's most important leaders: Frederick I (Barbarossa), the Holy Roman emperor; Philip II (Augustus) of France; and Richard I (*Coeur-de-lion*, the Lionheart) of England. Pope Gregory VIII preached a crusade after the great sultan of Egypt, Saladin (who ruled 1138–1193), recaptured Jerusalem. Although this Crusade met with mixed success, the leadership suffered precarious fates.

In 1190, Frederick drowned in Cilicia—certainly, a bad omen. Philip left after the Crusaders joined Guy of Lusignan and recaptured Acre, massacring its inhabitants (1191). Beha-ed-Din (a Saracen) gives a detailed account of the Acre slaughter, credited to betrayal by Richard I. He claims the Christians murdered three thousand Muslim prisoners who "were all bound with ropes . . . in cold blood." Another viewpoint calls this a retaliation for the Muslims' earlier actions against Christians.[34]

With Richard at the helm, it appeared they would retake Jerusalem, especially after taking Arsuf from the Muslims. The living conditions were so severe that Richard struck a truce with Saladin and left for home. The Crusaders had managed to secure Acre at the cost of many lives, and though Acre would endure longer than any other Crusader State, it would ultimately be in vain.

THE FOURTH CRUSADE This chapter's introduction has already mentioned the misguided and infamous Fourth Crusade, the pope's excommunication of the combatants immediately after it happened, and Pope John Paul II's apology for the massacre of Eastern Christians. These "martyrs" fall in a rather unique and unfortunate category—slaughtered in a greedy grasp of wealth by fellow Christians. Misguided crusaders from the Latin West raped, tortured, and killed Christian inhabitants to settle a debt. Ostensibly it was for the greater good of having money and transportation to retake Muslim-held Jerusalem. This was obviously criminal, resulting in martyrs of circumstance, who perhaps are not considered martyrs in the strictest sense of the word, but who died as Christians in a Christian fortress in a Muslim world knocking at their doors. The context for this debacle is summarized below.

The strongest medieval pope, Innocent II, strategized to retake Jerusalem from the Muslims by going through Egypt (1202). In a bizarre and unfortunate set of events, *doge* (Italian, "leader") Enrico Dandolo and the Venetians, who had provided transportation for the Crusaders, diverted to Zara, a Venetian city lost years earlier to the Hungarians. The Crusaders' inability to pay their fees due to an overestimation of numbers (and requesting too many ships) led to an agreement to sack this Christian port city, the source of oak for the Venetian ships. They moved next to Constantinople (1204) and sided with Byzantine exiles Emperor Isaac II and his son Alexius. This created further uprisings and also helped depose a Catholic king and papal vassal. For three days the Venetians and Crusaders sacked and pillaged Constantinople, permanently splitting instead of unifying Eastern and Western Christendom.[35]

The leader of the Crusade, Count Baldwin IX of Flanders, became the emperor of the East. Although Innocent had already excommunicated the participants, his political compass outweighed moral sensibilities when he realized that Latin Christianity now controlled both the patriarchy of Constantinople and the Greek Church. He absolved the Crusaders for their actions and for about fifty years Rome controlled Christendom. The spoils from the Crusade were immense, from mounds of golden objects and gems to the most prized possessions—relics.

Two of the most popular items were the alleged crown of thorns from Christ's crucifixion and doubting Thomas's finger. If they were real artifacts, it is all the more head-spinning. Christians slaughtering Christians, and then celebrating the theft of the very crown of Christ and finger of his disciple—reprehensible.

THE CHILDREN'S CRUSADES The Children's Crusades (1208 and 1212), enveloped in legend, became some of the more storied attempts to retake the Holy Land. It appears that two separate groups of German and French children made it to the Mediterranean, allegedly with some expectation that it would part all the way to the Holy Land. One group turned back and the other continued but was captured and sold into slavery. The recorded numbers range from a few thousand to thirty thousand. Stephen of Cloyes in France and Nicholas from Cologne led independent efforts. Stephen was only twelve, and created excitement when he insisted Jesus met him in the fields and handed him a letter commissioning him to lead the Crusade—a story King Philip rejected as folly. Undeterred, Stephen amassed a band of children and left. Thousands of boys and young men never returned and were unaccounted for in history after reaching Marseilles. Most of them likely died in slavery under the Saracens.[36]

DID YOU KNOW? *News of the Missing Children Crusaders*

From the various accounts of the Children's Crusades of 1212, it appears that at least seven ships full of young kids and a young priest set sail for the Middle East. The twelve-year-old leader, Stephen, thought this was a miracle. Although the miracle he prophesied didn't happen—the parting of the sea all the way to the Holy Land from

Marseilles—this indeed seemed to be divine provision. After all, it was free transportation. However, if tradition is correct, the very names of the captains who provided the "free" ships should have hinted of a shady deal—William the Pig and Hugh the Iron. Two of the ships crashed into San Pietro Island in a storm and all were lost. The other five ships sailed straight to a deal with Saracens, who transported them to slave markets in Algeria and Egypt. The whereabouts of these kids remained a mystery until the young priest was allowed to return to France in 1230. He reported that around seven hundred of the ill-advised Crusaders were still captives. A contingent ended up at the slave market in Baghdad, where eighteen of them were martyred for refusing to convert to Islam.[37]

THE LATER CRUSADES Historians' lists of Crusades often end in 1291 with the fall of Acre (the capital of what is often called the Second Kingdom of Jerusalem after it shifted during Jerusalem's demise). Some chronicle the "Later Crusades"—the Fifth through the Ninth.

The Fifth Crusade captured the key Egyptian port of Damietta in 1219. The Muslims offered to trade it for Jerusalem, but Pelagius, the papal legate, insisted instead on marching on Cairo. This backfired; he surrendered when trapped by the flooding of the Nile.

The Sixth Crusade was one of the more positive Crusades, and its fingerprints are visible in the look of the Old City of Jerusalem today—with its Ottoman walls. Emperor Frederick II spoke Arabic and obtained Jerusalem diplomatically with Saladin's son. In a bizarre sequence of events, the papacy excommunicated him for going, then later for leading the Crusade. In any case, his gains proved ephemeral. In 1244, the Latins lost Jerusalem to Asian Turks (under orders of the Egyptian ruler), and the city would remain in Muslim hands until 1917.

Louis IX of France launched two unsuccessful crusades, the Seventh Crusade against Egypt (1248) and the Eighth Crusade against Tunis (1270). He had to be ransomed after his capture in Egypt and died of dysentery on his second crusade. Throughout his reign, he was known for his approachability and sincerity with the poor. He also built one of the Church's prized possessions, the extant Sainte-Chapelle (Holy Chapel) in Paris. Its purpose was to house the reliquary for the alleged "Christ's Crown of Thorns" brought back from the Crusades. In keeping with his reputation for integrity and sincere faith, he actually purchased the relic instead of pilfering it.

Many Crusade lists omit the Ninth Crusade (1271), led by King Edward I of England, who had joined Louis for the previous one. His efforts in Syria were of little consequence, and they ended after a truce the following year.

While various campaigns in both Northern Europe and the Middle East could be charted, the fall of the Crusader States was actually the bookend to the long and storied sponsored Crusades. Jerusalem fell in 1244. The last three were taken back by the Muslims in less than fifty years: Antioch in 1268, Tripoli in 1289, and Acre in 1291 (a Crusader State that formed after Saladin had overrun much of the Kingdom of Jerusalem a century earlier).

The 14,000 Martyrs in Antioch (1260)

The Muslims continued their attacks during the time of these Crusades as well. In 1268, between the Seventh and Eighth Crusades, they sacked Antioch, one of the Crusader State capitals. One historian calls it "the single greatest massacre of the entire crusading era."[38]

The sultan of Egypt and Syria, Baibars, slaughtered 14,000 Christians and enslaved around a thousand other prisoners. This occurred three years after he massacred the inhabitants of Haifa, Caesarea, and Arsuf, and two years after doing the same in Galilee and Armenia (including the battle of Mari). The detailed accounts even give the prices of women, girls, and young children that were divided among the bounty.

The scene was gruesome. The people of Antioch certainly were aware of the Mamluks' brutality. Baibars was frustrated that the king had left the city, and had his secretary write a detailed account of the events.

> Death . . . came among the besieged from all sides and by all
> roads: we killed all whom you appointed to guard the city or
> defend its entrances. If you had seen your knights trampled under

the feet of horses, your provinces given up to pillage, your riches distributed by full measures, the wives of your subjects placed on the market for sale; if you had seen the altars and crosses overturned, the leaves of the Gospel torn and cast to the winds, and the sepulchers of your ancestors profaned; if you had seen your enemies, the Muslims, trampling upon the tabernacle and burning alive monks, priests, and deacons in the sanctuary; in short, if you had seen your palaces given up to the flames, the dead devoured by the fire of this world, the Church of St. Paul and that of St. Peter completely and entirely destroyed, certainly you would have cried out, "By Heaven, I wish that I had become dust!"[39]

Voices from the Past

Those who believe (in the Qur'an), and those who follow the Jewish (scriptures), and the Christians and the Sabians,—any who believe in God and the Last Day, and work righteousness, shall have their reward with their Lord; on them shall be no fear, nor shall they grieve.

QURAN 2:62

Those who believe (in the Qur'an), those who follow the Jewish (scriptures), and the Sabians and the Christians,—any who believe in God and the Last Day, and work righteousness,—on them shall be no fear, nor shall they grieve.

QURAN 5:69

Fight against those People of the Book [Jews and Christians] who have no faith in God [Allah] or the Day of Judgment, who do not consider unlawful what God and His Messenger [Muhammad] have made unlawful, and who do not believe in the true religion [Islam], until they humbly pay tax with their own hands [for being a non-Muslim]. Some of the Jews have said that Ezra is the son of God and Christians have said the same of Jesus.

Vintage Foxe

Forty-two persons of Armorian in Upper Phyrgia [in modern Turkey], were martyred in the year 845, by the Saracens, the circumstances of which transactions are as follows:

In the reign of Theophilus, the Saracens ravaged many parts of the eastern empire, gained several considerable advantages over the Christians, took the city of Armorian, and numbers suffered martyrdom. Flora and Mary, two ladies of distinction, suffered martyrdom at the same time. Perfectus [a gifted Christian orator from Cordoba] . . . took priest's orders, and performed the duties of his office with great assiduity and punctuality. Publicly declaring Mahomet an impostor, he was sentenced to be beheaded, and was accordingly executed, A.D. 850; after which his body was honorably interred by the Christians. Adalbert, bishop of Prague, a Bohemian by birth, after being involved in many troubles, began to direct his thoughts to the conversion of the infidels, to which end he repaired to Dantzic, where he converted and baptized many, which so enraged the pagan priests, that they fell upon him, and dispatched him with darts, on April 23, A.D. 997.[40]

CHAPTER EIGHT

The Persecutions in Bohemia

I tell you this, brothers: flesh and blood cannot inherit the kingdom of God, nor does the perishable inherit the imperishable. . . . For this perishable body must put on the imperishable, and this mortal body must put on immortality. **1 CORINTHIANS 15:50, 53**

And I, when I came to you, brothers, did not come proclaiming to you the testimony of God with lofty speech or wisdom. For I decided to know nothing among you except Jesus Christ and him crucified. And I was with you in weakness and in fear and much trembling, and my speech and my message were not in plausible words of wisdom, but in demonstration of the Spirit and of power, so that your faith might not rest in the wisdom of men but in the power of God.
1 CORINTHIANS 2:1-5

Do not believe I have taught anything but the truth. I have taught no error. The truths I have taught I seal with my blood. **JOHN HUSS, 1415**

I trust in the Lord God Almighty . . . that He will not take away from me the cup of His redemption, but I firmly hope to drink from it today in His kingdom. JOHN HUSS, 1415 (RESPONDING TO HIS PROSECUTORS' WORDS: "WE TAKE FROM YOU THE CUP OF REDEMPTION.")

When Martin Luther came across some sermons of the famous Bohemian martyr John Huss, they seemed to set his heart ablaze. You might say that Luther became obsessed with Huss's thoughts, life, and death. He immediately recognized that a century earlier, the Church had lost a great mind with an unrivaled passion for Christ. Yet religious leaders had burned Huss at the stake, declaring him a heretic. Many groups of Christians, like Luther a century later, were convinced to resist Rome, leading to the Hussite Crusades.

Reflecting on the impact of Huss's sermons early in his ministry, Luther wrote: "I was overwhelmed with astonishment. I could not understand for what cause they had burnt so great a man, who explained the Scriptures with so much gravity and skill."[1] We are fortunate that many of these sermons are still accessible today, along with dozens of his letters.

Huss was just one of countless martyrs in the rich history of Christianity in the area of the modern Czech Republic. His story, and that of his supporter, Jerome of Prague, who also suffered a horrific fate for his faith, helped John Foxe elevate that region's reputation for Christ—a region with a formidable pagan history.

The region suffered intense conflict between Christian and pagan leaders, like Ludmila and Drohimíra in the tenth century. Some Bohemian leaders would vie for support of the Carolingians—in the Christian lineage of Charlemagne (especially German and French territories). One such Bohemian leader was St. Ludmila, martyred on September 15, 920, in her castle at Tetin. She had been married to Borivoj, the first Czech prince to endorse Christianity.

From then until the present, a whirlwind of competing forces have been at play, sometimes as disparate as the Queen song "Bohemian Rhapsody," and unfortunately, today the Czech Republic is about as secular. Ever since the Battle of White Mountain (1620) between the Catholics and Protestants, the region has progressively declined in not only Christian followers, but religion overall. Church spires still dot the Czech landscape as a testimony to its Christian heritage, and twenty-seven crosses remain in the cobblestone of Prague's Old Town Square, representing the twenty-seven Protestant martyrs after the White Mountain loss. Though Prague had been the residence of some of the Holy Roman emperors, perhaps most notably Charles IV (who reigned 1346–1378), the majority of those in the region today are nonreligious, and only a small percentage claim Christianity.

An irony is that the lasting legacy of the Hussites came through the Moravians or the Unitas Fratrum ("Unity of Brethren"). The key theological proponent of this movement, credited with founding the Unity of the Brethren movement, is Petr Chelčický (ca. 1390–1460).[2] Why the irony? Huss and the majority of the Hussites in the next generation took up arms and fought viciously for their faith positions. However, the core of Chelčický's teachings—the hallmark, if you will—is nonviolence. This is a defining characteristic of the Unity of the Brethren movement and the Moravian Church.

LUDMILA AND WENCESLAS, SAINTS OF BOHEMIA Ludmila became a venerated saint of Bohemia, the modern Czechia, and her archrival, Drahomíra, became "the proverbial evil woman" and "in exile, branded a murderer."[3] The storyline is a bit dizzying, but it's a critical part of Bohemian history.

Accenting the tragedy of this martyrology is that St. Ludmila was Drahomíra's mother-in-law, and Drahomíra had a hand in both her death and her own son's. Ludmila's husband and two oldest sons, including Vratislav, who married Drahomíra, were both political and spiritual leaders of the country, strongly promoting Christianity and building many of the prominent churches in Bohemian history. The longest any of these men lived was to age forty, and what played out was high drama between the women—mainly on the part of Drahomíra, who sought power and supported paganism.

Ludmila had been put in charge of raising her grandson, Wenceslas, Drahomíra's oldest son. Tensions arose as Wenceslas began to express support for Christianity—especially since he became duke at age thirteen and Ludmila acted as his regent. Drahomíra's second son, Boleslav, endorsed paganism like his mother, and he became her favorite. Drahomíra's husband, Vratislav, had advocated for Christianity to her dismay; when he died in 920 and Wenceslas began his reign, Drahomíra ensured that Boleslav would be raised to venerate her pagan religion. In 921, Drahomíra had Ludmila executed. She ordered two men to do the deed at Ludmila's home. Ludmila allegedly asked the assassins to behead her so her blood could be of inspiration to the local Christians. Instead, they strangled her (one account details her strangulation with her own veil).

Wenceslas ruled until Boleslav and some nobles assassinated him at the feast of Saints Cosmas and Damian. Instead of a spiritual moment of celebration in the name of the Christian physicians, the murderers brutally cut Wenceslas apart with their knives before his younger brother finished him with his lance. Drahomíra was near the place of Wenceslas's murder. Though historical sources aren't clear about her role, she appears complicit.

The Christian majority in Bohemia aligned behind Ludmila and Wenceslas, and their deaths created even more support for Christianity.

Wenceslas's deep piety and benevolence, as well as his death at the hands of his pagan brother (AD 935), led the Bohemians to canonize him and worship him as Bohemia's patron saint. It is not known whether Drahomíra lived to see the effects of Wenceslas's martyrdom in galvanizing the Christians to eliminate the remaining pagans of Bohemia, for she fled north shortly after his murder. Boleslav succeeded his brother and remained duke of Bohemia until his death in 972.

In summary, we might say that Wenceslas was martyred en route to having mass, at the church door, and Ludmila helped her husband and oldest son open the door for the church in Bohemia.

She was generous with alms, persevering in nocturnal devotions, devout in prayers, and perfect in charity and humble among the unknowing. She was so willing in her care for God's servants that to those to whom she was unable to offer help during the light of day, she would send urgent help through her servants during the dark of night. . . . This mother to orphans, consoler to widows, and indefatigable visitor of the fettered and imprisoned was perfect in all good deeds.[4]

CULTURAL CONNECTION

The Bohemian Christmas Carol

What links the Beatles' 1963 Christmas album, *Hogan's Heroes*, *Dr. Who*, *The Muppet Christmas Carol*, *The Polar Express*, *The Simpsons*, *The Big Bang Theory*, *Game of Thrones*, and many, many other cultural icons? A story of a Bohemian martyr. At Christmastime in the Czech Republic, you can likely hear a nineteenth-century carol written to venerate St. Wenceslas, the Christian prince of Bohemia martyred at the church door. He was in his mid-twenties when his brother Boleslav the Cruel murdered him with the help of other assailants (AD 935). Due to the various accounts of miracles at Wenceslas's tomb, Boleslav, who had succeeded his brother (to his pagan mother's pleasure), transferred Wenceslas's remains to the Church of St. Vitus in Prague. It became a popular pilgrimage site in the Middle Ages as a cult-like quality quickly arose around it in both Bohemia and England. English hymn writer John Mason Neale wrote the following in 1853 about the venerated prince (whom the pope posthumously dubbed a king). Numerous renditions can be found online, including a lighthearted YouTube version by the Irish Rovers. We pick up the lyrics about halfway, as Wenceslas helped his page finish the journey to the mountains where the prince was delivering food to a starving peasant on St. Stephen's Day.[5] The NPR summary of this carol is spot on: "The history of this Christmas carol is a rich accumulation of music, image and legend that speaks beyond any one religious tradition. Its most basic message is summed up in its final lines: 'Ye who now will bless the poor / shall yourselves find blessing.'"[6]

"Bring me flesh and bring me wine, bring me pine logs hither: Thou and I shall see him dine, when we bear them thither."

Page and monarch, forth they went, forth they went together;
Through the rude wind's wild lament and the bitter weather.

"Sire, the night is darker now, and the wind blows stronger;
Fails my heart, I know not how; I can go no longer."
"Mark my footsteps, good my page. Tread thou in them boldly.
Thou shalt find the winter's rage freeze thy blood less coldly."

In his master's steps he trod, where the snow lay dinted;
Heat was in the very sod which the saint had printed.
Therefore, Christian men, be sure, wealth or rank possessing,
Ye who now will bless the poor, shall yourselves find blessing.

DID YOU KNOW? *St. Vitus Cathedral*

In the center of Prague, the capital of the Czech Republic and the historic capital of Bohemia, stands a castle, and within it the St. Vitus Cathedral. This was built on the spot of a Romanesque church to which Duke Wenceslas had gifted hand bones from St. Vitus—received from King Henry I of Germany (ca. 925). The bones of Duke Wenceslas, himself a martyr, were re-interred there a few years later. While the details of St. Vitus's martyrdom are lost, his name appears prominently in early lists under the Diocletian persecutions (AD 303), such as the Martyrologium Hieronymianum (Martyrology of Jerome, d. 420). Pope Gregory (sixth century) also mentions a church dedicated to him in Sicily, Vitus's home country. The loose legends around Vitus's martyrdom cast him as a boy (varying between seven and twelve years old) who resisted his own father's tortures to turn from his faith, and was then taken to Rome, where he rejected Diocletian's as well.

JOHN HUSS (JAN HUS, MARTYRED AD 1415) Some martyrdoms during the late Middle Ages seemed to loom larger than others. And some in *Foxe's Book of Martyrs* seemed to dominate its pages, accented by expensive woodcuts. The life, death, and legacy of John Huss is one of these. Part of this is his rags-to-righteousness journey, and the brazen public demonstration of political power against this pre-Reformation reformer.

His weighty words on theology and doctrine in his collected sermons, his popularity in the pulpit, and his martyrdom would inspire Martin Luther a century later. John Wesley would find direction and courage through his religious descendants, the Moravians. Hymnbooks throughout Europe and England would carry his message. And his followers remained so zealous that they would repel six Hussite Crusades against overwhelming odds.[7]

In the early 1400s, John Huss had become the leading voice in not only Prague, but also for many surrounding towns and areas. His fellow Bohemians were caught in a fight between German and Czech theological (and political) interests, and the Bohemians championed him. He was to Prague and its sympathizers what John Wycliffe and Martin Luther would become to England and Germany. For Christians in the twenty-first century to relate to Huss's place among the majority of Christians in Prague, think of some of the most popular preachers and writers today. The range is wide: Max Lucado, Satish Kumar, T. D. Jakes, David Yonggi Cho, Rick Warren, Greg Laurie, Prophet T. B. Joshua, Tim Keller, David Jeremiah, Joel Osteen, Joyce Meyer, Pope Francis, Tony Evans, Kevin Meyers, Beth Moore, Craig Groeschel, Charles Buregeya, Brian and Bobbie Houston, and a long list of others. It's almost impossible to separate the ones you know from their large flock of followers—Christians who worship under their care, often in a megachurch setting, or in many campuses with satellite messages. Warren and Saddleback. Groeschel and New Life. Houston and Hillsong. Meyers and 12Stone. Kumar and Calvary Temple. Most countries can claim such lists. And that was true of Prague—Huss and the massive Bethlehem Chapel.

During an imprisonment in 1412, Huss would reference the central role of the chapel:

> May God be with you, beloved lords and masters! I beg you in the first place to consider God's cause, to which great injury is being done; for certain persons desire to suppress His holy word, to destroy a chapel that is useful for the preaching of His word, and thus to hinder men from salvation.[8]

Huss was so popular that when he was finally imprisoned, the bishop moved him suddenly at night "fettered in a boat" and then had him escorted by 170 armed men—similar to the Roman escort of Paul from Jerusalem to Caesarea.[9]

Huss, far from timid, challenged authorities throughout his tenure. The Catholic Church excommunicated him four times, and authorities banned him from preaching on various occasions. He simply ignored them, and the majority of the citizens of Prague were behind him.

> Hus put these words into the mouth of Christ: "Everyone who passes by, pause and consider if there has been any sorrow like mine. Clothed in these rags I weep while my priests go about in scarlet. I suffer great agony in a sweat of blood while they take delight in luxurious bathing. All through the night I am mocked and spat upon while they enjoy feasting and drunkenness. I groan upon the cross as they repose upon the softest beds."[10]

The story of Huss was all too familiar to the Bohemians; he was one of them, born in Hussenitz in 1380. His poor parents helped him to get an education, and though he didn't excel, Huss managed to attend the University of Prague. His intention was to make a better life for himself as a priest—but a funny thing happens to many people who spend a lot of time studying the Bible. He started believing it. He became inspired to teach it, and to defend what he believed were orthodox teachings.

A large part of his energies would go to fight corruption among the clergy. His sermons and letters are filled with such sentiments. Three citizens who championed Huss's views against the selling of indulgences were beheaded by the Catholic Church. Huss's protégé, Jerome of Prague, led demonstrations against corruption, and then the public procession of their funerals to Bethlehem Chapel in Prague. Huss wrote:

> One pays for confession, for mass, for the sacrament, for indulgences, for churching a woman, for a blessing, for burials, for funeral services and prayers. The very last penny which an old

woman has hidden in her bundle for fear of thieves or robbery will not be saved. The villainous priest will grab it.[11]

The life and writing of John Wycliffe (d. 1384) had influenced Huss, as he found resonance with his own calls for reform of the Church and putting the Bible in the regular vernacular.

Early debates hinged on fine points of philosophy (the Czechs, with Wycliffe, were realists; the Germans nominalists). But the Czechs, with Huss, also warmed up to Wycliffe's reforming ideas; though they had no intention of altering traditional doctrines, they wanted to place more emphasis on the Bible, expand the authority of church councils (and lessen that of the pope), and promote the moral reform of clergy. Thus Huss began increasingly to trust the Scriptures, "desiring to hold, believe, and assert whatever is contained in them as long as I have breath in me."[12]

Observed John Foxe,

The English reformist, Wickliffe, had so kindled the light of reformation, that it began to illumine the darkest corners of popery and ignorance. His doctrines spread into Bohemia, and were well received by great numbers of people, but by none so particularly as John Huss, and his zealous friend and fellow martyr, Jerome of Prague.

The archbishop of Prague, finding the reformists daily increasing, issued a decree to suppress the further spreading of Wickliffe's writings: but this had an effect quite different to what he expected, for it stimulated the friends of those doctrines to greater zeal, and almost the whole university united to propagate them.

Being strongly attached to the doctrines of Wickliffe, Huss opposed the decree of the archbishop, who, however, at length, obtained a bull from the pope, giving him commission to prevent the publishing of Wickliffe's doctrines in his province. By virtue of this bull, the archbishop condemned the writings of Wickliffe: he also proceeded against four doctors, who had not delivered up the copies of that divine, and prohibited them, notwithstanding their privileges, to preach to any congregation. Dr. Huss, with some other members of the university, protested against these proceedings, and entered an appeal from the sentence of the archbishop.

The affair being made known to the pope, he granted a commission to Cardinal Colonna, to cite John Huss to appear personally at the court of Rome, to answer the accusations laid against him, of preaching both errors and heresies.[13]

At this and other intersections between Huss and the papacy, we see the wide support for this popular preacher. In an age with few celebrities, he was among the most famous people in the region. Though they couldn't prohibit the Roman pontiff from issuing multiple excommunications, the people stood in the gap for Huss on numerous occasions.

Like the journey of Martin Luther a century later to the imperial Diet of Worms, John Huss had also been promised safe travel. That promise was broken, and this was the last stage of his defiant crusade against papal corruption. The occasion was the Council of Constance in southern Germany in November of 1414. Sigismund of Hungary, heir to the Bohemian crown, called the gathering to dissolve tensions within the Church.

Sigismund ostensibly called the gathering to settle the dispute between the three popes—which sounds odd, but there was actually a major fight at the time, with three rival popes all vying for control. This further complicated most aspects of life for various regions, given the ramifications of each contender and their sponsors. But this was only one issue, and perhaps the overarching purpose of the council, which was to stop the Protestant Reformation.

John Huss was summoned to appear at this Council; and, to encourage him, the emperor sent him a safe-conduct: the civilities, and even reverence, which Huss met with on his journey were beyond imagination. The streets, and sometimes the very roads, were lined with people, whom respect, rather than curiosity, had brought together. He was ushered into the town with great acclamations, and it may be said that he passed through Germany in a kind of triumph. He could not help expressing his surprise at the treatment he received: "I thought (said he) I had been an outcast. I now see my worst friends are in Bohemia." As soon as Huss arrived at Constance, he immediately took lodgings in a remote part of the city. A short time after his arrival, came one Stephen Paletz, who was employed by the clergy at Prague to manage the intended prosecution against him. Paletz was afterwards joined by Michael de Cassis, on the part of the court of Rome. These two declared themselves his accusers, and drew up a set of articles against him, which they presented to the pope and the prelates of the Council.[14]

Huss would lose his freedom, and the false promise of safe passage became obvious.[15]

When it was known that he was in the city he was immediately arrested, and committed a prisoner to a chamber in the palace. This violation of common law and justice was particularly noticed by one of Huss's friends, who urged the imperial safe-conduct; but the pope replied he never granted any safe conduct, nor was he bound by that of the emperor. While Huss was in confinement, the Council acted the part of inquisitors. They condemned the doctrines of Wickliffe, and even ordered his remains to be dug up and burned to ashes; which orders were strictly complied with.

In the meantime, the nobility of Bohemia and Poland strongly interceded for Huss; and so far prevailed as to prevent his being condemned unheard, which had been resolved on by the commissioners appointed to try him. When he was brought before the Council, the articles exhibited against him were read: they were upwards of forty in number, and chiefly extracted from his writings.

John Huss's answer was this: "I did appeal unto the pope; who being dead, and the cause of my matter remaining undetermined, I appealed likewise unto his successor John XXIII: before whom when, by the space of two years, I could not be admitted by my advocates to defend my cause, I appealed unto the high judge Christ." When John Huss had spoken these words, it was demanded of him whether he had received absolution of the pope or no? He answered, "No."[16]

At this point we begin to see that Huss, regardless of whether he was in front of sacred or secular body, was uncompromising in his faith. It's crystal clear that these statements would bring down the wrath of his judges, but he continues:

Then again, whether it was lawful for him to appeal unto Christ or no? Whereunto John Huss answered: "Verily I do affirm here before you all, that there is no more just or effectual appeal, than that appeal which is made unto Christ, forasmuch as the law doth determine, that to appeal is no other thing than in a cause of grief or wrong done by an inferior judge, to implore and require aid at a higher Judge's hand. Who is then a higher Judge than Christ? Who, I say, can know or judge the matter more justly, or with more equity? When in Him there is found no deceit, neither can He be deceived; or, who can better help the miserable and oppressed than He?"[17]

Here we begin to see a radical change in the treatment of Huss. And it's not without notice that like the week following Christ's triumphal entry, Huss had gone from experiencing a celebrity's entrance with lined streets, to being mocked in a short span of time. The narrative continues:

While John Huss, with a devout and sober countenance, was speaking and pronouncing those words, he was derided and mocked by all the whole Council. These excellent sentences were esteemed as so many expressions of treason, and tended to inflame his adversaries. Accordingly, the bishops appointed by the Council stripped him of his priestly garments, degraded him, put a paper miter on his head, on which was painted devils, with this inscription, "A ringleader of heretics." Which when he saw, he said: "My Lord Jesus Christ, for my sake, did wear a crown of thorns; why should not I then, for His sake, again wear this light crown, be it ever so ignominious? Truly I will do it, and that willingly." When it was set upon his head, the bishop said: "Now we commit thy soul unto the devil." "But I," said John Huss, lifting his eyes towards the heaven, "do commend into Thy hands, O Lord Jesus Christ! my spirit which Thou has redeemed." When the chain was put about him at the stake, he said, with a smiling countenance, "My Lord Jesus Christ was bound with a harder chain than this for my sake, and why then should I be ashamed of this rusty one?" When the fagots [pieces of wood] were piled up to his very neck, the duke of Bavaria was so officious as to desire him to abjure. "No, (said Huss;) I never preached any doctrine of an evil tendency; and what I taught with my lips I now seal with my blood." He then said to the executioner, "You are now going to burn a goose, (Huss signifying goose in the Bohemian language:) but in a century you will have a swan which you can neither roast nor boil." If he were prophetic, he must have meant Martin Luther, who shone about a hundred years after, and who had a swan for his arms. The flames were now applied to the fagots, when our martyr sung a hymn with so loud and cheerful a voice that he was heard through all the cracklings of the combustibles, and the noise of the multitude. At length his voice was interrupted by the severity of the flames, which soon closed his existence.

Then, with great diligence, gathering the ashes together, they cast them into the river Rhine, that the least remnant of that man should not be left upon the earth, whose memory, notwithstanding, cannot be abolished out of the minds of the godly, neither by fire, neither by water, neither by any kind of torment.[18]

Earlier we saw the strong theological and philosophical connection between John Huss and John Wycliffe; Huss in Bohemia (but martyred in Germany), and Wycliffe in Lutterworth, England. Both have a connection to the Council of Constance in 1415. Though Wycliffe died in 1384, he also worked during an era in which the papacy was split between contenders. Both Wycliffe and Huss expressed issues with the papacy. Both rejected actions by clergy—calling for reform and access to the Bible in their own language. And both were officially condemned at Constance. Although Wycliffe's body had long been in the grave, the general council called for his bones to be dug up and burned, then to cast the ashes into the River Swift.

"Lord Jesus, it is for thee that I patiently endure this cruel death. I pray thee to have mercy on my enemies." JOHN HUSS, JULY 6, 1415; THE LAST WORDS ATTRIBUTED TO HIM WHILE TIED TO THE STAKE BEFORE BURNING

DID YOU KNOW? *The Bethlehem Chapel of Prague*

Throughout most of the Middle Ages, the largest gatherings were royal weddings and wars, but the Bethlehem Chapel in Prague was an exception—holding three thousand worshipers. It was built in 1391, and John Huss became its preacher three years later. From its inception it held services only in the native Czech language. Ironically, the historic site was restored by the Bohemian communist regime (1948–1989) after the pope closed the building, and it was repurposed for housing. The pulpit, outer walls, and some of the art remain from Huss's time.

Now imagine a modern megachurch suddenly losing its pastor—brutally and publicly tortured and then killed. It's the closest we can come to envisioning the impact of Huss's martyrdom in 1415. It was a societal earthquake invoking a type of collective trauma that was recounted for generations.

It did not escape his fellow Bohemians that Huss sang psalms as his body was burning. The preface of the *Hymnal of the Moravian Church* credits John Huss with their musical tradition, which takes a key role in their worship experience. (A service in 1732 celebrating the lives of two Moravians included over 100 hymns.) Written in 1501, the Moravian songbook is the first Protestant hymnal, containing 89 songs.

The Moravians' most famous hymn writer was Count Nicholas Zinzendorf (1700–1760), who wrote over 2,000 hymns and produced various collections including his first Moravian hymnal in 1735. His focus on "pure religion" and "Christianity of the heart" resonated with the Hussite descendants—the Moravians. Perhaps the most popular song became "Jesus, Lead Me On," translated into over thirty languages. However, the one best capturing his theology was "The Savior's Blood and Righteousness" (1739). The first of its thirty-three stanzas reads:

> The Savior's blood and righteous
> My beauty is, my glorious dress;
> Thus well arrayed, I need not fear,
> When in His presence I appear.[19]

Shortly before he died in Herrnhut, Saxony, Zinzendorf shared in Huss fashion the following words with his son-in-law:

> I am going to the Savior. I am ready. I am quite resigned to the will of my Lord. If He is no longer willing to make use of me here, I am quite ready to go to Him, for there is nothing more in my way.[20]

Four Moravian hymnals would be produced in England between 1742 and 1754, the last including 1,169 hymns. A completely new hymnal surfaced in 1755 known collegially as *The London Hymn Book*, containing over 3,000 hymns and including many of the hymns from the Unitas Fratrum.[21]

JEROME OF PRAGUE Perhaps the most ardent follower of Huss was Jerome of Prague, who had an exceptional giftedness in learning. A native of Prague and graduate of its university, he also traveled to other educational centers such as Paris, Heidelberg, Cologne, and Oxford. Richard II of England was tied to Bohemia through his wife, Anne, the sister of King Václav, which opened up scholarships at Oxford University for students like Jerome. His fame as a gifted lecturer gave him many opportunities, but also continued to raise concerns as he championed the views espoused by John Wycliffe years earlier.

Like Huss, he found Wycliffe's works not only engaging, but helpful in facilitating Bohemia's reform. With a penchant for languages, Jerome translated many of Wycliffe's works for his country. This was around forty years before the Gutenberg Press, so these were handwritten (or manuscripts—from the Latin *manu*-scriptus). In short, they were all the more priceless, especially for those of pre-Reformation leanings. Jerome became Huss's assistant upon returning to Prague, and these translations became key in enhancing the reformation's cause (or "Pre-Reformation" as this period is often called).

Jerome went to the Council of Constance to try to aid his mentor, even though Huss had strongly warned him to stay away. He slipped into the city around three months before Huss's pyre. He created a stir by tacking posters around the city, but soon learned the authorities knew he was the culprit. He was able to sneak away but was captured in Bavaria and illegally arrested by a friend of the Constance officials. A large posse came and "led Jerome in fetters by a long chain" behind the leader on horseback.

> Immediately on his arrival he was committed to a loathsome dungeon. Jerome was treated nearly in the same manner as Huss had been, only that he was much longer confined, and shifted from one prison to another. At length, being brought before the Council, he desired that he might plead his own cause, and exculpate himself: which being refused him, he broke out into the following exclamation: "What barbarity is this! For three hundred and forty days have I been confined in a variety of prisons. There

is not a misery, there is not a want, that I have not experienced. To my enemies you have allowed the fullest scope of accusation: to me you deny the least opportunity of defence. Not an hour will you now indulge me in preparing for my trial. You have swallowed the blackest calumnies against me. You have represented me as a heretic, without knowing my doctrine; as an enemy of the faith, before you knew what faith I professed: as a persecutor of priests before you could have an opportunity of understanding my sentiments on that head."

As you might imagine, Jerome was closing any door that may have opened. Although he would temporarily recant, he revisited his decision and became even more impassioned in his critique of the church officials. Parts of his claims are simply without merit, but it was obvious what he believed. During his travels he created commotion in most cities by inciting the hosts of large lectures with his Wycliffite views. In 1410 he was declared a heretic in Vienna, but skipped parole, and then wrote a condescending letter back to the judge. Jerome was not just an impassioned theologian, he was a kind of provocateur. And Jerome was about to pay the ultimate sacrifice for his firm belief—a belief that couldn't be denied because he had been so public with it. Not only was he going to be deemed a heretic, but he'd done significant damage to papal authorities because he'd spread his views among the crowds throughout the region. Though not without his own character issues, Jerome was a man of confident conviction and force-ful rhetoric, exclaiming in his defense,

> You are a General Council: in you center all this world can communicate of gravity, wisdom, and sanctity: but still you are men, and men are seducible by appearances. The higher your character is for wisdom, the greater ought your care to be not to deviate into folly. The cause I now plead is not my own cause: it is the cause of men, it is the cause of Christians; it is a cause which is to affect the rights of posterity, however the experiment is to be made in my person.

Perhaps the most amazing thing about this narrative is that one of the boldest and most confident proponents of the gospel would lapse even momentarily. He was well aware that there was no recourse for such statements. He seems to have planned to recant, then escape, but that was not to happen again like in Vienna.

This speech had not the least effect; Jerome was obliged to hear the charge read, which was reduced under the following heads: 1. That he was a derider of the papal dignity. 2. An opposer of the pope. 3. An enemy to the cardinals. 4. A persecutor of the prelates. 5. A hater of the Christian religion.

The trial of Jerome was brought on the third day after his accusation and witnesses were examined in support of the charge. The prisoner was prepared for his defence, which appears almost incredible, when we consider he had been three hundred and forty days shut up in loathsome prisons, deprived of daylight, and almost starved for want of common necessaries. But his spirit soared above these disadvantages, under which a man less animated would have sunk; nor was he more at a loss of quotations from the fathers and ancient authors than if he had been furnished with the finest library.

The most bigoted of the assembly were unwilling he should be heard, knowing what effect eloquence is apt to have on the minds of the most prejudiced. At length, however, it was carried by the majority that he should have liberty to proceed in his defence, which he began in such an exalted strain of moving elocution that the heart of obdurate zeal was seen to melt, and the mind of superstition seemed to admit a ray of conviction. He made an admirable distinction between evidence as resting upon facts, and as supported by malice and calumny.

Jerome had been a superstar from Prague. He was tall, with a dark beard, and had a striking presence. He had a gifted mind. Though considerably overconfident at times, his journey was one that could command admiration. However, eloquent speaking will not change the verdict on a view clearly deemed as heresy. Depending on which account of his trial you read, he's either a martyr (the view held by most Protestants), or a heretic who was changing official theology (according to most Catholic chroniclers of his time).[22] The Florentine humanist Poggio Bracciolini's famous letter about the trial seems preoccupied with Jerome's gifts. He concludes, "Yet I fear he was given all these gifts by nature for his own destruction."[23]

He laid before the assembly the whole tenor of his life and conduct. He observed that the greatest and most holy men had been known to differ in points of speculation, with a view to distinguish truth, not to keep it concealed. He expressed a noble contempt of all his enemies, who would have induced him to retract the cause of virtue and truth. He entered upon a high encomium of Huss; and declared he was ready to follow him in the glorious task of martyrdom. He then touched upon the most defensible doctrines of Wickliffe; and concluded with observing that it was far from his intention to advance anything against the state of the Church of God; that it was only against the abuse of the clergy he complained; and that he could not help saying, it was certainly impious that the patrimony of the Church, which was originally intended for the purpose of charity and universal benevolence, should be prostituted to the pride of the eye, in feasts, foppish vestments, and other reproaches to the name and profession of Christianity.

There was no surprise that as the trial ended he received the same sentence as Huss. The difference was that he was a layman and thereby sentenced to the "ceremony of degradation."

They had prepared a cap of paper painted with red devils, which being put upon his head, he said, "Our Lord Jesus Christ, when He suffered death for me a most miserable sinner, did wear a crown of thorns upon His head, and for His sake will I wear this cap."

The various accounts of Jerome's trial and two-day waiting period are nuanced differently. Some emphasize his recantation. Others include minor differences with Wycliffe and Huss. Others his firm zeal in the end. Ultimately, he stood firm against the cardinal of Florence's techniques to win him over to the Catholic view.

> In going to the place of execution he sang several hymns, and when he came to the spot, which was the same where Huss had been burnt, he knelt down, and prayed fervently. He embraced the stake with great cheerfulness, and when they went behind him to set fire to the fagots, he said, "Come here, and kindle it before my eyes; for if I had been afraid of it, I had not come to this place." The fire being kindled, he sang a hymn, but was soon interrupted by the flames; and the last words he was heard to say these, "This soul in flames I offer Christ, to Thee."
>
> The elegant Pogge [Poggio Bracciolini], a learned gentleman of Florence, secretary to two popes, and a zealous but liberal Catholic, in a letter to Leonard Arotin, bore ample testimony of the extraordinary powers and virtues of Jerome whom he emphatically styles, A prodigious man!

Vintage Foxe

When [Jerome of Prague's] whole body with his beard was so burned round about, that there appeared through the great burning upon his whole body certain great blisters as big as an egg, yet he continually very strongly and stoutly moved, and shaked his head and mouth, by the space almost of one quarter of an hour. So burning in the fire, he lived with great pain and martyrdom, while one minute easily could have gone from St. Clement's over the bridge to our lady church. After he was thus dead in the fire, by and by they brought his bedding, his straw bed, his boots, his hood, and all other things that he had in the prison, and burned them all to ashes in the same fire. Which ashes, after that the fire was out, they diligently gathered together, and carried them in a cart, and cast them into the river Rhone [Rhine], which ran hard by the city.[24]

JOHN ZISCA The aftermath of Huss's martyrdom brought a series of five Crusades against his followers, and all five were countered by what appeared to be inferior forces. Collectively historians call these the Hussite Crusades (1420–1431), which occurred about a century before the Protestant Reformation and Catholic Counter-Reformation. The Crusades were repelled by peasant armies commanded by John Zisca (Jan Žižka) and then Prokop Holý, who gave their lives in defending their Christian beliefs.

Zisca was born John de Trocznow in an established family in the court of Winceslaus, but the loss of an eye earned him the nickname "one-eyed," or *zisca* in Bohemian. Zisca had served the king of Poland against the Teutonic knights, gaining a reputation as a war hero. He became obsessed with vindicating the fate of his fellow Bohemians at the Council of Constance. Winceslaus IV (over Bohemia) and Zisca agreed to avenge the blood of Huss and Jerome if possible. And during one of his battles to avenge these deaths, an arrow pierced his remaining eye. "At Prague it was extracted, but, being barbed, it tore the eye out with it. A fever succeeded, and his life was with difficulty preserved. He was now totally blind, but still desirous of attending the army."[25]

Zisca began his stand against Rome (and Constance) by convening a large gathering of like-minded reformers at the castle of Wisgrade. Winceslaus gave his official blessing for them to take up arms for the cause of religious liberties. But this blessing became empty when Winceslaus died and his brother, Sigismond, tried annulling and removing such zealots. Sigismond had been king of Hungary and Croatia since 1387, and king of Germany since 1411, before becoming king of Bohemia in 1419. Zisca had his hands full with a forceful magistrate on a power-grabbing journey. Sigismond would later become Holy Roman Emperor (1433–1437).

Zisca and his friends, upon this, immediately flew to arms,
declared war against the emperor and the pope, and laid siege to

Pilsen with 40,000 men. They soon became masters of the fortress, and in a short time all the southwest part of Bohemia submitted, which greatly increased the army of the reformers. The latter having taken the pass of Muldaw, after a severe conflict of five days and nights, the emperor became alarmed, and withdrew his troops from the confines of Turkey, to march them into Bohemia.[26]

A long, bloody conflict ensued between Zisca's forces and Sigismond's imperial troops (aligned with the Catholic Church). The lives lost for the name of biblical purity were lost to the chroniclers, as slaughters were many during the ebb and flow of control. Referring to the biblical locale, Zisca had named his makeshift headquarters Mount Tabor.

At this point Zisca was going into battle blind, flanked on both sides with horsemen, and carrying a pole axe. In one battle his forces chased two thousand imperial troops (including many cavalrymen), who drowned when the ice broke while they were crossing the Igla River.

Our general had now leisure to attend to the work of reformation, but he was much disgusted with the gross ignorance and superstition of the Bohemian clergy, who rendered themselves contemptible in the eyes of the whole army. We find that "Zisca now began again to pay attention to the Reformation; he forbid all the prayers for the dead, images, sacerdotal vestments, fasts, and festivals. Priests were to be preferred according to their merits, and no one to be persecuted for religious opinions."[27]

However, doctrinal dissent was still a tricky thing as the Bohemians learned anew in a dispute over the Sacraments—nine of Zisca's men were killed, and then the populace turned on the magistrates and slew them. Zisca managed to make peace between the political and religious rivalries. Ironically, after all the bloodshed while en route to sign the peace agreement with Sigismond, Zisca succumbed to the plague in October 1424.

John Foxe observes, "Like Moses, he died in view of the completion of his labors, and was buried in the great Church of Czaslow, in Bohemia, where a monument is erected to his memory, with this inscription on it—'Here lies John Zisca, who, having defended his country against the encroachments of papal tyranny, rests in this hallowed place, in despite of the pope.'"[28]

THE HUSSITE CRUSADES With Zisca's death came a cascading and violent oppression of the Bohemians. The pope ordered the Roman clergy everywhere to excommunicate such as adopted their opinions, or commiserated their fate. Foxe's account of the Bohemian persecution is rather grim:

> At Prague, the persecution was extremely severe, until, at length, the reformed being driven to desperation, armed themselves, attacked the senate-house, and threw twelve senators, with the speaker, out of the senate-house windows, whose bodies fell upon spears, which were held up by others of the reformed in the street, to receive them.
>
> Being informed of these proceedings, the pope came to Florence, and publicly excommunicated the reformed Bohemians, exciting the emperor of Germany, and all kings, princes, dukes, etc., to take up arms, in order to extirpate the whole race; and promising, by way of encouragement, full remission of all sins whatever, to the most wicked person, if he did but kill one Bohemian Protestant.[29]

Keep in mind that the word *Protestant* is used anachronistically throughout this section, since those who "protested" the Roman Catholic Church and received this designation are generally linked to the work of Martin Luther.

Catholic chroniclers at the time considered this Crusade a great success against heretics. Protestant chroniclers saw thousands of martyrs. Though there were political and personal interests at play, the inciting differences were religious—differences that have all but dissipated today. Numerically, Christendom today is split somewhat evenly between Protestants and Catholics. The Second Vatican Council (1962–1965) even agreed with one of the main differences the Bohemians held—to allow the laity to partake of the cup at Communion (like the practice described in the New Testament). However, this doctrinal retreat came centuries too late to save the Bohemian martyrs cruelly thrown into the mines of Cuttenburgh and left to die.

A merchant of Prague . . . happened to lodge in the same inn with several priests. Entering into conversation upon the subject of religious controversy, he passed many encomiums [tributes] upon the martyred John Huss, and his doctrines. The priests taking umbrage at this, laid an information against him the next morning, and he was committed to prison as a heretic. Many endeavors were used to persuade him to embrace the Roman Catholic faith, but he remained steadfast to the pure doctrines of the reformed Church. Soon after his imprisonment, a student of the university was committed to the same jail; when, being permitted to converse with the merchant, they mutually comforted each other. On the day appointed for execution, when the jailer began to fasten ropes to their feet, by which they were to be dragged through the streets, the student appeared quite terrified, and offered to abjure his faith, and turn Roman Catholic if he might be saved. The offer was accepted, his abjuration was taken by a priest, and he was set at liberty. A priest applying to the merchant to follow the example of the student, he nobly said, "Lose no time in hopes of my recantation, your expectations will be vain; I sincerely pity that poor wretch, who has miserably sacrificed his soul for a few more uncertain years of a troublesome life; and, so far from having the least idea of following his example, I glory in the very thoughts of dying for the sake of Christ." On hearing these words, the priest ordered the executioner to proceed, and the merchant being drawn through the city was brought to the place of execution, and there burnt.[30]

The martyrdom of a Bohemian deemed to be a heretic had ramifications not just for the individual, but for the entire household, a dynamic that has played out in many centuries and regions, and we'll see it anew in our last section on modern martyrs.

Pichel, a bigoted popish magistrate [note Foxe's overt description], apprehended twenty-four Protestants, among whom was his daughter's husband. As they all owned they were of the reformed religion, he indiscriminately condemned them to be drowned in the river Abbis. On the day appointed for the execution, a great concourse of people attended, among whom was Pichel's daughter. This worthy wife threw herself at her father's feet, bedewed them with tears, and in the most pathetic manner, implored him to commiserate her sorrow, and pardon her husband. The obdurate magistrate sternly replied, "Intercede not for him, child, he is a heretic, a vile heretic." To which she nobly answered, "Whatever his faults may be, or however his opinions may differ from yours, he is still my husband, a name which, at a time like this, should alone employ my whole consideration." Pichel flew into a violent passion and said, "You are mad! Cannot you, after the death of this, have a much worthier husband?" "No, sir" replied she, "my affections are fixed upon this, and death itself shall not dissolve my marriage vow." Pichel, however, continued inflexible, and ordered the prisoners to be tied with their hands and feet behind them, and in that manner be thrown into the river. As soon as this was put into execution, the young lady watched her opportunity, leaped into the waves, and embracing the body of her husband, both sank together into one watery grave. An uncommon instance of conjugal love in a wife, and of an inviolable attachment to, and personal affection for, her husband.[31]

THE BOHEMIAN INQUISITION The manifestation of the Inquisition in Bohemia was among the darkest of days for an overreaching papacy and emperor Ferdinand II (Holy Roman Emperor, 1619– 1637) "whose hatred to the Bohemian Protestants was without bounds."[32] He was a Hapsburg, and held the kingships of Bohemia and Hungary. He had close ties with the Jesuits through his upbringing and education, and had vowed his allegiance to them. He enacted his systematic slaughter of the Bohemians somewhat as an extension of the Spanish Inquisition started in 1478 with Ferdinand II and Isabella. It would last in some form until 1834, spreading throughout much of Europe and "the new world." But the Inquisition against the Bohemians was far less restrained and regulated.

The emperor's rendition of the Inquisition was to send Jesuit judges ("reformers") throughout the territories with armed escorts and a roving high court. Another caveat proved the most lethal—the accused could not appeal. Carnage ensued.

This bloody court, attended by a body of troops, made the tour of Bohemia, in which they seldom examined or saw a prisoner, suffering the soldiers to murder the Protestants as they pleased, and then to make a report of the matter to them afterward.

The first victim of their cruelty was an aged minister, whom they killed as he lay sick in his bed; the next day they robbed and murdered another, and soon after shot a third, as he was preaching in his pulpit.

A nobleman and [a] clergyman who resided in a Protestant village, hearing of the approach of the high court of reformers and the troops, fled from the place, and secreted themselves. The soldiers, however, on their arrival, seized upon a schoolmaster, asked him where the lord of that place and the minister were concealed, and where they had hidden their treasures. The schoolmaster replied that he could not answer either of the questions. They then stripped him naked, bound him with cords, and beat him most unmercifully with cudgels. This cruelty not extorting any confession from him, they scorched him in various parts of his body; when, to gain a respite from his torments, he promised to show them where the treasures were hid. The soldiers gave ear to this with pleasure, and the schoolmaster led them to a ditch full of stones, saying, "Beneath these stones are the treasures ye seek for." Eager after money, they went to work, and soon removed those stones, but not finding what they sought after, they beat the schoolmaster to death, buried him in the ditch, and covered him with the very stones he had made them remove.

Some of the soldiers ravished the daughters of a worthy Protestant before his face, and then tortured him to death. A minister and his wife they tied back to back and burnt. Another minister they hung upon a cross beam, and making a fire under him, broiled him to death. A gentleman they hacked into small pieces, and they filled a young man's mouth with gunpowder, and setting fire to it, blew his head to pieces.[33]

In one of Foxe's most detailed and graphic martyrologies, we do not even learn the martyr's name.

As their [the Jesuit tribunal's] principal rage was directed against the clergy, they took a pious Protestant minister, and tormenting him daily for a month together, in the following manner, making their cruelty regular, systematic, and progressive.

They placed him amidst them, and made him the subject of their derision and mockery, during a whole day's entertainment, trying to exhaust his patience, but in vain, for he bore the whole with true Christian fortitude. They spit in his face, pulled his nose, and pinched him in most parts of his body. He was hunted like a wild beast, until ready to expire with fatigue. They made him run the gauntlet between two ranks of them, each striking him with a twig. He was beat with their fists. He was beat with ropes. They scourged him with wires. He was beat with cudgels. They tied him up by the heels with his head downwards, until the blood started out of his nose, mouth, etc. They hung him by the right arm until it was dislocated, and then had it set again. The same was repeated with his left arm. Burning papers dipped in oil were placed between his fingers and toes. His flesh was torn with red-hot pincers. He was put to the rack. They pulled off the nails of his right hand. The same repeated with his left hand. He was bastinadoed [beaten] on his feet. A slit was made in his right ear. The same repeated on his left ear. His nose was slit. They whipped him through the town upon an ass. They made several incisions in his flesh. They pulled off the toe nails of his right foot. The same they repeated with his left foot. He was tied up by the loins, and suspended for a considerable time. The teeth of his upper jaw were pulled out. The same was repeated with his lower jaw. Boiling lead was poured upon his fingers. The same was repeated with his toes. A knotted cord was twisted about his forehead in such a manner as to force out his eyes.

During the whole of these horrid cruelties, particular care was taken that his wounds should not mortify [become gangrenous], and not to injure him mortally until the last day, when the forcing out of his eyes proved his death.[34]

These tormentors considered themselves true Christians, yet we see here an evil bent towards the most inhumane of cruelties. A base creativity for pain. There can be no moral defense for their grotesque conduct—but only an attempt to explain it.

Unhappily, disagreements are inevitable for all who take the faith seriously. Both Eusebius [early church historian, d. AD 399] and Foxe have shown time and again that when the external heat is off, cantankerous Christians will provide heat on their own in conflict with one another. The Saints are sinners too, a phenomenon by no means limited to Christianity, as the deadly current struggle between Sunni and Shia Islam more than demonstrates.[35]

Foxe continues his narrative about these horrors.

Innumerable were the other murders and depredations committed by those unfeeling brutes, and shocking to humanity were the cruelties which they inflicted on the poor Bohemian Protestants. The winter being far advanced, however, the high court of reformers, with their infernal band of military ruffians, thought proper to return to Prague; but on their way, meeting with a Protestant pastor, they could not resist the temptation of feasting their barbarous eyes with a new kind of cruelty, which had just suggested itself to the diabolical imagination of one of the soldiers. This was to strip the minister naked, and alternately to cover him with ice and burning coals. This novel mode of tormenting a fellow creature was immediately put into practice, and the unhappy victim expired beneath the torments, which seemed to delight his inhuman persecutors.

A secret order was soon after issued by the emperor, for apprehending all noblemen and gentlemen, who had been principally concerned in supporting the Protestant cause, and in nominating Frederic elector Palatine of the Rhine, to be king of Bohemia. These, to the number of fifty, were apprehended in one night, and at one hour, and brought from the places where they were taken, to the castle of Prague, and the estates of those who were absent from the kingdom were confiscated, themselves were made outlaws, and their names fixed upon a gallows, as marks of public ignominy.

The high court of reformers then proceeded to try the fifty who had been apprehended, and two apostate Protestants were appointed to examine them. These examinants asked a great number of unnecessary and impertinent questions, which so exasperated one of the noblemen, who was naturally of a warm temper, that he exclaimed, opening his breast at the same time, "Cut here, search my heart, you shall find nothing but the love of religion and liberty; those were the motives for which I drew my sword, and for those I am willing to suffer death."

As none of the prisoners would change their religion, or acknowledge they had been in error, they were all pronounced guilty; but the sentence was referred to the emperor. When that monarch had read their names, and an account of the respective accusations against them, he passed judgment on all, but in a different manner, as his sentences were of four kinds, viz. death, banishment, imprisonment for life, and imprisonment during pleasure.

Twenty being ordered for execution, were informed they might send for Jesuits, monks, or friars, to prepare for the awful change they were to undergo; but that no Protestants should be permitted to come near them. This proposal they rejected, and strove all they could to comfort and cheer each other upon the solemn occasion.

On the morning of the day appointed for the execution, a cannon was fired as a signal to bring the prisoners from the castle to the principal market place, in which scaffolds were erected, and a body of troops were drawn up to attend the tragic scene.

The prisoners left the castle with as much cheerfulness as if they had been going to an agreeable entertainment, instead of a violent death.

Lord Schilik was about fifty years of age, and was possessed of great natural and acquired abilities. When he was told he was to be quartered, and his parts scattered in different places, he smiled with great serenity, saying, "The loss of a sepulchre is but a trifling consideration." A gentleman who stood by, crying, "Courage, my lord!" he replied, "I have God's favor, which is sufficient to inspire any one with courage: the fear of death does not trouble me; formerly I have faced him in fields of battle to oppose Antichrist; and now dare face him on a scaffold, for the sake of Christ." Having said a short prayer, he told the executioner he was ready. He [the executioner] cut off his right hand and his head, and then quartered him. His hand and his head were placed upon the high tower of Prague, and his quarters distributed in different parts of the city.

Lord Viscount Winceslaus, who had attained the age of seventy years, was equally respectable for learning, piety, and hospitality. His temper was so remarkably patient that when his house was broken open, his property seized, and his estates confiscated, he only said, with great composure, "The Lord hath given, and the Lord hath taken away." Being asked why he could engage in so dangerous a cause as that of attempting to support the elector Palatine Frederic against the power of the emperor, he replied, "I acted strictly according to the dictates of my conscience, and, to this day, deem him my king. I am now full of years, and wish to lay down life, that I may not be a witness of the further evils which are to attend my country. You have long thirsted for my blood: take it, for God will be my avenger." Then approaching the block, he stroked his long, grey beard, and said, "Venerable hairs, the greater honor now attends ye, a crown of martyrdom is your portion." Then laying down his head, it was severed from his body at one stroke, and placed upon a pole in a conspicuous part of the city. . . .

Lord Henry Otto, when he first came upon the scaffold, seemed greatly confounded, and said, with some asperity, as if addressing himself to the emperor, "Thou tyrant Ferdinand, your throne is established in blood; but if you will kill my body, and disperse my members, they shall still rise up in judgment against you." He then was silent, and having walked about for some time, seemed to recover his fortitude, and growing calm, said to a gentleman who stood near, "I was, a few minutes since, greatly discomposed, but now I feel my spirits revive; God be praised for affording me such comfort; death no longer appears as the king of terrors, but seems to invite me to participate of some unknown joys." Kneeling before the block, he said, "Almighty God! To Thee I commend my soul, receive it for the sake of Christ, and admit it to the glory of Thy presence." The executioner put this nobleman to considerable pain, by making several strokes before he severed the head from the body. . . .

Sir Gaspar Kaplitz . . . eighty-six years of age . . . addressed the principal officer thus: "Behold a miserable ancient man, who hath often entreated God to take him out of this wicked world, but could not until now obtain his desire, for God reserved me until these years to be a spectacle to the world, and a sacrifice to Himself; therefore God's will be done." One of the officers told him, in consideration of his great age, that if he would only ask pardon, he would immediately receive it. "Ask pardon?" exclaimed he, "I will ask pardon of God, whom I have frequently offended; but not of the emperor, to whom I never gave any offense; should I sue for pardon, it might be justly suspected I had committed some crime for which I deserved this condemnation. No, no, as I die innocent, and with a clear conscience, I would not be separated from this noble company of martyrs:" so saying, he cheerfully resigned his neck to the block. . . .

Tobias Steffick was remarkable for his affability and serenity of temper. He was perfectly resigned to his fate, and a few minutes before his death spoke in this singular manner, "I have received, during the whole course of my life, many favors from God; ought I not therefore cheerfully to take one bitter cup, when He thinks proper to present it? Or rather, ought I not to rejoice that it is his will I should give up a corrupted life for that of immortality!"

Dr. Jessenius, an able student of physic, was accused of having spoken disrespectful words of the emperor, of treason in swearing allegiance to the elector Frederic, and of heresy in being a Protestant. For the first accusation he had his tongue cut out; for the second he was beheaded; and for the third, and last, he was quartered, and the respective parts exposed on poles. . .

No person ever lived more respected or died more lamented than John Shultis. The only words he spoke, before receiving the fatal stroke, were, "The righteous seem to die in the eyes of fools, but they only go to rest. Lord Jesus! Thou hast promised that those who come to Thee shall not be cast off. Behold, I am come; look on me, pity me, pardon my sins, and receive my soul."

Maximilian Hostialick was famed for his learning, piety, and humanity. When he first came on the scaffold, he seemed exceedingly terrified at the approach of death. The officer taking notice of his agitation, Hostialick said, "Ah! Sir, now the sins of my youth crowd upon my mind, but I hope God will enlighten me, lest I sleep the sleep of death and lest mine enemies say we have prevailed." Soon after he said, "I hope my repentance is sincere, and will be accepted, in which case the blood of Christ will wash me from my crimes." He then told the officer he should repeat the Song of Simeon; at the conclusion of which the executioner might do his duty. He accordingly, said, "Lord, now lettest Thou Thy servant depart in peace, according to Thy word: For mine eyes have seen Thy salvation"; at which words his head was struck off at one blow.

When John Kutnaur came to the place of execution, a Jesuit said to him, "Embrace the Roman Catholic faith, which alone can save and arm you against the terrors of death." To which he replied, "Your superstitious faith I abhor, it leads to perdition, and I wish for no other arms against the terrors of death than a good conscience." The Jesuit turned away, saying, sarcastically, "The Protestants are impenetrable rocks." "You are mistaken," said Kutnaur, "it is Christ that is the Rock, and we are firmly fixed upon Him." . . .

Nathaniel Wodnianskey was hanged for having supported the Protestant cause, and the election of Frederic to the crown of Bohemia. At the gallows, the Jesuits did all in their power to induce him to renounce his faith. Finding their endeavors ineffectual, one of them said, "If you will not adjure your heresy, at least repent of your rebellion?" To which Wodnianskey replied, "You take away our lives under a pretended charge of rebellion; and, not content with that, seek to destroy our souls; glut yourselves with blood, and be satisfied; but tamper not with our consciences."

Wodnianskey's own son then approached the gallows, and said to his father, "Sir, if life should be offered to you on condition of apostasy, I entreat you to remember Christ, and reject such pernicious overtures." To this the father replied, "It is very acceptable, my son, to be exhorted to constancy by you; but suspect me not; rather endeavor to confirm in their faith your brothers, sisters, and children, and teach them to imitate that constancy of which I shall leave them an example." He had no sooner concluded these words than he was turned off, receiving the crown of martyrdom with great fortitude.[36]

+ Historic Sources

One of the many extant letters of John Huss, written in October 1412, reflects his common theme of encouraging those who worshiped at Bethlehem Chapel to persevere. Like other reformers during this era (and often in Foxe's works), Huss refers to the pope as the Antichrist. This should be differentiated from the faithful men who have graced that office through much of the Church's history—but Huss was dealing with his experiences, and those of likeminded followers. He was well aware that some of the pontiffs were especially brutal on dissenters. To compound matters, at times there were three competing popes. And some were guilty of many of the various shortcomings of some of the megachurch pastors who have been much in the news in the early decades of the twenty-first century. However, during Huss's time, the pope also had political and military powers and influences. The pontiff wielded religious authority (often ignored) over Sacraments and practices directly linked in most believers' minds to eternal consequences.

To the faithful who are zealous for the Lord Jesus Christ and His word, dwelling in the city of Prague: Master John Hus, a priest unprofitable, yet having a desire for their perseverance in the love of God.

Dear friends, it is because of my strong desire that I beseech you not to draw back from the truth, the knowledge of which the Saviour in His mercy hath generously bestowed upon you. I trust indeed that the Lord will perfect what He hath begun in you the elect, and will grant unto you perseverance when you are tempted. For myself, likewise, I trust in the kindly goodness of our Saviour, although now I can say with the apostle, that *to me to live is Christ and to die gain: and if to live in the flesh, this is to me the fruit of labour: and what I shall choose, I know not. But I am straitened between two, having a desire to be dissolved and to be with Christ, a thing by far the better. But to abide still in the flesh is needful for you.* So wrote the apostle to the Philippians, when confined in a Roman prison. In like manner, dearly beloved, I say to you, though not yet shut up in prison, that I would gladly die for Christ and be with Him; and yet I desire to labour for your salvation and *what I shall choose, I know not,* awaiting the mercy of God. I fear, however, that much ill may be wrought among you and that the faithful may suffer, while the wicked may lose their souls. The latter are now rejoicing and demanding that not only should the word of God be silenced within me, but also that the place of God's word—the Bethlehem—should be closed by force. But is it possible that the Lord Almighty will grant them what they are asking for? Even though He suffer them by reason of the crimes of wicked men, as He did in Bethlehem, where He was born, and in Jerusalem, where He redeemed us, let us still sound abroad the praise of His glory, humbling ourselves under His power; He is with those who love Him, and delivers them that suffer in His behalf and reserves His scorners for perpetual fire. Hence it is, dear friends in the Lord, that I beseech you not to fail through weariness, but rather to entreat the Saviour to grant to us perseverance in that which is good. Let us trust His unbounded goodness that He will liberate His word and give us help against Antichrist, against whom by the help of your prayers, please Christ, I will wage war with God's word for my weapon. Peace and love, advancement in all that is good, and hereafter eternal life in glory be unto you from our Lord Jesus Christ. Amen.[37]

DID YOU KNOW? *Defenestrations*

In this chapter, and certainly the previous one on the Crusades, we have found martyrs at times on the offensive, dying in service to their non-negotiables. Bohemians had another way of showing their defense for non-negotiables, like freedom of religion. That is through a "defenestration," or "[to throw one] out the window" (fenestration refers to a building's windows and doors). In May of 1618, Protestant leaders quickly tried and found guilty two imperial regents and tossed them and their secretary from the tower at Hradčany (Prague Castle). Their crime? Stopping the building of Protestant chapels, thus violating the *Letter of Majesty*'s guarantee of religious liberty. Though they survived the unwanted flight from the third-floor window, the Thirty Years War followed, in which around eight million people died.

CHAPTER NINE

The Persecution of Early European Reformers

Indeed, I count everything as loss because of the surpassing worth of knowing Christ Jesus my Lord. For his sake I have suffered the loss of all things and count them as rubbish, in order that I may gain Christ. **PHILIPPIANS 3:8**

As it is written: "For Your sake we face death all day long; we are considered as sheep to be slaughtered." No, in all these things we are more than conquerors through him who loved us. **ROMANS 8:36-37, NIV**

Lord have mercy on me. Pray, pray, good people, while there is still time. **WALTER MILL, BURNED AT THE STAKE IN ENGLAND IN 1558**

I am fully determined, with God's grace, to go to the bishop, and to his face tell him that what he does to me is insignificant. God will raise up teachers after me who will teach His people with more diligence and fruit than I have done. **ROWLAND TAYLOR, ENGLAND, QUEEN MARY'S THIRD VICTIM BURNED AT THE STAKE, 1555**

Access to the Scriptures seems the least of concerns for people in much of the West today and increasingly in the rest of the world. The introduction of the *YouVersion* Bible app in 2008 accented Bible access, already surpassing half a billion downloads—all free, offering 2,062 Bible versions in 1,372 languages. In light of this development, it seems unfathomable that for centuries thousands of people lost their lives for producing or obtaining copies of the Bible in their own language.

Many of the martyrs represented in this chapter died for their desire to study the Bible, and for questioning official Catholic interpretations (or laws—given Rome's military and political power). This chapter also includes a small representation included in John Foxe's original volumes—which were heavy on examples from the Marian persecution and the European Reformation, and were laden with anti-Catholic rhetoric. We believe the latter especially misses the host of Catholic saints who also died for their faith—in spite of the suspect and sometimes-dastardly actions of their leaders during this era of church history (not to mention counter measures by the Protestants, sometimes against other branches of Protestants).

We saw the differences over personal Bible study play out in the Hussite Crusades, especially over the basic teaching of the Sacraments. This was directly influenced by John Wycliffe (d. 1384), along with a desire to have access to the Bible in one's own language.

In a sense, it was all a call to return to the primitive church. The Bible had gone from its earliest languages—almost entirely in Hebrew and Greek—to some of the vernacular languages for people groups in their regions. During the early centuries after Christ, these included languages like Coptic for Egyptians and Syriac for those in much of the Middle East and even into Asia. But in the West, and even in the lands the Catholic monarchs would conquer in the New World during colonization, the Bible was only to be read in Latin—the official language of the Roman Catholic Church. The brilliant St. Jerome (d. AD 420) had translated the Bible into common or "vulgar" Latin, and it became known as the Vulgate, the prominent Bible translation of the Catholic Church to the present.[1]

After the Geneva Bible gained mass appeal, the Catholic Church would produce its own English version between 1582 and 1610, the

Douay-Rheims Bible (named after two cities in France where the Old and New Testaments were published). But this was long after many thousands of Christians had lost their lives for having copies of Scriptures in their own languages, accented by the works of Wycliffe, Tyndale, and Huss. Martin Luther, though not among those dying for translating into the German language, was in this lineage of translators.

At the end of the thirteenth century most Europeans could not read, or if so, barely. Within a century, much would change as written records and access became more important. The hope for access to these sources grew—especially in personal religion. Tyndale's printed Bible in English transformed religious life in the English isles, and Luther's translation into common German transformed a country. The King James Bible (1611, sometime erroneously called the Authorized Version) put a capstone on this era.

Before we discuss in more detail a representation of martyrs from this era, we should consider the reasons for the Roman Catholics' concerns. As stated in the last chapter, these were no excuses for the religious agents' grotesque treatment of people. Here we provide only a context to help explain this horrific chapter in church history. Foxe candidly and often called the pope the Antichrist, and declared that all his agents were of the devil. Though he had plenty of stated reasons for his candor, there were legitimate concerns prompting some of these otherwise evil deeds.

Chief among Rome's concerns was the protection of orthodoxy. One of the biggest fears throughout the Middle Ages and into the Enlightenment was fear of the uneducated masses. We have shelves of books today about cults and abuses carried out in the name of the Bible.[2] Also, Rome held to the firm belief in the authority of the papacy through the heritage of Peter (both biblically and historically). While these reasons seem valid, the next one seems the toughest to swallow today, especially given the fact that the fastest growing segments of Christendom globally endorse the very views martyrs died for. It was Rome's belief that torture and punishment might keep the "heretic" from eternal damnation, as well as the countless others he or she might influence. In a bizarre rationalization, it was a very real sense of duty in their minds to protect souls from hell.

Against this relentless and powerful persecution were seemingly endless voices for religious freedom and their bold commitment to Christ—reformers. The physical silencing of some of these reforming voices has fueled their legendary status as the movement reaches to the present. "The Reformers did not see themselves as inventors, discoverers, or creators. Instead they saw their efforts as rediscovery. They weren't making something from scratch but were reviving what had become dead."[3]

As history has played out, these martyrdoms indeed helped to revive some of the basics of the faith and preserve a biblical orthodoxy. Truly, the explosive evangelical growth in Asia and sub-Saharan Africa, and charismatic churches globally can be traced to these reformers. Their lives were not in vain, but the vein that tracks to the lifeblood of the gospel's spread today.[4]

Vintage Foxe

Previous to the persecution, the missionaries employed kidnappers to steal away the Protestants' children, that they might privately be brought up Roman Catholics; but now they took away the children by open force, and if they met with any resistance, they murdered the parents.[5]

JOHN WYCLIFFE AND THE LOLLARDS Although John Wycliffe had faced stiff opposition in his lifetime, he died of natural causes before his opponents could put him to flames. Many of his immediate followers were not so lucky. His ideas and their tangible expression in translation inspired them. His contemporaries labelled them "Lollards" after their constant praying (from *lollen*, meaning "to mutter"), which became a euphemism for "heretics."

Although there were many leading voices in the pre-Reformation theater, Wycliffe's was certainly center stage. He not only published the Bible in English (in manuscript form as printing would not become prevalent for some seventy years), but openly called the pontiff the Antichrist. Wycliffe's life has prompted thousands of books that often trace the line of influence between his work and that of reformers like Huss and Luther, and later John Wesley and others.

A significant aspect of the English Reformation was the progress that took place in the field of Bible translation. In 1382, John Wycliffe, desiring common people to have access to God's Word, translated the Bible from Latin into English. Authorities burned every copy of his Bible they could seize and banned the rest.[6]

Though there were various book burnings, they were not all seized. From the Museum of the Bible in Washington, DC, to the British Library, around 250 Wycliffe manuscripts survived. (In 2016, the late Dr. Charles Ryrie's Wycliffe Bible sold at Sotheby's for $1.4 million.) Wycliffe used Jerome himself to defend his English translation:

> For this reason Saint Jerome labored and translated the Bible from divers tongues into Latin that it might after be translated into other tongues. Thus Christ and his apostles taught the people in that tongue that was best known to them. Why should men not do so now?[7]

Wycliffe's influence stretched far beyond a vernacular Bible. He also challenged the alleged rights of priests to "withhold the cup" from the laity. Imagine Christians in the Middle Ages finally able to read the following New Testament passage, then being put to death for disagreeing with their local priest for only giving them the wafer (bread): "In the same way also he took the cup, after supper, saying, 'This cup is the new covenant in my blood. Do this, as often as you drink it, in remembrance of me'" (1 Corinthians 11:25).

Wycliffe differed with various Catholic interpretations. Withholding of the cup during Communion was one issue, and its actual meaning another. Wycliffe wrote: "The consecrated Host we priests make and bless is not the body of the Lord [as the Catholic Church claimed] but an effectual sign of it. It is not to be understood that the body of Christ comes down from heaven to the Host consecrated in every church."[8] Of course, the Church condemned his views as heresy, and many would either lose their lives or suffer lifelong persecution for such views.

Decades after Wycliffe's death, at the same Council of Constance (1414–1418) that deemed John Huss a heretic and called for his execution, the Catholic authorities also declared John Wycliffe a heretic. With precedent, they also ordered a bishop to dig up his bones, burn them, and then throw the ashes into the River Swift. Little did the Church realize that this would only enhance Wycliffe's legend and impact. William Wordsworth captures this in his sonnet "Wicliffe":

As thou these ashes, little Brook! wilt bear
Into the Avon, Avon to the tide
Of Severn, Severn to the narrow seas,
Into main Ocean they, this Deed accurst
An emblem yields to friends and enemies
How the bold Teacher's Doctrine, sanctified
By Truth, shall spread throughout the world dispersed.[9]

Then, we're told, "They burnt his bones to ashes and cast them into the Swift, a neighboring brook running hard by. Thus the brook conveyed his ashes into the Avon, the Avon into the Severn, the Severn into the narrow seas and they into the main ocean. And so, the ashes of Wyclif are symbolic of his doctrine, which is now spread throughout the world."[10]

William Sawtrey—The First Lollard Martyr

Sometimes martyrs died as "relapsed heretics," meaning the first time they were found guilty they recanted. But in the business of burning heretics, one strike was usually the warning death knell, two strikes meant death (many cases show a chance for "heretics" to recant and their lives spared— but the second time mercy and recanting was not an option).[11]

William Sawtrey was a parish priest in London at St. Scithe the Virgin Church. He had a disdain for the worshipping of idols, even if they were Christian symbols. This put him at odds with the wave of priests who bowed before crucifixes, and would result in various heretical charges against him. However, it was his rejection of Rome's view of the Eucharist that was the final straw. He didn't believe the elements were actually the body and blood of Christ (transubstantiation). He also rejected pilgrimages and the adoration of angels.

The edict to punish Sawtrey came from Henry IV. The authorities subjected him to degradation, and then burned him at the stake in Smithfield on February 26, 1401.

Voices from the Past

William Sawtrey, the first Lollard martyr (February 26, 1401), said, "Instead of adoring the cross on which Christ suffered, I adore Christ who suffered on it." He was burned in Smithfield, England.[12]

DID YOU KNOW? *Degradation*

When the church courts condemned priests like William Sawtrey as heretics, they usually went through degradation, a multistep process that officially removed their ordination. Being sentenced to prison, public shaming, and/or the stake sometimes wasn't enough. Sadly, some "heretics" also endured grotesque torture in the process. The bishop often subjected the accused heretic to a demeaning ceremony that "entirely and perpetually deprived of all office, benefice, dignity, and power conferred on him by ordination; and by a special ceremony is reduced to the state of a layman, losing the privileges of the clerical state and being given over to the secular arm." The very visible side of this was a colorful finale of the (alleged and condemned) heretic's official service. It was comprised of the bishop with the required six abbots, a lay judge, and an audience in ecclesiastical attire. The bishop would then remove from the priest, in order, each article of the sacred vestments.[13]

John Badby

Throughout England are reminders of the sacrifice of the saints—including Smithfield, the tournament grounds outside the old city walls in central London. It was here in 1409 that a bold Christian gave his life even though the Prince of Wales (future King Henry V) personally begged him to recant, and even stopped the fire thinking he heard him waver.

> The name of John Badby, a low and illiterate workman, well deserves to be recorded for the honour of divine truth. Arundel took serious pains to persuade him, that the consecrated bread was really and properly the body of Christ. "After the consecration, it remaineth," said Badby, "the same material bread, which it was before; nevertheless it is a sign, or sacrament of the living God. I believe the omnipotent God in trinity to be One. But if every consecrated host be the Lord's body, then there are twenty thousand gods in England." After he had been delivered to the secular power by the bishops, he was, by the king's writ, condemned to be burned. The prince of Wales, happening to be present, very earnestly exhorted him to recant, adding the most terrible menaces, of the vengeance, which would overtake him, if he should continue in his obstinacy. Badby, however, was inflexible. As soon as he felt the fire, he cried, Mercy! The prince, supposing that he was intreating the mercy of his judges, ordered the fire to be quenched. "Will you forsake heresy," said young Henry; "and will you conform to the faith of the holy church? If you will, you shall have a yearly stipend out of the king's treasury." The martyr was unmoved; and Henry, in a rage, declared, that he might now look for no favour. Badby gloriously finished his course in the flames.[14]

A version of the following Foxe account (1844) follows several pages of the official charges, and Badby's responses. This nineteenth-century account records his final words with more passion and detail.

> But this valid champion of Christ, neglecting in the prince's fair words, as also contemning [scorning] all men's devices, being fully determined rather to suffer any kind of torment, were it never so grievous, than so great idolatry and wickedness, refused the

offer of worldly promises, being no doubt more vehemently and inflamed with the Spirit of God, than with any earthly desire. Wherefore, when as yet he continued unmovable in his former mind, the prince commanded him straight to be put again into the pipe or tun [large cask or barrel, likely for wine], and that he should not afterwards look for any grace or favor. But as he could be allured by no rewards, even so was he nothing at all abashed at their torments, but as a valiant champion of Christ, he persevered invincibly to the end, not without a great and most cruel battle, but with much greater triumph of victory; the spirit of Christ having always the upper hand in his members, maugre [in spite of] the fury, rage, and power of the whole world.[15]

Following this event, the king passed a statute called "Ex Officio," which made it illegal for anyone to preach, teach, write, or do anything in the realm of religion without a license through their diocese.[16]

Vintage Foxe

A pious woman was burnt at Chippen Sudburne [ca. 1510], by order of the chancellor, Dr. Whittenham. After she had been consumed in the flames, and the people were returning home, a bull broke loose from a butcher and singling out the chancellor from all the rest of the company, he gored him through the body, and on his horns carried his entrails. This was seen by all the people, and it is remarkable that the animal did not meddle with any other person whatever.[17]

John Purvey and Nicholas of Hereford

John Purvey was Wycliffe's accomplice in translations and likely responsible for the Lollard Bible. He was languishing in prison, but recanted three days after Sawtrey's martyr's pyre. However, he returned to itinerant preaching of Lollard views. Like his mentor, he apparently died of natural causes instead of burning.[18] He couldn't shake his translation colleague's driving point that the Bible was "entirely true."

The Bible, he [Wycliffe] was convinced, had been conceived in God's mind before creation. It was therefore entirely true, and the exclusive criterion of faith and practice, far superior to church tradition [though he believed the church was also predestined by God, but had gone astray and become a "synagogue of Satan"]. Everyone ought to have access to its truth in his own language: "No man is so rude a scholar but that he may learn the words of the gospel according to his simplicity."[19]

Nicholas of Hereford had also assisted Wycliffe, and was among his brightest colleagues. His name is attached to the city and cathedral where he preached. He became excommunicated for his Lollard sermons, but would return after horrendous torture, years of imprisonment, and recanting. Ironically, he was made chancellor of Hereford, but in 1417 abandoned all of his posts and retired in a monastery (a move that indicates Wycliffe's views never truly left him).

Catherine Saube

The Roman Catholic officials lodged heresy charges against Catherine Saube only nine months after 1,500 townspeople marched with her to the nunnery. This had been in celebration of their local young girl requesting to be "shut up" in a cell. On October 2, 1417, according to the town records of Thou in Lorraine, France, she was burned at the stake. And in a rather brief and macabre passing comment in the records, we learn that all the nuns in the monastery on Lates Road where Saube had lived and proselytized were also burned. Allegedly, this occurred because she had "infected" them. The record from *Martyrs Mirror*:

> "That it is better to die, than to anger, or sin against God." Again, "That she [Catherine Saube] did not worship the host or wafer consecrated by the priest; because she did not believe that the body of Christ was present in it." Again, "That it is not necessary to confess one's self to the priest; because it is sufficient to confess

one's sins to God; and that it counts just as much to confess one's sins to a discreet, pious layman, as to any chaplain or priest." Again, "That there will be no purgatory after this life."[20]

The town records say:

Having pronounced this sentence upon her, the vicar of the inquisitor, M. Raymond, delivered her into the hands of the bailiff, who was provost or criminal judge of the city. The people entreated him much in her behalf, that he would deal mercifully with her; but he executed the sentence the same day, causing her to be brought to the place of execution, and there burnt as a heretic, according to law.[21]

Sir John Oldcastle

Sir John Oldcastle (Lord Cobham) also had Wycliffe leanings. He was publicly humiliated, strapped to a hurdle at the Tower and then taken to St. Giles's field. He had also unsuccessfully plotted to kidnap his friend, Henry V.

Upon discovery, they tried him both as a traitor (punished by hanging) and a heretic (by burning).

Upon the day appointed, Lord Cobham was brought out of the Tower with his arms bound behind him, having a very cheerful countenance. Then was he laid upon a hurdle, as though he had been a most heinous traitor to the crown, and so drawn forth into St. Giles's field. As he was come to the place of execution, and was taken from the hurdle, he fell down devoutly upon his knees, desiring Almighty God to forgive his enemies. Then stood he up and beheld the multitude, exhorting them in most godly manner to follow the laws of God written in the Scriptures, and to beware of such teachers as they see contrary to Christ in their conversation and living. Then was he hanged up by the middle in chains of iron, and so consumed alive in the fire, praising the name of God, so long as his life lasted; the people, there present, showing great dolor [sorrow]. . . .

How the priests that time fared, blasphemed, and accursed, requiring the people not to pray for him, but to judge him damned in hell, for that he departed not in the obedience of their pope, it were too long to write.

Thus resteth this valiant Christian knight, Sir John Oldcastle, under the altar of God, which is Jesus Christ, among that godly company, who, in the kingdom of patience, suffered great tribulation with the death of their bodies, for His faithful word and testimony.[22]

Oldcastle gives the following defense:

As for images, I understand that they be not of belief, but that they were ordained since the belief of Christ was given by sufferance of the Church, to represent and bring to mind the passion of our Lord Jesus Christ, and martyrdom and good living of other saints: and that whoso it be, that doth the worship to dead images that is due to God, or putteth such hope or trust in help of them, as he should do to God, or hath affection in one more than in another, he doth in that, the greatest sin of idol worship.

Also I suppose this fully, that every man in this earth is a pilgrim toward bliss, or toward pain; and that he that knoweth not, we will not know, we keep the holy commandments of God in his living here (albeit that he go on pilgrimages to all the world, and he die so), he shall be damned: he that knoweth the holy commandments of God, and keepeth them to his end, he shall be saved, though he never in his life go on pilgrimage, as men now use, to Canterbury, or to Rome, or to any other place.[23]

CULTURAL CONNECTION

Shakespeare and Sir John Oldcastle

A 1619 play intentionally misdated to 1600 carries William Shakespeare's name in the byline, though he didn't write it, or at least not directly. One thing that seems to be true of *The First Part of Sir John Oldcastle* is that the popular Shakespearean character John Falstaff is based on Sir John Oldcastle, the pre-Reformation martyr. Shakespeare changed his name to the fictitious Sir John Falstaff due to the political sensitivities. Falstaff is prominent in *Henry IV* (parts 1 and 2) and *Henry V*. A debate continues into modern scholarship on authorship. One key theory is that the play's authors "imagine Shakespeare's words not as what he penned but as what he *uttered*, as words spoken aloud at the moment of conception and also, in the prevalent seventeenth-century meaning of 'uttered,' as things offered for sale upon the market (*OED*)."[24] Shakespeare died in 1616.

CULTURAL CONNECTION

The Birth of Venus from a Martyr's Mentee

One of the most prominent paintings from the golden age of the Italian Renaissance is "The Birth of Venus." Or to be more precise, it should be called "Venus Landing on Shore after Being Born in the Sea." Sandro Botticelli painted it around 1480 in Florence, likely for the Medici family. The connection to our story is profound—his mentor was none other than Girolamo Savonarola, who led the bonfire of vanities before being martyred in the same plaza. Many of the very "vices" and moral failings that this radical friar preached against during his time in Florence (1490–1498) are found in this Botticelli classic. Mythological overtones, nudity, opulence, and ties to the very family he had criticized for leading the charge, the Medicis. Giorgio Vasari (d. 1574), the Italian artist who wrote about the lives of the artists and coined "Renaissance" in print, gives the following description of their relationship. Though he likely overstates the case (as many of Botticelli's paintings appear to date after Savonarola's martyrdom), it reflects the serious link to his religious mentor. It's amazing that *The Birth of Venus* has survived. "Botticelli was a follower of Savonarola's, and this was why he gave up painting and then fell into considerable distress as he had no other source of income. None the less, he remained an obstinate member of the sect, becoming one of the piagnoni, the snivellers, as they were called then, and abandoning his work; so finally, as an old man, he found himself so poor that if Lorenzo de' Medici . . . and then his friends and . . . [others] had not come to his assistance, he would have almost died of hunger."[25]

DID YOU KNOW? *Bonfire of Vanities*

Girolamo Savonarola figured out a way to deal with temptations—burn them. And that he did. Fueled by his apocalyptic sermons, and his vow of poverty and chastity as a Dominican friar, on February 7, 1497, thousands of items were burned in Florence's Piazza della Signoria, the same place where he was burned on a cross a year later. He began having regular "bonfires of vanities" in February of 1495 not long after his followers burned the Medici bank. They put to flame anything that represented opulence, greed, and other vices he dubbed luxuries from Renaissance culture. Months before the main 1497 bonfire, his followers, also called "Weepers," began collecting items their Florence friar considered social and artistic excesses. These were items like rare books and manuscripts, paintings, sculptures, carpets, musical instruments, cosmetics, mirrors, and a litany of shiny things. "Savonarola's followers adorned themselves with white gowns, garlands and red crosses and went door-to-door collecting objects for burning. An enormous pyre [sixty feet high] was erected in the Piazza del Signoria and it was surmounted by an image of Satan. Representatives of the different Florentine districts symbolically lit the pyre, obliterating the objects of vanity."[26]

GIROLAMO [JEROME] SAVONAROLA The Dominican friar and anti-Renaissance preacher, Girolamo Savonarola, championed opposition to several vices among both laity and clergy, and was eventually executed in 1498 at the same spot where he had held the bonfire of vanities. His life is a testimony to not only ardent beliefs and motivating masses through preaching, but also to having a profound influence on a city in a short time—his tenure in Florence was only from 1490 until his gruesome martyrdom.

The irony of his life is that his earlier patron and principal supporter, Lorenzo de Medici, was not only the former ruler of Florence but also a chief patron of the arts. Savonarola even attended his deathbed at his patron's request, but later attacked Lorenzo and the Medici family for their opulence and detachment from social ills.

He preached to overflow crowds at the Church of San Marco (in Florence), where he also relentlessly criticized Pope Alexander VI, the most infamous of the Renaissance popes. When Charles VIII of France successfully invaded Italy, he spared Florence at Savonarola's request. The popular preacher became the city's ruler in 1494.

His sermons targeted various sins, ranging from sodomy and papal abuses to more trivial matters. A key moral lapse Savonarola targeted was vanity, which convicted his follower Sandro Botticelli of the early use of his gifts. Botticelli, famous from his Sistine Chapel frescos and other commissioned work, allegedly helped burn thousands of manuscripts and items that drew attention to man rather than God—things such as cosmetics, mirrors, secular novels, paintings, false hair, fine clothing, and even chess pieces!

Aided by the Franciscans who disliked the Dominican leader, the city turned on Botticelli's religious mentor after Pope Alexander excommunicated him and threatened to put the city under interdict. This banned Florentines from mass, and in essence (according to Catholic doctrine), from salvation.

After considerable torture, the executioners cut off Savonarola's left arm but saved his right to sign a forced confession of heresy—then hanged him and two of his Dominican adherents (Sylvester and Dominic) in chains on a single cross over a bonfire. Like the aftermath of the Huss pyre and Wycliffe's remains, their ashes were gathered and tossed in the river of Arum.

Some consider Savonarola a precursor to Martin Luther. Similarities include passionate messages calling for personal and papal reform; a desire to reform—not secede from—the Roman Catholic Church; and messages that left audiences with clear choices.[27]

**EUROPEAN MARTYRDOMS IN THE CONTEXT OF PROT-
ESTANT REFORM** As we look more closely at Europe, we need to set
the martyrdoms against the backdrop of religious conflicts of the sixteenth
century. This period of reform was much broader than the church, though
the churchmen and the ecclesiastical issues were central to the movement.
These key developments include (1) the decline of the church, (2) the
spread of lay religion outside the official clergy, (3) the growth of northern
humanism, (4) the rise of monarchs who wished to control the church and
everything else within their kingdoms, and (5) the rise of the Hapsburg
Empire and Europe's fear of expansion.

The laboring poor grew disenchanted with ideas and practices that
had created an untenable social order. The local Catholic priest no
longer sufficed as their spokesperson due to the endemic dissatisfaction
with the church's wealthy and oppressive ruling class. From the laboring
poor emerged various religious sects. These are known historically as the
Anabaptists (precursor of the modern Baptists and various evangelical
groups), the Moravians, and the Mennonites.

The term "middle class" is used anachronistically here, but it helps us
frame a discussion of the masses whose place in society was above the poor
but below the wealthy. The imperial free cities were havens for this progressive group, and the middle class became a formidable force, especially in
Germany, Switzerland, and the Netherlands. Their ability to manage their
own business affairs influenced their desire to do the same in their religious
affairs. After all, the grand hierarchy of the Catholic Church was attached
to the monarchial system and was rather detached from their daily needs.

The papacy and landed families disputed a wide range of benefits,
policies, and positions throughout the Middle Ages. Monarchs and their
families—the royalty—especially ruling princes, were cognizant of the
Church's threat to their wealth and power, and increasingly considered
their countries or states as infringements. Eventually these rulers won the
decision to determine the religion in their realms, and the prominent win-
ners were Anglicans, Lutherans, and Calvinists.

Paramount among the reformers' concerns were, in their candid assessment, the moral, ethical, and religious failings of the Roman Catholic

Church. They began to concentrate their attacks on three particular disorders of the church. (1) Clerical immorality, including a long list of charges from sexual transgressions to gambling, drunkenness, and worldly dress (opulence). (2) Clerical ignorance, especially the lack of Latin—a major issue for liturgical services and study of the Vulgate. The softening of ordination requirements due to lack of candidates had ripple effects on many levels. Some accounts note priests mumbling to sound as if they knew Latin. (3) Clerical pluralism with related problems of absenteeism. Many clerics, especially higher ecclesiastics, held several offices simultaneously—each coming with a stipend. This created obvious logistical problems, as some ecclesiastics would seldom visit some of their offices (or positions in a geographic region).

Looming over all of these factors was the misuse of the papal office by some of the popes—a topic that runs through many of the reformers' letters and works, including Foxe's *Actes and Monuments*. The papacy's political maneuvers, economic pressures, and various social issues were a few of the factors that led to sharp divisions in Christian societies. Voices within the church called for reform, and not just those martyred and cast as outsiders. The Conciliarists called for the reform of the church "in head and members," a sentiment that aptly reflected public opinion. But even this group differed from one calling for the "constitutional" rather than "absolute" rule of a pope. Others rejected the whole hierarchical structure of the papal monarchy.[28]

Erasmus (himself living proof of clerical missteps—an illegitimate son of a priest and a servant girl) published *In Praise of Folly*, a work replete with biting commentary on clerical immorality and ignorance. The same candid condemnations are found in Martin Luther's Ninety-Five Theses and throughout many of his letters. It is important not to overlook such strong Catholic voices as that of Erasmus in this reforming effort. His printed Greek New Testament (1516) revolutionized Bible study for reformers, including Luther.[29] In another of his works, *Colloquies*, he championed the basic teachings of the gospel while challenging ecclesiastical Christianity. And in *Handbook of a Christian Knight* he espoused a thesis that resurfaced in the modern era in Bob Briner's *Roaring Lambs*. That is, that Christians can become effective agents of change in worldly affairs while retaining their beliefs. Both of these reformers were writing from within the church, with no desire to split its members. Erasmian virtues expounded in *Handbook* include a reasoned zeal for reform, gentleness, reasonableness, scholarship, tolerance, restraint, and a love of peace.

+ Historic Sources

MACHIAVELLI'S REFLECTIONS ON THE CHURCH
Niccolò di Bernardo dei Machiavelli was a diplomat and writer from Florence, and best known for his magnum opus, *The Prince*, written about 1513. It was a sort of handbook for tyrants to keep their power. Erasmus criticized it, and the Catholic Church banned it, placing it on the *Index Librorum Prohibitorum*. His last name has become synonymous with power politics or "the end justifies the means." His reflections below show another dynamic the reformers faced.

HUMBLE CHRISTIANS: THE WEAKNESS OF MODERN RELIGION
Pondering, then, why it can be that in those ancient times people were greater lovers of freedom than these, I conclude it came from the same cause that makes men now less hearty. That I believe is the difference between our religion and the ancient. Ours, because it shows us the truth, and the true way makes us esteem less the honor of the world; whereas the pagans, greatly esteeming such honor and believing it their greatest good, were fiercer in their actions. . . . Ancient religion . . . attributed blessedness only to men abounding in worldly glory, such as generals of armies and princes of state. Our religion has glorified humble and contemplative men rather than active ones. It has, then, set up as the greatest good humility, abjectness and contempt for human things; the other put it in grandeur of mind, in strength of body, and in all the other things apt to make men exceedingly vigorous.[30]

MARTIN LUTHER, ULRICH ZWINGLI, AND JOHN CALVIN
The Protestant Reformation realized a wave of martyrs, inspired by three key voices: Martin Luther (d. 1546), Ulrich Zwingli (martyred 1531), and John Calvin (d. 1564). And these men stood on the shoulders of many others like Wycliffe and Huss. While Zwingli was the only one of the three

key voices to die a martyr's death, they all are inextricably linked to the movement that would realize throngs of saints. Many under the influence of their teachings would die for dissenting from established Catholic rule (wielding religious and political power). Others died at the hands of some of these very dissenters (often in State Religion offices of Protestant territories, under "magisterial rule").

These leaders punished views they deemed heretical, such as Anabaptism. The latter (a "re-baptizing" as adults) might sound petty today. However, it concerned the heartfelt belief in "believers' baptism" and not "infant baptism." So Christians who fervently believed baptism was necessary for salvation had a massive issue with upstart Christian sects that denied the rite to children. A large portion of today's Protestants are Anabaptists in their theology.

With these huge movements in mind, and countless offshoots, we turn first to Martin Luther's role in the Protestant Reformation.

Luther came from a middle-class family in Eisleben, Germany, and his upbringing included tutelage by the Brethren of the Common Life. His journey led him through enrollment into the Order of the Hermits of St. Augustine, a doctorate in theology, and then a teaching position in Wittenberg. His struggle to understand the fullness of salvation would be central in launching the Protestant Reformation.

To help "the unlearned" understand true Christian liberty "and the bondage of the spirit," he set down the following two propositions: "A Christian man is a perfectly free lord of all, subject to none. A Christian man is a perfectly dutiful servant of all, subject to all." And that Christ "was at the same time free and a servant."[31]

While lecturing at the University of Wittenberg, he began to find inconsistencies between biblical passages and official church doctrine. It was in Romans 1 that he became liberated with the assurance of "justification by faith alone." This biblical injunction became the theological basis for the Protestant Reformation. He also began to uncover a litany of inconsistencies between biblical virtues and the actions of many church officials, along with the proper distinction between law and gospel. And when the unprincipled Dominican friar Johann Tetzel began selling indulgences to the poor, it would lead to Luther posting his Ninety-Five Theses to the church door in Wittenberg. What was intended for local discussion about his issues with shortcomings of the Roman Church created an international furor.

Luther would have to defend his views at the Diet of Worms in 1521. He was already under papal condemnation via *Pope Leo X against Martin Luther, papal bull, 1520* (referring to him as "a wild boar"). Luther responded with *Martin Luther against the Roman Catholic Church, 1521*. The next year he would produce his German translation of the New Testament, and the full Bible by 1534—that helped unify the German language and people.

The massive resistance against the Roman Church soon grew far beyond any one person, and those "protesting" (the Protestants) multiplied. It wasn't long before this resistance realized divisions and regional Protestant leaders surfaced.

Ulrich Zwingli, the cathedral priest in Zurich, Switzerland, endorsed most of Luther's views. They began to reject some of the church rituals, such as prohibitions against eating meat and certain other foods during Lent. Eventually, with support from the council of Zurich, Zwingli led a reformation of his own, and by 1525 the collection of the tithes had been abolished and clerical celibacy denounced.

Later on, Zwingli also repudiated worship of the saints, transubstantiation, the existence of purgatory, and the authority of the Pope. From Zwingli's idea emerged another Protestant group called the Anabaptists, noted earlier. Protestant preachers emerging from Zwingli's reform movement began arriving in the free city of Geneva, where John Calvin was to play such a vital role. In 1541, Calvin established a theocracy there (in simplest terms, a form of governance in which God rules through his designee, such as the priests or those specially anointed—like Calvin).

Calvin did not grant any power or free will to human beings because he argued that would detract from the sovereignty of God (the cornerstone for "predestination" and other tenets of Reformed theology).

While Luther subordinated the church to the state, Calvin made the state subordinate to the church. He succeeded in arousing Genevans to a high standard of public and private behavior. We are reminded of Savonarola's purging of "vanities" in Calvin's disdain for secular living. It was manifest in his civic policies. He stated, "Everything is in shameful confusion; everywhere I see only cruelty, plots, frauds, violence, shamelessness while the poor groan under the oppression and the innocent are arrogantly and outrageously harassed." Austere living, religious instruction for all, public fasting, and evening curfew became the order of the day. Dancing, card playing, fashionable clothes, and heavy drinking were strictly prohibited.

By many accounts, Calvin's Geneva became the model of Christian community for the sixteenth-century Protestant reformers. Refugees from France, England, Spain, Scotland, and Italy poured into the city. Subsequently, Calvin's church served as the model for the Presbyterian Church in Scotland, the Huguenot church of France, and the Puritan churches in England and New England. All of them would face oppression and claim their litany of martyrs.

Most of the long list of martyrs can be traced to these major challenges to the Catholic Church, and then the major divisions among the Protestants as well, especially involving the Anabaptists. Of these key leaders, Tyndale was martyred and Zwingli would die fighting the Catholics.

THE FIRST ANABAPTIST MARTYRS The term "Anabaptist" is likely unfamiliar to most readers today as a denominational or religious identifier, but they would likely know "Baptist" or "Mennonite" and "Amish." In short, those groups that baptize people after the age of accountability, not babies. These "radical" reformers were called Anabaptists because they "rebaptized" adults who had been baptized as children, according to Catholic and Protestant teaching. The Protestants became their main persecutors (one might contend that the majority of Protestants were persecuting fringe Protestants).

Although these views on baptism can be found in the early church, the movement itself started in the Reformation by three Swiss-born reformers. George Blaurock, Felix Manz, and Conrad Grebel met in Zurich in 1525 to address what they considered a waning of faith (and compromise) by followers of Luther and Zwingli. And they advocated for a more active faith—including baptism as adults. They lost a debate in Zurich with none other than Zwingli. The city council (basically the Zurich church) forbade them to teach, preach, or gather. During the fateful years of 1526–1529, Grebel (only twenty-eight years old), Manz, and Blaurock would pay the ultimate sacrifice for their ardent faith.

Almost immediately after the debate in Zurich they met, mutually baptized each other and others, and had thus committed a crime against the state. The nonconformist tradition among Protestantism was born.[32] The whirlwind of activity that occurred in Zurich after Zwingli's arrival is dizzying, complicated for Zwingli by this group of "Reformation storm troopers."[33] All three would die soon after, two martyred and the first, Grebel, worn out before reaching thirty years of age.

Conrad Grebel was born in the Zurich canton (likely Grüningen, ca. 1498), and died first. After being imprisoned twice and escaping the second time with the help of friends, he died a few months later from the plague at his sister's home in Maienfeld. He wrote his key text, a defense of Anabaptism, during his five-month prison time in Grüningen shortly before he passed. Around two months after his death, the leadership of Zurich executed his father, Jakob, ostensibly on ethics charges. He was a city magistrate and still in the Reformed tradition—but had recently challenged Zwingli on the harsh treatment of the Anabaptists (likely a factor in his sudden fall).

Perhaps it is an irony that Grebel's children were raised in the Reformed tradition after his death and assumed key posts in Zurich, and today some of their descendants are still in key civic positions.[34]

Felix Manz was arrested on various occasions, then finally sentenced to death by drowning—a common punishment for these "rebaptizers." They rowed him out onto Lake Lammat and sent him to his icy grave (January 4, 1527) as he walked the plank bound and weighted—encouraged by his mother and brothers to remain strong. Engraved in his cell were the words, "I praise Thee, O Lord Christ in heaven, that Thou dost turn away my sorrow and sadness . . . already before my end has come, that I should have eternal joy in Him."

George Blaurock was hounded during this last days, beaten but released the day of Manz's martyrdom. As he fled this foreign country of Switzerland, he was arrested in four cities, but released. He landed in Austria, where he replaced pastor Michael Kürschner, who had suffered martyrdom at the stake. In August 1529, the Innsbruck authorities arrested Blaurock and his assistant, Hans Langegger, and burned them at the stake on September 6, 1529, near Klausen in northern Italy. Two of Blaurock's hymns survive, preserved in *Ausbund*, the oldest Anabaptist hymnal still used by North American Amish congregations. A verse seems prophetic from his "Gott, dich will ich loben" ("God, I Want to Praise You"):

Forget me not, O Father,
Be near me evermore;
Thy Spirit shield and teach me,
That in afflictions great
Thy comfort I may ever prove,
And valiantly may obtain
The victory in this fight.

The litany of Anabaptist martyrs is unfortunately long and diverse. The movement began with three keen minds and passionate souls who were attracted to Zurich by Zwingli's teaching. They separated from the Catholic Church and eventually from Zwingli for not being conservative enough. In the end, both religious groups hunted them.

The Anabaptists were diverse and decentralized, extending from Holland to Hungary. With their many passionate personalities, the Anabaptists represented a variety of emphases. But uniting them was a shared vision that distinguished the radicals from the other reformers and gave Anabaptism lasting impact.

The Legendary Fate of the Anabaptist Martyrs

The listing of all the Anabaptist martyrs is not only beyond the scope of this volume, but also impossible because oftentimes the records give only general numbers of the saints, not their names. Often, the leaders' names are mentioned, followed by a number of "others." More macabre were the mass executions, like the "three hundred and fifty" in Alzey, Germany, slain at the emperor's command. After the Second Diet of Speiers in 1529, the death sentence for Anabaptists enhanced the carnage. In Swabia, the police force tasked with hunting and slaughtering Anabaptists was increased from four hundred to a thousand due to the demand.[35]

But in many cases, like that of perhaps the leading Anabaptist theologian, Dr. Balthasar Hubmaier, we have extended accounts. His prolific nature and forceful presence resulted in numerous confrontations, including at least one major recantation and a major public challenge to Zwingli himself who expected a full account of his apology. This led to dueling pulpits as Zwingli jumped up in the other pulpit and the two argued until the guards escorted Hubmaier away. He wrote his *Short Apology* in 1526, but as the only Anabaptist at the time with a theology doctorate, his main contribution was a systematic defense of their views. Ferdinand of Austria's forces captured him, and after enduring the rack and refusing to recant, Hubmaier was burned at the stake in Vienna on March 10, 1528, while his wife exhorted him to face the last test with courage. Three days later they threw his wife into the Danube River, weighted.

An eyewitness gives the following account of Hubmaier's last moments:

While his clothes were being removed: "From thee also, O Lord, were the clothes stripped. My clothes will I gladly leave here, only preserve my spirit and my soul, I beseech thee!" Then he added in Latin "O Lord, into thy hands I commit my spirit," and spoke no more in Latin.

As they rubbed sulfur and gunpowder into his beard, which he wore rather long, he said, "Oh salt me well, salt me well." And raising his head, he called out "O dear brothers, pray God that he will give me patience in this my suffering."[36]

Around a year earlier, in February 1527, the Prince of Bavaria reluctantly ordered George Wagner burned at the stake for his Anabaptist views. Though his wife and children were brought before him to attempt a change of mind, Wagner persisted and en route to his pyre in Munich exclaimed,

"Today I will confess my God to all the world!" As if God was making a statement, the henchman (executioner) died in his sleep that night.

Michael and Margaretha Sattler were both Anabaptist martyrs, and both had renounced their vows and followed Zwingli. Michael had been a Benedictine monk, and Margaretha a nun—but Zwingli's preaching drew them to Zurich and fueled their passion for a more primitive Christianity.[37] However, Michael's "rebaptism" views and growing disillusion with Zwingli's "compromises" caused his expulsion with other Anabaptists in 1525. In the end, he was tried as a relapsed heretic after he had played a key role forming the Schleitheim Confession (February 1527), the most comprehensive expression of Anabaptist beliefs. His group was captured on the journey home, with the actual confession ("Brotherly Union") documents in hand.

During Michael's trial in Rottenburg, his desire to debate with the judges brought both laughter and contempt. The court secretary retorted, "You rascal of a monk, should we dispute with you? The hangman shall and will dispute with you!" Within ninety minutes the judges passed sentence on the Sattlers, and nine other men and eight women.

> Michael Sattler shall be committed to the hangman, who shall
> take him to the square and there first cut out his tongue, then
> chain him to a wagon, tear his body twice with hot tongs there
> and five times more before the gate, then burn his body to powder
> as an arch-heretic. [Sattler prayed for those executing him a
> quarter mile outside of town. The following would have been
> severely distorted without his tongue. Sattler prayed,] "Almighty,
> eternal God, Thou art the way and the truth; because I have not
> been shown to be in error, I will with Thy help on this day testify
> to the truth and seal it with my blood."[38]

They tied a sack of gunpowder around his neck and then tossed him into the fire. He eventually raised his hands as the ropes burned through and as if in victory, prayed, "Father, I commend my spirit into Thy hands."

The persecutors then burned three more of his male colleagues. They drowned Margaretha eight days later in the adjacent Neckar River.[39]

The martyrdom of young Patrick Hamilton in the summer of 1527 was a miserable sight. As if burning at the stake for one's Anabaptist views wasn't enough, it took him six hours to die. The executioners made the pyre at St. Salvator's College in St. Andrews out of green wood that didn't burn very well. Accenting his sad state was the failure of the gunpowder bags strapped in his armpits to explode. They merely burned hotter, causing increased pain. Hamilton, related to Stuart King Charles V, was a new member of St. Andrew's University faculty, at nearby St. Leonard's College. He joined only in 1524, but had already distinguished himself in various ways, and was honored with delivering his own musical composition for mass. He was friends with Erasmus and Luther, an acquaintance of Melanchthon, and recently married. James Beacon, the archbishop of St. Andrews, lured him to St. Salvator's (the founding college in St. Andrews) for what Hamilton thought was going to be a fun debate or exchange. Rather, the archbishop and his judges quickly filed charges and burnt him immediately to prevent his influential friends from interceding. But the plan backfired, or rather, barely fired.

Hamilton wrote a series of essays which his supporters posthumously called "Patrick's Places," which helped introduce Lutheran and Anabaptist views to Scotland. His initials are monogrammed in the flagstones of the cobblestone street outside St. Salvator's Chapel. The students help perpetuate his legend with their superstitions about stepping on them. An additional sad note about his treatment at the hands of the Catholic prelates was their public double standards.

Perhaps the most visible example of these moral shortcomings is none other than David Beaton, among other things a persecutor of Protestants. He received various church titles, including cardinal (1538), archbishop of St. Andrews (1539), King James V's ambassador to France many times, and papal legate to Scotland (1544). However, he also had eight children with his mistress, Marion Ogilvy, and lived openly with her in Ethie Castle.

Hamilton's testimony was tied to the martyrdom of his admirer, Henry Forest. He was a Benedictine monk who began referencing Hamilton's life and teachings. Archbishop Beaton sent a spy (a friar) into the confessional, and used what was supposed to be private for proof of heresy. The outcry over Hamilton's death prompted Beaton to order Forest smothered in a dreary jail cell (1529).

But Cardinal Beaton's disdain for the reformers would cost him his own life. He had the popular preacher George Wishart strangled and burned on March 1, 1546. This event saw the well-educated Wishart escorted after his capture from the castle at Elphinstone to Edinburgh and finally to St. Andrews. Wishart had translated into English the *Helvetic Confession of Faith* and had strong Protestant support, especially from John Leslie of Parkhill. Along with two colleagues he attacked Cardinal Beaton on May 29, 1546, only three months after Wishart's martyrdom. They displayed his pulverized body from a window in St. Andrew's castle.

Various memorials commemorate Wishart, including the prominent Martyrs Memorial in St. Andrews (honoring Patrick Hamilton and other martyrs as well), the Wishart memorial, possibly St. Andrews' old city Cowgate (allegedly with the "Wishart Arch"), and various facilities. Like Hamilton and other martyrs, his initials also mark his site of execution. The blue plaque at the site reads:

George Wishart, 1513-1546.

A powerful protestant preacher, he was betrayed to Cardinal Beaton, brought here, put in the sea tower, condemned for heresy and burnt at the stake on 1 March. The lettering G W on the roadway marks where he died. His friends conspired against the cardinal, and on 26 May gained entry to the castle, killed him and hung his body from the battlements. Then together in the castle they created the first congregation of the Protestant church in Scotland.

ULRICH ZWINGLI (BATTLE OF KAPPEL, 1531) Zwingli was instrumental in forming the Reformed Defensive Alliance, which he envisioned as an attempt to unite all Protestant countries and cities against Rome. When the five Romish cantons learned of these plans they struck hard.

> Persecution was increased. . . . The Reformed people were fined, imprisoned, tortured, scourged and banished; their goods were confiscated; their pastors had their tongues cut out, or they were beheaded or burned. Bibles and evangelical books were taken away and cast into the flames. Refugees from Austria were given up to their mad pursuers. And still the gospel won more and more believers. The bishop of Constance wrote to the five cantons that if they did not act more vigorously, the whole country would embrace the Reform.[40]

They began their burnings with the parson James Keyser, "the Locksmith of Utznach." They wanted to make a statement, and sent smoke signals from the pyre in Schwytz. A condescending judge said, "Go and tell them at Zurich how he thanks us." This infuriated Zwingli and he assumed a role akin to a general. After preaching strong war messages, he mounted up and left Zurich amongst crowds who cheered, though reluctant to lose their preacher. Although they would agree on a truce, eventually Zwingli would ride off to battle knowing his forces had little chance.

> Near to a pear tree, in a meadow, Zwingli stood at the post of danger, the helmet on his head, the sword at his side, the battle-axe in his hand, and the sword of courage on his lips.[41]

He had been struck by rocks on four different occasions, but managed to rise each time. But on the last effort, he was mortally wounded.

> A lancer gave him a thrust and sent him reeling to the earth. "What evil is it?" he exclaimed. "They may kill the body, but they cannot kill the soul." These are said to have been his last words. Under the pear tree he was found lying, with hands clasped and eyes upturned to heaven, not yet dead. Some marauders came to

him when the battle ceased, saw that his breath was not entirely gone, and they asked, "Will you confess? Shall we fetch a priest?"

A shake of the head told them as eloquently as his tongue had last proclaimed in the cathedral, "No I shall not deny my Savior."

"If you cannot speak," they said, "at least think in thy heart of the mother of God and call upon the saints." He shook his head and still gazed heavenward. The soldiers began to curse him. "No doubt," said the ignorant of his name, "you are one of the heretics of the city."[42]

He met an inglorious death by battle standards. Pitiful. The mercenaries fighting for the Catholics didn't even realize they had maimed Zwingli until they were camping and pulled his face up to the fire.

A veteran captain, a papist and a pensioner, then came near, saying, "Zwingli! What, that vile heretic Zwingli, that rascal, that traitor!" The captain then struck the dying Christian Reformer on the throat with a sword, exclaiming, "Die, obstinate heretic!"[43]

Zwingli's death is unusual on a few accounts—a golden-tongued reformer, heralded by the masses, undertook a military role and became the unlikeliest of commanders. Also unique to his martyrdom is what transpired after his death. He was indeed a celebrity martyr. The following is the account from pastor Heinrich Bullinger who followed Zwingli at Grossmünster.

Later that day a crowd of wild young men collected, including pensioners and mercenaries, whom Zwingli had vigorously attacked and who were equally incensed against him. They considered dividing Zwingli's body into five parts, sending one portion to each of the Five States [the cantons of their alliance]. Others disagreed: who would want to carry round or send forward a heretic? He should be burnt. Some of the leaders, like Schultheiss Golder and Amman Doos, came forward, saying that a dead man should be left in peace. This was not the place for action of this sort. No one could tell how it was going to be settled—some talked about the need for luck, and so on. To this the noisy gang replied that they had discussed the matter fully and they wanted some action to be taken. So injustice triumphed, and when the leaders saw that there was nothing to be done they went off.

The crowd then spread it abroad throughout the camp that anyone who wanted to denounce Zwingli as a heretic and betrayer of a pious confederation, should come on to the battlefield. There, with great contempt, they set up a court of injustice on Zwingli which decided that his body should be quartered and the portions burnt. All this was carried into effect by the executioner from Lucerne with abundance of abuse; among other things he said that although some had asserted that Zwingli was a sick man he had in fact never seen a more healthy-looking body.

They threw into the fire the entrails of some pigs that had been slaughtered the previous night and then they turned over the embers so that the pigs offal [entrails or unused inside parts of animals] was mixed with Zwingli's ashes. This was done close to the high road to Scheuren.

Verdicts on Zwingli from scholars and ignorant alike were varied. All those who knew him were constant in their praises. Even so there were still more who were critical either because they really did not know him or, if they had known him a little, were determined to show their resentment and spoke ill of him.[44]

MIGUEL DE MOLINOS Hindsight is not always 20/20, as religious traditions might disagree how to label the death of the seventeenth-century Italian Catholic quietist Miguel de Molinos. He advocated for a vibrant personal (but quiet) faith, and many influential members of the Catholic Church sought his spiritual direction. Born to Spanish nobility, he chose a contemplative priestly life. His *Il Guida Spirituale* (1675) drew a considerable following, which seemed to be part of his undoing[45]—he coached the laity into deeper spirituality in ways contrary to some established church practices. But whatever his institutional history, it's clear that he attempted to challenge all Christians to "walk by faith" in complete submission to God's will.[46]

He was offered residence within the Vatican because of influence,[47] and had twice received favorable rulings from the pope and the Inquisitors, finding his writings "in agreement with the faith of the church and with Christian Morality."[48]

However, the Quietist movement he led wasn't quiet enough for some. What seems to be as much a power struggle as a doctrinal battle persisted, leading to another investigation in 1684 and then a heresy indictment. A papal bull of 1687 states, "We have condemned . . . Michel de Molinos as guilty, convicted, and confessed, and, although penitent, as a formal heretic, to the punishment of a narrow and perpetual prison, and to salutatory penances, to which he will be held to submit after having made a formal abjuration according to the form which will be prescribed to him."[49]

In life, in death, and in history he remains a martyr in the middle. He allegedly died in prison—which likely reflects his conflicted place within his own community (instead of being sentenced to the stake). As one biographer states, "He was, after all, a totally orthodox Catholic advocating that every person who sought a deeper walk with God also restrict himself to total obedience to his Spiritual director."[50]

CHAPTER TEN

Martyrs of Sixteenth-Century England

Why are you cast down, O my soul, and why are you in turmoil within me? Hope in God; for I shall again praise him, my salvation and my God. **PSALM 43:5**

You are my hiding place and my shield; I hope in your word. **PSALM 119:114**

It is impossible that anyone should write well of it [the Christian faith] or well understand what is correctly written of it, unless he has at some time tasted the courage faith gives a man when trials oppress him. But he who has had even a faint taste of it can never write, speak, meditate, or hear enough concerning it. **MARTIN LUTHER, ON CHRISTIAN LIBERTY**

Thou shalt be delivered from sins, and be freed from the acrimony and fury of theologians. . . . Thou shalt go to the light, see God, look upon his Son, learn those wonderful mysteries which thou hast not been able to understand in this life. **PHILIP MELANCHTHON, SPEAKING OF HIS WEARINESS AND IMMINENT DEATH**

Before Martin Luther's stand in Germany (1521) and William Tyndale's martyrdom in England (1536), the legacies of many earlier martyrs set the stage for the wider Protestant Reformation, and for Tyndale and Luther. These two Reformers helped to categorize specific movements in their own countries of Germany and England, and influenced religious history across the known world. We have been introduced to both of them, and here want to represent those martyrs concurrent with or in the shadow of their reforming notions.

Those saints martyred in the two centuries before Tyndale and Luther died during what historians call the "pre-Reformation." This groundswell for religious change played out differently in various countries—with England having its own complex story attached to monarchial changes and key personalities. Generally, the pre-Reformation runs from the fourteenth-century through Luther's posting of the Ninety-Five Theses in 1517, and encompasses events and people in line with the later Protestant leanings of the sixteenth century.[1]

We also chronicled the earlier work of John Wycliffe, and how his views influenced groups in many countries—which the Council of Constance (1414–1418) emphatically condemned. Many European reformers learned of his views while studying at Oxford and Cambridge. In turn, English scholars learned of Zwingli, Luther, and Calvin (Reformers who all thrived in the early to mid-sixteenth century) during European visits.

The first martyrdom recounted in this chapter represents well this inter-continental exchange, and for many the traceable link between the pre-Reformation and Reformation thinkers. John Frith (d. 1533) had studied under William Tyndale in Oxford, and then translated Patrick Hamilton's work while in Marburg, Germany—and suffered consequences in both places. Imprisonment in the former case and death in the latter. And Hamilton, as noted on the plaque at his martyrdom site in St. Andrews, had been to "the Continent [where] he had been greatly influenced by Martin Luther." And Luther by Huss, and so forth.

Besides this cross-pollination of reforming notions, the dynamics of martyrdoms in England were closely linked to the religious sentiments of its kings and queens. Lollard sentiments lingered, Tyndale's numerous pamphlets and brilliant English translation of the Bible were well known, and Luther's views were much discussed. However, the monarchial marital morass framed the most overt religious changes.

> The Reformation in its early stages was not anti-Catholic, but it resulted rather from the desire of Henry VIII for a male heir. Despite the break with Rome he remained, at least in his own opinion, a Catholic, but after 1534 there was no place for the pope in his version of the Christian faith.[2]

We can trace the religious implications of each of the subsequent English monarchs' beliefs—those of Edward VI, Mary I, Elizabeth I, and James I. One enduring tangible legacy of this era is the King James Bible (1611); produced halfway into James's reign (1603–1625), it followed horrendous stretches in which Christians from all occupations and persuasions died for their fervent beliefs. During the eras of Wycliffe and Tyndale, a major issue was access to the Bible in English. Other differences involved the presence versus symbolism of Christ in the Communion elements (bread and wine), and a litany of other theological differences with Catholic doctrine. But by 1611, the very words of William Tyndale rang through the translation funded and commissioned by King James. In many regions of the British Isles and Europe, the very beliefs for which martyrs died had become articles of faith within a century (if not a decade).

The martyrs of the English Reformation included some of England's best minds. The Martyrs' Memorial greets visitors as they approach downtown Oxford. The limestone tribute is prominently located next to Balliol College, one block from Cornmarket Street and the city center. It features statues of three English leaders: Hugh Latimer, Nicholas Ridley, and Thomas Cranmer. It is inconceivable today in most western countries to think of executing (let alone publicly torturing and burning) prominent intellectuals for almost any cause, especially religious views. Unfortunately, this is not true of all countries. Followers of Christ still face rampant persecution and martyrdoms (discussed at the end of this book).

The English Reformation effectively began with Henry VIII's claim in 1534 that he was the supreme head of the Church (the first Act of Supremacy), a designation long claimed by the pope. In essence, this was the beginning of the Anglican Church (Anglican meaning "of England"), with its doctrines articulated in the Ten Articles (1536) and the Thirty-Nine Articles (1563 and 1571—after various iterations). A viable ending point for the English Reformation is the Elizabethan Settlement in 1559.

While the origin of the Protestant (or European) Reformation in 1517 is commonly known, there are various contenders for its terminus. One viable option is the Peace of Westphalia (1648) which ended the Thirty Years War (and for the most part, European wars of religion).[3]

Therefore, we frame the English Reformation from 1534 to 1559, and the general Protestant Reformation from 1517 to 1648. A *New Yorker* article on the Reformation's five hundredth anniversary claims, "The Reformation wasn't led, exactly; it just spread, metastasized."[4] Moreover, it reminds us of the power of written arguments and expository biblical reflections. "Luther led the movement mostly by his writings. . . . Luther's collected writings come to a hundred and twenty volumes. In the first half of the sixteenth century, a third of all books published in German were written by him."[5]

The Protestant Reformation means many different things to various groups, and the Catholic Church had its Counter-Reformation. Throughout these events, many of the reformers were priests or monks, or else educated by them. Many martyrs during this time still professed a Catholic faith, as ardent in their Christian beliefs as Catholic defectors. Before we move into a closer look at the lives and deaths of martyrs during this period, the following summary paints well the context—complex, multifaceted, and an unavoidable reality.

> The Protestant Reformation was the 16th-century religious, political, intellectual and cultural upheaval that splintered Catholic Europe, setting in place the structures and beliefs that would define the continent in the modern era.
>
> In northern and central Europe, reformers like Martin Luther, John Calvin and Henry VIII challenged papal authority and

questioned the Catholic Church's ability to define Christian practice. They argued for a religious and political redistribution of power into the hands of Bible- and pamphlet-reading pastors and princes. The disruption triggered wars, persecutions and the so-called Counter-Reformation, the Catholic Church's delayed but forceful response to the Protestants.[6]

The irony of the Protestant Reformation is in part that it propelled the Catholic Church into a major Catholic Reformation that helped preserve it to the present in parts of Europe. "Though in the 1530s and 1540s it appeared as if Europe might become Protestant, a century later the picture was reversed—Catholicism had ended its decline and was showing a vigour and dynamic that compared favourably with a now rigid Protestantism."[7] It's the rigidity among Protestants that led to the martyrdoms of many who had broken from the Catholic Church.

JOHN FRITH, ANDREW HEMET, AND SIR THOMAS MORE

Many martyrs were indicted as much for what they owned as what they said, and John Frith was no exception. The bright young theologian was caught with "heretical books" and imprisoned with nine others. It must have been an unusually rancid time in a makeshift subterranean prison—a cave somewhere under or near Christ Church, Oxford, where salt fish were stored. Some of the prisoners died from an infection.

Foxe gives high praise for the intellectual capacity of Frith, whom he sees as "so learned and excellent a young man [around age 30]; which had so profited in all kind of learning and knowledge, that scarcely there was his equal amongst all his companions." At one point he won his freedom from the stocks (being mistaken in that town for a vagabond) by wooing the local schoolmaster with his Latin and Greek. But his ingenuity (and many disguises) protected him only so long before Sir Thomas More (High Chancellor for Henry VIII) intercepted him and sent him to the Tower of London. Foxe writes that they carried him from the Tower "into Smithfield to be burned." He continues,

And when he was tied unto the stake, there it sufficiently appeared
with what constancy and courage he suffered death; for when
the faggots and fire were put unto him, he willingly embraced
the same; thereby declaring with what uprightness of mind he
suffered his death for Christ's sake, and the true doctrine, whereof
that day he gave, with his blood, a perfect and firm testimony.
The wind made his death somewhat the longer, which bare away
the flame from him unto his fellow that was tied to his back: but
he had established his mind with such patience, God giving him
strength, that even as though he had felt no pain in that long
torment, he seemed rather to rejoice for his fellow than to be
careful for himself.

This truly is the power and strength of Christ, striving and
vanquishing in his saints; who sanctify us together with them,
and direct us in all things to the glory of his holy name! Amen.[8]

Martyred with Frith was Andrew Hemet, a twenty-four-year-old tailor.
Several times during his "trial," he deferred to Frith's stance, along with
rejecting various attempts to persuade him to change his theological views.
Much like the way Tyndale had been captured, Hemet trusted men who
would in turn ensnare him. The key culprit was William Holt, "foreman of
the king's tailor," who plotted for a private social gathering to gain access to
Hemet's belongings. He found an opportunity "to show forth some fruit of
his wickedness" and betrayed Hemet. Hemet managed to escape his chains
with a file slipped to him, only to be recaptured. He would burn at the
stake with Frith in 1533.

The bishops used many persuasions to allure this good man from
the truth, to follow them; but he, manfully persisting in the truth,
would not recant. Wherefore on the fourth day of July, in the
afternoon, he was carried into Smithfield with Frith, and there
burned.

When they were at the stake, one Doctor Cook, a parson in
London, openly admonished all the people, that they should in

no wise pray for them, no more than they would do for a dog; at which words Frith, smiling, desired the Lord to forgive him. These his words did not a little move the people unto anger, and not without good cause. Thus these two blessed martyrs committed their souls into the hands of God.[9]

The timing for Frith and Hemet was rather unfortunate, given the state of affairs with Sir Thomas More and Henry VIII. We will never know if they would have escaped persecution given the changing tides of religious views in Hampton Court and Windsor Castle. More had been Henry's important counselor, and they spent considerable time together, even sharing a mutual interest in astronomy. More had long been pursuing "heretics" like Frith—those who opposed papal claims—but now found himself in the King's crosshairs on June 1, 1533, only a month before Frith and Hemet burned. However, More's downfall took two years to play out and three until his own execution.

More had angered Henry when he refused to attend the coronation of Anne Boleyn, formerly Henry's young mistress (and sister to his former lover). More had resigned as Lord Chancellor to avoid such a conflict with the King but to no avail. The jilted Queen Catherine (Henry's first wife who had reigned twenty-three years) was a devout Catholic and a favorite of More (and the people). Henry banished Catherine until her death on January 1, 1536, only six months before More's execution. Catherine's daughter Mary never forgot this treatment by the "Protestants" (or whatever classification is afforded Henry VIII). Ironically, in 1521 Pope Leo X had labeled Henry "The Defender of the Faith" for his rebuke of Luther's views, and mainly for his defense of the Seven Sacraments—especially the sacramental nature of marriage. Fifteen years later, More went to the chopping block refusing to acknowledge biblical grounds for Henry's divorce from Catherine—endorsing the same views for which Henry had received papal praise—and for refusing separation from "the vicar of Christ" in Rome.

More claimed to his interrogator, Thomas Cromwell, to have left the King's service to "study upon the passion of Christ" and his "passage out of this world." He refused to "meddle with any matter of this world." We have these words from a letter he wrote (May 2–3, 1535) to his sister from his imprisonment in the Tower. This was nearly two full years after the pyres of Frith and Hemet.

> As if sensing that his words would be preserved for posterity, More defiantly declared on the final page [of the letter to his sister], "I am, quoth I, the King's true faithful subject and daily bedesman [humble servant] and pray for his highness and all his and all the realm. I do nobody harm, I say none harm, I think none harm but wish everybody good. And if this be not enough to keep a man alive in good faith I long not to live." It certainly wasn't enough for Henry, who demanded More's full submission; anything less was unacceptable.[10]

More himself was killed for standing firm on his religious beliefs— beheaded at the King's order on Tower Hill (instead of hanged, drawn, and quartered—the usual punishment for "traitors"), July 6, 1536. This devout Catholic who pursued Protestant reformers is now deemed in England as a Reformation martyr.

JOHN LAMBERT A friend of Frith and Tyndale, John Lambert met the same fate—burned at the stake. The three of them had spent time in Antwerp, enjoying long chats with humanist theologians at the White Horse Tavern. His journey went from the highest of accolades to the pyre. Catherine of Aragon had named him a fellow at his alma mater, the prestigious Queens College, Cambridge. But Lambert had to flee his privileged position at Cambridge over theological differences, espousing views more in line with the tavern talk. And when the duke of Norfolk finally captured Lambert back in England, his sympathies for Queen Anne Boleyn didn't help.

Lambert appealed to Henry VIII, perhaps assuming the king sym-pathized with Protestant leanings because of the break from Rome (and Anne's beliefs). Henry made an example of him—and besides parading before dignitaries at the trial like a gifted theologian, he called for harsh treatment of the accused.

Lambert's main heresy charge? He rejected transubstantiation (the real presence of Christ's body and blood in the bread and wine at Communion). They took him to Smithfield, chained him to a stake, and proceeded to torture him in the most inhumane of ways. His dying words as he raised his hands—fingertips burning and his legs burned to stumps: "None but Christ! None but Christ!"[11]

Once again, we find grotesque treatment even in the already horrendous execution of a devout Christian. Though his legs had been incinerated, the tormentors allowed the fire to burn to a single coal and prolonged his pain. Then the guards hoisted him on their halberds (a two-handed axe on a six-foot pole). They raised him until the chains prohibited any more, then dropped him into the flames, where he perished. Lambert died in 1538, just two years after Tyndale and four years after Frith.

ANNE ASKEW In 1546, Henry VIII was trying to align himself and England more directly with Rome, and fear of the rising reformers threatened this. In hopes of finding names of more prominent voices within this movement, he followed his advisors' plan of examining (under torture) any who would betray such people. His plan backfired as his examiners placed twenty-four-year old Anne Askew into the flames, having been crippled from her torture on the rack.

It seems that if your plan were to quiet a religious rebellion, the last thing you would allow is an established author, the first known English woman poet, to write about her treatment from her cell! They twice put her on the rack. The first time she fainted from the pain. Her tormentor, the lieutenant, appealed to be relieved of his duties due to the pitiful sight. Her screams were so loud that those in the castle's gardens could hear—including the lieutenant's wife and daughter. However, she gave up no names. The second time, the replacement tormentors turned the crank so hard it pulled her shoulders and hips from their sockets and dislocated her knees and elbows.

She went to the stake at Smithfield, burned with three men, and never gave up names of other "heretics." Due to the injuries from the rack they had to carry her in a chair—but her physical condition didn't soften her bold manner as she criticized the sermon at the ceremony. Foxe calls her a "blessed sacrifice unto God," and a "singular example of Christian constancy for all men to follow" and records her answer to John Lacel's letter:

O friend, most dearly beloved in God! I marvel not a little what should move you to judge in me so slender a faith as to fear death, which is the end of all misery. In the Lord I desire you not to believe of me such wickedness: for I doubt it not, but God will perform his work in me, like as he hath begun. I understand the council is not a little displeased, that it should be reported abroad that I was racked in the Tower. They say now, that what they did there was but to fear me; whereby I perceive they are ashamed of their uncomely doings, and fear much lest the king's Majesty should have information thereof; wherefore they would no man to noise it. Well! their cruelty God forgive them. Your heart in Christ Jesus. Farewell and pray.[12]

Anne's prayer:

O Lord! I have more enemies now, than there be hairs on my head: yet, Lord, let them never overcome me with vain words, but light thou, Lord, in my stead; for on thee cast I my care. With all the spite they can imagine, they fall upon me, who am thy poor creature. Yet, sweet Lord, let me not set by them that are against me; for in thee is my whole delight. And, Lord, I heartily desire of thee that thou wilt of thy most merciful goodness forgive them that violence which they do, and have done, unto me. Open also thou their blind hearts, that they may hereafter do that thing in thy sight, which is only acceptable before thee, and to set forth thy verity aright, without all vain fantasies of sinful men. So be it, O Lord, so be it!
　　By me, ANNE ASKEW[13]

THE RUTHLESS YEAR OF 1555 UNDER QUEEN MARY Queen Mary I ruled from 1553 to 1558, and though we could highlight a few different years of martyrdoms, 1555 was especially busy.

Some martyrs were of low means and lived otherwise obscure lives, like James Trevisam, burned at the stake on July 3, 1555. He had severe physical challenges, and had long been bedridden. One night as his servant was reading the Bible to him in the privacy of his home, Berd the Promoter happened to visit and, overhearing the reading up the stairway, proceeded up to find several listening. He immediately arrested James and carried him on a cart to jail (against neighbors' pleas). Within days James was sentenced by the bishop of London to be burned and his body cast into a ditch—not put in a coffin or buried in the cemetery. Besides the Bible reading, Trevisam's main offense was denying transubstantiation. The local priest had to fight with Trevisam's widow to prevent her from retrieving the body, discarded in the ditch wrapped only in a sheet. The local landowner found the corpse, by this time naked, and buried it. As fate would have it, that landowner was then called before the courts, but Foxe's account breaks off with no resolution.

Less than two weeks later, the pyres would move from the obscure to the celebrated. The fear of violent retribution among Protestant families must have been heavy across England, especially in London, where fires seemed to dot the horizon.

The day of July 12, 1555, burns in infamy. We begin with John Bradford, a former lawyer during Henry VIII's reign, and chaplain under his son Edward VI. Bradford later became a popular preacher, and served on staff at St. Paul's.

Bradford was burned for one of the more curious offenses—calming a crowd and escorting bishop Bourn of Bath from his stage to safety. The bishop had riled a crowd at St. Paul's Cross, London, with his demeaning comments about the late king. Even another bishop and the mayor could not curtail the riot, but Bradford succeeded. He stepped forward from the back of the stage, calmed the crowd, and with the help of the sheriff's men helped escort the bishop to an adjacent house, shielding him from behind after one dagger had already been thrown. One rioter yelled, "Ah Bradford,

Bradford, thou savest him that will help to burn thee. I give thee his life. If it were not for thee, I would (I assure thee) run him through with my sword."[14] This indeed played out as some deceitful souls turned on the popular Bradford and blamed him for the uproar.

Two days later, Queen Mary summoned Bradford to the Tower of London, where she was staying (in the royal quarters, of course), and charged him with sedition and, curiously, for preaching at that event without authority. It's dizzying logic, since Bradford had actually saved a Catholic priest. He refused the queen's pardon since it would mean a compromise of his own faith, and he lingered for two years before his translation to eternity. As he was about to be burned and the charges recounted, there was actually an argument about whether he was saving the priest or elevating himself. The priest himself wasn't even present to vouch for Bradford's heroism.

Foxe records long dialogues and court hearings, including numerous responses from Bradford. This is one among many:

> The Lord, before whom I stand as well as before you, knoweth
> what vain-glory I have sought, and seek in this behalf: his mercy
> I desire, and also would be glad of the queen's favour, to live as
> a subject without clog of conscience. But otherwise, the Lord's
> mercy is better to me than life. And I know to whom I have
> committed my life, even into his hands which will keep it, so
> that no man may take it away before it be his pleasure. There are
> twelve hours in the day, and as long as they last, so long shall no
> man have power thereon: therefore his good will be done. Life,
> in his displeasure, is worse than death; and death, with his true
> favour, is true life.[15]

He preached twice a day and drew crowds to his cell. The night before he was burned at Smithfield, they tried to transport him at midnight to avoid popular support. When word leaked out, huge crowds greeted him. By 4:00 a.m., massive crowds were present at Smithfield. A friend had made him such a nice shirt that people were shocked at his pleasant appearance.

He burned around 9:00 a.m. Bradford was around forty-five years old, and tied to the stake with young John Leaf, only twenty years of age.

Upon Friday before Palm Sunday, he [Leaf] was committed to the Compter in Bread-street [a small English prison], and afterward examined and condemned by the bloody bishop.

It is reported of him, that, when the bill of his confession was read unto him, instead of pen, he took a pin, and pricking his hand, sprinkled the blood upon the said bill, desiring the reader thereof to show the bishop that he had sealed the same bill with his blood already.[16]

Some records state that Bradford comforted him at the stake, reminding him that on that very night they would be dining with Jesus.

On that same fateful day of July 12, 1555, four martyrs were burned at Canterbury. Two were clergy, John Bland and John Frankesh, and they were joined by Nicholas Shetterden and Humphrey Myddleton. The case of John Bland is especially troublesome, as he was promised that his discussion of Scripture would not be used against him in a later meeting—and the meeting was actually to try him for his very words. In his defense, he repeatedly made statements like the following: "I am not ashamed of my faith: for I believe in God the Father, in Jesus Christ his only Son, and all the other articles of the creed. And I believe all the holy Scriptures of God. I will declare no more than this." Like so many of these martyrdom accounts during Queen Mary's reign, to waver on a clear endorsement of the actual presence of Christ's blood and body in the Sacraments was deemed heresy and a ticket to the flames. All four were strapped to two poles and burned in the same fire.

The day after Bradford and Leaf died for their faith, another martyr was named thirty-two miles outside London in Maidstone. A priest, William Minge, died in the local prison with "great constancy and boldness."[17] Apparently, this was not long before his scheduled execution.

The next week, July 22 and 23, 1555, Dirick Carver and John Launder went to the stake at Lewes and Stenning (Steyning)—towns about twenty miles apart near the southern city of Brighton. Launder, a husbandman (tenant farmer or small landowner), openly objected to most of the key liturgies and practices of the church. The presiding bishop charged that "he doth believe and confess that auricular confession is not necessary to be made to any priest, or to any other creature, but every person ought to acknowledge and confess his sins only to God; and also that no person hath any authority to absolve any man from his sins."[18] Also, for salvation a person merely needs to be sorry and ask for forgiveness from God, not "make any auricular confession of them to the priest, either to take absolution for them at the priest's hands."[19]

Dirik Carver had gained considerable wealth, though being imprisoned by the "greedy raveners" left his wife and kids destitute. He was deemed guilty by his open association with others, "Bishop Hooper, Cardmaker, Rogers, and others of their opinion, which were of late burned."[20] Foxe affords us a good glimpse of the issue with reading Scripture in English, the main issue that we saw with James Trevisam.

> He [Carver] saith that since the queen's coronation he hath
> had the Bible and Psalter in English, read in his house at
> Brighthelmstone divers times, and likewise since his coming into
> Newgate: but the keeper, hearing thereof, did take them away; and
> saith also, that about a twelvemonth now past, he had the English
> procession said in his house, with other English prayers.[21]

As Carver was about to be put into the barrel (likely a wine tub), the sheriff threw his English Bible into the barrel. After Carver stripped and stepped into the barrel, he threw the Bible to the crowd—which brought a strong rebuke from the sheriff. Anyone keeping it and not throwing it into the fire would have to join it.

> Dear brethren and sisters, witness to you all, that I am come
> to seal with my blood Christ's gospel, because I know that it is
> true. . . .
> And he said further in his prayer as followeth:

"O Lord my God, thou hast written, He that will not forsake wife, children, house, and all that ever he hath, and take up thy cross and follow thee, is not worthy of thee. But thou, Lord, knowest, that I have forsaken all, to come unto thee: Lord, have mercy upon me, for unto thee I commend my spirit; and my soul doth rejoice in thee."

These were the last words of that faithful member of Christ, before the fire was put to him. And after that the fire came to him he cried, "O Lord, have mercy upon me;" and sprung up in the fire, calling upon the name of Jesus, and so ended.[22]

Two weeks later (August 2) another martyr added to the tally of charred corpses credited to the bishop of Norwich. The young James Abbes had recanted, influenced by the bishop's bribe. However, Foxe captures his change of heart. "The bribe lay so heavily upon his conscience, that he returned, threw back the money, and repented of his conduct."[23] In one version Foxe states "his conscience began to throb."[24] And as fate would have it—or irony, since his body was burned—his pyre was in the city of Bury (near Manchester). Abbes had stripped and given his clothes to the poor as he approached the fire pit. Foxe records that a sheriff's servant who had verbally accosted him earlier went mad during the event and also stripped, then ran around repeatedly yelling, "Thus did James Abbes, the true servant of God, who is saved but I am damned."[25]

LINES IN MEMORY OF JOHN BRADFORD, MARTYR

Lament we may both day and night
For this our brother dear;
Bradford, a man, both just and right,
There were but few his peer.
For God's true servant he was known
In every city and town:
His word amongst them he hath sown
Till it was trodden down. . . .

From God's true word he would not slide,
Though it was to his pain;
But in the truth he did abide,
All men might know it plain.
The wicked men, they did him take,
And promise him much store,
To cause him this his God forsake,
And preach the truth no more.

But he, for all that they could say,
Would not his God displease;
But trusted, at the judgment clay,
His joy would then increase.
And where they punished him therefore,
Full well he did it take:
He thought no pains could be so sore
To suffer for Christ's sake.

Alas! the people did lament,
When that they did hear tell
That he in Smithfield should be burnt,
No more with us to dwell.
His preaching was both true and good,
His countenance meek and mild;
Alas! the shedding of his blood
Pleas'd neither man nor child: . . .

In going to the burning fire,
He talked all the way:
The people then he did desire
For him that they would pray.
And when he came unto the place
Whereas then he should die,

Full meek the fire he did embrace,
And said, "Welcome to me."

A servant true of God, I say,
With him that time did burn;
Because in God's word he did stay,
Not willing to return.
But quietly were both content
Their death to take truly;
Which made the people's hearts to rent
Their deathful pangs to see.[26]

CULTURAL CONNECTION

Thomas More and *A Man for All Seasons*

The Richard Bolt play *A Man for All Seasons* was released at London's Globe Theatre (now the Gielgud Theatre) on July 1, 1960. Drafts had been performed on BBC Radio (1954) and on television (1957), and it appeared on Broadway in the United States in 1961. Bolt presents Sir Thomas More as a man of unflappable conscience. In the gripping dialogue between More and the third duke of Norfolk (Thomas Howard), his close friend begs More to lighten up on the principles of Henry VIII's annulment from his first wife, Catherine of Aragon, in order to marry Anne Boleyn (Norfolk's niece). He urges More to save himself from certain death and remain in the fellowship of his friends. More responds, "And when we stand before God, and you are sent to Paradise for doing according to your conscience, and I am damned for not doing according to mine, will you come with me, for fellowship?"[27] In 1966 the movie made from this script won multiple Academy Awards, and another film of the same name was released in 1988, with Charlton Heston as More. John Gielgud, progenitor of the former Globe Theatre, portrayed Cardinal Wolsey.

CULTURAL CONNECTION

The Oxford Martyrs in *Fahrenheit 451*

Oftentimes writers and other artists employ references that are only useful if the audience knows the source. For example, using the phrase "Good Samaritan" assumes familiarity with the story in Luke 10:25-37. It is little wonder that readers queried the following phrase in *Fahrenheit 451*, a 1953 novel by bestselling author Ray Bradbury (with various film adaptations, including one in 2018). After authorities declare reading illegal, an elderly woman who owns a house with many books decides to burn herself with her collection rather than to live without reading. Before she drops the match on the kerosene spread by the firemen, tasked with burning all books, she says, "Be of good comfort, and play the man, Master Ridley; we shall this day light such a candle, by God's grace, in England as, I trust, shall never be put out!" It shows she has read one of the classics, *Foxe's Book of Martyrs*, and that she was going to be a candle for her cause. The main character, Guy Montag, becomes enticed with books and though a third-generation firefighter, begins reading to find answers to his life's emptiness.

THE OXFORD MARTYRS The most famous martyrs of the English Reformation are the Oxford Martyrs.[29] Two were burned at the stake together in 1555: Nicholas Ridley and Hugh Latimer. Thomas Cranmer was burned at the same place five months later on March 21, 1556. All three Oxford martyrs died in the persecutions under Mary Tudor, who reigned over England and Ireland as Mary I from 1553 to 1558. Though she is often dubbed as "Bloody Mary," this is misleading compared to the massive number of executions under other Protestant and Catholic rulers.

Nicholas Ridley was the bishop of London (and Winchester), and besides his doctrinal differences with Queen Mary's court, had signed the papers for Lady Jane Grey to be Queen. Hugh Latimer was the bishop of Worcester, and was all too familiar with "heretic" burnings. In 1538, prime minister Thomas Cromwell ordered him to preach the parting sermon before the burning of John Forest, a Franciscan friar who refused to acknowledge Henry VIII's claim to be head of the church.

> Ridley went to the pyre in a smart black gown, but the grey-haired
> Latimer, who had a gift for publicity, wore a shabby old garment,
> which he took off to reveal a shroud. Ridley kissed the stake
> and both men knelt and prayed. After a fifteen-minute sermon
> urging them to repent, they were chained to the stake and a bag of
> gunpowder was hung round each man's neck. The pyre was made
> of gorse branches and faggots of wood. As the fire took hold,
> Latimer was stifled by the smoke and died without pain, but poor
> Ridley was not so lucky. The wood was piled up above his head,
> but he writhed in agony and repeatedly cried out, "Lord, have
> mercy upon me" and "I cannot burn." Cranmer, who was made
> to watch, would go to his own death the following year.[30]

Latimer had also been greatly affected by the martyrdom of Thomas Bilney in Norwich (1531), a Catholic who challenged teachings such as pilgrimages, venerating saints, and relics. Bilney's time of confession with Latimer factored in opening Latimer's eyes. Ironically, it came shortly after Latimer had received a standing ovation for his Bachelor of Divinity Act refuting Philip Melanchthon's *The Rhetoric* (1519).[31] Latimer wrote about the confession:

> Bilney sought me out, and he came to me afterwards in my
> study and desired me for God's sake to hear his confession:
> and to say the truth, by his confession I learned more that

afore in many years. So from this time forward I began to
smell the Word of God and forsook school doctors and all such
fooleries.[32]

Bilney was one of dozens to die in "the Lollard pit" at Norwich, just
outside Bishopsgate in the chalk pits.[33]

Latimer was also influenced by James Bainham's burning. The eminent martyr reminded Latimer the night before his execution at Smithfield
(1532) to be strong. Both were burned at the stake, Bainham in London
and Latimer in Oxford three years later. Latimer was not new to controversy, as his views cost him his bishopric, and he thrice found himself in
the Tower of London (1539, 1546, and 1554).

At sixty-eight years of age, Latimer was still witty and bold—encouraging
Ridley amid the flames to "play the man," and that they would be "candles"
to the ages.

Paying homage to Latimer, Clara Stuart says,

We burn no heretics today. Instead of too many guidelines there
often seem to be none. Spiritual darkness is as deep now as
then. Social and moral evils grow even worse in our permissive
age. The things for which Latimer stood could be relevant still.
Today's preachers may find light from the candles he lit over four
centuries ago:

- The candle of devotion to the Scriptures, by which every belief
  and practice is tested.
- The candle of certainty that justification is by faith in Christ
  and his finished work on the cross.
- The candle of insistence on holiness of life, accepting no
  compromise with sin.
- The candle of faithfulness in preaching the Word as primary
  responsibility.
- The candle of compassion for one's fellow men and the
  willingness to labor in their behalf.

- The candle of fearlessness in speaking out against the evils of the day, wherever found, in places high and low.
- The candle of an exemplary personal life, against which the sternest critics can find little to speak.
- The candle of courage in standing for the truth, at whatever cost, be it opposition, imprisonment, or death.[34]

Such brilliance was prematurely snuffed from this world in these heresy trials, as testified anew in the burning of Thomas Cranmer. He had faithfully served the waffling Henry VIII, though often disagreeing. The king had appointed him archbishop in 1552. Cranmer declared Henry's marriage to Catherine void from the beginning, and then helped depose Anne Boleyn for alleged infidelity. Cranmer helped secure Henry's marriage to Anne of Cleves, which proved problematic when Henry jilted her over her looks.[35] Cranmer went on to serve Edward VI after Henry's passing, and then helped install Lady Jane Grey in 1553—an alliance that cost him his head after Mary ended Jane's term just nine days later. For nearly three years he lingered in prison, and was finally martyred in 1556.

Cranmer's journey to the platform saw many twists and turns. Cranmer was the very person who had drafted the founding document of Anglicanism and *The Common Book of Prayer*. Twice he signed documents recanting his Protestant leanings and endorsing the papacy in order to save his life, but he headed to the stake nonetheless. After the public embarrassment of degradation, he was given time to speak at the church before his pyre. Instead of following through on his faux endorsement of the pope in his final effort to survive, he jolted the crowd with his about-face and legendary last words:

I come to the great thing that troubleth my conscience more than any other thing that I ever said or did in my life. All such bills which I have written or signed with my own hand [are] untrue. And as for the pope, I refuse him as Christ's enemy and antichrist, with all his false doctrine.[36]

You might imagine the fury of his persecutors and the speed with which they dragged him away and fastened him to the stake—in the same place as the other Oxford martyrs. Today a metal cross marks this spot on Broad Street outside the porter's station of Balliol College (though in the mid-sixteenth century it would have been a ditch outside the city gates).

As the fire began to burn, he held his right hand in the flames and burnt it to a stub. In reference to signing his recantations, he yelled while keeping his hand in the flames, "This hand hath offended." Shortly before his translation to heaven, he said, "Lord Jesus, receive my spirit!"[37]

NICHOLAS BURTON Martyrs come from all professions, and often their captors interrupted their business routines. Many martyr stories represent a Christian who happened to be in the wrong place at the wrong time—but these future martyrs sometimes saw such situations as providential, and a chance to share their faith with others. That was the fate of English merchant Nicholas Burton, who was in Cádiz, Spain, during the reign of Philip II. It was a time in which the Spanish Inquisition had transitioned from a church-led to a state-led purge.[38] Being tricked to reveal the location of his loaded ship, Burton suddenly found himself languishing in the Cádiz prison where he began preaching to other inmates and leading them to a relationship with Christ. Though the Roman Catholic Church and Protestants served the same Jesus of the Bible, the institutional role in such matters created an issue for the prison preacher. On November 5, 1560, he met his end for his open faith.

The grand Inquisitor had moved him to Castle of San Jorge in Seville, the headquarters of the Inquisition. They brought him before an *auto de fe*, a ceremony to punish heretics. They made him wear garments with images of the devil torturing souls. They also tied a stick to his tongue to prevent speech while they pronounced his death sentence—to be burned with others outside the city.

During the human inferno, witnesses state that Burton remained peaceful, even cheerful. His inquisitors claimed this as proof he was demon possessed and oblivious to earthly pain. And they kept his ship—raising suspicion about their real motive but not his relentless faith (allegedly

✠ THE NEW BOOK OF CHRISTIAN MARTYRS

heretical). He became one of an estimated 32,000 Protestants killed during the Spanish Inquisition.[39]

Vintage Foxe

Afterward, the 20th of December, they brought the said Nicholas Burton, with a great number of other prisoners, for professing the true Christian religion, into the city of Seville, to a place where the said inquisitors sat in judgment which they called Auto, with a canvass coat, whereupon in divers parts was painted the figure of a huge devil, tormenting a soul in a flame of fire, and on his head a copping tank of the same work.

His tongue was forced out of his mouth with a cloven stick fastened upon it, that he should not utter his conscience and faith to the people, and so he was set with another Englishman of Southampton, and divers other condemned men for religion, as well Frenchmen as Spaniards, upon a scaffold over against the said inquisition, where their sentences and judgments were read and pronounced against them.

And immediately after the said sentences given, they were carried from thence to the place of execution without the city, where they most cruelly burned them, for whose constant faith, God be praised.

This Nicholas Burton by the way, and in the flames of fire, had so cheerful a countenance, embracing death with all patience and gladness, that the tormentors and enemies which stood by, said, that the devil had his soul before he came to the fire; and therefore they said his senses of feeling were past him.[40]

MISPLACED CREATIVITY, HORRENDOUS TORTURES Every martyrdom we have read represents a terrible death, whether it's the anticipation of the axe or the more common walk to the pile of wood and the death stake. Bishop John Hooper was burned in Gloucester with bladders of gunpowder between his legs and under his arms. After three attempts to start the fire, the bags finally blew but didn't kill him. Finally, his arms fell off and he fell forward, suspended only by the iron around his waist and perished (February 9, 1555).

The same day, Dr. Rowland Taylor died in Hadley. After the guards placed him in a pitch barrel, the persecutors faced an awkward pause when they could not find anyone in the crowd to light the fire beneath their beloved pastor. Finally, someone stepped forward.

Bishop Edmund Bonner examined large groups of saints, deemed them heretics, and then parceled them out for burning. In March of 1555, Bonner used a bizarre and cruel method on Thomas Tomkins, a weaver from Shoreditch, in the Diocese of London. Bonner was known for his cruelty and was called many names by the accused and oppressed, such as "butcher" and "bloodsucker."[41] In an effort to persuade Tomkins of the pain ahead at the pyre, and perhaps eternal flames, the bishop took him by the fingers and held his hand over a candle with multiple wicks. Instead of being dissuaded, the prisoner, while his hand was engulfed in flames, said, "O Lord, unto thy hands I commend my spirit." Master Harpsfield (who accompanied Tomkins) was so visibly moved that he begged the bishop to stop. Tomkins was spared further torture at that time, and the bishop sent him to Smithfield, where they burned him on March 16.

John Laurence was the last to burn among six martyrs examined together by Bishop Bonner. The heavy prison chains and food deprivation rendered him too weak to walk to the stake on March 29, 1555. So there in Colchester they carried him on a chair, and burned him on it.

George Marsh suffered a horrible death as they put a cask of hot tar above him that dripped on him while the fire burned him from below.

> After that, he began to speak to the people showing the cause of his death, and would have exhorted them to stick unto Christ, but one of the sheriffs prevented him. Kneeling down, he then said his prayers, put off his clothes unto his shirt, and was chained to the post, having a number of fagots under him, and a thing made like a firkin, with pitch and tar in it, over his head. The fire being unskilfully made, and the wind driving it in eddies, he suffered great extremity, which notwithstanding he bore with Christian fortitude.

When he had been a long time tormented in the fire without moving, having his flesh so broiled and puffed up that they who stood before him could not see the chain wherewith he was fastened, and therefore supposed that he had been dead, suddenly he spread abroad his arms, saying, "Father of heaven have mercy upon me!" and so yielded his spirit into the hands of the Lord. Upon this, many of the people said he was a martyr, and died gloriously patient. This caused the bishop shortly after to make a sermon in the cathedral church, and therein he affirmed, that the said "Marsh was a heretic, burnt as such, and is a firebrand in hell."[42]

In the bizarre case of John Tooley, he was hanged for robbing a Spaniard at St. James. Although this was an unusually steep penalty for his crime, he faced it as a repentant and courageous Christian, and began preaching anti-papal sentiments. Then he called for the three hundred or so present to shout "Amen!" and they did. When Cardinal Poole and Bishop Bonner learned of this, they had his body dug up and burned—the requisite fate for heretics.

WOMEN MARTYRS DURING THE ENGLISH REFORMATION

Numerous women are listed among the martyrs, often only in name or association with their spouse. However, other times they were as openly defiant of their accusers—courageous to the end. And in several instances, the women martyrs are burned together. During the reign of Queen Mary I, at least fifty-six of the recorded martyrs were women (nearly 20 percent).[43] Agnes Potten and Joan Trunchfield died tied to the same stake—burned in Ipswich for showing kindness to martyr Robert Samuel six months earlier. Some cases like this one include curious details. A dozen or so expenses are recorded for the execution (the expense of three sergeants riding from their homes, a gallon of wine, transport of prisoners, the wood, carrying the wood to the site, preparing documents, and even the expense of the stake itself).[44] We also know a bit about the martyrs' families and their community, and the martyrs' last words and actions. One important context is that at the time of Queen Mary I's early death, around eighty people in the Ipswich region were on the condemnation list. We also know that Joan's husband, Michael Trunchfield (a shoemaker), and another relative (John Trunchfield) were listed as condemned at the time of the women's martyrdom, February 9, 1556.

The husband of one of these women, most likely Agnes Potten, was described as "a carnal man," which kept her from fleeing at the advice of a young friend due to her children's care. Thus, she would "stand for the love of Christ and his truth . . . to the extreme of the matter." Foxe notes that both martyrs were exemplary wives and mothers, and references their eternal reward accordingly. "The one was a brewer's wife, the other a shoemaker's wife, and now both are espoused to a new husband Christ."[45] The women vacillated from high anxiety to extreme joy, and faced death solid in their faith.

The woodcut from Foxe of the four women burned with John Lomas is as defining of the times as any—and among the more memorable images. Anne Albright, Joan Catmer, Agnes Snoth (a widow from the Smarden parish), and Joan Sole spent their last moments chained to two separate stakes, singing psalms and praising God until their bodies expired from the heat. The account notes that Sir John Norton could not contain himself at the sight and wept aloud.

Joan Catmer of the Hythe parish had already been through the toughest of times, witnessing the martyrdom of her husband, George Catmer, the previous September at Canterbury. As in her march to Zion, George also was burned in one big fire with four others. Mrs. Catmer had twelve months to reflect on his adamant stance during his trial, that Christ, "sitteth in heaven, on the right hand of God the Father; and therefore I do not believe him to be in the sacrament of the altar. But he is in the worthy receiver spiritually; and the sacrament, as you use it, is an abominable idol."

Anne Albright was especially candid in her response to her accusers:

. . . saying, "that she would not be confessed of a priest;" and added moreover, speaking unto the priests, "You priests," said she, "are the children of perdition, and can do no good by your confession."

And likewise speaking unto the judge and his assistants, she told them that they were subverters of Christ's truth.

And as touching the sacrament of the altar, she said it was a naughty and abominable idol, and so utterly denied the same sacrament. Thus, persisting and persevering in her former sayings and answers, she was condemned the said eighteenth day of the said month, with the others above mentioned; with whom also she suffered quietly, and with great comfort, for the right of Christ's religion.[46]

The end of this account lists those responsible for this heinous act. For some, their only mention in historical record is complicity in the inhumane treatment of others—burning courageous brothers and sisters in the same faith they hold.

In Muchbently in Essex several relatives were burnt in two waves in March of 1557. Alice Munt, her husband, William, and their daughter Rose Allin all died together. Edmund Tyrrel, of the line of Tyrrel who killed Edward V, hunted them down. In response to Rose's bold defense he burned the back of her hand until it sizzled. When she wouldn't recant, he said, "Why whore wilt thou not cry?" When he asked her if she needed mending, she sealed her fate with her direct response, "Mend it? Nay, the Lord mend you and give you repentance, if it be His will. And now if you think it good, begin at the feet and burn to the head too. For he that set you a work shall pay you your wages one day."[47]

Five months later in August 1557, the examiners took Rose, her family, and several others in their association (some found in their same hiding place) and burned them near the town wall of Colchester. One martyr died in prison and ten others burned in two different burnings in the same spot—half were women, and two other women followed a month later. At the first burning between six and seven o'clock in the morning, the officer striking the nail in the stake missed and smashed Elizabeth Folk's shoulder with his mighty swing. She had just taken hold of the stake and said, "Welcome, love." Rose burned in the afternoon with three men. Two others from their group were burned on September 17, 1557, Agnes Bongeor and

Margaret Thurston (whose husband had died in prison). The jailer errantly had previously left one behind and a clerical error omitted the other (a sad testimony to the number of cases).

Mistress Joyce Lewes was born and died "a Gentlewoman," with a throng of friends who actually drank with her before her execution—which imperiled their own lives. After a year in the "stinking" prison, the fresh air startled her, and friends called for wine to help her. They joined her and she toasted them: "I drink to all them that unfeignedly love the gospel of Jesus Christ, and wish for the abolishment of papistry." They responded in their toast with "Amen!"

Her main offense that started her examination was turning her back on the holy water during Mass. The local martyrdoms had greatly disturbed her, especially the burning of her brother, Robert Glover, in September 1557.

Her husband, Thomas Lewes of Mancetter, had no desire to risk his own fortune by attempting to save her.

> And so, like a murderer of his own wife, he carried her to the bloody bishop, where she was examined, and found more stout than she was before death was threatened. And to begin withal, she was sent to such a stinking prison, that a certain maid which was appointed to keep her company, did swoon in the same prison.
>
> Being thus kept in prison, and oftentimes examined, and ever found stout, at the length she was brought in judgment, and pronounced a heretic worthy to be burnt.[48]

Her popularity played out at the execution, as the locals made sure her suffering was not prolonged (December 18, 1557):

> When she was tied to the stake with a chain, she showed such a cheerfulness that it passed man's reason, being so well coloured in her face, and being so patient, that the most part of them that had honest hearts did lament, and even with tears bewail the

tyranny of the papists. When the fire was set upon her, she neither struggled nor stirred, but only lifted up her hands towards heaven, being dead very speedily: for the under-sheriff at the request of her friends had provided such stuff, by the which she was suddenly despatched out of this miserable world.[49]

Perhaps the most horrific of the Marian martyrologies involving women is the case of Perotine Massey, her sister Guillemine Gilbert, and mother Catherine Cauchés. Collectively they became known as the Guernsey martyrs (July 18, 1556). In their heroic steadfastness in their faith we see Foxe's penchant for presenting strong women (unlike the more passive depictions of the Renaissance).[50] Massey's husband was a Norman Calvinist minister (in London at the time), which likely set the stage for a series of despicable incidents by the Catholic authorities.

A woman from the Guernsey isle community stole a silver goblet, which Massey identified and purchased to give back to its rightful owner—but authorities charged her for possession. During the questioning, she went from the temporal courts to the religious since her Protestant religious views surfaced. Because she lived with her sister and mother, all were put in prison at Coronet Castle and examined, and in short order their possessions inventoried for sale.

In the end, the thieving felon (also a woman) was released with a whipping and her ear maimed for her crime, and banished from the isle. Foxe's details are graphic, and though accused later of embellishing, Foxe successfully defended his account with numerous interviews from eyewitnesses and contemporary sources:

> The time then being come, when these three good servants and
> holy saints of God, the innocent mother with her two daughters,
> should suffer, in the place where they should consummate their
> martyrdom were three stakes set up. At the middle post was the
> mother, the eldest daughter on the right hand, the youngest on
> the other. They were first strangled, but the rope brake before they
> were dead, and so the poor women fell in the fire. Perotine, who

was then great with child, did fall on her side, where happened a rueful sight, not only to the eyes of all that there stood, but also to the ears of all true-hearted Christians that shall read this history. For as the belly of the woman burst asunder by the vehemence of the flame, the infant, being a fair man-child, fell into the fire, and eftsoons [immediately] being taken out of the fire by one W. House, was laid upon the grass. Then was the child had to the provost, and from him to the bailiff, who gave censure that it should be carried back again, and cast into the fire. And so the infant, baptized in his own blood, to fill up the number of God's innocent saints, was both born and died a martyr, leaving behind to the world, which it never saw, a spectacle wherein the whole world may see the Herodin cruelty of this graceless mutilation of catholic tormentors.[51]

Though it's no consolation, after Queen Mary's reign, those in charge of these hearings were all severely punished (petitions were made to Queen Elizabeth). The case of the Guernsey martyrs from that fateful day in mid-July of 1556 factored in public support for the rise of Calvinism in the Channel Islands.

Cicely Ormes, much like Mistress Joyce Lewes and others, was moved by the cruel treatment of martyrs and her own religious beliefs. The doings at Lollards Pit left an indelible impression and would move her to the same fate in 1557.

Then she came to the stake, and laid her hand on it, and said, "Welcome the cross of Christ." Which being done, she, looking on her hand, and seeing it blacked with the stake, wiped it upon her smock; for she was burnt at the same stake that Simon Miller and Elizabeth Cooper was burnt at. Then, after she had touched it with her hand, she came and kissed it, and said, "Welcome the sweet cross of Christ;" and so gave herself to be bound thereto. After the tormentors had kindled the fire to her, she said, "My soul doth magnify the Lord, and my spirit rejoiceth in God my Saviour." And in so saying, she set her hands together right against her breast, casting her eyes and head upward; and so stood, heaving up her hands by little and little, till the very sinews of her arms did break asunder, and then they fell. But she yielded her life unto the Lord as quietly as if she had been in a slumber, or as one feeling no pain; so wonderfully did the Lord work with her: his name therefore be praised for evermore. Amen![52]

CULTURAL CONNECTION

The Bloody Mary Cocktail

A popular drink known internationally as the "Bloody Mary" is a mixture of vodka, tomato juice, and an assortment of spices. Its origin seems to trace to the 1920s, possibly to a bar Ernest Hemmingway would later frequent in Paris (and later renamed Harry's New York Bar in Paris). One version has the drink named for the girlfriend (Mary) of a frequent patron. Ferdinand Petiot, the Parisian bartender and alleged inventor, claims his customer met Mary in the "Bucket of Blood" cabaret.[53] But the leading possibility is that directly or indirectly it was named for Queen Mary I because of the moniker John Foxe gave to her in *Actes and Monuments*. However, many historians note that the macabre nick-name seems rather unfair in the wider scope of royal actions. Mary put to death around three hundred Protestants during her five-year reign (1553–1558). But this pales in comparison to the number of executions credited to Henry VIII during his thirty-seven-year reign (of Protestants and Catholics, depending on his religious leanings at the time—or rather, that of his favored consort). These numbers vary widely, from 57,000 to 72,000 executions. Even on the conservative end of this, his tally comes to 1,405 per year (including those executed for treason), compared to around 60 per year for Queen Mary.[54] We could well have had a drink named Bloody Henry, or for that matter, given its Parisian club origin, Bloody Harry.

DID YOU KNOW? *Utopia*

Sir Thomas More was declared a Catholic saint in 1935 and a Reformation martyr. In 1516, twenty years before his martyrdom and the year before Luther posted his Ninety-Five Theses, More published a classic work of literature, *Utopia*, which underwent five editions in its first five years. This fictional political satire has two main characters, a fictional role for himself as narrator, and a gregarious and verbose traveler, the fictional Raphael Hythloday. The plot, with humor that isn't entirely innocent,[55] weaves in historical characters like Pieter Gilles and explorer Amerigo Vespucci, engaging readers in a believable manner. It also protects More from the views Hythloday is sharing about the Utopians, whom he criticizes. Nonetheless, though Hythloday is critical of the somewhat egalitarian and prescriptive societal arrangements, and the fictional More calls many of them absurdities, the Utopian ideas are put before sixteenth-century readers in plain view of the Catholic Church.

Section one begins with a dinner party at the table of the Archbishop of Canterbury. Hythloday (fictional) describes the culture of a remote island country he discovered named Utopia (which actually can mean "nowhere"). Its founder, Utopus, had managed to cut a fifteen-mile channel, cutting off the island from the continent. This is important, implying that Utopia is a creation of human will and ingenuity. In section two, he spends the final chapter describing the many religions of Utopia. The one common requirement is all religions must espouse the idea of one Supreme Being. However, much of the chapter is Hythloday's harsh criticism of the religious systems and church hierarchy of Tudor England. The title page of the original volume reads: "A truly golden little book, no less beneficial than entertaining, on the best state of a commonwealth, and on the new island of Utopia. By the distinguished author Thomas More, citizen and undersheriff of the famous city of London."

Utopia reflects a bit of disdain similar to Savonarola's in criticizing opulence, and the tongue-in-cheek poking at the bumbling monks and priests of *In Praise of Folly*—which Erasmus dedicated to More. Erasmus's title itself may be a play on More's name, as *moria* is Greek for *folly*.

The irony for the historical More is that he was executed on an island country, that once remote place that the Romans found mysterious and barbaric—an island where Christianity was at a crossroads that caught him, a statesman and principled Roman Catholic, in its political crosshairs. In Utopia, nothing was private (including property), and citizens even left their doors open. More had tried to live out his life in privacy—but he wound up in the public eye, and his unwillingness to condone an ill-advised and unbiblical marriage led ultimately to his demise.

CULTURAL CONNECTION

The Book of Common Prayer

Thomas Cranmer is largely responsible for *The Book of Common Prayer* (BCP), both its original version in 1549 and the more "Reformed" version in 1552. It seems inconceivable that within a year of publishing this English literary treasure, he would be imprisoned, and within four years beheaded. Though sidelined during both the reign of Queen Mary I and the English Civil War (1642–1651), the BCP was reaffirmed and reissued in 1662. That version has become a mainstay in English worship. It is among the four most influential books in the formation of the modern English language. The others are the King James Bible (1611), the works of Shakespeare, and *Pilgrim's Progress*. Below are some of the key phrases from the BCP that have become idioms in modern English, followed by one of its "collects" or prayers. The BCP is used in over 150 countries in over 50 languages.[56]

From the Marriage Liturgy
- "Speak now or forever hold your peace"
- ". . . so long as ye both shall live"
- "To have and to hold from this day forward, for better for worse, for richer for poorer, in sickness and in health, to love and to cherish, till death us do part"
- "With this ring I thee wed"
- "Those whom God hath joined together let no man put asunder"

From Other Prayers and Blessings

- "He is risen. The Lord is risen indeed" (*Morning Prayer*)
- "All sorts and conditions of men" (Order for Morning Prayer)
- "Give peace in our time, O Lord" (*Mattins and Evensong, Versicles*)
- "Earth to earth, ashes to ashes, dust to dust; in sure and certain hope of the Resurrection unto eternal life" (*Prayer of Commital from the Order for Burial of the Dead*)
- "Glory be to the Father, and to the Son, and to the Holy Ghost; As it was in the beginning, is now, and ever shall be, world without end. Amen." (*Gloria Patri*)
- "The peace of God, which passeth all understanding, keep your hearts and minds in the knowledge and love of God, and of his Son Jesus Christ our Lord." (*Blessing*)

A collect (daily prayer for a special week or service) written by Archbishop Thomas Cranmer for Advent says:[57]

> Blessed Lord, who hast caused all holy Scriptures to be written for our learning; grant that we may in such wise hear them, read, mark, learn, and inwardly digest them, that by patience and comfort of thy holy Word, we may embrace, and ever hold fast, the blessed hope of everlasting life, which thou hast given us in our Savior Jesus Christ. Amen.

Vintage Foxe

Although the rage and vehemency of this terrible persecution in Queen Mary's days did chiefly light in London, Essex, Norfolk, Suffolk, and Kent, as hath been partly already declared; yet, notwithstanding, besides the same, we find but few parts of this realm free from this fatal storm, but some good martyrs or other there shed their blood.[58]

The Colonization of Peoples through the Cold War (AD 1991)

From the Encomienda to the Russian Gulags

LORENZO RUIZ

Some martyrdom accounts become all the more real because of vivid literary and film accounts. Such is the case of Lorenzo Ruiz. Shūsaku Endō's novel *Silence* (1966) is a riveting account of the Tokugawa shogunate's persecution of Roman Catholic Japanese Christians. Martin Scorsese's 2016 film adaptation brought Endō's historical fiction to the big screen. But unlike Endō's main character, a Jesuit priest who commits apostasy (after horrific treatment), real-life hero martyrs from this era abound, including Lorenzo Ruiz from the Philippines. After prolonged torture, he died upside down in Nagasaki on September 29, 1637. Pope John Paul II beatified him on February 18, 1981, and canonized him on October 18, 1987.[1]

Ruiz's childhood in Binondo, Manila, was a journey of growing commitment to Christ, including membership in the Dominican Confraternity of the Most Holy Rosary, a collective prayer effort to produce the "Perpetual Rosary."[2] He even married a woman named Rosario.

However, in June of 1636 the life of this professional calligrapher radically changed. He was implicated in the killing of a Spaniard and had to flee. He found himself with three Dominican priests bound for Japan, where the Tokugawa shogunate arrested them within days.

They endured water tortures and guards jumping on boards on their stomachs which forced water out of their nose and mouth. Two priests recanted Christianity after bamboo skewers were forced under their fingernails, and Lorenzo almost followed.

He endured the Okinawa prison for two years before being transferred to Nagasaki. Lorenzo was repeatedly asked to recant his faith, but he refused. After tortures failed, the shogun subjected him to "tsurushi"—hanging upside down with one's head and torso in a pit, with feet tied tightly to slow circulation and prolong the pain. Lorenzo also endured rocks tied to his waist that enhanced the ankle pressure. One practice Scorsese's film captures with vivid intensity is when the guards "would make cuts in the prisoner's head every few hours to allow blood buildup to escape."[3]

Some otherwise brave priests succumbed and recanted, but like the hero in *Silence*, Ruiz did not. His last words were, "I am a Catholic and wholeheartedly do accept death for God. Had I a thousand lives, all these to Him I shall offer. Do with me as you please."[4] The shogun burned his body to further desecrate it, and then deposited his ashes in the harbor.

CHAPTER ELEVEN

The Costs of Colonialism in the Americas

Your brother's blood cries out to me from the ground.

GENESIS 4:10, NIV

For you, O Lord, are my hope, my trust, O Lord, from my youth.

PSALM 71:5

We at *Christianity Today* deeply love the church. Serving the bride of Christ, growing her love for God, and telling the story of her redemptive and transformative work in the world is the heart of what we do. We do not revel in the history of her sin. But we cannot love our brothers and sisters well if we cannot tell their story in truth. And we cannot tell their story in truth if we cannot confess our participation in it. The Bible is honest about the flaws of even the most remarkable people. We should follow its example.[1]

TIMOTHY DALRYMPLE, EDITORIAL IN *CHRISTIANITY TODAY*

During Europe's Protestant Reformation, the world was expanding elsewhere—at least in the eyes of Western Christians. While the upstart "protesters" were preoccupied with reforming the Roman Catholic Church, the church in the West was growing rapidly in territories and in number of "converts." Indeed, for Protestants, the price of the Reformation was Latin America.[2] While Protestants were fighting for Europe, Catholicism was unchecked in much of the New World.

Unfortunately, the cost to the indigenous people of Latin America was oppression or enslavement. For many it meant near obliteration of their ethnic identity, and for some, actual extinction. The conquest and exploitation of Latin America was a travesty for native inhabitants, and a precarious position for many Christian missionaries and conscientious Christian merchants and explorers.

For many indigenous cultures (like the Aztecs and Incas), religion played a prominent role in their pre-Columbian culture. This made it easier for the conquistadores to establish their religion as the governing authority. And in turn, for the monarchs—especially the Spanish crown—to endorse the same.[3]

The earliest days of European visitors gave indications that not all would go well for indigenous peoples. From Christopher Columbus's Caribbean touchdown in 1492, to exploits of F. Hernández de Córdoba in the Yucatan peninsula in 1517 and Hernán Cortés's campaigns in 1519, the stage was set for the conquistadores and oppression—and the pandemics of the 1600s brought by the foreigners.

Many among the Catholic ranks would lead revolts against the Spanish—like the parish priest of Dolores, Miguel Hidalgo y Costilla, who called for independence on September 16, 1810, Mexico's Independence Day.

Though it is no recompense for centuries of inhumane treatment, these people oppressed by colonial powers found hope in the Bible through the work of some heroic priests and missionaries. These indigenous believers would eventually adopt the Bible and the faith as their own, not some filtered version from foreigners. People groups around the world have similarly embraced God's Word for themselves, but the effect has been striking in Latin America, where Christianity is currently experiencing explosive growth.

What happened in the Americas from the sixteenth to the nineteenth centuries has further ramifications in these regions today. In 2020, for instance, the worldwide protests, riots, and violence during the spring and summer—ignited after George Floyd's horrific death in Minneapolis, Minnesota—had roots in Europe's colonization of the Americas.[4]

This chapter and overall section help show the expansion of Christianity during these controversial times of colonialization. Amid the chaos and oppression of peoples, Christians gave their lives so that others might believe in Christ (often an evangelism through their deeds as much as their sermons). We include here a representation of both the bad and the good acts carried out in Christ's name during this overall sad era in human history.

Slavery itself was millennia old by the age of colonization, and not a respecter of any race—most ethnic groups have it in their history, as perpetrators or as victims. However, during this era, the story is rather clear that colonialism in the Americas was anathema to indigenous or settled peoples and an excruciating, extended experience for enslaved African communities.

While European Protestants were fighting for survival against the popes and their ecclesiastical machine, and then against other Protestants, Catholic monarchs were dividing the "New World" and claiming it for crown and pope. The same year Cortés defeated the Aztecs, 1521, the Catholic Church condemned Martin Luther at the Diet of Worms—a major development in launching the Protestant Reformation (i.e., protesters).

The Catholics were conquering landmasses and islands newly discovered (at least by them). Many in the West thought these were uncivilized regions, and often considered their inhabitants subhuman. Some missionaries in 1830 concluded that the conversion of these groups was impossible and wrote, "The perverse levity and awful depravity of these savages appear to be unequalled in the history of man."[5] From "noble savages" to nonhuman, many Westerners totally disregarded the precious souls of those they were mistreating. Temporal objectives, not eternal ones, carried the day, the decades, and even the centuries.

But other missionaries and Christian leaders, those we honor in this volume, fought for the indigenous peoples and saw them rightly as precious to God. Many among the "three battalions" of missionaries—Dominicans, Franciscans, and Augustinians—demonstrated a sincere commitment to spiritual goals above others.[6] (Their roles were initially as military chaplains, friars, and then the mixture of friars joining the "apostolic missionaries.")

The conquerors' best army was the "army of missionaries." In the battle for the people's minds and hearts, the cross could achieve "a conquest far more effective than the one achieved by the sword."[7] While the priests had one agenda, often their military and royal leaders had another. Not unlike the Russian invasion of Ukraine in 2022, regardless of what the church officials and staff had in mind—and sometimes the soldiers themselves—the political leaders' ultimate objective was to subjugate the conquered.

Much of what we know about the earliest days of post-Columbian America is most likely skewed in the *Florentine Codex*, or perhaps because of it—trying to rationalize or excuse the relatively easy conquest of the huge Aztec empire.[8] However, a case can also be made for the traction of the gospel message in spite of it all. That traction came through life sacrifices of a host of faithful Christians across the centuries.

+ Historic Sources

THE CROSS ON NEW WORLD SHORES

Not to be lost in this discussion of martyrs in the Americas is that the sign of the Christians' arrival was often the cross, the symbol of the ultimate martyr. The Aztec sun stone—more formally the Cuauhxicalli Eagle Bowl—is replete with indigenous religious symbols like rabbits, flowers, and numbers representing gods. Their world was suddenly shaken by invaders flanked by priests wearing and carrying new symbols, ornate crosses. The Europeans' power, backed of course by gunpowder and steel, is often cast in Western accounts to represent stronger gods. But the conversion of native people, whether coerced or sincere, was far from easy, and apparently not all was as it was recorded. "In the first few years after the conquest was complete [1521], the Aztecs exhibited few signs of believing that gods walked in their midst."[9]

It is important to realize that likely the majority of these men—soldiers as well as clerics—were not hypocrites. Most truly believed that they were sanctioned by God. They were indignant, even incensed, when the inhabitants of the land could not perceive the superiority of Christianity. The European conquerors established regular Masses spoken for the salvation of local people's souls.

As he lay dying, a victim of a conspiracy among his fellow conquistadores, Francisco Pizarro, the cruel conqueror of the Inca empire, drew a cross with his own blood so he could die contemplating the cross. Hernán Cortés, the conqueror of Mexico, kissed the hem of the robes of the first Franciscan missionaries arriving at the newly conquered land. Obviously, to say that they were sincere does not mean that they were good—and even less that what they did was good. It does mean that they were convinced that in their deeds they were serving not only their greed and lust for violence but also God.[10]

THE INSTITUTIONAL BACKDROP OF COLONIZATION

Even as merchants and monarchs established or enabled the horrific Middle Passage slave trade supplying labor to the colonized regions, Europe was undergoing religious and political transitions. Religious wars and colonization were not merely the norm, but the nemesis of true evangelists.[11] The pure in heart wanted to share the Good News, yet conquest and colonialism usually (and understandably) created barriers in reaching the indigenous peoples.

On either side of the Atlantic, many Christians were caught in conflicts' crosshairs and died for their faith. Again, we look at the fallout of colonialism (the route of Christianity's spread) and connections to present events. However, our focus in this text is on the martyrs, and historical events and movements are given here for the context of heroic efforts to reach and assist unsaved inhabitants (indigenous and immigrant).

Overlapping the events of colonization in the Americas were the philosophical movements of the Renaissance and the Enlightenment, and of course the Protestant Reformation (1517–1648). Aspects of the Renaissance and Enlightenment influenced how Christians thought and how their actions were both articulated and rejected.

The Renaissance ran from the fourteenth to the seventeenth centuries and "promoted the rediscovery of classical philosophy, literature and art."[12] Many Renaissance figures are considered some of history's greatest thinkers. From Dante, Chaucer, and Giotto to Milton, Hobbes, Descartes, and Galileo, religion played a key role in their contributions. Religious influence is clear in the artistic genius of Michelangelo, Botticelli, Titian, and Raphael. And the works of scholars like Erasmus both provoked an assessment of religion, via *In Praise of Folly*, and provided revolutionary scholarship through his printed Greek New Testament (1516).

The movement usually discussed in tandem with the Renaissance is the Enlightenment (or Age of Reason) that occurred during "the long 18th century" (1685–1815).[13] The Enlightenment was not a single unified movement, but a diverse set of movements in different countries. The High Enlightenment across a wide swath of regions dates to 1730–1780. It was a time in which the thinkers thought the universe could be "demystified and catalogued." Two of the prominent and classic attempts to do so are Voltaire's *Philosophical Dictionary* and the opus of the era, Diderot's *Encyclopédie*.

> Enlightenment thinkers in Britain, in France and throughout
> Europe questioned traditional authority and embraced the notion
> that humanity could be improved through rational change. . . .
> The American and French Revolutions were directly inspired
> by Enlightenment ideals and respectively marked the peak of its
> influence and the beginning of its decline. The Enlightenment
> ultimately gave way to 19th-century Romanticism.[14]

However, the Enlightenment reshaped or crumbled many Christian institutions and traditions as these thinkers asserted their rationality, and deists joined materialists in seeing the universe and history like a giant clock running itself.

Against this complex backdrop, we open section 3 with this chapter on the move to new territories. It's a time of conquistadores conquering people from other religious backgrounds and "converting" them—often through coercion or force. Ironically, two of the world's hotspots for Christianity's growth in the twenty-first century are Latin America and southern Africa—both part of the colonial onslaught centuries earlier. Indeed, the indigenous and resettled peoples of those regions adopted the Bible as their own, and gave rise to their own martyrs in that cause.

MARTYRS DURING COLONIZATION Four types of martyrs surfaced in this global land grab. Most discussions of the definition of martyrdom outline various categories and nuancing. Augustine cautioned not to highlight the painful death of a person, but rather the cause for dying. Pope Benedict XVI noted that martyrs died for both direct and indirect hatred of the faith. One theologian writes, "As is clear in the writings of recent pontiffs, it is critical that martyrdom be an act of innocence standing against power, even at the price of one's death."[15]

The first group of martyrs during the colonization period were like many throughout history—killed by people of other faiths, or by those of none at all.

Second, some martyrs of this period were indigenous people who became sincere Christians and were killed by Christian overlords for renouncing the denominational affiliation of their conversion. This was usually for endorsing a version of Christianity unacceptable to a new wave of European governors and landowners. Pope Francis canonized three children martyred in sixteenth-century Mexico who refused to renounce Catholicism after anti-Catholic rulers came into power. At the ceremony, Pope Francis said: "The robe they wore daily was the love of Jesus, that 'mad' love that loved us to the end and offered his forgiveness and his robe to those who crucified him."[16]

Third, there were Christian servants who died serving others on missions in these new lands, or in unique circumstances. Some fell exhausted in service and others by the sword. This category includes the indefatigable Pedro Claver in Cartagena, Colombia (d. 1654). Some in the first part of this category, dying of exhaustion, are not included on stricter lists of martyrs. However, we include them here under this broader definition of martyrdom, as the spread of Christianity is only understood in the Americas through them.

And the fourth category of martyrs in the colonial period mirror the religious battles in Europe: those European Christians in the colonies who either changed their views while there (sometimes prompted by the church's treatment of local peoples), or originated from a religious tradition not accepted by those in charge of the territories.

The story of Christian beginnings in the Caribbean and the Americas can be "thoroughly bleak. Power-hungry monarchs. Greedy and violent conquistadores. Horrible people doing hellish things in the holy name of Christ."[17] Regardless of the religious sincerity of many of the invaders and the priests they brought, their arrival caused an estimated 25 million deaths among the inhabitants.

[handwritten margin note: Lowest estimate. 8m total inhabitants in Americas in 1492]

[handwritten note: Insane. Source?]

Though the record is both appalling and embarrassing, it shouldn't be surprising. From start to finish the Bible makes clear that our fallen world is marked by evil and darkness and populated by sinners. The New Testament further shows that among those who claim the name "Christian," we will always find immature believers, worldly believers, and, yes, even "make-believers." Not the best advertisements for the gospel! But always, in every generation, we also find a remnant that possesses extraordinary faith—men and women who really do live—and love—like Jesus.[18]

Today we can trace the thriving Latin American church to these faithful saints from its first centuries—priests who bucked the system, or at least the norm, and prioritized the well-being of the indigenous people and those enslaved and brought in bondage.

Francisco de Vitoria

Vitoria was a public intellectual and chair of theology at Spain's top educational institution, the University of Salamanca. The horrifying stories out of Latin America sickened him, and he spent the rest of his life advocating for the people there.

He stunned the West and especially the Catholic world when he rejected the Requerimiento document, arguing that the Pope had no authority over Indian aborigines (or any other unbelievers), especially seizing their possessions if they failed to recognize him.[19] His pioneer work advocating for the humanness (instead of subhuman categorization) of the Indians is a benchmark in the field. He didn't die for his faith per se, but endured relentless criticism for his unpopular views.[20]

Bartolomé de las Casas

Las Casas became to Latin America what the names Washington, Lincoln, Tubman, and Martin Luther King Jr. are in the United States. Chroniclers single him out for praise, such as in this account of the fall of Santiago:

> This city for more than three centuries had been the Spaniards'
> own; round it were centered some of the proudest memories
> of the race. In its history were great dates [events], mighty
> names—Balboa, Cortez, Columbus, Las Casas *the humane, the
> almost saintly* [emphasis added]. From this harbor sailed on their
> memorable expeditions, Cordova, Grijalva, Cortez; at this port
> had touched De Leon, Pizarro, De Soto, and Christopher Estévan,
> in those old days when the New World was new.[21]

Like Vitoria, the name Las Casas is synonymous with humanitarianism. However, he began as a dreaded *encomendero* in Hispaniola and Cuba. An *encomienda* was a farm worked by the indigenous population who had little choice but to stay for their own safety and survival (sometimes from other local tribes). However, they ended up with little freedom and were often worked to death by the owner, the *encomendero*. In 1514 (at age forty), Las Casas became profoundly convicted spiritually about profiting on the backs of these people. He shocked the colonists with his about-face and open defense of them.

After joining a Dominican order and becoming the bishop of Chiapas,

Mexico, he challenged local *encomenderos*, even in his congregation. His opus, *A Brief Account of the Destruction of the Indies*, gives vivid descriptions of the atrocities:

> [The Spanish] snatcht young Babes from the Mothers Breasts, and then dasht out the brains of those innocents against the Rocks; others they cast into Rivers scoffing and jeering them. . . .
>
> The Lords and Persons of Noble Extract were usually expos'd to this kind of Death; they order'd Gridirons to be placed and . supported with wooden Forks, and putting a small Fire under them, these miserable Wretches by degrees and with loud Shreiks and exquisite Torments, at last Expir'd.[22]

Las Casas' exhaustive work on behalf of the Indians (and several trips to Spain), led to the New Laws intended to thwart abuse of Indians. A hallmark of his fight for Native American Indian rights in the New World occurred in Valladolid, Spain (1550). He debated the famous philosopher Juan Ginés Sepúlveda at the request of King Charles V, and prevailed.[23]

Pedro Claver

Claver became the "Mother Teresa" of seventeenth-century Colombia, leaving his native Spain in 1610. He would declare himself "the slave of the slaves forever," and during his forty years of ministry baptized over 300,000 enslaved people, who "called him their master, their protector, their father; never thinking they did enough to express their gratitude."[24] It is perhaps the greatest of tributes that the Roman Church canonized Claver in 1888—the same year African slavery was abolished in Latin America.[25]

> With grim regularity slave vessels came and went, containing in their foul-smelling holds hundreds of kidnapped Africans. Some of these captives—often up to one-third—were already dead by the time the ships arrived. The rest—at best exhausted and emaciated, at worst diseased—often wished they were dead.

Fortunately, the first face seen by most of these terrified Africans was the kindly face of Father Claver. As soon as a ship docked, he (together with his interpreters and helpers) would board, go down into the hold, and begin ministering to the souls in chains. As the slavers unloaded their "human cargo," Claver and company would distribute water, clothing, fruit, and food. They bound wounds, offered brandy, administered medicine, and showed basic dignity. Only after such tangible expressions of love did Claver dare talk of God's love. He believed, "We must speak to them with our hands by giving, before we speak to them with our lips."[26]

Claver wore out his body serving the enslaved and disenfranchised. Like many martyrs, he died in a distant land in a dingy room. And perhaps the biggest of ironies, cared for by an uncaring slave! He allegedly was often found filthy and in horrid condition. Like saints of old, as it became obvious he was about to enter heaven, people wanted relics—anything associated directly with Claver. One church authority took the very crucifix from his hands before he passed. However, a mélange of well-meaning pilgrims would make their way to his room—free and enslaved Africans, priests and civil magistrates, rich and poor.

Antonio de Valdivieso

Though not as heralded as Las Casas for his work among the indigenous population, Valdivieso was martyred for his relentless defense of the Nicaraguan Indians.[27] A common theme in Latin America among martyrdoms is the interruption of the profit stream for the Europeans. Valdivieso was an ordained member of the Order of Preachers, and during Pope Paul III's papacy, Bartolomé de las Casas consecrated him bishop of Nicaragua (1544). As he challenged the unfairness of the *encomienda*, he incurred the wrath of many of those raping the country, including the governor, whose son eventually incited a riot to attack and fatally stab the priest in his house (February 26, 1550).

Antonio Ruiz de Montoya

Montoya defended the Indians, attempting to use *reductions*. These theo-cratic communities (Spanish *Reducciónes*, Portuguese *Reduções*) were the Jesuits' attempt to protect local peoples from enslavement (even forming Indian military units to resist the slave traders). The term "reduction" is from the Latin "to lead back," and reflects the missionaries' belief that the gospel had at one time been revealed to local populations, but they had for-gotten it. Thus, the Jesuits went into the wooded areas of Argentina, Brazil, Colombia, Paraguay, and Uruguay to establish these model communities. Their actions also led to the conquistadores' and European slavers' resent-ment of the Jesuits for stymying their economic interests.[28] Also, the Pope had given much of the territories to Spanish and Portuguese monarchs, and the Jesuits brought Vatican authority too close to their New World interests.

Montoya was "one of the most distinguished pioneers of the original Jesuit mission in Paraguay, and a remarkable linguist."[29] He baptized over 100,000 Indians, and added thirteen reductions to the twenty-six already in place. In one of the more remarkable escapes in history, Montoya and another priest evacuated 15,000 Christian Indians as Brazilian slavers were approaching (using seven hundred rafts and canoes and navigating thick jungles). He risked his life and exhausted his personal energies. Before his death in 1652, he was able to secure special provisions from Philip IV to protect the Indians from the Brazilians.

Miguel Hidalgo y Costilla

Though today Costilla is considered the father of Mexican independence, and his name graces many places and structures throughout the country, his ambition was not fame. Rather it was justice for oppressed and starving natives whom the Europeans had trapped and practically enslaved in their own country.

Mexico was under *Patronato Real* (Royal Patronage), which mandated that the Spanish monarchs (not the Catholic Church) would appoint the bishops. This created quite a gap between bishops and the local priests in touch with the people. Many priests, like Costilla, supported the rebellion and Mexican independence openly opposed by the bishops (who thus had to return to Spain after independence).

Costilla's efforts to help his parishioners were fueled not only by theological and justice claims, but heritage—that is, those born in Mexico of mixed Spanish descent were often at odds with the Iberian-born Spanish who controlled much of the economy.

Many of the Spanish were *creoles*—born in the Americas to European ancestors—who would align with indigenous groups. Most were "patriots" vying for independence, but some remained creole royalists like the *Peninsulares*, Spaniards living in the Americas who were actually born in Spain. They had claimed Spain via the actions of Pope Alexander XVI, who was born in Spain. He signed two decrees in 1493 and the Treaty of Tordesillas in 1494, giving most of South America to Spain. Portugal retained the east coast of Brazil.

On September 16, 1810, Costilla rang the church bell in the town of Dolores as Spanish troops were approaching. He then gave his famous "Cry of Dolores" speech, legendary in Mexico's history.[30] Today the Mexican president will traditionally shout some version of its phrases from the National Palace's balcony on the eve of Independence Day, "Viva México! Viva la independencia! Vivan los héroes!"[31] Costilla began with this small Indian and mestizo parish and amassed tens of thousands to rebel. ("Mestizo" refers in period literature to those of mixed race having indigenous American and European descent. The term is still used in recent Pew Research reports.[32]) They marched under the banner of Our Lady of Guadalupe and took numerous cities along the way to the gates of the capital before the resistance fractured and waned.

On January 17, Costilla lost the battle of Calderón Bridge near Guadalajara and failed in his attempt to retreat to the United States for safety.[33] A Spanish firing squad executed him on July 30, 1811. But his efforts weren't in vain; Mexico would become a republic with its own constitution in 1824, and Costilla's humanitarian efforts represented the noble aspects of Christian service to millions.[34]

The full name of Mexico's second largest airport, Miguel Hidalgo y Costilla Guadalajara International Airport, reveres a martyred Roman Catholic priest, Miguel Hidalgo y Costilla (d. 1811). However, if authorities had used his full name when they opened the facility in 1966, they would have needed much larger signs: *Miguel Gregorio Antonio Francisco Ignacio Hidalgo-Costilla y Gallaga Mandarte Villaseñor Guadalajara International Airport.*

THE MASSACRE OF PRIESTS IN THE CRISTERO REBELLION (1927-1929) We can hardly imagine modern Mexico without thinking of an active and vibrant Christian community—both the long-standing Catholic presence from colonial beginnings and the charismatic explosion among the Protestants. However, beginning in the 1920s, atheist leaders launched a major effort to stamp out Christianity. Church doors were bolted, celibate priests were forced to marry, and common religious practices were banned—largely enforced through the Calles Law, signed into effect in 1926 by and named for president Plutarco Elías Calles.[35]

Before the rebellion (or war) ended, national forces killed at least forty priests under the auspices of keeping the church and state separate. By 1934, less than a decade later, the priesthood in Mexico had shrunk from 4,500 to 334. Those who didn't emigrate lost their licenses to practice or faced harsh fines and punishments for minor infractions, such as wearing priestly attire or vestments.

Two of the priests who helped lead the armed resistance were Aristeo Pedroza and José Reyes Vega.

THE APOSTLES OF MEXICO We jump forward in our narrative four centuries from Bartolomé de las Casas, and three from Pedro Claver to Archbishop Óscar Romero of San Salvador (d. 1980). Any discussion of Latin American Christian history would have to include this important hero. He's a bona fide martyr, "the voice of the voiceless." He wrote:

In less than three years over fifty priests have been attacked, threatened, calumniated. Six are already martyrs—they were murdered. Some have been tortured and others expelled [from the country]. Nuns have also been persecuted.[36]

Assassins gunned him down during Mass at an El Salvador hospital chapel, captured on audio the day following his radio broadcast.[37] He was attempting to soften the violent tactics of El Salvador's military government against the people in maintaining their rule. On his final broadcast he charged:

In the name of God, in the name of this suffering people whose cries rise to Heaven more loudly each day, I implore you, I beg you, I order you in the name of God: Stop the repression![38]

A twelve-year civil war would follow, claiming more than 75,000 Salvadoran lives. Only six days after Romero's assassination, 250,000 Salvadorans attended his funeral on Palm Sunday (1980). The junta attacked, killing dozens and injuring more than two hundred.

In his death, Romero became a symbol of the best of incarnational Christian theology and self-sacrifice. Beloved by oppressed masses everywhere, it was only a matter of time (2015, to be precise) before the Roman Catholic Church declared Romero a martyr and beatified him. Three years later, the first pope ever from Latin America—Pope Francis—wore Romero's bloodstained sash from 1980 in the ceremony that canonized the Salvadoran as a saint.

Ondina and Justo Gonzalez speak of "the two faces of the church in Latin America." One was the "dominant face" that "justified what was being done in the name of evangelism." The other was the face protesting injustice, "particularly against injustice in the name of Christianity" and "voices of prophetic protest that were seldom matched in the British colonies."[39]

This second face of the church—the brave men and women who spoke out against the Europeans' harsh oppression of indigenous peoples and who condemned the exploitation of natural resources—are to be thanked for the nurturing and growth of Christ's Kingdom in Latin America.[40]

Historians liken the martyrdom of Jesús Emilio Jaramillo Monsalve (Bishop Jaramillo) in 1989 to that of Romero in both its national impact and its brazen violence. The National Liberation Army stopped Jaramillo's car in Colombia, abducted him, and then deposited his body in a rural area. Fr. José Muñoz Pareja witnessed the abduction and only left due to Jaramillo's insistence (out of "obedience"). Muñoz found his mentor's body the next day. It was face up in the form of a cross, with two shots to his head from an assault rifle.[41]

In 2017, Pope Francis held a special beatification ceremony in Villavicencio, Colombia, honoring Father Jaramillo and Pedro María Ramírez Ramos (Father Ramírez). They were two of the more "high pro-file" victims among the 220,000 who died during the fifty-two-year war. Pope Francis had raised a question in similar ceremonies: "What does the church need today?" He answered, "Martyrs and witnesses, those everyday saints, those saints of an ordinary life lived with coherence. But it also needs those who have the courage to accept the grace of being witnesses to the end, to the point of death."[42]

During a political upheaval in Colombia in 1948 called "the Violence," a mob dragged Father Ramírez from his church in Armero and hacked him to death with a machete in the town square. Oftentimes the clerics were linked closely with the central church in Rome, the largest landowners in Latin America (and thus, many high clerics tended to be conservative—siding with Rome). Well-meaning, benevolent clergy like Father Ramírez and Bishop Jaramillo were caught in these social and political crosshairs. A contemporary *New York Times* article states that these two priests "remain potent symbols among Catholics of a war that seemed to spare no one, not even clergymen."[43]

DID YOU KNOW? *The Praying Indian Towns*

Missionaries like the heralded English Puritan John Eliot (d. 1690) founded and supported fourteen "praying Indian towns." They planned these communities for indigenous tribes like the Algonquin in the New England area. The hope was to protect them from further oppression and to teach them Christian culture and the structure of Christian society. Eliot gave his missionary life for the conversion and well-being of these tribes and for their education, along with that of Africans brought to the Americas. Among his most famous work is the first printed Bible in British North America, the *Mamusse Wunneetupanatamwe Up-Biblum God*—or more commonly called the Eliot Indian Bible (1663).

ANNE HUTCHINSON (1591-1643) John Winthrop, a founding voice and governor of the Massachusetts Bay Colony, helped bring the martyred Anne Hutchinson legendary status in his popular account *Short Story* (1644).[44] By the nineteenth century, she became an icon for religious liberty, and her statue stands outside the Massachusetts State House. Its inscription ends, "Killed by the Indians / at East Chester New York 1643 / Courageous Exponent / of Civil Liberty / and Religious Toleration."

Some declare her the inspiration for Hester Prynne in Nathaniel Hawthorne's *The Scarlet Letter*. In 1994, Anne Hutchinson was inducted into the National Women's Hall of Fame. She lived an eventful life and took courageous stands for her beliefs, long before women's voices were accepted by the church or by society at large.

Hutchinson was a fiery preacher and challenged the prevailing views of the Puritan clerics. Perhaps her unorthodox views on faith and works may have incurred lesser charges, but she also claimed to hear God's voice directly. Historian Edwin Gaustad observes, "Worse, during her trial, Hutchinson admitted to having heard 'voices,' private revelations beyond the public revelation of the Bible. For Puritans, this was the ultimate presumption to be so arrogant as to claim that God spoke directly to her. She was denounced as an enthusiast—literally, one filled with God, or at least proudly pretending to be."[45]

This prompted the religious leaders of the Massachusetts Bay area to expel her large family. Anne's husband died in Rhode Island, and she then moved to the area of New Netherland that is today the Bronx in New York City. She had befriended the Narragansetts (of the Algonquin tribe in Rhode Island), but died in 1643, killed by men of the Siwanoy tribe who were unfamiliar with her. Mistaking her for one of the despised Dutch (who had massacred some of their tribe), they pretended to befriend Anne. Later they returned, asked Anne to tie up her dogs, and proceeded to scalp her and her children, along with her helpers.[46]

> The Siwanoy warriors stampeded into the tiny settlement above Pelham Bay, prepared to burn down every house. The Siwanoy chief, Wampage, who had sent a warning, expected to find no settlers present. But at one house the men in animal skins encountered several children, young men and women, and a woman past middle age. One Siwanoy indicated that the Hutchinsons should restrain the family's dogs. Without apparent fear, one of the family tied up the dogs. As quickly as possible, the Siwanoy seized and scalped Francis Hutchinson, William Collins, several servants, the two Annes (mother and daughter), and the younger children—William, Katherine, Mary, and Zuriel. As the story was later recounted in Boston, one of the Hutchinsons' daughters, "seeking to escape," was caught "as she was getting over a hedge, and they drew her back again by the hair of the head to the stump of a tree, and there cut off her head with a hatchet."[47]

Not all of Anne Hutchinson's children died during the massacre. Nine-year-old Susanna was out picking blueberries. One account described her hiding in the ancient landmark Split Rock when the Indians found her. Speculation is that her red hair may have saved her, and she lived among the Siwanoy for several years before her relatives were able to barter for her. She joins her mother in the statue outside the Massachusetts State House.

> Less involved observers can regret that this woman of unusual spiritual intelligence did not live longer to promote her distinctive interpretation of the Puritan faith, for it was a reading that would be echoed time again in North America. Throughout its entire history, liberation by God's grace, apprehended through faith,

has been the heart of the Christian message. But an enduring problem, especially for the most ardent Christian communities, has also been the construction of religious institutions and religious regulations that seem to quench the faith they are put in place to embody. As elsewhere, so too in America, the delicate balance between law and gospel defined by the apostle Paul proved difficult to maintain.[48]

Vintage Foxe

Since it is the will of the Almighty that we should suffer for his name, and be persecuted for the sake of his gospel, we patiently submit, and are joyful upon the occasion; though the flesh may rebel against the spirit, and hearken to the council of the old serpent, yet the truths of the gospel shall prevent such advice from being taken, and Christ shall bruise the serpent's head. We are not comfortless to confinement, for we have faith; we fear not affliction, for we have hope; and we forgive our enemies, for we have charity. Be not under apprehensions for us, we are happy in confinement through the promises of God, glory in our bonds, and exult in being thought worthy to suffer for the sake of Christ. We desire not to be released, but to be blessed with fortitude, we ask not liberty, but the power of perseverance; and wish for no change in our condition, but that which places a crown of martyrdom upon our heads.[49]

CANADIAN MARTYRS OF THE SEVENTEENTH CENTURY

Some of the most daring and intrepid of all Christian missionaries have been Jesuit priests of the Roman Catholic Church. Since its founding by St. Ignatius Loyola and St. Francis Xavier in 1534, this religious order of highly trained intellectuals has been sending members to the farthest reaches of the known world. For nearly five hundred years, no distance has been too great, no cultural gap too vast for the Jesuits to traverse in the name of the gospel.

The Jesuits' adventurous spirit and their emphasis on extensive academic training have led them to firsts of one kind or another in many of the world's most forbidding contexts. They have tended to be not only passionate evangelists, but also world-class linguists, translators, and cultural ambassadors. Because of this, countless people around the world, especially from the sixteenth through the eighteenth centuries, had their first access to the Bible, and other Christian texts, through the work of this order.

The first to introduce Western science and astronomy in sixteenth- and seventeenth-century China? The Jesuits.

The first translation of Scripture into a language native to India? The Jesuit Ignacio Arcamone in 1667.

The first to write Christian hymns in the Native American Huron language? Again, a Jesuit missionary—Jean de Brébeuf, who wrote "The Huron Carol," the first Canadian Christmas song:

Oiling His scalp many times, saying, "Hurray!"
"We will give to Him honor to His name."
"Let us oil His scalp many times, show reverence for Him,
As He comes to be compassionate with us."
It is providential that you love us, and think
"I should make them part of My family."

The list could go on.

After its founding, the Society of Jesus (the official name of the Jesuit order) quickly established a reputation as a uniquely swashbuckling arm of Christian evangelism. Ignatius of Loyola was the order's primary founder—a former soldier whose military career ended when his right leg was shattered by a cannonball. The order became known for undertaking expeditions that no other Christian group at that time could, or would.

Many of these expeditions look today, as they must have looked then, essentially like suicide missions from which there was no reasonable hope of returning. The Society of Jesus has made mistakes, often in the direction of its militaristic origins, as we have seen earlier in this text with the Spanish Inquisition. However, it has also blessed the church—and world—with a veritable army of fearless teachers and evangelists whose stories it is an honor to share. In one account after another, they simply poured out their lives, like the blood and water of Jesus' side (see John 19:34), in the hostile climes of the world's still unfolding frontiers.

As striking as any in this category is the group of seventeenth-century Jesuits remembered today simply as the Canadian martyrs, though some prefer North American martyrs, since territories of many of their deaths are now in parts of the United States.[50]

Caught in the Crossfire

In the 1630s and 1640s, while Pedro Claver was becoming the "Mother Teresa" of Colombia and offering himself as "the slave of the slaves forever," his fellow Jesuits were navigating the cold winter waterways along the modern-day border between Canada and the United States. Because Philip II of Spain had banned the French Huguenots (Protestants) from immigrating to the new world—slaughtering 350 Huguenots at Fort Caroline in Jacksonville, Florida—the French curbed such efforts in Florida. This also led to French Catholics dominating the Canadian provinces, or New France.[51]

The Jesuits arrived in the New World at a time of ongoing conflict between local tribes and with all of the baggage of seventeenth-century colonial expansion. The so-called Beaver Wars between the Iroquois confederacy and its rivals defined the socio-political life of the region, and Jesuit attempts to broker peace in these wars ended in failure and, in many cases, the death of these missionaries. Dutch traders had provided muskets to the Mohawks (part of the Iroquois confederacy), which resulted in their dominance over the Huron warriors.

The first to die was René Goupil (1608–1642), a French surgeon who had come to New France from Paris in 1640 to treat the sick and wounded at the Saint-Joseph de Sillery mission, located in modern-day Quebec City.

Most frontier surgeons at that time were so-called "barber-surgeons," all-purpose practitioners with minimal academic training. Goupil's formal training as a physician and surgeon set him apart on the Canadian frontier.

On August 3, 1642, Goupil was traveling in a Huron flotilla of twelve canoes when Iroquois forces captured and tortured the entire group.

Various captives died during these proceedings. After his torture, Goupil made the traditional sign of the cross over an Iroquois child. An Iroquois warrior witnessing this act became enraged by it, perhaps mistaking it for a tribal curse, and struck Goupil in the head with a hatchet.

Incidentally, Goupil is venerated today in the Roman Catholic Church as the patron saint of all anesthetists, in tribute to a life spent relieving physical pain on the frontier. A section of a Fordham University (New York) dormitory, Martyrs Court, is also named after Goupil. The other two sections of Martyrs Court are named after the two Canadian martyrs who followed Goupil in giving their lives four years later, in 1646—Isaac Jogues and Jean de Lalande.

Jogues had accompanied Goupil and survived captivity among the Mohawks—though not without cost. He would become the most famous of these martyrs caught in the crosshairs of the Indian war. "Perhaps no missionary to North America ever had a more adventurous or more torturous experience. Jogues . . . enjoyed ministry success among the Huron Indians north of the Great Lakes. Among their bitter enemies, not so much."[52]

Father Jogues knew well the risks of leaving fortified or protected areas, and indeed was captured near Ft. Orange (modern-day Albany) during one of his excursions to secure needed supplies. Jogues was captured in Goupil's traveling party noted above, and then tortured before and after his friend's murder. The captives had been paraded through Iroquois villages and arrived at their place of judgment, the village of Ossernenon in today's upstate New York, with broken bones and exposed wounds.[53]

During Jogues's months of torture, the Mohawk severed his thumb to keep him from being able to use a musket against them, ate some of his fingers, and pulled fingernails from others.

Jogues managed to escape, but not before becoming conversant in the language of his captors. After receiving kind treatment from the Dutch at New Amsterdam, Jogues returned to France, where he was given a hero's welcome, and where, with papal permission, he was permitted to celebrate mass (another priest had to hold the communion elements for him).

✠ THE NEW BOOK OF CHRISTIAN MARTYRS

In 1646, dismissing his prior experience, Father Jogues returned . . . to northern North America and resolved to reach out to his former captors. Initially, the Mohawks [in Ossernenon] received him, but when hardships came in the form of crop failure and some sort of viral epidemic, the tribe blamed Jogues and his companions.

The missionaries were apprehended, stripped bare, beaten, and slashed with knives. Finally, Jogues was killed with the blow of a tomahawk. When the news of his death reached Quebec, his fellow missionaries celebrated a massive Thanksgiving rather than a requiem Mass for the repose of his soul. The Catholic Church later declared Isaac Jogues and his brothers martyrs and saints.

The story is told that a group of Frenchmen later captured a certain Mohawk, and took him to Three Rivers where he boasted that he had been Jogues' killer. This confession infuriated some members of the Algonquin and Huron tribes there, prompting the Jesuits to take the man into protective custody. After a few weeks in their care, the man asked for Christian baptism, and expressed a desire to take Isaac Jogues' name. The Jesuits complied.[54]

A few days after the baptism, the new convert also became a martyr. Some Algonquin tribe members, seeking revenge, captured the converted Mohawk and executed him. One of the Jesuits allegedly said, "God willing, there are now two Isaac Jogueses in heaven."[55]

Jogues wrote the following to a fellow priest before his final return to the Mohawk village: "My heart tells me that if I am the one to be sent on this mission I shall go but I shall not return. But I would be glad if our Lord wished to complete the sacrifice where He began it. Farewell, dear Father. Pray that God unite me to Himself inseparably."[56]

Jean de Lalande had followed Jogues back into Iroquois territory in 1646 and remained with him to the end of his life. When Jogues was murdered, Lalande attempted to retrieve his body and was himself killed in this effort before both bodies were dumped in a nearby river.

Also, among the North American martyrs were Antoine Daniel (1648),

Jean de Brébeuf (1649), Noël Chabanel (1649), Charles Garnier (1649), and Gabriel Lalemant (1649), who each have their stories of faithfulness in remote places, under extreme duress. The story of Brébeuf can serve as an exemplar of the sacrifice and impact of these martyrs and their collective contribution to the global church.

Jean de Brébeuf died March 16, 1649, with escaped co-captives verifying accounts about his bravery. He also became the patron saint of Canada. He had the distinction of being venerated by his captors for his bravery— for his stoic acceptance of what God had for him, and for his concern more for the other captives, including Gabriel Lalemant. Father Brébeuf endured the ritual and excruciating torture, and additional pain. "Brébeuf endured stoning, slashing with knives, a collar of red-hot tomahawks, a 'baptism' of scalding water, and burning at the stake."[57] However, the Iroquois drank his blood and ate his heart hoping to absorb some of the courage that a divine source (or spirit) had evidently placed upon him.[58]

CHAPTER TWELVE

The Nineteenth Century:
Martyrs in an Age of
Alleged Progress

He was pierced for our transgressions; he was crushed for our iniquities; upon him was the chastisement that brought us peace, and with his wounds we are healed. ISAIAH 53:5

I want to be found in the battle when He comes, and I want to be an instrument in the hands of God in saving souls from death.[1]
"MISS TROYER," APPLYING TO SERVE WITH THE CHINA INLAND MISSION, LATER MARTYRED IN CHINA IN 1900

Lord, send me anywhere, only go with me. Lay any burden on me, only sustain me. Sever any ties save the tie that binds me to Thy heart.[2] **DAVID LIVINGSTONE, MISSIONARY TO AFRICA**

The surge of martyrdoms in the nineteenth and twentieth centuries generated a historical disconnect. While major changes were taking place during a period dubbed the Age of Progress (1789–1914), especially in the West, massive inhumane actions persisted, both in Western territories and in other parts while Westerners remained silent, impotent, or in some cases, complicit.

The killings in pogroms belie the claims of progress.

In history's long timeline, we find certain eras dominated by prominent developments. These ages receive nicknames, such as Renaissance and Reformation. The same is true of the nineteenth century: the Age of Progress and the Industrial Age, both of which spanned from the late eighteenth century through the early twentieth century.

This time frame saw the advancement of math, engineering, business, and economics on the one side and humanities and spiritual needs on the other. "The most significant development in modern history occurred not in the political but in the economic realm. . . . Because of industrialization, hardly any corner of the globe was left untouched by Western economic and political power."[3]

Consequently, the massive shifts to industrialized cities begat radical responses such as the fomenting of communism and socialism, and conversely Christian humanitarianism. The former would eventually exploit and murder hordes of the very people they claimed to help. The latter would launch evangelical humanitarian networks such as the Salvation Army and the YMCA, along with robust missionary groups around notables like Adoniram Judson, William Carey, Samuel Crowther, and Hudson Taylor. Suffice it to say, this was a busy century.

In 1859, smack-dab in the middle of this era, Charles Dickens penned the following words—among the most famous opening lines of any literary work. They begin his classic *A Tale of Two Cities*, staged within the tumultuous times of the French Revolution and the Reign of Terror, 1789 to ca. 1793, the beginning of our era under discussion:

> It was the best of times, it was the worst of times, it was the age of wisdom, it was the age of foolishness, it was the epoch of belief, it was the epoch of incredulity, it was the season of Light, it was the season of Darkness, it was the spring of hope, it was the winter of despair, we had everything before us, we had nothing before us, we were all going direct to Heaven, we were all going direct the

other way—in short, the period was so far like the present period, that some of its noisiest authorities insisted on its being received, for good or for evil, in the superlative degree of comparison only.[4]

The world Dickens describes was just across the English Channel from his desk, a few decades earlier. Is it little wonder that the "justified" execution of thousands in a self-proclaimed civilized society is the precursor of a century steeped in martyrdoms? Maximilien Robespierre, shifting French religion temporarily to his new Cult of the Supreme Being, also espoused his operational justification of Jean-Jacques Rousseau's "general will" (in *The Social Contract*) with these chilling words:

> If virtue be the spring of a popular government in times of peace, the spring of that government during a revolution is virtue combined with terror: virtue, without which terror is destructive; terror, without which virtue is impotent. Terror is only justice prompt, severe and inflexible; it is then an emanation of virtue; it is less a distinct principle than a natural consequence of the general principle of democracy, applied to the most pressing wants of the country.[5]

The form of "virtuous" progress Robespierre espoused brought a sudden end to his ability to do so. On the one hand, he was a champion of abolishing slavery in the French colonies, and of ending the de-Christianization of France and the Cult of Reason (in which martyrs of the Revolution replaced Christian martyrs). On the other hand, his notion of terror and an ambiguous Cult of the Supreme Being seemed to bring hands to the guillotine ropes. Parisians beheaded him and ninety of his companions in 1794.

Progress is in the eye of the beholder, and countless eyes (at least for chroniclers) were forced early to an eternal perspective. While often "progress" is inextricably linked to industrial advances, much has been written to challenge this label.[6] "The Age of Progress," a song of 1860, includes a final stanza that gives a glimpse of society's blissful outlook.

The age of priceless knowledge, –
The scholar's jubilee!
The land all dotted over
With institutions free.
Our public schools! O, hail them!
They offer treasures cheap:
The boys and girls are scaling (hailing),
Science's rugged steep.[7]

The song's penultimate stanza reflects on the snapped "cable of the deep," and notes "But we will mend it. We have no time to weep." The confidence. The joy. The total unawareness or eclipsing of countless martyrs dying in several countries. The entire nineteenth century, the heart of both the Age of Progress and the Industrial Age, give us plenty of reason to weep.

The main or first Industrial Revolution (1760–1840) shifted England to the forefront of world power. As economic engines changed and social pressures mounted, the British Parliament outlawed the slave trade in 1807. Obviously, it was a long overdue but positive step. However, another generation of people remained displaced, stolen, or worked to death until 1833 when Parliament freed all slaves throughout the Empire.

For some missionaries trying to address these rapacious actions, like John Smith, much like in the days of the encomienda in Latin America, it was too late. His missionary work in British Guiana (Guyana) overlapped closely with this delay between outlawing slave trade and freeing the slaves.

The London Missionary Society sent Smith to this Caribbean island in 1817, ten years after the law to end the slave trade was enacted. There, plantation owners forbade him to teach their slaves how to read. However, it became a natural (and pastoral) priority for him to help his church leaders read the books he had distributed from his mission. As they began to understand the ramifications of the 1807 British mandate, they launched an unsuccessful armed rebellion. In turn, Smith received a mock trial by a military tribunal, which sentenced him to hang for alleged complicity. British religious leaders were in an uproar and frenzy trying to save him, but he died of pneumonia, a lonely martyr's death in a foreign jail. It was 1824, and his parishioners would have to weather another decade of the conditions against which he had struggled.[8]

For others, like David Livingstone, the persistence of the slave trade by other countries proved his main obstacle to evangelism of African communities and the planting of colonies. He preached "Christianity and commerce," legal, productive, and ethical trade.[9]

His successors from the London Missionary Society, especially John Mackenzie, carried on this fight against racism. Mackenzie's aggressive work on behalf of justice in southern Africa reflects the complexities of the Industrial Age. He especially attacked the racism of the Boers, farmers of Dutch, German, or Huguenot descent—today's Afrikaners. Though many of his views and "humanitarian policy" were not followed, his efforts helped to form the Bechuanaland Protectorate (1885), the country known today as Botswana. "Mackenzie's importance does not lie so much in what he did as in what he said [humanitarian scheme]." Because the British did not follow most of his proposals, "his prophesies of doom came true with dramatic suddenness."[10]

While engines turned and machines transformed farms and towns, Christian humanitarians set up schools and hospitals to provide needed care. Social changes like biblical teachings and literacy had far-reaching ramifications. Sociologist Robert Woodberry observed, "Areas where Protestant missionaries had a significant presence in the past are on average more economically developed today, with comparatively better health, lower infant mortality, lower corruption, greater literacy, higher educational attainment (especially for women), and more robust membership in nongovernmental associations."[11]

John Mackenzie, among a host of other missionaries, fought for both the souls of the indigenous peoples and their betterment while still on earth.[12] Although he escaped martyrdom, the context of his missionary activity reveals the danger in many countries throughout this century. In his book *Austral Africa*, Mackenzie argues that the acts of aggression to control new lands weren't some new notion of independence for those of European descent (the Boers) but "a desire common to both races, to obtain cheaper and better land, and to secure an easier and pleasanter life."[13] He also writes in this same discussion:

> The brute-force frontier-man, calling the black his natural enemy, would know only the advance of conquest. He would seize all the land of the natives, disqualify them from owning an acre of it, and only allow them to remain on it as vassals, in practical servitude on account of their colour. This doctrine is hateful to an English-speaking man, and indeed to every man of European education.[14]

While the economies and urban centers were transformed, many Christians were still dying for their faith. Ongoing persecutions were not factors in measuring "progress." After all, many of these martyrdoms took place in colonized lands or remote territories. These were regions Western mission boards labelled "uncivilized," like the territories of modern Guyana, Vietnam, Indonesia, many African countries, and others. Indigenous peoples speared some Christians. Butchered some. And ate others. Yet heroic missionaries still went forth, knowing the risks.

The Voice of the Martyrs is a leading resource for learning about those who have endured these persecutions and for supporting efforts to help this generation's oppressed Christians. Its stated mission: "Serving persecuted Christians through practical and spiritual assistance and leading other members of the body of Christ into fellowship with them."[15] One of the ministry's resources is an updated version of *Foxe's Book of Martyrs*. Though different in scope and purpose from this present book, its section on "Persecution during the Industrial Revolution: 1790–1902" highlights many of the same martyrs. It also summarizes well this current discussion:

> The Industrial Revolution [Age] redirected Western religious aspirations from world evangelism to wealth, from sacrifice to a regime of efficiency, and from geographic churches to widespread acceptance of the notion that people must live and work together with different faiths in order to reap the benefits of progress and products promised by new machines.[16]

In the previous chapter we saw major religious wars in the West, while Catholics and Protestants were flooding the "New World" with missionaries and military troops. In this chapter we find the West in an economic war and societal transformations as missionaries are still going to the ends of the earth.

Historian Ronald Wells calls this era "a test of a worldview," and prefers to define it as "economic modernization." He writes in his *History through the Eyes of Faith*: "In sum, in seeing the transition from traditional society to modern society we see a process of development from agricultural to industrial, from simple to complex, from rural to urban, from local to national and international."[17]

The major philosophies of economic systems accept at their core the Enlightenment worldview with its emphases on "science, rationality, natural law, and—above all—progress." Wells adds, "Most of us sense—almost more than we know—that the idea of progress is more rhetoric than reality except in simplistically material terms. . . . If the world is getting better every day it escapes our notice as we endure political and economic instability, terror, and famine."[18]

As the nineteenth century unfolded, there were indeed signs of moral progress, a veneer of Enlightened success. Russian serfs, British Empire slaves, and those in major slave economies like the United States and Brazil finally gained freedom. Though international conflicts played out short term, there were no world wars or global conflicts between 1815 and 1914.

However, a "secular religion" of sorts undergirded the Industrial Age with its Enlightenment precepts. According to Wells, this newly minted secular religion "intends to supplant the dominant religion in the West, Christianity," adding,

> It is sometimes said, especially in North America, that Christians must put away pious theories and live in the "real" world. But, what passes for the "real" world must be called by his actual name—a fallen world. The way that things have worked out in so-called reality is not the way the Lord of lords intended them to work out.[19]

So we find radical missionaries giving their lives for their ardent belief in the gospel, while their home nations operate on materialistic principles that are "*inherently* unacceptable" to Christianity. These are economic systems based on Enlightenment ideology, "in which the Christian can find no legitimate place."[20]

The Industrial Age indeed saw nations change the way they did business, and the way those performing repetitive production tasks interacted with the community and the church. But missionaries were still about the Lord's business, and still risking their lives to share the gospel message. For them, that was worthwhile progress.

Perhaps the nineteenth century's main lesson for us is the need for action on behalf of the persecuted. To support ministries like Open Door to help address pressing needs before it is too late for our suffering brothers and sisters. To remind people while they sing songs about "giant progress" that giant persecutions are taking place. We will end this introduction with reminders from John Smith's trials—one while he was languishing in a sordid cell in Guyana, where he died in 1824, and the other back in London to clear his good name. Even with the robust London Missionary Society and some prominent voices trying to rescue him, he died in a remote part of the world while elsewhere progress was allegedly moving forward.

William Wilberforce, the noted abolitionist, spoke in Smith's defense to clear the name of this martyr who died incarcerated, killed four months prior not by the indigenous people—but his own, on British soil. This is indicative of a century cast as one of progress, while educated people couldn't or didn't stop the persecution of Christians. The forceful Wilberforce argued:

> Let us thereby manifest our determination to shield the
> meritorious, but unprotected, Missionary [John Smith], from
> the malice of his prejudiced oppressors, however bigoted and
> powerful. Let us shew the sense we entertain of the value of such
> services, and prove, that, whatever may be the principles and
> feelings which habitual familiarity with the administration of a
> system of slavery may produce in the colonies, we in this House,
> at least, have the disposition, and judgment, and feelings, which

justice and humanity, and the spirit of the British constitution, ensure from the Members of the House of Commons.[21]

While not everyone can go to foreign countries to help minister to those in need and to share the gospel, countless have done so and continue to. We find in Wilberforce's efforts an indictment of letting distance filter and often thwart principles. As we turn more directly to stories of nineteenth-century Christians who exhausted their energies on fulfilling the Great Commission, we are prodded by that question, "What would Jesus do?" Several years ago this was associated with trending T-shirts and wristbands. However, the question first came into popularity at the end of the complex and important nineteenth century through one of the all-time bestselling books, *In His Steps: What Would Jesus Do?*

The novel, based on the fictitious weekly stories delivered by Congregational minister Charles Monroe Sheldon, continues to prompt millions to think through their Christian duties. The story begins with a pastor in Raymond (a railway town, indicative of the Industrial Age) brushing off a jobless man's plea for help. A couple of days later, on Sunday morning, the man walks onto the pastor's church platform and shares his situation. Not having received any needed help from the congregation, he then collapses and dies. The pastor is deeply moved, clearly regretting his uncaring response to the man's need. The next week, the pastor addresses the congregation: "Let us pledge not to do anything without first asking, 'What would Jesus do?'"[22]

As we continue our study of martyrs, now into the modern era, Sheldon's question is *a priori*. He gives us the same guiding principle on the minds of those hearing the machete's path to their necks, or seeing the spear approaching or the rifles raised—we must walk "in His steps."

THREE MARTYRS FROM THE NINETEENTH CENTURY The prolific English author Elizabeth Rundle Charles penned the account of *Three Martyrs of the Nineteenth Century: Studies from the Lives of Livingstone, Gordon, and Patteson.*[23] The very title proclaims the fame of these men, only using surnames. In the case of General Charles George Gordon, this is especially noticeable as other martyrs with the same last name died horrific deaths, one also named George (the others are Ellen, his wife, and James, their son—remarkable testimonies also included below).

David Livingstone in Zambia

David Livingstone died on the mission field in northern Zambia, where his African servants found him as if kneeling in prayer at his bedside. His body was sent 1,500 miles back to a hero's celebration in London, but first his heart was removed and buried "beneath a mupundu tree in the middle of Zambia. In 1899, locals believed the tree was diseased, cut it down, and shipped back to London a section of the trunk that had been engraved with Livingstone's name."[24] In Zambia, Livingstone's legacy lives on, or as it's been said, "Livingstone's heart has taken root."[25]

Livingstone has been described as brilliant but a "frail, temperamental human being with serious personality flaws."[26] Regardless of such perceptions and despite any shortcomings, he became the most famous missionary to Africa.

Many debate whether he should be listed as an explorer rather than a missionary—since the former preoccupied him and as to the latter, he only records one convert (Sechele, chief of the Bakwain, who later reverted back to paganism). Nor did Livingstone establish lasting Christian institutions. "Yet it was his extraordinary discoveries (Lake Ngami, Victoria Falls) and his extraordinary courage (some would say recklessness) that left an indelible impression on the British public."[27]

Though Livingstone was partially driven by a desire to create a British colony, his primary ambition was to expose the slave trade and cut it off at the source. The strongest weapon in this task, he believed, was Christian commercial civilization: "He hoped to replace the 'inefficient' slave economy with a capitalist economy: buying and selling goods instead of people."[28] He had pressed farther into Africa than any European, with the noble goal of finding waterways that would enable legitimate commercial trade to counter the slave trade. Livingstone wrote, "If Christian missionaries and Christian merchants can remain throughout the year in the interior of the continent, the slave trader will be driven out of the market."[29] His oldest son, Robert, found his own way to fight against the slave trade like his father. He went to America and fought for the North in the Civil War, where he died in 1864.

David Livingstone came across as the swashbuckling hero, the type legends are made of—but the stories of his exploits are true. He has been described as "Mother Teresa, Neil Armstrong, and Abraham Lincoln rolled into one."[30]

Various reports of David Livingstone's adventures and "success" as a missionary circulated back home. He had already been mauled by a lion and survived an accident—limiting use of his left arm. He returned December 9, 1856, as a national hero, lectured at Cambridge, and published works that inspired generations. However, two years later, against the advice of friends, he returned to the dangerous African adventures. He would suffer further loss as his wife died in Shupanga on the Zambezi. (Decades later the republic of Malawi was formed from the fruits of their early work there.) He considered the great Zambezi River "God's Highway" for missionaries and Christian merchants to the interior. Livingstone returned to England for a couple of years before his major departure in 1866.

His death seven years later was not at the end of a spear, but from sickness. He almost died earlier when a deserter left his camp and stole his medicine box. The reach of Livingstone's influence is hard to quantify.

In his 30 years of travel and Christian missionary work in southern, central, and eastern Africa—often in places where no European had previously ventured—Livingstone may well have influenced Western attitudes toward Africa more than any other individual before him. His discoveries—geographic, technical, medical, and social—provided a complex body of knowledge that is still being explored. In spite of his paternalism and Victorian prejudices, Livingstone believed wholeheartedly in the African's ability to advance into the modern world. He was, in this sense, a forerunner not only of European imperialism in Africa but also of African nationalism.[31]

Livingstone is indeed a legend—one who died trying to open all of Africa to the gospel. His life efforts to establish God's Highway led him to his straight and narrow road to heaven—but one with a lot of adventure along the way.

During the present cancel-culture era, efforts are in place to efface most colonialists. And there is indeed division in the West over Livingstone. But in many parts of Africa, the history books and native historians seem to paint him a different hue than other colonialists. His statue still watches over Zambia's capital, and his name graces institutions, media outlets, and cities. Likewise, his worldview seems to underpin that of Zambia, whose constitutional preamble states, "We, the people . . . declare the Republic a Christian Nation while upholding a person's right to freedom of conscience, belief or religion."[32] At Victoria Falls, "a massive statue of David Livingstone continues to watch over Zambia. He actually faces the country while standing in Zimbabwe."[33] At the statue's feet are the words "Missionary. Explorer. Liberator."[34]

DID YOU KNOW? *Dr. Livingstone, I Presume?*

Late in his missionary service, some of David Livingstone's adversaries reported him dead—and indeed he was out of touch with the West and his mission board for two years. Europe grew curious. A reporter from the *New York Herald* searched for and found him, then allegedly greeted Livingstone with the now famous words, "Dr. Livingstone, I presume?" The journalist and world adventurer, Henry Morton Stanley, made the missionary "immortal."[35] "Stanley stayed with Livingstone for five months and then went off to England to write his bestseller, *How I Found Livingstone*. Livingstone, in the meantime, got lost again—in a swamp literally up to his neck. Within a year and a half, he died in a mud hut, kneeling beside his cot in prayer [May 1873]."[36] After its long journey home and a twenty-one-gun salute, his body was buried at Westminster Abbey. His gravestone reads: "Brought by faithful hands over land and sea, here rests David Livingstone, missionary, traveller, philanthropist. For thirty years his life was spent in an unwearied effort to evangelize the native races, to explore the undiscovered secrets, to abolish the desolating slave trade."[37] Years later, Livingstone's tombstone epithet would inspire a depressed Cameron Scott, about to give up, to return and found the Africa Inland Mission.

Charles George Gordon in Sudan

General Gordon was a larger-than-life leader. Hordes of Africans would follow him through the streets out of admiration. Mothers sought him out to touch ill children, hoping for a miracle. Enemies on the battlefield feared him—especially after his exploits in Asia against overwhelming odds that earned him the moniker "Chinese Gordon."

Whereas Livingstone, whether correctly or not, was described as "frail" and "unbalanced," no such descriptions were cast Gordon's way—at least with any hint of accuracy. Perhaps "gentle," "sacrificial," and "gentlemanly" would be fitting. What the two intrepid men did have in common was a Christian core and an overriding life purpose, a resolute determination. And exhausting themselves on foreign soil for Christ.

In their own ways, they both died miserable deaths far from home.

In August he [General Gordon] had written—"there is one bond of union between us and our troops; they know that if the town is taken they will be sold as slaves. And we must deny our Lord if we would save our lives."

Natives who escaped describe him as having been killed in coming out of his house to rally his faithful troops, who were taken by surprise. They were cut down to a man. For hours the town was given up to a merciless massacre.

A later account speaks of him having been called on to become a Mussulman [Muslim] or die, and so literally having the choice of dying as a martyr for the faith of Christ given to him and accepted.

Yet such literal details matter little. As a martyr for Christ and for justice and mercy he lived, and lived on to that last act of his life which we call dying.[38]

Gordon had rejected orders to return to Britain, remaining out of commitment to the people whom he had served. He also felt abandoned by the country he had dedicated his life to protect—as they delayed sending reinforcements. He held the city of Khartoum for a year against larger forces. The Mahdists killed him on January 26, 1885, just two days before the arrival of liberating forces.

The accounts of his final moments vary, including "being shot while attempting to run for safety; or, the most sensational of them all, Gordon being decapitated while still alive. The most prevalent story of the time was that of Gordon being speared. It is also the description referenced in most biographies and in the official account provided in the comprehensive history of the war."[39]

Gordon's service was indeed to God and country, and in God was his hope to protect the lives of the people he had served, many of whom had become Christians. Some historians have preoccupied themselves with his sexuality, making much of his decision never to marry, his efforts for the well-being of a group of boys, and his demeanor in various situations. Whether revisionism is correct or not, it's clear that he was a Christian serving his Lord, and at times feeling alone and abandoned apart from God. He wrote on October 6, 1878, about our created state of being children of God but in earthen vessels:

> You cannot evade it: we are each composed of two beings—one
> of which we see, which is temporal, which will fulfil certain works
> in the world; and one unseen, eternal, and which is always in
> conformity with God. One is sometimes uppermost, sometimes
> subdued, but rules in the long run, for it is eternal, while the
> other is temporal.[40]

✛ Historic Sources

The death of General Charles George Gordon shocked and saddened the world. The poet laureate Tennyson called him "the great simple soldier," and his relationship and earlier conversations with General Gordon had led to the posthumous establishment of Gordon's dream (named in his

honor), the Gordon Boys' Home. The princesses of Great Britain and Ireland, the Peeresses of the Realm, and the wives of bishops and members
of the House of Commons presented Gordon's family members with a
forty-five-page volume of tributes. Gordon's service had reached all levels
of citizens, as "forty of those pages were filled with signature cards from
some of the most well-known women in Britain, ranging from the Princess
of Wales, who was the first signature, to Florence Nightingale, the last."[41]
Space here is limited for the tribute for Gordon, and we include here only
two contemporary glimpses of the widespread admiration for his service
as a leader and as a person.

All Christendom turned its eyes to that lonely Englishman ready to ransom the
lives of his black people by his own blood, and comprehend that the story of the
Divine Founder had a new illustration.[42] *Daily Telegraph*

General Gordon died as he had lived, true to his trust and faithful to the end.
Nor will any one who can get out of his eyes the dust of the present say that
he has died in vain. His immediate effort has been foiled, and his purpose has
failed, and the city he strove for has fallen; but it is still true that "the grandest
heritage a hero can leave his race is to have been a hero." His memory, the
memory of a soldier whose life was willingly laid down for the people he went
to save, and whose strength through life was his strong trust in God, may yet be
a source of inspiration to the generations unborn.[43] *Tablet*

As with David Livingstone's death, General Gordon's may not fit
some definitions of martyrdom. He certainly was defending the lives of
many Christians when the Muslims killed him. Moreover, his religious
views were very clear and documented. Stephanie Laffer chronicles well
both the events of his death, and this discussion of his martyrdom. She
summarizes:

These interpretations helped shape the so-called myth of Gordon. One popular
view on Gordon was to portray him as a Christian martyr, a view aided by
the lack of a body. Those who supported Gordon as a Christian martyr took
their evidence from his life, especially his time spent at Gravesend and the
beliefs he held, comparing the struggles in Gordon's life to that of another
martyr, Jesus Christ. These comparisons were strengthened with Gordon's
death at the hands of a Muslim enemy. Beyond his portrayal as a Christian

martyr, he was also remembered as a second type of martyr: an imperial martyr, whose death served his country. This concept of martyrdom was compounded by the public's belief that his death could have been avoided. This argument places the blame and responsibility for Gordon's martyrdom on the Prime Minister and his Cabinet, making Gordon a martyr to politics, rather than to religion.[44]

John Coleridge Patteson in the Solomon Islands

Bishop John Coleridge Patteson is the third of Charles's nineteenth-century martyrs. With at least fifteen biographies, stained-glass windows, churches, a host of articles, and various other tributes—we have plenty of reminders of his self-sacrifice and legendary status.[45]

Patteson's ministry colleagues found him dead in 1871, floating at sea with a palm branch in his hand. When the indigenous people of the Solomon Islands killed him, he was only forty-four years old. He had learned over twenty of the greater South Sea Islands' approximately two thousand languages.[46]

He packed a lot into his brief life—another one cut short because of the slave trade. While it's not certain why the islanders killed him, it appears they mistook him for a slaver. (Slavers would sometimes impersonate missionaries to deceive the islanders, or say that Patteson asked them to visit.)

On September 20, 1871, he traveled to Nukapu on the far east of the Solomon Islands. He knew the risks but had expressed no fear about journeying to visit these most ferocious of the tribes. He left alone for shore in a canoe belonging to chiefs he knew, but others of his team awaiting offshore were attacked. And about forty-five minutes later, the bishop drifted back toward the main vessel, butchered. Slavers had recently abducted five of the Nupaku men, and Patteson had five hatchet wounds in his chest—which seems much more than a coincidence. Some of his colleagues died shortly after from the infection from arrow wounds. A firsthand account is rather vivid, picked up here as his canoe (with a bundle in it) was brought to the main boat:

On removing the matting, we found the right side of the skull completely shattered. The top of the head was cloven with some sharp weapon, and there were numerous arrow-wounds about the body. Beside all this havoc and ruin, the sweet face still smiled, the eyes closed, as if the patient martyr had had time to breathe a prayer for these his murderers. There was no sign of agony or terror. Peace reigned supreme in that sweet smile, which will live in our remembrance as the last silent blessing of our revered Bishop and our beloved friend. We buried him next day at sea.[47]

As inspirational as his courage was, his journey through the trail of martyrs in Oxford was almost as remarkable.

He graduated from Balliol College in Oxford in 1849. This college is adjacent to the very spot where authorities during Queen Mary's reign burned the three Christian martyrs in 1555/6. In fact, there is a cross in paving stones marking the bonfire spot, just outside of Balliol's gate through which he would have passed every day.

The huge Martyrs' Memorial greets visitors entering city center from that side, next to Balliol and intersecting Broad Street, and a short jog from Cornmarket Street. Furthermore, there allegedly are burn marks on the college's gate from the martyrs' pyre.

You likely see the picture. A young Patteson was in the presence of martyrs' memories. Every day he would walk over or next to the cross in Broad Street. And most days he couldn't avoid the prominent memorial to the three local martyrs.

While reflecting on his proficiency for languages and his training for the mission field, he often talked about "one thing helping another," like similar languages leading to an easier understanding of the next. Charles recounts this playing out in his "one continuous life" with overlapping influences:

Most interesting is to trace, as far as outside human eyes can trace, those deep inward workings, the gradual emerging of introspective struggles into unconscious love; the growth of the strenuous striving to be humble into the humility which forgets itself through looking up in adoration and around in ceaseless service.

Within, from his baptism and early home training to his martyrdom, as without, from St. Alban, the first British martyr, to John Patteson, it is all one continuous life.[48]

Patteson heard Bishop Selwyn (from New Zealand) lecture at Oxford in 1852. The bishop was calling for South Sea missionaries, for which Patteson's heart had long been primed. (One key account recalls in detail a sermon from the same bishop when Patteson was only fourteen, and it is one Patteson recalls often.) His third interaction with the bishop was in August 1854, and this time he accepted the call. A witness of his sending-off party said it was reminiscent of a funeral—and his father was resolved that it would be. The two never saw one another again after Patteson's departure. His father had said to Bishop Selwyn, "Mind, I give him wholly, not with any thought of seeing him again. I will not have him thinking he must come home again to see me."[49]

Nineteen years later, following the "one continuous life" motif, the same Bishop Selwyn would go and reconcile the Nukapu islanders to Patteson's memory, as their friend.

DID YOU KNOW? *Diversity and Inclusion*

Bishop Patteson clung to the Bible of his youth, and even had it at his ordination. It was his guide to life, and included guidelines on how to treat all people. Long before whole college departments and curricula were established, he had figured out that appearance and "foreign" culture can never make a person unequal or somehow less of a human being. The following is a passage from Charles's *Three Martyrs* book, which was written just a few years after his martyrdom: "'Savages' he would never call them. . . . The 'wild fellow' . . . is probably intelligent, respectable, and not insensible to the advantage of hearing about religion. It only wants a little practice to overcome one's English feelings about dress, civilization, etc., and that will soon come."[50]

THÉOPHANE VÉNARD IN VIETNAM For many of us reading this book from the comfort of our own homes, a running theme of these pages is horror and tragedy that we cannot imagine enduring ourselves. The courage and resilience of the martyrs can look almost otherworldly—and indeed, in one sense we believe that it is.

Even by these standards, Théophane Vénard's composure in the days before his execution is striking. It was said of the Roman Catholic priest in his dark and dirty cell, "Though in chains, he is as gay as a little bird."[51] During much of his four months in captivity, his captors often kept him in a small, narrow cage, though popular support for him eventually garnered him a bit larger one with a mosquito net.

Before Vénard's teen years, the story of Father Cornay's martyrdom in Vietnam had inspired him to go there and serve, and likely be martyred. His life unfolded to that end. His father was convinced his oldest son would indeed be martyred. During their send-off meal, his father said, "My dear son, receive this blessing from your father, who is sacrificing you to the Lord. Be blessed forever in the name of the Father, and of the Son, and of the Holy Spirit."[52]

Vénard had left seminary in Paris on September 19, 1852, for missions in Hong Kong and a short time later traveled to northern Vietnam, where he would spend the rest of his life. In late 1860 he was arrested and sentenced to death for defying the national ban on Christian evangelism, which had been instituted by the Emperor Minh Menh. A Vietnamese website for martyrs summarizes his journey:

> Shortly after Father Vénard's arrival a new royal edict was issued against Christians, and bishops and priests were obliged to seek refuge in caves, dense woods, and elsewhere. Father Vénard continued to exercise his ministry at night, and, more boldly, in broad day. On 30 November, 1860, he was betrayed and captured. Tried before a mandarin, he refused to apostatize and was sentenced to be beheaded.[53]

When his executioner attempted to barter for his clothing in exchange for a quick and easy death, he replied simply, "The longer it lasts the better it will be." We can only assume his frustrated executioner took him at his word. One account notes that as the brutish, inebriated man swung his axe, Vénard sang "The Magnificat" (song of Mary, usually followed by "Gloria Patri").[54] They also executed thirty-three of his converts.

DID YOU KNOW? *Mary's Song of Praise*

History tell us that Théophane Vénard sang "The Magnificat" en route to his beheading, or at the event itself. The lyrics are taken from Luke 1:46-55 (see below). This song is usually followed in Roman Catholic liturgy by "Gloria Patri" ("Gloria to the Father" or "Glory Be"). The Roman Rite version is given below Mary's song. In the opening lines of Mary's song is the clear focus on who Jesus is, and the lasting honor of being associated as one who loved him—"from now on all generations will call me blessed." For Théophane Vénard, though considered frail and sickly in his youth, there certainly was no faltering in his faith or the subject of his gaze.

THE MAGNIFICAT

And Mary said,
"My soul magnifies the Lord,
    and my spirit rejoices in God my Savior,
for he has looked on the humble estate of his servant.
    For behold, from now on all generations will call me blessed;
for he who is mighty has done great things for me,
    and holy is his name.
And his mercy is for those who fear him
    from generation to generation.
He has shown strength with his arm;
    he has scattered the proud in the thoughts of their hearts;
he has brought down the mighty from their thrones
    and exalted those of humble estate;

he has filled the hungry with good things,
   and the rich he has sent away empty.
He has helped his servant Israel,
   in remembrance of his mercy,
as he spoke to our fathers,
   to Abraham and to his offspring forever."

GLORIA PATRI

Gloria Patri, et Filio, et Spiritui Sancto,
Sicut erat in principio, et nunc, et semper, et in saecula saeculorum.
   Amen.

Glory to the Father, and to the Son, and to the Holy Spirit,
As it was in the beginning, and now, and ever shall be, world without
   end. Amen.

VANUATU: MARTYRS AT THE ENDS OF THE EARTH One of
the more remote destinations for Christian missionaries in the nineteenth
century was the Vanuatu archipelago, just over 1,000 miles east of northern
Australia. However, this island chain's prized natural resources had connected it to the rest of the world. As with colonialism in the New World
and the Opium Wars in China, missionaries were caught in the crosshairs
of aggressive and inhumane commercial tactics.

The discovery of sandalwood on the fourth largest island in this archipelago, Erromango, attracted scores of European traders in the 1830s
and 40s, eager to exploit the island's resources. This is the world's second
most expensive wood, prized for its medicinal and aromatic oil—popular
for centuries in India and China, and even for embalming the dead in
ancient Egypt.[55]

When these sandalwood traders deliberately exposed the natives to
measles, the Erromangan natives blamed the missionaries who had followed these traders to the region.[56] After all, the missionaries lived among
them. The strange religious rituals of these outsiders could easily be mistaken for tribal curses.

The following are a few representatives of the many missionaries who served and died in these remote islands.

John Williams and James Harris

Although countless martyrs suffered innumerable types of persecutions and martyrdoms, among the worst is that horrific and dreaded fate of being eaten by cannibals. That was the plight of legendary missionary John Williams in 1839, along with his partner, James Harris. They had the misfortune of arriving a couple of days after foreign sandalwood traders on Erromango had killed two of their tribe members. The locals clubbed Harris to death, and after clubbing Williams filled him with arrows while he tried running into the sea.

> The good missionary [Williams] . . . was cruelly murdered
> and eaten by the savages of one of the South Sea Islands [i.e.,
> indigenous people]. When the news of his dreadful death reached
> our country and Great Britain, it filled the hearts of Christians
> with bitter sorrow, for he was one of the best and most useful
> missionaries ever sent to the heathen.[57]

Williams's life seemed destined for missionary legend from the start. He was born in England in 1796, the same year the London Missionary Society sent its maiden voyage of missionaries to the South Sea Islands. Thirty-nine missionaries traveled on their ship, *Duff*, to Tahiti, Tonga, and the Marquesas Islands.

At age twenty, Williams and his new bride, Mary, headed for Oceania. They soon sold their schooner, *Endeavor*, to pay their bills. However, his teenage years as an ironmonger and his acuity for building helped him to build his own ship, *Messenger of Peace*, so he could hop around the islands sharing the gospel. This was against the wishes of his senders—the London Missionary Society. He allegedly managed to visit every island within two thousand miles of Tahiti and earned the title "Apostle of the South Seas." On a furlough back in England he wrote *Narrative of Missionary Enterprises in the South Sea Islands.* He died only two years after returning to the islands, but his book and story would influence a wave of missionaries. Also, the London Missionary Society had recognized its earlier error in not supporting his personal vessel, and commissioned an entire fleet of missionary ships.

Christianity Today aptly titles its article on Williams, "Bringing Peace to Paradise."[58] His *Peace* ship also facilitated his philosophy of training indigenous missionaries and working through new converts like King Auura of Rurutu. The latter came to Tahiti with many of his people, fleeing an epidemic. After converting, Auura asked for assistance in returning to share the gospel before the epidemic claimed their lives.

> Williams honored Auura's request and sent a few Tahitian deacons along with him on an English merchant ship.
>
> Williams also sent with Auura a boat of his own and a Tahitian crew to bring back word of how the mission fared. "After an absence of little more than a month, we had the pleasure of seeing the boat return," Williams wrote, "laden with the trophies of victory, the gods of the heathen taken in this bloodless war, and won by the Prince of Peace." The people of Rurutu rejected their "idols" and embraced the Christian faith before a European ever stepped onto the island.[59]

In 1837, Samoa boasted 20,000 Christians, half its population. This was after a mere seven years. Once again, Williams sent indigenous missionaries and focused on the conversion of the chief and other leaders. "What emerged was Polynesian [Christianity] with British overtones rather than British Christianity in Polynesian garb."[60]

In 2009, various descendants of the cannibals who killed Williams (the Uswo-Natgo clan) attended a ceremony commemorating this event. After a reenactment of the 1839 murders, a long line of the island descendants asked Williams's great-great grandson, Charles Milner-Williams, and seventeen other Williams descendants for forgiveness. Milner-Williams relayed the details of the murders, as recorded in the eyewitness account of the captain of the missionary ship *Camden*:

Harris, who was the furthest inland, was clubbed down and killed. John Williams turned and ran towards the sea. They caught up with him on the seashore. They clubbed him and shot him with arrows and he died there in the shallows. It was a Royal Navy ship that went back to the island. The islanders then said that yes they had killed and eaten both Harris and Williams.[61]

The BBC covered this event, including the comments from then president of Vanuatu, Iolo Johnson Abbil: "Since we claim to be a Christian country it is very important that we have a reconciliation like this." This was especially true since many citizens, according to Abbil, believed Erromango was under a curse for having killed these missionaries.

The country also symbolically renamed the site of the massacre, changing it from Dillons Bay to Williams Bay. Ironically, Dillons Bay was named after a sandalwood trader, Peter Dillon, who "discovered" the sandalwood bonanza in 1825, which started the wave of foreign ships. Besides the sandalwood, these traders would carry off most of the population for various types of oppressive labor. Through this "blackbirding" practice of deceiving the indigenous people with promised work, coupled with introducing various diseases, Erromango's population dipped from many thousands to below four hundred before the century's end.

Throughout this time of inhumane deportations and viral slaughter, other missionaries would enter the arena. Harris and Williams would not be the last to be murdered by the very peoples they had gone to serve.

Ellen Catherine Powell, George Gordon, and James Gordon

Ellen Catherine Powell and George N. Gordon (her husband) became two of the most prominent missionaries on Erromango, arriving from the Presbyterian Church of Nova Scotia. His language skills, coupled with his hearty constitution and ingenuity, served him well in that early missionary environment. Within two weeks, he translated the Ten Commandments into the Erromangan dialect of Melanesian, and with only a few helpers he constructed several buildings—including the church and his home.

However, the missionaries would soon pay with their lives for the sandalwood traders' treachery of purposefully spreading measles to the islanders. The disease decimated the native population, as planned, and the evangelists on the island began to brace for the worst. Two of the chief's sons were among the casualties. These human losses overlapped with a cyclone that decimated the crops—all of which factored into their spiritual assessment of these foreigners and their God.

Shortly before George Gordon's murder, two notes alerted him to the likely fate ahead:

> Dear Sir,—One of my Tanna men was killed and eaten yesterday by some of the people of the river, without any reason that I can learn. I am really at a loss to know what to do.

> Mr. Gordon,—Please let me know if you have heard about the natives going to attack us to-day or to-morrow. One of the natives that is trading for us told me this morning they were going to kill all the whites on the island on account of the ships bringing this disease. I believe they are going to commence to-day.[62]

Shortly after receiving these letters, on May 20, 1861, the people of the island followed through. The Gordons refused to go to safer zones and were killed in two coordinated attacks, in different parts of the village, mere minutes apart. Both died quickly, by axe wounds to the head and neck.

> "They killed Mrs. Gordon [Ellen Catherine Powell] with equal barbarity. Poor Lamb!" [R]epresented by Dr. Turner as "quiet, amiable, intelligent, and possessing a heart *full* of love to the heathen," what had she done to incur their resentment or savage ferocity? Her name, too, must have been on the death-list previous to the starting of the murderers for Dillon's Bay.[63]

The remaining natives who had shown sympathies to Christian teachings, whether converts or seekers, were given strict orders to burn their western clothes, and especially all Christian books and symbols. Allegedly, some hid Bibles and held secret services.

Hearing of his brother's murder, James Gordon traveled to Erromango to continue George's translation of the New Testament. He was surprised to find a church when he arrived. He ministered there for eight years before following his brother into martyrdom. On Thursday, March 7, 1872, he died on the floor of his study with a hatchet in his face. He had just finished translating the seventh chapter of the book of Acts—the story of Stephen, the first Christian martyr.

JAMES CHALMERS IN PAPUA NEW GUINEA Robert Louis Stevenson, author of classics like *Treasure Island* and *The Strange Case of Dr. Jekyll and Mr. Hyde,* referred to James Chalmers as "a man that took me fairly by storm for the most attractive, simple, brave, and interesting man in the whole Pacific."[64] Chalmers so impressed the author that Stevenson promoted the missionary's memoirs among readers in England, calling him a hero.

Chalmers was known for his humor and humility, and his native name among the Papuan tribe is a subtle example of both traits. They called him "Tamate" (pronounced Tama-ty), which was not a lofty title or even a native word. It was simply what the first acquaintance from Papua called him when he was unable to pronounce the name "Chalmers." Rather than correcting this, Chalmers was tickled by it and cherished this name to the end of his life. This small, simple gesture captures the playful spirit that colored his ministry and calls to mind Paul's approach:

> To the weak I became weak, that I might win the weak. I have become all things to all people, that by all means I might save some.
> 1 CORINTHIANS 9:22

Chalmers was uninterested in the pronunciation of his own name, and wholly consumed with the articulation of the gospel. But unfortunately for Chalmers and the rest of the Christian world, the people who lived on the island found this gregarious Westerner to be as dangerous as Stevenson found him charming.

After years of successful diplomacy with these remote warrior tribes, he sailed to an especially violent tribe that had remained unreached. He brought with him his young assistant Oliver Tomkins, who had refused to leave his side. They landed on April 8, 1901, for the occasion of a native feast they had been invited to join, but until they arrived the meal was incomplete—the people were cannibals.

When Chalmers and Tomkins failed to return, recovery expeditions were sent out. But they returned only with the story, from an indigenous warrior, of what had happened:

> When they got ashore, the whole party was massacred, and their heads cut off. The boat was smashed up, and the clothing, etc., distributed. All the bodies were distributed and eaten, Tomkins being eaten at the village of Dopima (where they were all killed), and the body of Tamate being taken to Turotere. His Excellency informs me that the fighting chief of Turotere was the man who killed Tamate. No remains of the bodies could be found, though we searched diligently for them; but we found Tamate's hat, and pieces of the smashed boat.[65]

When Chalmers first arrived in New Guinea it was almost entirely cut off from the rest of the world. Today, the Independent State of Papua New Guinea is 95 percent Christian and the national anthem includes praises and the words

Thanks to the good Lord above
For His kindness, His wisdom and love [66]

ROBERT THOMAS IN KOREA Reports may differ about the method of Robert Jermain Thomas's execution in August 1866 outside a small village in Korea. But whether he was decapitated by a violent swing of a machete or burned alive, all accounts agree that he spent his life in service to his Savior.

He was perhaps the first Protestant missionary to Korea, visiting briefly in 1865, but he lacked Korean materials and "resolved to return."[67]

That same year an edict allowed missionaries to enter legally, and Horace Underwood and Henry Appenzeller walked ashore shoulder to shoulder at Inchon so that neither of their denominations (Presbyterian and Methodist, respectively) could claim to have arrived before the other.

The Catholics had seen considerable success in Korea in the 1700s, though this did not help open a door for Thomas. The Korean leaders found the growth threatening, a sign of foreign influence, and in 1866 slaughtered thousands of Christians.[68] Thomas was not entering a land friendly to the gospel, and his own translation to heaven occurred during the year of the fiercest political opposition to all things considered Western.

He had been sailing as a translator on a non-missionary vessel, a former US navy ship called the *General Sherman*, led by a reckless captain who repeatedly ignored Korean orders to turn back. The captain followed that blunder with another when he sailed onto a sandbar and lodged his ship between two riverbanks.

The locals attacked the ship from both sides. The helpless Westerners lacked any leverage to negotiate their way out. So for around two weeks, the ship's crew fought off these attacks with rifle and cannon fire.

Eventually, the locals sent burning barges against the ship that set it on fire and caused all surviving passengers to jump overboard. When they did, they were captured and killed. Somehow the Bibles Thomas brought made it ashore, and his most enduring missionary legacy in Korea lies in . . . wallpaper.

Thomas never had the opportunity to preach the gospel to the Koreans himself on that trip before he was killed, but one witness recounts him urgently handing his captors a copy of the Bible in the Korean language before this man killed him. One way or another, the Bible reached a government official, who rather than reading it, wallpapered his house with it. Twenty years later it was still covering the walls on the inside of his home, where all visitors might read it. The wallpaper was discovered by a later Christian missionary to Korea, Samuel A. Moffett, who had been inspired by Thomas's story and followed him to this so-called "hermit kingdom." In 1886, two decades after Thomas's fateful arrival, Moffett baptized his first Korean converts, fulfilling the martyr's dream and continuing his legacy.

THE CATHOLIC MARTYRS OF KOREA During the nineteenth century, between 8,000 and 10,000 Christians in Korea were executed for their faith. Most of them were Catholic, and these executions occurred in waves, with major slaughters occurring in 1839, 1846, and 1866. At various times, the Catholic Church canonized groups of them, including 103 martyrs in 1984.[69]

In 2014 Pope Francis did the same for Paul Yun Ji-Chung and his 123 companions. Yun was the first of the modern Korean martyrs, killed in 1791. Yun had provoked condemnation from his noble family for burning the family plates used in ancestral rites, following the orders of the Catholic bishop in Beijing to reject pagan practices. Xenophobia has many faces, and Yun's actions were not only foreign to Korean culture, but rejected as coming from foreigners and their God.

Yun also honored his mother's wishes for a Catholic funeral, and within a decade of his conversion and five years of his baptism, he gave his life. One of his first converts, his cousin Kwon Sang Yeon James, endured tortures alongside him before the officials beheaded them.

The deaths of Korean converts brought sadness and mourning. The slaughter of European priests in 1866 brought warships.[70] In the end, Koreans themselves were most responsible for evangelizing Korea.[71]

The Korea that Robert Thomas visited, and where Paul Yun Ji-Chung and thousands of others died for their faith, had actually received Christian guests as early as the seventh century, as attested by archaeological sources.[72] We also have record of the famed Matteo Ricci's Christian books reaching Korea in the early 1600s through a Korean visitor to Beijing. But the road to true tolerance was serpentine, as the Korean king labelled Catholicism evil in 1758 and outlawed the religion. After the aristocrat Yi Seung-hun converted and was baptized in Beijing in 1784, he returned and founded the first Korean church.

However, the tables began to turn with Yun's challenge to the ancestral rites. And they turned even more abruptly at the beginning of the nineteenth century with Queen Jeongsun. She ordered the execution of more than three hundred Catholic Christians.

Witnessing this atrocity was a Christian woman by the name of Columba Kang Wan-suk. She belonged to a group called the "Unmarried Virgins," mostly affluent women who refused marriage or otherwise bucked familial societal norms by living in community and practicing celibacy. When Columba hid a priest from the authorities—so that area Catholics might be able to celebrate holy communion—she was arrested, tortured, and executed as part of what came to be known as the Sinyu Persecution (1801). Once again, Christianity was prohibited in Korea.[73]

Amid the trade wars and political maneuverings, several more persecutions broke out. The Kihae mass executions were a retaliation for informing the French of three executions of priests. When three battleships appeared off his coast, the Korean king knew he had a mole and proceeded to execute suspects among the Christian community.

At the end of the persecution in the 12th month of 1840, 54 Catholic[s] had been beheaded, while those who were hanged, beaten to death, or died of an illness in prison numbered more than 60. Apostates who were released numbered 450.[74]

The Pyongin Persecution proved the most devastating and occurred in four stages, from 1866 through 1871. These attacks on Christians began as the Koreans feared the advance of the Russians. There appeared to be hope for the Christians as the bishop was trying to negotiate with the French to assist against the Russians.

The Korean regent called for a meeting with Catholic leaders, generating a false sense of relief. After all, he had branded their religion as "evil doctrine that has neither father nor king."[75] In response,

the Catholic church members believed that their long-cherished desire of religious freedom had already been fulfilled, and intoxicated with bliss, rather than promptly taking action [and getting word to Bishop Berneux out in the countryside], they even informed the believers in the countryside and gathered in Seoul to perform a mass of gratitude.[76]

It was indeed a faux festival, or premature at best. As the Russian threat subsided, King Kojong's father, Taewŏn-gun, personally interrogated Bishop Berneux. He refused to recant his faith and leave the area (Chosŏn), so the Korean officials beheaded him on the Noryangjin execution ground. That same day, the bishop's colleagues and the respected leaders of Korean Christians, Nam Chong-sam and Hong Pong-ju, lost their heads on the execution ground outside the Sŏsomun Gate.

This was just the beginning of a wave of martyrdoms. Queen Dowager Cho issued a nationwide order to burn all Catholic books, and to

enforce the five-household mutual surveillance system, reward those who report heretics and punish those who hide them, and to strengthen the guarding of the Hwanghae Ch'ungchŏngdo coast. Thus began an unprecedented full-scale persecution of Catholicism throughout the nation. The missionaries who had been caught up to the 7th day of the 2nd month were all executed, and executions were carried out in Seoul and Pyŏngyang and elsewhere in the countryside. In addition to the massive slaughtering of Chosŏn Catholics, the execution of nine French priests, and the deaths of refugees from diseases and starvation, there were many others, who, though innocent, were killed by corrupt and false charges leveled by corrupt government officials.[77]

French warships achieved a minor victory when some troops overwhelmed defenders of a government building on Kanghwa Island. But the French had merely enjoyed a Pyrrhic victory, and were roundly defeated in the next battle.

After defeating the French warships, the Taewŏn'gun [d. 1898, father of the Korean king, Kojong] erected *Ch'ŏkhwabi* (Stele Rejecting Reconciliation) throughout the nation and further spurred on the persecution of Catholicism. He swore that the land polluted by the Western barbarians should be washed clean with the blood of pursuers of the Western Learning, and thus he continued to execute numerous Catholic believers.[78]

After these intense times with Russia, the debacle of the Opium Wars, and the horrific casualties of the Taiping Rebellion in China (which ended in 1871), Korea reopened to missionaries.[79] The Presbyterian Church experienced "phenomenal growth" in Korea after applying the "Nevius method." The American Presbyterian missionary to China, John L. Nevius, accepted an invitation to review the Korean missions in 1890. They subsequently applied his indigenous and self-sustaining strategy found in his book, *Planting and Development of Missionary Churches* (1886). Roman Allen (1868–1947), the Anglican missionary to China, would champion this "three-self" approach (self-governing, self-supporting, and self-propagating). "This strategy [the three-self approach] proved to be decisive in the church in the non-Western world that has taken place in the twentieth century."[80] That is, a shift to missionary efforts becoming self-sustaining via indigenous leadership, and therefore not perpetually dependent on foreign help.

The regent Taewŏn-gun and his son, King Kojong, tried to eradicate the Christian movement, but it was their dynasty that came to an end. The Chinese kidnapped Taewŏn-gun in 1882, and in 1885 Kojong declared himself emperor and renamed the country "Great Han" to peeve his captors. But after the Japanese conquest of the Korean peninsula, and the subsequent annexation, Kojong was impotent and allegedly died of poisoning.

DID YOU KNOW? *The Boxers*

The name "Boxer Rebellion" comes from the nickname for the revolutionaries trained in the martial arts. They had grown weary of foreign influence within Chinese culture—accentuated in their minds by Christianity and spearheaded by missionaries. These revolutionaries formed a movement called the Society of the Righteous and Harmonious

Fists. In 1900, they indeed used brute force to decapitate nearly all Christian missionaries and converts they could find in northern China.

THE MARTYRS OF CHINA'S BOXER REBELLION (1900)

As the centuries passed since Christ's death and resurrection, his enemies abounded in every nation, frontier, and era. Not at all times in all places, but at some places in every era. Those resisting his teachings, and at times his very historicity, did so out of hate, envy, and fear of Christ's power. Persecution and rejection of Christians would indeed surface "to the ends of the earth." And still does.

The Industrial Age saw many champions of "progress" who certainly missed the boat, so to speak, on the fallen nature of humankind. The Chinese revolutionaries who slaughtered thousands of missionaries in 1900 were a manifestation of anything but progress.

The martyrs of the Boxer Rebellion came from every stripe of Christian tradition, from the Methodists and Presbyterians to the Plymouth Brethren, as well as the long-standing Catholics. The numbers vary widely. Some sources claimed the Boxers and government soldiers killed only 200 missionaries and around 500 converts in 1900. However, in the Shanxi province in northern China, the Chinese (likely the governor with a "bitter hatred") killed at least 2,000 Christians.

The latter was the Tiayuan Massacre, July 9, 1900, which one journalist called "the greatest single tragedy in the history of Christian evangelicalism."[81] One contemporary update cites the *London Times*: "During July [1900] from 15,000 to 20,000 native converts were massacred in the northern provinces."[82]

The same source reveals the scanty information that was reaching families and friends of foreign missionaries. Imagine fasting and praying for weeks, and this short telegram changes everything: "Mr. J. Young, Mrs. Young murdered July 16th; with Mr. G. McConnell party."[83] Also, consider the hundreds affected by the single following telegram:

Reliable educated native has brought news from Shansi: Pigott party arrested Sheo-yang; driven on foot in chains to T'ai-yuen

Fu; shared fate other missionaries. Mission houses, T'ai-yuen Fu, burned, except Farthing's. Missionaries fled there 29th June; escorted Ya-men 9th July; promised safety, immediately massacred; altogether 33 Protestants:—Pigott (3), Duval, Robinson, Attwaters (2), Stokes (2), Simpsons (2), Lovetts (3), Coombs, Beynon (4), Wilsons (3), Farthings (5), Whitehouse (2), and four others. Hoddle, Underwood and Stewart have not been mentioned. Also 10 Catholic priests: others not known. Probable total, 51 foreigners, besides many natives. Hsin-cheo, 6 persons escaped mountains, horseback, probably Dixons, McCurrachs, Renaut, Eannals; fate unknown.[84]

A historical treatment of the events of 1900 gives a helpful summary. The evil governor of Shanxi, Yu-Hsien, had acted on the Empress's mandate to squelch the Christian movement and foreign intervention. She reminded her people that their sheer determination and numbers could overwhelm any outside force. He immediately shut the city gates and blocked the river escape routes. He didn't want to expel them. Rather, he wanted to trap and behead them. And except for the few who escaped, he did so. Men, women, and children. Foreign and native. All remnants of anything from outside their indigenous culture. And though Christianity by this time had reputable tenure in the territory, it was still considered foreign.

> The first riot occurred on June 27, when Miss Coombs was killed and Dr. Edwards' hospital destroyed. A messenger brought this information in a letter written by Dr. Miller Wilson, and sewn into the sole of one of the messenger's shoes.
>
> On July 9 the Governor, Yu-Hsien, having taken the precaution to have the gates of the city closed and carefully watched, commanded all the foreigners in the city to appear before him, sending armed soldiers to enforce his orders.
>
> The Europeans, driven to the Yamên [an office of public officials], were received in audience by Yu-Hsien, who had by his side the Prefect and Sub-Prefect of the province, while a number

of servants, five hundred soldiers, and a crowd of murderous individuals, surrounded the foreigners.

When all had been brought up, Yu-Hsien enjoined the Europeans to prostrate themselves at his feet, accusing them of bringing vice, evil, and unhappiness in the Empire of Heaven. There was only one remedy for such evil, and that was to behead them all. The order was to be carried out in his presence.

Two Roman Catholic Bishops and three other missionaries were then led out, and were the first to be decapitated on the spot. Then one and all—men, women, and children—were mercilessly beheaded in the courtyard of the Yamên. . . . To satisfy their superstitious curiosity, the soldiers are said to have pounced on some of the bodies, still throbbing, of these unfortunates, and cut their hearts out for inspection by the bonzes [Buddhist monks] and other learned men.

Insult—no greater could be given in China—was added to injury by taking the bodies outside the city walls and leaving them to the dogs instead of burying them. Great credit should be given to the local native Christians, who, with admirable pluck and faithfulness, to say nothing of the danger to themselves, surreptitiously secured the bodies by night and buried them. Partly on account of this charitable deed two hundred native Christians were put to death five days later (July 14).

In despatches sent by the local officials to various Yamêns it is stated that 37 foreigners and 30 native converts were massacred on July 9; but it is not known for certain whether that figure includes children, or only adults. A report from a city in the neighbourhood of Tai-yuen-fu places the number at 550, quite a number of Yu-Hsien's officers being so horrified at the Governor's orders that they sent the foreigners under their charge to him, that he might carry out his vengeance personally.[85]

Earlier martyrdoms had warned of this outbreak, such as the eleven Anglican missionaries killed in Huashan on August 1, 1895. Decapitations were the swift ends to most of these children and adults. Whole families entered heaven together as, in a figurative sense, the Yellow River ran red.

Once again, xenophobia was also at play. The Chinese authorities suspected the foreigners—primarily seen as linked to the god of the Europeans—of infiltrating their economies and leading the immoral support of the opium trade and wars. In the Shan-si Province, for example, a missionary talks about his "opium-refuge work." He notes in his 1890 report to the China Inland Mission that fourteen Chinese were "breaking off their opium," and a long line was awaiting room for treatment.[86]

And reciprocal xenophobia only exacerbated the situation. The United States had passed the Chinese Exclusion Act in 1882, leading many Chinese to conclude: *"American Christians want to save our souls . . . but apparently only on our soil."* [87]

Due to this storm of frustrations, many generations of missionary work seemed extinguished.

> Painful beyond words was the news that practically all their
> converts, the result of patient work of centuries, and of untold
> hardships and privations, had been murdered. No less than fifteen
> to twenty thousand native Catholics had been massacred, and
> whole villages and small towns of Christians exterminated by
> the Boxers, in the northern provinces and in Manchuria, where
> Roman Catholicism had made great strides.[88]

After nearly two thousand American troops squelched the Boxer Rebellion, China actually realized more foreign intervention—the opposite of the revolutionary goals. Missionary work resumed, along with an aggressive reparations initiative. In a memorable selfless act, with Christ's work firmly in the forefront of his mind, pioneer missionary Hudson Taylor refused the significant compensation for the damages and pain suffered by China Inland Mission (CIM). The funds, instead, helped build Chinese universities. Taylor responded to the money offer: "Had I a thousand pounds China should have it. Had I a thousand lives China should claim every one."[89] It is little wonder that before he passed in 1905, through CIM (which he founded in 1865), he helped bring around 800 missionaries to China. CIM became Overseas Missionary Fellowship (OMF) in 1964, and lives on today as OMF International.

THE MARTYRS OF NAMUGONGO, UGANDA (1886) An annual holiday throughout Uganda celebrates the funeral pyres of at least forty-five young men in 1886. The Bugandan king Kabaka Mwanga II had retaliated against these relatively new Christians. They were pages, ages thirteen to thirty, in his personal service who had refused his homosexual advances. The head of the royal household, Joseph Mukaso, was martyred for encouraging his pages' steadfastness.

> They were marched to Namugongo, where, bound with ropes, shackles, iron rings, and slave yokes, they waited for one week. During that time the martyrs prayed and sang hymns; the Catholics among them recited morning and evening prayers, grace before and after meals, as well as the Angelus and the rosary, in preparation for their deaths. On June 3, before the execution of the rest of the young men, Charles Lwanga was put to death by the king's men. He was wrapped tightly in a reed mat, a yoke was hung on his neck, and he was thrown onto a pyre. Taunting his executioners, Charles is said to have shouted, "You are burning me, but it is as if you are pouring water over my body!" Before he died he cried out, *"Katonda,"* or "My God."[90]

Hundreds of thousands of pilgrims from various countries gather near shrines in their honor every June 3. The Catholic basilica in Namugongo, around ten miles northeast of Kampala, is built on the site of many of the twenty-two martyrs' deaths, whom Pope Paul VI canonized in 1964. Charles Lwanga was a key leader among these heroes of faith. He encouraged the other pages during their imprisonment, and requested and received baptism on the night the king's men killed Mukaso.

Around two miles away is the main Anglican shrine where the king burned several Anglican missionaries. Shrines and memorials, stained glass tributes, schools, and other inclusion of martyrs' names dot the landscape.

In 2015, an estimated two million pilgrims participated in the annual festivities. Annually, at least a half million celebrate the main feast, and many of the ceremonies are broadcast nationally.

BERNARD MIZEKI IN RHODESIA (1896) Witch doctors led attackers to end the life of a selfless servant in Rhodesia (modern Zimbabwe), the first martyr recognized by the Anglican Church in this region. The locals had risen up against what they considered oppression under the British, particularly the British South Africa Company. Famine and plagues heightened the tension. Under the strong rule of Chief Mangwende, the people Bernard Mizeki had served attacked him, described in the following account. His life and death inspired both his contemporaries and modern-day Christians, with shrines, college departments, and even liturgical dramas recalling the inexplicable events surrounding his death.[91]

> During the Mashona rebellion of 1896 Mizeki was warned to flee, since local African Christians were regarded as agents of European imperialism rather than as independent agents. Mizeki would not leave the Christian community for which he assumed responsibility and, on the night of June 18, was speared outside his hut. His wife and another person racing to find food and blankets to keep him alive saw a blinding white light and heard a rushing wind on the hillside where they had left him. On their return, the martyr's body had disappeared. The place of his death has become a site for Protestants and Catholics to worship, and each year on the anniversary of his death pilgrims come from many parts of South Africa [and other countries] to pray and to commemorate his life.[92]

Although originally from Mozambique and educated in Cape Town, Mizeki's Anglican ordination identified him with the "enemy." He had a reputation for strong teaching and service, but he likely became a target when he peeved the witch doctors and other traditional spiritualists. He refused to placate evil spirits and even cut down some of the trees where they allegedly resided.

Perhaps local memory of Mizeki's impeccable service factored in the undisturbed nature of his hut when Father E. W. J. Crane arrived thirty-seven years later (in 1933). And perhaps fear of some type of ramification of an evil spell from the witch doctors. In any case, it was remarkably preserved for over three decades. Since there was no known shrine for Catechist Father Bernard Mizeki, they erected one on the positively identified mud hut floor, incorporating the simple items found there.[93] The daily items include a Huntley and Palmers biscuit box used to hold Mizeki's pencils and one of the slate pencils. Within the next few years a concrete platform was built atop the near perfect mud hut floor, and then various additions and a cross on the adjacent hillside from the side of his attackers' approach.

On the fiftieth anniversary of Mizeki's martyrdom (1946), the Anglican magazine *The Link* noted that "common citizenship and common blood" came from "the fruit of the seed which was sown by a martyr's blood."[94]

DID YOU KNOW? *The Cowley Fathers*

When Bernard Mizeki moved to Cape Town, he worked menial jobs to survive, and caught the attention of a patron, the German Baroness von Blomberg of Madenburg. She became sort of a surrogate mother and funded Mizeki's education with the Cowley Fathers. This is the nickname for a group founded in Cowley, Oxford, in England in 1866. Its official name is The Society of St. John the Evangelist (SSJE), and though only a few brothers of this society are left in the UK, it remains a registered charity in that nation. It has members around the world, including around 1,000 in the United States. The SSJE was the original community of men in the large Anglican Communion (now 85 million members), and at one time had numerous buildings in Oxford, which were later sold and repurposed as St. Stephens House, and operations were moved to Westminster, London. Many key leaders benefited from the Cowley Fathers, from missionary martyr Bernard Mizeki in the mid-1800s to C. S. Lewis in the mid-1900s.[95]

PRATULIN MARTYRS IN POLAND The Russian Imperial Army killed thirteen Christians on January 24, 1874, for trying to block the entrance to their small Catholic Church in the village of Pratulin in modern Poland. Troops gunned down these men and boys outside the church.[96]

Though the tsar had implemented a full-scale rejection of Catholics, these martyrs and their families gathered outside the church, well aware of the tsar's deportation of clergy and lay leaders. Surviving believers were marched off in long columns, likely to a perilous fate in Siberia. It was an obvious Russification of the church, forcing all Christians to join the official (and state-controlled) Russian Orthodox Church.

Pope John Paul II beatified the martyrs in 1996 and gave a homily about their legacy in 1999 that is perhaps our best tribute to their legacy:

> Like Christ, who offered himself in sacrifice for them, to consecrate them in the truth—so did they offer their lives for the sake of faithfulness to Christ's truth and defence of the Church's unity. These simple people, fathers of families, chose at the critical moment to suffer death rather than yield to pressure in a way untrue to their conscience. "How sweet it is to die for the faith"— these were their last words. . . .
>
> The new evangelization needs true witnesses of faith. It needs people rooted in the Cross of Christ and ready to accept sacrifice for the sake of the Cross. Authentic witness to the life-giving power of the Cross is given by those who, in its name, overcome in themselves sin, egoism and every evil, and want to imitate the love of Christ to the very end.
>
> As in the past, the Cross must continue to be present in our lives as a clear pointer to the path to follow and as a light which illumines our whole being. May the Cross, the very form of which unites heaven and earth and men among themselves, flourish in our land and become a great tree laden with the fruits of salvation. May it bring forth new and courageous proclaimers of the Gospel, who love the Church and take responsibility for the Church, true heralds of the faith, a breed of new men. May they be the ones to

light the torch of faith and to carry it burning brightly across the threshold of the third millennium.

> Cross of Christ, to you be praise.
> We hail you in every age,
> from you there spring power and strength,
> in you our victory![97]

+ Historic Sources

Amid these horrific and heroic episodes in the long line of nineteenth-century Christian martyrs, faithful servants of Jesus demonstrated not only great resolve and expectation, but joy and confidence as well. A missionary's report from Shensi province, China, expresses his passion for the souls of the Chinese and his hope for remarkable years ahead.

SHENSI PROVINCE
FROM MR. BLAND

Feng-tsiang Fu, March 29th.—By GOD's grace we are keeping the main thing well to the front, *i.e.*, telling out the message of salvation to poor benighted heathen. We have splendid audiences as a rule, and some listen with evident interest. You will praise GOD for this, and more still for the fact that at least two are enquiring the way. We shall value your prayers at this time, for only the SPIRIT can cause these dry bones to live, and we need to plead, too, that those who are interested may not be hindered by the enemy from coming out brightly for JESUS. We are happy in the work, and more than satisfied with our inn accommodation, especially as we see a great deal of Chinese life, and are in continual contact with the people more than we could be in our hired house.[98]

Vintage Foxe

Those who were taken experienced the most cruel tortures the infernal imaginations could invent; and, by their constancy evinced that a real Christian can surmount every difficulty, and despise ever danger to acquire a crown of martyrdom.[99]

CHAPTER THIRTEEN

Millions of Martyrs in the Twentieth Century

Remember those who are in prison, as though in prison with them, and those who are mistreated, since you also are in the body.
HEBREWS 13:3

The Bible tells us that God did not originally make the world to have disease, hunger, and death in it. Jesus has come to redeem where it is wrong and heal the world where it is broken.[1] **TIMOTHY KELLER,** *THE REASON FOR GOD*

When people are being persecuted and oppressed, they tend to have a different perspective on God, the world, and the Bible from those who have positions of power in state-supported universities or churches.[2] **ALAN KREIDER, "GOD'S LEFT WING: THE RADICAL REFORMERS"**

In the twentieth century, persecution and war eclipsed "progress." As the Boxer Rebellion ended, mission organizations, denominations, and countless families grieved the significant loss of lives among their ranks. Rampant decapitations cast a macabre pall over foreign missions. But the heroism of the faithful fueled applications to replace the fallen. There was renewed hope of reaching the Asian populace for Christ.

The tide had turned in many corners to protect missionaries, even efforts to compensate them financially. The United States' Open Door Policy of 1899 seemed prima facie to help open doors for the missionaries. United States Secretary of State John Hay ushered this Open Door Policy proclamation to the major European powers to have equal trading with China and to protect China's sovereignty.

Overlapping these events was the work of the China Inland Mission. In 1865, long before the Boxer Rebellion, Hudson Taylor had marshalled considerable personnel and resources for reaching China. During the Boxer Rebellion, he went through the gut-wrenching, violent loss of dozens of the missionaries working alongside him and his leaders. Afterward, there was much work to do to rebuild—along with other mission agencies. And rebuild they did. Taylor died in 1905, hopeful, but the same realist as when he began.

> China is not to be won for Christ by self-seeking, ease-loving men and women. . . . In short, the men and women we need are those who will put Jesus, China [and] souls first and foremost in everything and at all times: life itself must be secondary.[3]

However, in the end, not all went well on the international diplomacy front. The Robert Burns–John Steinbeck phrase seems apropos, "the best laid plans of mice and men." The economic strategy of the Open Door, however protective it appeared of Chinese independence, was inherently flawed—its planners had failed to include Chinese leaders. The humiliation was not short lived. The already awkward climate for missionaries was enhanced by Russian advances into Manchuria, then Japanese aggression, compromises, and secret treaties, not to mention Lenin, the Bolshevik Revolution, and two world wars.

The twentieth-century annals of Christianity's spread and survival are best painted in red hues. The blood of millions of martyrs flowed alongside that of so many other victims of philosophical, political, and personal power grabs.[4]

Communism in China took hold in earnest in 1949, as its leaders forced out the Nationalist Party (the KMT went to Taiwan), and established Communist China (People's Republic of China today). The twentieth century saw a rise in the alarming reality of pogroms—of Christians—in many regions. Millions of Christians died for their belief in Christ, and millions of Jews also died for their heritage and belief in God as expressed in the Hebrew Bible—the Christian Old Testament.

Once again, claims of human "progress" seemed smothered in corpses—an attack on religious groups that continues today. Lists of Christian martyrs from the twentieth century highlight saints from numerous countries. They are but a fraction of the faithful fallen. The innocent victims. The slaughtered and maimed. No list can capture the lost names of executed and persecuted Christians under regimes like the Russian Revolution (1917–1923), Stalin's Great Purge of 1937–1938, and the Chinese Cultural Revolution (1966–1976), to name just a few of the great persecutions of Christians in the twentieth century.

The execution tallies are dizzying. Though the following quotes differ in their estimates, in both cases the totals are staggering.

During this [twentieth] century, we have documented cases in excess of 26 million martyrs. From AD 33 to 1900, we have documented 14 million martyrs.[5]

More than 70 million Christians had been martyred over the last two millennia, more than half of whom were killed in the twentieth century under fascist and communist regimes. The average annual rate at the end of the twentieth century was estimated to be about 160,000 martyrs per year (or 1.6 million over the decade 1990–2000). This included large numbers of Christians killed in the Rwandan genocide and the Sudanese civil wars.[6]

The scholars behind the second quote above helped to establish widely used parameters for counting martyrs. Their five criteria include the helpful qualification that the Christians died because of "human hostility [which] takes a variety of forms, including war, conflict, random killing, and genocide, and can be conceptualized as either individual or communal (such as by governments)."[7]

As the world struggled through two world wars, the capacity for evil seemed limitless. Author Eric Metaxas observes, "Hitler had made the true reality of the human condition less avoidable; evil had stepped to the center of the world stage and removed its mask."[8] Monsters in leaders' attire must have appeared as the Antichrist in the eyes of the millions taking the long march of no return into Siberia, or in line to killing fields and mass graves, or staring at Boxers with machetes or Red Army soldiers with rifles, or enduring the smell and sound of whole villages being annihilated in Africa.[9]

For example, hundreds of priests and bishops died during the Russian Revolution, not including the undocumented disappearance of religious staff at many of the nearly six hundred monasteries. The Soviet Union era (1917–1991) brought dark days for Russian believers, with estimates as high as 12 to 20 million slain.[10] Stalin, who had himself attended seminary from 1894 to 1899, killed untold numbers of Christians during his regime (1922–1953). During the Great Purge of 1937–1938, Stalin slaughtered between 680,000 and 1,200,000 of his people (with some estimates drastically higher). During Stalin's Great Terror, he had over 100,000 Russian clergy killed in his effort to remove challenges to his *secular atheism*.

So we remember the Christian martyrs of the twentieth century with humility and with the knowledge that an untold number of Christians died—during crowded executions and buried in trenches, on a lonely road in a small village, or like John Smith in the previous century, in a filthy cell, gradually decomposing before taking the last breath. This chapter affords but a small representation of the violence against Christ followers.

While Hudson Taylor had hope for the gospel's spread when he died in 1905, and it continued to spread via China's underground church, he would have been heartbroken to know of the slaughters still ahead. Or to know that in that same year of his passing, the Turkish government would begin its massacre of nearly two million Christians (1905–1918). Sudanese leaders would kill hundreds of thousands of Christians (and other non-Muslims) by 1979, the end of the reign of terror. By the century's end, tens of thousands of Christians in southern Mexico would flee their homes in Chiapas, leaving behind hundreds massacred for their faith.

David Neff wrote the following in 1996, near the end of the tumultuous twentieth century. He captures well the context of the accounts ahead in this chapter, as well as this book's final section, covering the most recent and ongoing martyrdoms of the twenty-first century:

> Most American Christians do not lead typical Christian lives. The typical Christian lives in a developing country, speaks a non-European language, and exists under the constant threat of persecution—of murder, imprisonment, torture, or rape.
>
> The persecutor's sword dangles by a hair over Christians in the still-communist countries and in lands where the rising tide of Islamism overwhelms political efforts at fairness, tolerance, and due process. Human rights and religious liberty are high-sounding abstractions. . . .
>
> Indeed, the church is the community of those "who are persecuted and martyred for the gospel's sake," according to a memorandum drawn up in preparation for the writing of the Augsburg Confession.
>
> Interacting with, working for, and praying on behalf of suffering believers in intolerant lands reminds us that it is they who live the normal Christian life and we who exist in a parenthesis of toleration. While we work and pray for their liberties, may we be strengthened to resist the more subtle and seductive attacks of the enemy in this time and in this place.[11]

Most readers of this book (itself a tribute to the millions of martyrs) are indeed living in history's "parenthesis of toleration" for Christians—at least in some mitigated sense in our home countries. Many, even in the United States, are realizing how easily even these once-bold parentheses can disappear.[12]

TURKEY'S ORGANIZED KILLING OF CHRISTIAN MASSES

The apostle Paul, Ignatius of Antioch, Emperor Constantine, and a litany of others were instrumental in launching Christianity and the organized church in Asia Minor, a region that is today part of Turkey. This accentuates even more the horrific and nearly unbelievable Turkic massacre of Christians, perhaps "the worst organized killings of Christians in this [twentieth] century."[13] In his book *Their Blood Cries Out*, Paul Marshall says,

> Although Turkey is now a country with relatively few Christians, this was not always the case. Less than one hundred years ago, Turkey, or rather its Ottoman predecessor, was about 30 percent Christian. This situation changed when some two million ethnic Armenian Christians were massacred between 1905 and 1918, a genocide which the Turkish government still denies. Many of the remaining Christians fled immediately. Others, facing death threats, systemic harassment, and discrimination, followed them later.[14]

The twentieth century brought increased tensions between Muslims and Christians in Turkey as the Ottoman Empire waned and ended. The movement to a pan-Islamism curtailed some long-enjoyed freedom among Christians.[15] The "equality" policies of the Ottomans for non-Muslim religions, though not without their taxes and issues, were lost. Christians became caught in the crosshairs, or some would say they became scapegoats.[16] During the First World War, toleration of non-Turkish (and non-Muslim) groups abated and massacres ensued. In the decades following, Islamic control tightened, creating untenable conditions for most Armenian Christians. More recently, according to Open Doors, "the main religion, Islam, is enmeshed with fierce, fanatical nationalism."[17] One author wrote in 2019, "The percentage of Christians in Turkey declined from nearly 25% in 1914 to less than 0.5% today."[18]

Chrysostomos (1922)

For Christians, the city of Smyrna (in modern-day Turkey and now called Izmir) is inextricably linked to one of our earliest martyrs—Polycarp. He was martyred in AD 155, a story covered in chapter 3. Even after the days of Emperor Constantine, Smyrna would continue to be a stronghold of Greek Orthodox Christianity, and in 1922 it was unique with its Christian majority within a Muslim nation. It was also the wealthiest city in Turkey.

However, Polycarp was by no means the last martyr there, or the last bishop publicly executed. Among the most horrific acts during the Turkish massacres of Christians was the 1922 bludgeoning of Chrysostomos, the metropolitan (high-ranking bishop) of the city.

After the end of World War I, Greek forces marched on Turkey without any major allies, and failed in their attempt to establish a Greek territory. As the Muslim forces repelled them and approached Smyrna, Chrysostomos refused to flee. He had openly and aggressively championed Greek nationalism in his sermons, so his chances of surviving the Turkish army were slim. But in the end, his demise came at the hands of an angry mob, not the troops, who stood down. Eyewitness accounts from a soldier and other sources note that he survived the initial inhumane violations and died after they dragged him to another street. One account has him constantly raising his hands and his face toward heaven, and a soldier claims to have cut off his hand. Another said his attackers dragged him behind a car. And one soldier notes it was such a pitiful sight he finally shot him twice in the head.

> The mob took possession of Metropolitan Chrysostom and
> carried him away [and paused a short time later] . . . in front
> of an Italian hairdresser named Ismail . . . they stopped and the
> Metropolitan was slipped into a white hairdresser's overall. They
> began to beat him with their fists and sticks and to spit on his
> face. They riddled him with stabs. They tore his beard off, they
> gouged his eyes out, they cut off his nose and ears.[19]

The assistant to Chrysostomos, Thomas Voultsios, provides details through his lens. When the soldiers approached the cathedral and insisted that the bishop report to the garrison, he said his goodbyes, then calmly followed their instructions. He also welcomed the garrison with a glass of cherry juice. But Voultsios wasn't there, and in fact did not know what had happened until the next day, by his own admission.

One of the soldiers tried to appease his conscience by telling another of the prisoners what had transpired. The following is directly from a respected teacher and leader of the cultural and athletic life of the area, G. Mylonas of Smyrna. He was a friend of Chrysostomos and had been incarcerated the same night as the executions. He shared this on the sixtieth anniversary of the martyrdom.

We were so surprised to hear the Turk say: "I will not kill you, I will save you. Tonight all the prisoners will be executed because we need to make room for new inmates who have just arrived. I will save you today and I hope this will help me forget a terrible scene which I witnessed and took part in."

And he went on: "I have witnessed the slaying of your Bishop. I was among those who blinded him, uprooted his eyes and dragged him from his beard and hair while he was bleeding through the Turkish neighborhood. We hit him, swore at him and cut off pieces from his skin. I was deeply impressed by his attitude. He neither begged, screamed or cursed while he endured all the tortures. His pale face, covered with the blood of his eyes, was constantly looking up towards the sky and he continuously mumbled something which could not be heard. Do you, teacher, know what he was saying?"

"Yes, I know," I replied. "He was saying: 'Holy Father, forgive them, for they do not know what they are doing.'"

"I don't understand what you are saying, teacher, but it does not matter. Every now and then, whenever he had the strength to do so, he would raise his right arm and bless his persecutors. A Turk realized what the Bishop was doing; he got so furious that he cut off the Bishop's hands with his sword. He fell on the ground in a lake of blood and sighed. It was more a sigh of relief rather than a sigh of pain. I was so sorry for him at that moment, that I shot him twice in the head and that finished him off. That's my story. Now that I have said it to you, I hope that I will find my peace of mind. That's why I am saving your lives."

"And where did they bury him?" I asked with agony.

"No one knows where they threw his chopped-up body."[20]

Chrysostomos stated in his last sermon, "It is during the high seas that the good sailor stands out, and it is during [the] time of tribulations that the good Christian does the same."[21] Although people considered 1922 a time of *advanced* civilization, much of the world stood by as the troops who let the mob tear apart the bishop, in turn, raped, tortured, and killed unconscionable numbers. While the billows of smoke rose around the hordes of the slaughtered, twenty-seven Allied warships also stood down.[22] But even as nations held back, individuals stepped forward. A preacher from upstate New York, Rev. Asa K. Jennings, with the help of naval officer Lt. Commander Halsey Powell, orchestrated the remarkable rescue of hundreds of thousands of those fleeing Smyrna.[23]

CULTURAL CONNECTION

Smyrna

Around forty cities in the United States are named Smyrna, after the Turkish city of numerous martyrs, most notably Polycarp and Chrysostomos. There are Smyrnas from Alabama and Alaska to those in Washington, West Virginia, and Wyoming.

In 1933, when there were already twelve American towns named Smyrna, Dr. Esther Lovejoy noted that "godfathers" probably sponsored them because they "knew the 'tribulations' of the ancient city over which she has triumphed gloriously century after century."[24]

Smyrna was that beacon of orthodoxy via its early association with Bishop Polycarp, whom the Romans said, "is the teacher of Asia, the father of the Christians, and the overthrower of our gods."[25] Greek bishop Irenaeus (died ca. AD 202) wrote that Polycarp "always taught the things which he had learned from the apostles, and which the Church has handed down, and which alone are true. To these things all the Asiatic Churches testify, as do also those men who have succeeded Polycarp."[26] You likely see the pattern—Smyrna was more than a strategic port city like Ephesus to the south, it was a city known as a seat of Christian teaching. Tertullian (ca. 208) held the heritage of Smyrna's church as a standard for the heretics to envy: "Anyhow the heresies are at best novelties, and have no continuity with the teaching of Christ. Perhaps some heretics may claim Apostolic antiquity. We reply: Let them publish the origins of their churches and unroll the catalogue of their bishops till now from the Apostles or from some bishop appointed by the Apostles, as the Smyrnaeans count from Polycarp and John, and the Romans from Clement and Peter; let heretics invent something to match this."[27]

GRAND DUCHESS ELIZABETH OF RUSSIA (1918) The journey of Queen Victoria's granddaughter, Elizabeth, is engaging—from German Lutheran to Anglican leanings, and then to full-fledged Russian Orthodoxy. Her transition to Windsor, under Victoria's care after being orphaned, then to St. Petersburg after her marriage, is intriguing. In 1884, Elizabeth married the fifth son of Tsar Alexander II, Grand Duke Sergei Alexandrovich. Leaving the gorgeous confines of Windsor became not only a departure from security, but also a path to sainthood.

Although Elizabeth—known as Ella—was beloved by the Russian people, the Grand Duke appears to have treated her harshly at times. Nonetheless, she remained committed, even shielding him from assassination attempts.[28] After revolutionaries succeeded in assassinating the Grand Duke in 1905, her strong religious commitments eventually put her at odds with the Bolsheviks and their militant revolution in 1917.

Her strength and commitment to service for the church is perhaps a precursor to the role of women in the modern Russian Orthodox Church.[29]

This [her husband's death] marked a turning point in Elizabeth's life. Now she gave away her jewellery [*sic*] and sold her most luxurious possessions, and with the proceeds she opened the Martha and Mary home in Moscow, to foster the prayer and charity of devout women. Here there arose a new vision of a diaconate for women, one that combined intercession and action in the heart of a disordered world. In April 1909 Elizabeth and seventeen women were dedicated as Sisters of Love and Mercy. Their work flourished: soon they opened a hospital and a variety of other philanthropic ventures arose.[30]

These fruitful years of humanitarian service and worship offer a stark contrast to her last hours in a dark mineshaft. Her martyrdom is both inspirational and sad—yet another reminder of human capacity for evil.

The Bolshevik party was avowedly atheistic, and it saw in the Orthodox Church a pillar of the old regime. In power, it persecuted the Church with terrible force. In time, hundreds of priests and nuns were imprisoned, taken away to distant labour camps, and killed. Churches were closed or destroyed. On 7th May 1918 Elizabeth was arrested with two sisters from her convent, and transported across country to Perm, then to Ekatarinburg, and finally to Alapaevsk. On 17th July the Tsar and his family were shot dead. During the following night Elizabeth, a sister from SS Mary and Martha [monastery] named Varvara, and members of the royal family were murdered in a mineshaft.[31]

Elizabeth's final days and hours were fraught with the type of sinister activity expected in a horror film. Her captors took her and others from their holding cell at night, blindfolded them, and tied their hands behind their backs. Then they loaded her and her colleagues on carts and began to transport them—allegedly to a former factory building for imprisonment.

However, the cart stopped about two hours later near a sixty-foot-deep mineshaft. They threw in Elizabeth first, and then the others. Perhaps the water at the bottom saved them from instant death. Elizabeth crawled to a ledge, obviously suffering from earlier beatings and the crush of the fall. She reached out to another woman struggling. An eyewitness noted that the dastardly deed seemed complete, until they heard worship songs rising from below.

One of the henchmen then threw in a grenade, which still failed to kill all of them. Next, they stuffed down a bunch of wood and torched it. When the locals exhumed the bodies around three months later (October 8), it appeared that Elizabeth actually died of starvation, having somehow survived the violent murder attempts. They carted the bodies in simple wooden coffins to the local cathedral, and eventually Elizabeth's sister Victoria arranged to have her body interred at the Church of Mary Magdalene in Jerusalem.

MANCHE MASEMOLA IN SOUTH AFRICA (1928) As people enter Westminster Abbey's Great West Door, ten statues greet them. These represent twentieth-century martyrs from across the world, and none is more striking than the likeness of Manche Masemola. She was only around fourteen or fifteen years old when she died in 1928.

Individuals reach maturity at different ages. Some never attain it, and some, like Mary (mother of Jesus) and Manche, exhibit it in their early teens. Manche died at the hands of her parents—advised by the local witch doctor in their northeastern province of South Africa.

When a teenager is firm enough in her belief in Christ to forecast being baptized in her own blood rather than recant her beliefs, it's little wonder she gains international acclaim. In the face of imminent death for her stand against her parents' faith (and that of her tribe, the Pedi), missionary records credit her with various statements, such as:

> "I am sorry, but from now on, I am going to stand by myself."
> "If they cut off my head, I will never leave my faith."
> "I may be baptized with a better baptism."[32]

Manche could not read or write, but she learned the gospel story through the preaching of Father Augustine Moeke of the Anglican Community of the Resurrection. Although the chief of her Pedi people (at Ga-Marishane in the Transvaal) welcomed missionary groups, and Christians would become a minority within the tribe, Manche's parents remained distraught. Besides considering this foreign religion linked to their country's famine, they also thought her conversion would keep her from marrying, or worried she would leave and they would lose her work on the farm, work which their culture relegated to women.[33] Her mother resorted to following her with a spear and whip. She also hid Manche's clothes to keep her from attending more Christian classes. In one account, Manche clearly committed to working the fields and instructed her cousin (and Christian follower) Lucia to do the same. Lucia reflected after Manche's martyrdom, "Manche's mother said she would force us to leave the church. She beat Manche every time she returned from church."[34]

Eventually, Manche's parents did what for most Westerners is unthinkable (but for them, a last resort to protect their people). "Eventually, in about February 1928, her parents took her to a lonely place and beat her to death, because she refused to give up her allegiance to Christ and her desire for baptism."[35]

Perhaps the best reflection on the significance of her death, put squarely into its local context, comes from Dr. Madipoane Masenya (ngwan'a Mphahlele), professor of Old Testament Studies in the Department of Biblical and Ancient Studies at the University of South Africa, and an advisor to the *Dictionary of African Christian Biography* project:

> What attracted me to the difficult story of a young Pedi girl
> whose strange and controversial death turned her not only into a
> local, national, and international icon, but also more importantly
> for the purposes of this brief introduction, into a martyr? First,
> coming from the Anglican tradition, residing then in the northern
> Transvaal, not far from Manche's gravesite, I once, as a secondary
> school pupil, participated in a pilgrimage to Manche's grave in the
> year 1972. Second, unlike the many relatively older heroes and
> heroines whose lives are celebrated in the *Dictionary of African
> Christian Biography*, Manche's narrative presents a unique case of
> a faith commitment by a young rural girl. Third, being part of the
> Pedi people and cognisant of the strict gender and age hierarchies
> between parents and children as well as the difficult relationship
> that I sometimes had with my parents, especially my father, on

account of my newly found faith, Manche Masemola's story hits close to home.[36]

For nearly forty years after killing her daughter out of hatred for the alleged magic of Western Christianity, Manche's mother would swear and harass the throngs of pilgrims visiting Manche's grave. However, on the forty-first year, in 1969, she chose to follow Christ. Archdeacon John Tsebe baptized her, and records the account. The big church in her hometown of Ga-Marishane was packed. The only problem was, Manche's mother wasn't there. "The old lady crept to the church two hours before the service" to be baptized.[37] She defended her eagerness: "When one keeps a tryst with God one needs no company."[38] However, she took the biblical name Magdalene and the crowd enjoyed quite a celebration afterward. Each August, thousands of Christians make the pilgrimage to Manche's grave, and no longer under the harangue of her mother.[39]

DID YOU KNOW? *Statues of Modern Martyrs*

Whether we stand in the center of St. Peter's Square and look at the statues atop the Vatican structures, or trace the names of the saints dotting niches in the side of Germany's Cathedral of St. Peter and Mary in Cologne, we realize that behind each figure is a story worth studying. This could not resonate more than with those whose statues fill the long-empty niches above Westminster Abbey's Great West Door. These gothic niches had remained empty since the sixteenth-century completion of the lower level of the towers, and the eighteenth-century completion of the upper. After the restoration of these towers in 1995, the planning commission decided to fill them.[40]

> Above the Abbey's Great West Door stand ten statues to modern martyrs—Christians who gave up their lives for their beliefs. The martyrs are drawn from every continent and many Christian denominations and represent all who have been oppressed or persecuted for their faith. . . . St. Maximilian Kolbe from Poland;

Manche Masemola from South Africa; Janani Luwum from Uganda; Grand Duchess Elizabeth from Russia; Dr. Martin Luther King Jr., a civil rights leader who was assassinated; St. Oscar Romero, Archbishop in El Salvador who was assassinated; Dietrich Bonhoeffer, from Germany, killed by the Nazis in 1945; Esther John from Pakistan; Lucian Tapiedi from Papua New Guinea; and Wang Zhiming, a pastor killed during the Chinese Cultural Revolution. . . .

The statues, carved from French Richemont limestone, were unveiled on 9th July 1998 by the Archbishop of Canterbury.[41]

From filicide in Manche's case, to the murder of the Grand Duchess in a mineshaft, to the Nazis' noose for Bonhoeffer, each martyr's story is a precious account of faithfulness, courage, and the sovereignty of God. All of these martyrs are included in this chapter, with the exception of Oscar Romero, whom we discussed earlier in connection with Latin America. These are but a representation of the millions slain for the gospel in the twentieth century.

JOHN AND BETTY STAM IN CHINA (1934) The Communists decapitated John and Betty Stam only three months after they arrived in China's Anhui Province. The swift martyrdoms of these recent Moody Bible Institute graduates rocked much of the Christian world—and had an adverse effect on the Communists' efforts to cut down the Christian causes. Instead, hundreds more missionaries signed up for service.[42]

This eastern area of China had a much different image than its peaceful landscape paintings, which often depict low-hanging clouds in the rugged granite Huangshan Mountains. The Red forces advanced on Christian outposts through hidden trails among those granite outcroppings, surprising villagers. A prisoner released to make room for the Stams stepped in to save their baby, Helen, only to be hacked to death. Later, a doctor tried to help them, but when a Bible and hymnal were found in his house, they killed him as well.

The last hours for the Stams were both horrific and legendary—though inspirational. John was permitted to write the following letter the night before his decapitation (though he realized it had no chance of making a difference):

> My wife, baby and myself are today in the hands of the communists, in the city of Tsingteh. Their demand is twenty thousand dollars for our release. . . . We were just too late.
>   The Lord bless and guide you, and as for us, may God be glorified whether by life or by death.[43]

At the post office on that fateful trip, the postmaster who recognized them asked, "Where are you going?" John answered, "We do not know where they are going, but we are going to Heaven."[44]

The captors carted off the Stams without their coats, hands tied tightly behind them. Betty was allowed to use a horse for part of the trip due to inflammatory rheumatism issues. Their last night was in an abandoned manse, with John tied to the bedpost.

> The next morning the young couple were led through town without the baby [Betty had hidden little Helen in bedding with a note, supplies, and two five dollar bills]. . . . John walked barefoot. He had given his socks to Betty. The soldiers jeered and called the town's folk to come see the execution. The terrified people obeyed. . . . John pleaded for the man's life [the Christian doctor]. The Red leader sharply ordered him to kneel. As John was speaking softly, the Red leader swung his sword through the missionary's throat so that his head was severed from his body. Betty did not scream. She quivered and fell bound beside her husband's body. As she knelt there, the same sword ended her life with a single blow.[45]

An amazing part of this story is the survival of baby Helen. A Chinese evangelist named Lo rescued the baby with the help of other local believers. Betty's hidden provisions were just enough to help them smuggle Helen to safety, and eight days later—carried in a rice basket on a shoulder pole—they reached a safe haven. She would live out her life, funded through college years by Wilson College in Pennsylvania, Betty's alma mater.[46]

PAVEL FLORENSKY IN RUSSIA (1937)

For a brief account of the life and death of Pavel Florensky, we might turn to an admirer of his—the Nobel Peace Prize–winning author and political prisoner Alexander Solzhenitsyn, who was nearly a Christian martyr himself.

Florensky was a well-respected scientist, philologist, art theorist, philosopher, physicist, and mathematician—a true polymath. Above all, he was a beloved priest of the Russian Orthodox Church.[47]

Solzhenitsyn followed Florensky's career from afar and remembered him in his monumental *The Gulag Archipelago* as "perhaps one of the most remarkable men devoured by the Archipelago of all time."

> Well-informed people say of him that he was a scholar rare for the twentieth century, who had attained a professional mastery of a multitude of knowledge. He was educated as a mathematician, and in his youth he had experienced a deep religious conversion and become a priest. The book he had written in his youth, *The Pillar and the Affirmation of the Truth*, is only today coming into its own. He had to his credit many essays in mathematics (topological theorems, proved much later in the West), in art history (on Russian icons, on religious drama), and on philosophical and religious subjects. (His archive has been in the main preserved and has not yet been published. I have not had access to it.)
>
> After the Revolution he was a professor at the Electrical Engineering Institute (where he delivered his lectures in his priest's robes). In 1927 he expressed ideas anticipating those of Wiener. In 1932 he published in the magazine *Socialist Reconstruction and Science* an essay on machines for the solution of problems which were close in spirit to cybernetics. Soon after that he was arrested. His prison career is known to me only at several separate points,

which I list with trepidation: exile in Siberia (in exile he wrote works and published them under a pseudonym in the works of the Siberian expedition of the Academy of Sciences), Solovki, and after Solovki was shut down the Far North, and according to some sources the Kolyma. In the Kolyma he studied flora and minerals (in addition to his work with a pick). Neither the place nor the date of his death in camp is known. But according to some rumors he was shot during wartime.[48]

The rumors Solzhenitsyn heard were true. Initial reports suggested a "natural" death in the harsh climate of Siberia, but it was later revealed that after years of forced labor, a sham tribunal finally executed Florensky.

As Solzhenitsyn noted, Florensky would lecture and attend scientific meetings in the Soviet Union in his priestly robe, which inevitably caught the attention of government officials in the image-conscious Soviet party. Florensky certainly didn't look the part of the secular scientist, and at one early meeting Leon Trotsky leaned forward and asked, in genuine confusion and perhaps a smidge of annoyance, "Who is that?"[49]

Florensky's study of flora and minerals in the Kolyma region afforded him some respite from the boredom of the gulag, but it was a far cry from his former life in the Russian academy. A central part of Florensky's life had always been the marriage of faith and science, only one of which was acceptable under the brutal Soviet regime.

Trotsky soon knew Florensky's name, and his reputation continued to grow in the Soviet scientific community. As frustrated as they were with his insistence on wearing his priestly garb, Florensky was too valuable to persecute. He would soon write the official Soviet textbook for electrical engineering, which was still in use twenty years after his death.

But Soviet patience with this defiant priest eventually wore out; they tired of his flouting communist conventions; they tired of his backwards, clerical wardrobe, his large pectoral crosses, and his insistence that higher mathematics speak eloquently of Christian truth.

So on a December night in 1937, one of the greatest minds of the twentieth century was marched into the woods outside the city of St. Petersburg and executed with a single shot to the back of his head. His body, still wearing the priestly robe he refused to take off, was dumped with two other men into a growing mass grave.

Multiple times over the course of Florensky's imprisonment, the Soviets had offered him exile in Paris, rather than the string of prison and labor camps that eventually led him to the forests of St. Petersburg, but with that stereotypically Russian genius for suffering, he refused. He chose to suffer with his people, for his people, as Christ had done two thousand years before. He remains today a model of not only the compatibility of religious and scientific worldviews, but also of the perils of exploring and professing that compatibility in the modern world.

MAXIMILIAN KOLBE IN AUSCHWITZ (1941) Amid the millions of Christians suffering persecution and death during the 1900s, in 1982 Pope John Paul II declared one as "The Patron Saint of Our Difficult Century." The Polish Catholic priest Maximilian Kolbe had lived a life of aggressive missions, but one iconic act seared his name into heroic lore. At the Auschwitz concentration camp, he volunteered to die in the place of a stranger.

> In July 1941 there was an escape from the camp. Camp protocol, designed to make the prisoners guard each other, required that ten men be slaughtered in retribution for each escaped prisoner. Francis Gajowniczek, a married man with young children, was chosen to die for the escape. Maximilian volunteered to take his place, and died as he had always wished—in service.[50]

The punishment was starvation in an underground bunker. According to an eyewitness (a janitor), Father Kolbe was always praying when they checked on the status of the condemned. Eventually they had all starved to death, except him. After three weeks in this death hole, the Nazis injected him with a lethal dose of carbonic acid. He raised his arm to his tormentors as if to assist in their task. They cremated his remains the next day, August 15, 1941. Francis Gajowniczek, on the other hand, lived in Poland until his death in 1997.

In 1927, Father Kolbe, though enduring several bouts of debilitating health issues, including tuberculosis, founded perhaps the world's largest monastery at Niepokalanów, the City of the Immaculate. Around 800 brothers resided in the self-sufficient monastery near Warsaw, and during World War II it sheltered 3,000 refugees (including 2,000 Jews). Its main publication, the *Knight of the Immaculate*, would reach a peak production of 750,000 monthly copies. Its Catholic newspaper, the *Little Daily*, reached 225,000 copies on Sundays and holy days, and 137,000 on weekdays.[51]

The Catholic Church celebrates this saint (canonized in 1982) as the patron saint of drug addiction, drug addicts, families, the incarcerated, journalists, political prisoners, prisoners, and the pro-life movement. Father Kolbe wrote the following in his last issue of the *Knight*, which proved somewhat prophetic. Though quoted in various sources, the *Catholic Voice* perhaps introduces it best—"From the heart of the 20th Century Holocaust when all the proud boasts of secularism were revealed for what they are, Max K[olbe] still speaks to us:"

> No one in the world can change Truth. What we can do and
> should do is to seek truth and to serve it when we have found
> it. The real conflict is the inner conflict. Beyond armies of
> occupation and the hecatombs of extermination camps, there are
> two irreconcilable enemies in the depth of every soul: good and
> evil, sin and love. And what use are the victories on the battlefield
> if we ourselves are defeated in our innermost personal selves?[52]

MAY HAYMAN AND LUCIAN TAPIEDI IN PAPUA NEW GUINEA (1942) The Japanese invaded Papua New Guinea (PNG) in 1942 to establish a base for attacks on Australia. Local indigenous religious leaders helped them locate and slaughter over three hundred Christians.[53]

Anglican leader Bishop Philip Strong's radio broadcast urged missionaries not to abandon the local churches by evacuating, and the missionaries agreed. At that time, PNG was a diocese of the ecclesiastical Province of Queensland. Strong declared, "Whatever others may do, we cannot leave. . . . If we are fools, we are fools for Christ's sake."[54] However, it soon became obvious that their days were numbered, and church leaders changed their stance. Within nine months, all were encouraged to escape.

To capture the memory of this cloud of witnesses, we highlight two individuals who chose not to leave the islands. These faithful believers are honored in the Westminster Abbey and Beeson Divinity School statue displays of twentieth-century martyrs.

May Hayman and another nurse refused to leave. But local men betrayed their hiding place in the forest, and the Japanese captured, caged, and tortured them. On September 2, 1942, the troops executed them and threw their bodies in a trench near Orla Bay. Today, pilgrims and local Christians share Communion at a commemorative stone in her honor on the anniversary of her martyrdom.[55]

Hayman had the double angst of trying to save herself while knowing her fiancé was also in hiding. He, Vivian, spent his last few weeks on earth hiding in the bush while still trying to minister to his flock. Embogi, a local sorcerer, betrayed him to the Japanese. "[Lucian] Tapiedi . . . pleaded for Vivian's life and was brained with an ax. Vivian and other Christians, including a six-year-old boy, were beheaded, their corpses cast into the sea."[56]

Tapiedi was a Papuan Anglican teacher and evangelist in Sangara—in the southeast part of PNG. In one account, which is corroborated by later actions on the part of his alleged assassin, Hivijapa from the Orokaivan tribe, his pursuers bashed in his skull with an axe, likely decapitating him. This seems to be the authentic view, as Hivijapa later repented and became a Christian. He also built a church in Lucian Tapiedi's honor. The statue of Tapiedi at Westminster Abbey captures his strength and youth—he was only twenty-one years old when he died.

JOHN WILLFINGER IN BORNEO (1942) The Japanese invasions of the Pacific Islands also ended the life of a missionary in Borneo, the largest of the islands. John Willfinger and his translation partners for the Murut version of the New Testimony, the Lenhams, initially retreated further inland among their Murut friends, more generally the Lun Dayeh ("upriver people" or "people of the interior"). The collective term is the "Dayaks."[57]

When the names Willfinger and Lenham appeared on "the most wanted list," they decided not to put their indigenous friends in peril and turned themselves in. This decision would cost them their lives.

The missionaries had been offered protection by the Dayak tribe, a group popularized in *National Geographic* and noted as the last to renounce headhunting. However, the Japanese forces evidently deemed the Christians' religious beliefs and national origin more of a threat than some of the fiercest people known in the world.

Willfinger wrote a letter to a Menadonese Christian official, Mr. Makahanap, explaining he could not put them at risk—knowing that even though they said they could hide him in unknown places, the invaders would torture their family members for clues. His letter became part of their sacred treasures.

> If I hide, naturally the saints will be forced to lie, to disobey orders
> if they hide me. In short, I would be forced to drag them into sin,
> whereas my intention upon leaving my country and my family
> was only to make mankind righteous and not to bring them into
> sin, even though I pay for it with my life.[58]

He also wrote a letter to the Christian and Missionary Alliance headquarters, resigned in his fate and faith: "I have decided to go to the enemy, trusting God as to the ultimate results. . . . Kindly send my love . . . to my family and my sweetheart, Miss Mary McIlrath."[59]

Willfinger and the Lenhams planned to turn themselves in to the nearest Japanese outpost. The Lenhams went directly, while John toured eastern Borneo encouraging Christian groups. Like the apostle Paul and St. Ignatius, in a sense John appealed to Caesar and then visited churches along the way. However, he disappeared, and only after the war was his body recovered. His captors had taken him to a Japanese internment camp and decapitated him on December 28, 1942, around two months after he disappeared during his church tour. After the war they found his Bible, which includes the following poem he copied on the inside cover—the first and last paragraphs of "Christ Is God," which appeared in the *King's*

Business newsletter from the Bible Institute of Los Angeles (today known as Biola University):

No mere man is the Christ I know
But greater far than all below;
Day by day His love enfolds me,
Day by day His power upholds me.
All that God could ever be
The Man of Naz'reth is to me. . . .
No mere man can my strength sustain
And drive away all fear and pain,
Holding me close in His embrace
When death and I stand face to face.
Then all that God can ever be
The unseen Christ will be to me.[60]

Perhaps as powerful as this old poem is Willfinger's inspirational comment written below the poem: "Hallelujah, this is real."[61]

Two years later, when nine US aviators from a crashed B-24 became stranded on the island, the Dayak recognized that their US insignia matched that of their fallen missionary friend. Out of respect for Willfinger—who sacrificed his life for them—they hid the troops out of sight, saving their lives.[62]

FRANZ JÄGERSTÄTTER IN GERMANY (1943) Terrence Malick's 2019 film, *A Hidden Life*, tells the story of the prosecution and death of Franz Jägerstätter, a Christian dissenter in Nazi Austria during the Second World War. Jägerstätter was a devout Catholic who stood alone against the rise of Nazism in his small mountain village in upper Austria.

The closing epigraph of *A Hidden Life* would be a fitting one for this volume of martyrology:

The growing good of the world is partly dependent on unhistoric acts; and that things are not so ill with you and me as they might have been, is half owing to the number who lived faithfully a hidden life, and rest in unvisited tombs.[63]

This quotation comes from George Eliot's novel *Middlemarch*, and in the case of Malick's film, it carries a sense of irony: Because of *A Hidden Life*, Jägerstätter's life is no longer hidden. But as Malick tells the story, this martyr's motives are still somewhat unclear.

The film portrays Jägerstätter's stance against the Nazi officials, but Jägerstätter's inner world remains somewhat obscured. We can read the dilemma in his face, to serve his government or his God, but the film cannot fully elucidate the reasons for his misgivings.

A deeper look into this moment in history helps us understand. In March of 1938, Nazi troops invaded his native Austria in an attempt to absorb it, with all other lands of German-speaking peoples, into one pan-Germanic state—the Third Reich of the German Republic.

Less than a month after this occupation, on April 10, 1938, a vote was held throughout Austria regarding this Nazi takeover and 99.7561 percent of respondents were alleged to have voted for its ratification.[64] Jägerstätter voted no and was the only man in his village to do so. Previously, during the takeover in April, the German army offered Jägerstätter the position of mayor of Sankt Radegund, which he rejected on principle. He was off on the wrong foot immediately.

Confronted with the overwhelming Christian support for Nazism in his homeland, Jägerstätter lamented in his journal and personal letters, "I believe there could scarcely be a sadder hour for the true Christian faith in our country."[65]

In the face of such overwhelming odds, he knew he would change little by resisting, commenting:

We frequently hear it said today that we can do nothing more, that it would bring us only imprisonment and death because we can change nothing much in world events. . . . I am aware, of course, that speaking publicly today about all of this would accomplish very little other than imprisonment.

It is not good that our spiritual leaders have remained totally silent for many years. Words teach, and they gain weight by personal example. Isn't it the case that people today are looking for Christians who will bring clarity, comprehension, and certainty into the darkness, for Christians who stand with the purest freedom and courage amid the absence of peace and joy, amid the self-seeking and the hatred?[66]

Jägerstätter felt called by God to be one of these people. And while his village and government officials criticized him for his resistance to the Nazi regime, he called these same people to task for their support of all the evils of the Nazi regime.

As early as 1942, he wrote in his notebook,

Oh, we are a poor people, blinded by our megalomania. Shall we regain our use of reason? . . . We German-speaking people are fighting against almost all of the earth's peoples. . . . Through the radio, newspapers, public rallies, etc., we knew almost everything that Hitler planned on accomplishing with his N.S. [National Socialist] agenda.[67]

Jägerstätter was particularly appalled at what he had heard of the Aktion T4 initiative, in which Nazi officials systematically exterminated the inhabitants of mental hospitals and psychiatric wards, in order to purify the gene pool and relieve themselves of the expense of caring for such "defective" and "unproductive" people.

But even as Jägerstätter protested and condemned these programs, he never passed judgment on his fellow Christians for their sins.

I am not throwing stones at our bishops and priests. They are human beings of flesh and blood as we are, and they can be weak. Perhaps they are even more tempted by the evil foe than we are. Perhaps, too, they were too little prepared to take on this struggle and to decide for themselves whether to live or to die.[68]

Yet he asked of these Christian leaders,

> Is it not more Christian for someone to give himself as a sacrifice than to have to murder others who possess a right to life on earth and who want to live in order to save their lives for a short while?[69]

The painful irony, from Jägerstätter's perspective, was that the Roman church to which he belonged had spoken clearly on all these issues. The Pope had almost immediately condemned Aktion T4, on December 2, 1940, and as early as January 21, 1933, had declared,

> It is impossible to be a good Catholic and a true National Socialist (Nazi) at the same time.[70]

But German-speaking Catholics were not listening. Their deeper allegiance, by and large, was to their ethnic community, known as the German *Volk*, or "folk," and to the increasingly sinister National Socialist party. Witnessing this incredible lack of nerve and faithfulness in his local church, Jägerstätter felt compelled to make himself a sacrifice, in order that the true church might be seen.

The last straw was Jägerstätter's conscientious objection to serving in the Nazi military and his refusal to take the so-called "Hitler oath" required of military personnel:

> I swear to God this holy oath that I shall render unconditional obedience to the Leader of the German Reich and people, Adolf Hitler, supreme commander of the armed forces, and that as a brave soldier I shall at all times be prepared to give my life for this oath.

Of course, Jägerstätter could never say such a thing. His only unconditional obedience was to God. He was incarcerated at Tegel prison, the same facility holding Lutheran pastor Dietrich Bonhoeffer at that time, though there is no evidence the two men ever met.[71] On August 9, Jägerstätter was transferred to the notorious Brandenburg-Görden Prison and beheaded that same day by guillotine.

His final journal entry, written the month of his execution, August 1943, opens with a comment surprisingly upbeat, though in a tenor now familiar among our Christian martyrs:

> Now I'll write down a few words as they come to me from my heart. Although I am writing them with my hands in chains, this is still much better than if my will were in chains.[72]

Jägerstätter closes this final essay with a comment on heaven, and an anecdote from ancient Christian history:

> It would likely become a moment of dizziness if one were to think about the eternal joy of heaven. We are fortunate when we experience a little joy in this world. But what are the short moments of joy in this world in relation to that which Jesus has promised us in his kingdom? No eye has seen, nor ear heard and no human heart has grasped what God has prepared for those who love him [see 1 Corinthians 2:9]. One time, when St. Augustine wanted to write a book about the joy of heaven, St. Jerome—who had just died—appeared to him and said: "Just as there is little in this world that you can grasp with your hands, so there is little about the joy of heaven that you can express in a book. You are not yet at that place to which you are diligently trying to go." If the joy of heaven is so great, shouldn't we dismiss all of this world's delights?[73]

DID YOU KNOW? *The Confessing Church*

When persecution of any people group appears in a society, all groups are threatened—and Christians are called to action. The Confessing Church arose to fight against a government-sponsored and controlled church (a "unified" Protestant church). During the rise of the Nazi regime, Christians throughout Germany were fractured. The group called "German Christians" actually were pro-Nazi. The Pastors Emergency League, which grew into the Confessing Church, opposed Nazi sentiments and propaganda, and especially a Nazi-supported church that called for state control.

Some of the key voices of the Confessing Church were Karl Barth, Dietrich Bonhoeffer, and Martin Niemöller. Barth wrote the Barmen Declaration calling the German church not to swear allegiance to the state or its leader—and he mailed this document directly to Adolf Hitler. This led to Barth's removal from his professorship at the University of Bonn and his return to his native Switzerland. Dietrich Bonhoeffer was especially vocal, challenging the Confessing Church to go further, not just standing for independence in doctrine and governance, but fighting for the humane treatment of the Jews.[74] He died in the death camps. Niemöller barely avoided execution during his internment in the concentration camps, but realized Bonhoeffer was correct, and out of guilt and shame, wrote the following prose and supported the Stuttgart Declaration of Guilt. Niemöller reminds Christians of the need to take a stand while they can, for both persecuted Christians and those from other backgrounds.

> First they came for the socialists, and I did not speak out—
>> Because I was not a socialist.
> Then they came for the trade unionists, and I did not speak out—
>> Because I was not a trade unionist.
> Then they came for the Jews, and I did not speak out—
>> Because I was not a Jew.
> Then they came for me—and there was no one left to speak for me.[75]

DIETRICH BONHOEFFER IN GERMANY (1945) The staggering multitude of martyrs—of both Jews and Christians—during the Nazi campaigns is well known. The images of these pogroms are seared into our collective recollection of these dark years.

Adolf Hitler's dictatorship over Germany began in 1933. He took the title Führer in 1934, and in a decade he would ravage Europe and shake the world's confidence in justice, or at the least, their confidence in the triumph of good. Noteworthy books like *Night* (1960) and *The Boy in the Striped Pajamas* (2006) are but two among many that provide a fuller picture of the German government's horrific actions.

Only three weeks before Hitler took his own life in an underground bunker on April 30, 1945, he ordered the execution of one of Germany's greatest minds and most courageous Christians, Dietrich Bonhoeffer.

Bonhoeffer was hanged on April 9, 1945, in Germany's Flossenbürg concentration camp about twelve hours after his arrival from another camp.

Imagine the despondency of throngs of Germans, so desperate for recovery from World War I and severe economic depression that the self-serving and inhumane Hitler seemed to be a savior. But we don't have to imagine, as records document what transpired. For example, German pastor Hermann Gruner preached the following: "The time is fulfilled for the German people of Hitler. It is because of Hitler that Christ, God the helper and redeemer, has become effective among us. . . . Hitler is the way of the Spirit and the will of God for the German people to enter the Church of Christ."[76]

A key devotional book for a large swath of Christians today emerged from this dark era: Dietrich Bonhoeffer's *The Cost of Discipleship*. This fact has as much to do with its content as the author's courage. In 1939, Bonhoeffer's American friends had arranged to shield him from the Nazis' reach by scheduling a speaking tour in the United States. At age twenty-four (1930–1931), he had studied under Reinhold Niebuhr in New York and appreciated the ministries at Abyssinian Baptist Church in Harlem—and the emphasis on social justice.[77] However, his return to the US was brief. After only a month at Union Seminary in New York City, he chose to return to his homeland to help people remain true to the teachings of Jesus. He was targeting those in the Confessing Church, to address the inhumane actions enveloping the country.

He wrote to Niebuhr, "Christians in Germany will face the terrible alternative of either willing the defeat of their nation in order that Christian civilization may survive, or willing the victory of their nation and thereby destroying our civilization. I know which of these alternatives I must choose; but I cannot make that choice in security."[78]

Bonhoeffer was a Lutheran pastor and theologian who took a strong stance against the Nazis. He helped found the Confessing Church to resist the Nazis' puppet religious organization, the National Reich Church,[79] an attempt to subsume all Protestants. Christians were split between these two groups, with a large number silent and uncommitted, trying to avoid either choice. Within two days of Hitler's rise to chancellor he denounced Bonhoeffer on public radio as a "seducer of the German people." Bonhoeffer writes:

> It is precisely here, in our attitude toward the state [Nazi Germany], that we must speak out with absolute sincerity for the sake of Jesus Christ and of the ecumenical cause. It must be made quite clear—terrifying though it is—that we are immediately faced with the decision: National Socialist or Christian.[80]

Bonhoeffer also became involved in a complex double agent scheme, one in which the German intelligence (*Abwehr*) recruited him ostensibly to spy for Hitler. However, they also wanted his help to overthrow the Führer. Most of those involved were caught and executed—some alongside of Bonhoeffer.

Most of the details of Bonhoeffer's last two months, and his last hours, come from the British intelligence officer Captain Sigismund Payne Best, recorded in his *The Venlo Incident*.[81] The henchmen came for Bonhoeffer just after he finished giving his Sunday homily on April 8, 1945, the first Sunday after Easter. He was still being held at a schoolhouse in Schönberg. The Scriptures for that day were Isaiah 53:5 and 1 Peter 1:3. Best records:

> He had hardly finished his last prayer when the door opened and two evil-looking men in civilian clothes came in and said:

"Prisoner Bonnhöfer. Get ready to come with us." Those words "Come with us"—for all prisoners they had come to mean one thing only—the scaffold.

We bade him good-bye—he drew me aside—"This is the end," he said, "For me the beginning of life."[82]

He had actually been taken to Schönberg by mistake, and the officers had to travel a hundred miles to fetch him in time for a "summary trial" at Flossenbürg. This was Hitler's bizarre attempt to have a pretense of order, even as his demonic plans were unraveling. Bonhoeffer was hanged within twenty-four hours of giving his last homily.

H. Fischer-Hüllstrung, the camp doctor at Flossenbürg, realized Bonhoeffer's importance years later and recorded the following:

Through the half-open door in one room of the huts I saw Pastor Bonhoeffer, before taking off his prison garb, kneeling on the floor praying fervently to his God. I was most deeply moved by the way this lovable man prayed, so devout and so certain that God heard his prayer. At the place of execution, he again said a short prayer then climbed the steps to the gallows, brave and composed. His death ensued after a few seconds. In the almost fifty years that I worked as a doctor, I have hardly ever seen a man die so entirely submissive to the will of God.[83]

The crematorium was out of commission. They tossed Bonhoeffer's corpse onto a pile of other corpses, and burned them. A commemorative granite plaque at this site reads, "In resistance against dictatorship and terror, they gave their lives for freedom, justice, and humanity." Bonhoeffer's words from a sermon he had preached at the Deutsche Evangelische Kirche in Sydenham, London (where he preached between 1933 and 1935), are a fitting tribute to his intense courage and resolve at Flossenbürg:

No one has yet believed in God and the kingdom of God, no one has yet heard about the realm of the resurrected, and not been homesick from that hour, waiting and looking forward joyfully to being released from bodily existence. . . . Death is hell and night and cold, if it is not transformed by our faith. But that is just what is so marvelous, that we can transform death.[84]

Bonhoeffer left a myriad of quotable reflections. Along with *The Cost of Discipleship*, his *Life Together* is also a devotional classic. Perhaps one of his most cited quotes is about his notion of "cheap grace":

Cheap grace is preaching forgiveness without requiring repentance, baptism without church discipline, Communion without confession. . . . Cheap grace is grace without discipleship, grace without the cross, grace without Jesus Christ, living and incarnate.[85]

DID YOU KNOW? *Founders of The Voice of the Martyrs*

The Voice of the Martyrs, one of the most prominent organizations advocating for persecuted Christians worldwide, was itself founded by individuals who knew what it meant to follow Christ in the face of dire consequences.

In 1945, Communist forces in Romania established a new government that was intensely hostile to Christianity. Facing extreme repression, Pastor Richard Wurmbrand continued his ministry to the underground church. Romanian authorities arrested him twice, and Wurmbrand was imprisoned and tortured for a total of more than fourteen years. During his imprisonment, his wife, Sabina, continued his ministry and was herself incarcerated for three years.

During Richard Wurmbrand's testimony before the US Senate in 1966, he exposed his torso to reveal numerous scars from his torture—physical, tangible evidence of intense persecution in his home country.

In 1967, Richard and Sabina Wurmbrand founded The Voice of the Martyrs, traveling widely to set up offices that would provide aid for Christians facing persecution. They encouraged and admonished the church around the world, reflecting the biblical mandate for the church: "Remember those who are in prison, as though in prison with them, and those who are mistreated, since you also are in the body" (Hebrews 13:3).

MAURICE TORNAY IN TIBET (1949) In some ways, Maurice Tornay may have had the most exotic of journeys from childhood to martyrdom at age thirty-nine. The seventh of eight children, he was raised in an idyllic setting in the Swiss Alps. His parents' solid Catholic convictions helped ground him in his faith and in stories about service and martyrdoms.[86]

He also worked with Saint Bernard dogs, made famous through their affiliation with Canons Regular of Grand Saint Bernard. Tornay was among the Canons asked by the Church to serve in the Himalayas on the Tibetan border. His upbringing in high altitudes was a key factor for selection.

As with many missionaries during these times, the Japanese invasion in 1939 complicated his work. In Tornay's case, it emboldened the Buddhist lamas where he served in southeast Tibet. He had been given charge of a boys' orphanage and then served as parish priest in Yerkalo. Within only a few days, forty lamas raided his house and forced him elsewhere. He realized that his best recourse was to make the long trek to meet with the Dalai Lama, but the aggressive and jealous lama from Yerkalo, Gun-Akhio, sent forces to intercept his caravan. They shot Father Tornay by the Choula Gorge near China's border.

On May 16, 1993, during the beatification service for Father Tornay, Pope John Paul II said that "in the spirit of his order, in which everyone risks his life to save people from storms, [Father Tornay] tried every means possible to rescue these pilgrim Christians of the 'Asiatic Alps.'"[87]

THE ECUADOR FIVE (1956) The Huaorani (or Waodani) tribe of Ecuador's tropical rain forest speared five American missionaries on January 8, 1956. The five men's wives, close associates and partners in this mission, never received the planned 4:30 p.m. call on their short-wave radios. And they wouldn't know their husbands' fate until the next morning.

The missionaries (husbands and wives) were aware that this group of approximately 600 indigenous people had a history of violence. They had killed rubber traders and Shell Oil staff earlier that century. They killed other tribes who appeared to threaten their safety or livelihood. And sometimes they even killed daughters when sons died or buried children alive with their fathers.[88] However, a passion to share the gospel "to the ends of the earth" drove these young men and women, bringing a simultaneous sense of trepidation and inspiration.

A reconnaissance flight at 9:30 the morning after the incident reported the sighting of their stripped missionary plane on "Palm Beach," a sandbar on the Curaray River near Huaorani settlements. Within hours, international broadcasts carried news of the martyrs' likely deaths. The world soon became very familiar with these five young men—the Ecuador Five.

Within three weeks of their deaths, the foremost publication of the day, *Life* magazine, published ten full pages with thirty stunning photos.[89] Two are haunting images of fallen missionaries still floating in the water—Jim Elliot and Roger Youderian. The photo of the latter shows one of the two spears still protruding from his body. The other three martyrs were Nate Saint, Ed McCully, and Peter Fleming, all brutally cut down in their youth.

Nate Saint, the missionary pilot, was the oldest at age thirty-two, and Ed McCully the youngest at twenty-seven. They all were married, and all had children except Peter Fleming, who had married only eighteen months before his death.

The rescue team found all five bodies, and some revealed violent machete blows. These weapons were likely among the tools and other gifts the missionaries had dropped during earlier flights. This was a rare moment of ministry passion and martyrdom playing out before the world—both Christian and non-Christian. The human story proved gripping. Amid the tragedy was also a story of tremendous hope in the making.

The missionaries had launched Operation Auca in 1955. (Today, they would have given it a different name, as *Auca* is a derivation of the pejorative word for "savages.") Nate Saint made various flyovers of the area beginning in September 1955, dropping the first gifts on October 5. The Huaorani began tying reciprocal gifts to the rope Saint used to lower the packages, taken as a sign of gratitude. This gesture prompted the missionaries' landing, and building a makeshift campsite and treehouse on Palm Beach.

They would only get to use the campsite seven nights, going from ecstatic expectations to martyrdom in the span of a week.

The five missionaries had learned enough of the Huaorani language to communicate truncated messages, yelling friendly phrases over a loudspeaker. These included an invitation to their campsite, which eventually worked. After regular contact with the tribe, they relayed increasingly positive reports back to their wives. Nate even gave one of them, Nankiwi, an airplane ride over his village. Nankiwi actually waved to those on the ground, and on January 8, the missionaries were fully expecting many of the villagers to arrive for their turn.

What only became apparent through later interviews with the Huaorani is that Nankiwi had lied to his tribe, claiming they had been attacked. In reality, he was caught walking with his (assumed) girlfriend alone through the forest (without tribal escort). The charge was serious enough in their culture for him to deflect the blame to the foreigners who dropped out of the sky.

On January 7, Nate had spotted a group headed toward their camp, and fully expected a celebration of sorts the next day when they arrived. He planned to give numerous plane rides, and talked with his wife on the radio about it at 12:30 p.m. The Huaorani arrived at 3:00 p.m., and he would never make his promised call at 4:30.

Instead, the Huaorani lured two of the missionaries across the river with two girls who were pretending to want to chat with them. Other Huaorani awaited in different places and attacked them—slaughtering all of them. Both the men and women attacked. Fleming kept yelling questions in their language—basically, "Why are you killing us?"

After spearing and hacking them all to death, the attackers threw their bodies into the river, ripped the cloth from the airplane, and retreated. Anticipating a counterattack, they destroyed their own village and moved into the jungle.

We know these details through a remarkable turn of events. Elisabeth

Elliot, Jim's widow, and Rachel Saint, Nate's sister, would return to the Huaorani people to minister (1958–60).

One of the most amazing stories from these martyrdoms is that of Mincaye Enquedi, one of the attackers of the Ecuador Five and likely the one who killed both Nate Saint and Ed McCulley. He became not only a Christian, but a preacher, church elder, and close friend of Nate's son, Steve Saint. Steve was born on the mission field, and was five years old when his father died. Enquedi and Steve Saint collaborated on the 2005 feature film *End of the Spear*, which presents the story of the attacks through their eyes.

Jim Elliot kept extensive journals from his time at Wheaton College forward. While various books and films tell his story, perhaps a single line from one of Elliot's journals is the most piercing and oft-quoted:

> He is no fool who gives what he cannot keep to gain that which he cannot lose.[90]

DID YOU KNOW? *The Huaorani Legacy*

Rachel Saint, sister of the martyr Nate Saint, went to Ecuador and adopted as a sister a Huaorani girl, Dayuma, a refugee from her tribe who taught Rachel the language. The two traveled to various gatherings in the United States to give testimonies—and raised considerable funding for Elisabeth's and her sending mission, the Summer Institute of Linguistics.

By 1969, Rachel and Dayuma had helped protect the Huaorani through gaining official "reservation" status. An entire movement began around their newly formed camp, Tihueno, which grew to around 500 before they decided in 1976 that it was changing Huaorani culture, and stopped funding it. The Huaorani became Rachel's life calling, which meant going independent of her longtime sending mission in order to stay.[91] She died in Ecuador at age eighty and is buried in Toñampare, among the Huaorani whom she served.

Through Gates of Splendor

The Christian world seemed to stand still with the murder of the Ecuador Five in 1956. There was a collective pause to read the account from Elisabeth Elliot, widow of Jim Elliot. People had heard the news via international radio, and outlets like *Life* magazine published photojournalistic reports. She endeared herself through her article in *Christianity Today*, "Through Gates of Splendor," and her bestselling book by the same title that year (1957). In 2005, the book went into its fiftieth anniversary edition with Tyndale House Publishers.[92] She represented all the missionary families involved and built her narrative on their letters and interviews, and the pulse of her own heart. The title comes from a line in the song "We Rest on Thee," by Edith G. Cherry, which had a special place in the lives of the five widows and their families. It was the hymn sung in the missionaries' send-off on their first Ecuador trip in September of 1955. This was the launching of Operation Auca, a mission to the Huaorani.[93] The song's first and last stanzas follow:

> We rest on Thee, our Shield and our Defender!
> We go not forth alone against the foe;
> Strong in Thy strength, safe in Thy keeping tender,
> We rest on Thee, and in Thy Name we go. . . .
>
> We rest on Thee, our Shield and our Defender!
> Thine is the battle, Thine shall be the praise;
> When passing through the gates of pearly splendor,
> Victors, we rest with Thee, through endless days.[94]

ESTHER JOHN IN PAKISTAN (1960) Qamar Zia was born in India. When she was seventeen, her father transferred her from a public to a Christian school. There her teachers' faith captured her attention, and then her heart and mind. Passages of Scripture, especially in Isaiah, spoke to her spiritual interests and prompted her belief in Christ.

It was a tense time in the region for all non-Muslim religions. India (and Britain) partitioned off Pakistan in 1947 for Indian Muslims—and they established their own constitution in 1956. Meanwhile, India remained mostly Hindu. Zia's parents had made the transition to the Muslim region, and Zia moved with them from Madras, India, to become refugees in Pakistan, the new Muslim country.

Zia's mentor from Madras helped her to connect with a Christian in Karachi, Pakistan—Marian Laugesen, who miraculously found Zia among the throngs of refugees. Laugesen gave Zia a pocket New Testament that she read privately for years before she left home—and according to Zia's friend Vivienne Stacey, she read it through twenty-seven times.

After leaving home, Zia served in an orphanage in Karachi, and during this time changed her name from Qamar Zia to Esther John. She endured constant pressure to come back home and marry a Muslim to whom her family had pledged her, and to recant her faith. Instead, she moved to the Punjab to work at a mission hospital in Sahiwal, protected by Pakistan's first Anglican bishop.

Then, sensing a vocation to teach, she studied at Union Bible Training center. After completing her studies in 1959, she lived with Presbyterian missionaries in Chicawatni.

Esther John rejected various pleas from her Muslim relatives to return home. Instead, she remained in the Punjab area, several hundred miles away—and presumably much safer for Christians.[95] But in a country replete with radical Islamism, this passionate Christian missionary found no safety.

She rode her bicycle to women in villages and taught them to read. And through this, she was teaching them about Christ while often staying several nights with them in their tents.

Vivienne Stacey shares about her friend: "Everyone loved her. She and I often went together to visit homes in the villages around. She would speak of her experience of Christ and I would teach a little from the Bible."[96]

When she was just thirty years old, Esther John was brutally murdered while asleep in her bed. Her assassins remain unidentified, but the circumstances elevated her immediately to martyr status. Today pilgrims attend a chapel in her honor at the Sahiwal mission hospital. Vivienne Stacey also adds the following:

> The police officer, going through her possessions looking for clues, [said], "This girl was in love with your Christ." God had already prepared me for this terrible news. I had noted in my diary a comment in a book by Geoffrey Bull that the early Christians were not concerned with living long but in dying at the right time. I knew that God would use this lovely woman's life and death for his glory. "She still speaks, even though she is dead" (Heb. 11:4, NIV).[97]

PAUL CARLSON IN THE DRC (1964) Paul Carlson served as a medical missionary doctor in what is today the Democratic Republic of the Congo, where rebels shot him in 1964. He had served there in various capacities in missions, including at a large hospital and a leper colony.

With degrees from North Park, Stanford, and George Washington universities, he had many doors open to him in the United States. However, after a six-month missionary trip in 1961, he couldn't get the needs of the Congolese out of his mind, and he moved with his wife and two children to the DRC in 1963.[98]

They arrived during a time of acute unrest, the Simba Rebellion (1963–1965). Communist-aided rebels led an insurgency, and Dr. Carlson managed to evacuate his family to the Central African Republic, but then he chose to return to his hospital to tend to the needs of his people. He mistimed his return, however, and was soon captured—falsely accused of spying for the Americans—and sentenced to death. The rebels had taken all white people hostage, retaining around 1,500 people. As the Congolese army approached, "the savage rebels threatened to roast all the hostages alive and eat them."[99]

The rebels succeeded in leveraging their captives' lives in negotiations with the Americans. Chaos erupted, however, as Belgian paratroopers dropped in (flown in by US forces), and rebel fire riddled the crowd. They rescued all but fifty of the hostages.

As the captives ran for the wall, Dr. Carlson helped a pastor to climb ahead of him. The rebels fatally shot Dr. Carlson in the back as he climbed behind the pastor. Like the Ecuador Five, prominent publications highlighted his story. *Time's* cover features a close-up illustration of Dr. Carlson's face and the title "The Congo Massacre." *Life's* cover reads "Congo Martyr" with a picture of him serving the Congolese, and its feature is titled, "Congo Ransom: A Good Man's Life." It begins:

> Everywhere Dr. Carlson went, the Congolese called him
> *Monganga Paulo*—"my doctor Paul." He was a missionary doctor
> serving 100,000 people, and he did so with a genuine love of
> God and God's people. His patients responded to his warmth.
> And then he was caught up in a burst of wanton savagery that
> stunned the civilized world—and he paid for his work with
> his life.[100]

Shortly before his capture, Dr. Carlson sent an audio tape to be played for First Covenant Church of Los Angeles.[101] Much of the message is about the continued growth of the church where he was serving in the Congo, in the city of Wasolo. However, he paused to talk about martyrdom:

> Continue to uphold us in prayer. Pray that through the trials
> we face here we may be an effective witness for Christ and
> that through the trials being faced, we may see growth in the
> Congolese church.
> It is always very hard to know what to say to [the Congolese]
> because they do not realize what has gone on elsewhere in the
> world. They do not realize that in this century more people have
> died for Christ than died in the early centuries, which we think of
> as the days of martyrs.[102]

MARTIN LUTHER KING JR. IN THE UNITED STATES (1968)

The life and death of Rev. Dr. Martin Luther King Jr. is among the most familiar accounts of modern martyrs in the United States. By his death at age thirty-nine, he had already become "a symbol of progressive change in policies concerning race relations and poverty."[103]

What is often overlooked, however, is that this American hero was a pastor first and to the end, and his actions stemmed from his biblical beliefs. This is not missed in David J. Garrow's Pulitzer Prize–winning book, *Bearing the Cross: Martin Luther King, Jr., and the Southern Christian Leadership Conference* (1986). In a 2003 interview, he contended, "Dr. King, if he were alive today, probably would simply be a minister, a pastor. His initial intent was, indeed, just to be a preacher. He didn't have any egotistical desire or need to be a public figure or celebrity. He got drafted—or, really, dragged into it—initially in Montgomery."[104] From the Montgomery bus boycott (beginning December 5, 1955, after Rosa Parks refused to stand) until his death, his gifts and passion thrust him onto the world stage.

King's life and assassination continue to frame much of the United States' discussion on social justice,[105] and he is commemorated by an American federal holiday on the third Monday of January (around the date of his birth, January 15, 1929).[106]

His very name reflects his family's heritage, and that of Protestantism. His father, Rev. Michael King Sr. changed his son's name in 1934 from his birth name of Michael, after a trip to Germany. The Ebenezer Baptist Church of Atlanta sent his father to a Baptist World Alliance meeting in Berlin that year. After touring German sites associated with the Protestant Reformation, Rev. King became awestruck with Luther's influence on the Church and world history.[107]

Dr. King would give his life, literally and figuratively, for humanitarian causes in line with biblical doctrines, and he cited Scripture and used biblical imagery throughout his ministry. He described his call as "an inner urge calling me to serve humanity."[108] Among his many campaigns, challenges, time in the Birmingham jail for his protests, and numerous writings and talks, Martin Luther King is best known for his brilliant speech at the National Mall, known widely as "I Have a Dream." Besides this speech's themes that resonate with biblical wisdom, its heralded prose contains four direct or indirect Scripture references:

- Amos 5:24 (NIV): "But let justice roll on like a river, righteousness like a never-failing stream!"
- Isaiah 40:4 (KJV): "Every valley shall be exalted, and every mountain and hill shall be made low: and the crooked shall be made straight, and the rough places plain."
- Psalm 30:5 (NIV): "Weeping may stay for the night, but rejoicing comes in the morning."
- Galatians 3:28 (NIV): "There is neither Jew nor Gentile, neither slave nor free, nor is there male and female, for you are all one in Christ Jesus."[109]

On April 3, 1968, the night before his assassination, Dr. King gave another iconic speech at Mason Temple in Memphis, Tennessee: "I've Been to the Mountaintop." He posed a scenario in which God asked, "Martin Luther King, which age would you like to live in?" Dr. King eloquently posed highlights from the beginning of history to the present and then answered, "Strangely enough I would turn to the Almighty and say, 'If you allow me to live just a few years in the second half of the twentieth century, I will be happy.'" He saw in his century, riddled with persecution and rampant martyrdoms in other countries, hope in helping the oppressed to be free. He ended the speech with words that proved prophetic:

Well, I don't know what will happen now. We've got some difficult days ahead. But it doesn't matter with me now. Because I've been to the mountaintop. And I don't mind. Like anybody, I would like to live a long life. Longevity has its place. But I'm not concerned about that now. I just want to do God's will. And He's allowed me to go up to the mountain. And I've looked over. And I've seen the promised land. I may not get there with you. But I want you to know tonight, that we, as a people, will get to the promised land. And I'm happy, tonight. I'm not worried about anything. I'm not fearing any man. Mine eyes have seen the glory of the coming of the Lord.[110]

He met the Lord the next day, gunned down while in Memphis to support the oppressed sanitation workers.

Allegedly, James Earl Ray aimed his pump-action hunting rifle, a Remington Model 760 Gamemaster, and assassinated Dr. King while he stood on the second floor balcony of Memphis's Lorraine Motel. Ray was "a confirmed racist and small time criminal" originally from Alton, Illinois, and an escaped convict from the Missouri State Penitentiary the previous year. He pled guilty, having allegedly positioned himself in a boarding house's second-floor bathroom at the rear of the building across Mulberry Street from the hotel, then dropped his gun in flight. Later he asked to retract his plea, saying a man named Raoul was actually the assassin.[111] Numerous conspiracy theories abound, easily found online and in books. Many in Dr. King's family voiced concerns about either Ray's guilt or his ability to act alone, and even met with him in prison. One sensational theory even alleges J. Edgar Hoover and the FBI were involved. The bullet fragment removed from Dr. King's body cannot be linked to the alleged rifle due to lack of markings, so a cloud of uncertainty remains. Ray died in 1998, still incarcerated.[112]

WATCHMAN NEE IN CHINA (1972) One of the most famous Christians in China's history, and "probably the most influential Protestant preacher in China in the early twentieth century," was Watchman Nee.[113] However, he spent all but one of his last twenty years incarcerated. He died at age sixty-eight, with no outside contact except with his wife, Charity, until her death the year before his passing, and thereafter only with her oldest sister. Nee was brilliant, intense, and controversial at times, while founding and fueling the massive local church movement before his arrest. He died alone in a labor camp, not long after being transferred there from prison to deflect any blame for his imminent passing. Even his grandniece received a tardy notice about his cremation.[114] But his life's work seemed to amplify with each passing year.

Nee had been prolific, utilizing his library of three thousand books to help him articulate his God-given plans for the body of Christ. We have numerous writings and countless stories from Nee. All of these, along with his business involvements (saving and enhancing his brother's pharmaceutical company), presented threats to the Communist leaders, who took over during his key ministry years.[115] His profits were going back into his ministry. His freedom would last for only three more years after the 1949 regime change, as the Communists arrested him on a litany of falsified charges on April 10, 1952.

However, Nee's founding of the local church movement (commonly called the Little Flock) and the concurrent launching of the self-governance philosophy of the "three-self" anchored explosive growth among Chinese Christians, resulting in at least seven hundred churches.

In the spring of 2022, the Museum of the Bible (Washington, DC) opened a yearlong exhibit of Watchman Nee's works with a riveting filmed testimony of his cellmate of nine years, You Qi Wu (interviewed by this text's authors).[116] Wu was converted during his time with Nee, and would spend twenty years as well in prison or on a labor farm. He saw Nee again shortly before his death. To hear Wu's impassioned recollection of his time with Nee, on film or in person, is to catch a glimpse of Nee himself.

Nee's work, and that of this original self-governance effort, is not to be confused with the Communist-initiated "Three-Self Patriotic Movement," which demanded socialist allegiance and anti-imperialistic rhetoric. Under the false impression that the government would afford churches the freedom to evangelize and baptize, Nee initially encouraged Little Flock leaders to sign "The Christian Manifesto" of 1950 that aligned many Protestants with Communism, and to support the Three-Self Patriotic Movement. However, once the veneer of openness was stripped away, Nee not only countered this but would ultimately pay the ultimate sacrifice for the free expression of faith.

Following the Communist leaders' expulsion of all foreign missionaries, Nee launched the Ecumenical Campaign in 1951, uniting four key groups and seeing rapid growth. These were the China Inland Mission churches (suddenly without foreign help), the Jesus Family, independent churches, and denominational churches in good standing with his movement.

Nee also began to realize the true stakes, as the government began claiming large properties for collective farms—and many were his or those of the Little Flock. Tensions within and without the Little Flock grew, as it became clear the two philosophies—evangelical Christianity and Communism—were diametrically opposed. The Communist authorities arrested him in 1952 but did not try his case until 1956.

What cost Nee his life was full and unabashed commitment to Christ, and never to the Maoist regime. The Little Flock "strongly believed that they were called out of this world to follow and serve Jesus Christ and that they could exist outside of politics yet coexist with the Communist government in the post-1949 era."[117] The changing nature of the relationship between the Little Flock and Communist leaders is complex, but suffice it to say it eventually drove the church underground.

In typical Communist fashion, it recruited some of Nee's church members to become informants. In turn, many Little Flock members would face arrests similar to Nee's, dying in labor camps or worse. The government held numerous public gatherings, or denunciations, calling on Christians to declare their view of Watchman Nee. (Knowingly or otherwise, those in agreement risked severe punishment.) Massive campaigns against the Little Flock appeared to work, and by the Great Leap Forward of 1958 (a social and economic campaign of the Chinese Communist Party), the Three-Self Patriotic Movement seemed to have control of the large Little Flock movement. The handwriting was on the wall for those choosing Christ over Communism—that is, in public.

Nee's grandniece wrote the following:

In June 1972, we got a notice from the labor farm that my granduncle had passed away. My eldest grandaunt and I rushed to the labor farm. But when we got there, we learned that he had already been cremated. We could only see his ashes. . . . Before his departure, he left a piece of paper under his pillow, which had several lines of big words written in a shaking hand. He wanted to testify to the truth which he had even until his death, with his lifelong experience. That truth is—"Christ is the Son of God who died for the redemption of sinners and resurrected after three days. This is the greatest truth in the universe. I die because of my belief in Christ. Watchman Nee." When the officer of the labor farm showed us this paper, I prayed that the Lord would let me quickly remember it by heart. . . .

My granduncle had passed away. He was faithful until death. With a crown stained with blood, he went to be with the Lord. Although God did not fulfill his last wish, to come out alive to join his wife, the Lord prepared something even better—they were reunited before the Lord.[118]

While large swaths of Christians still read several of Nee's books, his best known is *The Normal Christian Life* (1957). His thesis is clear and is based firmly on Paul's words in Galatians 2:20, "I have been crucified with Christ. It is no longer I who live, but Christ who lives in me. And the life I now live in the flesh I live by faith in the Son of God, who loved me and gave himself for me." Nee states in his introduction to *The Normal Christian Life* that Paul is "presenting God's normal for a Christian, which can be summarized in the words: I live no longer, but Christ lives his life in me."[119]

WANG ZHIMING IN CHINA (1973) As the young Red Army rose up during China's Cultural Revolution (1966–1973), all things old seemed in peril. And their view held Chinese religion as ancient and Christianity as new and imported. They closed churches and other places of worship, arrested and often killed clerics and other religious leaders, and strove to bring about what they considered a better world.

The goal may have been a pipe dream, but the ramifications were all too real. The beatings were often public. Christians and Muslims had to meet in secret. Preachers like Wang Zhiming had to navigate the contentious terrain. He lived and served in China's Yunnan region, in Wuding County, home to around 2,800 Christians. Though he was careful to show loyalty to the state, helping with allegiance to the Three-Self Patriotic Movement, he refused to concede to the public denunciation meetings. Wang said, "My hands have baptized many converts, and should not be used for sinfulness."[120] These forced public (state) meetings were much like the meetings Watchman Nee endured. Crowds of people ridiculing you, conscripted or pressured, or in this case, in frenzied agreement with the youthful atheists.

They arrested Wang in 1969 and didn't try him until 1973. During these years, over twenty other Christian leaders were arrested and many of them beaten. This delay between arrest and trial became a pattern, with key years of lives spent hidden in dire conditions and then being killed anyway.[121] In 2007, one of his sons, Wang Zisheng, spoke about his father's imprisonment.

> We could visit the detention center but were not allowed to see him. . . . They wouldn't give us any information about his physical condition. We were constantly taunted by the revolutionary soldiers: "Your old man was a bad guy. He believed in God. Why don't you draw a clear line with him?" "God is not the savior. Chairman Mao and the Communist Party are the saviors of the people. Do you believe in God or in Chairman Mao and the Communist Party?"[122]

On December 28, 1973, officials informed family members that Wang Zhiming would be executed the next day. The narrative of their last encounter with their father, after four years of absence, is touching—with "the above" used as code for "God."

> We finally saw our father. His hair had turned gray; he was thin, like a skeleton. Each time he moved, the shackles around his ankles clanked loudly. As he hobbled toward us, we all cried. . . . Seeing our whole family crying & sobbing, one guard howled at us: "Stop crying! Hurry up and talk to your father one by one. Time is limited."
>
> My mother nodded at my father and said, "You are the one who used to do all the talking. We listen to you first." My father smiled. . . . "I haven't been able to reform my thinking," my father said. "Since I cannot be changed, I am responsible for, and

deserve, what I receive. But for all of you, don't follow me. Listen to what 'the above' tells you."[123]

The Red Army amassed a rally of 10,000 people, but things didn't go as planned. Many Christians in the crowd attacked the leaders and pandemonium broke out.[124]

My father, with his hands & legs tied with ropes, stood in the middle of the stage, the two other criminals on either side. There was blood at the corner of his mouth. We learned later that a guard had used his bayonet to slash his tongue so he wouldn't be able to shout or preach. Some former church members and leaders went up on the stage and denounced my father's crimes. After that was over, a leader grabbed the microphone & announced, "Wang Zhiming has been sentenced to death; the execution will be carried out immediately." Soldiers raised Father into the air so everyone could see him. The crowd roared. They raised their fists high and shouted, "Down with . . . ," "Smash . . . ," and "Long live Chairman Mao." . . .

The soldiers put a wooden sign on his back—a "death sign," it was called. It listed the 5 crimes my father was said to have committed. His name was also there, with a big red X over its characters. The soldiers carried him to a truck and pushed him in with the other prisoners, bending his head low. Two cars led the way. My father's truck was in the middle. Another truck with fully armed soldiers followed, a machine gun was perched on its roof. They paraded my father around the streets for half an hour before taking him to an old airport where he was shot.[125]

The family had to remain at the assembly area, with hands on heads and backs to the stage like they were supposed to be while their father was there (but they peeked when guards looked away). Soldiers tied them together with a rope, led them to his cell, and yelled at them to take home his belongings. Though the official had bragged they would blow up their father's body (to prevent veneration), in the end someone outside the family convinced him to release it. However, guards stood around their house to prevent people from paying respects.

Decades later, a different image of Wang Zhiming prevails than the shriveled, maimed, berated figure his oppressors thought would be the last fading memory of a detractor.

Today Wuding County can boast something novel—"the only monument known to commemorate a Christian killed in the Cultural Revolution."[126] The monument is of Wang Zhiming, and another statue of this hero is among those of the twentieth-century martyrs at Westminster Abbey. The following words are on the monument's base:

> As the Scripture says of the Saints, "They will rest from their labours for their deeds follow them."[127]

Wang's wife and three sons suffered greatly—they were also imprisoned in 1969. His wife served three years in prison, two of the sons served nine, and the third seems to have committed suicide. In the end, the government's efforts to stamp out religion not only failed, but also seemed to backfire. In 1980, it considered Wang posthumously rehabilitated, and extended compensation to his family (only the equivalent of $250). The number of Christians in Wuding County grew to 30,000, and churches increased to 100![128]

JANANI LUWUM IN UGANDA (1974) When esteemed historian Mark Noll spoke at a ceremony honoring modern martyrs at the Beeson Divinity School (Samford University), he chose Janani Luwum as his prime example. A reflection on his talk notes that Luwum's "suffering and death encouraged many Ugandans and others to turn to Christ." The article adds,

> "Luwum teaches us not to brush over the aftermath of violence," said Noll, who had cited scripture from Habakkuk, which references that the earth shall be filled with the knowledge of the glory of the Lord, as the waters cover the sea.[129]

Dictator Idi Amin had been ruthless, killing the former prime minister he had supplanted, Milton Obote, and the entire population of the man's home village. Frustrated over one of Luwum's sermons against him, Amin ordered a raid on the bishop's house. The soldiers arrested Luwum on trumped up charges on February 16, 1977, then claimed he died in a jeep wreck trying to take over the steering. However, when his body arrived in Mucwini in Kitgum, on February 19, the locals saw bullet holes that told the real story.[130] Archbishop Luwum had been shot in an attempt to silence religious dissent. His wife and children fled to Luwum's home village in Kenya around 500 km away. On these same dates in 2020, the Church of Uganda organized a pilgrimage, and seventy-six Christians walked this same journey.[131]

Luwum's martyrdom was not the first in Uganda, whose Christians had faced mass executions between 1885 and 1887, known as "The Ugandan Martyrs," introduced in the previous chapter. Luwum and others a century later remained inspired by their rich heritage.

DID YOU KNOW? *Samford's Memorial Statues*

Statues of martyrs watch over one of the most stunning buildings of this century on any college campus, Hodges Chapel at Beeson Divinity School. This memorial display is a showpiece of the Samford University campus in Birmingham, Alabama. More importantly, it venerates the gospel story and the heritage of the church. Prominent crosses symbolizing the ultimate martyr dominate the space. A tribute of shields to the apostles line the nave; all are martyrs but John. Carved by an English company, they represent "the Church Militant" against the powers of darkness.

Among the four prominent cherrywood carvings of great ministers surrounding the pulpit, two are martyrs (Chrysostom and Jan Hus). A great cloud of witnesses look down ninety feet from the stunning mural lining the domed ceiling. Among the images of sixteen witnesses are martyrs Perpetua and Felicitas, Thomas Cranmer, and Lottie Moon—an amazing Southern Baptist missionary in northern China who had an impact far greater than her four-foot, three-inch stature. She exhausted herself at age seventy-two, dying in 1912 en route home and weighing only around fifty pounds—in large part from giving much of her food and funds to help others. She transformed the commitment to take furloughs to extend one's health, and successfully implemented the important opportunities for women to reach other women in Chinese culture. She "symbolizes not only the women's organization among Southern Baptists but also the missionary soul of the denomination itself."[132]

The most prominent celebration of martyrs is embodied by the six statues of twentieth-century martyrs, one from each inhabited continent. Rómulo Sauñe from Peru was gunned down by the Shining Path after visiting the grave of his grandfather, who had also been brutally murdered by the same. When the Japanese invaded Papua New Guinea in 1942, they murdered May Hayman and another missionary nurse in 1942. They buried them in a coffee plantation trench. Bishop Haik Hovsepianmehr "mysteriously disappeared" in Iran in 1994 for successfully bringing international attention to persecuted pastors. Dictator Idi Amin killed Archbishop Janani Luwum in 1977, among many other Ugandans raising voices against his brutality. After a faux military trial, Luwum "was never seen alive again." His funeral was held in the capital of Kampala, and he was buried next to one of the first martyrs of the Ugandan church, Archbishop James Hannington (1885). The next June, 25,000 Ugandans made a pilgrimage to these graves to celebrate the centennial of the first sermon in their country. Another statue represents Dietrich Bonhoeffer—martyred for his active resistance against Adolf Hitler and his treatment of the true church and of the Jews. Bill Wallace, a surgeon from Knoxville, Tennessee, died in Wuchow, China, after serving there seventeen years. The communists framed and convicted him for spying, and he died alone in his cell after excruciating treatment.[133]

Vintage Foxe

Princes, kings, and other rulers of the world have used all their strength and cunning against the Church, yet it continues to endure and hold its own.[134]

SECTION FOUR

Martyrs of Recent History

From Terrorists' Beheadings to School Shootings

ANGAELOS'S STORY

Angaelos was a Coptic Christian from the area of Ismailia—a beautiful city at the midpoint of the Suez Canal, on the northwestern bank of Lake Al-Timsah in northeastern Egypt.[1] Though considered to be the "Garden City" or the "Little Paris of Egypt," evil ripped through its beauty. Angaelos's death proved to be one of thousands that literally reflected the biblical command found in Matthew 16:24:

> Then Jesus told his disciples, "If anyone would come after me, let him deny himself and take up his cross and follow me."

Angaelos was returning from work among the Bedouin with his friend, a Muslim, when he met both evil and his Maker within minutes. His wife, Mariam, shared some of the details of his martyrdom in an in-person interview for this book on April 22, 2017. Sitting in her home, and joined by her sister and brother-in-law, Mariam showed the cross tattooed on her wrist and shared these piercing words about his murderers: "Like the devil, they get nervous when they see the cross."

Angaelos stopped their car that fateful day for two Army trucks. However, instead of soldiers, terrorists from the mountains emerged and asked for their IDs, which in Egypt would also indicate the bearer's religion.

Mariam shared, "The Muslim man, he just gave them his ID, and my husband . . . gave them the ID—he was *so* brave—and said, 'I am Christian.'" She said Angaelos knew these men were terrorists.

The terrorists yelled at Angaelos, "Okay, get out of the car!" His Muslim friend stayed in the car, and they never asked him to get out. "Bow down on your knees!" Angaelos bowed down.

Mariam emphasized that they pressured him, "Say the two words [phrases]. There is no God except Allah, and Muhammad is the prophet of Allah."

And the terrorists urged Angaelos again, "Say it!"

"No, I will never say that! I am Christian, and here is the cross!" he responded, pointing to the small tattoo of the Coptic Orthodox cross on his wrist.

His proud widow continued, "They shot him with a bullet here [pointing to her head], and then about *fourteen* here," pointing to her wrist tattoo of the cross. "He was so brave."

Mariam spoke of the risks he took daily. "He was so brave and he was always telling [the Bedouin in his work] . . . and the Bedouin are so aggressive . . . and they are like kind of fanatical Muslims, but he kept telling them about Jesus and about the Bible."

She was always worried and afraid for him. She would often caution him, saying, "What are you doing?! How are you just telling them about the Bible and about Jesus, because this is unsafe for you."

He usually responded, "We will not be afraid, we should be brave" and "I don't worry and am not afraid of anybody, except God. No one but God . . ."

The Bedouin he was witnessing to "asked him for a Bible because he kept telling them about stories from the Bible and Jesus and such."

For whoever would save his life will lose it, but whoever loses his life for my sake will find it. For what will it profit a man if he gains the whole world and forfeits his soul? Or what shall a man give in return for his soul?

MATTHEW 16:25-26

Mariam has a very clear answer for how her husband, a heroic martyr, answered Christ's questions.

A Note from the Authors on Our List of Modern Martyrs (After 1989)

The last decade of the twentieth century and the first two decades of the twenty-first century were some of the bloodiest in modern Christian history.

On nearly every continent, Christians—and especially Christian leaders—were killed in grotesque ways for their faith alone. The sheer scale of these persecutions, which came mainly at the hands of Islamic extremists and communist governments, present a terrible challenge for any author trying to pick and choose which among countless possible stories ought to be included in a book like this. So we solicited the help of friends and advisors to select a representative sample of martyrs over the last century.

Volumes upon volumes of stories could be compiled from 2010–2020 alone, but we have chosen approximately fifty reports, organized geographically, to represent the thousands we could not chronicle here. We have also selected accounts that demonstrate different types of persecution. This includes what you'd expect (beheadings at the hands of Islamic extremists, for instance), but also what you might not expect (Christians killed for standing up to corruption and injustice). We have included stories of foreign missionaries who gave their lives in service to a country in which they weren't born, and we've documented stories of indigenous local Christian communities. We have also included some stories which are connected to one another, demonstrating how martyrdom can affect a whole community or family over generations.

This section also presents a departure from the previous sections in two ways.

First, unlike the rest of this book, where we have gone to great lengths to describe the history surrounding the accounts, we have foregone *some* contextualization in order to focus on these stories. So here, and not unlike the original *Foxes' Book of Martyrs*, we'll assume you know more about our shared living memories to help you place each account in its appropriate region, historical setting, and political context. You'll simply find one story after another. The stories will, we believe, inspire you and give you pause as you continue to reflect on the enormity of these sacrifices.

Second, this section is entirely and intentionally ecumenical. It includes stories of Orthodox, Catholic, and Protestant (including evangelical) Christians who have died for their faith. One of our great challenges in presenting this *New Book of Christian Martyrs* has been to integrate appropriately (albeit selectively) the original Foxe's text while acknowledging that other branches of the Christian church also deserved the accolades Foxe denied them through his unabashed Protestant emphasis. In this section, we aim to make a point about the unity of the church today because of persecution. There is, as Pope Francis said so poignantly at the height of the ISIS atrocities in Iraq and Syria, "an ecumenism of blood" uniting a once divided church. Those who come to kill Christians don't ask first if the Christians are evangelicals or Catholics or anything else. They just look for a cross.

We hope these stories impact your life as they have ours.

CHAPTER FOURTEEN

From the Soviets in Europe and a Caliphate in the Middle East

---

We are hard-pressed on every side, yet not crushed; we are perplexed, but not in despair. **2 CORINTHIANS 4:8, NKJV**

We, Christians of Mesopotamia, are used to religious persecution and pressures by those in power. After Constantine, persecution ended only for western Christians, whereas in the east threats continued. Even today we continue to be a church of martyrs.[1]
PAULOS FARAJ RAHHO

From the very beginning of the life of the Church, Christians have always believed that the blood of martyrs is a seed for Christians, as Tertullian said. Today too, in a dramatic way, the blood of a great number of Christian martyrs continues to be shed on the field of the world, with the certain hope that will bear fruit in a rich harvest of holiness, justice, reconciliation and love of God. But we must remember that one is not born a martyr. Archbishop Romero remarked, "We must be willing to die for our faith, even if the Lord does not grant us this honor. . . . Giving life does not only mean

being assassinated; giving life, having the spirit of martyrdom, means offering it in silence, in prayer, in the honest fulfillment of one's duty; in this silence of everyday life, giving life a little at a time."[2]
POPE FRANCIS

The fall of the Berlin Wall in 1989 led evangelist Billy Graham to declare that "Russia could be on the verge of the greatest religious revival in the history of the Christian faith."[3] Not long thereafter Graham held an evangelistic crusade in the Olympic Stadium, just a short walk from the Kremlin, the seat of the Soviets' authoritarian, atheistic government. It was 1992 and thousands came to hear the gospel message. Everyone attending was given a copy of the book forbidden for decades—the Bible. Soviet Christian leaders called the event an "unbelievable miracle."[4] It seemed that atheist Communism, which two generations of Christians had seen as the gospel's ultimate enemy, was losing its stranglehold on the gospel message.

Within thirty years of the fall of the Berlin Wall and Graham's pronouncement, the global church had helped to rebuild Eastern Europe by planting thousands of churches, training tens of thousands of workers, and conducting extensive humanitarian projects. A Pew Research Center survey reported that religion had reasserted itself across the Central and Eastern European countries where communist regimes had previously outlawed religious worship. Today, most citizens in those nations identify with some sort of orthodoxy, often as part of their national identity, even if they don't often attend a place of worship. Fully 86 percent of the people in those nations are unashamed to say they now believe in God.[5]

As the collapse of Communism led to a decrease in Christian persecution in some places, that same era produced massive worldwide Islamic extremism that unleashed new deadly force against Christians. In addition, India experienced a new, fiercely political Hinduism, and many African nations came under the authoritarian rule of deadly dictatorships. For Christians around the world, a new fight was on.

Nations that had not been actively Islamic abruptly changed. In 1994, a major Islamic push caused Turkish political candidates to pledge their support for a return to Islam from the secular stance the nation had adopted in the 1920s. Within one decade, Turkey's politicians were mostly Islamic, and the nation emerged from its long secular sleep as a major force for Islam—and sometimes, extremism.

Iran started its push toward extreme Islam in 1979 under the Ayatollah Khomeini. The "mullahcracy" he started continued when a 1989 constitutional amendment downgraded the qualification for Supreme Leader and cleared the way for Ali Khamenei to take over. Khamenei's Iran has continued to persecute its Christian minority, and exports weapons to destabilize neighboring nations such as Iraq and Syria. This paved the way for the Islamic State (IS) to declare, albeit briefly, a hugely destructive caliphate in swaths of land otherwise controlled by traditional nation states. Islamic violence continues to escalate against non-Islamic people in a global "jihad." Though IS, ISIL, and ISIS adherents exploit divisions between Islamic groups and fight each other, their main target is clear. The ISIS magazine, at the height of their rise, was adorned with a picture of Vatican Square with an ISIS flag superimposed atop its famous obelisk.

CULTURAL CONNECTION

Fall of the Berlin Wall

East Berlin built the Berlin Wall in 1961, ostensibly to keep the West from entering the East. It instead became a de facto prison wall, keeping people in the East from defecting to the West. On November 9, 1989, a Communist spokesperson for East Germany announced that the wall would open for free travel. Starting at midnight that night, and continuing all weekend, two million people crossed what had been the modern world's most formidable barrier. Three figures are most responsible for the fall of the Berlin Wall: Pope John Paul II, Margaret Thatcher, and Ronald Reagan. Reagan's iconic speech in front of the wall was punctuated by these famous words, "Mr. Gorbachev, tear down this wall!"

Refuseniks were Jews whom the Soviet Union would not allow to leave. There was often no explanation given for why an emigration visa was denied, beyond a vague attribution to "state security." Vladimir Slepak, a leading Jewish activist, was held because he had once been an engineer and might divulge Russian secrets to the West, although any "secrets" he knew years earlier were by that time common knowledge.[6] Refusenik Benjamin Bogomolny waited from 1966 to 1986 to leave, and became listed as "most patient" in the Guinness Book of World Records. Once refuseniks applied to leave, they were fired from their jobs and forced to accept whatever job the government was willing to give them. Highly educated people might become street sweepers. The government confiscated money sent from outside. Because of tenacious activism on their behalf, about two million Soviet Jews moved to Israel, the United States, and other countries between 1990 and 2015.[7]

FATHER ALEKSANDER MEN Aleksander Men was born to an agnostic father and a Jewish mother in Moscow in 1935. When he was seven months old, his mother secretly arranged to have him baptized as a Christian and was herself baptized at the same time.[8] In his childhood, Men's mother and aunt constantly read to him and introduced him to other languages.[9] The priest who baptized him also tutored him, feeding his hungry intellect and borrowing more books once Men had devoured the priest's library.[10] As a child, Men's interests were wide but his higher education was interrupted when he was expelled from studying biology because of his religious convictions. Instead, he started a correspondence course in theology. He eventually graduated from the Leningrad Theological Seminary, and then earned a doctorate at the Moscow Theological Academy.

Aleksander Men was born during the Stalinist purge, in which 24,000 Moscow-area residents, including nearly all the priests and monks, were executed.[11] He grew up during difficult times. His father was arrested, and his mother and aunt fled with him. They faced constant danger from nearby fighting during World War II and had to work hard to keep from starving. The bright eyes of young Aleksander Men saw all of this. One of his most dramatic early memories was a clandestine Mass celebrated in a forest where, to his child's eye, all of nature praised God. As he studied, Men appreciated church tradition, and yet also believed that in looking forward, not back, a person could realize his potential and, ultimately, his destiny.

Under the Soviet regime, Christians in Men's generation had been besieged with propaganda that resulted in spiritual poverty. The Orthodox Church under Soviet influence had become essentially a branch of the government, an anachronism without influence, removed from the world of common people. Men's studies led him to reconnect the Orthodox tradition to the daily concerns of real people.

By the time he was ordained a priest in 1958, Men was anything but spiritually impoverished. After flailing his way through two parish assignments, he was sent to the rural parish of Novaya Derevnya, where he finally mastered his ministry skills. The little parish soon acquired a reputation because of Men's incisive teaching. People found he could not only address the needs of parishioners and connect them to the traditions of the church, but he could also minister to the needs of the highly educated and talk to them on their own terms.

Men made close friends of intellectuals and yet, his messages made Christianity relevant to poor, uneducated parishioners as well as intellectuals. He used examples from nature and history, referred to church fathers and philosophers, and always directed people into the truths of the faith. As a result of his powerful messages, he was criticized by church leaders who rightly called him "non-Orthodox," and he was persecuted by the KGB, the foreign intelligence and domestic security agency of the Soviet Union.

In the 1980s, Men's parish messages became nationally known. Mikhail Gorbachev opened up Soviet society beginning in 1986, and Men was called on as a television commentator and lecturer. He became a national celebrity overnight. Although he lectured extensively, he never tired of listening to and answering people's questions. He was at ease with himself and with people, whether on a stage or one-on-one. Even when the KGB brought him in for questioning after one of the many times his house was raided, he was not irritated. Someone asked if the police interrogation exhausted him. Men replied, "Not at all. I enjoy talking with people."[12]

In 1989, Aleksander Men gave one of the greatest sermons of his life, titled, "Two Understandings of Christianity." The sermon was about the church and the world around it and the practices that make Christianity vital to it. Men explained we need both. At the time, the Communist party was increasingly discredited, which left a vacuum of thought. Men was purposeful in his speech, reacquainting his audience with Russian history to offer a framework on which the church could build a future, effectively moving Russian audiences away from Communist ideology while offering intellectual solutions that satisfied minds taught to prioritize rational thought. Soon, people saw a deep appeal in the church and began supporting its revival in order to regenerate Russia.

All the while, Men wrote prolifically. His most popular work was *The Son of Man*. He also wrote a trilogy on *Life within the Church*, catechisms for children and adolescents, a six-volume study on pre-Christian spirituality, manuals of prayer for adults, and 1,790 articles later used in Russian seminaries.[13] He became one of the founders of the Russian Bible Society in 1990. That same year, he founded the Open Orthodox University.

On September 9, 1990, Russian Orthodox priest Aleksander Men set out from his home outside Moscow to catch the early train to Novaya Derevnya. The path to the train station was bordered by trees. As he walked, someone jumped behind him and struck an axe into his skull. Men dragged himself back to the cottage. His wife rushed him to the hospital, where he died. He was fifty-five years old.[14] The president of the USSR and the president of Russia ordered an investigation, but no arrests were ever made, and the murder remains unsolved.[15]

Some of Men's greatest contributions, besides his personal life of faith, were to bring intellectual relevance to the church and to challenge the church in Jesus' own words, "You are called to freedom, brethren."[16] Aleksander Men exercised that freedom and paved the way for many Russians to believe, even under a totalitarian system.

The Russian Orthodox Church in Modern Russia

First-century missionary apostle Andrew founded what became the Greek Orthodox Church. In the ninth century, Greek Orthodox missionaries in turn founded a church in Kyev, Ukraine that became the first Russian Orthodox Church. As Russia came out from under Mongol rule in the mid-1400s, the Russian Orthodox Church named its own metropolitan, thereby becoming *autocephalous*, an independent extension of Eastern Orthodoxy.

Centuries of power struggles ensued with Russian czars exerting or relinquishing control, and Christians were forced underground for long periods, until the Russian Church found an unexpected champion. The ruthless dictator Joseph Stalin freed the church to elect its own officials, as part of his effort to get patriotic support for World War II. Stalin, of course, deserves no credit, for his purpose was to exploit the church, but his policy led to a period of expansion, church planting, and building theological institutions. Starting in 1959, Nikita Khrushchev and Leonid Brezhnev reversed Stalin's policy, resulting in widespread Christian persecution and church closures. Stalin stabbed the church in the back while his successors stabbed them in the front.

Mikhail Gorbachev's leadership and the 1991 collapse of the Soviet Union changed everything. A flood of missionaries built churches and seminaries across the nation. Lest Westerners think the work is done, studies show that although Orthodox Russians believe in God, they don't regularly attend worship services. Sociologist Grace Davie famously called it "believing without belonging."[17] Still, the Russian Orthodox Church continues to be a major presence throughout the nation.

FATHER JACQUES HAMEL Father Jacques Hamel spent fifty-eight years in the priesthood before his life came to a sudden and brutal end in the summer of 2016.

Hamel was born in Normandy in 1930 to parents who were unhappy enough to scandalize their Catholic parish with a divorce. His mother,

Jeanne, was a weaver, and barely able to provide for the family. She cleaned the parish church and often prepared meals for nuns who lived nearby. However, the stigma of divorce never left. At Hamel's 1958 ordination, Jeanne watched while hiding behind a church pillar.[18]

Hamel grew up timid, impoverished, and in love with the church. Although he struggled with poor health, he sang in the choir and helped the priests in any way he could. In his private playtime, he acted out the Mass. His sister said that despite his difficulties, he didn't complain, but seemed to enjoy a deep inner peace.[19] In his early adulthood, his ill health didn't prevent him from being conscripted into the army and sent to French Algeria. The brutality of the Algerian War deeply impacted him. Perhaps it was in Algeria that he began to fully appreciate what he had learned in the Bible about man's capacity for evil or the belief that Satan was roaming the earth seeking whomever he could devour.[20]

To stand against that enemy, he answered the call to the priesthood. Hamel was rooted in the working class at a time when most priests came from the middle class, so his choice was unusual but not unexpected. In seminary, his superiors showed concern at his diffidence and ill health. When he asked to become a missionary to Africa, they declined. He was assigned instead to a parish in the Archdiocese of Rouen. He never left.

His church in Saint-Étienne-du-Rouvray, France, is situated neatly between the River Seine and a national forest that is tucked inside the city limits. Across the street, children play in the outdoor playground of a nursery. On the road are cafés, businesses, and shops. The woman in the flower shop was taught her catechism by the town's gentle priest, Father Jacques Hamel, as were most of the adult Catholics living nearby.[21]

Hamel's ordinariness, the frailties he wore on his sleeve, lent an aura of trust, and parishioners leaned on him when the unspectacular rural life they led became troubled. His fellow priests said he was clumsy rather than charismatic. He could be cantankerous or simply stay silent, as he often did at clergy meetings. But his silence was a felt presence. He was a good listener, adaptable, considerate. Each week he handwrote homilies. Five hundred carefully worded messages for religious services, baptisms, marriages, and funerals remain. In them, he showed his determination to portray a clear gospel message, often focused on holiness. He regularly said, "Don't be afraid of sanctity!"[22]

In 2006, Hamel stepped down from his position, having reached the official retirement age of seventy-five, but he never stopped working. If anyone asked why he was still conducting baptisms or visiting the sick or grieving, he would say, "I made a vow of obedience and I will go on to the end."[23]

In his early eighties, Hamel saw a change in France as terrorist attacks made international headlines. As he approached his eighty-fifth birthday, he read the news of jihadist suicide-bombers and gunmen killing people in Paris, and a jihadist mowing down civilians in Nice with a truck. Hamel admired the Algerian martyr Charles de Foucauld, a desert priest who was killed by Islamic extremists. The 1996 beheadings of the Cistercian monks by Islamic fanatics in Algeria had moved him enough to see the film about them called *Of Gods and Men* in 2010. No doubt these martyrs reminded him in vivid detail of the savage war he'd once been forced to join.

In 2016, Hamel told his sister that he was having a recurring nightmare. In it he would leave his little church to go home and be ambushed by a group of strangers who beat him. He would look for help, but the streets were deserted.

Speaking of the martyrdom of Algerian monks by Islamist fanatics, Jacques once commented to his sister, "How is it that these men [who killed the monks] could act with such vicious violence against [those] who had lived in their community doing nothing but serving the poor, feeding the hungry, and caring for the sick? Is it because the devil had entered into their hearts and minds, and they became numb to all charity and compassion?"[24]

On the night before his death, Hamel told family members that the terrorists who carried out such butchery in "the name of God" were "men without souls, nor faith, nor law."[25]

The next morning, July 26, 2016, proved warm and fair as Hamel awoke, read, ate his breakfast pastry, and left home to conduct the nine o'clock Mass. Three Catholic sisters, a layperson, and a married couple named Guy and Janine Coponet joined him there.[26]

The little group was startled when the doors burst open and two men armed with knives, Adel Kermiche and Abdel Malik Petitjean, began shouting at the gathering, "'*Vous, les chrétiens, vous nous supprimez!*' [You, the Christians, we will do away with you!]." They made Jacques get on his knees before the altar, yelling "*Allahu Akbar!*"[27] They forced a video camera into the hand of Guy Coponet to record the assassination of the priest. Hamel clearly called back, "*Va t'en Satan!*" ("Get away, Satan!") The attackers slit his throat.[28]

As the priest's blood soaked the floor, one of the attackers asked Sister Hélène Decaux, "Are you afraid to die?" She said, "No . . . I believe in God, and I know I will be happy." He retorted, "I believe in God, too, and I am not afraid to die. Jesus is a man, not God!"[29]

The bizarre conversation provided time for police to arrive. As the terrorists attempted to leave the church, they were immediately shot dead.

In death, the gentle faith of Father Jacques Hamel was readily seen. Although he sought to draw all people into a personal, loving relationship with God, he held a dogged, stubborn love for all those whom he could not persuade. They loved him in return. Who would have ever imagined that a simple, faithful parish priest would become a famous martyr meriting the admiration of Christians around the world?

The Communist mayor of Saint-Étienne-du-Rouvray openly wept as he announced the murder to the world.[30] Large numbers of Muslims wept with their Christian neighbors at memorial Masses. In the community, the mosque condemned the attack and professed solidarity with its Catholic neighbors. Guy and Janine Coponet publicly expressed forgiveness for the two young men. Father Jacques's own sister was seen consoling crying Muslims during a prayer service.[31]

Father Jacques Hamel's last words were taken from Matthew's Gospel. A lifelong student of God's Word, he would have known by heart the entire passage in which Christ rebuked the devil. "Away from me, Satan! For it is written: 'Worship the Lord your God, and serve him only'" (Matthew 4:10, NIV). The beloved priest, no longer timid and sickly, spoke with the authority and power of his Lord as he knelt before the altar renouncing evil and worshiping God with his dying breath. This last defiant act reflects the hope expressed in Scripture: "Where, O death, is your sting?" (1 Corinthians 15:55, NIV).

Mother Teresa was born Agnes Gonxha Bojaxhiu on August 26, 1910, in Skopje, North Macedonia. She was the youngest of three children born into an Albanian family that settled in the former Yugoslavia. By age twelve, little Gonxha felt a passion to train as a missionary and help the poor. At age nineteen, she took her vows and joined the Sisters of Loretto, an Irish community of nuns in Kolkata, India. For the rest of that century, Mother Teresa and her Missionaries of Charity rehabilitated slum dwellers and built children's homes, homes for the dying, clinics, a leper colony, and more. As her work spread through Asia, Africa, and South America, her reputation spread worldwide. The woman known as one of the world's greatest humanitarians died September 5, 1997. The Mother Teresa Memorial House now stands at the site of the church where Gonxha Bojaxhiu was baptized, received her first communion, and sang in the choir.[32]

While Mother Teresa was not a martyr, her ministry—universally admired in India and around the world—faced persecution from a division of the government of India in 2021. The ministry was barred from receiving foreign donations four days before Christmas. Persecution often makes a person think of martyrdom or imprisonment, but in many countries of the world, persecution is the result of governments using regulatory regimes to punish those they oppose.[33]

MARTHA MYERS "Bury me in Jibla," was the last wish of Dr. Martha Myers, speaking of the city in Yemen where she served as an obstetrician for over twenty-five years. Friends from 1963, when she was only an undergraduate freshman, remember she was "as clear as crystal" that her future was medical missions.[34] On a mission trip to Yemen during her last year of medical school in 1971, Myers saw the mission field where she wanted to serve.

In Yemen, a country with an average of 7.6 births per woman, only one in four women receive prenatal care, and one in thirteen women die during childbirth. The infant mortality rate is sixty-two per 1,000 women.[35]

Myers's father, a doctor and state health officer in Alabama, said his daughter saw the great need in Yemen. "This is what she felt she ought to be doing," he said, "and she did it."[36]

Myers could have gone anywhere. Her biology professor at Samford University said, "She was a brilliant, hard-working person, good in things other than [just] biology," he said. "She sang in the a cappella choir and edited the literary magazine, but there was never any doubt among the faculty that she was headed to the medical mission field."[37]

When Myers left the United States for good, she gave her reasoning in a video posted on the International Mission Board's website. She said, "No prayers are wasted on Yemen . . . because the needs are so great. And I would say the fields are white unto harvest and we need to pray to the Lord of the harvest to send out folks to help."[38]

Her specialty was obstetrics and gynecology, but Martha Myers treated men and children too. One Yemeni said she would get out her medical bag "and set up a clinic on the side of a rocky road until every person had been treated."[39] As she drove her Toyota Land Cruiser around the nation to immunize children or dispense medications, people would recognize her and shout, "Dr. Martha!"

When family and friends visited and tried to sightsee, she was recognized—and needed—everywhere. Her sister, Joanna Kingery, said she always carried her medical bag, and people flocked to her for help. "She felt that we need to grab every opportunity to get to know people, find out where they are and share with them," Kingery said. Often she took visitors on her medical visits. "We couldn't keep up with her," Kingery said. "It's like she always runs on more than a full tank."[40]

Every few years when she returned to the United States, Myers stayed just as busy, talking to church groups about her work and gathering medical supplies and other items needed. On a couple of visits, she collected enough supplies to fill fifteen large suitcases to send back to Yemen.[41] Myers also spent hours online with people all over the world discussing the work in Yemen. "I used to refer to her as the Energizer bunny," her father said. "I don't think she slept in her bed the last time she was home for more than one or two nights."[42]

Myers discovered her gift for serving at a young age. Her father said, "She took care of her brother [Grady] who was 13 months younger than she was even when she was in nursery school." Joanna Kingery said family pictures often show her, the little sister, in Myers's arms. In those early years, Myers also became interested in medicine, sometimes imitating medical procedures on Grady. When she became a Christian as a child, she practiced meeting the needs of others further.[43]

After Myers completed her medical training, friends and family found it only natural when she left for London to receive seminary training and lessons in Arabic. Her long quest was realized when she joined the Jibla Baptist Hospital as one of only a few obstetrician-gynecologists in Yemen.[44]

Martha Myers's adopted home was a nation of 60 million guns and 20 million people. Shootouts and kidnappings are common. Her brother Grady said, "They had a place in the hospital where you check your weapon when you go in. I guarantee that if she had been shot and wasn't killed, she would not come home. She was just that dedicated."[45]

In 1998, four armed men hijacked Myers's Toyota and forced her to lie down in the back. They growled that they'd kill her if she spoke and she replied, "Well, I'll be in heaven." The vehicle then stalled, and the men abandoned it.[46] Even after this incident, the idea of leaving Yemen apparently never crossed her mind. Joanna Kingery recalls Myers saying if she were lucky, she'd be in Yemen "until her dying day."[47]

Call it luck or God's grace or an abominable tragedy, Martha Myers's wish came true when, at age fifty-seven, she was in a meeting with coworkers when a gunman smuggled a weapon into the hospital and shot her and her two coworkers in the head.

Forty thousand Yemenis jammed the streets to mourn the death of "Dr. Martha" on the day of her funeral. Government documents may have listed her place of ministry as "Jibla Hospital," but Yemeni newspapers called it the "Hospital of Peace."[48]

After Myers's death, her father said, "I am certain that if she knew that this was going to happen to her, that would not have deterred her. [But] she would be embarrassed about the amount of coverage that this has been given."[49]

Humble, brilliant, and gracious, "Dr. Martha" literally loved the people of Yemen unto death.

DID YOU KNOW? *The First Christian Missionary to Iraq*

Nestled in the "fertile crescent" of the Tigris and Euphrates riverbeds, Nineveh is the oldest city of the ancient Assyrian empire in the region known today as Iraq. Ancient Nineveh was just north of today's Mosul.

While the prophet Jonah was the first known missionary God sent to the people of Nineveh, the apostle Thomas in the first century was the first Christian missionary to the area. Large churches and Christian communities grew over the centuries, even amid periods of great persecution. For the last 1,400 years, Christian proselytizing has often been forbidden, yet ancient Christian communities enjoyed long periods of stability, living at peace with their Muslim neighbors.

Only in the modern era, since the 1990s, have Iraqi Christians faced extinction. They have been forced to flee by the tens of thousands to escape unfair taxation, persecution, slavery, and execution. Most flee northward, through ancient Nineveh, where makeshift refugee camps provide little relief. Although some reports declare that Iraqi Christianity risks extinction, remarkably the gospel is still being preached by faithful and tenacious Christian leaders, and the church perseveres.[50]

KAREN WATSON "I wasn't called to a place; I was called to Him," Karen Watson wrote. "To obey was my objective, to suffer was expected, His glory was my reward."[51]

Watson, age thirty-eight, was killed in Iraq on March 15, 2004. A year earlier, she penned a poignant letter to her pastor, Phil Neighbors, that went viral when he released it to the world after her death.

Karen Watson was described by friends and colleagues as radiant, alive, talkative, bright, sweet, and likable. She loved movies, shopping, enchiladas, her church, Jesus, and the missions trips he sent her on during every vacation.

"She was friendly and funny," said Sheriff Lt. Kevin Wright, her boss when she worked at the Kern County Jail. But he also called her "stern and by-the-book."[52] Wright described her as "a straight shooter," adding, "She was the kind of person you wanted on your side when the going got rough."[53] The inmates liked her, too, because she was compassionate.

Wright said, "I never knew her to be melancholy, downcast or distraught. And even with her letter, she wasn't being mystical. She wasn't expecting to die. She was aware of the dangers. . . . She was just taking care of business." The secretary at Watson's church described her as "fun-loving and great" and observed that "she wanted to help the people in Iraq and show them that God loved them."[54]

In March 2003, Watson took a leave of absence from her job to start her new career as a missionary. She went all-in. She sold her house, her car, and almost everything else. She stuffed her remaining earthly possessions into a single duffel bag, threw it over her shoulder, and headed for Iraq. After Watson's sister, Lorraine, dropped her off at the airport, she turned to her husband and said, "I'm never going to see her again."[55]

That same month, the United States military invaded Iraq and deposed Saddam Hussein. Relief agencies, such as the International Missions Board, swooped into the vacuum to help rebuild the country, not realizing that it would descend further into lawlessness and violence. Into that mix, a mature, sensible woman chose to place herself, fully aware of the dangers.

She had already had a colorful life. One close friend said as a young person, Watson had been "pretty wild." She was born in Bakersfield, California. She suffered a broken home and "devastating losses of loved ones" that led to years of depression and emotional pain which she wasn't afraid to share in order to help others.[56] Watson was twenty-nine years old and running a pool hall when she had a powerful encounter with Jesus. She invited him not just into her life, but to take over her life. Within a year, she took the job at the jail, and soon after, started volunteering at church and serving on missions trips throughout the world.

Erich Bridges, an author who worked for the International Mission Board, pored over Watson's journals and interviewed her friends after her death. He said her journals were like "a series of love letters from God to Karen, and from Karen to God, recording her pursuit of Him with all of her mind, body, and soul. . . . She packed a lifetime of loving Jesus into the nine years she knew Him as Savior before her death."[57]

As Watson worked through the summer in Iraq, threats and attacks on foreigners increased. She was almost killed by bombings in the Baghdad area, and she regularly awoke at night to the sounds of gunfire. Eventually, she left with other relief workers for a season. She journaled about the temporary retreat, "Lord, in all my weakness I need Your strength for the future."[58]

After decompressing with friends, prayer, and Bible study, Watson voluntarily returned to the war zone. She used her training in leadership and organization as the International Mission Board distributed thousands of food boxes, rebuilt schools, and (her favorite) helped illiterate Iraqi women learn skills that could provide them with an income.

On March 15, 2004, Watson and four other aid workers were helping a village get a water purification system, so they would not be dependent on the dirty trucked-in water so common in Iraqi communities at the time. As the mission team drove away, gunmen pulled alongside their car and opened fire. Sitting in the back seat, Watson was an easy target. She died instantly, as did her coworkers Larry and Jean Elliott. Of the other two in the car, David McDonnall died hours later and his wife, Carrie McDonnall, later recovered from multiple gun wounds.[59]

News of the missionaries' death quickly spread across the world. Pastor Neighbors received a call and found the letter Watson had left in an envelope that read: "Only open this letter in the case of my death."[60]

March 7, 2003

Dear Pastor Phil & Pastor Roger,
You should only be opening this letter in the event of death.
*   When God calls there are no regrets. I tried to share my heart with you as much as possible, my heart for the Nations. I wasn't called to a place. I was called to Him. To obey was my objective, to suffer was expected, His glory was my reward, His glory is my reward.*

One of the most important things to remember right now is to preserve the work. . . . I am writing this as if I am still working among my people group.

I thank you all so much for your prayers and support. Surely your reward in Heaven will be great. Thank you for investing in my life and spiritual well-being. Keep sending missionaries out. Keep raising up fine young pastors.

In regards to any service, keep it small and simple. Yes simple, just preach the gospel. If Jason Buss is available or his dad have them sing a pretty song. Be bold and preach the life-saving, life-changing, forever eternal GOSPEL. Give glory and honor to our Father.

The Missionary Heart:
Care more than some think is wise.
Risk more than some think is safe.
Dream more than some think is practical.
Expect more than some think is possible.
I was called not to comfort or success but to obedience.

Some of my favorite Scriptures are: Isaiah 6, you know the one, 2 Cor. 5:15-21, 1 Peter 1:3, Col. 4:2-6, Romans 15:20, Psalm 25 and 27. You can look through my Scofield and see where it is marked. Please use only what you want or feel is best.

There is no Joy outside of knowing Jesus and serving Him. I love you two and my church family.

In His care,
Salaam, Karen[61]

Watson's friends remembered that in a surprising move, the very thrifty missionary who lived on "next to nothing" had purchased a gold ring with small diamonds before she returned to Iraq. A friend had worn a wedding band when she was single to remind herself that she was married to Christ. She asked Watson if that's what she was doing. "Yes," she replied with a radiant smile. "I guess that's it." At the news of Watson's death, her friend remembered the ring. "It was her wedding day," her friend said. "Christ had so prepared her as a bride that she was completely without blemish. I don't know if I have ever been with anyone who was more ready to meet Him face to face."[62]

Karen Watson experienced trying times before having faith in Christ, and even scarier times after, as she adventured with him. Such things were swallowed up in her love for him. "I'm not going to give anything to my Lord that will cost me nothing," she wrote in 1998.[63]

She paid with everything she had in laying down her life, and in doing so, she inspired a generation of Christians in their own faith.

RAGHEED GANNI Like all young Iraqi men from the largely Christian city of Mosul during the Saddam Hussein regime, Ragheed Aziz Ganni served in the military. He completed his degree in civil engineering, then entered the seminary and was sent to Rome in 1996 for further study. In Rome, he played soccer for the Pontifical Irish College and celebrated his first Mass at the college chapel. He spent summers with friends in Ireland and made a name for himself. The Irish leaders offered him a parish after he was ordained in 2001. Ganni declined. He knew he'd be needed in Iraq. War seemed imminent at home and he feared that Iraqi Christians would be targeted and persecuted. By the time Ganni arrived home, his fears had become realities.

Father Ragheed put to use his fluency in Arabic, Italian, French, and English as a correspondent for the international agency "Asia News" of the Pontifical Institute for Foreign Missions. He told the world what was happening in his homeland. He had every opportunity to flee, but he said, "That is where I belong, that is my place."[64]

In June 2004, his nineteen-year-old sister, Raghad, was carrying a pail of water to wash the church floor when two men drove up and threw a grenade into the church. It landed just a few yards from Raghad.

For Ganni and his community, he said, "My sister's wounds were a source of strength so that we, too, may bear our cross." He explained to church leaders in Rome the next year, "Mosul Christians are not theologians; some are even illiterate. And yet inside of us for many generations one truth has become embedded: without the Sunday Eucharist we cannot live."[65]

When a car bomb struck St. Paul Church after an evening Mass, killing two and wounding more, Ganni proclaimed it a miracle because only one bomb in the car had gone off. Had they all exploded, more of the four hundred worshipers would have been killed or injured. By mid-2004, churches were being destroyed, young Christians were targeted, and families began to flee.

Ganni's words gained him an international following. He was constantly begging for prayer. His church and his house had been blown up. But Ganni pressed on, saying Mass in the church basement. Once, while leading children in the makeshift basement church, loud gunfire broke out. The children were terrified, but Ganni remained calm. He explained away the noise, saying it was fireworks to celebrate their First Communion.[66]

"There are days when I feel frail and full of fear. But when, holding the Eucharist, I say 'Behold the Lamb of God, Behold him who takes away the sin of the world,' I feel his strength in me," he said. "When I hold the Host in my hands, it is really he who is holding me and all of us, challenging the terrorists and keeping us united in his boundless love."[67]

On Trinity Sunday, June 3, 2007, Father Ragheed Ganni celebrated Mass and left Mosul's Holy Spirit Chaldean Church with three subdeacons—his cousin Basman Yousef Daud, Wahid Hanna Isho, and Gassan Isam Bidawed—plus Isho's wife, Balah. She later reported,

We were stopped by four gunmen with masked black suits and Kalashnikov rifles. Two of them pointed the guns at Father Ragheed's car, and the other two pointed their guns at our car. They shouted at Father Ragheed to get out of the car. Father Ragheed asked them who they were, they replied that they were Ansar al-Sunna.

"How many times did we tell you to close the church? How many times did we tell you not to pray in the church?" the masked men shouted. "How could we possibly close the house of prayer, and the place that helps poor people?" the priest replied.[68]

The attackers shot down Father Ragheed and Daud. Bidawed and Isho went to their aid and "they fell in a pool of their own blood." When shots were fired again, Balah and her husband Isho ducked, but the gunmen opened fire on them, shouting "Allah Akbar."[69] The killers set one of the cars with explosives, so it would take several hours before the bombs could be defused and the bodies recovered.

The next day, thousands of people attended the funeral. The Vatican Secretary of State, Cardinal Bertone, telegrammed on behalf of the Pope that "Ragheed's sacrifice will inspire in the hearts of all men and women of good will a renewed resolve to reject the ways of hatred and violence, to conquer evil with good and to cooperate in hastening the dawn of reconciliation, justice and peace in Iraq."[70]

During Ragheed Ganni's fight to keep churches open and ministering to people, he said, "The terrorists might think they can kill our bodies or our spirit by frightening us, but, on Sundays, churches are always full. They may try to take our life, but the Eucharist gives it back."[71]

KAYLA MUELLER Kayla Mueller was born in 1988 to parents who were told they would never conceive. Her arrival unleashed unbridled happiness in their home. Her mother, Marsha, often called her "Kaylala" due to "the music and joy in my heart when I think of her."[72] Growing up, Kayla showed a gift for helping, whether working with animals or encouraging children. At an early age, she felt called to volunteer and encouraged others to do the same. In an eighth-grade speech, she said, "So start volunteering, be a good person, always have love in your heart and think before you do."[73]

Mueller launched into her own journey of service after college, working in India, Israel, Guatemala, and at home in an HIV/AIDS clinic. In 2012, she went to the Syria-Turkey border to help Syrian refugees fleeing a bloody civil war. The crisis deeply affected her. She reflected in her blog, "Anger, sadness, and fear are the best composts for compassion."[74]

In May 2013, Mueller shared her experiences with a Kiwanis club in her hometown of Prescott, Arizona. "For as long as I live," she said, "I would not let this suffering be normal, become something that we just accept."[75]

In August 2013, Mueller joined a Syrian friend in Doctors Without

Borders to deliver communications equipment to a hospital in Syria. On this trip, she was captured by the terrorist group ISIS. A Swedish refugee worker held in captivity with her for six weeks said Mueller was making friends. In particular, one older guard "would keep her company. . . . He tried to cheer her up by giving her chocolate and oranges."[76]

Later, Mueller's situation worsened. She was repeatedly raped by Islamic State leader Abu Bakr al-Baghdadi, who treated her as a sex slave. Even while she suffered, she wanted to help others. She became a mother figure to teenage Yazidi girls who were captured and held with her for months. When two of them had a chance to escape, Mueller refused to go because having a foreigner with them might endanger them while they were on the run.[77]

Kayla Mueller's tears were not just for herself and the others in captivity; her heart was broken for her family. In a letter that was smuggled out, she wrote to her parents saying, "If you could say I have 'suffered' at all throughout this whole experience it is only in knowing how much suffering I have put you all through. . . . I have come to see there is good in every situation, sometimes we just have to look for it. . . . Please be patient, give your pain to God. I know you would want me to remain strong. That is exactly what I am doing. Do not fear for me, continue to pray as will I."[78]

Eighteen months into her captivity, her life ended violently.

Her grief-stricken family recalled the amazing twenty-six years of Kayla Mueller's life in a statement saying, "We are heartbroken to share that we've received confirmation that Kayla Jean Mueller has lost her life. Kayla was a compassionate and devoted humanitarian. She dedicated the whole of her young life to helping those in need of freedom, justice, and peace."[79]

Mueller's legacy of strength in the face of adversity and kindness in the face of danger inspired millions. Her testimony was even on the lips of the president of the United States when he announced that Abu Bakr al-Baghdadi had died during a US military operation. The elite soldiers who carried out the mission had dedicated it to Kayla Mueller.[80]

VASILIOS HAVIAROPOULOS In the shadow of the Hagia Sofia, the great Orthodox cathedral commissioned by Emperor Constantine, stands a simple, unassuming building, the Shrine of Therapon. Housed within its walls is a holy spring that is believed to have healing properties. The spring's namesake, Therapon, a Cyprian bishop, was a martyred saint who died professing Christ ca. AD 259. In the ninth century, Therapon's relics were moved from Cyprus to Constantinople, modern-day Istanbul. A church was built around the relics. To this day, believers seeking healing visit the shrine and partake of the holy waters.

It was to this sacred space, full of hope and prayer, that Vasilios Haviaropoulos, would come every Monday to distribute those waters to the faithful. A caretaker of the holy relics, he was faithful in his service. It was a place of peace and hope, until the night of Monday, January 12, 1998. Early in the evening, the Ecumenical Patriarchate of the Greek Orthodox Church was notified that the shrine had caught fire. As windows in the building shattered and smoke poured out of the shrine, the fire department worked to eliminate the blaze. An hour later, with the fire extinguished, the ecumenical members entered the shrine. They found multiple relics missing, along with a blessing cross and an antique Bible. The sacred well had been closed. There was no sign of its caretaker, Haviaropoulos.

This was not the first time in Turkey that a sacred shine or holy place was vandalized. Violent attacks targeting the Greek Orthodox Church have occurred intermittently over the last seventy-five years—destruction of sacred places, stolen icons, desecration of cemeteries and shrines, and the murder of innocents.[81] Such crimes often occur without reprisal, and the lives of those following Orthodox practices are in peril.

After the fire at the Shrine of Therapon, Vasilios's son, Father Iakovos Haviaropoulos, a Greek Orthodox priest, went to the Patriarchate with his brother-in-law and a friend. His father had not come home from work. Gravely concerned, he had checked all the hospitals in the area, but without success. The Patriarchate called on the police to investigate his disappearance further. Authorities unsealed the door on the shrine and conducted a thorough search.

Bloodstains were found on the floor in front of Therapon's holy icon. When Haviaropoulos was not located, a member of the patriarchate pressed for a search of the storage area where the candles and holy oil were kept. When this hunt yielded nothing, they asked that the well itself be searched.[82]

The police were reluctant to disturb the well at first, feeling that the opening to it was not large enough to fit a body, but they finally sent for the fire department to conduct a search. Small items were pulled up from the well. A sweater. A pair of shoes. A packet of cigarettes. Finally, Haviaropoulos's broken body was pulled from the well. The coroner, district attorney, and crime squad were all summoned.

While there was some question as to how he had died, by beating or by drowning, it was clear that Vasilios Haviaropoulos had suffered in the moments before his death. Bruised and bloodied, with a fractured skull, the body served as evidence that he had been tortured, bound hand and foot, then thrown into the well.[83]

The Patriarchate issued a formal statement saying that it was "grieving, shocked and anxious at this crime." Their fear was that this vicious act of violence "will result in the further departure of our people and will weaken this sacred institution of the Ecumenical Patriarchate, the rampart of Orthodoxy and our pious faithful."[84] Only time will tell if the anti-Orthodox crimes in Turkey will increase or subside. But one thing is certain, Vasilios Haviaropoulos, faithful caretaker of the healing spring, found himself in the company of the great martyrs, professing Christ and laying down his life in service to others.

BISHOP LUIGI PADOVESE On April 3, 2010, Bishop Luigi Padovese had no idea that the words of his letter to Sister Chiara Laura Seroboli, abbess of the Monastery of St. Clare of Camerino, Italy, would be prophetic.[85] Celebrating the upcoming canonization of Blessed Camilla Battista, the founder of the abbess's order, Padovese noted the parallels between Camilla's thirteenth-century Italy and his own present-day Turkey, where he served as Apostolic Vicar of Anatolia. Political tension, religious intolerance, and persecution linked the two across five hundred years. He referenced this is in his letter, saying that "tragic political events that affected Camilla Battista's family, going so far as the killing of her loved ones and her exile, even in their tragic nature, did not defeat this woman. She had the inner strength to pray for her enemies to the point of transforming the hatred of which she was the object into an occasion of forgiveness and heroic love."[86]

While serving in Turkey, Padovese faced the same challenge: to love and forgive in the face of persecution. Bishop Padovese asked his sisters in Christ to pray that "this martyred land may transform so much pain into an invocation for peace and proclamation of forgiveness."[87] Exactly two months later, Bishop Padovese would join the ranks of those who had given their lives in service to Christ.

Like Blessed Camilla, Luigi Padovese was Italian. Born in Milan on March 31, 1947, he entered the Order of Capuchin Friars Minor of the Province of Lombardy in 1965 and was ordained as a priest in 1973. He continued his theological studies at the Pontifical Gregorian University and the University of Würtzburg (Germany). His scholarship was evidenced in his writing of articles and papers, as well as his professorships from 1977 to 1995. His theology and faith were tested in new ways in 2004 when he arrived in Turkey. Faith, forgiveness, and peace intertwined to weave a common thread throughout his time in Iskenderun.

In Turkey, the tension between the Muslim and Christian communities is centuries old. In the first century, Turkey welcomed Christians who were fleeing persecution in Jerusalem. Constantinople, modern-day Istanbul, is home to the Hagia Sophia, once the largest cathedral in the world, which served as a center of worship for Eastern Christianity from the sixth to the fifteenth centuries.[88] The Ottoman Empire established Islam but continued treating Christians with tolerance. The fall of this same empire in 1923 ushered in bursts of unrest and hostility towards followers of Jesus.

After the 2006 martyrdom of Father Andrea Santoro,[89] Padovese accompanied Santoro's body back to Rome.[90] "It's the anti-Christian climate that has been produced in Turkey," Padovese said. "There's a strong current of religious extremism, and that climate can fuel this sort of hatred. It's passed along in families, in schools, in the newspapers. . . . There were several million Christians in Turkey at the fall of the Ottoman Empire. How is it possible that in the arc of just seventy or eighty years we've become merely 60,000 or 70,000? . . . There are zones of Turkey which are completely 'Islamified,' where it is dangerous to be a Christian."[91]

In spite of this tension, Padovese expressed how deeply he "loves the Turkish people," most of whom "are good people who want dialogue."[92] That dialogue was the focus of his leadership style. Jesuit Father Tom Michel, an expert on Islam, spoke of Padovese's gifting in this area. "More than any other, he was the bishop in Turkey who truly believed in the importance of dialogue. . . . He had good relations with many Muslim leaders. He had a strong personal friendship with the Turkish Ambassador to the Holy See, and good ties with the Ministry of Religious Affairs in Turkey. They issued a glowing tribute to him after the news broke that he had been killed."[93]

Padovese's premature death would come at the hands of one of those ordinary people that he held dear, his own driver, Murat Altun. On June 3, Padovese was attacked and stabbed repeatedly by the twenty-six-year-old man in his summer home garden. Following the attack, neighbors heard shouts of "I killed the great Satan! *Allah Akbar!*" At his trial, he was bereft, stating he "was sorry for killing *Monsignore* Luigi, who was the last person who could harm him. At that moment, I was not in control of myself."[94] Padovese's death was a shocking loss to his community. Vatican spokesman Father Federico Lombardi said, "The tragedy of this event shows the difficulty that the Christian community endures in the Middle East region."[95]

Bishop Padovese claimed that Blessed Camilla Battista modeled the virtues that were needed in the world today. In troubled times, she was "an example of reconciliation and an occasion to rediscover hope by going to the source of the passion of Christ."[96] Bishop Padovese modeled those same virtues, clinging to the hope of reconciliation and peace in a land of martyrdom.

ARCHBISHOP PAULOS FARAJ RAHHO Paulos Faraj Rahho, archbishop of Mosul, called Iraqi Christians "a church of martyrs."[97] His relatives recalled him saying, "I belong to the Church."[98] He loved his people and gave his life for this Church.

His hometown, the northern city of Mosul, had become plagued by terrorists and religious militias. Extremists demanded Rahho close his parish, the Cathedral of the Holy Spirit sometimes called "The Ship." He kept it open. As a result, it was attacked at least ten times. In 2008, four other Mosul churches were attacked with car bombs and other explosives, and another four in Bagdad.[99]

Rahho stood fast, publicly decrying the violence. On one occasion, he was threatened in the street by men with guns, but he walked away, daring them to shoot. Another time, terrorists pulled him from his home, bound him, then forced him to watch as they burned down his house.[100] One of his parish's priests was driving home from church with three deacons when masked men with machine guns stopped the car and opened fire, killing all four men.[101] Their martyrdom shocked the Christians in the city. Yet despite the grief and the terror around him, Rahho continued to minister. His passion for his work and his people trumped everything else.

On February 29, 2008, the sixty-five-year-old archbishop had just finished leading the Way of the Cross, a meditation practice focused on the fourteen events that take place during Jesus' passion death. As he drove home from the church, kidnappers loaded his vehicle with bullets, wounding Rahho in the leg. They abducted the priest, then killed his driver and two companions in the car.[102]

The kidnappers sped away with Rahho in the trunk, but the intrepid archbishop pulled out his cell phone and called the church. He told them under no circumstances to pay any ransom, caring for his flock even in this moment of greatest distress. That was the last time anyone heard his voice.

The kidnappers repeatedly made ransom and political demands. World leaders demanded Rahho's release. On March 13, two weeks after the kidnapping, church leaders followed a lead that indicated where to find Rahho's body. The final cause of Rahho's death was never known. He'd been injured in the kidnapping but also required daily medication for a heart issue. Nor did anyone discover how long he had been dead before he was found. His body had been dumped in a shallow grave outside the city.[103]

In both life and death, Rahho echoed the passion of Jesus and his radical, all-encompassing love.

Paulos Faraj Rahho had traveled far and studied widely. He was the eighth and last child of a family of Chaldean Catholics, the largest Christian sect in Iraq. During his ministry, he built the Church of the Sacred Heart in Mosul's Christian district of Telkif, and in 1989 he founded the Charity of Joy and Brotherhood home for orphans and people with disabilities. He would eventually become the beloved pastor of more than 20,000 Christians in Mosul.[104]

Rahho was known as a sociable, humble, loving man, and a man of wit. An accomplished raconteur, he was famous among his peers for his jokes. But he was also known as a man of courage. Christians were concerned about the rise of Islamic radicals; Rahho publicly condemned the violence.

When the Iraqi constitution was rewritten, the ever-fearless Rahho publicly expressed concern that it included sharia law and pronounced Islam as the national religion.[105] Rahho's public declarations may have led to his death. Eventually the Iraqi government announced that an al-Qaeda leader known as Abu Omar was sentenced to death for Rahho's murder.[106] Most Christians didn't want to speak about it, and some officially condemned the murderer's execution.[107] But everyone now knew that in Mosul, terrorists and criminals too often had the "freedom to target Christians with impunity."[108]

Rahho's passion for people was not just for fellow believers, but for all people. He followed the teaching of Jesus and urged others to love all their neighbors, including those of other religious groups. In doing so, he earned the respect of Arabs, Jews, Sunnis, Kurds, and others in his community. Rahho was so successful at building bridges that when his house was set ablaze, a local imam offered refuge in a mosque.

In his will, Rahho urged Christians to continue the work. "I call upon all of you to be open to our Muslim and Yazidi brothers and to all the children of our Beloved Homeland, to work together to build solid ties of love and brotherhood among the children of our Beloved Country, Iraq."[109]

Thousands, people of all faiths, ignored the danger and jammed the services for his memorial in the ancient Christian village of Kremlis.

Every Iraqi Christian would agree with Rahho's words, "We, Christians of Mesopotamia, are used to religious persecution and pressures by those in power. . . . We continue to be a church of martyrs."[110]

Archbishop Louis Sako of Kirkuk spoke of his friend's ultimate sacrifice. "Above all, [he was] a pastor. Despite all the risks to his life, he stayed in the city. He gave up his life for his people and for his church."[111]

Rahho's own words reflected his convictions. In his will, he wrote, "Life means fully placing oneself in the hands of God."[112] Archbishop Rahho, anchoring his life in love for his people and community, displaying the passion of Jesus at all costs, did just that.

RUEL JANDA Joining the Overseas Filipino Workers, Ruel Janda became one of the millions of expatriates from all over the world living and working in Saudi Arabia.[113]

Although little is known about his life, Ruel Janda's death gained international attention. On April 7, 1995, Saudi police officers charged Janda with forceful armed robbery. According to a Saudi newspaper, he and Arnel Beltran attacked a store employee with an iron bar, striking the man in the head. Both men vehemently denied the attack. The government was unrelenting.

When Janda arrived at the prison, he and Beltran shared a cell with a Christian named Donato Lama. Lama says that Ruel Janda was terrified and depressed. "Ruel must have come straight from the hospital since he was still wearing a hospital gown and smelled of medicine. . . . He [had] tried to commit suicide by drinking poison. Ruel wanted to take his life because of so many problems at home and at his work. I took pity on the man as I could easily see his loneliness and confusion. Only the Lord could meet his needs."[114]

Despite Ruel Janda's circumstances, this encounter became a dramatic turning point for him. Early the next morning, he cried out to the Lord, confessing his sins and placing his faith in Jesus.

Janda, Beltran, and Lama formed a deep friendship as brothers in Christ, even hosting Bible studies with other Filipino prisoners. For over a year, they suffered together, enduring ferocious beatings and, at one point, sharing a cell with a lunatic for two months.[115]

The Saudis eventually released Donato Lama after serving many months and receiving seventy lashes. Although weak and in poor health, Lama flew home to the Philippines, where he reunited with his family. Ruel Janda and Arnel Beltran, however, were beheaded.

According to one Christian Filipino inmate, Rene H. Camahort, the authorities likely executed Janda because of his faith. "He was the one who started Bible studies here. As you know, it is prohibited for us Christians to even pray here. Nevertheless, he was not intimidated, despite countless times that he was put in isolation cells."[116]

Lama recalled, "He was given the offer to renounce his faith, embrace Islam, and he would be released. But he remained faithful to the Lord until his last breath."[117] Amid torture, cruelty, and impossible circumstances, Janda found comfort in his salvation. And at his death, that salvation led him straight into the arms of his Father in heaven.

HAIK HOVSEPIAN MEHR Born in Tehran on January 6, 1945, to a middle-class Armenian family, Haik Hovsepian Mehr was only a teenager when he began pastoring a church in Tehran. After his mandatory military service, Bishop Hovsepian—as his congregation called him—started pastoring a church he had planted in Gorgon at the ripe age of twenty-two, while still enlisted. In 1969, Mehr and his wife, Takoosh, were in a car crash that killed their eldest child and seriously injured the two of them. Pressing through the pain of loss and recovery, Mehr threw himself into the study of God's Word. Mature at a young age, he became a beloved pastor, a bold apologist and evangelist, later a denominational official, and an outspoken critic of the government.

Mehr experienced the upheaval of the 1979 Islamic Revolution, during which his church was only saved from destruction by a friendly Muslim cleric.

After the Revolution, Mehr worked to increase the collaboration between evangelical churches within Iran. In 1981 he moved his family to Tehran to lead the seven Assemblies of God churches in the country and establish five more. Soon Mehr was recognized for his leadership and elected president of the Council of Protestant Churches. He would become known as one of the boldest Christian church leaders in the country and a defender of Christian rights.[118]

Most of Mehr's Assemblies of God congregations consisted of Farsi-speaking former Muslims. In time, outraged Islamic groups banned church publications and closed churches, and in 1990 they executed a pastor.

In 1993, Mehr refused to sign two declarations: one stating that he would not allow Muslim converts to attend his churches, and the other stating that Christians enjoyed full rights in Iran. Only one other pastor refused with him.[119] Instead, Mehr compiled a dossier detailing Iran's violations of religious freedom. In a relentless attempt to inform the world about the fate of Iranian Christians, Mehr sent the dossier to the United Nations Special Representative to Iran with an invitation to come see the violations for himself.

In spite of numerous threats, Mehr consistently refused the government's intervention in the churches and criticized the Islamic regime's actions against Christians. He met with the Minister for Islamic Guidance for Minorities and demanded minority religious rights that were provided in the 1979 Constitution. In response, the government cracked down on Assemblies of God churches, ordering them not to preach in Farsi, to issue membership cards, restrict attendance only to members, release membership records to the government, add new members only after the government was notified, and worship only on Sundays but never on Fridays, the holy day for Muslims.

Mehr responded, "Never would [he or his ministers] bow down and comply with such inhumane and unjust demands. Our churches are open to all who want to come in."[120]

In 1993, even as Mehr protested the treatment of Christians, his good friend and colleague Mehdi Dibaj, who had been kidnapped in 1985, was finally tried and received a death sentence for the crime of apostasy. Mehr brought Dibaj's plight to the attention of the international community. Pressure on Iran came from human rights groups, the international community, and the United Nations. The Iranian government temporarily relented and released Dibaj on January 16, 1994. Dibaj had been tortured and beaten in prison. At home, his wife had been forced to divorce him and marry a Muslim man.[121]

Three days later, on Wednesday, January 19, 1994, Mehr was kidnapped. He apparently died the next day. On January 30, the family was shown photographs, from which they identified his body. Police had already claimed not to know his identity and buried him in an Islamic cemetery. The family arranged a Christian reburial, and discovered his chest was riddled with stab wounds.[122]

By this time, Bishop Mehr had become a prominent leader in Iran's churches and a world-renowned advocate for religious rights. His sudden death made global headlines. The Islamic government denied any knowledge of the murder, but Iranians, along with Christians around the world, quickly claimed Hovsepian was killed for his faith in Christ.[123] Five months later, on June 24, 1994, Mehdi Dibaj was found stabbed to death in a park.

In a letter penned the day before he was abducted, Mehr had written, "I am ready to die for the cause of the Church so that others will be able to worship their Lord peacefully and without so much fear."[124] The kind of boldness that Mehr showed came from having already died to flesh and living only for Christ, giving his life for the bride for which Jesus also gave his life.

All these years later, Iranian Christians remain among the most persecuted believers on the planet.

TILMANN GESKE, NECATI AYDIN, AND UGUR YUKSEL

Tilmann Geske was from Germany, but he loved Turkey. Malatya was the city he had called home for ten years with his dear wife, Susanne, and their three young children.

He worked as a translator for a local Christian publishing house, and he had been pleased to meet several young Muslims in his community who had expressed an interest in his faith.

Geske wanted everyone to know the love of Jesus as he did. He invited his young friends to a Bible study at the publishing house with himself and two Turkish believers, Necati Aydin and Ugur Yuksel. He opened his heart in the spirit of Jesus, but these young men were on a different kind of mission.

When they arrived for the Bible study, they locked the door from the inside. They proceeded to brutally massacre Geske, Aydin, and Yuksel.

Geske was stabbed over 150 times. All their throats were cut, sacrificed for their faith in Jesus.

It is hard to understand why those who were offered the hand of friendship would react so violently. Many years later, when the perpetrators were eventually tried, they "insisted they were trying to stop the 'harmful activities' of Christian missionaries who they claimed were trying to destroy Turkey and the honour of Islam."[125]

Geske's death was not the end of his story. His wife, Susanne, reeling from his death, took his offer of friendship and Jesus' love one step further. Her response captivated the media in Turkey and all around the world.

The day after her husband's murder she found herself in her home filled with Christians from the entire community. They had come to grieve with her over the loss of Geske. "Then, someone came and said that the media is in front of the door and they want to talk to you," Susanne Geske told the *Christian Post* in 2017. "I was like, 'No way. What on earth do I say to them?' . . . [Then] a switch flipped inside to make me move. I was like, 'Okay! But what do I say?'"[126]

Saying a prayer, she walked outside to find the Turkish television station ATV. She looked at the camera and said a few powerful words, "Father, forgive them, for they know not what they do."[127]

At a moment when she could barely see through her own tears, she preached a sermon that was heard throughout the entire Islamic world.

Susanne Geske didn't feel like loving anyone at that moment. In fact, the day before, in the wake of her devastating loss, she had been treated cruelly by those in authority. She said, "They sent me to the police office. . . . I sat there for two hours not knowing what I am doing there and have this television on. I asked if they could [shut it down] because they all were just telling lies about us and what horrible people we are. I didn't want to watch that conversation."[128]

Yet, despite being maligned even in the hours after her husband's death, she managed to pronounce her faith in Jesus, showing the same spirit of love and determination that her husband had.

Ten years later, the murder trial faced delay after delay, prolonging the terrible injustice committed against her husband. Susanne's heart had not changed. She said again to the Turkish press, "Some people think that I am still angry and I haven't been able to forgive them. I want to say again, ten years have passed, and I have truly forgiven those five youths. Maybe someday if there is an opportunity, I will go to the prison; I want to tell them themselves that I have forgiven them."[129]

Geske's sacrifice and his wife's heart of forgiveness paint a powerful picture of Jesus' love at work in Turkey, offering mercy and freedom to all who embrace him.

RAMI AYYAD Of all the lands mentioned in the Bible, perhaps Gaza is the most drenched in blood. It was Samson's adopted homeland, then came under King David's rule as Israel expanded. Gaza was ruled by the Philistines, Egypt, Alexander the Great, Rome, the Crusaders, and the Ottoman dynasty, finally coming under British rule during World War I. Israel won Gaza during the 1967 Six-Day War, then ceded it to the newly formed Palestinian Authority in 2005. Hamas won the 2007 elections, and life in an already difficult place became exponentially harder.

"The heart of the matter is that Gaza is a place overrun with violence," writes Philip Rizq, an Egyptian German based in Gaza who writes for the *Palestine Chronicle* website.[130]

Amid the harshness of life, civil war, terrorist attacks, restrictions, and the constant threat of persecution, Christianity thrived, and Christians needed resources. In 1998, the Palestinian Bible Society opened Gaza's only Christian bookstore, The Teacher's Bookshop, in downtown Gaza City. Rami Ayyad, a cheery Greek Orthodox Christian who worshiped in a Baptist church, managed the store. In addition to selling Christian resources, his store served as an internet café and offered computer and language lessons. The warm and kind Ayyad flashed a brilliant smile as soon as anyone's foot crossed the store's threshold. He generally knew everyone who entered, but if not, he knew them before they left. Friends would find him in his ever-present swivel chair "laughing and joking no matter how depressing life became."[131]

And life could often be depressing. In 2006 and 2007, Gaza suffered a wave of bombings. Forty bombings occurred before October 2007—most claimed by "The Righteous Swords of Islam," a small group attempting to enforce Islamic law.[132] On February 3, 2006, a few days after the Palestinian Hamas won victory in parliamentary elections, two pipe bombs destroyed the shop's front doors. A note was left demanding that the store close. The Bible Society soon reopened it. On April 15, 2007, Ayyad's shop was bombed again, blowing out windows and burning shelves of resources.

In June 2007, when Hamas seized control of Gaza, life for the three thousand Christians living there changed "180 degrees."[133] Hamas leader Sheik Saqer promised that Christians could continue to live safely in Gaza only if they accepted Islamic law, and all Christians who engaged in missionary work would be "dealt with harshly."[134] Ayyad's wife, Pauline, later said that Ayyad didn't receive personal threats, but she now thinks they should have noticed the signs of increasing danger. A man posing as a customer one day asked Ayyad why he was not Muslim. Ayyad answered, "Because I believe in Jesus." Before leaving the shop, the man had said, "I know how to make you become a Muslim."[135]

Instead of being intimidated, Ayyad and Pauline continued to faithfully follow Jesus. The ever-smiling Ayyad continued to respond to violence with laughter, love, and peace.

On Thursday, October 4, he was locking up the store and saw a bearded man watching him. The next day, both Ayyad and the taxi driver taking him home noticed they were being followed by a car without license plates. The car parked near Ayyad's house and he could see the driver had a similar beard.

On Saturday afternoon, as Ayyad closed the shop, the stalkers struck. Ayyad was kidnapped. He called his wife from his mobile phone, evidently while in the kidnappers' car, and said he was going to be late, but if he wasn't back within two hours, he would not be back for a very long time. "He sounded a bit tense, but not afraid," said Pauline.[136] It was the last time she would hear his voice. He never came home.

Friends and family searched for him late into the night. At 5:30 on Sunday morning Ayyad's beaten body was found. His wallet, ID, and watch were gone. Witnesses later said the attackers stopped a few blocks from the shop. Three armed men, two in masks, beat him publicly with clubs and the butts of their guns. After they beat him, they shot him. Later, security sources said signs of torture were found on Ayyad's body.[137]

Three hundred Muslims and Christians attended his memorial service. One Christian remarked, "If somebody thinks this murder will make Christians leave, they are mistaken. This is our homeland."[138]

In February 2008, Pauline gave birth to Ayyad's third child, a girl she named Sama, which means *heaven* in Arabic. Pauline said she chose the name "because her father is in heaven."[139] Years after her husband's murder, Pauline saw a picture of the murderer in the newspaper. She said that at first she was angry. But the Holy Spirit helped her forgive. She placed a picture of the news article on Facebook with the words, "I forgive this man."[140]

Ayyad's life had been a beacon of perseverance and joy. And even his death, horrific though it was, became an example to all believers—not of despair or grief, but of forgiveness and gratitude.

ANDREA SANTORO Father Andrea Santoro was a man of prayer. On February 5, 2006, while kneeling to pray in his church in Trabzon, Turkey, he was shot twice in the back. The Bible he held slipped from his hands.

Father Santoro had first visited Turkey in 1993. He stayed in the city of Antioch, fascinated by the Christian history of the city, and his heart was won over by this historic, beautiful land and its people. On his return to Rome, he asked to be sent back as a missionary. He longed to be a "'small light' in the midst of a small flock and 'Jesus' presence' in Arabic and highly Islamic lands."[141] The historic church he served had a small congregation of fifteen people, but his heart beat for the whole region. He wanted the people of Turkey to know the love and salvation of Jesus.

Santoro struggled with the language but appreciated that it kept him humble and stripped down his homilies to only the most essential truths. He was known in the community for his kindness. His willingness to serve and his love for the marginalized, the poor, and those caught in sex trafficking and prostitution motivated him. He advocated on their behalf. His care and recognition caused backlash from those in the sex trafficking industry. He received threats, but Santoro kept caring anyway.

In 2003, he started Window for the Middle East, an association grounded in study and prayer, meant to bridge the Middle East and the Western world.[142] He wanted to "rediscover the sap that flows from the Jewish roots into the Christian tree, encourage a genuine and respectful dialogue between Christianity and Islam, and [this enabled] him to bear witness with his life and feelings, above all through prayer, the study of the Holy Scriptures, friendships based on listening, talking, simplicity, his sincere believing and the way he lived."[143]

A church worker who knew Santoro said, "He was a man full of determination and earnestness. Although I met him only a few times, for brief moments, when we did meet, our interaction was always intense, straightforward, centered on God, His Word, and Jesus Christ."[144] Father Santoro said, "'I am convinced that in the end there are no two ways, only one way that leads to light through darkness, to life through the bitterness of death. Only by offering one's flesh is salvation possible. The evil that stalks the world must be borne and pain must be shared until the end in one's own flesh as Jesus did."[145] Santoro lived out the life and the death of Jesus until his own dying day, when a radicalized sixteen-year-old boy, looking to avenge the controversial Danish Muhammad cartoons that had been published in 2005, found the priest in prayer, shouted "Allah Akbar!" and gunned him down.[146]

PASTOR HOSSEIN SOODMAN When Hossein Soodman was a seven-year-old, he threw a stone to break a Christian woman's water pot. As he ran from her, he fell and cut his knee. The woman approached to help him but he recoiled, expecting her to hit him. Instead, she cleaned him up and gave him sweets. That was Soodman's first encounter with a follower of Christ. The second came when he was hospitalized while serving in the army. An Armenian Christian nurse prayed for him and gave him a cross. That night he dreamed of Jesus and awoke healed, a miracle that changed his life.

At the time, Christian conversion and evangelism were still legal in Iran. Soodman located a Christian church in Tehran that discipled him in the early 1960s. He attended Bible courses taught by a Presbyterian missionary. Although his family disowned him because of his new faith, he became an outspoken witness for Christ. The Bible Society enlisted him to sell Bibles across the nation. In Isfahan, he stayed to work for the Christian Institute for the Blind, where he met his wife, Mahtab Noorvash. Soodman openly shared the truth of Christ and became an associate pastor at a church.

Following the 1979 Islamic Revolution, the regime of the Ayatollah Khomeini began to repress Christians with a new intensity. The first martyr under that regime was the minister who had officiated at Soodman's wedding. By this time, Soodman and Mahtab had moved with their four children to Soodman's former hometown of Mashhad, where they planted a church in their basement. Authorities persecuted them and demanded Soodman renounce his Christianity. He wouldn't. The authorities shut down his church, but he secretly continued to disciple believers. Iran's radical Islamic regime finally arrested Soodman in 1990 for converting from Islam, a "crime" that hadn't been a crime thirty years earlier when he'd received Christ. His church group, the Assemblies of God, campaigned on his behalf. After a month of torture and solitary confinement, he was released.

Months passed and again, Soodman was arrested. The family was allowed to visit him once. Then two weeks passed without news. A pastor friend went to the religious police and learned that he'd been executed by hanging. No constitutional law said Soodman's conversion from Islam to Christianity was illegal. But sharia law, imposed by the new regime, outlawed it. Soodman could have avoided the death penalty by renouncing his Christian faith, but he refused.

Soodman left behind a family that was bold in their witness for Jesus. His son Ramtin was imprisoned in 2008. His daughter Rashin received asylum in the West, where she has continued speaking out against the persecution of Christians.[147]

Soodman had friends who fled Iran. Shortly before he died, he wrote to them, "By following the example of the Great Shepherd of the flock, the Lord Jesus Christ, I am willing to sacrifice my life for my sheep. My escape from these dangers would weaken the flock of God and discourage them. I don't want to be a bad example to them, so I am ready to go to jail again and, if necessary, even to give my life for them."[148]

MISSIONARIES OF CHARITY: SISTER ANSELM, SISTER JUDITH, SISTER MARGUERITE, AND SISTER REGINETTE

The nation of Yemen hugs the southern border of Saudi Arabia, separating the Saudis from the Gulf of Aden. In 2000, the Gulf of Aden made headlines when terrorists attacked the destroyer the USS *Cole* there. The attack was indicative of a long history of violence in Yemen. Most recently, a bloody civil war that started in 2015 has killed tens of thousands.[149] In March 2015, Shia Houthi terrorists, supported by the Iranian regime, sought to oust Yemen's Sunni-led government. In the Battle of Aden, Saudi-led fighters recaptured the ruined city from the Houthi, leaving a power vacuum. According to the *New York Times*, Aden has "descended into lawlessness."[150]

In the less turbulent times of the 1990s, Sister Teresa's Missionaries of Charity adopted a home for the elderly and disabled at the request of the government. As civil war broke out twenty years later, most Christians fled the country. A handful of priests and nuns from the Missionaries of Charity stayed to continue loving and serving.[151]

On the morning of March 4, 2016, gunmen told the Missionaries of Charity gatekeeper they had come to see their mothers in the home. Upon entering, the men immediately shot the gatekeeper to death. The killers then hunted for the nuns as the workers shouted, "Don't kill the sisters! Don't kill the sisters!"[152]

It was clear that the Missionaries of Charity were specifically targeted for being "the only Christian presence" in Aden. A report of the attack said, "ISIS wants to get rid of all Christianity."[153]

As they searched for the nuns, the gunmen went room to room, and when they found workers, they bound them and then shot them in the head. The terrorists found four of the five nuns, Sister Anselm from India, Sister Judith from Kenya, and Sister Marguerite and Sister Reginette, both from Rwanda. As with the rest of the workers, the killers systematically tied each woman to a tree, shot them in the head, and crushed their skulls.[154] None of the hospital's eighty patients were harmed, but the priest, Father Tom Uzhunnalil was kidnapped. He was kept in captivity for the next eighteen months.

In the two-hour killing spree, sixteen people lost their lives. The superior, Sister Sally, was one of the few who escaped harm. That evening, she recounted the events to a regional superior in the Middle East, Sister Rio, who faxed the account to the Missionaries of Charity Superior General. "The ISIS men were already getting to the convent," the report stated, "so she went into the [refrigerator] room since the door was open. These ISIS men were everywhere searching for her as they knew they were 5. At least 3 times they came in the [refrigerator] room. She did not hide but remained standing behind the door—they never saw her. This is miraculous."[155]

Each of the remarkable women who gave their lives knew the dangers, but they stayed because of their commitment, born out of various life experiences that had brought them to the feet of Jesus.

Sister Anselm from eastern India had fallen into a seventy-two-foot-deep rock-lined well when she was in eighth grade. Her brother said miraculously, she missed the rock walls and landed in the water. When friends and family members pulled her up using ropes and sticks, she had only a few scratches. "After the accident, she used to tell us that she wanted to become a nun and dedicate her life for Christ," one neighbor recalled. A friend noted Sister Anselm's experiences with "enormous difficulties, such as poverty and disease," adding, "those experiences must have made her strong enough to stick with her mission even at the cost of her life."[156]

Sister Judith was one of eight children from the remote Kenyan town of Kitise. Her father died when she was young and her impoverished mother was forced to relocate the family to Nairobi. At a young age, Sister Judith pledged to help those in unfortunate circumstances. That desire landed her in Yemen, her first and last mission.

Sister Marguerite was one of ten children. When her mother died, she took her siblings into her home. As a nun, she was quick to see the needs of others. She was "joyful and responsible," according to a friend. "She stood for the truth, was hard-working, and had zeal for souls and love for the poor."[157]

Sister Reginette at age sixteen "disappeared" from her Rwandan home for a month. When the family finally found her, she had been caring for a hospitalized friend. With such compassion, it's understandable why she turned down a government job to serve on the mission field. When she renewed her vows, she said, "In my spiritual life I deepen the knowledge of Him by allowing the Spirit to lead me, Jesus to heal my fears, supporting me in difficulties, remembering that I am finite—unable of anything without Him."[158]

Steadfast to the end, these four nuns died because of their faithfulness and dedication to Christ. As Sister Sally's friend reported that evening, "They were so faithful. . . . And because of their faithfulness, they were in the right place at the right time and were ready when the Bridegroom came."[159]

JIN-WOOK KIM In 2019, Jin-Wook Kim, a Korean evangelist, moved with his pregnant wife and four-year-old son to the city of Diyarbakir, Turkey, to work with a small house church there. Kim was ministering to a community of Christians, spreading the truth and love of God. He often shared with others about his faith in Jesus.

On November 19, Kim left his house, telling his wife he was going to evangelize. Those were the last words he ever spoke to her.[160] While walking through the downtrodden Baglar district near his home, Kim was attacked and stabbed three times by a sixteen-year-old.[161] Bystanders on the street called the police and summoned an ambulance.

The teenager who had stabbed Kim had a criminal history and struggled with drug addiction. He said he was trying to steal the pastor's cell phone when he stabbed him.[162] But Christians in the community feared that this wasn't an isolated incident. In the wake of Kim's death, a Turkish evangelist received threats. He said, "This wasn't just a robbery; they came to kill him. We always get threats. They know that I am trying to spread the gospel, so they may target me too. This may be a sign."[163] Other Christians raised similar concerns, pointing to billboards in the city of Konya "warning citizens not to befriend Christians and Jews, quoting a verse from the Quran."[164]

Claire Evans, the Middle East regional manager for International Christian Concern, shared the feelings of the believers in the area. "The grief among Turkey's Christian community is strongly felt, along with great shock and fear. Just this year, we have seen a significant increase in incidents proving how the environment has grown more hostile toward Christianity."[165] Despite the Turkish President's claims that he is "sensitive" to the problems of believers in Turkey, there is a growing climate of violence in the country.[166] Christians do not feel protected or heard.

When Jin-Wook Kim arrived at the Selahaddin Eyyubi State Hospital, he was treated immediately, but doctors' efforts were in vain. Kim died later that night.

One Korean Christian who attended Kim's memorial said, "We know this will cause more prayer for Turkey. . . . The Christians of Korea and around the world will pray more because of this!"[167] The pain of his death was felt keenly by family. Kim's mother, brother, mother-in-law, and sister-in-law flew in from Korea to support his wife during his memorial service in Diyarbakir on November 21. Three days after the funeral, Kim's wife gave birth to their beautiful baby girl and named her Sevinc, which means "joy" in Turkish.

In the last moments of his life, Pastor Jin-Wook Kim had one thing on his mind—sharing the life-giving power of Jesus with those in his neighborhood. He shared the essence of God's all-encompassing truth: the willing sacrifice of love.

FATHER FRANS VAN DER LUGT Frans van der Lugt was a Dutch Jesuit who, during fifty years on the mission field in Syria, captured the hearts of everyone he encountered—Christian, Muslim, pro-regime, or opposition.

In the 1960s, Van der Lugt first arrived in Syria. He became fluent in Arabic and adopted Syria as his home, not a temporary church assignment. In the 1980s he led his parish students on an eight-day cross-country hike across the Jebal Ansariya, the coastal range of Syria that descends into the Mediterranean. It turned into an annual excursion.

"The hike brings people together," Van der Lugt explained in later years. "They share the common experience of fatigue, of sleeping and eating together, and this builds a link between people. After the hike it is not important that you are Christian or Muslim, it is important that you are present."[168]

In the early 1990s, Van der Lugt was given some flat agricultural land just southwest of Homs, Syria. He named it Al-Ard, meaning "the earth," a site founded on simplicity. A dirt road led to the center, passing through olive groves and vineyards that sprang up from a blanket of wildflowers. In the center of the grounds grew a vegetable garden, tended by volunteers who found solace digging their hands into the red dirt.[169]

Van der Lugt typically navigated the narrow roads of Homs on a bike, like most residents. But as Al-Ard grew, he reached out to people with disabilities whose families typically hid them in shame. Each morning, he would drive his old VW van to pick up the disabled, the young, the marginalized. Each volunteer learned to accept Van der Lugt's value system, as part of "a community that values everybody."[170] As the vineyards became economically viable, these helpers became employees.

When simple lodging was provided, some volunteers came to live on the grounds. Those who didn't stay often came to spiritual retreats led by Van der Lugt. During the retreats, his Jesuit colleagues would complain that he worked too hard, spending the whole night hearing confessions, giving spiritual advice, or just listening, then getting up early in the morning to start his meditation. "For me," this man of God said, "it is important to start from the human meeting. Not to start with religion."[171]

Van der Lugt tried to build a basic human experience that would lead people to accept the "common place of being." For that reason, Al-Ard had no outward appearance of being a Christian space. Instead, it became a place that attracted young people and all walks of life as he preached simply about living a life of love.

Syria descended into a civil war that eventually left Homs in the center of conflict, "the cradle of rebellion" against the government.[172] The Islamic government responded to the rebels in Homs by putting the city under siege. Starting in May 2011, conditions in Homs deteriorated until people were starving.

Van der Lugt risked his life in staying to provide help to all victims of the conflict. He reported the cruelties of the siege through social media, YouTube, and emailed reports. He wrote, "The interaction with the circumstances of our lives here does not produce optimism, but we know that all the Syrian people are suffering—and we are part of them. Let's help each other to cross this difficult stage, living out solidarity and interdependence in our search for new horizons."[173]

"No food has entered our besieged region for more than 15 months," he wrote in 2013 . He said local warehouses and abandoned homes were scavenged and empty. People suffered from "hunger, cold, lack of electricity and water." With no oil or gas, people had only wood for heating but the supply was dwindling. The furniture of abandoned homes had all been burned. "There is no access in and out of our region. . . . Then there is the deteriorating health condition of people in our community. . . . Disease has captured some of us and is knocking on the door of others."[174]

Journalists followed Van der Lugt's posts as he spoke on behalf of the trapped population. "If these people are suffering now I want to be in solidarity with them," he told one reporter. "As I was with these people in their good times, I am with them in their pain."[175]

In February 2014, the *Economist* reported that Frans van der Lugt was likely the last European left in the city.[176] He declined evacuation during a UN operation in 2014 that saved 1,400 people from the besieged city.[177] "'There is nothing more painful than watching mothers searching for food for their children in the streets,' he said in a video released in February. 'We love life, we want to live. And we do not want to sink in a sea of pain and suffering.'"[178]

Just days before his death, Van der Lugt posted on the Facebook page he used to spread news: "Christians in Old Homs are asking themselves: 'What can we do? We can't do anything!' But God will take care of us; we are paralyzed, though we believe that God is with us, especially in these circumstances. . . . God will never forsake us, he knows us, and knows our suffering. . . . We see evil is trying to find his way among us, but . . . we need to fight to keep this flame in our hearts."[179]

On Monday, April 7, 2014, at 9:30 a.m., masked extremists called the Al-Nusra Front abducted Frans van der Lugt and executed him by gunshot. One friend recalled that Frans "never missed the chance, [one] generation after another to inspire Syrian Jesuits to continue their journey. . . . I can hear you, now in the midst of my course, saying to me: 'Move forward, Tony, and continue the work of the church in Syria.'"[180]

Van der Lugt wrote before his death: "There is an atmosphere of love, openness and interaction and those of us who remain feel that we are one group. It's hard to live in painful circumstances alone, and it is possible that these conditions become harder and harder. Each one of us needs to do more and more to help each other. A person has to pay much attention to the needs of another, to the point of forgetting one's own needs."[181]

Frans van der Lugt was a priest who preached only what he practiced. He forgot his own needs in the darkest and most desperate time, to meet the needs of the people he loved. The power of that love and his sacrifice for the people he loved endure.

Vintage Foxe

A good Christian is bound to relinquish not only goods and children, but life itself, for the glory of his Redeemer: therefore I am resolved to sacrifice everything in this transitory world, for the sake of salvation in a world that will last to eternity.[182]

CHAPTER FIFTEEN

From Atheists and Religious Zealots in Asia

Therefore take up the whole armor of God, that you may be
able to withstand in the evil day, and having done all, to stand.
EPHESIANS 6:13, NKJV

More persecution, more growth! That is the history of the Church![1]
SAMUEL LAMB

I want God to give me long life to see one million arrows sent out to
establish one million churches. I always love seeing God use ordinary
orphans to do extraordinary gospel work. I do pray and desire for
a martyr's death. I want to see the nations in the 10/40 window
come to accept the saving knowledge of Jesus Christ and be saved.[2]
M. A. THOMAS

I will endure all the suing, trials and arrests. Numerous predecessors
have endured similarly.[3] **CARDINAL ZEN**

In 1980, China's Deng Xiaoping met with US President Jimmy Carter and signed accords that gave the People's Republic of China full diplomatic recognition by the United States. During that historic meeting, Carter made religious freedom demands on Deng: reopen churches that had been closed, allow the printing of Bibles, and allow Western missionaries. Deng agreed to the first two but not the third. Churches reopened and didn't lack for missionary fervor, leading to exponential growth in conversions.[4]

But waves of change began crashing across Asia. The Chinese church's reprieve came to an end. Hundreds—perhaps thousands—of young demonstrators were gunned down in Tiananmen Square in 1989. That same year, Chinese Party leaders saw Poland defy Communist Soviets and secure free elections. They watched as Romanians threw off the Communist reign of Nicolae Ceaușescu in a bloody street battle that ended with Ceaușescu's execution on Christmas Day. With Communism under attack worldwide, Deng and his leaders rescinded their promised reforms, and persecution of Chinese citizens started rising again.

In 1990 the people of Pakistan elected and then quickly dismissed Benazir Bhutto, the most "Western" leader in its history. This ushered in a ten-year identity crisis for the nation, during which it began a decades-long fight with India over the Kashmir Valley. India, meantime, elected and dismissed its leader within one year as well. The vacuum emboldened the political wing of India's extremist Rashtriya Swayamsevak Sangh (RSS), who loudly insisted that to be Indian is to be Hindu. Their movement gained momentum and is today a determining factor in elections and public policy.

Indonesia, home of the world's largest Muslim population, became a recruiting ground for al-Qaeda during the 1990s. At the same time, angry mobs began attacking Christians in this part of Asia. Even hostile government and police forces had to intervene because the mob violence was so great.[5]

In recent decades, the "new normal" in Asia is for Christians to be maligned and persecuted on a scale unprecedented for centuries.

Christianity's Growth in China

The numbers of Chinese Christians are multiplying so rapidly that China may become home to the world's largest Christian population within ten years. Chinese Communists are understandably alarmed. Estimates place the Christian population anywhere from 130 to 300 million with traditional Buddhism at 185 million. The Communist Party has fewer than 100 million members.

The allure of Christianity is varied. Chinese people in impoverished rural communities tend to resonate with a gospel that meets needs and with a God who answers prayer. In more prosperous cities, Chinese workers are more drawn to spiritual nourishment, and the freedom of speech and human rights that the Judeo-Christian tradition reflects. In many communities, Chinese Christians build enormous crosses and some light them at night to be beacons of hope.

The Communist Party has a hard time policing these outbreaks of Christianity among its 1.4 billion citizens. To quash the growth, the government has enacted new laws that instigated hundreds of attacks on churches and the demolition of tens of thousands of crosses.[6]

DING CUIMEI China has a plan to "beautify" itself. However, Christian churches and crosses evidently do not qualify as beautiful.[7] For years, legal Chinese churches have placed crosses on their structures, with full government permission. Now thousands of crosses are being removed from structures across the nation. In southern China, China Aid founder Bob Fu estimates 2,000 churches were forced to take down their crosses in the year 2016 alone.[8]

That same year, thousands of legally operating churches across the country have been demolished and dozens of pastors were arrested on false corruption charges.[9]

Pastor Li Jiangong and his wife, Ding Cuimei, were shocked to see bulldozers outside their church on April 14, 2016. With government permission, the couple had openly pastored Beitou Church in Zhumadian, Henan Province, China. They were one of the fortunate Chinese churches that had its own land and building.[10] Yet when a local developer made an offer to the authorities for the land, the government agreed and sold it out from under them.

The developer that "purchased" the land said he wanted the site cleared. The government complied. Authorities sent a government demolition crew to destroy the church.

As if reenacting the iconic scene from Tiananmen Square, the pastor and his wife jumped in front of the bulldozers. They tried to wave the heavy machinery to a stop. To no avail. The driver did not stop.

"Bury them alive for me," a demolition worker reportedly said. "I will be responsible for their lives."[11]

The bulldozer crew relentlessly bore down on the two, shoving them into a pit. The crew continued to work and covered the pastor and his wife with soil. Pastor Li, still conscious, cried for help and struggled to dig his way out of the debris. Ding suffocated before she could be rescued.[12] Eventually her body was pulled from the rubble. Her red shirt and blue pants were not marred. There simply was no life left in her body.

The murder caused international outrage. "Bulldozing and burying alive Ding Cuimei, a peaceful and devout Christian woman, was a cruel, murderous act," Bob Fu said. "This case is a serious violation of the rights to life, religious freedom and rule of law. The Chinese authorities should immediately hold those murderers accountable and take concrete measures to protect the religious freedom of this house church's members."[13]

Pastor Li said the "police took an uncommonly long time to arrive at the scene after a report of the murder was filed."[14] Then the Chinese government tried to walk back the murder. On April 17, a China Aid reporter said authorities had detained two people from the demolition team and a criminal investigation was forthcoming, but no one was charged.

On April 25, the government backpedaled further, reversing itself and designating Pastor Li's church land as a site for religious use. The authorities also issued a report to acknowledge that the church owned the land. For church parishioners the news brought both "joy and sorrow" since "we had to mourn one of our sisters to have justice."[15]

The martyrdom of Ding Cuimei underscores the Chinese government's increasing persecution of religious minorities, and specifically Christians. A little more than 5 percent of China's 1.4 billion people are believed to be Christians. David Curry, president and CEO of Christian advocacy group Open Doors USA, said the Chinese government appears determined to lower the profile of the church. "There was a time when they [Christians] were being recognized as productive members of society. The government treated them fairly," Curry said. "But that has changed."[16]

The death of Ding Cuimei is indicative of the callous treatment of Chinese Christians nationwide. The Chinese government has shifted from removing church spires to rezoning church properties and now, as in the case of Pastor Li's church, sending in demolition teams. Pastor Li and his congregation have courageously rebuilt on the spot where a brave woman boldly stood her ground, trying to protect the right of Chinese people to worship the Lord Jesus. This precious sister embodied the words of Ephesians 6:13: "Having done all, to stand firm." The world saw Ding Cuimei take a stand and will not easily forget her sacrifice.

MARIAM VATTALIL Samandar Singh, a hired killer, sat in prison alone, guilty of murder for brutally stabbing and mutilating a nun on a public bus. In August 2002, Singh's frequent visitor Father Michael Porattukara came as always, but brought a terrified young nun with him this time, Sister Selmy Paul. Singh may not have been terrified, but he was nervous, not knowing what to expect.[17]

After introductions, Selmy reached out and tied a traditional Hindi "Rakhi" to Singh's hand, the symbol of a brother-sister relationship.[18] In Hindi, it means "the bond of protection" and symbolizes the man's duty and honor to protect the woman. The meeting had been hard for Father Michael to arrange. The nun who had shown Singh this act of grace was the younger sister of the nun he had murdered.

Selmy's elder sister had been born in 1954 in Kerala, roughly 800 miles south of Mumbai. Born Mariam Vattalli, she joined the Franciscan Clarist Congregation at Kidangoor and assumed the name of Sister Rani Maria as she made her final vows in 1980. Sister Rani remained in a northern convent before being assigned to work among the poor within the Diocese of

Indore in the state of Madhya Pradesh. Numbering less than one percent of the area's population, Christians commonly face discrimination, yet Sister Rani was undaunted.

Sister Rani encouraged the landless poor to insist on a living wage from their greedy employers. She taught poor tribal farmers better agricultural methods. She encouraged families to give up drinking, send their children to school, and establish savings accounts. Sister Rani also organized women's groups to pool their money so they could provide assistance in emergencies. Ultimately, her goal was to help poor people avoid taking cash advances from moneylenders who were often their own property owners. She often received threats, but with great boldness and dedication, she pressed on with her work. As a result, the property owners arranged to have Rani assassinated.

On February 25, 1995, Sister Rani woke up early for Mass then hurried to the bus stop. The plan was to get some work done, then catch the train to visit her aging parents at home in Kerala.

The bus moved along the country road with passengers hopping on and off. Then three men got on, sat next to her, and started cussing at her, taunting and insulting her. More than fifty passengers watched as Rani remained silent. Then one of the men pulled out a large knife and stabbed her in the stomach. The men forced the bus driver to stop and tried to drag Rani off, but she held on to the door until they cut her hands. As those on the bus watched in horror, Rani was stabbed fifty-four times. They heard her repeating the name, "Jesus, Jesus, Jesus" until finally the attacker that held the knife slit her throat.

At the news of the attack, Selmy raced to find her sister's mutilated body and covered it with kisses. A large crowd gathered around the bloody remains of the body to pay respects. The nation was shocked. Thousands of people, both Christians and non-Christians, overflowed the cathedral church in the city of Indore for Rani's funeral. Everyone wanted to pay homage to a nun who was, as one bishop stated, "a model for us, as she was ready to shed her blood for the sake of the poor and downtrodden."[19] Cardinal Baselios Cleemis called Sister Rani Maria "a model for heroic life, a model for proclaiming the gospel in a pluralistic country," adding that she was "a symbol of the deep Christian commitment to the service of the poor and marginalized."[20]

In the aftermath, Sister Rani's family struggled through their grief and the knowledge that it was their Christian duty to forgive her killer. It was obvious that Sister Rani would have forgiven him. Finally, in 2002, Sister Selmy mustered the courage to go with Father Michael to visit Singh, the assassin who had plunged his knife fifty-four times into her sister. Selmy expressed her forgiveness and their family's forgiveness.

Singh was overwhelmed with shock, grief, and finally, repentance. He asked, in turn, for Selmy to forgive him. The following year, the sisters' aging mother visited Singh and kissed both his hands. This expression of Christian forgiveness eventually led Singh himself to Christ and he asked to be baptized. "I was overcome with grief and remorse for killing an innocent nun, who only selflessly worked to uplift the poor people and make our nation progress," Singh said later.[21]

In 2006, Rani's family petitioned the court for Singh's pardon, and he was released. A 2013 documentary film about the assassination, *Heart of a Murderer*, won the top prize at the World Interfaith Harmony Film Festival.[22]

On November 4, 2017, Sister Rani Maria was beatified in Indore. At the ceremony, Singh told reporters, "I accept full responsibility for my heinous murder of Sister Rani Maria. . . . I will regret my actions till the day I die. In my own small way, I try to follow her example, helping those who are less fortunate than me, like tribal Christians and all those who are marginalized."[23] Sister Rani's sacrifice paved the way for her murderer to know the unbelievable transformative love of Christ, and for all of us to understand a deeper kind of forgiveness.

DID YOU KNOW? *The First Missionary to India*

According to church tradition, in AD 52 the apostle Thomas went to Kerala on the southwestern tip of India, to introduce the gospel. Kerala's climate of searing heat and drenching monsoons is well known for producing spices. Historians presume that even before Christ, ancient trade routes took spices from Kerala throughout the world. The frequent trading ships would have provided Thomas with an excellent opportunity to spread the message of Jesus. Some Christian families in Kerala claim to be direct descendants of Thomas, much like the Mayflower Society of the United States—only ten times older and much harder to prove. Whether or not they are directly descended, Kerala Christians create huge celebrations for St. Thomas's Feast Day to honor their founder. Thomas is amply honored the rest of the year on buildings, avenues, businesses, and especially churches that carry his name.

DR. TOM LITTLE Some individuals simply look at people, while others *see* people truly. Dr. Tom Little saw people as image bearers of God.

Dr. Little, an American optometrist, led a team of medical professionals who worked with the International Assistance Mission (IAM) Nuristan Eye Camp, a Christian humanitarian organization that has provided eye care for the people of Afghanistan for over forty years.[24]

Little married his high school sweetheart, Libby, and in 1978 the two traveled to Afghanistan. Initially, they planned to stay in Afghanistan for several months. Little was an aid worker at the time, and he and Libby wanted to help wayward young people get out of jail and return home safely. A year after they arrived in Afghanistan, however, the government cancelled their visas, which meant that Little needed to find something else to do. Since his father was an ophthalmologist, he decided to work at an eye care hospital in the region.

Ultimately, Little became an optometrist, spending the next thirty years in Afghanistan, despite the changes in leadership and escalating danger.

Dr. Little's faith in Jesus compelled him to serve the people of Afghanistan. He saw himself as a neighbor to the Afghans, not an outsider who had come to set things right. For instance, rather than performing surgeries himself, he trained local Afghans to do them.

Dr. Little *lived* his faith, and as a result, he built trust with people from all occupations, enabling him to accomplish things that larger NGOs could not do.

Over time, Dr. and Mrs. Little raised three daughters in Afghanistan, consistently demonstrating the love of Jesus to some of the poorest people on earth. Dr. Little and his team offered medical relief and eye care throughout the Russian invasion, various civil uprisings, and the rise and fall of the Taliban.

He and Libby recalled the brutality of war in several interviews; at one point, they said, the US Embassy told their loved ones in America that the Little family had likely died.[25]

In August 2010, during Dr. Little's fifth trip to the Nuristan province, Taliban insurgents massacred his ten-member team, accusing them of "spying for the Americans" and "preaching Christianity."[26]

In 2011, he was posthumously awarded the Presidential Medal of Freedom.[27] He persisted in the face of peril because he believed that God *sees*—and *loves*—people.

After Little's death, officials presented Libby Little with her husband's blood-stained notebook, containing a devotional that Tom had presented to the team, reminding them of 2 Corinthians 2:15: "For to God we are the fragrance of Christ among those who are being saved and among those who are perishing" (CSB).[28]

Three months after her husband's murder, Libby Little addressed a crowd of four thousand people in Cape Town, saying, "Go spread the aroma of Christ in hard places."[29] Her husband had done the same. Dr. Tom Little carried out the work of his Savior to the end, sharing the gospel of peace and giving sight to the blind.

TAHIR IQBAL In 1988, some outgoing Christians in Pakistan befriended Tahir Iqbal, a twenty-eight-year-old Muslim who was said to be a direct descendant of the prophet Muhammad. The Christian community was overjoyed when Iqbal gave his heart to Christ. A few years earlier, an illness had left him paralyzed from the waist down. As a result, his family abandoned him.[30] But Iqbal's new Christian family continued to accept him, and his enthusiasm was irrepressible. From his wheelchair, he became a bold witness of a God who accepted him as he was and loved him.

The imam at Iqbal's former mosque became irate. Feeling the pressure to return to Islam, he declared, "They want me to say that I was forced to change my beliefs, that it was because of money, or for a good job, or to get a wife. They must know that I only changed my faith because I did find the Truth."[31]

A local mullah accused Iqbal of underlining sections of the Quran and writing in the margins, thereby desecrating it. The offense is punishable by death under Pakistan's infamous blasphemy laws. On December 7, 1990, Muslim leaders whipped a crowd into a frenzy that set out to murder Iqbal. Police said the only way to protect him was to move him to prison. After the "rescue," he was charged with the crime of blasphemy and kept imprisoned for the rest of his life.

For years, human rights activists have accused the Pakistani government of using blasphemy laws as an "arbitrary instrument of intimidation."[32] The government is quick to state that no one has been executed based on the law, yet many of those accused of blasphemy have died from mysterious "natural causes," and many more have watched their lives ebb away in prison. Others have also been burned alive by mobs, killed by angry zealots, and stabbed, beaten, or tortured to death in front of or by the police. After one such incident, a human rights activist argued that "anyone who is charged under [the blasphemy laws] ought to be protected until he gets a fair trial" but not sent to prison because so many die there.[33] Such was the case with Tahir Iqbal.

In prison, Iqbal's wheelchair was taken away. In cold weather, he was not provided with a blanket. He was often deprived of food, water, electricity, or toilet facilities. Lawyers fought for his release, but the court refused to set bail. Iqbal received no medical care when his left side became numb. Even with the testimony of a prison medical officer, the court would not release him. Iqbal complained of death threats.[34] But it all fell on deaf ears. One judge said his apostasy—leaving Islam to convert to Christianity—was an offense with "serious implications."[35]

On July 13, 1992, Iqbal was finally given a court hearing and his trial was set for July 21, 1992. He never made it to his court date. On July 20, Tahir Iqbal mysteriously died in Kot Lakh Pat District Jail in Lahore. Other prisoners said he vomited blood before he died. Poison was speculated. Prison officials claimed that Iqbal died after a sudden illness.[36]

Iqbal's estranged stepmother claimed his body and buried him with Islamic rites in Faisalabad. The burial ceremony was performed by the same Muslim cleric who had demanded the death penalty. Iqbal's stepmother declared, "Allah never forgives those who blaspheme against his holy prophet. Tahir received what he deserved."[37]

Tahir Iqbal may have been young in his faith, but he was deep. He refused to renounce Christ and refused to stop talking about him. When threatened with death, he referred to the teenager Mona, who was to be executed by the Islamic Republic for her faith. At her execution, she kissed the rope, then put the noose around her neck. In prison, Iqbal said emphatically, "I'll kiss that rope, but I'll never deny my faith."[38] The brutality of his treatment revealed the depths of his faith. In the darkness of his cell, Tahir clung to the light of Jesus' love.

MARTIN BURNHAM As a boy, all Martin Burnham wanted was to get through high school, become a pilot, and get rich. God fulfilled all three of young Martin's goals but with riches far beyond the child's understanding. Martin Burnham did become a pilot, then spent his life making exciting flights over the jungles of the Philippines in a rich life dedicated to serving others. He and his wife made international news when they were kidnapped by terrorists linked to Osama bin Laden. In that season of crisis, Martin had the opportunity to show the world what true riches really are. Shortly after the 9/11 suicide attacks by religious fanatics, Burnham displayed just how much his values had been transformed—he devoted his life to honoring God by serving others with a pure, passionate love, even at the expense of his own life.

In Sunday school, Martin had made a personal commitment to Christ before he ever dreamed of flying. In 1970, his parents herded their children aboard the *Philippine Corregidor* freighter to move their family from Kansas to Manila for missionary service. Traveling home from his boarding school, Burnham sometimes got to fly on a mission plane. He fell in love with flying. That's when he set his life goals: flying and fortune.

His parents didn't dissuade him, but insisted that after high school, he first attend the New Tribes Bible Institute in Jackson, Michigan. From there, he moved to Wichita, Kansas, and joined the Cessna Flying Club. In the process, his goals changed from planes and money to planes and ministry.

Martin Burnham taught in the Calvary Bible College flight department while he completed college. There, he was smitten by a fellow student, Gracia Jones. They married in Kansas City on May 28, 1983, and started preparing for a life of missions. In early 1986, Martin and Gracia went to the Philippines to work with New Tribes Mission. Martin served as a jungle pilot and Gracia aided in support roles while homeschooling their children. Martin had a big heart for the missionaries he served and for the local tribes as well. He delivered supplies to missionaries and transported sick and injured people to medical care.[39]

On May 26, 2001, Martin and Gracia decided to get away for a brief but much-needed break to celebrate their eighteenth wedding anniversary. They chose the beautiful Dos Palmas Resort on secluded Palawan Island that featured bungalows on stilts over the water. After midnight, their rest ended when someone banged repeatedly on their door. Martin opened the door expecting to help someone in need but instead was met by young gunmen. Martin and Gracia dressed quickly in shorts and flip-flops, then were herded onto a boat.

A radical Muslim faction called the Abu Sayyaf Group (ASG) abducted the Burnhams, along with one other American and seventeen Filipinos. As it turned out, they would behead the other American the next month. The group first took the hostages to the ASG stronghold on Basilan Island. Martin's first prayer for the hostage group was, "Lord, all of this doesn't surprise you. You know where we are, even though we don't. We know that people are worried about us. But you hold us in your hands. Give us the grace to go through this trial. We're depending on you."[40]

That prayer would be repeated often during the coming months as Martin and Gracia saw several hostages killed or set free. Soon, only the Burnhams and a Filipino nurse named Ediborah remained in captivity. They spent months in constant danger. Moving from camp to camp to evade capture, the hostages endured gun battles, sickness, and other atrocities of harsh treatment in the jungle. The 9/11 terror attack heightened the global interest in the ASG because of its ties to Osama bin Laden. The Burnhams' plight, the attempted rescues, and expert opinions of what was really happening fascinated and horrified the public and made a feeding frenzy for international news agencies.[41]

More than a year after their kidnapping, on June 7, 2002, intelligence officers received a tip that at least one of the Burnhams was being held near a fishing village in the southern province of Zamboanga del Norte. As if following the narrative of a Tom Clancy novel, US-trained Light Reaction Company fanned out through coconut groves and farms outside the village. With US forces backing them, hundreds of elite Filipino troops rushed into the jungle camp to rescue the missionaries. A gun battle with the rebels ensued, claiming many casualties before it was all over: Ediborah, the Filipino nurse held hostage with the Burnhams, was shot and killed, as were four of the kidnappers, and Martin was shot in the chest. He died afterward as a result of the wound.[42]

The Burnham family had hoped for a peaceful, rather than violent, resolution, but Martin's parents, Paul and Oreta Burnham, revealed the incredible grace and courage that comes from a life of missionary service. They immediately stated, "Obviously, this is not what we wanted, but we will get through this. . . . the Lord will give us the strength."[43]

Gracia was taken immediately to a military hospital in the southern city of Zamboanga for surgery on a bullet wound in her right thigh. She returned home under a national spotlight and later commemorated Martin's sacrifice in a *New York Times* bestselling book, *In the Presence of My Enemies.*

Every morning after the abduction, Burnham family and friends had gathered at the Rose Hill Bible Church outside of Wichita to pray. In the jungle, Martin and Gracia were constantly in prayer. Often Gracia would ask, "How can these people be so cruel?" Martin would answer, "I think God is gracing these guys with one more chance to turn to him, to finally get it right."[44] Martin "got it right" and in so doing, laid down a challenge for the rest of us to treasure life's true riches.

Christianity in the Philippines

The Philippines is known as the only "Christian nation" in Asia. Islam had taken hold of the island nation in the fourteenth century. Two hundred years later, colonial Spain introduced Christianity and ensured the quick spread of Catholicism, which remains the dominant religion on the archipelago nation. Protestant missionaries arrived after the United States rose in power at the start of the twentieth century. Unlike in other postcolonial nations, Christianity has become almost fully indigenized in the Philippines. Now Filipino Christians take the light and message of Christ all over the world, including the Middle East, where many homes and businesses are staffed by multinational Filipinos who work abroad to support their families at home. It isn't unusual for a Muslim leader in government or in religion to have many Filipino Christians as professional accounting staff or as facility or culinary managers.

GRAHAM, PHILIP, AND TIMOTHY STAINES What started with a slideshow and an innocent correspondence between two pen pals ended with the horrific deaths of a father and his two sons.

In 1941, Graham Staines was born in the suburban town of Palmwoods in Queensland, Australia. He became a Christian at the age of ten, but it was later, when he heard missionary Vera Stevens speak about her time abroad, that he took an avid interest in India. Her slideshow depicted the suffering of destitute lepers. He envisioned the hopelessness that surrounded the outcasts as they passed from a life of misery into an eternity without Christ.

His tender heart and care for the lost deepened as he grew into adulthood. While Staines was reading his devotions one day, he paused at Mark 1:39-42, the story of Jesus' encounter with a man with leprosy. The Lord's compassion moved Staines to tears, and he realized that God was asking him to leave the comfort of home and move to the mission field where he, too, would minister to people with leprosy.

Staines enrolled in Brisbane Missionary Institute in 1963 and developed a long-distance friendship with an Indian engineer, Santanu Satpathy of

Baripada, with whom he shared a birthday. Two years later, Staines decided to visit his friend, where he fell in love with the people of India and saw firsthand the anguish of the sick and outcast.

He moved to India and immersed himself in ministry. Staines worked faithfully at the Mayurbhanj Leprosy Home, and he eventually became the superintendent and secretary, responsible for the housing and welfare of its residents. He spent his time preaching, planting churches, counseling church leaders, helping translate the Bible into the Ho dialect, and arranging conventions. He spoke three local languages, sharing the love of Jesus everywhere he went. He was a beloved, highly respected member of the community.

After twenty years on the mission field, Staines met his wife, Gladys, a nurse who had also heeded God's call to serve abroad. They had three children, Esther, Philip, and Timothy.

Then on January 21, 1999, Staines and his sons said goodbye to Gladys and Esther and headed to a village where they planned to hold a jungle camp to offer health and hygiene instruction. After a productive day, they decided to sleep in the car since the makeshift church was so crowded.

Staines covered the roof with a straw pad to block the cold winds, then just after midnight, a mob of enraged Hindu extremists attacked. They pierced the tires with *trishul*, or tridents, then broke the car windows. They ruthlessly beat Graham and his sons, spearing each one with the tridents. Then the men stuffed straw beneath the car, poured gasoline on the vehicle, and set it ablaze. Staines and his two sons, Philip (ten) and Timothy (seven) were burned alive.[45]

Although shocked and heartbroken, Gladys and Esther extended forgiveness to the murderers. At the funeral, Gladys and her daughter sang a familiar chorus: "Because He lives, I can face tomorrow." Their faith stands as a testament to the love that Graham, Philip, and Timothy Staines proclaimed to society's outcasts.

One of the lepers who knew Staines and his family said, "Our world was darkness. . . . we were left to die in the jungles all alone, like worms . . . Then came Staines Dada and his friends . . . They stretched forth their hands in mercy and took us to the Leprosy Home. . . . There we saw the love of God."[46] Staines and his sons lost their lives in the service of Jesus, but the love and hope that they shared will last for generations.

SHAHBAZ BHATTI Pakistani Minorities Minister Shahbaz Bhatti had chosen to live a simple life. He told an interviewer, "I have not married because I know that I will be killed, and I am willing to be a martyr for Christ. I would even find it to be a big honor to be killed for my faith in Jesus Christ. I'm ready to give my blood for that."[47]

Bhatti had been asking for additional security in recent weeks, even requesting a bulletproof car because of threats against his life. According to senior officials, Bhatti had been assigned police and paramilitary troops but had declined their assistance. Bhatti disputed the claim, confirming to a friend, "I haven't been given any extra security. It's just the same as it has been since I became a minister."[48]

Bhatti advocated reforming the country's blasphemy laws. The blasphemy law was originally aimed at all religions with a small sentence attached. But the Islamic government changed it to carry a death sentence for anyone who insults Islam or the prophet Muhammad. Christians and other critics point out that it is unfairly applied and hinges on witness testimony, which is often based on grudges, and amounts only to persecution.[49]

"This law is being misused," Bhatti said in a magazine interview. "Many people are facing death threats and problems. They're in prison and are being killed extra-judicially."[50] Bhatti's brother-in-law, Yousaf Nishan, said, "In this society you can't open your mouth, even if you want to say something good, because you're afraid who you might offend."[51]

Bhatti, who was the only Christian serving in the Islamic state's government, began receiving increasing threats. In November 2010, Bhatti advocated for the release of Asia Bibi, a Christian woman sentenced to death for blasphemy. Another politician, Punjab governor Salman Taseer also advocated for her. Taseer was assassinated by one of his bodyguards in broad daylight in front of a café on January 4, 2011.[52] In an interview following that assassination, Bhatti said he would defy death threats and continue his efforts to reform the blasphemy law.

In 2010, Bhatti had predicted his death at the hands of the Taliban or al-Qaeda.[53] He recorded a video to be broadcast if he died. "It's sort of his testimony to the world," said Johan Candelin, who worked for the religious freedom advocacy group First Step Forum and worked with Bhatti for seven years. Candelin said that Bhatti "had very much come to terms with the prospect of his own murder."[54]

On Wednesday morning, March 2, 2011, Bhatti left the home he shared with his mother in a quiet Islamabad neighborhood. His driver picked him up for work, but without a guard or the additional security vehicle that would generally accompany a Pakistani minister. Bhatti's driver had driven a quarter of a mile when a white Suzuki car pulled in front and forced them to stop. Two gunmen jumped out and sprayed Bhatti's car with bullets. The attackers then opened the door, dragged the driver out, and continued firing on Bhatti through a side window.

After putting eight bullets into Bhatti, the gunmen scattered pamphlets on the road written by Taliban al-Qaeda Punjab, saying Bhatti was a "Christian infidel" and that President Asif Ali Zardari had put him in charge of a committee to review the blasphemy laws. "With the blessing of Allah, the mujahideen will send each of you to hell," it said.[55]

Mariam, Bhatti's twenty-two-year-old niece, arrived at the scene and wept next to his body. "I said 'uncle, uncle' and tried to take his pulse. But he was already dead," she said when she was interviewed at Bhatti's house, filled with the wailing of mourning women. Her hands were still stained by his blood.[56]

Bhatti's body was taken to Shifa Hospital where he was pronounced dead on arrival. He was forty-two years old.

After Bhatti's death, his video was released on television and online. It showed Bhatti saying that "the forces of violence" were prepared to kill him because "they want to impose their radical philosophy in Pakistan." He said he would never stop speaking for Christians and other marginalized minorities. "I'm living for my community and suffering people, and I will die to defend their rights. So these threats and these warnings cannot change my opinions and principles."[57]

In his farewell address, Bhatti made the most honorable statement any Christian can utter, the martyr's oath: "I believe in Jesus Christ who has given his own life for us, . . . and I am ready to die for a cause."[58] Bhatti honored the name of Jesus to the end of his life by standing up for those who could not speak for themselves.

IRIANTO KONGKOLI Irianto Kongkoli clasped the hands of his wife, Rita, and their four-year-old daughter as they got out of their car to head into the store in Palu, the capital city of Central Sulawesi province in Indonesia. Their two other children were not with them. The family knew that living openly as Christians was dangerous in their hostile area of Sulawesi, Indonesia's fourth largest island and the site of a major brawl in December 1998 that led to religious clashes between Christians and Muslims lasting until 2001 and leaving more than a thousand dead. Despite the hostilities, Kongkoli and his family bravely and openly identified themselves as followers of Jesus.

On October 16, 2006, they were shopping at the Sinar Sakti hardware store. As the trio headed back outside, someone called Kongkoli back into the store. Immediately, two masked men fired two bullets at near point-blank range into his head.[59] The killers sped away on a motorcycle. Kongkoli was rushed to the hospital but succumbed to his wounds.

The governor of Central Sulawesi said he believed that the killing might have been linked to an event the previous month. Three Christians accused of leading a Christian militia had been convicted and sentenced to death for killing several Muslims during inter-faith clashes in 2000. Minority leaders and human rights activists pointed out that the population is 80 percent Muslim and said the trial was "unjust" due to pressure from Muslim fundamentalists.[60]

In the month following the executions, at least two people were killed during several bomb attacks. At the same time, Kongkoli was named to head the Central Sulawesi Christian Church. He replaced a leader who stepped down after being unable to secure the release of the three Christians who were eventually executed.

The governor reminded reporters that Kongkoli "was an outspoken priest who many times led Christian protests against the executions."[61] It was true that Kongkoli was a strong religious figure who had been a critic of police and government authorities. He struggled for peace and harmony in the region and supported interfaith dialogue. Kongkoli helped create the Poso Humanity Forum with various key Islamic figures, as a further effort to foster stability in the region.

Kongkoli's leadership was ideally suited to his times. He had completed theological training in Christianity and studied Islam at the Yogyakarta State Religious Institute. He spoke Javanese fluently and Arabic as well. He worked as a peace broker during those years of violence and was a signatory on the Malino peace agreement.

After his death, the government downplayed the religious tension, saying the murder was not indicative of hostility between Christians and Muslims. But news reports and popular opinion demonstrated that the relationship between the two groups had become extremely tense over the previous month.[62]

When Kongkoli was buried at the Talise cemetery in Palu, five thousand people attended his funeral.[63] Irianto Kongkoli is remembered for his steadfast love for people of all faiths. He was a bringer of peace, sent by the Prince of Peace, to his island home for his appointed time, and his legacy lives on among the martyrs of history.

CHELSEA DECAMINADA AND THE EASTER SUNDAY MARTYRS

Around the world, Easter Sunday attracts the largest attendance at worship services. On April 21, 2019, it was no different in Sri Lanka as the faithful traveled to celebrate together the holiest Christian day. While tourists in resort hotels relaxed in beautiful breakfast locations overlooking the sparkling Indian Ocean, local churches were packed.

As the innocent ate or attended church, nine suicide bombers made their way to six assigned locations. The targets were three churches—in Colombo, Negombo, and Batticaloa—and three Colombo luxury hotels: the Shangri-La, Kingsbury, and Cinnamon Grand.

The first report of a blast came at 8:45 a.m. Soon the entire nation was feared to be under siege as smoke rose. Screams and mourning were heard throughout the three cities where attacks occurred. Rescuers rushed to help, stepping over strewn body parts to get to the wounded and the dead. "You can see pieces of flesh thrown all over the walls and on the sanctuary and even outside of the church," reported a priest at a bombed church.[64] Six blasts attacked the first six locations. Smaller blasts continued later outside the zoo, in a car, and in a house being raided for the crime.[65]

Chelsea Decaminada was one of the wounded. A Duke University graduate with a degree in public policy and international comparative studies, Decaminada had studied in South Africa, where she used her French language skills to volunteer weekly with Francophone refugees. She later interned at the Clinton Foundation and Creative Associates International, then spent two years in the Peace Corps. She was hired by the US Commerce Department as an international program specialist. On assignment in Sri Lanka, she was staying at the Shangri-La Hotel and attending Mass in Colombo when the bombs went off. She had to be airlifted to Singapore for treatment for critical wounds. For two weeks, Decaminada and the medical staff fought for her life, but on May 4, 2019, she died. The total death toll would eventually rise to 269.[66]

A local radical cell of the Islamic State called National Thowheeth Jama'ath claimed responsibility for the bombings. Islamist preacher Zahran Hashim, the suspected ringleader, was one of the suicide bombers.[67] Sri Lankan authorities arrested or killed the remaining jihadists responsible.

In Sri Lanka, attacks on Christians had surged in 2018. "We are witnessing that communities are being mobilized in an increasing manner against Christians," reported a lawyer working with the National Christian Evangelical Alliance of Sri Lanka.[68] In August 2018, the Sri Lanka Supreme Court ruled that proselytizing was not protected by the constitution.

Sri Lanka's minority Christian community appeared to be the main target of the attack that Sunday. The NYPD Deputy Commissioner of Intelligence and Counterterrorism, John Miller, called it "an attack directed at Christians specifically with a tinge of economic targets." He said intelligence agencies had been "waiting for that shoe to drop" since leaders of al-Qaeda and ISIS called for revenge for a shooting attack at a mosque in New Zealand a month earlier.[69]

International leaders poured out commendations and sympathies for Chelsea Decaminada's dedication, talent, courage, and spirit. US Secretary of Commerce Wilbur Ross remarked on Decaminada's devotion to public service, stating, "her dedication and spirit were a model for all of us at Commerce. She served her country with distinction."[70]

Decaminada was mourned by close relatives and friends at a funeral Mass in St. Joseph Parish in Somers, New York. The priest who conducted it recalled a question he had asked priests on the night before Easter, "I wonder where Catholics will be attacked tomorrow." He later wrote, "The vicious persecution of the Church is almost expected in Egypt, India, Sri Lanka, Nigeria, the Middle East, Indonesia, Pakistan, China, especially on major feast days."[71]

The priest who conducted Decaminada's funeral reflected, "What dawned on me at Chelsea's funeral was how dramatically the thugs had failed. It was Chelsea and the other martyrs who had conquered. Not only did their martyrdom because of their faith assure them of eternal life, but the crowd at St. Joseph's Parish in Somers left more convinced than ever that Chelsea's way—loyalty, love, service, friendship, family, faith—was the only true route to happiness, in this life and the next."[72] Chelsea Decaminada spent her life serving others, and in a final act of sacrifice, she gave her life in service to her Savior.

Perhaps American Christians connect with her the most, and her death certainly received the most coverage in her home country, but herein we reflect our own bias. Were the lives of the 268 others who died any less meaningful? The terrorists that day targeted Sri Lanka's Christians, killing forty-five foreigners as they did. We remember families like the Fernando family. Rangana died with his wife, Denadiri and their three children: Biola (six), Leona (four), and eleven-month-old Seth. Ramesh Raju saved countless lives when he ran a bomber out of Zion Church that morning only to lose his own life in the ensuing explosion. Raju left behind a wife and two children. Also killed in Zion Church were twelve-year-old Sharon Santhakumar, along with his younger sister, Sarah. Thirty-three-year-old Bennington Joseph died with his wife, Subramaniam, and their three young sons. The list goes on and on.[73]

Hundreds of martyrs lost their lives that Easter in the barbaric attack. In their death, as in their life, they proclaim Christ.

RUFUS HALLEY Halley was born and raised in Waterford, Ireland, then attended the Benedictine Glenstal Abbey outside of Limerick. He joined the Catholic Columban missionary order, pledging to support the poor and stand against injustice. In 1969, Halley was ordained and the same year was assigned to the remote coastal town of Jala-jala, fifty miles from the Philippine capital of Manila.

Reverend Rufus Halley remained in the Philippines his entire adult life. A gifted linguist, he mastered many of the nation's languages and dialects. After a brief time in the Manila area, Halley chose a mission post at the Diocese of Marawi, in the nation's Islamic stronghold. Located on the island of Mindanao, his new home was devastated by corruption and in constant upheaval. But Halley quickly learned the local languages and mingled with his Muslim neighbors as easily as with Christians. How much he was loved and revered became evident when he was asked to serve as a peace broker in a conflict between two Muslim factions. The negotiations were tense, but Halley earned the respect of the nation when he was ultimately successful in creating a lasting settlement.[74]

Halley had found his niche. He spoke the languages like a local, navigated rough roads, and managed the difficulties in traveling from island to island. Halley attacked his work with determination, even when it made him uncomfortable. When he saw members of the army acting in disrespectful ways in his Muslim community, he called them out. When he was needed to help reconcile opposing factions, he showed up.

As Halley traveled home from a Christian-Muslim meeting at Our Lady of Peace parish church in Malabang on August 28, 2001, four men armed with M16 assault rifles and wearing ski masks flagged him down on his motorcycle.[75] Witnesses saw the men try to drag him away, evidently in a kidnap attempt. When Halley resisted, the men, who were later found to be Islamic extremists, shot him in the head and then sped away in a van. Halley died on the spot. His death is still commemorated by Christians, as well as the Muslim community in the region.

Halley was buried in the Columban plot in Cagayan de Oro, the twenty-fourth martyr of the Columban order.[76] Two thousand people, Muslims and Christians, packed the Church of the Immaculate Conception for his funeral.[77] In a eulogy, a friend remembered how he handled living in a lonely post through prayer and meditation. Halley had often been threatened, but his peace was found in his total dependence on Christ. In a letter, Rufus had written what summed up his philosophy of fearlessly giving his all to Christ:

> This life which we love so much is God's gift to us—that, as Isaiah says, he has carved us in the palm of His hand. . . . Each of us is called to live out, in imitation of Jesus, . . . the total offering of ourselves back to God. . . .When God so chooses to accept back this gift which we voluntarily offer, well it is up to him.[78]

Carved in the palm of God's hand, Halley offered up the gift of his life, imitating the life of the Savior he loved.

SEIJA JÄRVENPÄÄ AND KAIJA-LIISA MARTIN An unidentified woman wrote of her experience in Afghanistan,

> I'm often asked what I wear in Afghanistan and what it's like to wear a veil. It's freedom. Freedom to have a bad hair day, freedom to arrange my *chadar* to conceal the curve of my breasts and backside, freedom to not be an expatriate for a little while. It means freedom to hide even on the street from the Afghan men's eyes which seem to strip me naked.
>
> When I relax my shoulders and walk less purposefully, less confidently, my eyes downcast and covered by sunglasses, I pass for an Afghan woman. I hear the men whisper in Dari, "Is she a foreigner or local woman?" I chuckle but am silent.
>
> On the street, I'm also a free target . . . freely exposed to groping, sexual innuendos whispered to me as a man bicycles by, free to have stones thrown at me, freely seen as no one's wife, daughter, sister, mother, friend, or boss. I step inside my gate and remove my *chapan* and *chadar*. Now I'm someone's boss, motherhood returns to me as little steps run to greet me, and

I receive a kiss from my adoring husband. Now I'm free to his loving and gentle eyes, which know and enjoy my curves, free to once again be under the protective umbrella of being a wife, mother, friend, colleague, boss, niece, sister, daughter, *woman*.[79]

For Finnish expatriates like Seija Järvenpää and Kaija-Liisa Martin, working in Afghanistan meant taking serious risks every day. Both women served with International Assistance Mission (IAM), a Christian organization that has offered health and economic development assistance to the Afghans since 1966. Järvenpää worked with mental health patients, while Martin helped low-income women improve their lives through business opportunities.

In 1998, the two women moved to Afghanistan. Seija Järvenpää traveled to Herat to join IAM as part of their Community Development Project (CDP). Kaija-Liisa Martin came to work in various senior administrative roles within IAM in Kabul and Herat. She served alongside Järvenpää in Herat, while also assisting the organization's Business Development Services (BDS) to raise the standard of living for low-income women.[80]

In 2006, Järvenpää returned to Finland to continue her studies in social work, ministering to Afghan refugees there. Her passion for the people of Afghanistan prompted a return to Herat in 2013, where she piloted a social work project for mental health patients and their families. Martin had also left and returned to Herat in July 2014 to become the regional team leader of IAM.

One neighbor recalls Kaija-Liisa Martin as a "sweet, soft-spoken, kind Finnish woman."[81] Both women were too passionate to stay home when they knew of a need they could fill.

On July 24, 2014, Järvenpää and Martin sat in a taxi on a street in Herat. ISIS insurgents had targeted them.[82] As the two women sat waiting, two armed men on a motorcycle drew close to the taxi and opened fire at point blank range. Järvenpää and Martin were killed instantly.

These women embraced God's call wholeheartedly, and like the apostle Paul, who understood firsthand the cost of Christian discipleship, they echo the truth he wrote:

I eagerly expect and hope that I will in no way be ashamed, but will have sufficient courage so that now as always Christ will be exalted in my body, whether by life or by death. For to me, to live is Christ and to die is gain.

PHILIPPIANS 1:20-21, NIV

CHERYL BECKETT Ten aid workers had been helping northern Afghan villagers, particularly mothers and their children, with eye care and other medical needs. Then one day red-bearded gunmen lined up the workers and shot them one by one, including Cheryl Beckett, age thirty-two. The only survivor was the Afghan driver, who was reciting the Quran.[83] Their Land Rovers, riddled with bullets, were found next to the ford of a swollen river. In an official Taliban statement in Pashto, at the time claiming responsibility, a key charge was the claim they found Dari language Bibles.[84]

According to Beckett's parents, and her heartfelt journal entries, she graduated from Indiana Wesleyan University with a global passion for love and justice. Having already visited numerous countries before Afghanistan, she developed a clear call to spread Christ's love—a call which led her to a village near Kabul in 2005.

The sponsoring group was the International Assistance Mission, a Christian charity group that was "a bedrock institution in Afghanistan" since 1966.[85] It reported that she had joined the medical team for their three-week trip as a translator, helpful as a Pashto speaker for the local women. Her family's release states, "Cheryl loved and respected the Afghan people. She denied herself many freedoms in order to abide by Afghan law and custom."[86]

Her father, Reverend Charles Beckett, had little doubt about her driving faith. After her death, he read her journals and reflected:

She wrote in her journal, which has been a spiritual oasis for me. Over and over again I read this theme: no longer my own, I've been bought by Christ, with His own blood. I want to know Him better.

And then she wrote, "I want to die to myself." And then she asked the question to herself, "What does that look like? How do I make that tangible?" That is what she devoted her life to, knowing Him but knowing Him by sacrificially suffering in order to show Him.[87]

THE ALL SAINTS CHURCH BOMBING On Sunday, September 22, 2013, fifty-two-year-old Khalid woke up happy. He had been severely ill for several months and unable to attend church with his beloved friends, but finally, he was well enough to attend.

"He had made a promise to God that when he got better, he would go to church," said Khalid's twenty-year-old son Joel Fakhar. "He was looking forward to seeing his friends."[88]

Khalid moved through the streets of the old section of the walled city of Peshawar, Pakistan, that morning, along with hundreds of faithful congregation members who came from all directions. They passed the historic Kohati gate, then filed under the Oriental arches of the 130-year-old All Saints Church. Entering through its tall wooden doors, most stopped to take off their shoes according to local tradition.

After the service, Khalid and roughly six hundred fellow members spilled out of the church to mill in the courtyard in animated groups. Children squealed and laughed. Under a clear blue sky, the church dome gleamed with its minaret-type turrets and black cross, creating a picturesque backdrop for the mingling crowd.

While parishioners enjoyed their fellowship, the joyous midday peace was broken with the approach of two men wearing suicide vests—bombs designed for maximum carnage. The first blast sent shockwaves through the crowd, then came the second, even stronger than the first.[89] People screamed and fell. Windows in neighboring buildings shattered from flying shrapnel. The force of the ball bearings packed inside the bombs even pocked the outer walls of the church and surrounding buildings.

Khalid and more than one hundred others became the largest number of Christian martyrs in one attack in Pakistani history.

Immediately, friends and relatives searched for their loved ones and began to wail. Among the first found dead were thirty-seven children.[90] Many others were maimed or orphaned.

Doctors and paramedics rushed to the scene. One doctor who arrived moments after the blast estimated that many more died than would be reported, because their bodies were recovered by relatives before they could be counted.[91] Officials first reported that 85 people had been killed and more than 100 injured. But a week later they confirmed that the toll was 127 people dead and another 170 injured.[92]

Graphic news images of the dead and dying, wailing adults and bewildered children, captured the attention of the nation. By afternoon, images of coffins and gravediggers were added to those of the blast site. The roads of Peshawar became jammed with emergency vehicles, as well as stunned, angry residents and very active, vocal Christians. In the major cities of Lahore, Islamabad, and Karachi, Christians joined their Peshawar brothers and sisters in spirit, taking to the streets in huge crowds to demonstrate their resolve not to back down from their faith.

"'It's not safe for Christians in this country,' said Mano Rumalshah, the bishop emeritus of Peshawar, who was standing in the courtyard, comforting sobbing parishioners who clasped his white robes. 'Everyone is ignoring the growing danger to Christians in Muslim-majority countries.'"[93]

The next day, national protests continued. In the meantime, several groups were blamed for the attacks, and others proudly took credit for killing Christians. One Pakistani intelligence official said, "There were warnings of a coming attack. Unfortunately, no one could predict where this attack was going to take place." He attributed the attack to a "hard-line Sunni Muslim militant group known to be loyal to al-Qaeda and the Taliban." Another unnamed official said, "All the indications suggest that this was an attack by the Taliban."[94]

At the church, with the bodies cleared from the blast area, only a pile of blood-soaked shoes remained, along with scores of bloody patches on the cobblestones of the courtyard. Coffins had been lined up on a nearby school playing field, allowing hundreds of mourners to pay their respects. Men hugged coffins, women wailed and wept, friends and relatives clutched each other. Many mourners were overwhelmed by the sight.

"A grave injustice has been done today," said a young woman. "All these people inside the church had innocently gathered to say their prayers."[95]

The tragedy was at the time the deadliest attack ever conducted against Pakistani Christians, who make up less than 2 percent of the population. Politically, these resilient faithful are considered a very weak minority group. But there was nothing weak about their resolve on the streets of Pakistan following the incident.

Some people suggested that the only safe option for Christians was to leave Pakistan. But most Christians vowed to remain, intent on showing they were unafraid.[96] They blocked major streets. They held candles, built bonfires, carried crosses. Young Christians mourned the dead and chanted Christian slogans outside the hospital where the injured were taken.[97]

The church's founders had once written, "In no way will [the building] be regarded as a successful effort, unless spiritual stones are added thereto."[98] One hundred and thirty years later, a poster in the protests that followed testified to the rock-solid faith of the Pakistani believers: *Live as Christian, Die as Christian, Proud to be Christian.*[99]

JOHN JOSEPH On May 6, 1998, rioting broke out after Bishop John Joseph ended his own life with a gunshot to his head. A note left at the scene indicated his death was intended as a protest against Pakistan's blasphemy laws that condemned to death another Christian, twenty-five-year-old Ayub Masih. Masih's sentence was suspended, which makes Joseph's sacrifice appear to be, in essence, the laying down of his life to save the life of another.[100] Controversy and rumors swirled about his sudden and shocking action. To stop the rumors, the Vatican confirmed the death in a statement, as did the Pakistani church. Many Pakistani Christians now believe his death was no common suicide, but that Bishop John was a martyr. "We should not call it suicide," said Lahore Archbishop Emmanuel Yousuf Mani. "He sacrificed his life fighting against injustice."[101]

Regardless of what happened in his death, Joseph's life left an indelible mark. Born into a Catholic community in the Christian village of Kushpur, he trained in Rome and at age fifty-two fulfilled a boyhood ambition to become the first native-born Pakistani bishop. Growing up, he was an excellent athlete but an even better student. His elder sister, already a nun when Joseph was a boy, said he "studied, studied, studied" in the school where his elder brother, Lazarus, was headmaster.[102] After his ordination, Joseph was appointed rector of Christ the King Seminary in Karachi and translated many Christian works into Urdu. His ordination as Bishop of Faisalabad came in 1984. There, in a highly unusual move, Joseph opened his home two nights per week to anyone, especially to anyone who wanted to dialogue about faith.

Throughout his life, Joseph was a champion of justice. When he saw that Muslim children had to walk miles to cross a river to get to school, he recommended a bridge be built—Muslims starting from their side, and Christians starting from theirs. When a bulldozer was poised to destroy a Christian shantytown, he blocked the bulldozer. When identity cards unfairly identified minorities for discrimination, he went on a hunger strike to protest.

Colleagues knew him as man with deep feelings for the poor and marginalized, one who became for them a symbol of peace and justice and who introduced interfaith dialogue in Faisalabad. He formed the National Commission for Justice and Peace (NCJP) for human rights and with his huge capacity for leadership, motivated people to join him.

Of all his accomplishments, it was Joseph's fight against Pakistan's blasphemy laws that would eventually claim his life. "It is extremely sad that his decision has taken away the best of the best from the human-rights movement in Pakistan, but his message comes through very clearly," said a spokesman for the Catholic Church of Pakistan.[103]

The original blasphemy laws were written under British rule in the 1860s and applied to all religions with a maximum sentence of two years. The recently revised version was limited to remarks about Islam and carried the death sentence. Christians consider the strict blasphemy law Pakistan's best method to persecute Christians. One of the most famous arrests came in 1993, when three Christians were sentenced. While leaving the courthouse, they were fired on and one died. At the funeral of the man who died, Bishop Joseph promised that no one else would lose their lives to blasphemy laws, then kissed the dead man's feet and said, "The next blood to be shed for these laws will be mine."[104]

Instead, the next five years brought one injustice after another, including murders and unjust arrests. On February 6, 1997, someone took pages from a Quran, wrote on them, and threw them in a deserted mosque in a Christian village called Shantinagar. Between 30,000 and 50,000 Muslims attacked the village—looting, burning, gathering all the Bibles in heaps and setting fire to them, razing more than 1,000 houses. One resident said, "Nothing was left." They burned crops, cows, buffaloes, trees, vegetable gardens. Loudspeakers from area mosques egged them on shouting, "Destroy the [infidels]. It is your duty, fulfill it—now!"[105]

Months later, Joseph held a huge rally in Islamabad condemning the violence. "We do not accept a Pakistan that discriminates among its citizens on the basis of religion," he thundered. "We reject all discriminatory laws. We demand immediate withdrawal of the death sentence from the blasphemy law."[106] When Ayub Massih was sentenced on April 27 of the following year, Joseph threatened to protest Massih's death sentence in an "astonishing" way.[107] The sixty-five-year-old bishop went to a prayer meeting for Massih in Sahiwal on May 6, and then entered a hallway to the courthouse where Massih was sentenced to death. Joseph was found there, dead from a gunshot wound.

Immediately, thousands of Christians began protests against the laws, spreading across the country. About 1,500 Christians marched through Karachi, thousands more gathered around his home in Khushpur. Ten thousand mourned at his funeral on May 8. In reaction, five hundred Muslim militants rampaged through a Christian neighborhood, screaming slogans and burning homes. Christians in the village attacked police for not responding.[108]

Pakistani bishops, priests, and nuns in Vatican City said they hoped Joseph's death would "stir the consciences of all the brothers and sisters of the country."[109] Fourteen years later, Nisar Barkat, diocesan director for the NCJP, said, "We are still determined to carry on his mission towards protecting the rights of religious minorities in Pakistan."[110] In a gathering in Joseph's honor, his friends and followers vowed again to "continue the mission of the 'martyr bishop.'"[111]

Joseph had hoped to end, once and for all, the atrocities being perpetrated against the tiny Christian community of Pakistan. He wrote prior to his death: "I shall count myself extremely fortunate if in this mission of breaking the barriers, our Lord accepts the sacrifice of my blood for the benefit of his people."[112]

The blasphemy laws remain intact and persecution in Pakistan continues, yet many people are inspired by his faithful and courageous example. And while Joseph's death remains controversial, his life was not. One journalist concluded that Joseph's life is one reason why, "for all the bloodshed, for all the killings, for all the death and persecution, the light of the church in Pakistan has not been put out."[113]

SHAHZAD AND SHAMA MASIH An anti-terror court in Pakistan sentenced five people to death for the mob violence that killed two Christians. The young couple was lynched and burned in a kiln after being falsely accused of blasphemy. Their six-year-old son described the ordeal to reporters. He said that "many, many people beat up his *amma* [and] *abba*." He explained that his amma and abba "were tied behind a tractor and dragged through the village before they were burnt."[114]

The incident united the nation in outrage, even as it sent many Christian families fleeing the area in fear for their lives.

Pakistan's blasphemy laws carry the death penalty for anyone who speaks directly or indirectly against Islam in any way. Even unproven accusations can stir up violence. Critics accuse the laws of unfairly targeting Christians, and being used for personal vendettas.

Pakistani Christians are vulnerable for several other reasons. The Christian population of about three million is dwarfed within the fifth largest nation on earth that numbers over two hundred million. Christians are not just one of the smallest but also one of the poorest groups in Pakistan.[115] The Chuhra caste of sweepers, which was the lowest level of South Asian society, was evangelized in the nineteenth century. British missionaries hoped to help change their social status, but that low standing continues to the present day. As a result, 4.5 million laborers are indentured in that lower class, many of them Christians. Trapped in the system, if they even try to get out, someone can just bring an accusation against them, keeping them in their place.

Such was the case of twenty-six-year-old Shahzad Masih and Shama Bibi, twenty-four, who lived in the village of Kot Radhakishan, just south of Lahore. The couple was crippled religiously, economically, and educationally—like most of the lower-class Pakistani Christians, they were illiterate. Yet they were accused of tossing pages of the Quran into the kiln where Shahzad worked. Only after their deaths were the allegations proven false. Shahzad's father had used pages of inscriptions for his work. When he died, the couple had no need for what they couldn't even read, so they burned the pages. In the ensuing court case, Nadeem Anthony, an investigator with the Human Rights Commission of Pakistan, was emphatic: "Let me be clear that there was no burning of the Quran there." He said it was paper with an Arabic *taveez* [a local charm], not verses of the Quran.[116]

The accusation came allegedly through someone finding a few pages of the Quran outside their mud hut. The village imam announced the crime through loudspeakers, and hysteria ensued around the region. The couple locked themselves into their mud hut, but a crowd broke down the door. The angry mob beat them with fists and sticks, then dragged them across the village with their little son looking on.

At the brick kiln where Shahzad worked, the couple were set ablaze and thrown in. Eye witnesses said they were still breathing when they were burned. Shama's clothing didn't burn fast enough for the frenzied crowd, so they pulled it off and wrapped her in fast-burning cotton. Muhammad bin Yameen, a local police official, claimed that police were too outnumbered to stop the crowd. However, police in Pakistan are not known for clamping down on mob violence.[117]

Prosecutors seeking justice for the couple discovered the attack was instigated at the behest of a kiln owner, who feared they would default on a debt of less than $1,000.

A total of 103 people were charged with the crime, but a court acquitted ninety, including the kiln owner. Forty-five were arrested, eight were given two-year sentences, five were given the death sentence.[118] Many questioned if the death sentences would be carried out. "Consistent failure by the government to tackle violence in the name of religion has effectively sent the message that anyone can commit outrageous abuses and excuse them as defense of religious sentiments," said David Griffiths, Amnesty International's deputy Asia-Pacific director.[119]

Christians in Pakistan suffer, and Shama and Shahzad suffered more than most, as will their little boy for the rest of his life, after witnessing their torture and murder. Their martyrdom was tragic, but perhaps their legacy is that this one time in Pakistani history, the entire nation agreed that the actions against this young, illiterate, underserved couple were intolerable, and justice had to be served.

HAN CHUNG-RYEOL Pastor Han Chung-Ryeol led hundreds of people in a church on the Chinese side of the China-North Korea border from 1993 to 2016. A North Korean defector once estimated that Pastor Han shared the gospel with at least one thousand North Koreans.[120] Others have estimated it was many more. North Koreans passing through the border town had heard they could get help from a building with a cross on it. It was Pastor Han's church that fearlessly displayed the cross.

When the church started in 1993, North Koreans were fleeing a famine in their country. Pastor Han helped every person he encountered—orphans, sex-slave victims, soldiers, and starving refugees. He provided food, shelter, and clothing, and he shared the gospel with each person. He encouraged them to share Christ with others. North Koreans aimlessly knocked on the doors of other houses, so Pastor Han trained local residents to help them. A Christian leader reported that Pastor Han planted churches in North Korea and was sending deacons to do the work.[121]

Pastor Han spent his life serving people until the day it cost him his life. On Saturday, April 30, 2016, the forty-nine-year-old pastor left his church at 2:00 p.m. and headed up the mountain near the border town of Changbai where he lived. On the side of the mountain, his lacerated body was found at 8:00 that night "with knife and axe wounds in his neck."[122]

A murder was no surprise. Pastor Han had not hidden his Christianity but emblazoned his faith across his city. Over the years, many people had become targets for North Korean hit squads. In 2000, North Korea murdered a US pastor, Kim Dong-shik, for aiding fleeing refugees; in 2009, North Korea sent hit teams to murder Chinese and South Korean human rights activists.[123] Since 2003, Pastor Han had been on Pyongyang's most-wanted list.[124] Finally, they carried out their threats.

North Koreans said they could see Pastor Han's heart. In their culture, a North Korean would only enter into a trust relationship, close enough to be led into the Kingdom of God, if they could see your heart.[125]

One of the North Koreans Pastor Han helped was Sang-chul. In a short documentary with The Voice of the Martyrs, Sang-chul explains, "In primary school, we were taught that all missionaries were terrorists. They told us that a missionary will be nice to you at first, but when they get you into their homes, then they will kill you and eat your liver."[126]

Sang-chul said that he didn't have a way to earn money for food, so he sneaked across the mountains into China. As he went, he picked mushrooms in hopes of selling them. In China, he met Pastor Han, who said he'd sell them for Sang-chul and give him the money. When Pastor Han didn't cheat him, Sang-chul asked him why he was willing to help, when it was so dangerous.

"It is because I am a Christian," Han said. Sang-chul recoiled in fear at the word, but Pastor Han continued. "God is real. There is hope for every person."

"I could not believe he would say that word, 'God,'" Sang-chul says. "Nobody says that word. We know that it is an act of treason . . . [and] can lead to soldiers coming in the night."

Eventually, Pastor Han gave Sang-chul a Bible. Sang-chul, his wife, and best friend all became Christians as a result of Pastor Han's bold proclamation of the gospel.

"Pastor Han gave his life, but he gave hope to me and to many other North Koreans," Sang-chul says. "And despite the ever-present danger, many of us will continue to share the message that God is real."

Sang-chul says, "We hope that our sacrifice, when the day comes, will be worthwhile, just like it was for Pastor Han."[127] Pastor Han's bravery, wisdom, and compassion will never be forgotten by the thousands of people whose lives he reached directly or through others.

Billy Graham's beloved wife, Ruth Bell Graham, was born in Qingjiang, Kiangsu, in the Republic of China on June 10, 1920. She was sent to boarding school in Pyongyang, located in modern-day North Korea. Her parents, Dr. and Mrs. L. Nelson Bell, were medical missionaries to China. Under their leadership, Ruth developed a desire to pursue full-time ministry. She moved to the United States to enroll at Wheaton College. There she met the strapping young man the other students called "Preacher." After some struggles as to whether she would engage in a ministry on her own or marry a man and adopt his ministry as her own, Ruth married Billy Graham. She was his first and most important member of his ministry for the next sixty-three years, until her death.

Vintage Foxe

His astonishing constancy during these trials, and serenity of countenance while under such excruciating torments, gave the spectators so exalted an idea of the dignity and truth of the Christian religion, that many became converts upon the occasion.[128]

CHAPTER SIXTEEN

From Criminals in North and South America

Do not fear, for I have redeemed you; I have summoned you by name; you are mine ISAIAH 43:1, NIV

I am not going to apologize for speaking the Name of Jesus. . . . If I have to sacrifice everything . . . I will. RACHEL SCOTT

My desire was to tell [the church], "My brothers and sisters, let us rise in arms. Let us fight." But the words from my mouth came, "Our fight is not against flesh and blood." I was . . . looking at the bodies of my brothers, my uncles, my cousins, my nephews. . . . For the first time in my life, I understood that . . . the militants are not my enemies. God is asking me to forgive them because they are people that need Jesus Christ.[1] JOSHUA SAUÑE, SURVIVING FAMILY MEMBER OF THE SAUÑE MARTYRS

Many Christians in open societies find it easy to believe persecution of Christians occurs far from home. But the situation for Christians has deteriorated globally in the past decade, and this period has also marked a dramatic rise in persecution worldwide, including in the Americas.

Even the United States, whose founding fathers created the First Amendment to protect citizens' rights, has seen persecution rise in recent court rulings, confirmation hearings, and violence against religious establishments, regardless of Constitutional protections. Religious profiling is not uncommon.[2] Those who claim the name of Christ are most often reported to be bigots, and local churches are frequently found to be ethnocentric, although the church worldwide is one of the most diverse movements in history.[3] In fact, Christianity itself has played an indispensable role in addressing racism and other injustices. It was, of course, the faith of the likes of Martin Luther King Jr. that animated their activism. As we have noted throughout this book, the church is far from perfect on any of these fronts and has too often been itself the means to deploy anti-biblical ideas. Yet, it is also true that the church is severely persecuted as it stands for both biblical truth and biblical justice.

School environments for America's young Christians reflect all of these rising sentiments. Students are sometimes targeted and publicly ridiculed for their faith.[4] Millennials have grown up with the threat of school shootings; such incidents rarely occurred earlier. The deaths of two martyrs at Columbine captured the eye of a generation. The trauma of that shooting has been repeated, as school attacks have explicitly targeted Christian students.[5]

In South America, gangs and drug lords have routinely ordered the assassination of priests and ministers. Missionaries standing up for poor farmers are targeted by poachers and other criminals. Terrorist organizations, guerrillas that have the tacit approval of corrupt governments, and gangs are a constant threat in many nations. In Colombia alone, 13 percent of Christian leaders have received death threats, with many more being harassed, extorted, and even murdered.[6]

DOROTHY STANG Dorothy Stang was born in Dayton, Ohio, one of nine lively siblings in a devout Catholic family. She entered the Sisters of

Notre Dame de Namur, intent on making her life one of service to others. In 1953, when she was twenty-two years old, she took her first assignment—teaching children, serving the poor, and working at a church in Sunnyslope, Arizona. While there, she applied for an overseas post, writing on her application, "I want to be a missionary in China."[7] Instead, in 1966, Stang was assigned to help the poorest of the poor in Brazil. So devoted was she to her mission that she eventually became a naturalized Brazilian citizen.

Stang's work in Brazil galvanized her when she realized the poor farmers had no chance to build independent futures for themselves and their families. Laborers were promised land, then driven off by more powerful entities—loggers, ranchers, land speculators, agribusiness, and the criminal gangs they often hired. Since the government didn't intervene to protect the farmers, Stang decided she would do it, and lived in destitution as she fed the hungry, built community, and founded a center for women. She taught farmers sustainable farming methods, as well as how to read.

Stang studied the law and advocated for poor farmers. She passed on what she learned, teaching the population their rights, the law, and their responsibilities to the law. Emboldened by her new knowledge, Stang often barged into government offices, lodging complaints. The president of the human rights commission for Brazil's lawyer association, Mary Cohen, recalled Stang's determination to pressure government agencies to take action. Cohen said, "She once slept on the steps of the Institute for Agrarian Reform so they would talk to her."[8] The lawyer association gave Stang a human rights award two months before her death.

While studying the region, Dorothy learned that the rain forest surrounding her was called the earth's lungs and was critical to maintaining earth's stable environment. She began wearing a favorite T-shirt emblazoned with "The death of the forest is the end of our lives."[9]

In spite of her activism, the lives of the farmers Stang served did not improve. Their rain-forest lands were increasingly exploited and stripped of rich natural resources. The destruction of the forest and theft of land from those farmers undermined the self-sufficient communities she was trying to build. Frustrated, Stang repeatedly said, "You don't need to cut down the forest to obtain your livelihood from it."[10]

In return, government officials got frustrated with Stang. By 2002, a mayor in a nearby town reportedly said, "We have to get rid of that woman if we are going to have peace."[11] A kill list emerged with bounties. At the top was "Stang, $20,000."[12]

Undaunted, Strang pressed on in her mission. "I don't want to flee, nor do I want to abandon the battle of these farmers who live without any protection in the forest. They have the sacrosanct right to aspire to a better life on land where they can live and work with dignity while respecting the environment."[13]

As the danger increased, she said, "I know that they want to kill me, but I will not go away. My place is here alongside these people who are constantly humiliated by the powerful." A few months before her death, she told her sister, "I just want to sink myself into God." Upon her return, she faced trumped-up charges for "organizing armed rebellion."[14]

During that trial, she continued working, pleading with Brazil's human rights secretary to protect the farmers. A few days after that meeting, she walked down a dirt road to meet some rural farmers who were being harassed by illegal loggers and ranchers. Perhaps she was meditating on the words she'd shared with a novice earlier that week: "I look at Jesus carrying the cross and I ask for the strength to carry the suffering of the people." Or she may have been reflecting on what she'd told friends the day before: "If something is going to happen, I hope it happens to me, because the others have families to care for."[15]

Gunmen approached. She took her Bible out of her bag and read from Matthew, "Blessed are the poor in spirit. . . . Blessed are those who hunger and thirst for justice. . . . Blessed are the peacemakers . . ." Then she looked up at the assassins and said, "God bless you, my sons."[16] The hired assassins shot her six times.

Stang's assassination triggered outrage among Christians, environmentalists, and world leaders. With Stang gone, two issues emerged. First, an increased recognition of the need to preserve the rain forest, and second, the danger to advocates trying to save it. In the time between Stang starting her studies and her death, the world's rain forests were depleted by 50 percent.[17] To this day, the threat of assassinations continues to intimidate farmers, keeping them enslaved to debts they can never repay.

After Stang's death, President da Silva put twenty thousand square miles of rain forest near the Anapu region under federal protection. The move allowed the Sisters of Notre Dame de Namur and others to continue Stang's work. And her legacy lives on in other media as well. Notre Dame de Namur University created the Sr. Dorothy Stang Center for Social Justice and Community Engagement. *They Killed Sister Dorothy*, a documentary about her life, received awards at the South by Southwest Festival.[18] Composer Evan Mack, inspired by a lecture about Sister Dorothy, wrote *Angel of the Amazon*, an opera about her life and work.[19]

In a letter penned to her family, Dorothy once said, "That I've been able to live, love, be loved and work with the Brazilian people, help them find confidence in themselves, to profoundly sense God's presence in their lives and then be a creative influence in society from which a more human society can be born, I thank all of you."[20] Her gratitude had grounded her in life. She had remained devoted to her Lord, fulfilling Proverbs 19:17: "Whoever is kind to the poor lends to the LORD, and he will reward them for what they have done" (NIV). Stang's love for people, care for the poor, and courage to confront injustice were the trademarks of her life. Her struggle for justice and hope continues to echo throughout the Amazon.

CULTURAL CONNECTION

Rise of Evangelicalism in Brazil

An unabated political crisis has gripped the nation of Brazil for many years, with a parade of politicians taking key positions, only to topple due to corruption. Since 2010, the minority of politically conservative Brazilians has turned into a majority, with citizens favoring more law and order. It seems the emergence of this political conservatism is also connected to a biblical conservatism embodied by the rise of the evangelical church in Brazil. Evangelical Protestant and Pentecostal churches have experienced massive growth. In 1980, 6.6 percent of the population claimed to be evangelical; by 2010, that figure had grown to 22.2 percent, and was estimated to be 31 percent of the population in 2020.[21] If the Catholic Church continues its decline, estimated at 1.2 percent per year, experts believe the majority of Brazilians will claim to be evangelicals in only a few years.[22] Whether evangelical or Catholic, followers of Jesus are everywhere you look in Brazil—it may very well be the most Christian country on earth.

RACHEL SCOTT Rachel Scott was a vivacious seventeen-year-old, with a passion for Jesus and a love for her fellow students. An aspiring actress and playwright, she had a flair for the dramatic and loved being in front of the camera. She was active in her youth group, but despite being bullied for her faith throughout her school career, Rachel wasn't afraid to stand up for what she believed.

In a 1998 talent show, Rachel performed in a pantomime dance, portraying Simon of Cyrene, the man who carried Jesus' cross to His crucifixion. The sound tech that day was Dylan Klebold, a classmate since kindergarten. He saved the show with a reserve tape deck when the sound went down.[23] But there was no one to save the day on April 20, 1999, when Dylan and his friend, Eric Harris, opened fire on the students and faculty of Columbine High School, near Denver, Colorado.[24] Rachel was one of the first victims. The dance she performed at the talent show would later be re-enacted at her funeral.

Rachel was sitting on the grass near the west entrance of the school eating lunch with her friend Richard Castaldo when Dylan and Eric began shooting. Victims of bullying themselves, the shooters were taking revenge. They chose random targets, picking off students one by one. Rachel was hit several times and fell to the ground. When she tried to get up, one of the killers shot her at point blank range in the chest, arm, leg, and head.

Rachel's brother, Craig, who was in the library during the shooting, was miraculously unharmed, while other students hiding there perished. He didn't know if Rachel had been killed or escaped the mayhem. Her family feared the worst. Their fears were confirmed when her name was included on the list of those confirmed dead.[25]

The loss was devastating to both family and friends. Her car, sitting in the parking lot of the school, became a memorial site, as friends bedecked it with flowers and notes, mourning her death. Her friend Lauren Beachem said, "In my eyes, she was just one of those kinds of people you know you won't ever meet again. She was the kind of person only born once."[26]

Rachel had longed for all of her friends at Columbine to know about Jesus' love. In one of the journals her family found, she shared the types of attitudes that she wanted to develop in herself and encourage in others, traits like empathy and compassion. Her brother said, "She was talking about . . . things like not judging or labeling other people, looking for the good in others and being a leader, showing mercy and forgiveness."[27] In a paper for a school assignment, Rachel wrote, "I have this theory that if one person can go out of their way to show compassion, then it will start a chain reaction of the same."[28]

Rachel penned the prophetic words, "I am not going to apologize for speaking the Name of Jesus. . . . If I have to sacrifice everything . . . I will."[29] In Rachel's moment of sacrifice, God answered the prayer of her heart. Her words, her actions, and her love for others have inspired others and have been used for His purpose and glory. After her death, Rachel Scott's mother and father, Beth Nimmo and Darrell Scott, wrote a bestselling book entitled *Rachel's Tears* (2000), and her father wrote another bestselling book, *Rachel Smiles* (2002). Both inspired tens of thousands of Christian young people to stand for Christ.

JUAN JESÚS POSADAS OCAMPO Netflix isn't often a source of Christian news, but in the first season of *El Chapo*, episode 4, producers suggested that the assassination of Cardinal Juan Jesús Posadas Ocampo was a government conspiracy, not the accidental death of a bystander caught in the crossfire of a drug war.[30]

Posadas Ocampo had been born, raised, and educated in Mexico. A native of Salvatierra, he studied at the nearby Seminary of Morelia. He was ordained in 1950 and served in various posts in Morelia, Tijuana, and Cuernavaca. In 1987, he became Archbishop of Guadalajara, one of Mexico's most influential dioceses. On June 28, 1991, Pope John Paul II elevated him to cardinal.[31]

On May 24, 1993, the driver of Cardinal Posadas Ocampo's white 1993 Grand Marquis was stopped in front of the Guadalajara airport, an isolated location thirty minutes from downtown. Around twenty gunmen piled out of three large SUVs in the airport parking lot and opened fire. When the attack ended, Posadas Ocampo's car had fifty-two bullet holes. Posadas Ocampo, who had exited the car, was shot fourteen times at such close range that the shots left a gunpowder stain on his chin. The driver and five other people were also killed.

Mystery and controversy immediately enveloped the murders. Early police reports stated that Posadas Ocampo was caught in the crossfire between two drug cartels. A police lieutenant told reporters that the gunmen fled, but two suspects were in custody. Later information would reveal that only one gunman had been arrested that day for the murder, and that a flight was delayed for twenty minutes to allow eight gunmen to leave the city. None of them were arrested when they returned.[32]

Most people did not initially believe Posadas Ocampo was deliberately murdered. Blame for Posadas Ocampo's death soon shifted to the Tijuana gang of the Arellano Félix brothers. The government alleged the gang had intended to kill El Chapo (given name, Joaquín Guzmán) and mistook Posadas Ocampo for the drug kingpin. Neither the church nor the people of Guadalajara believed this implausible narrative. The plump, gray-haired cardinal dressed in clerical vestments was twenty-four years older than the slightly built, black-haired El Chapo. The story shifted to him being mistaken for El Chapo's bodyguard, then again to his car being mistaken for El Chapo's car.[33]

Rumors flew that Posadas Ocampo could even have been targeted by his own church.[34] A conservative cleric, he continually countered liberal religious influences. Some speculated he could have been killed by the government he was unafraid to criticize. The cardinal was a nationally known opponent of the drug trade that kept a choke hold on Mexico. A report submitted to the United States government said the cardinal denounced "not only the traffickers, but those in authority, as well, who either turned a blind eye, or were themselves complicit in this plague that devastates so much of our society today."[35] As a result, he was threatened and stalked, and his phones were tapped. But he was not quiet. Posadas Ocampo had served the people of Mexico his entire life, and they were grateful. After his death, followers jammed the Guadalajara Cathedral, where his body lay in state. Some organized a march through the city.

But after the physical attack took his life, news sources briefly initiated a moral attack on his character, linking the cardinal to drug trafficking. An anonymous twenty-six-page dossier accused high-ranking members of the church, including Pope Paul VI, of receiving money from the infamous drug lord Pablo Escobar. After an eight-month investigation that diverted the nation's attention from solving the real crime, the bogus accusation was exposed, and the reputation of Posadas Ocampo restored.

After his forty-three years of ministry, Posadas Ocampo's largest legacy may yet be realized through his murder. In 1999, the government finally reported that the attack was indeed intended to kill the cardinal. In 2006, a member of the Mexican parliament for the Jalisco State reported to the United States House of Representatives that the cardinal was most likely murdered because he possessed information about drug trafficking and prostitution that included high-profile politicians on their payrolls. The cardinal would have been able to expose this information.[36]

Yet, in more than a quarter of a century, no one has been convicted for the cardinal's murder. Internationally, the assassination has become "emblematic of severe shortcomings in Mexico's justice system and its respect for the rule of law."[37] The murder spotlights Mexico's chronic inability to solve crime due to the infiltration of drug gangs into the federal judicial system. If the Mexican government were to prosecute Cardinal Posadas Ocampo's murder, it might well expose and bring to justice the drug traffickers that the cardinal had fought against, even at the expense of his own life. In both life and death, Cardinal Posadas Ocampo invested all that he had in love for his people and their fight for truth and justice.

Catholicism in Mexico

Mexico, the largest Spanish-speaking country in the world, has the second largest number of Catholics of any nation (Brazil has the most). While many Catholics in other Latin American countries have converted to Protestant denominations, and some have left Christianity completely, Mexico has kept strong ties to its Catholic faith. More than 80 percent of the population claims the Catholic faith, which is passed on through generations as part of a cultural identity. The Catholic Church has been seen as a catalyst for positive change in Mexico, rather than preserving a status quo. As sociologist and legal scholar Gabriel Le Bras said, "To ignore what happens inside the churches is to ignore a remarkable part of the spirit of the century and the factors of national life."[38]

DID YOU KNOW? *The World's Richest Man*

Carlos Slim Helú is not a household name worldwide, yet his wealth has at times exceeded that of well-known multibillionaires Warren Buffett and Bill Gates.[39] For decades, he has been one of the wealthiest men in the world, often ranking number one. And he's a Christian. Slim, born and raised in Mexico, was instilled with Christian values from his parents who were Lebanese Maronite Christians. (Maronite Christians are Eastern Orthodox who function with the Catholic Church in Rome.)

Slim's father emigrated from Lebanon and built a substantial business. Every Sunday, Slim's father would give him a five-peso allowance and require him to record his purchases in a ledger. By age eleven, Slim was putting into practice the lessons he learned from his father, and he soon started investing. As Slim continued to build his empire, his business ventures expanded far beyond Mexico. When Slim began investing in US companies, the joke among businessmen became that it was "because there was nothing left to acquire in Mexico."[40] Although Slim's extensive holdings are run by computer professionals, he has continued to track his businesses with written ledgers rather than a computer. Slim has never strayed from the lessons of his father, continuing to follow both his business acumen and his faith. His philanthropy is legendary.[41]

JUSTINIANO QUICANA When Joshua Sauñe, the leader of over two hundred Ecuadorian churches, speaks about his grandfather Justiniano Quicana, he speaks with pride, affection, and reverence. Quicana was one of the first people in Peru to accept the gospel when Protestant missionaries came to the area in the 1950s.[42] Before meeting those believers, Quicana believed that Christians would only come up into the hills of Peru to kill his people. But hearing the missionaries' words of love and truth, he began to understand that giving his life to Jesus was the only thing that would save him. Quicana, a direct descendant of the Inca people, began to share the love of Jesus with his neighbors. He and his family began planting churches high in the Peruvian hills.

Quicana raised his family in the knowledge of God. They ministered to the Quechua people. His son and several of his grandchildren followed in his footsteps, becoming pastors and evangelists. He spent his days encouraging others in the Lord, but it was not an easy task.

Christians in Peru were being severely persecuted. In the early 1980s, the Communist Party of Peru, called the Shining Path, was trying to overthrow the government. They used fear tactics and torture to subdue the Peruvian people. They saw Christians, who wouldn't join or fight with them, as barriers to their goal of domination.[43] The Shining Path murdered over 800 pastors during their reign of terror. They obliterated entire congregations. The government claims that somewhere around thirty thousand to a hundred thousand Peruvians lost their lives to their violence.[44] Quicana lost his home when they burned it to the ground. His wife was beaten and left for dead. He was on the Shining Path's Most Wanted List, so Quicana knew that it was only a matter of time before they would come for him.

Many times while Quicana was praying, the Holy Spirit had warned him that they were coming for him and he was able to escape. One Sunday, Quicana stood in front of his congregation and told them he would not be with them any longer. He said, "My brothers, next Sunday I'm not going to be here because the Lord has called me home." The next day, the Shining

Path came to take him away. Quicana didn't cower with fear. He didn't run and hide. He did the one thing he knew how to do. He offered the terrorists hope and a different kind of power. He said, "My sons, the only way we can change our country, the only way we can change the heart of our people is through Jesus Christ, and you must accept Jesus Christ."[45]

Quicana's statement infuriated the thugs who were trying to arrest him. They began to beat him and he fell to the ground, where he kept asking them to accept Christ as their Savior. In a violent fury, wanting to stop his words, they cut out his tongue. As his wife watched, they proceeded to gouge out his eyes, and cut his beating heart from his chest—the heart that beat with love for the people of Peru and for Jesus.[46] He died defending Christ and offering the hope of heaven to his murderers. Even though his life was lost high in the Andes, Quicana's heart beats on. His children and grandchildren continue to preach the love of Jesus to the Quechua. His grandsons Romulo and Joshua are proof of that.

ROMULO SAUÑE Romulo Sauñe had a way with words. A linguist with a heart for the Quechua people in his native Peru, he was honored on June 23, 1992, with the Religious Liberty Award from the World Evangelical Fellowship for his courage in bringing the Good News to his people.[47]

Years earlier, Sauñe started splitting his time between Peru and the United States to work on a dream God had given him—to translate the Bible into his native tongue. He grew up high in the Andes Mountains and understood the deep need for God's Word to be available in the Quechua language. On his mother's side of the family, he descended from Incas. Now, as a third-generation Christ-follower, Sauñe felt the love of Jesus and service to his people embedded just as deeply in his DNA as his ethnic roots.

Sauñe also understood that it would be up to the churches to spread the gospel. With his wife, Donna, they founded Runa Simi in 1983 to support the Quechua churches in his homeland, and especially the translation efforts. The Wycliffe Bible translating organization helped in what turned out to be a fourteen-year effort to translate the Bible. Finally, in 1987, Sauñe's dream had come true. The Bible translation was complete. But he was not done.

Sauñe started working on a recording of the Scripture for the many illiterate people who could never read what he had written, but who still longed to know God's Word. Yet Sauñe had an even bigger vision. He started translating hymns that could be sung and played with indigenous instruments.

Passion for Christ and love for his people drove Sauñe. But some of his countrymen disapproved. A group of Communist guerillas had killed his grandfather, Justiniano, in 1989. Now they became aware that the grandson, Romulo Sauñe, also was responsible for leading Quechan people toward Christ. To the guerilla fighters, the Cross of Christ served as a roadblock in their quest to overthrow the Peruvian government.

These Communists, known as the Shining Path, or Sendero Luminoso, grew in power throughout the 1980s and 1990s. Eventually they became infamous around the world as the deadliest guerrilla network in the Western Hemisphere.[48] The Shining Path would eventually take the lives of thousands upon thousands of Christians—men, women, and children. To escape the brutality of these killers, many Quechua Christians ran to the hills to hide in caves, often without food. The idea of dying of starvation was less dreadful than dying at the hands of these butchers.

In May 1992, at his home in Arizona, Sauñe told his brother Joshua that he felt the need to return to their people. Sauñe was concerned at how the Shining Path was stalking the Quechua church. He wanted to encourage them and show them that God remembered and cared for them. Ten weeks later, he headed back to Peru, leaving Donna safe in Arizona. Upon arrival, Sauñe joined his extended family who had fled to the hills. And then, he was gone.

Romulo Sauñe's brother Joshua remembers receiving a terrible call on September 5 from his sister-in-law, Donna. The Shining Path had ambushed Sauñe, along with his parents, his brother Ruben, and three nephews. His parents were forced to stand just yards away and watch as their sons and grandsons were savagely murdered.[49]

Joshua hung up the phone, heartbroken and enraged. *How could God have let this happen? How could a powerful God who loved so well let his family be killed?* When Joshua arrived in Peru for his brothers' and nephews' funerals, he was filled with anger and wanted to avenge his family's deaths. He expected his mother to be beside herself with grief. Instead of being dressed in the dark clothes of mourning, she met him at the airport wearing her brightest, most beautiful dress. She said, "Joshua, there is no time of crying or grief. It is a time of rejoicing because your brothers have reached heaven already."[50]

When Joshua looked at the bodies of his brothers and nephews, God changed his heart. He realized that his fight wasn't against the Shining Path; it was against Satan. The only way to win the fight was to share the love of Jesus with those who so desperately needed him. In spite of the danger, more than five thousand people attended the funeral for the Saune family. Joshua told them, "The people who killed my brothers need Christ just as you and I do."[51]

A legacy of love and literacy followed Romulo Saune's death. Joshua and his wife left Arizona for Peru so they could help carry on Romulo's work, evangelizing and partnering with the mission he had formed, Runa Simi. Donna took their four children and raised them high in the Peruvian mountains that Romulo had loved.[52] She decided to run a literacy program for women. Two of Romulo Saune's children continued in the ministry their father had started. Romulo Saune Schools eventually served more than 15,000 children who had been orphaned by the Shining Path.[53]

Joshua says of his brother, "He believe[d] and he follow[ed] our Lord Jesus Christ with all his life." Romulo knew the cost. He used to tell Joshua, "We are immortals until the day and the hour and the moment the Lord will say, 'It's time for you to come home.' Bullets will pass us. [They] will never hit us, but the day the Lord says it's time for you to come home, the bullet will hit us in the heart." Joshua says, "That's exactly how he [gave] his life, with a bullet in his heart."[54] The man with a love for words and a heart for Jesus died remaining faithful to the Word he loved most of all.

The rate of Bible translation has accelerated since 1990. At the beginning of this period, experts estimated that all major language groups would have at least a portion of a written Bible in their own tongue by 2150. With improvements in technology, this estimate is now as early as 2035.[55] And translation agencies are working to finish the job even sooner.[56] In Latin America, at least 200 languages are being targeted for Bible translation by agencies such as Wycliffe. In Colombia alone, there are twenty-one active language translations currently underway.[57] The IllumiNations exhibit in the Museum of the Bible (Washington, DC) provides a vivid display of the world's Bible translations. These are represented both in color-coded volumes by level of translations in languages, and via advanced technology displays. One of the clear takeaways is the number of languages remaining to receive some portion of the Bible and the challenges to achieving this goal. The goal is attainable within twenty years.

CASSIE BERNALL Cassie Bernall was a young woman who was transformed by the power and love of Jesus. It was a miraculous shift from the troubled girl she had been in her early high school years. Cassie had struggled with personal challenges as well as overt rebellion against her family's values. She experimented with drugs and alcohol and struggled with her mental health. Mona, her best friend at the time, encouraged this darkness. Cassie's mom, Misty, found letters from Mona, littered with occultist symbolism. Other letters were rife with sexual language, talk of drug use, and Mona's desire to kill one of her teachers, inviting Cassie to join her.

The letter that gripped Misty with fear instructed Cassie to kill her parents and included crude drawings portraying the killing. Her parents pulled her from school and enrolled her in a private school. To say that Cassie was lost in darkness was an understatement. There was a battle being waged for her soul. It was during this frightening time that Cassie met a new friend. Her name was Jamie.

Cassie's parents didn't think that Jamie looked like your average Christian girl, with her grungy look, heavy chains, and bleached blonde hair. But there was more to Jamie than her looks. Jamie was all about Jesus and his love. Her passion for reaching others influenced Cassie. Cassie had told Jamie that she felt gripped by a powerful darkness and couldn't break free.

Jamie invited Cassie to go on a retreat with her youth group. It was on that retreat that Cassie came face to face with the life-altering love of God and his care for her. The hope and light of the retreat's worship service broke through the darkness in her spirit. Cassie broke down in tears, asking Jesus for forgiveness. Jamie could see the change in her face. Cassie's life began to change in that moment. Her parents said that they got their daughter back. Cassie saw that day—March 8, 1997—as the day of her rebirth.[58]

In the fall of 1997, Cassie transferred from her private school to Columbine High School in Littleton, Colorado, telling her mom that she would be able to reach more people for Jesus at a public school. Although life wasn't perfect, it was a fresh start for Cassie. She thrived at her new school and in her youth group. There was no way to know that just a year and a half after her transfer, tragedy would strike.

On April 20, 1999, Cassie found herself huddled under a table in the school library, hiding from two classmates on a shooting rampage. Dylan Klebold and Eric Harris, targets of bullying at school, were meting out a violent reprisal against the student body. After their homemade bombs failed, they were shooting random students, and striking terror into the hearts of both students and faculty.

When Eric Harris entered the library where Cassie was hiding, he asked one of the students if she believed in God. Witnesses said that Cassie answered yes. After shooting several students, Eric Harris slapped the table that Cassie and another student were under, twice, and said, "Peekaboo," then shot her in the head. She died instantly.[59]

Mourning her daughter's death and celebrating her life, Misty wrote Cassie's story, *She Said Yes*, sharing the transformative effect of Jesus at work in Cassie in her final years. During Cassie's last days, her thoughts and prayers had centered on Jesus. The day before she died, Cassie had written a note to a friend, including a postscript, "P.S. Honestly, I want to live completely for God. It's hard and scary, but totally worth it."[60] That thought must have surrounded her as she hid in the library. Those are the words inscribed on her grave. Cassie Bernall died living completely for God, knowing the powerful, freeing love of Christ at work in her life.

SHARONDA COLEMAN-SINGLETON In a June vigil held for the murdered members of Mother Emanuel AME Church in Charleston, South Carolina, a single sentence captivated the nation and the world.

"Love is stronger than hate," said Chris Singleton, son of one of the victims, Sharonda Coleman-Singleton. He added, "So if we just love the way my mom would, then the hate won't be anywhere close to where the love is."[61]

Sharonda Coleman-Singleton was a speech and language pathologist and head coach for girls track at Goose Creek High School. She distinguished herself through dedication, competence, and a huge smile. The school principal said. "Her number one concern was always the students. She made a difference in the lives of children. She cannot be replaced at this school."[62]

Sharonda was an ordained minister, working part-time with young adult ministries at Emanuel AME. That's where she was June 17, 2015, when a white supremacist named Dylann Roof joined a prayer service, then opened fire on the congregation gathered there. Survivors reported that at 9:05 p.m., Dylann took a pistol from his fanny pack and shot a twenty-six-year-old woman, then systematically shot eight more people, including Sharonda. The victims became known as the Charleston Nine.[63]

Roof fled the church and was arrested after a national manhunt. Roof later explained that he was trying to start a race war.

Sharonda's greatest pride was always her sons and daughter: Christopher, Caleb, and Camryn. She was the type of parent who raised a son, Chris, who electrified the nation at the vigil for the victims, and nailed it again in an ESPN *E:60* episode called "Love Is Stronger." Producer Ben Houser said Chris was "one of the strongest people we have ever featured on the show." In it, Chris said his mother gave him the ability to forgive the shooter,

Dylann Roof. "I chose to forgive him, because that's what my mom would do," he said.[64]

Chris again made a lasting impact at the 2018 dedication of the Singleton Baseball Complex at Charleston Southern University. The words "Love is always stronger" are engraved outside the sports complex.

Chris summed up his mother's forty-five years on earth. "When I think about this building, I smile about how awesome my mom was," he said. "If there was an Awesome Award, my mom would have won it forty-five years straight. Every day when I wake up, I ask the Lord to give me strength and wisdom so I won't let my mom down."[65]

CULTURAL CONNECTION

Church Shootings in the USA

Christians feel increasingly like targets even in North America. Since 1999, roughly 100 churchgoers have died in church shootings in at least 22 reported incidents.[66] A 2007 Colorado shooting rampage extended from the Youth with a Mission complex in Arvada to New Life Church in Colorado Springs. The armed gunman walked through the church parking lot and into the church before being apprehended. Some church members said they thought he was taking part in a drama and didn't think to report him. This attack spurred many churches across North America to invest in security measures and training, including asking congregants to report all weapon sightings and teaching that a gun will never be used in a drama. At the same time, American churches are becoming more armed than ever. In a December 2019 attack at West Freeway Church of Christ, a churchgoing firearms instructor shot the gunman and saved many lives. With the increase in attacks, more churches perceive a need to be more proactive and vigilant for future attacks.

Vintage Foxe

Those who were taken experienced the most cruel tortures the infernal imaginations could invent; and, by their constancy evinced that a real Christian can surmount every difficulty, and despise ever danger to acquire a crown of martyrdom.[67]

CHAPTER SEVENTEEN

From a New Jihad in Africa

When the Lamb broke the fifth seal, I saw under the altar the souls of all who had been martyred for the word of God and for being faithful in their testimony. REVELATION 6:9, NLT

We live [years of persecution] with a sense of resilience, but we have never fallen into a state of victimhood or triumphalism. We realize that it is the cross of Christ. . . . It's not the end of the road because there is a resurrection that comes after the cross and the empty tomb. And so it is in that hope that we continue to live. And it's in that hope that we continue to carry that cross, knowing that it will be removed from us.[1] ARCHBISHOP ANBA ANGAELOS

I have never been discouraged, because all conditions that one finds himself is in the hands of God. . . . By the grace of God, I will be together with my wife, my children, and all my colleagues. And if the opportunity has not been granted, maybe it is the will of God. All people close and far . . . be patient, don't cry, don't worry. But thank God for everything. NIGERIAN PASTOR LAWAN ANDIMI, IN HOSTAGE VIDEO BEFORE HE WAS BEHEADED ON JANUARY 21, 2020

The last century has witnessed the Christians of Africa expand from less than 10 million, 7 percent of the total population, to nearly 700 million people, almost half the continent's population.[2] To put it in perspective, 25 percent of all Christians on the planet today are African Christians, and they will soon make up 40 percent of all Christians worldwide.[3]

Some of this expansive growth is due to the rise of African church movements. One such denomination, for example, the Redeemed Christian Church of God, was started by an illiterate farmer in Nigeria. The movement has grown to more than five million members around the world, including over seven hundred congregations in the United States, all planted by African missionaries sent to the West.[4]

Another growth factor is the rapid exodus from Islam to Christianity. This falling away is so prevalent, researchers have common abbreviation: MBBs (Muslim Background Believers). Some Muslims overreport the number of MBBs to stoke religious fervor among Muslim parents and motivate them to keep their children from apostasy. One Muslim leader claimed Muslims convert to Christianity at a rate of 667 every hour, 16,000 every day, and six million every year.[5] He might be overstating it, but the real numbers are still staggering. A 2015 study estimates that 2,161,000 African Muslims have converted to Christianity.[6] Experts identified four major reasons for Muslim conversions: (1) The "massive increase in prayer" for Muslim people, (2) a "far greater involvement of Christian outreach" specifically for Muslims, (3) globalization providing Muslims with new ideas and interactions, and (4) "social and political turmoil in the Muslim world" causing them to question their faith.[7]

It is no wonder that the growth of Christianity is accompanied by persecution. Outraged Muslim extremists, such as the infamous Boko Haram and Al-Shabaab movements, regularly harass, kidnap, enslave, and kill Christians. One million Christians were killed in the decade ending in 2010, and 900,000 in the following decade.[8] With the large Christian population in Africa, and the widespread tribalism and other religions on that continent, much of the Christian persecution in the world occurs in Africa. One research team estimates that in 2015, 4,028 out of 7,100 Christian martyrs were from just one African nation,

Nigeria. Another expert claims that 70 percent of all Christian martyr-doms occur in Africa.[9]

Two-thirds of the world's Christians live in regions of war, conflict, and violence, an apt description of much of the continent of Africa. There are no signs that persecution in this region is on the decline, and all indicators point toward an increase. Yet the growth of the African Church appears unstoppable.

ARCHBISHOP YVES PLUMEY Yves Plumey from Vannes, France, was a pioneer of evangelization in Africa. Initially intending to go to Brazil, he instead saw the need in Cameroon. He answered the call in 1946 as part of a massive Christian effort to evangelize a nation being overtaken by Islamic influences.

Christians from all backgrounds sent resources, providing health care, economic development, and education. The country prospered. Among the most successful efforts were those led by the Catholic Church, and by Plumey himself. By the time of Cameroon's independence in 1961, the nation appeared healthy, and Catholics were well on the way to eventually claim adherents of almost 40 percent of the population.[10]

Success did not come without a price. When Plumey accepted the call to lead the Missionary Oblates of Mary Immaculate, he wrapped his life and love around the nation. In 1955, he was appointed Archbishop. In 1957, he ordained Cameroon's first black African priest. Plumey built Mazenod College in the town of Ngaoundere. Mazenod educated many leaders, including Cameroon's second president, Paul Biya. In retirement, he wrote a book on the gospel in Cameroon.

Beloved in his adopted homeland, the bespectacled priest never returned to France, but eventually retired in Cameroon. Tragedy struck in September 1991. Plumey's violent murder shocked the nation and the church. The mystery surrounding it was never solved. His house had been ransacked. He was tied to his bed by strips of curtains from his home and strangled. Some said he died of a heart attack in a struggle with burglars. Others said he was killed by thieves looking for money given him by President Paul Biya of Cameroon, who had recently visited. Church leaders said there was no sign of a break-in so they believed he opened his door late Monday night to people he knew. Police brought in his cook and his driver for questioning. They were imprisoned the next day, but the investigation was never completed.[11]

Unfortunately, Cameroon has a long history of Christian persecution. Following Cameroon's independence in 1961, the country's first president was Muslim. Under President Ahidjo's administration, Muslim politicians actively obstructed the growth of Christian churches. Christians in the north who refused to convert to Islam faced discrimination. In 1982, the same year Plumey became Archbishop, Ahidjo mistook sickness for a life-threatening illness and relinquished control to his protégé, Paul Biya.

The year of Plumey's death, 1991, saw Christian advances with the opening of three campuses of the Catholic University of Central Africa. It was also a year of political upheaval, aimed at forcing a more democratic government. Cameroon historians wrote that the failed campaign was followed by "wanton violence, looting, rape and arson, torture and horrendous murders."[12] The National Bishops Conference of Cameroon boldly opposed the violence and pressed for justice, resulting in a string of high-profile clergy murders, all unsolved, including mutilation, poisoning, and assassination. The year after Plumey's death, more were martyred, starting with the murder of two French nuns.

Plumey paid the ultimate price for people he loved. He had written instructions to Christian leaders who would come after him, "Go and teach! That is the watchword that the Lord gives to us who continue the work started by the Twelve. . . . In the bush and in the centers we have to sow the truth, the Word of God, which has in itself the power of light and strength to conquer."[13]

CULTURAL CONNECTION

The Islamic/Christian Line in Africa

Imagine the map of Africa as an ice cream cone. Pick up the cone, with your hand extending up to the middle of Nigeria. The cone flares out at the top to hold the ice cream. The single scoop on the top is northern

Africa. At the very highest point are Algeria and Tunisia, with Morocco on one side and Libya on the other. The ice cream is warmer where it meets the cone, so it drips down one side, covering Somalia and the east side of nations such as Kenya and Tanzania. The ice cream and where it has dripped are the nations that are predominately Muslim. The cone features the nations that did not convert to Islam as it spread during the seventh and eighth centuries. Along the line where the ice cream meets the cone are the hot spots of conflict.

The Islamic-Christian Line extends roughly along the tenth parallel, 700 miles north of the equator, in a 4,000-mile-long swath from Senegal on the Atlantic Ocean to Somalia on the Indian Ocean. The line is a path of dangerous tensions, persecutions, and wars. So common are the disturbances along this divide that although they are reported, they rarely make headlines. A seventy-seven-year-old nun is beheaded in the Central African Republic.[14] In Burkina Faso, one of the world's most dangerous places, gunmen burst into a Sunday Mass, killing twenty-four worshipers.[15] A half million residents have streamed out of Burkina Faso, seeking to escape the terror and find safety for their families.[16]

Along the Line, charities and NGOs are overwhelmed and underfunded, Christians are persecuted, and entire people groups are displaced. It is the global frontline for escalating Christian persecution.

JEAN-MARIE BENOÎT BALLA Bishop Jean-Marie Benoît Balla of Bafia, Cameroon, was loved and respected. A year after his disappearance and murder, church leaders were still celebrating his life and demanding justice for his death. A fisherman found Balla's body floating in the Sanaga River June 2, 2017, three days after he disappeared. The body was discovered miles from the Sanaga River bridge where his SUV was found abandoned. In it, a note scribbled in French read, "Do not look for me! I am in the water."[17] Church leaders immediately cried foul, saying it could not be a suicide, but was a murder.

"Papa Benoît," as his followers called him, had just turned fifty-eight and was about to celebrate thirty years in the priesthood. Born in 1959, he was ordained in 1987 and consecrated Bishop of Bafia in 2003. A Cameroon reporter said he was far from ordinary: "He had forged an image of an upright spiritual leader of national and international repute."[18] He was known especially for his care for the sick and marginalized. As well as serving in a parish, he was appointed to lead one seminary even while teaching at another.

Balla's nephew, Alexis, said his uncle's death shattered the family, that he had been their "pillar."[19] In a statement, bishops said the tragic death "shocked and upset the People of God, all Cameroonians and international opinion."[20]

After Catholics and many other Christians spent a tense three days searching for Balla, their hopes and prayers had turned to sudden grief. At the discovery of his body, they immediately demanded an investigation. Reports regarding his death were confusing. An initial autopsy leaked to the press within a week of Balla's death indicated torture and murder. It concluded he had been dead before entering the water and was only in the water four hours before being discovered.[21] Weeks later, INTERPOL determined the bishop died by drowning.[22] A month later, a new autopsy by the government dismissed his death as a drowning.[23]

Church leaders rejected all possibilities of accidental drowning or suicide. They delayed holding a funeral for two months, pending an investigation.[24] Cameroon's president of the Chamber of Criminal Experts, Steve Francis Olinga, believed Balla was murdered and insisted the results of the investigation be made public.[25] No results were forthcoming. No arrests were made.

The murder would be the latest in a long string of unsolved clergy killings in Cameroon going back thirty years. A group of bishops called Balla's death "one too many" murders by "obscure diabolical forces."[26]

His slaying unleashed grief and righteous anger among colleagues and fellow citizens. The Catholic Church "came out of its characteristic reserve" and announced that Balla was the latest victim of Cameroon's clergy killings.[27] Cameroonian bishops stated they had evidence Balla was "brutally assassinated." Balla's friend Monsignor Joseph Akonga Essomba said flatly, "The Catholic Church has come under attack."[28]

Emmanuel Ngah Obala, a close friend and Cameroonian who now resides in Italy, said, "For decades, there have been mysterious killings of priests, religious and Catholic laity. After the murder of Monsignor Balla, however, something has changed in the perception of people: they are starting to rebel and ask for justice."[29]

A year after Papa Benoît's death, his friends, fellow bishops, and members of the Bafia diocese gathered at a memorial Mass on the banks of the Sanaga River to commemorate the anniversary of his death. Bishops threw flowers in the water in his honor. He was known to be a pastor of the people, loving, kind, and protective. Jean Paul Ahanda, a resident of Bafia, said, "We have lost a great pastor, who gave himself to the service of others."[30]

CULTURAL CONNECTION

The Role of African Tribes

European nations haphazardly carved Africa into sections during the colonization of the nineteenth and twentieth centuries. As African countries gained independence from those powers, instead of moving boundaries to reflect linguistic or cultural groups, they (for the most part) kept the colonial boundaries. But while political entities are de jure law (officially recognized by government), tribal ties are de facto law (true in fact but not formally recognized). When given a choice, loyalties often fall to the tribe, its customs and beliefs. This presents problems both for governments and for tribes. Tribal rule sometimes runs counter to government rule, and sometimes tribes that are united in language and culture find themselves separated by arbitrary political borders running through their territory.

In Nigeria, tribes have made the nation a "killing field of defenseless Christians."[31] Although the nation is home to the continent's largest Christian population, Nigeria's Christians are often minorities in the parts of the country where extremists commit their atrocities. Boko Haram has killed countless thousands. Becoming even deadlier are certain Fulani herdsmen who are carrying out a jihad specifically aimed at Christian communities, killing on average five Christians each day.

According to one account more than 11,500 Nigerian Christians were murdered between 2015 and 2020.[32]

In Rwanda, tribal warfare broke out in 1994 when 800,000 people of the minority Tutsi tribe were slaughtered within 100 days by Hutus and their compatriots. Some "church" sects were in league with the Hutus. More people died while seeking shelter within churches than anywhere else. However, faithful Christians provided shelter and trauma care after the massacre. Rwanda is now considered a Christian nation, with 95 percent of the population claiming the Christian faith. In a 2012 Rwandan census, 44 percent were Catholic, 38 percent Protestant, and another 13 percent adhering to "church" sects of various kinds. A mere 2 percent were Muslim.[33]

THE ANCHA VILLAGE MASSACRE As of this writing, Nigeria ranks as the seventh worst country for Christian persecution due to attacks by Islamist terrorist groups, though these figures are in constant flux.[34] The infamous Boko Haram operates in the northeast, but other Islamist-incited groups such as Fulani herdsmen in the north central states are helping to spread persecution against Christians nationwide.[35] In the violence of the area, where herdsmen compete with farmers for fertile land, herdsmen have justified their attacks. As a result, thousands of Christians have been killed. In most cases their properties are then looted and burned, including hundreds of churches.

Martha Sunday and her family live in a Christian farming community in the Middle Belt of Nigeria. She and her husband raise their children in an area dotted with chicken farms, lined by fields of maize and wheat, with rows of staples such as beans, red peppers, potatoes, tomatoes, carrots, cabbages, and melons. Christianity gained a foothold in the region more than one hundred years ago, when missionaries built churches, schools, and hospitals.

However, the father of the Nigerian church was a Nigerian himself, Samuel Crowther.

The Sunday family's Christian village is typical—clannish, family-oriented, and hospitable. Local herdsman often leave their own leaf-plastered huts to visit with friendly faces and enjoy a good meal in the Christian villages.

When schools let out for summer break in August 2017, Martha Sunday sent her children, Ishaya and Emmanuel, to visit their grandparents in nearby Ancha, a Christian village of fifty homes occupied by three family clans. When school was about to resume in September, Martha and her husband made plans to pick up the children. Then the unthinkable happened. The Sundays were informed that all the children and the grandparents had been killed in a night attack on the village.

On Friday, September 8, 2017, shortly after midnight, Fulani tribesmen attacked and killed twenty-four Christians in Ancha. Nine were children, ranging from three months to seventeen years old. Among them were six-year-old Emmanuel and eight-year-old Ishaya Sunday, Martha's only two children.

Witnesses said when the attackers came, mothers ran into the bush for safety, dragging their children with them. Some escaped. Others were killed on the way, and still others were caught in their homes, where they were sliced to death.

One family patriarch, seventy-four-year-old Goh Rohu, lost his wife and fifteen relatives in the attack—five brothers, four of their wives, and six children. Surviving family member Baba Rohu said the attack was well planned, with attackers separating into groups. He said they went house to house for thirty minutes without resistance. Evidence showed they entered many houses and shot bullets through others.

Another villager, Lami Ishaya, lost her husband, four children, and three other family members. She wailed, "I don't know where to start now that all I laboured for in my entire life has been taken away in one night." [36]

"My heart is terribly heavy. I haven't been able to sleep," said Rev. Nanchwat Laven, pastor of Salama Baptist Church.[37] The church lost twenty members in the attack.

After the attack came a mass burial, and then the questions. The first question was the number of martyrs. While police reported that nineteen were killed, other reports said only seven children died and five people were injured.[38] Miango Chief Aka definitively declared the death toll at twenty-four, with nineteen dying in the village, others in the bush and hospital.[39]

The second question was, "Why and what would be done about it?" A Fulani boy had been found killed and decapitated in a neighboring village, and many believed this attack was a reprisal. Local Christians wondered why they were targeted since the boy's murder took place elsewhere. Christians had apologized to the Fulani on their knees for the boy's murder and even gave police five potential suspects. Police Commissioner Peter Ogunyanwo admitted the evidence for the massacre was against Fulani herdsmen, and yet no arrests were made.[40]

The larger question was whether the government would intervene at all to prevent Christian persecution. Nigeria's President Muhammadu Buhari gave an appeal on the day after the massacre, asking for calm and stating the local security authorities have pulled the state back "from the brink of anarchy and senseless killings."[41] Critics claim that because the president is a Fulani Muslim, and the attacks are predominately on Christian communities, he's not willing to crack down.[42]

The Chairman of the Northern Christian Association of Nigeria, Rev. Yakubu Pam, called on warring groups to "lay down their arms [and] embrace dialogue and the mechanisms put in place by the state government towards peaceful resolution of all issues of conflict."[43]

Samson Ayokunle, president and CEO of the Nigerian Baptist Convention (NBC), pleaded "for prayer 'for the future of the church in Nigeria,' declaring that Christianity is under attack in the country, the most populous in Africa."[44]

In an interview, Sunday Abdu, the president of Irigwe Development Association, said, "I have lost count of the casualties because it is being done almost every day. The villages that were attacked were up to five and houses burnt were over 200. The deaths were also many but, as I told you earlier, I have lost count of the dead bodies."[45]

Because of the attacks, eight of Nigeria's thirty-six states have been called "gory killing fields."[46] Nigeria ranks second in the number of Christians killed for their faith, behind Pakistan.[47] Locals call the Fulani Muslims "killer herdsmen." Believers must be cautious, though, about attributing the massacres to the Fulani as a whole. The Fulani are the largest tribe in all of Africa and the terrorists among them represent a very small minority, yet they are decimating the region without serious repercussions from the authorities. The herdsmen now rank as the fourth deadliest terror group in the world. In 2016, the year before the Ancha Village massacre, they were responsible for more deaths than Boko Haram.[48]

Christian Solidarity International (CSI) has now issued a genocide warning for Nigeria because of the violence directed against Christians. The CSI International Management chairperson said, "The increasingly violent attacks and the failure of the Nigerian government to prevent them and punish the perpetrators are alarming. CSI therefore calls on the permanent members of the U.N. Security Council to take swift action to uphold this commitment to genocide prevention in Nigeria."[49]

Area resident Dung Tabari, speaking for persecuted, peace-loving Christians, said, "We will continue to show them love as taught us by our Lord and Savior, Jesus Christ. We will remain resolute as Christians, and nothing shall separate us from the love of Christ."[50]

CULTURAL CONNECTION

The Story of Samuel Ajayi Crowther

Samuel Crowther was born in what is now Nigeria. Muslim traders raided his town, and he was sold as a slave at least six times, the final owners being Portuguese slave-traders. He wrote, "I was sold to the Portuguese, at whose first touch I almost trembled to death. Being embarked from the town in canoes in an evening about seven o'clock, to be shipped early the next day, we gave ourselves up totally for lost. We could not tell where our miseries would end, especially as we thought there was no safety in the land nor on the sea."[51]

The Portuguese slave ship was boarded by a British antislavery patrol, who freed the enslaved people there, taking Crowther to Freetown. He wrote, "We six boys had the luck of being taken into the *Myrmidon* where we were very kindly treated. The number of all the slaves was I think 189, out of whom 102 perished in the sea. When we were landed at Sierra Leone, we were placed in a school under the care of the Church Missionary Society."[52]

He was baptized in 1825, went on to study in London, and became both a priest and linguist. Starting in 1841, he spent decades traveling on missions trips throughout Nigeria. In 1864, he became the first African bishop for the Anglican Church and took the name Samuel Crowther. He died of a stroke in 1891. As a linguist, Crowther had translated the entire Bible into his native Yoruba language, setting a standard for future African translations. The colonial missionaries failed in their attempt to evangelize Nigeria, and then Africa. It took Crowther, a Nigerian by birth, whose life was barely saved, to lead his own people to faith. Now, despite their persecution, Nigeria has one of the largest Christian populations in the world and some of the world's largest churches.

CHRISTOPHE MUNZIHIRWA MWENE NGABO "There are things that can be seen only with eyes that have cried." This was the favorite saying of Archbishop Christophe Munzihirwa Ngabo of the Democratic Republic of the Congo.[53] In the Africa Munzihirwa knew, hardly a dry eye was left. Born in 1926, Munzihirwa studied social sciences and economics, and then joined the Jesuits in 1963 before returning to his home area in 1969. After holding several other positions, he was appointed archbishop on March 24, 1994.

The primary killing fields for Christians had shifted to Africa during the 1990s. As danger grew, Munzihirwa became a symbol of hope and resistance.

At the start of the Rwandan genocide, millions of refugees flooded into the eastern region of Congo, where Munzihirwa served. A courageous leader, he confronted the governments of Rwanda, Burundi, and the international community. He insisted his region wanted peace. When the genocide continued, he took up the cause for Hutu refugees crossing the border into Congo. He knew some were likely guilty of atrocities but that most were innocent. Years later, when civic leaders fled the city in fear of the oncoming Rwandans, Munzihirwa stood fast. He realized he was the only one standing between the soldiers and the refugees.

Munzihirwa had a history of taking such stands. When the DRC's president, Mobutu Sese Seko, forcibly enrolled university-age students in the military during a crackdown in 1971, Munzihirwa embarrassed the government by insisting on being enlisted alongside his seminarians.

In the mid-1990s, Munzihirwa resisted his own government several times. Once, he objected to the arrest of some humanitarians and a missionary and demanded their release. Military officials chided him for not being a "friend" of President Mobuto, hinting at a bribe. Munzihirwa said he would sleep outside the cell of the detainees until they were freed. Their release came that evening.

Another time, President Mobutu ordered violence on the city, but Munzihirwa challenged the military, "Stop troubling the people! I ask you, I order you: Stop it!" When the commander threatened to arrest Munzihirwa, he answered, "I am ready. Arrest me."[54] Other clergy stepped in to prevent the arrest.

Munzihirwa knew what was at stake. Just six weeks before his death, another archbishop had been executed in nearby Burundi.

Munzihirwa himself was executed at the start of what would be called the First Congo War. Rwandan troops invaded his city of Bukavu, on the eastern border of Congo, formerly called Zaire. As the Rwandans took hold of the city on October 28, 1996, Munzihirwa broadcast a desperate plea for help. He said, "We hope that God will not abandon us and that from some part of the world will rise for us a small flare of hope."[55]

The next day, Munzihirwa surrendered himself to Rwandan soldiers, in hopes that two of his friends would be able to escape. Munzihirwa was executed and his body was dumped in the streets among the many corpses the soldiers had left behind. His two companions were also caught and killed. The next day, a small group of seminarians recovered Munzihirwa's body to bury him.

The two archbishops' deaths were only the beginning. In the two decades after Munizhirwa's death, the region where he had ministered saw between seven and eight million deaths due to wars, rebel groups, and martyrdom.[56] Pope John Paul II called these African heroes the "new Christian martyrs" and remarked, "There are so many of them . . . countless unknown soldiers who fought for the great cause of the gospel."[57]

Munzihirwa might have rejected the title of "martyr." Another African mission leader explained that "martyrdom" is often just being in the wrong place at the wrong time, but Christians make that choice to place themselves in harm's way. He added, "Presence is the key point. It's a gospel principle."[58]

Munzihirwa knew martyrdom was a possibility. In a 1994 homily, Munzihirwa wrote, "God's mercy, which breaks the chain of vengeance, is hurtful to militants on every side. But in reality, that is the only thing that can definitively shatter the infernal circle of vengeance."

For Easter, Munizhirwa wrote, "Despite anguish and suffering, the Christian who is persecuted for the cause of justice finds spiritual peace in total and profound assent to God, in accord with a vocation that can lead even to death."

He concluded, "In these days, when we continue to dig common graves, where misery and sickness appear along thousands of kilometers, on routes, along pathways and in fields . . . we are particularly challenged by the cry of Christ on the Cross: 'Father, forgive them.'"[59]

DID YOU KNOW? *The Ancient Christianity of Ethiopia*

Nearly half of all Ethiopians are members of the Ethiopian Orthodox Church.[60] Archaeologists recently found the oldest known Christian church in sub-Saharan Africa, uncovering proof of the heritage of Ethiopian Christianity, which traces its history all the way back to Philip in the book of Acts.[61] With the discovery of the church in an ancient port city on the Red Sea, the Ethiopian claim of early Christian faith moved from tradition to fact. The location was part of Axum, an ancient trading empire once ruled by the Queen of Sheba, who visited Solomon. Axum grew into a trade center of the ancient world, starting in the first century. It was geographically and politically significant because it linked the Roman Empire 3,000 miles away with eastern Africa and western Arabia.

Scientists estimate the unearthed church was built in the fourth century, the same century in which Roman Emperor Constantine I legalized Christianity. It corresponds to the reign of Axum King Ezana, who ruled between AD 330 and 356, and who declared Christianity to be the official religion of the nation.

In the seventh century, a tiny religion called Islam formed right across the Red Sea from Axum. Its adherents soon encountered persecution and fled to Axum where King Negus sheltered them. Today Ethiopian schoolchildren learn about wise King Negus who treated early Muslims with dignity.

The sixty-by-forty-foot basilica uncovered by archaeologists in 2019 features a wall inscribed with a prayer asking "for Christ [to be] favorable to us."[62] Though the nation has seen its share of disaster, there is one way God has answered that prayer: Ethiopia is the only African country to remain continuously independent since antiquity.

THE COPTIC 21 When a sports team takes the field before a game, a cheer rises from the stands. Frenzied fans break into chants for the team and screams for their favorite players. Faces painted in team colors flash enormous smiles, and below them, hands, elbows, fists, chests, bump in affirmation. Such was the scene in the crowd when twenty-one stouthearted men marched out on a beach, single file, in orange uniforms, hands behind their backs.

They didn't shout or strut as they walked. Each man's face reflected grace and peace, the dignity of a champion with nothing to prove, all jaws set in determination to do what he had trained to do. Not one tried to draw attention to himself. Each man walked in humility, obedience, "absolute resilience."[63] They marched in a steady, steadfast rhythm, each step proof that they were ready to go all in on the beach that day.

The twenty-one men assumed the starting position, kneeling with their heads leaning forward, looking down at the earth for a final time, furtive eyes locking in quick sidelong glances as if congratulating each other ahead of their assured victory. The beach was hushed as masked handlers standing behind each man raised enormous swords. Then in unison, as a final act of what was in their collective team spirit, the men let out a shout of song. Three words, three notes, their team song. The swords struck. The strains of the Coptic Christian refrain hung in the air, "Ya Rabbi Yassu,"

"Oh my Lord Jesus." Twenty-one heads toppled off the orange jumpsuits and tumbled to the ground.[64]

Heaven let out a roar, angels shouted, the elders and creatures bowed before the throne. King Jesus stood and welcomed home his team, looking each one in the eye and saying, "Well done, son, well done." For the men, the mingled smell of the ocean, sweat, and blood was replaced by the fragrance of heaven, an aroma wafting off their own robes, a sacrifice that filled the nostrils of the living God as they lifted their eyes to behold Him. For the King of Kings, the death of these saints was precious, costly, invaluable, priceless, a treasure.

On earth, the scene was remarkably different. In the blue light of monitors, phones, and television screens in every nation, millions of hands flew over mouths that hung agape with horror. Tears squeezed out of a million squinted eyes that did not want to see what they were witnessing but found it hard to look away. Millions of ears rejected the news. Surely, they'd heard an exaggeration. Throats choked with emotion. Surely not, assuredly not. Minds brimmed with disbelief. Surely, the video was a hoax, doctored to make it look real.

A slow reality check followed the sunrise around the earth on the morning of February 16, 2015, as the world came to realize that the Islamic State had really and truly beheaded twenty-one Coptic Christians lined up on a Libyan beach. Worse, the terrorists recorded it and posted it online, where every phone, every computer, every television could transmit this abomination across the world to shock, scare, and terrorize. But their objective backfired.

Twenty-one men—twenty Coptic Orthodox Christians from Egypt and one Ghanaian.[65] The Egyptians were all day laborers, very poor men from very poor villages who came to Libya in search of work. The Ghanaian, Matthew, was also a poor migrant worker. The kidnappers told Matthew they would let him go because he was not a Christian. Matthew refused to leave his friends.

The 21, as they came to be called, were captured and held for a long time, during which their captors tried to break them and make them convert to Islam. Instead, far from being broken, the young Egyptian Christians led Matthew to faith in Christ. In a short time, Matthew became such a believer that he was willing to die with them. Ultimately, believing was the crime that cost all of them their lives. They would not renounce their Christian faith.

Coptic Archbishop Angaelos of London said the men displayed a "godly peace" in the moments before their deaths.[66] On the day the world watched the video with alarm, Archbishop Angaelos prayed for the victims' families on Twitter and added a hashtag, #FatherForgive.[67] The news media picked it up. The Archbishop was called into interview after interview, and each time testified of Christ's forgiveness. "I think that was a way of expressing our spirituality and theology," he said. "We're a church that is very rooted in martyrdom."[68]

In many interviews, the archbishop explained the fascinating history behind the young men's deaths. Mark, the writer of the second Gospel, first brought Christianity to Egypt, but in AD 284, Egyptian Christians suffered a terrible wave of martyrdom. Then came an era when, for long periods, Egyptian Christians and Muslims lived well together. In the 1950s, Egypt freed itself of British rule, and the nation became increasingly Islamized and increasingly dangerous for Christians. Martyrdoms rose. Angaelos estimates that Coptic Christians account for about 15 percent of Egypt's population, and about 80 percent of the entire Christian population in the Middle East.[69] Right next to Egypt, Libya won independence later than Egypt. Then, in 2011, the fall of Libya's Muammar Gaddafi brought an immediate increase in attacks on the country's Christian minority.

"We've had Coptic Christians killed in church bombings and shootings in targeted attacks," Archbishop Angaelos said. "Tragically, we also know this isn't the end; there will be others to come."[70]

The archbishop attributes the strength of Coptic Christians' faith to a century-long "strong Sunday school movement" and "a very strong youth ministry" that affects how Coptic children and young people view the church. "I think it is incredibly effective and powerful," the archbishop said.[71] The faith in which The 21 were raised was effective enough not just to make a hero of a single outstanding person who would go to his death with boldness, but twenty young men who would go, and even bring a new convert with them.

Archbishop Angaelos said that Egyptian Christians have long experienced persecution, adding, "The interesting thing is, we live with a sense of resilience, but we have never fallen into a state of victimhood. . . . We do not, cannot, and will not hate. Our hearts cannot be changed by what we're experiencing."[72]

The families of the martyrs spoke publicly in the same way, giving grace to the killers, honor to the fallen, and forgiveness to all. This outpouring of Christian forgiveness amazed the world. A literary writer and German Catholic, Martin Mosebach, was so moved that he went to Egypt to meet the families.

Mosebach expected to see grief, mourning, or anger. He was surprised to find families that were proud of how their brave young men faced persecution with courage, just as they had been taught. He didn't find any unforgiveness or bitterness, talk of revenge or retaliation, nor any question of justice. No issues of Muslim-Christian opposition came up in Mosebach's interviews. Mosebach was amazed that the families didn't even blame the killers. Remarkably, Mosebach said the families only blamed the killings on the devil. And everywhere, Mosebach saw The 21 depicted in art as if they were church icons and "crowned like kings." Even as the community grieved their loss, they showed enormous gratitude that their sons were chosen to become martyrs.[73]

In his book *The 21*, Mosebach explained how he watched the video repeatedly. As he moved from one family to the next, one small concrete house to another, the families repeatedly showed what was supposed to have been a propaganda video to instill fear but instead reinforced their faith. On iPads, phones, and computers, they would replay what millions of eyes could scarcely watch. With eyes wide open, brimming with tears of tremendous pride, family members would point out their loved one on the screen. Mosebach watched again and again the brave men on the beach in front of families who watched with "quiet pride."[74]

The terrorists' video, in short, was a spectacular failure. Perhaps no piece of propaganda has ever backfired so completely. The video did not show Islamic domination, but showed the power and strength, courage and honor, faith and peace of the Christian faith. In a moment that was supposed to show Christianity's weakness, the only men who appeared weak were the masked executioners who were too ashamed or afraid to show their faces.

Coptic Christians now *celebrate* February 15. On that date, they commemorate all the church's martyrs.[75] An Egyptian Christian tradition to tattoo a cross on the inside of the wrist has resurfaced. The move reportedly dates back centuries when people were marked for their faith. Today, Christians all over the world, from Orthodox to fundamental evangelicals, have been inspired by The 21 to get tattoos of the cross on the inside of their wrists.

The families recognize their loss as heaven's gain in a profound way, far beyond what could be a familiar phrase spoken at a funeral. "I wanted to see Milad come back from Libya on his feet after his struggle and hard work to earn a living in a harsh life abroad," said Zaki Hanna, the father of one of the martyrs. "But thanks be to God, he died a hero. [He] did not beg anyone to spare his life, and he and his brothers, the martyrs, did not abandon their faith or homeland."[76]

Angela Georgy, 37, a Coptic Christian woman from New Jersey, reflected on the lives of The 21 in a way shared by many. "Their martyrdom encourages me," she said. "Our faith is not cheap."[77]

The proud mother of one of the martyrs shared, "I never prayed during his captivity that he may come free. I prayed, 'God, let him stay firm.' And he stayed firm."[78]

ANNALENA TONELLI On Sunday night, October 5, 2003, "Somalia's Mother Teresa" quietly moved through one of the tuberculosis hospitals she had founded. It was after dark, a dangerous time in Borama, Somalia. Out of habit and devotion, Annalena Tonelli refused to return to her walled house with its permanent guard until she had visited all 377 patients. From the ward, she moved outside to visit the exterior huts built for nomads. There, a man approached and put a gun to her head. In her thirty-four years living with the poorest of the poor in Africa, Annalena Tonelli often encountered life-threatening situations, famine, stonings, brutality, and once even a massacre, where she was the only person to care for the injured and bury the dead.[79] Once again, she would reject fear and respond with love, even as the gunman pulled the trigger. Twice. And love she did, right into her Savior's arms.

As a teenager, Tonelli had a tenacious—some would say stubborn—commitment to serve the poor. Controlling her fear, she would bike through dark streets of Forlì, Italy, which her parents condemned because of the horrors they'd witnessed there during World War II. In university, she befriended a prostitute in the city's most dangerous slum, Casermone. She would go, day and night, to serve the people she met there, whenever she saw a need.

"She was in love with people and with Jesus Christ," her brother Bruno said. That love powered her entire life. She learned from Francis of Assisi to call her body "Brother Donkey." In her youth, she disciplined herself to sleep only four hours each night and never to eat a full meal. "She never wanted to take more than the poor would have," Bruno said.[80]

Her relentless dedication as a young person surprised people. Roberto, a fellow student in a Christian university club, said, "Our study was a serious, academic study—until the arrival of Annalena. . . . With Annalena, we began to work with, and live near, the poor. This was shocking. But every one of us recognized that Annalena was an example of the gospel, of Christianity."[81]

Tonelli was a superior student but she finished university with a law degree only at her mother's insistence. She and her university friend Maria Teresa were eager to leave their hometown to engage with the poor, not projects. They longed to interact with individuals with names, rather than numbers on a chart. Maria Teresa said they wanted "a place where we could live poor, literally, among the people. Not to assist them but to share with them—the poverty, the risks of life, the diseases."[82]

Degree in hand, Tonelli left on her life quest at her first opportunity. She first entered Kenya in 1969 as a teacher, then saw another need—desert Somali nomads routinely dying of tuberculosis. Nomadic culture was not conducive to treatment, which took over a year of repeated sessions. In

Somalia, the culture fought even the diagnosis. People were discarded if they admitted to having the disease. An infected person could infect ten to fifteen people per year, which is why tuberculosis is history's deadliest disease.

Although Tonelli was not a medical professional, she developed a way to treat tuberculosis among nomadic peoples. Naturally gifted in organization, she established a manyatta system involving huts for outpatient treatment. Although she shunned recognition or publicity, four months before her murder, Annalena Tonelli accepted the Nansen Refugee Award from the United Nations. She did so only so she could refocus the world's attention on Somalia. In the world of medicine, she will forever be known for developing the precursor to the "directly observed treatment, short-course" (DOTS) for tuberculosis.[83]

After witnessing a massacre carried out by the Kenyan government in 1984, Tonelli was forced to leave, and spent her remaining years in Somalia among the same nomadic people group. There, she found more need. UNICEF Polio Officer Capobianco recalled, "During the Somalia famine, she saved the lives of thousands of Somalis who would have otherwise starved."[84]

In 1996, she founded the hospital where she would eventually be killed. She created a research facility for tuberculosis, supporting HIV/AIDS prevention and control. It is believed by many that suspicions of her caregiving were the root cause of her death. Rumors turned to hatred as people misunderstood her treatments, believing she was infecting people, not curing them.

Undaunted, Tonelli pressed on. In the last two years of her life, she developed a campaign led by local leaders to eradicate female genital mutilation, which is practiced by 99 percent of Somalia's population. Her campaign successfully ended the circumcision profession in the city where she died.

Before turning sixty the year she died, Annalena Tonelli had established homes for the deaf, as well as "eye camps" where five hundred young people with eye problems could be seen by surgeons. She advocated for literacy and worked to solve malnutrition.

"She wasn't a saint," her childhood friend Maria Teresa insists. But Tonelli accomplished her mission. Her radical poverty was noticed by all. "She did not have any property except for her few clothes," recalls World Health Organization leader Akihiro Seita. "She dedicated her entire life for the care of patients."[85] Even in death, Tonelli did everything she set out to do. Biking past a cemetery one day, she had once said, "How many times did I dream of being buried in a remote, isolated place?"[86]

At her memorial, a UN refugee official said, "She overcame prejudice and hate by her deep love of others. This love was like a spark that enflamed others around."[87] "Annalena was a visionary, a remarkable individual," said UNICEF Somalia Representative, Jesper Morch. "[Her] whole life represented service to others."[88]

As "a servant of the sick and poor," wrote *USA Today* columnist Tom Krattenmaker, her life "demonstrated, to an almost incomprehensible degree, what it means to love the least of these."[89]

Former First Lady of Somalia Mariam Mohamed said Annalena Tonelli's life challenges people to believe we can "choose acts of kindness and love even during difficult circumstances. Her courage inspires us to challenge evil: everyone can make a difference."[90]

"I'm a nobody," Tonelli often said, and yet out of love for the Savior of the world, she taught the world what it means to put faith in practice and be a "somebody" for Jesus.

PIERRE CLAVERIE Bishop Pierre Claverie of Oran, Algeria, knew his life mission was hazardous—to be a "guest in the house of Islam," being a friend to Muslims, without compromising his Christian identity. He wanted, in his words, to overcome "the abyss that separates us." His quest led many Muslim mourners at his funeral to describe him as "the bishop of the Muslims too."[91]

Living among a tiny Christian minority within an Arab society, he wrote during the year before his death, "Reconciliation is not a simple affair. It comes at a high price. . . . An Islamist and a *kafir* (infidel) cannot be reconciled. So, then, what's the choice? Well, Jesus does not choose. He says, in effect, 'I love you all,' and he dies."[92]

A fourth generation *Pied-Noir*, meaning "French settler," Claverie grew up in Algeria's "colonial bubble."[93] Eight months before his death, he still mourned his early blindness to the Arab population all around him. He wrote, "I asked myself why, throughout my entire childhood as a Christian . . . and hearing sermons on the love of one's neighbor, I had never been told that the Arab was my neighbor. Perhaps I had been told but hadn't been listening."[94]

"We were . . . indifferent, ignoring the majority of the people in this country," he wrote. "They were a part of the landscape of our outings, the background of our meetings and our lives. They never were equal partners."[95]

Claverie's death at the hands of those whose friendships he cherished was one of nineteen clergy killings in Algeria during the 1990s. The carnage became a template for radical extremists elsewhere. But such Muslim extremism does not reflect the history of the nation.

Algeria was Christianized before Western Europe and is the birthplace of saints such as Augustine, whose famous *Confessions* is still revered. When Islam overtook Algeria in the eighth century, they protected Christian communities. But during France's conquest of Algeria in the 1800s, Christianity, for most Muslims, became synonymous with colonialism. The French government opposed the church by condemning proselytizing while favoring slavery.

Claverie studied at the famed Dominican LeSaulchoir outside of Paris, briefly interrupting his schooling for a short stint in the military. When he was ordained in 1965, Algeria had gained its independence and Claverie's family had fled Algeria, part of a mass exodus of *pieds-noirs*. Returning in 1967, he plunged into his "Algerian vocation" by mastering Arabic, studying Islam, and learning the Berber language and culture. He knew he had chosen a dangerous path.

In the diminished church Claverie returned to, Archbishop of Algiers Léon-Étienne Duval was denouncing France's torture of Arab nationalists and was working toward "fraternal love" between religious groups. Even in the deteriorating political environment, Claverie followed suit and adopted an "apostolate of friendship."[96] However, by the 1970s, a cultural revolution accelerated Islamization. Church leaders were under suspicion. Claverie was even questioned for his interest in the Berber language.

Claverie worked tirelessly, believing Christians could not permit "our love to be extinguished despite the fury in our hearts, desiring peace and building it up in tiny steps, refusing to join the chorus of howls, and remaining free while yet in chains."[97] At his 1981 appointment as Bishop of Oran, Claverie addressed Muslims. "I have learned above all to speak and to understand the language of the heart, that of brotherly friendship. . . . I believe that this friendship comes from God."[98]

In his efforts to befriend Muslims, Claverie rejected being fashionable or politically correct. He believed statements such as "We are all children of Abraham" or "We believe in the one God" glossed over the real differences in beliefs.[99] As a young Dominican, Claverie had already encountered liberal Dominican works but "was never swept up in . . . revolutionary currents."[100]

Claverie was deeply respected, lecturing at the Diocesan Institute of the rue des Glycines, forming deep friendships with all classes of Algerians and remaining in, and identifying with, Algeria. He was a prolific writer and preacher. His gift of relationship, clear-eyed analysis, openness to debate, and deep prayer life all attracted people to him. Claverie maintained his pursuit of a "dialogical Islam" that accepted differences without compromising one's beliefs, and in 1987 he was selected to serve on the Pontifical Council for Interreligious Dialogue.[101] He remained steadfast to his mission, "to establish, develop, and enrich a relationship, always, everywhere, and with everyone."[102]

Mohamed Boudiaf, a leader in Algeria's war for independence, became president in 1992 and was assassinated the same year. Immediately, writers, artists, educators, and clergy became targets for assassination. The people were easily swayed, in part because at the time of Algeria's independence, 90 percent of Muslims were illiterate, stemming from the lack of Arab education under French rule. In the violence, Claverie declared that Algerian Christians were "in the right place—at the foot of the Cross" and Islamic extremists were cowards that "kill in the shadows."[103]

Four missionaries were assassinated in 1994, followed by three religious sisters in 1995. Then seven Trappist monks were beheaded in 1996, stirring an international outcry. In 2010, the monks were memorialized in the film *Of Gods and Men*, which won the Cannes Film Festival's Grand Prix.

At the end of his life, Claverie knew he would never be accepted. "In the Muslim world it is not nationality that confers belonging, but religion," he wrote. "The longer I live in Algeria, the more I realize, in spite of the strength and quality of my Algerian ties, that I remain a stranger here."[104] Yet he insisted, "I cannot abandon Algeria to the Islamists."[105]

Claverie did not abandon those whose friendship he sought but paid for that friendship with his life. He was killed when a remote-controlled bomb exploded as he entered his residence with his Muslim driver, Mohamed Bouchikhi.

Claverie wrote, "Dialogue permits the disarming of fanaticism in us and in others. It is for this we are called to express our faith and love of God. . . . Brothers and sisters, this is our mission."[106] Claverie's mission was never realized on a national scale but his successful mission of love was witnessed when more Muslims than Christians attended his funeral.

A CHURCH IN BURKINA FASO As they prepared for Christmas in December 2019, Christians in Burkina Faso were on alert for jihadist attacks but no one was "overly fearful."[107] No one thought it particularly dangerous when roughly thirty people formed a new Protestant church in an eastern village near the border with Niger. Hantoukoura was a small place, barely accessible by just one road. Most members that gathered on Sunday, December 1, were young teenagers. Only one was over forty. The young people had a worship leader but no pastor. Still, they met to sing and worship.

As their service concluded that morning and members began filing out, twelve unidentified armed men encircled them. The attackers separated the members, ordering the women and girls back inside. Men and boys were ordered to get on the ground. The jihadists covered the men's heads with cloth and began the killing. Fourteen died, many more were wounded. Most of the martyrs were young, aged ten to fourteen.

Security forces reported that soldiers searched for the attackers, who had fled on motorcycles. Some reports said they had come from Niger. No motive was apparent other than religion, and hundreds of people had recently been killed by jihadists.

Burkina Faso's population is mostly Muslim, and until recent years the nation enjoyed a culture of religious tolerance. That changed in 2015 when jihadists began attacking various locations, including churches, mostly spilling over from neighboring Mali in the north. Most attacks came from groups aligned with al-Qaeda.[108]

The attacks increased, spreading to the east, and the counts were staggering. Thirty people were killed in a January 2016 hotel raid in Ouagadougou. Dozens were killed in assaults on security bases in August and November. Fifteen also died in an attack on a mosque in October, as jihadists often target fellow Muslims who are not on board with their religious extremism. In November, thirty-seven died in an attack on a mining company.

Such attacks were "totally new and traumatic for Christians," according to Illia Djadi, Open Doors' senior analyst for sub-Saharan Africa. "To see young people become radicalized, turn violent, and attack Christians and other civilians is a dramatic about-face."[109]

International alarm worsened the conditions. When the US State Department issued a warning on travel, foreign aid and missions efforts had to scale back. The impoverished nation's economy weakened. With little equipment, training, or resources, the nation's security forces were no match for the jihadists. President Roch Marc Christian Kaboré condemned "the barbaric attack" on the church and offered his "deepest condolences to the bereaved families and wish a speedy recovery to the wounded."[110] But there was little he could do. In desperation, the federal government diverted resources from education to the military, forcing two thousand schools to close.

Hundreds of Christians fled. Westerners, including missionaries, sent their children away. In the growing humanitarian crisis, mission agencies began begging for prayer.

Henri Yé, president of the Federation of Evangelical Churches and Missions in Burkina Faso (FEME), said Catholics and evangelicals are "closer together than before, because we face the same attacks, the same threats, the same hardships." He called on churches to "use fasting and prayer as first weapons." To church members, Yé said to be cautious "but there is no self-defense. . . . Just pray that the Lord, the Prince of Peace, rescues Burkina Faso from terrorism—from threat and fear. The Lord will give us victory over those who oppress us."[111]

Burkina Faso citizens joined in, calling the nation to fight for justice on behalf of the victims. "God is a God of justice . . . he will render justice to the height of the crime," one wrote. "Let us be vigilant and redouble all efforts at all levels so as not to leave any fault to the enemy."[112]

Illia Djadi asked prayer for Burkina Faso. "Don't abandon that church. Don't abandon that area. Don't give up. . . . Pray that they would remain firm in their faith and that they would not give in to the temptation to retaliation, because that's part of [the terrorists'] strategy: to divide people with violence."[113]

"We would like Christians around the world to join us in prayer," said Yé. "There is no need for the church in Burkina Faso to be fearful; no need to be angry nor to complain. Our values of tolerance, forgiveness, and love were violated. The freedom of worship enshrined in our Basic Law has been trampled on. However, it is in the love of God and our neighbour, in unity and solidarity, by ridding ourselves of all spirit of fear and revenge, that we will eventually overcome."[114]

Before their deaths that morning, the small gathering of young people who were martyred had been singing praise to the God who loved them completely and wholly. In those moments of pain and suffering, he surrounded them with that love and ushered them into his presence.

LEONELLA SGORBATI Sister Leonella Sgorbati, a Catholic nun from Piacenza in northern Italy, lived out the words of the apostle Paul, "To the weak I became weak, to win the weak. I have become all things to all people so that by all possible means I might save some. I do all this for the sake of the gospel, that I may share in its blessings" (1 Corinthians 9:22-23, NIV). The gospel of God's love compelled her to service within her community—the Somali people, whom she loved unto death. Referring to Sgorbati, Sister Joan Agnes Matimu affirmed, "She said there was no problem of working with people of other culture and religion as long as there is respect."[115]

Born in 1940, Rosa Maria Sgorbati made her first vows as a Consolata Missionary Sister at the age of twenty-five, taking the name "Sister Leonella."[116] Sister Leonella earned her diploma in nursing science. This qualification opened the door for her to practice nursing in Kenya. She worked as a midwife for thirteen years, caring for new moms and babies. Her excellent skills led to her promotion. In 1985, she became the head of Kenya's Nabuk Hospital of Meru. She treated her rural nursing students with professionalism, respect, and Christian love. In 1993, Sister Leonella stepped away from nursing when she was elected the Superior of the Consolata in Kenya. But her passion for caring for others stayed with her.

In 1999, when her term was up, Sister Leonella relaunched her nursing career in war-torn Somalia. In the capital city of Mogadishu, she realized that learning a nursing profession could provide young people a way to improve their lives and avoid the lure of joining terrorist groups. Sister Leonella's hope was to launch a nursing school, then give it to qualified Somalis who could manage and expand the training. Once again, she felt her heart beating for nursing and for people.

At a time when the entire nation of Somalia had only one hospital, Sister Leonella founded the Hermann Gmeiner School of Registered Community Nursing in 2002. At the first graduation, the World Health Organization certified the thirty-four new nurses. Sister Leonella then took four nurses with her to Kenya to provide them with additional specialized training, intending to return to Somalia after a brief break. Somalia was unstable and growing increasingly dangerous, having been without a government following its independence in 1980. For two decades, insurgents had vied for control.

Sister Leonella was aware of the danger but throughout her life, she had come to accept that following Jesus Christ might one day cost her life. "I know there is a bullet with my name on it," she reportedly said in a March 2006 interview. "I don't know when it will arrive, but as long as it does not arrive, I will stay [in Somalia]."[117] Her heart and conviction kept her focused on Somalia even in the midst of violence. Sister Leonella simply said, "I cannot be afraid and at the same time love. I choose to love."[118]

That love defined her in life and death. Sister Leonella returned to

Mogadishu on September 13, 2006. Four days later, on September 17, she left the hospital where she had been teaching a group of nurses. She was crossing a street with her bodyguard when two gunmen in a nearby car fired several shots. As Leonella fell to the ground, her bodyguard shielded her with his body. He was killed instantly. As she lay wounded and dying, witnesses heard her repeat, "I forgive, I forgive, I forgive."[119]

Rushed to the hospital with seven gunshot wounds, she died later that day. Sister Leonella's last words revealed the common threads of her life: hope in a loving Savior, love and forgiveness for all of mankind, and a solid belief that no matter what, God's love, not fear, will change people and in turn, the world.

PADRE PIETRO TURATI Francesco Turati was born into a godly home, and from an early age, he felt the Lord calling him to the mission field. At sixteen, Francesco entered Italy's Collegio Serafico Missionario, the College of Angelic Missionaries. He was a caring young man with a heart for both people and his Savior. His superiors took notice of him, saying, "The young Turati is good, obedient and humble."[120] Years later when he joined the Convent of Rezzato, he adopted the clothing of the "Friars Minor" and took the name Padre Pietro.

Padre Pietro chose the name because *Peter* means "rock," and he viewed himself as a stone in God's hands—one to be shaped, molded, and crafted in his Savior's image. Padre Pietro's superior saw that the name fit. He noticed Padre Pietro's "spirit of prayer and devotion," his "firm character," that Padre Pietro was "docile towards superiors, charitable towards companions, (and) diligent in work."[121] His compassion for the poor and his desire to show them the love of Christ would set the course of his life.

In his final year of theological studies, Padre Pietro wrote to his provincial minister and told him, "Being a missionary is my vocation."[122] He completed his theological studies in Milan and was ordained on June 27, 1948. Padre Pietro felt extreme compassion for the people of Somalia. As an Italian, he understood the importance of ministering to the people his country had enslaved in colonial conquest. Rather than exercising power, he desired to humble himself before his Somalian brothers, even in times of upheaval. Padre Pietro wrote a request that he be appointed as a missionary to Somalia. His superior agreed.

Arriving in Mogadishu, Somalia, Padre Pietro first worked as secretary to Bishop Filippini. Desiring to serve among the people, it was not the kind of ministry that he had envisioned, but Padre Pietro applied himself to his duties without complaint. Gradually, Padre Pietro began to assume more responsibility, starting with the Mission of Merka, where he ran a boarding school for orphans. He also ministered to locals and expatriate Italians living in the area.

It seemed that whatever capacity he served in, Padre was drawn to the most vulnerable: the children, the sick, the displaced, and the heartbroken. In 1973, Padre Pietro supervised a mission in Gelib, Kisimayo, where he was able to devote his time to orphans, abandoned children, lepers, and the poor. For nearly twenty years, Padre Pietro served in this ministry among Muslims and others who opposed Christianity. An expert mason, capable electrician, plumber, mechanic, and painter, he put hands and feet to his ministry, using his skills to serve those around him. He helped to rebuild the Sacred Heart Church and the Cathedral at Mogadishu in 1974. Despite hardship, he traveled more than seventy miles to Kisimayo each week to celebrate Mass.

Padre Pietro worked closely with the Sisters of the Consolata, taking food and medicine to lepers. Social outcasts called Padre Pietro the Santone Bianco, or "White Holy Man." One of the Sisters of the Consolata said, "Padre Pietro was a true Franciscan, because he gave all that he received. For him, he did not take anything, his joy was in giving."[123] Day by day, month by month, year by year, Padre Pietro poured out his life.

Padre Pietro continued to work quietly, caring for society's sick and destitute castaways. His willingness to sacrifice everything for the Somali people was evident. On December 29, 1990, he arrived in Mogadishu carrying the body of an Italian man who had died a few days earlier. In life, the man had been abandoned by everyone. He had died alone in Padre Pietro's arms. Not wanting to abandon him to a pauper's grave, Padre brought the body to a cemetery where Franciscan missionaries and the Consolata Sisters were laid to rest. He used his own casket, the one that missionaries bring with them for their own burial, to lay the man to rest. He lovingly placed a cross at the head of the grave.[124]

Father Pietro lived out the words of Jesus found in Matthew 25:40: "Truly I tell you, whatever you did for one of the least of these brothers and sisters of mine, you did for me" (NIV). Padre Pietro Turati understood this truth, applying selfless compassion to every area of life. He loved the least of these.

Padre Pietro spent his final days during a time of great political unrest. Rebel factions were warring with government soldiers. On February 8, 1991, Padre Pietro was standing in front of the former Mission of Gelib and was caught in the crossfire of rebel bullets. His life ended but the love he had for the Somalis lived on, crossing all cultural, ethnic, and religious lines. In the midst of the violent atmosphere, the head of the Muslim village arranged for the Christian missionary's burial. The village sang a song of Muslim piety in Padre Pietro's honor. He was buried in his bloodstained suit, but Padre Pietro entered eternity surrounded by love and clothed in Christ's righteousness.

NEIMA ABIAD IDRIS Ascending from the desert floor, the Nuba Mountains in southern Sudan climb to an elevation of 3,000 feet. Across the hills flowed the sweet tunes of the "Peace Singer," Neima Abiad Idris. Idris's songs, all in the Koliib language, were filled with faith, prayer, and hope for the Nubian people.

Idris's people farm the same small plots as their ancestors. They live in *tukuls*, houses built with circular rock walls with roofs made of tree branches or dried sorghum sheaves. They struggle to keep children fed and schools open. Muslims attend mosque-like meetings, devout Christians build churches, other religions such as animism are passed from parent to child. It's not a bad life, but it's not an easy one either.

During Idris's teen years, Sudan passed sharia law in northern Sudan, and by the time she had six children of her own, Sudanese Arab militias were active in the Nuba Mountains. They scoured the countryside for political enemies and alleged violators of this new legislation, and they ruthlessly dealt with Christians and Muslims alike. Those that weren't killed began to starve, unable to work their fields because of the conflict. To make matters worse, the Sudanese government sealed the Nuba Mountains from receiving international aid. Human rights organizations called it genocide.[125] All the while, Neima continued to sing her aspirations for her people, providing strength and hope. Soon, every household throughout this huge mountainous region knew the name of the woman they called the Peace Singer.[126]

Many Nubians left their mountain homes and joined resistance forces in what is now the nation of South Sudan. To protect what was left of their safety and liberty, they fought together against the hard-line Islamic government of the north. But Idris stayed with her six children in rebel-controlled Dellami county, having never seriously considered leaving her home for a safer location. Her people needed her. She kept on singing, making recordings in which the titles alone engendered hope, *Faith Is Essential to Achieve Our Goals* and *Building Peace, Forgiveness & Reconsiliation.*

In a 2002 ceasefire between Sudan's north and south regions, Nubians were excluded, and they were once again at the mercy of the very government they'd just fought a war to stop. Predictably, the Sudanese government cracked down, forcibly moving tens of thousands of Nubians from their mountain homes to so-called "peace villages." In these "peace villages" the government-backed militia known as the Popular Defense Force often raped and murdered the people they were hired to protect.[127]

In 2011, when South Sudan became its own nation, its brothers-in-arms from the north, the Nuba warriors, were left behind as part of Sudan. Although they'd fought for independence, the Nubian people were not allowed, under the terms of this new agreement, to secede. So they picked up arms again and continued to fight for their lives against the oppressive Khartoum government. In the meantime, Idris's family was starving, along with the rest of the nation. But she continued to hold fast, living with great courage under the daily threat of death by the Islamic authorities.

In December 2011, the Famine Early Warning Systems Network warned that humanitarian conditions were deteriorating and that by March 2012, the Nuba Mountains would be just one designation short of famine—entirely manmade, because of the conflict.[128] Human rights groups pressured the international community to step in and save the Nubian people.

Advocates as diverse as actor George Clooney and Samuel Totten, professor emeritus from the University of Arkansas, risked their lives to bring supplies to the region and film what had become full-fledged genocide. "It's a consistent, constant drip of terror," Clooney stated, "keeping [people] from planting, keeping from farming, and keeping from surviving."[129]

The people of the Nuba Mountains grew accustomed to empty stomachs and ferocious bombs as Russian-made Antonov bombers and Sochki 24 fighter jets flew daily sorties over the region. Those who avoided death still often lost limbs or suffered other debilitating injuries. The tukuls dotted across the mountainsides that once provided protection from the elements now provided clear targets for these bombers.

In 2014, a congregation stopped their worship service when they heard planes pass over, so that the congregation could flee outside. When the bombs landed on their church, the structure was reduced to rubble, but the worshipers were saved.[130] In perhaps the same series of attacks, on November 6, 2014, a bomb dropped by an Antonov plane struck Idris's home village of Kadir. Neima Idris was hit by shrapnel and killed. She was forty-nine years old.

Idris was immediately hailed as a hero and martyr. When others fled, she refused to run from the daily terror, fulfilling her ministry of song to her people. Christians around the world noted the death of the Peace Singer who was sent by God to one small part of the globe to bring hope and peace to a targeted group of people. One persecution watch ministry stated it simply: "She is a hero and a martyr."[131] Along with her legacy of fearless faithfulness, Neima Idris left behind her music, songs that continue to ring through her beloved mountains.

DID YOU KNOW? *Genocide in Darfur*

On September 9, 2004, US Secretary of State Colin Powell declared the human rights atrocities in Darfur, Sudan, to be "genocide." This was the first time the term was used by the executive branch of the United States government.[132] The genocide started in 2003 when two rebel groups arose against the mainly Arab government of President al-Bashir, a military general who grabbed power in 1989 through a coup. The government responded by attacking the rebels and its own citizens, as well as unleashing the brutality of a militia known as "men on horse-back," or "Janjaweed."

Al-Bashir, the Janjaweed, and members of the Resistance Front were tried in absentia by the International Criminal Court for genocide that was waged mainly against non-Arab populations, for war crimes, and for crimes against humanity. Specific charges include mass killing, rape, murder, destruction of property, pillaging, persecution, forcible trans-fer of population, inhumane acts, imprisonment, severe deprivation of liberty, torture, and extermination.[133] Most of those they targeted were Christians. Numerous Christians were killed or subjected to various indignities.

From the start of the conflict to the present day, rape is a primary tool of terror used by the fighting factions. The Janjaweed routinely burn villages, loot resources, pollute water, and murder, rape, and torture civil-ians.[134] Children are treated as easy targets for brutality. According to a Sudan expert, by 2005 more than one million children have been "killed, raped, wounded, displaced, traumatized, or endured the loss of parents and families" since the violence began.[135] Reporters and relief workers were not allowed in the country, so statistics are difficult to come by. Estimates in the first half of 2014 alone said 400,000 individuals were displaced.[136] In 2016, it was estimated that more than 2.7 million people had been displaced.[137]

Out of this crisis in one of the poorest nations on earth has come one of the most innovative technological answers. A Google employee whose family includes Holocaust survivors from Germany wanted to raise awareness of the genocide. By partnering with the United States Holocaust Memorial Museum, she developed a method whereby Google Earth viewers could see the effects of the Sudanese genocide with images that "graphically convey the mayhem that has been inflicted on the people of the region."[138]

President al-Bashir was convicted of war crimes in international court in 2009 and in 2019 was removed from office. A Sudanese court sentenced him to two years in detention for money laundering and corruption.[139]

In 2018, UN Deputy Secretary-General Amina Mohammed said that $16 billion has been invested in peacekeeping in Darfur, plus the humanitarian funding sent to alleviate suffering. In a colossal understatement, she declared it was time to "step up and make sure Darfur moves towards peace and prosperity."[140] In one of the most unlikely events of the modern era post al-Bashir, Sudan has been undergoing a massive reform that includes the elimination of blasphemy laws, the promotion of religious freedom, and even talk of normalizing relations with their archenemy, Israel. Sudan's terrorist ex-president, al-Bashir, awaits trial by his own people.

LAWAN ANDIMI The World Watch List ranks Nigeria as one of the world's most violent countries for persecuted Christians, second only to Pakistan.[141] In 2021, Nigeria was ranked ninth in the top fifty countries where it's hardest to be a Christian and leads the world in Christian martyrdoms. Confirmed deaths numbered 3,530 in 2021.[142] The terrorist group Boko Haram is a major contributor, famous for abducting 276 girls from a school in Chibok. In March 2018, 104 schoolgirls were released but the terrorists refused to release a girl named Sharibu because she would not recant her Christianity. As of this writing, one hundred girls are still missing.[143]

In December 2019, it became evident that attacks against Christians were increasing from Boko Haram and its faction called the Islamic State West Africa Province (ISWAP), which is aligned with ISIS. Four abducted aid workers were killed. On Christmas Eve, ISWAP beheaded eleven Christian captives. On Christmas Day, they killed nine Christians and two other captives. On January 2–3, 2020, Boko Haram led attacks in Michika town. The next day, they attacked the home of the chairman of a local chapter of the Christian Association of Nigeria and abducted Pastor Lawan Andimi.[144]

On January 5, 2020, the terrorists released a video in which Pastor Andimi turned the tables on his captors by making the video a sermon. "By the grace of God, I will be together with my wife, my children, and my colleagues," Andimi said. "If the opportunity has not been granted, maybe it is the will of God. . . . Be patient, don't cry, don't worry. But thank God for everything."[145] Andimi followed hostage video protocol by appealing to denominational leadership and the Adamawa governor to intervene for his release. But without showing any of the usual signs of desperation, Andimi made clear his hope lay elsewhere.[146]

Gideon Para-Mallam, an ambassador for the International Fellowship of Evangelical Students, said Andimi was targeted in order to "annihilate the Christian faith" by eliminating its leaders. He remarked on Andimi's brave witness saying, "From the lion's den, he said to death: 'To hell with you, I'm not afraid.'" Para-Mallam added, "This is completely different from most hostage videos. . . . [Andimi] appeared as one who has already conquered death, saying to his abductors and the rest of us that he is ready to die for his faith in Christ."[147]

Some persecution watch agencies were hopeful for Andimi's release, but others were not. Even as Andimi was being held, eleven kidnapped Nigerian Christians were executed by ISWAP. Then on January 20, 2020, ISWAP released a video showing a masked child shooting a pistol to kill a twenty-two-year-old Christian student. The boy said, "We have not forgotten what you have done to our parents and ancestors and we are telling all Christians around the world, we have not forgotten and will not stop. We must avenge the bloodshed that has been done like this one."[148]

On January 21, the news came that Pastor Andimi had been executed. A video was released to Nigerian journalist Ahmad Salkida showing Andimi being beheaded. Salkida wrote in a tweet, "Rev. Andimi was a church leader, a father to his children and the community he served."[149]

The Christian Association of Nigeria (CAN) declared three days of prayer and fasting, and condemned the "brutal murder" of Andimi as "a shame to the Nigerian government."[150] CAN called for Nigerian Christians to remain calm but challenged Nigerian president Buhari "to be more proactive about effort to get rid of the continuous siege on Nigeria and end the wanton killings and destructions of lives and property."[151]

"We cannot lose hope on divine protection and the power of our Lord Jesus Christ to expose those behind the sponsorship of terrorism in Nigeria and to get Nigeria safe from the arms of the criminals," stated Kwamkur Samuel Vondip, CAN director for legal and public affairs.[152]

Said Nathan Hosler, director of the Church of the Brethren's Office of Peacebuilding and Policy, "Though the world has paid less attention to Boko Haram, the situation in the region still is dire for those plagued by this radical insurgency. This fact somberly rings true today. . . . In remaining aware of the violence that our brothers and sisters in Nigeria face daily, let us walk alongside one another in joy and loss."[153]

President Buhari condemned Andimi's slaying, calling it "cruel, inhuman and deliberately provocative."[154] He tweeted, "I am greatly saddened by the fact that the terrorists went on to kill him even while giving signals of a willingness to set him free by releasing him to third parties."[155]

"Rev. Andimi died a martyr and therefore no doubt a Christian hero," said Para-Mallam. "The blood of martyrs is the seed which waters and grows the gospel of peace as good news to a broken and hurting world which Jesus Christ called us to proclaim. Rev. Andimi's blood will water the spread of the gospel in the North East, Nigeria, and other parts of the world. No doubt about this."[156]

Andimi's death will be most remembered by his words spoken in the video that serves as a testimony to his life.

As Andimi prepared for eternity, he left a mark of Christian courage and a reminder for us all. "I have never been discouraged, because all conditions that one finds himself is in the hands of God—God who made them to take care of me and to leave [me with] my life."[157] And it was into God's hands and care that Rev. Andimi was ushered the moment that he died.

MARY SAMEH GEORGE Mary Sameh George was a lover of Jesus and a lover of people. A Coptic Christian in Egypt's Orthodox Church, she was a woman who served her community by putting feet to her faith. Beautiful and upbeat with a winning smile, she was a favorite of church youth as well as the elderly. Every Friday she would drive into the Muslim neighborhood of Ain Shams, Cairo, and park by the Virgin Mary and Archangel Michael Coptic Orthodox Church to deliver medicine and meals to the elderly Muslims and Christians who lived there. Her car sported a cross dangling from her rearview mirror that reminded her as she drove of the One who inspired her care for others.

At twenty-four years of age, she had earned a bachelor's degree in law from Ain Shams University and had begun work at a communications company. She had also fallen in love and was planning to become engaged in the spring of 2014. Beloved by friends and family, to the eyes of all, Mary was thriving.

On Friday, March 28, 2014, Mary got into her car to drive to Ain Shams, but the Cairo she was driving toward was not the same Cairo where she'd grown up. President Morsi had been removed from office, causing unrest across the city. Morsi had been the Muslim Brotherhood presidential candidate whose promise of social justice and economic reform won the election by a narrow margin.[158] But after a single turbulent year in office, he was overthrown for reneging on his political promises and under suspicion of yielding power to the Islamist Brotherhood. Now Morsi supporters were outraged over the announcement that General Sisi, who had removed the president from office, would be running for that office himself. Sisi would later be heralded by most of Egypt as having saved their great country from the Islamists who dreamed of turning it into an extremist state inspired by Iran.

On the afternoon Mary George was driving into Cairo to take care of the elderly, a pro-Morsi group called the National Coalition for Legitimacy had called for protests after afternoon prayers. Human rights reports have shown that an "overwhelming majority of attacks on Egypt's Christians occur on Friday—the day when pious Muslims meet in mosque for prayers and to hear sermons."[159] Unbeknownst to Mary, she was on a collision course with an enraged, uncontrollable mob.

Mary pulled up in front of a private school near the church in the neighborhood she had visited many times before. As she parked, the sight of the swinging cross above her dashboard caught the eye of protestors nearby. Protestors started screaming at her, inciting the crowd into a frenzy of violence. Eyewitness accounts said that the protestors swarmed over her car to the point where it could not be seen under the crush of bodies.[160] As the car roof collapsed, the crowd wrenched open the car door and pulled

Mary out onto the street, taking turns hitting and kicking her. Vicious hands grabbed handfuls of beautiful, curly hair and ripped it out with pieces of her scalp still attached. Others tore at her clothes. Her cries were lost among the shouts of "Allahu Akbar! Allahu Akbar!" Mary tried to cover her face with her hands, which exposed her back. She was stabbed in the back repeatedly. A lethal blow went through to her heart. A pair of hands pulled her lifeless head back, exposing her neck, and slit her throat. Mary died in the street, right next to a church that could have offered sanctuary. When she was dead, the protesters continued to satiate their bloodlust by torching her car and burning it to the ground.

Onlookers, in danger of losing their own lives, watched helplessly, unable to assist. Mary's death by mob violence was given little notice by Cairo news sources, but the Australian Coptic Movement Association shared its outrage with the world. They stated, "Mary George was targeted for her faith in what is becoming an increasingly intolerable and inhospitable region for Christians; given that Ain Shams is a known stronghold for the Muslim Brotherhood. The Egyptian government must send a clear message that this behavior will not be tolerated and that the culprits will be held to account under the full force of the law."[161]

A friend who had spoken to Mary only a few hours before, heard about her death from the media. She wouldn't presume to know Mary George's last thoughts or words on that fateful Friday afternoon, but said, "She was a sincere servant, she loved the Lord from her deep heart."[162]

VINCENT MACHOZI Father Vincent Machozi was born into a family of thirteen children in the Democratic Republic of the Congo. His mother, having lost several of her children at birth, chose the name Vincent for him, which means "son of tears." Machozi would become a priest from the house of the Augustinians of the Assumption, and would never be a stranger to tears.

Machozi's father died when he was just fifteen years old. The country he was born into was rampant with political strife and violence. In the war-torn region where he was raised, as many as three quarters of the women in some villages were raped by soldiers.[163] Men, women, and children were regularly forced into slavery, mining for the mineral coltan, which is found in nearly every cell phone across the globe. Daily atrocities occurred because people were seen as disposable. In a country shaped by despair and violence, Father Machozi longed to bring spiritual freedom, social justice, and global awareness to the plight of his people.

Father Machozi began his religious studies at the age of seventeen and was sent abroad by the Assumptionists to study in Lille, France. After graduating, he returned home to work with the youth in his community. He left the DRC again in 2003 to attend Boston University (BU). He received his master's degree in 2006 and enrolled in a PhD program, studying social ethics. He was fascinated by those who had transformed the world they lived in, men like Dr. Martin Luther King Jr., who had also attended BU. Father Machozi wanted to grow in his knowledge of how to bring about social change. He found work at an African Studies Center and built a wonderful community away from home. He began to minister at the Immaculate Conception parish in Everett, Massachusetts, serving a diverse immigrant community. Father Machozi was beloved by the congregation, and many looked up to him as a role model. But the tragedy and hardship of home always pulled at him. His people were never far from his thoughts. All the while Father Machozi lived in the United States, his heart bled for Africa.

The region of Kivu in Northern DRC, where Father Machozi was raised, had been wracked by war for over two decades. The Council on Foreign Relations reported that those northern communities were regularly terrorized by as many as seventy different armed groups.[164] Following the 1994 end of the Rwandan genocide, over 5.4 million Congolese lost their lives to starvation, disease, and violation.[165] For Father Machozi, his real home was a nation in crisis. Like a modern-day Moses, he heard the cries of his people ringing in his ears. He couldn't stay still. He couldn't just do nothing. Father Machozi decided he had to act.

Father Machozi built a website called "Beni Lubero Online" with a plan to foster awareness and outrage in the global community. Beni and Lubero are two territories that sit high above Lake Edward in Northern DRC, but Father Machozi didn't want to show pictures of the verdant lake district that promoted tourism. Instead, he showed a much different Beni-Lubero area.

The site was populated with grim pictures of the atrocities that were taking place in his homeland and the names of the militant groups responsible. People in the DRC took notice. They started texting Machozi's iPhone even more graphic videos or photos of death and destruction. Father Machozi uploaded them all to the website. In his own version of an "underground railroad," he recruited informants who would sneak him the grisly photos from internet cafés and report which militant groups committed the crimes. Teams of two would visit the cafés, one to upload pictures and one to stand as a lookout. If anyone entered the café, the person on the computer would switch to a different website.[166]

Father Machozi wanted the full force of justice to be visited upon those who were killing the people he loved. He wanted peace for his community and hope for his land. His studies in social ethics fueled his desire to make a difference for the Congolese. However, his website raised concerns with his superiors. Father Claude Grenache said, "He was always careful to publish the website under his own personal name, because if he did that in the name of the congregation, everybody would be in danger. Even in this country [the United States], we could have run into problems."[167]

While Beni Lubero Online did receive some recognition, Father Machozi was frustrated. Change was not coming fast enough. People he loved were still being murdered. Children were still being forced into conscripted labor to mine coltan ore. Consumers were still buying cell phones, unaware of what it cost his people to provide coltan ore for the phones. In 2012, Father Machozi decided to return home. He wanted to be with those he loved and stand with them, seeking justice and providing support on the ground. He told his friend and fellow alumnus Shandirai Mawokomatanda, "I have to go back for my people. My people need me and I need them. If I don't do this, no one else will."[168]

Even though he was in danger, Father Machozi's friends and colleagues knew he had to go. Mawokomatanda said, "He felt that as a Christian and a priest, he had a higher calling—to share in the ministry of peacemaking. He was like Jesus. He was a peacemaker and a justice seeker in the Congo."[169]

Father Machozi returned to the DRC and continued to carry on his dangerous work with his website. He told an interviewer, "I want to bring the story of the Congo to the world through the continued development of the website."[170]

At home in the DRC, Father Machozi began shepherding a congregation and developed a community center. He felt a great sense of hope in 2013 when he was elected to a three-year term as the president of the Nande community of eight million people. His dreams of changing his community seemed to be bearing fruit. Behind the scenes, he continued to document the horrors of the militant groups that wreaked havoc on his people, calling them out, putting names to the death that surrounded him. He was not immune to the danger. Seven separate attempts were made on Father Machozi's life.

In 2016, he posted more damning photos and stated that the Congolese government was complicit in the acts of violence. The corrupt leaders set a trap. While waiting to attend a peace talk, Father Machozi found himself sitting in a courtyard with his laptop. Ten military men carrying guns surrounded him. He lost his life to the violence he abhorred, dying in a shower of bullets.[171]

The people of the DRC rose up to honor him, their champion, the man who sacrificed his life to fight for their freedom and protection. Thirty thousand Congolese citizens accompanied his body to the church. Father Machozi's love for Jesus had determined the course of his life. His love for his people had dictated his actions. He could have lived in safety and used his degree in an administrative position for social justice. Instead, he answered a higher calling to fight for the oppressed. In answering that call, Father Machozi poured out his life as a sacrifice and demonstrated how to live a life of righteousness, pursuing justice without caving.

Vintage Foxe

My Lord Jesus Christ, for my sake, did wear a crown of thorns; why should not I then, for His sake, again wear this light crown, be it ever so ignominious?[172]

Notes

INTRODUCTION

1. *Eusebius—The Church History: A New Translation with Commentary*, trans. Paul L. Maier (Grand Rapids, MI: Kregel Publications, 1999), 107.
2. For the image of this cover page, see Gordon Campbell, *Bible: The Story of the King James Version, 1611–2011* (New York: Oxford University Press, 2010), 98.
3. This is a key point made by John L. Allen Jr., *The Global War on Christians: Dispatches from the Frontline of Anti-Christian Persecutions* (New York: Image, 2013). Also, see websites from the following organizations: Center for the Study of Global Christianity (CSGC), Gordon-Conwell Theological Seminary, https://www.gordonconwell.edu/center-for-global -christianity/; The Voice of the Martyrs, https://www.persecution.com/; and Open Doors International, https://www.opendoors.org/en-US/. For a list of how Christ's early apostles died, see David B. Barrett and Todd M. Johnson, *World Christian Trends AD 30–AD 2200: Interpreting the Annual Christian Megacensus*, Part 4: Martyrology (Pasadena, CA: William Carey Library, 2001), 229.
4. George Weigel, "Rediscovering the Martyrology," *First Things* (February 4, 2014), https://www .firstthings.com/web-exclusives/2014/02/rediscovering-the-martyrology.
5. See also Johnnie Moore, *The Martyr's Oath: Living for the Jesus They're Willing to Die For* (Carol Stream, IL: Tyndale House, 2017).
6. "Seminal Historical Text Now Online in Culmination of 20-Year Project," News archive of University of Sheffield, July 15, 2011, https://www.sheffield.ac.uk/news/nr/john -foxe-1.174306.
7. Taken from The Voice of the Martyrs website, reflecting on the passion of its founders, Richard and Sabina Wurmbrand: https://www.persecution.com/about/. See also https://www .barnabasfund.org.
8. See https://www.opendoorsusa.org/christian-persecution/world-watch-list/.
9. See Under Caesar's Sword homepage, http://ucs.nd.edu/ (last accessed Nov. 8, 2017). See also "What Is to Be Done? Responding to the Global Persecution of Christians," National Press Club, Washington, DC, April 20, 2017, http://ucs.nd.edu/public-events/launch/.
10. Stating any definitive number for martyrs evokes debate; these are conservative numbers. See counterpoints to the estimates like 900,000 in the last decade, e.g., Ruth Alexander's "Are There Really 100,000 New Christian Martyrs Every Year?" BBC News, November 12, 2013, http://www.bbc.com/news/magazine-24864587.

11. A prime example is the apostle John, whom Foxe includes, noting that Emperor Domitian imprisoned him on the island of Patmos. (He also includes stories of various trials, hardships, and miracles.)

12. Justin Martyr, *Dialogue with Trypho*, 110.

13. The essence of the statement isn't in question—that martyrs' deaths strengthened the resolve of fellow Christians—but scholars differ on whether modern research supports Tertullian's claim, calling into question the staying power of Christianity in places where Muslims have driven nearly all Christians from their territories—often their ancient centers that grew amid martyrdoms. However, Emperor Julian seemed to realize that his predecessors' persecution of Christians only contributed to their growth, and thus resorted to oppressive measures instead. For a fuller discussion of Tertullian, including the original wording of this statement, see Morgan Lee, "Sorry, Tertullian," *Christianity Today* (December 4, 2014), https://www .christianitytoday.com/ct/2014/december/sorry-tertullian.html.

14. Stanley Fish, *Save the World on Your Own Time* (Oxford, UK: Oxford University Press, reprint ed., 2012), and Gary A. Olson, *Stanley Fish: America's Enfant Terrible* (Carbondale, IL: Southern Illinois University Press, 2016). See also Jerry Pattengale, "What Are Universities For? The Contested Terrain of Moral Education," *Books and Culture* (July-August, 2010); and Pattengale, "The Big Questions: Have Our Colleges and Universities Lost Sight of Their Purpose?" *Books and Culture* (November-December, 2009), a review of Anthony T. Kronman, *Education's End: Why Our Colleges and Universities Have Given Up on the Meaning of Life* (New Haven, CT: Yale University Press, 2007).

15. The following was published as part of this response to the government's request, "Determining the Difference between Noble and Ignoble Causes," *RE Today Magazine* [for all UK schools], April 2016.

16. This film is based on Shūsaku Endō's book, *Silence*, trans. William Johnston (New York: Picador, 1966). Makoto Fujimura gives a helpful reflection of this work and the Japanese context in *Silence and Beauty: Hidden Faith Born of Suffering* (Downers Grove, IL: IVP Books, 2016).

SECTION ONE: THE NEW TESTAMENT THROUGH THE BATTLE OF TOURS (AD 732)

1. David C. Downing, *Into the Region of Awe* (Downers Grove, IL: InterVarsity Press, 2005), 60.

2. A legendary report found in various stories.

3. Peter Kirby, "Historical Jesus Theories," *Early Christian Writings*, accessed February 1, 2019, http://www.earlychristianwritings.com/srawley/polycarp.html.

4. Kenneth Berding, "John or Paul: Who Was Polycarp's Mentor?" *Tyndale Bulletin* 59, no. 1 (May 1, 2008): 135–43, https://tyndalebulletin.org/article/29251-john-or-paul-who-was -polycarp-s-mentor.

5. St. Colluthus of Egypt, a Coptic physician, gave nearly the same phrase at his martyrdom. See Jerry Pattengale, *Benevolent Physicians in Late Antiquity: The Cult of the Anargyroi* (Oxford, OH: Miami University dissertation, 1987), 130–32.

CHAPTER 1: NEW TESTAMENT MARTYRS

1. Emerson (1803–1882) is quoted here for his brilliant prose, not to be mistaken as a voice for Christian orthodoxy. He became a leading proponent of transcendentalism—a philosophy criticized broadly, including by Edgar Alan Poe in "Never Bet the Devil Your Head" (1841) and Nathaniel Hawthorne in *The Blithedale Romance* (1852).

2. In addition to biblical accounts of some of the Christian martyrs on this list and the context behind religious-political tensions, we have a wealth of tradition passed down to the present. From robust Roman Catholic sources chronicling Christian saints, familiar in liturgy through

The Roman Martyrology, to the various versions of *Acts and Monuments* (or *Foxe's Book of Martyrs*), many names are in common on the lists. One of these sources perhaps ranks next to the Bible in importance for the Mennonites and the Amish, i.e., Thieleman J. van Braght's book *Martyrs Mirror*, or more formally by its full title, *The Bloody Theater or Martyrs Mirror of the Defenseless Christians Who Baptized Only upon Confession of Faith, and Who Suffered and Died for the Testimony of Jesus, Their Saviour, from the Time of Christ to the Year AD 1660* (Holland: 1660). See Nanne van der Zijpp, Harold S. Bender, and Richard D. Thiessen, "Martyrs' Mirror," Global Anabaptist Mennonite Encyclopedia Online, November 2014, https://gameo.org/index.php?title=Martyrs%27_Mirror. Like the writings of John Foxe, Braght's work surfaced posthumously in other editions by other editors. He died in 1664 and the noble second edition appeared in 1685. See also "Martyrs Mirror of the Defenseless Christians," homecomers.org, accessed July 8, 2021, https://www.homecomers.org/mirror /index-mirror.htm. For a short introduction to persecution, see Everett Ferguson, "Persecution in the Early Church: Did You Know?," *Christian History*, originally published in "Persecution in the Early Church," *Christian History*, no. 27 (1990), http://www.christianitytoday.com /history/issues/issue-27/persecution-in-early-church-did-you-know.html. A suggested chronology of early martyrdom also appears in the same *Christian History* series, dating Stephen's death to approximately AD 35, and those of Peter and Paul to AD 65. See "Persecution in the Early Church: A Christian History Timeline," *Christianity Today*, accessed July 8, 2021, https://www.christianitytoday.com/history/issues/issue-27/persecution-in -early-church-christian-history-timeline.html.

3. William H. C. Frend, "When Christianity Triumphed," *Christianity Today*, originally published in "Persecution in the Early Church," *Christian History*, no. 27 (1990), https://www .christianitytoday.com/history/issues/issue-27/when-christianity-triumphed.html; William G. Bixler, "How the Early Church Viewed Martyrs," *Christianity Today*, originally published in "Persecution in the Early Church," *Christian History*, no. 27 (1990); Jolyon Mitchell, *Martyrdom: A Very Short Introduction* (Oxford: Oxford University Press, 2012).

4. Adapted from "Christian History Timeline: Persecution in the Early Church," Christian History Institute, originally published in *Christian History*, no. 27 (1990), https://christianhistoryinstitute .org/magazine/article/persecution-in-early-church-timeline. The main sources for the timeline listed in *Christian History* are W. H. C. Frend, *The Rise of Christianity* (Philadelphia: Fortress, 1984); Michael Walsh, *The Triumph of the Meek* (London: Roxby, 1986); Ray C. Petry, ed., *A History of Christianity* (Englewood Cliffs, NJ: Prentice-Hall, 1962). These corroborate Early Church and medieval history sources with the biblical narrative.

5. For a deeper discussion of these and other examples, and images, see Jerry Pattengale, Tim Dalrymple, et al., "John the Baptist," *The Bible's Impact on Western Culture* (Washington DC: Museum of the Bible, 2019).

6. "Tomb of Apostle Philip Found," *Bible History Daily* (blog), Biblical Archaeology Society, August 6, 2017, https://www.biblicalarchaeology.org/daily/biblical-sites-places/biblical -archaeology-sites/tomb-of-apostle-philip-found/.

7. This account is generally not considered historical, but is early and reflects the church's ardent belief in Matthew's persecution. The term *Ante-Nicene* refers to those church fathers before the First Council of Nicaea (AD 325), the source of the Nicene Creed endorsed by many factions of Christians to the present.

8. The depiction was ordered by Cardinal del Monte, carrying out terms of the will of Cardinal Contarelli, the progenitor of Contarelli Chapel in the Church of San Luigi dei Francesi in Rome, where the painting hangs (one of three of Caravaggio's on St. Matthew).

9. Rachel Hachili and Ann Killebrew, "Jewish Funerary Customs During the Second Temple Period, in the Light of the Excavations at the Jericho Necropolis," *Palestine Exploration Quarterly* 115, no. 2 (1983), 109-39, https://doi.org/10.1179/peq.1983.115.2.109.

10. Jodi Magness, "Ossuaries and the Burials of Jesus and James," *Journal of Biblical Literature*, vol. 124, no.1, 2005, pp. 121–54. Also see Gordon Govier, "Trial on Antiquities Fraud Ends, But Not the Controversy," *Christianity Today* (March 14, 2012), https://www.christianitytoday.com/news/2012/march/trial-fraud-controversy.html. The ossuary raised numerous discussions and claims, but it appears that this bone box came from the Talpiot burial site where other first-century names appeared on ten other ossuaries (and in the New Testament), though speculation that Jesus' bones were also in the box at one point is completely unfounded: Tia Ghose, "New Controversy Surrounds Alleged 'Jesus Family Tomb,'" *Live Science* (April 9, 2015), https://www.livescience.com/50434-jesus-family-tomb-geology.html.

11. Eusebius, *Ecclesiastical History* (AD 323), bk. 2, chap. 23.

12. Much of the account of Andrew's martyrdom comes from the third-century apocryphal account of *Acts of Andrew*, published by Constantin von Tischendorf (1821). See Hans-Josef Klauck, *The Apocryphal Acts of the Apostles: An Introduction*, trans. Brian J. MacNeil (Waco, TX: Baylor University Press, 2008).The church fathers mention various places of service for Andrew, including Scythia. See Eusebius, *Church History*, bk. 3, chap. 1.

13. Thomas C. Oden, *The African Memory of Mark: Reassessing Early Church Tradition* (Downers Grove, IL: Intervarsity Press, 2011). See also Ed Smither, "Review of Oden's African Memories of Mark," *Criswell Theological Review* (Spring 2012): 91–93; Oasis International, *Africa Study Bible* (Carol Stream, IL: Tyndale, 2017).

14. Eusebius, *Church History*, bk. 2, chap. 24.

15. John Foxe, *Actes and Monuments*, 1570 edition, bk. 1, 52. See *The Unabridged Acts and Monuments Online* (Sheffield: Digital Humanities Institute, 2011), https://www.dhi.ac.uk/foxe/. For a helpful introduction to St. Mark in early sources, see "St. Mark," *Catholic Encyclopedia*, vol. 9 (New York: Robert Appleton, 1910), https://www.newadvent.org/cathen/09672c.htm.

16. According to Jacobus de Voragine, *The Golden Legend* (circa AD 1260; London: William Caxton, 1483), his death was recorded by Marcellus, Pope Linus, Hegesippus, and Pope Leo. The complication comes with the Pseudo-Marcellus document that seems to gather various accounts of this martyrdom. See *The Golden Legend of Jacobus de Voragine*, trans. Granger Ryan and Helmut Ripperger (London: Longmans, Green, 1941), 330–41. Dionysius is also much quoted. An online version is available via the Internet History Sourcebooks Project, Fordham University, http://www.fordham.edu/halsall/basis/goldenlegend.

17. Jacobus de Voragine, *The Golden Legend of Jacobus de Voragine*, trans. Granger Ryan and Helmut Ripperger (London: Longmans, Green, 1941), 330–41.

18. Voragine, *Golden Legend*, 330–41.

19. This letter is referred to as *Epistle of Pseudo-Dionysius the Areopagite to Timothy* (*Ep. Tim. Dion.*), and was written in late antiquity or the early middle ages; Clavis numbers ECCA 908; CANT 197.

20. A common phrase used by professor Glenn Martin at Indiana Wesleyan University during his long tenure (d. 2004). See Jerry Pattengale, "The Capitol Offense: A Christian Professor's Warning 50 Years Ago," *Religion News Service* (January 27, 2021), https://religionnews.com/2021/01/27/the-capitol-offense-a-christian-professors-warning-50-years-ago/.

21. Abdias, an apocryphal writer, was allegedly the first bishop of Babylon and wrote an account of the apostles' deaths in ten books, *History of the Apostolical Contest*. However, many scholars place its composition much later—in the ninth century—and actually from a different author. Nonetheless, the ten books on the lives of the apostles (in Foxe credited to Abdias) show reliance on the earlier works, and are the only place some stories or legends survive.

22. Foxe, *Actes and Monuments*, 1583 ed., bk. 1, 58, *Unabridged Acts and Monuments Online*, https://www.dhi.ac.uk/foxe/. Foxe challenges one aspect of Abdias's account—that milk flowed from Paul's neck instead of blood. That story seems, according to Foxe, to be borrowed from another hagiographic account but is referenced by Ambrose in sermon 68.

23. Voragine, *Golden Legend*, 330–41.

24. The New Testament portion of the Douay-Rheims Bible was published in 1582 in Rheims, France. The Old Testament at the University of Douai in 1609 and 1610 (two volumes). A common iconic representation shows Jude holding the Edessa Image, a cloth with an image of Christ—with traditions of its origin ranging from the first to sixth centuries. Another tradition places his death in (modern) Beirut by an axe, along with Simon the Zealot.

25. This is Theodorus Lector, an early sixth-century reader (lector) at the Hagia Sophia at Constantinople (modern Istanbul). For an introduction to *The Golden Legend*, see: Kevin Di Camillo, "What Was 'The Golden Legend' and Why Is It Relevant Today?" *National Catholic Register*, July 12, 2017, http://www.ncregister.com/blog/dicamillo/what-was-the-golden-legend -and-why-is-it-relevant-today.

26. Alban Butler, *The Lives of Fathers, Martyrs, and other Principal Saints*, vol. 8 (London: John Murphy, 1815), 331. This resource morphed into the handy *Butler's Lives of the Saints*, now available in various versions, including a concise version (331 pages, 2005), and a more robust, well-edited, four-volume set with Herbert J. Thurston and Donald Attwater, eds. (Westminster, MD: Christian Classics, 1956).

27. For a helpful introduction to this debate, see Sean McDowell, "Did the Apostle Thomas Die as a Martyr?" Sean McDowell (website), blog, February 25, 2016; http://seanmcdowell.org/blog /did-the-apostle-thomas-die-as-a-martyr.

28. Michael Walsh, ed., *Butler's Lives of the Saints*, rev. ed. (New York: HarperCollins, 1991), 342. See also Nicholas Wade, "'Body of St. Luke' Gains Credibility," *New York Times*, October 16, 2001, https://www.nytimes.com/2001/10/16/world/body-of-st-luke-gains-credibility.html.

29. Thieleman J. van Braght, "Luke, the Holy Evangelist, Hanged on a Green Olive Tree, in Greece, AD 93," *Martyrs Mirror*, 95, https://www.homecomers.org/mirror/martyrs012.htm.

30. Foxe, *Actes and Monuments*, 1570 ed., bk. 1, 78, *Unabridged Acts and Monuments Online*, https://www.dhi.ac.uk/foxe/.

31. In his popular edited version, William Byron Forbush lists only crucifixion, and only his death in Britain, *Foxe's Book of Martyrs: A History of the Lives, Sufferings, and Triumphant Deaths of the Early Christian and the Protestant Martyrs* (Peabody, MA: Hendrickson, 2004), 6. This reflects accurately the short representation in Foxe's original: see Foxe, *Actes and Monuments*, 1570 ed., bk. 1, 52, *Unabridged Acts and Monuments Online*, https://www.dhi.ac.uk/foxe/.

32. Foxe, *Actes and Monuments*, 1570 ed., bk. 1, p. 56, *Unabridged Acts and Monuments Online*, https://www.dhi.ac.uk/foxe/.

33. Isidorus (Latin) is Archbishop Isidore of Seville, ca. AD 560–636.

34. F. L. Cross and E. A. Livingstone, eds., *Oxford Dictionary of the Christian Church*, 3rd ed. (New York: Oxford University Press, 2005), s.v. "Barnabas."

35. This is Rhabanus Maurus (d. 856), a student of Alcuin in Charlemagne's empire who became archbishop of Mainz; a prolific writer of many works, including an encyclopedia, *On the Nature of Things*.

36. John Foxe, *Foxe's Book of Martyrs: The Acts and Monuments of the Church* (London, 1851), 26. See also https://www.exclassics.com/foxe/foxe1pdf.pdf.

37. Thieleman J. van Braght, *Martyrs Mirror* (Holland: 1660, trans. Joseph F. Sohm, 1886), "Summary of the Martyrs of the First Century," 68, http://www.homecomers.org/mirror /martyrs010.htm#68.

CHAPTER 2: THE GREAT PERSECUTIONS

1. This includes all levels of NCAA and NAIA football, averaging 12,888 in 2017. With minimal attendance, the Roman spectacle would far surpass this number. See "2017 Football Attendance," NCAA, accessed July 11, 2021, http://fs.ncaa.org/Docs/stats/football_records /Attendance/2017.pdf.

2. Sandra Sweeny Silver, "Colosseum in Ancient Rome," *Early Church History*, accessed July 21, 2021, https://earlychurchhistory.org/entertainment/colosseum-in-ancient-rome/.

3. Maurice Hassett, "The Coliseum," *Catholic Encyclopedia*, vol. 4 (New York: Robert Appleton, 1908), http://www.newadvent.org/cathen/04101b.htm.

4. For a general history, see "Colosseum," History.com, updated June 6, 2019, https://www.history.com/topics/ancient-history/colosseum. For a more detailed look, see Michele Renee Salzman, *On Roman Time: The Codex-Calendar of 354 and the Rhythms of Urban Life in Late Antiquity*, (Berkeley: University of California Press, 1991).

5. Anna McCullough, "Female Gladiators in Imperial Rome: Literary Context and Historical Fact," *Classical World* 101, no. 2 (Winter, 2008): 197–209, http://www.jstor.org/stable/25471938.

6. John Foxe, *Actes and Monuments*, 1570 ed., lists Justin's martyrdom under both Antonius Pius and Marcus Aurelius.

7. "Justin Martyr," *Christianity Today*, accessed July 21, 2021, https://www.christianitytoday.com/history/people/evangelistsandapologists/justin-martyr.html.

8. Chaucer, *Parlement of Foules*, lines 309–10.

9. Nicolai von Kreisler. "Bird Lore and the Valentine's Day Tradition in Chaucer's *Parlement of Foules*," *Chaucer Review* 3, no. 1 (Summer 1968): 60–64, https://www.jstor.org/stable/25093071.

10. *Analecta Bollandiana* 11 (1892): 472; Hippolyte Delehaye, "Les martyrs d'Interamna," *Bulletin d'ancienne littérature et d'archéologie chrétiennes*, 1 (1911): 161–68.

11. "St. Valentine Beheaded," History.com, accessed July 11, 2021, https://www.history.com/this-day-in-history/st-valentine-beheaded.

12. "Butler's Lives of the Saints—Saint Valentine, Priest and Martyr," CatholicSaints.Info, (February 12, 2013), https://catholicsaints.info/butlers-lives-of-the-saints-saint-valentine-priest-and-martyr/.

13. *Encyclopedia of the Early Church*, vol. 2, ed. Angelo Di Berardino (New York: Oxford University Press, 1992), s.v. "Valentinus."

14. Charles Colson with Catherine Larson, "Valentine's Dynamic Love," *Christianity Today*, February 12, 2010, https://www.christianitytoday.com/ct/2010/february/19.57.html. The various legends attaching Valentine to romantic notions are many and without convincing historic corroboration, and the holiday notions in America today come from somewhat disconnected and late notions. The first Valentine note was actually sent from the Tower of London by the duke of Orléans to his wife in 1415; see Ted Olsen, "Then Again Maybe Don't Be My Valentine," *Christianity Today*, February 1, 2000, https://www.christianitytoday.com/ct/2000/februaryweb-only/11.0a.html.

15. Théodoret of Cyrrhus, *Cure of Pagan Ills* 8, 10–11, ed. Pierre Canivet, Sources Chrétiennes, collection dirigee par H. de Lubac et J. Danielou, SC, 57; see also *Théodoret de Cyr, Histoire des moines de Syrie*, tomes 1–2, eds. Pierre Cavinet and Alice Leroy-Molinghen (Sources Chrétiennes: 1977, 1979), SC 234, 257.

16. For the martyrology record, see Kevin Di Camillio, "The Roman Martyrology Shows What It Means to Die Like a Christian," *National Catholic Register*, October 26, 2017, http://www.ncregister.com/blog/dicamillo/the-roman-martyrology-shows-what-it-means-to-die-like-a-christian; Hippolyte Delehaye, "Martyrology," *Catholic Encyclopedia* (New York: Robert Appleton, 1910), accessed July 16, 2021, http://www.newadvent.org/cathen/09741a.htm.

17. The Latin comes from *code* (from tree, especially trunk) and reflects an early form of wooden tablets.

18. Quoted in Kevin Di Camillo, "Roman Martyrology Shows What It Means to Die Like a Christian," *National Catholic Register* (blog), October 26, 2017, https://www.ncregister.com/blog/the-roman-martyrology-shows-what-it-means-to-die-like-a-christian.

19. John Foxe, *Acts and Monuments*, 1570 ed., bk. 1, 138. Accessed at https://www.johnfoxe .org/index.php?realm=text&gototype=&edition=1570&pageid=150.

20. In addition to biblical accounts of some of the Christian martyrs on this list, and the context behind religious-political tensions, we have a wealth of tradition passed down to the present. For a short introduction to persecution, see Everett Ferguson, "Persecution in the Early Church: Did You Know?" *Christianity Today*, originally published in "Persecution in the Early Church, 1990," *Christian History*, no. 27 (1990), http://www.christianitytoday.com/history /issues/issue-27/persecution-in-early-church-did-you-know.html. A suggested chronology of the early martyrdoms also appears in the same Christian History series, dating Stephen's death to approximately AD 35, and those of Peter and Paul to AD 65. From robust Roman Catholic sources chronicling Christian saints, familiar in liturgy through "The Roman Martyrology," to the various versions of *Acts and Monuments* (or *Foxe's Book of Martyrs*, with mixed levels of reliability), many names are in common on the lists. One of these sources perhaps ranks next to the Bible in importance for the Mennonites and the Amish, i.e., *Martyrs Mirror*, or more formally by its full title, *The Bloody Theater or Martyrs Mirror of the Defenseless Christians Who Baptized Only upon Confession of Faith, and Who Suffered and Died for the Testimony of Jesus, Their Saviour, from the Time of Christ to the Year AD 1660*, Thieleman J. van Bright (Holland: 1660). Like the work of John Foxe, Bright's work surfaced posthumously in other editions by other editors. He died in 1664 and the noble second edition appeared in 1685. A searchable index is available online at: http://www.homecomers.org/mirror/index-general.htm. See Nanne van der Zijpp, Harold S. Bender and Richard D. Thiessen. "Martyrs' Mirror," Global Anabaptist Mennonite Encyclopedia Online. November 2014. Web. 19 Mar 2018.

21. Tacitus, *Annals*, 15.44.3–8, in *A New Eusebius: Documents Illustrating the History of the Church to AD 337*, 2nd ed., ed. J. Stevenson, revised by W. H. C. Frend (London: SPCK, 1987), 2–3.

22. Alvin J. Schmidt, *How Christianity Changed the World*, (Grand Rapids, MI: Zondervan, 2004), 26.

23. W. M. Ramsay, *The Church in the Roman Empire before AD 170* (London: Hodder and Stoughton, 1904) 259.

24. A helpful discussion of the Revelation passage and the entire Domitian debate on persecution is found in Arthur M. Ogden and Ferrell Jenkins, "Did Domitian Persecute Christians? An Investigation," online ed. (Ogden's Biblical Resources and BibleWorld by Ferrell Jenkins, March 1999), 8, http://www.historytimeline.org/docs/pdfs/did_domitian_persecute_christians.pdf.

25. Justo L. González, *The Story of Christianity: The Early Church to the Dawn of the Reformation*, vol. 1, 2nd ed. (New York: HarperOne, 2010), 48.

26. Origen, *Contra Celsum* 3.8.

27. Eusebius, *History of the Church*, bk. 3, chaps 17, 19; *History*, 80–82.

28. Silver, "Colosseum in Ancient Rome"; see also Sandra Sweeny Silver, *Footprints in Parchment: Rome Versus Christianity 30–313 AD* (Bloomington, IN: AuthorHouse, 2013), 123–24.

29. Pliny to Trajan, quoted at Stephen Tomkins and Dan Graves, "#102: Pliny's Letter to Trajan," Christian History Institute; accessed July 17, 2021, https://christianhistoryinstitute.org/study /module/pliny.

30. Andrea Lorenzo Molinari, "Women Martyrs in the Early Church:Hearing Another Side to the Story," *Priscilla Papers* 22, no. 1 (Winter 2008), 5–10, https://www.cbeinternational.org/resources /article/priscilla-papers/women-martyrs-early-church.

31. Robert G. Clouse, Richard V. Pierard, and Edwin M. Yamauchi, *Two Kingdoms: The Church and Culture through the Ages* (Chicago: Moody Press, 1993), 46.

32. Commodus: *Reign of Blood* (season 1) premiered November 11, 2016, Netflix. It focuses on Marcus Aurelius's son, Emperor Commodus (r. 180–192), after the first few episodes. Though it indeed highlights carnage in the border wars with the Germanic tribes, executions after Aurelius's death (AD 180) due to Commodus's paranoia (and self-defense), and huge gladiatorial games to please the citizens, the plight of the Christians is overlooked.

33. Like many martyrdom accounts, scholarship stretching back more than a century debates the details or occurrence of these stories. In this case the debate is mainly over the emperor Eusebius depicts since Marcus Aurelius receives more favorable treatment from earlier church writers. See James Westfall Thompson, "The Alleged Persecution of the Christians at Lyons in 177," *American Journal of Theology* 16 (July 1, 1912), https://archive.org/details/jstor-3154941.

34. Larry Hurtado, "Marcus Aurelius and Christians," Larry Hurtado's Blog, October 16, 2016, https://larryhurtado.wordpress.com/2016/10/13/marcus-aurelius-and-christians/.

35. Paul Keresztes, "Marcus Aurelius a Persecutor?" *Harvard Theological Review* 61, no. 3 (July 1968): 321–41, http://www.jstor.org/stable/1509154.

36. Eusebius, *History of the Church*, bk. 5, chap. 1, Medieval Sourcebook: The Persecution and Martyrdoms of Lyons in 177 AD, Internet History Sourcebooks Project, Fordham University, accessed July 17, 2021, https://sourcebooks.fordham.edu/source/177-lyonsmartyrs.asp.

37. Tertullian, *Apology*, chap. 18.

38. John Foxe, *Foxe's Book of Martyrs*, ed. William Byron Forbush (Peabody, MA: Hendrickson Publishers, 2004, ninth printing, 2016), 30.

39. Clouse, Pierard, and Yamauchi, *Two Kingdoms*, 48.

40. John Foxe, "The Eighth Persecution, under Valerian, AD 257," *Foxe's Book of Martyrs*, Bible Study Tools, accessed July 17, 2021, https://www.biblestudytools.com/history/foxs-book-of-martyrs/the-eighth-persecution-under-valerian-a-d-257.html.

41. Eusebius, *The History of the Church from Christ to Constantine* [*Ecclesiastical History*], trans. G. A. Williamson, ed. Andrew Louth, rev. ed. (1965; London: Penguin Books, 1989), 263–64.

42. Foxe, *Foxe's Book of Martyrs*, ed. Forbush (2004), 32–33, accessed at http://kotisatama.net/files/kotisatama/Tekstit_ja_kirjat/foxe.pdf.

43. W. H. C. Frend, *The Rise of Christianity* (Philadelphia: Fortress, 1984), 601.

44. Frend, *Rise of Christianity*, 604.

45. Julian, Letter XXII. Cited from Frend, *Rise of Christianity*, 601.

46. Origen, translation in Frend, *Rise of Christianity*, 289. Origen also wrote *Exhortation to Martyrdom* (AD 236).

47. Cf. Peter Brown, *The Cult of the Saints: Its Rise and Function in Latin Christianity* (Chicago: University of Chicago Press, n.d.), 10, cf. n. 45, p. 136.

48. Jerome, *Contra Vigilantium* 12.

49. Cf. Hippolyte Delehaye, "Loca Sanctorum," *Analecta Bollandiana* 48 (1930): 5–64; *Les origines du culte des martyrs*, Subsidia hagiographica, no. 20 (Brussels: Société des bollandistes, 1933); Hippolyte Delehaye, *Sanctus. Essai sur le culte des saints dans l'Antiquité, Subsidia hagiographica*, no. 17 (Brussels: Société des bollandistes, 1927).

50. Commonly cites as *Graecarum affectionum curatio*, or *The Cure of Greek Diseases*. The actual architectural structure of churches holding these remains is discussed in the next chapter under "martyria."

51. Théodoret, quoted in Josiah H. Gilbert, *Dictionary of Burning Words of Brilliant Writers* (New York: 1895), 263.

52. Théodoret of Cyrrhus, *Cure of Pagan Ills*, 8.10–11, Sources Chrétiennes, SC 57; see also *Theodoret de Cyr, Histoire des moines de Syrie*, tomes 1–2, SC 234, 257.

53. Foxe, *Actes and Monuments*, 1570 ed., bk. 1, 137–38, https://www.dhi.ac.uk/foxe/.

CHAPTER 3: MARTYRED LEADERS OF THE GROWING CHURCH

1. This is perhaps Bonhoeffer's most famous quote from *The Cost of Discipleship*, rev. ed. (Nashville: Holman Reference, 1999), cited on the sixty-fourth anniversary of his martyrdom by John Piper, "Dietrich Bonhoeffer Was Hanged Today," *Desiring God*, April 9, 2009, https://www.desiringgod.org/articles/dietrich-bonhoeffer-was-hanged-today.

2. Cornelius Tacitus, *Annals of Tacitus*, trans. Alfred John Church and William Jackson Brodribb (New York: Macmillan, 1921), 305.

3. Alvin J. Schmidt, *How Christianity Changed the World* (Grand Rapids, MI: Zondervan, 2004), 23–24. Rodney Stark's much-cited book, referred to here, is *The Rise of Christianity: A Sociologist Reconsiders History* (Princeton: Princeton University Press, 1996), and Schmidt cites from page 164.

4. Schmidt, *How Christianity Changed the World*, 234.

5. Jennifer Hevelone-Harper, "Saint Colluthus and Coptic Christian Syncretization of Greco -Roman Healing Cults in Egypt" (NEH paper, 1991).

6. E. A. E. Reymond and J. W. B. Barns, *Four Martyrdoms from the Pierpont Morgan Coptic Codices* (Oxford: Clarendon, 1973), 146.

7. "President Obama Shows His Coptic Cross from Ethiopia," *Tadias*, January 16, 2016, http://www.tadias.com/01/16/2016/video-president-obama-shows-his-coptic-cross-from-ethiopia/.

8. Some of these modern martyrdoms are shared in the final section of this book.

9. *Claremont Coptic Encyclopedia*, vol. 5, s.v. "Liturgical Vestments," ref. no. 1475a–1479a, https://ccdl.claremont.edu/digital/collection/cce/id/1221/rec/1.

10. Peter Sinthern, "Zum Kult der Anargyroi," *Zeitschrift fur Katholische Theologie* 69, no. 3 (1947): 354–60.

11. Jerry A. Pattengale, "Benevolent Physicians in Late Antiquity: The Cult of the Anargyroi," (PhD diss., Miami University, 1993), 127–30.

12. Owsei Temkin, *Hippocrates in a World of Pagans and Christians* (Baltimore, MD: Johns Hopkins University Press, 1995), 114.

13. William A. Fitzgerald, "Medical Men: Canonized Saints," *Bulletin of the History of Medicine* 22, no. 5 (September 1948): 639.

14. St. Cyril of Alexandria, "Oratiunculae Tres in Translatione Reliquiarum SS. Martyrum Cyri et Joannis," in *Patrologia Graeca*, ed. J. P. Migne, vol. 87, cols. 1099–106. See also Hippolyte Delehaye, *The Legends of the Saints: An Introduction to Hagiography*, trans. Virginia Mary Crawford (New York: Longmans, Green, 1907), 132–33.

15. Delehaye, *Legends of the Saints*, 48–49, n. 109; Butler, *Lives of the Saints*, 213.

16. François Halkin, *Bibliotheca hagiographica graeca, Subsidia hagiographica*, no. 8a (Brussels: Société des bollandists, 1957), 21; Bollandists, *Bibliotheca hagiographica Latina* (Brussels: Société des bollandists, n.d.), nn. 1370–80; Fitzgerald, "Medical Men: Canonized Saints," 639–40. For St. Blaise's legendary throat cures, cf. Butler, *Lives of the Saints*, vol. 1, 239.

17. Fitzgerald, "Medical Men: Canonized Saints," 641.

18. Pattengale, "Benevolent Physicians," 136.

19. Merchants, Roman citizens, and various slaves from Phrygia and Asia settled in the Rhone Valley. See Henry Chadwick, *The Early Church*, Pelican History of the Church, vol. 1 (Baltimore: Penguin Books, 1967), 63.

20. W. H. C. Frend, *The Rise of Christianity* (Philadelphia: Fortress, 1984), 195.

21. Eusebius, *History of the Church [Ecclesiastical History]*, bk. 5, chap. 1. Translation in Paul Keresztes, *Imperial Rome and the Christians: From Herod the Great to about 200 AD* (New York: University Press of America, 1989), 187–88.

22. *The Martyrdom of Polycarp*, trans. J. B. Lightfoot, quoted at Stephen Tomkins and Dan Graves, eds., "#103: Polycarp's Martyrdom," accessed July 19, 2021, Christian History Institute, https://christianhistoryinstitute.org/study/module/polycarp.

23. Fitzgerald, "Medical Men: Canonized Saints," 638.

24. "St. Theodula of Anazarbus in Cilicia," Antiochian Orthodox Christian Archdiocese of North America, accessed July 19 2021, http://ww1.antiochian.org/node/17489.

25. "St. Theodula of Anazarbus in Cilicia." Also see Per Einar Odden, trans., "Saint Theodula of Anazarbus and Three Companions (d. 303)," *Der katolske kirke*, October 25, 2104, http://www.katolsk.no/biografier/historisk/theo3anaz.

26. *Encyclopedia of the Early Church*, ed. Angelo Di Berardino, vol. 2 (New York: Oxford University Press, 1992), s.v. "Pantaleon." The section on Panteleimon relies heavily on Pattengale, "Benevolent Physicians," 134–35.

27. "Greatmartyr and Healer Panteleimon," Orthodox Church in America,, accessed July 19, 2021, https://oca.org/saints/lives/2000/07/27/102099-greatmartyr-and-healer-panteleimon.

28. "Greatmartyr and Healer Panteleimon."

29. Ignatius of Antioch to the Romans, section 4 in *The Early Christian Fathers: A Selection from the Writings of the Fathers from St. Clement of Rome to St. Athanasius*, trans. and ed. Henry Bettenson (London: Oxford University Press, 1956), 62.

30. Robert G. Clouse, Richard V. Pierard, and Edwin M. Yamauchi, *Two Kingdoms: The Church and Culture through the Ages* (Chicago: Moody, 1993), 46.

31. "Ignatius of Antioch: Earliest post-New Testament Martyr," *Christianity Today*, accessed July 19, 2021, https://www.christianitytoday.com/history/people/martyrs/ignatius-of-antioch.html.

32. Ignatius of Antioch to the Romans, section 5, in *A New Eusebius: Documents Illustrating the History of the Church to AD 337*, 2nd ed., ed. J. Stevenson, revised by W. H. C. Frend (London: SPCK, 1987), 12–13.

33. Eusebius, *HE*, 6.3.

34. Eusebius VI.3.

35. See Jerry Pattengale, "Self-Maiming: Why Many Have Lost More than the Pulse of Scripture," in *Is the Bible at Fault? How the Bible Has Been Misused to Justify Evil, Suffering, and Bizarre Behavior* (Franklin, TN: Worthy Books, 2018), especially 41–42.

36. John Foxe, *Foxe's Book of Martyrs* (Project Gutenberg, August 25, 2007), https://www.gutenberg.org/files/22400/22400-h/22400-h.htm.

37. Justin Martyr, cited at "Justin Martyr: Defender of the 'True Philosophy,'" *Christianity Today*, accessed July 19, 2021, https://www.christianitytoday.com/history/people/evangelistsandapologists/justin-martyr.html.

38. Justin Martyr, cited at "Justin Martyr."

39. Peter Brown, *The Cult of the Saints: Its Rise and Function in Latin Christianity* (Chicago: University of Chicago Press, 1981, 2015), 88.

40. Eusebius, *Ecclesiastical History*, IV xv.

41. Maximus of Taurin, sermon 12.1–2, translation from Robert Markus, *The End of Ancient Christianity* (Cambridge: Cambridge University Press, 1990), 143.

42. Foxe, *Actes and Monuments*, 1583 ed., bk. 1, 58, *Unabridged Acts and Monuments Online*, https://www.dhi.ac.uk/foxe/.

CHAPTER 4: WOMEN MARTYRS IN THE EARLY CHURCH

1. Christian Askeland, "Coptic Manuscripts and the Rise of Egyptian Christianity," Museum of the Bible, Oklahoma City, Oklahoma (November 16, 2015); accessed at https://youtu.be/KJDGOY6MCPA.

2. Evelyn Stagg and Frank Stagg, "Jesus and Women," *Christianity Today*, originally published in "Women in the Early Church," *Christian History*, no. 17 (1988), https://www.christianitytoday.com/history/issues/issue-17/jesus-and-women.html.

3. Matthew Henry comments on this passage in Luke 23: "Daughters of Jerusalem, weep not for me. Not that they were to be blamed for weeping for him, but rather commended; those hearts were hard indeed that were not affected with such sufferings of such a person; but they must not weep for him only (those were profitless tears that they shed for him), but rather let them weep for themselves and for their children, with an eye to the destruction that was coming upon Jerusalem, which some of them might live to see and share in the calamities of, or, at least, their children would, for whom they ought to be solicitous. Note, When with an eye of faith we behold Christ crucified we ought to weep, not for him, but for ourselves. We must

not be affected with the death of Christ as with the death of a common person whose calamity we pity, or of a common friend whom we are likely to part with. The death of Christ was a thing peculiar; it was his victory and triumph over his enemies; it was our deliverance, and the purchase of eternal life for us. And therefore let us weep, not for him, but for our own sins, and the sins of our children, that were the cause of his death; and weep for fear (such were the tears here prescribed) of the miseries we shall bring upon ourselves, if we slight his love, and reject his grace, as the Jewish nation did, which brought upon them the ruin here foretold." *Matthew Henry Commentary on the Whole Bible*, Luke 23, Bible Study Tools, accessed July 19, 2021, https://www.biblestudytools.com/commentaries/matthew-henry-complete/luke/23.html.

4. James A. Borland, "How Jesus Viewed and Valued Women," Crossway, March 8, 2017, https://www.crossway.org/articles/how-jesus-viewed-and-valued-women/.

5. Stagg and Stagg, "Jesus and Women."

6. Robert G. Clouse, Richard V. Pierard, and Edwin M. Yamauchi, *Two Kingdoms: The Church and Culture through the Ages* (Chicago: Moody, 1993), 52–53.

7. Following the approach of John Foxe, martyr accounts are included based on their acceptance or recognition by Christian communities, whether through contemporary ancient sources or later traditions—and are entered here as such. This is in the latter category. The wheel as a torture device was known through numerous ancient sources, such as Demosthenes, Aristophanes, and Plutarch.

8. The following account is based on a combination of these later accounts.

9. Carthage, modern Tunis (in Tunisia), is about the same distance from Alexandria (near Cairo) as Sicily is from Cyprus.

10. *Encyclopaedia Britannica*, s.v. "St. Catherine of Alexandria: Egyptian Martyr," accessed July 19, 2021, https://www.britannica.com/biography/Saint-Catherine-of-Alexandria.

11. "St. Catherine of Alexandria," *Catholic News Agency*, accessed July 19, 2021, https://www .catholicnewsagency.com/saint/st-catherine-of-alexandria-398. This Catholic site also states, "Devotees relished tales of her rejection of marriage, her rebuke to an emperor, and her decision to cleave to Christ even under threat of torture. Pope John Paul II restored the celebration of her memorial to the Roman Catholic calendar in 2002. Catherine's popularity as a figure of devotion, during an era of imaginative hagiography, has obscured the facts of her life. It is likely that she was of noble birth, a convert to Christianity, a virgin by choice (before the emergence of organized monasticism), and eventually a martyr for the faith. Accounts of Catherine's life also agree on the location where she was born, educated, and bore witness to her faith."

12. J. Cardinal Gibbons, Archbishop Baltimore, "Introduction to the Roman Martyrology," 1916, *Boston Catholic Journal*, http://www.boston-catholic-journal.com/roman-martyrology-complete -in-english-for-daily-reflection.htm.

13. "Catherine" at Mom.com, accessed June 2, 2022, https://mom.com/baby-names/girl/19936 /catherine.

14. Check for "Catherine," "Katherine," and "Delilah" at the website of the Social Security Administration at https://www.ssa.gov/cgi-bin/babyname.cgi.

15. Sebastian Brock, "Codex Sinaiticus Syriacus," Saint Catherine Foundation, accessed July 19, 2021, https://www.saintcatherinefoundation.org/codex-sinaiticus-syriacus.

16. Caroline Alexander, "Two of a Kind," review of *The Sisters of Sinai*, by Janet Soskice, *New York Times*, September 1, 2009, https://www.nytimes.com/2009/09/06/books/review/Alexander-t .html.

17. Jerry Pattengale et al, *The Book: The Narrative, History, and Impact of the Bible*, vol. 1, *Genesis to Ruth* (Washington DC: Museum of the Bible, 2017), 115.

18. Aziz S. Atiya, "The Monastery of St. Catherine and the Mount Sinai Expedition," *Proceedings of the American Philosophical Society* 96, no. 5 (October 15, 1952), 578–86.

19. "Manuscripts in St. Catherine's Monastery, Mount Sinai," Library of Congress, accessed July 19, 2021, https://www.loc.gov/collections/manuscripts-in-st-catherines-monastery-mount -sinai/about-this-collection/. These were recorded, filmed, and the list published in 1949 and 1950. Since then, various initiatives have discovered more, and ongoing work continues— including with the Museum of the Bible (which assisted the Eastern Orthodox Church, owner of the monastery, with a high digital scanner, 2017).

20. Clement of Alexandria, *Stromateis* 7.11. See also the discussion in Christian Cochini, *The Apostolic Origins of Priestly Celibacy*, trans. Nelly Marans (San Francisco: Ignatius Press, 1990), 66.

21. St. Asterius of Amasea (d. 410), quoted at "Euphemia, St.," Encyclopedia.com, accessed January 30, 2019, https://www.encyclopedia.com/religion/encyclopedias-almanacs-transcripts -and-maps/euphemia-st.

22. All citations of *The Acts of the Scillitan Martyrs* in this section are from Livius, *Acts of the Scillitan Martyrs*, Livius.org, last modified October 26, 2018, https://www.livius.org/sources /content/acts-of-the-scillitan-martyrs/translation/.

23. Livius, *Acts of the Scillitan Martyrs*.

24. Livius, *Acts of the Scillitan Martyrs*.

25. Tertullian, *The Passion of the Holy Martyrs Perpetua and Felicitas*, chap. 5, accessed July 20, 2021, http://www.tertullian.org/anf/anf03/anf03-54.htm.

26. *The Passion of Perpetua and Felicity*, trans. W. H. Shewring (London: 1931), "Saturus' Account," Medieval Sourcebook: St. Perpetua: *The Passion of Saints Perpetua and Felicity* 203, Internet History Sourcebooks Project, Fordham University, accessed July 20, 2021, https://sourcebooks.fordham.edu/source/perpetua.asp.

27. Perpetua, quoted at "Perpetua: High Society Believer," *Christianity Today*, accessed July 20, 2021, https://www.christianitytoday.com/history/people/martyrs/perpetua.html.

28. *The Passion of Saints Perpetua and Felicity* 203, "Perpetua's Account," https://sourcebooks .fordham.edu/source/perpetua.asp.

29. *Passion of Saints Perpetua and Felicity* 203, "Narrative of Martyrdom."

30. Tertullian, *Passion of the Holy Martyrs Perpetua and Felicitas*, chap 6, http://www.tertullian .org/anf/anf03/anf03-54.htm.

31. This represents a common hagiographic topos—a literary device indicating that later editors have added touches that appear in various accounts, such as beasts refusing to attack them.

32. Eusebius, *The History of the Church from Christ to Constantine* [*Ecclesiastical History*], trans. G. A. Williamson, ed. Andrew Louth, rev. ed. (1965; London: Penguin Books, 1989), 147.

33. Tertullian, *Acts of the Martyrs*, trans. S. Thelwall, chap. 2, accessed July 20, 2021, http://www .tertullian.org/anf/anf03/anf03-52.htm.

34. Eusebius, *History of the Church*.

35. John Foxe, *Actes and Monuments*, 1570 ed., bk. 1, 130. See *The Unabridged Acts and Monuments Online* (Digital Humanities Institute, 2011), https://www.dhi.ac.uk/foxe/.

36. This is adapted from Foxe, *Actes and Monuments*, 1570 ed., bk. 1, 130.

37. This is adapted from Foxe, *Actes and Monuments*, 1570 ed., bk. 1, 131.

38. This is adapted from Foxe, *Actes and Monuments*, 1570 ed., bk. 1, 131.

39. Foxe, *Actes and Monuments*, 1570 ed., bk. 1, 131.

40. Foxe, *Actes and Monuments*, 1570 ed., bk. 1, 132.

41. Foxe, *Actes and Monuments*, 1570 ed., bk. 1, 132.

42. These are the words of Agnes Smith Lewis, a great Victorian scholar aptly named after Agnes of Rome. The document that John the Recluse erases and writes over is none other than Syriac Sinaiticus, one of the world's earliest and most-complete copies of the Gospels—rediscovered by Agnes Lewis at St. Catherine's Monastery. Agnes Smith Lewis, *Select Narratives of Holy Women from the Syro-Antiochene or Sinai Palimpsest*, Studia Sinaitica 9 (London: C. J. Clay

and Sons and Cambridge University Press, 1900), p. v, https://archive.org/stream/selectnarratives00johnuoft#page/n7/mode/2up.

43. Her martyrology in the *Martyrologium Hieronymianum* records her death by fire, though a conflicting account records a beheading. The latter was sometimes a late edit which allowed for the creation of relics, or to account for relics already known.

44. Foxe, *Acts and Monuments*, 1570 ed., bk. 1, 85.

45. "Caecilia, St., Roman Lady," *Dictionary of Early Christian Biography*, eds. Henry Wace and William C. Piercy (London: 1911; Peabody, MA: Hendrickson: 1999), accessed July 20, 2021, Christian Classics Ethereal Library, https://www.ccel.org/ccel/wace/biodict.html?term=Caecilia,%20st.,%20Roman%20lady.

46. Foxe, *Acts and Monuments*, 1570 ed., bk. 1, 89.

47. John Chapman, "Dionysius of Alexandria," *Catholic Encyclopedia*, vol. 5 (New York: Robert Appleton, 1909), http://www.newadvent.org/cathen/05011a.htm.

48. C. H. Spurgeon, "Stephen's Martyrdom," *Metropolitan Tabernacle Pulpit*, vol. 13, sermon 740 (March 17, 1867); accessed at https://www.spurgeon.org/resource-library/sermons/stephens-martyrdom#flipbook/.

49. See the discussion of the Roman Colosseum in chapter 2, "The Great Persecutions."

50. *Church History*, bk. 6, chap. 5, trans. Arthur Cushman McGiffert (New York, 1890), New Advent, ed. Kevin Knight, accessed July 20, 2021, http://www.newadvent.org/fathers/250106.htm.

51. "John Huss: Pre-Reformation Reformer," *Christianity Today*, accessed July 20, 2022, https://www.christianitytoday.com/history/people/martyrs/john-huss.html; see also "Jan Hus: Incendiary Preacher of Prague," *Christianity Today*, originally published in *Christian History*, no. 68 (2000), https://www.christianitytoday.com/history/issues/issue-68/.

52. John Foxe, *Acts and Monuments*, Book 5 (1570), 764–65, *The Unabridged Acts and Monuments Online*; accessed at https://www.dhi.ac.uk/foxe/index.php.

CHAPTER 5: THE RISE OF ISLAM

1. For a summary of the territorial map of these kingdoms, see Philip Jenkins, "Persia's Christian Roots," *Anxious Bench* (blog), Patheos, May 15, 2005, https://www.patheos.com/blogs/anxiousbench/2015/03/persias-christian-roots/.

2. John Foxe, *Acts and Monuments*, 1576 ed., bk. 1, 125, and bk. 6, 711. See *The Unabridged Acts and Monuments Online* (Sheffield: Digital Humaniaites Institute, 2011), https://www.dhi.ac.uk/foxe/.

3. Bernard Lewis, *The Political Language of Islam* (Chicago: University of Chicago Press, 1991), 93.

4. Robert G. Clouse, Richard V. Pierard, and Edwin M. Yamauchi, *Two Kingdoms: The Church and Culture through the Ages* (Chicago: Moody, 1993), 137–38.

5. Michael Philip Penn, *Envisioning Islam: Syriac Christians and the Early Muslim World* (Philadelphia: University of Pennsylvania Press, 2015), 9–10.

6. Christian C. Sahner, *Christian Martyrs under Islam: Religious Violence and the Making of the Muslim World* (Princeton, NJ: Princeton University Press, 2018), 1, 3.

7. Sahner, *Christian Martyrs under Islam*, 1–2.

8. Sahner, *Christian Martyrs under Islam*, 1–7.

9. Foxe, *Acts and Monuments*, 1576 ed., bk. 3, 191.

10. Robert Louis Wilken, "Christianity Face to Face with Islam," *First Things*, January 2009, https://www.firstthings.com/article/2009/01/christianity-face-to-face-with-islam. Wilken is the William R. Kenan, Jr. Professor of the History of Christianity emeritus at the University of Virginia, an elected fellow of the American Academy of Arts and Sciences, past president of the American Academy of Religion, the North American Patristics Society, and the Academy of Catholic Theology.

11. George W. Bush, "'Islam is Peace' Says President," September 17, 2001, Islamic Center, Washington, DC, The White House, https://georgewbush-whitehouse.archives.gov/news /releases/2001/09/20010917-11.html.

12. Philip Jenkins, *The Lost History of Christianity: The Thousand-Year Golden Age of the Church in the Middle East, Africa, and Asia—and How It Died* (San Francisco: Harper One, 2008), 143.

13. Jenkins, *Lost History of Christianity*, 143–44.

14. Wilken, "Christianity Face to Face with Islam."

15. Philip Jenkins, *God's Continent: Christianity, Islam, and Europe's Religious Crisis* (New York: Oxford University Press, 2007), 1.

16. Riay Tatari Bakri, quoted at Tracy Wilkinson, "Islam's Claim on Spain," *Los Angeles Times*, January 18, 2005, https://www.latimes.com/archives/la-xpm-2005-jan-18-fg-granada18-story .html. Bakri is a Syrian-born imam at Madrid's Abu Bakr mosque.

17. Sahner, *Christian Martyrs under Islam*, 171.

18. The dating of the Quran (discussed below) also factors into the likelihood of the *hiraba* standard in the earliest phases of the *futūh*.

19. John Sanidopoulos, "Holy Hieromartyr Peter of Capitolias (+715)," Mystagogy Resource Center, October 4, 2017, https://www.johnsanidopoulos.com/2017/10/holy-hieromartyr-peter -of-capitolias-715.html.

20. There remains a debate on how early the Quran was involved in establishing practices; the standard Islamic story of the Quran's formation is that allegedly the archangel Gabriel revealed it to Muhammad in visions (AD 610 to 632). His companions compiled these, both through memory and written texts, and Muhammad's son-in-law Uthman and third great caliph (d. 656) created the standardized version. Although the supernatural and spiritual claims are separate matters for the textual researchers, many agree with this timing, and inscriptions at the Dome of the Rock and the Birmingham manuscript (including Carbon-14 texts) seem to attest to this earlier date. See Joseph E. B. Lumbard, "New Light on the History of the Quranic Text?" *Huff Post*, July 24, 2015, https://www.huffpost.com/entry/new-light-on-the -history_b_7864930. A whole school of revisionists dispute these, noting the earliest copy is in the next century. See Fred M. Donner, *Muhammad and the Believers: At the Origins of Islam* (London: Belknap Press of Harvard University Press, 2010). The dating of the Quran also becomes important for our assessment of *hiraba*'s enforcement.

21. Adriano Duque, "Claiming Martyrdom in the Episode of The Martyrs of Córdoba," *Collectanea Christiana Orientalia* 8 (2011), 34.

22. "The Life of St. John the Almsgiver," from *Three Byzantine Saints: Contemporary Biographies of St. Daniel the Stylite, St. Theodore of Sykeon and St. John the Almsgiver*, trans. Elizabeth Dawes (London: 1948), Internet History Sourcebooks Project, Fordham University, accessed July 21, 2021, https://sourcebooks.fordham.edu/basis/john-almsgiver.asp.

23. "Life of St. John the Almsgiver," chap. 13.

24. Zacharias of Jerusalem, *Patrologia Graeca*, ed. J. P. Migne, vol. 86.2, cols.:3227–34.

25. "Zacharias, Patriarch of Jerusalem," Encyclopedia.com, accessed July 21, 2021, https://www .encyclopedia.com/religion/encyclopedias-almanacs-transcripts-and-maps/zacharias-patriarch -jerusalem.

26. "Saint Sophronius, Patriarch of Jerusalem," Orthodox Church in America, accessed July 21, 2021, https://oca.org/saints/lives/2016/03/11/100777-st-sophronius-the-patriarch-of -jerusalem. With the bloodless Muslim conquest of AD 637, the Jews were allowed to worship again in Jerusalem after a 400-year prohibition.

27. Sahner, *Christian Martyrs under Islam*, 44.

28. John Sanidopoulos, "Synaxarion of the Holy Martyrs Andrew, John, Peter and Anthony of Syracuse," Mystagogy Resource Center, September 23, 2017, https://www.johnsanidopoulos .com/2017/09/synaxaarion-of-holy-martyrs-andrew-john.html.

29. Sanidopoulos, "Synaxarion of the Holy Martyrs Andrew, John, Peter and Anthony of Syracuse."

30. John L. Esposito, *Islam: The Straight Path*, 3rd ed. (New York: Oxford University Press, 1998), 34.

31. Kristin Romey, "Archaeologists Stumble across a Hoard of Gold," *National Geographic*, February 20, 2015, https://news.nationalgeographic.com/news/2015/02/150219-gold-hoard-coins-dinars -israel-fatimid-caesarea-archaeology/. These coins, now in Israel's National Museum, are from one of the twenty-three ships discovered in these breakwaters.

32. Ruth Schuster, "This Day in Jewish History 1009: The 'Mad Caliph' Destroys Jewish, Christian Sites in Fatimid Empire," *Haaretz*, October 18, 2016, https://www.haaretz.com /jewish/.premium-1009-the-mad-caliph-attacks-christian-sites-in-fatimid-empire-1.5450335.

33. For a simple overview of the church, see "Church of the Holy Sepulchre," Church of the Holy Sepulchre (website), accessed July 21, 2021, https://churchoftheholysepulchre.net/. The church has an uneven history—destroyed by the Persians (614), adapted in part for a mosque (ninth century), surviving a fire in the dome (966), the al-Hakim destruction, the Turkish occupation, Crusader occupation, Muslim re-conquest of Jerusalem (1187), earthquake damage (1927), and the fighting among Christian groups.

34. Peter Brown, cited in Jon Davies, *Death, Burial and Rebirth in the Religions of Antiquity* (London: Routledge, 1999), 191.

35. Davies, *Death, Burial and Rebirth*, 193.

36. Sahner, *Christian Martyrs under Islam*, 42.

37. Vahan M. Kurkjian, *A History of Armenia* (New York: Armenian General Benevolent Union of America, 1958; Indo-European Publishing, 2018), 276.

38. Nina Garsoïan, "The Arab Invasions and the Rise of the Bagratuni (640–884)," in *The Armenian People from Ancient to Modern Times: The Dynastic Periods: From Antiquity to the Fourteenth Century*, vol. 1, ed. Richard G. Hovannisian (New York: St. Martin's Press, 1997), 133.

39. "St. Vahan of Goghtn," Armenian Church: Eastern Diocese of America, accessed July 21, 2021, https://armenianchurch.us/the-saints/st-vahan-of-goghtn/.

40. Sahner, *Christian Martyrs under Islam* (2018), 44.

41. Adapted from Charlotte Allen, "Christian Martyrs to Islam, Past and Present," *Wall Street Journal* (May 22, 2013).

42. *Free Library*, s.v. "Obscure Text, Illuminating Conversation: Reading The Martyrdom of 'Abd al -Masih (Qays al-Ghassani)," para. 3–4, originally published in Mark N. Swanson, *Currents in Theology and Mission* 35 (2008): 374–81, accessed July 21, 2021, https://www.thefreelibrary .com/Obscure+text,+illuminating+conversation:+reading+The+Martyrdom+of. . .-a0186594231.

43. *Free Library*, "Obscure Text," para. 18.

44. *Free Library*, "Obscure Text," para. 20.

45. *Free Library*, "Obscure Text," para. 21.

46. *Free Library*, "Obscure Text," para. 22.

47. *Free Library*, "Obscure Text," commentary point 5.

48. *Free Library*, "Obscure Text," para. 23.

49. See Sahner, *Christian Martyrs under Islam*, 49–53. Sahner provides an excellent summary of this account, and the various nuances and possible interpretations of the events. This section relies heavily on his detailed assessment for its summary.

50. Amir Harrak, "Piecing Together the Fragmentary Account of the Martyrdom of Cyrus of Harrān," *Analecta Bollandiana* 121, no. 2 (2003): 297–328.

51. Michael Philip Penn, *Envisioning Islam: Syriac Christians and the Early Muslim World* (Philadelphia: University of Pennsylvania Press, 2015), 174–76. *The Life of Cyrus* (London: Religious Tract Society, 1847) in the British Library records his martyrology.

52. Roy Jackson, *What Is Islamic Philosophy?* (New York: Routledge, 2014), 173.

53. Asma Afsaruddin, "Islamist Militants Carry Out Terror, Not Jihad," *Religion News Service*, June 9, 2017, https://religionnews.com/2017/06/09/islamist-militants-carry-out-terror-not-jihad/.

54. Jane Peters, "Christian Martyrs in the First Islamic States," review of *Christian Martyrs under Islam: Religious Violence and the Making of the Muslim World*, by Christian C. Sahner, Russell Kirk Center, November 4, 2018, https://kirkcenter.org/reviews/christian-martyrs-in-the-first -islamic-states/.

55. Afsaruddin, "Islamist Militants Carry Out Terror."

56. Sahner, *Christian Martyrs under Islam*, 101–5.

57. Sahner, *Christian Martyrs under Islam*, 147.

58. Duque, "Claiming Martyrdom in the Episode of The Martyrs of Córdoba," 28. Duque makes the salient point that hagiographers would often "reinterpret Byzantine hagiographic material" to present martyrdoms under Islam (like at Cordoba) "as a rallying declaration of religious orthodoxy" (Duque, 48).

59. Sahner, *Christian Martyrs under Islam*, 147.

60. Sahner, *Christian Martyrs under Islam*, 148.

61. Sahner, *Christian Martyrs under Islam*, 148.

62. Sahner, *Christian Martyrs under Islam*, 150–51.

63. Christian C. Sahner, "Swimming against the Current: Muslim Conversion to Christianity in the Early Islamic Period," *Journal of the American Oriental Society* 136, no. 2 (April–June 2016): 276, https://www.academia.edu/28388644/_2016_Swimming_against_the_Current_Muslim _Conversion_to_Christianity_in_the_Early_Islamic_Period.

64. World History Encyclopedia, s.v. "Etchmiadzin Cathedral," by James Blake Wiener, June 8, 2018, https://www.ancient.eu/Etchmiadzin_Cathedral/.

65. Steven Gertz, "How Armenia 'Invented' Christendom," *Christianity Today*, originally published in "The Council of Nicaea: Debating Jesus' Divinity," *Christian History*, no. 85 (2005), https:// www.christianitytoday.com/history/issues/issue-85/how-armenia-invented-christendom.html.

66. See "Agathangelos," Livius.org, last modified October 12, 2020, https://www.livius.org/sources /content/agathangelos/. This is a useful site that collects texts in the public domain—the host, Bill Thayer, posts such a mission as well as no claims of being an authority on the texts collected. The preceding text is from Agathangelos, *History of St. Gregory and the Conversion of Armenia*, books 1 and 2 (1.21–2.20).

67. St. Gregory the Illuminator (d. AD 330), cited in Agathangelos, *History of St. Gregory and the Conversion of Armenia* 2.25, mid-fifth century.

68. Laurence E. Browne calls the Islamic conquests an "empty conquest" because they had a "bankrupt" faith, and "From the fifteenth century Islam had no religious contribution to give to the world." In Browne, *The Eclipse of Christianity in Asia* (Cambridge: Cambridge University Press, 1933; New York: Howard Fertig, 1967). Cited in Philip Jenkins, *The Lost History of Christianity: The Thousand-Year Golden Age of the Church in the Middle East, Africa, and Asia— and How It Died* (San Francisco: Harper One, 2008), 258. Jenkins puts such statements in their historic context, and here Browne's minority position among modern scholars. He calls Browne's view "a then-common Western view of Islam as a spiritual and cultural dead end" (Jenkins, 258).

69. Adapted from John Foxe, *Actes and Monuments*, 1576 ed, bk. 2, 148. See *The Unabridged Acts and Monuments Online* (Sheffield: Digital Humanities Institute, 2011), https://www.dhi.ac.uk /foxe/.

SECTION TWO: THE LATE MIDDLE AGES THROUGH THE KING JAMES BIBLE (1611)

1. Lawrence H. Schiffman and Jerry Pattengale, eds., *The World's Greatest Book: The Story of How the Bible Came to Be* (Franklin, TN: Worthy, 2017), 196. This represents the Tyndale account

in the earliest version of Foxe's *Acts and Monuments*, including his final statement that also appears in various woodcuts.

2. John Foxe, *Foxe's Book of Martyrs*, XII, "The Life and Story of the True Servant and Martyr of God: William Tyndale."

3. John C. Olin, ed., *Christian Humanism and the Reformation: Selected Writings of Erasmus*, 3rd ed. (New York: Fordham University Press, 1987), 97.

4. Patrick Collinson, *This England: Essays on the English Nation and Commonwealth in the Sixteenth Century* (Manchester: Manchester University Press, 2011).

5. Schiffman and Pattengale, *World's Greatest Book*, 192.

CHAPTER 6: CHRISTIANS MARTYRED AT DIVERSE HANDS

1. Author unknown, but likely a Christian apologist of the late second century as *Mathetes* is used in the text (*disciple* in Greek). The last surviving copy of this text was lost in a fire in Strasbourg in 1870.

2. Nestorianism takes it name from Nestorius, a fifth-century patriarch of Constantinople. He taught that Christ actually came to earth as two separate persons—both divine and human (as opposed to the orthodox doctrine of one person who is simultaneously wholly human and wholly divine). Monophysitism was also deemed heretical because this sixth-century doctrine taught only a divine nature. The word comes from the Greek words *monos* (*alone*, or in this case, *one*) and *physis* (meaning *nature* in this usage). The heretical doctrine of Monothelitism surfaced in the late seventh century, ironically as an attempt to unify the earlier factions over Christ's nature—by focusing on "one will." The easiest way to digest these various views is to study them alongside the Nicene Creed, the simplest and widest-held representation of orthodoxy.

3. Earle E. Cairns, *Christianity through the Centuries: A History of the Christian Church* (Grand Rapids, MI: Zondervan, 1954, 1967), 247.

4. John Foxe, *Foxe's Book of Martyrs*, ed. William Byron Forbush (Peabody, MA: Hendrickson, 2004, 2016), 57.

5. Cairns, *Christianity through the Centuries*, 247.

6. John Foxe, "Persecutions from about the Middle of the Fifth, to the Conclusion of the Seventh Century," *Foxe's Book of Martyrs*, ed. William Byron Forbush, Bible Study Tools, https://www .biblestudytools.com/history/foxs-book-of-martyrs/persecutions-from-about-the-middle-of-the -fifth-to-the-conclusion-of-the-seventh-century.html.

7. Evagrius Scholasticus, *Ecclesiastical History: A History of the Church in Six Books, from AD 431 to AD 594*, trans. E. Walford (1846), bk. 2, chap. 8, The Tertullian Project, http://www.tertullian .org/fathers/evagrius_2_book2.htm.

8. Foxe, "Persecutions from about the Middle of the Fifth," Bible Study Tools.

9. Foxe, "Persecutions from about the Middle of the Fifth," Bible Study Tools.

10. Pope Pius VII, *Diu Satis* (1800), Papal Encyclicals Online, https://www.papalencyclicals.net /pius07/p7diusat.htm.

11. Foxe, "Persecutions from about the Middle of the Fifth," Bible Study Tools.

12. "Saint Killian," CatholicSaints.Info, last updated July 4, 2020, https://catholicsaints.info/saint -killian.

13. This is a legend with many variations. See Matthew Sewell, "Thor, St. Boniface, and the Origin of the Christmas Tree," ChurchPOP, December 24, 2014, originally posted on Mountain Catholic, https://www.churchpop.com/2014/12/24/thor-st-boniface-and-the-origin-of-the -christmas-tree/.

14. Fabian Bruskewitz, "The Martyrdom of St. Boniface," Catholic Exchange, February 15, 2007, https://catholicexchange.com/the-martyrdom-of-st-boniface.

15. Foxe, "Persecutions from the Early Part of the Eighth, to Near the Conclusion of the Tenth Century," *Foxe's Book of Martyrs*, ed. William Byron Forbush, Bible Study Tools, https://www.biblestudytools.com/history/foxs-book-of-martyrs/persecutions-from-the-early-part-of-the-eighth-to-near-the-conclusion-of-the-tenth-century.html.

16. Foxe, "Persecutions from the Early Part of the Eighth."

17. Michael Swanton, trans., ed., *Anglo-Saxon Chronicle* (New York: Routledge, 1998), 142. Italics in the original.

18. John Foxe, "Persecutions in the Eleventh Century," *Foxe's Book of Martyrs*, ed. William Byron Forbush, Bible Study Tools, https://www.biblestudytools.com/history/foxs-book-of-martyrs/persecutions-in-the-eleventh-century.html.

19. Alban Butler, *The Lives of the Fathers, Martyrs, and Other Principal Saints*, vo. 2, ed. F. C. Husenbeth (London: Henry, 1857) 391, https://books.google.com/books?id=DosEAAAAQAAJ&pg=PA391&dq=gerard+chonad&hl=en&newbks=1&newbks_redir=0&sa=X&ved=2ahUKEwiikpLA5uflAhXkmq0KHQjMBHQQ6AEwAHoECAIQAg#v=onepage&q=gerard%20chonad&f=false.

20. Butler, *Lives of the Saints*, 392.

21. John Foxe. Accessed at https://www.biblestudytools.com/history/foxs-book-of-martyrs/persecutions-in-the-eleventh-century.html.

22. Butler, *Lives of the Saints*, 392.

23. Francis Mershman, "St. Stanislaus of Cracow," *Catholic Encyclopedia*, vol. 14 (New York: Robert Appleton, 1912), http://www.newadvent.org/cathen/14246a.htm.

24. *Encyclopaedia Britannica*, s.v. "Saint Stanislaus of Kraków," (April 7, 2019), https://www.britannica.com/biography/Saint-Stanislaus-of-Krakow.

25. John Foxe. Accessed at https://www.biblestudytools.com/history/foxs-book-of-martyrs/persecutions-in-the-eleventh-century.html.

26. "St. Stanislaus," Catholic News Agency, feast day April 11; accessed at https://www.catholicnewsagency.com/saint/st-stanislaus-433.

27. "Peter Waldo," *Encyclopedia of World Biography*, Encyclopedia.com, updated June 27, 2018, https://www.encyclopedia.com/people/philosophy-and-religion/protestant-christianity-biographies/peter-waldo. The name "Peter" was added to Valdes's name around 1368 to place in ilk of the disciple Peter.

28. John Foxe. Accessed at https://www.biblestudytools.com/history/foxs-book-of-martyrs/an-account-of-the-persecutions-of-calabria.html.

29. John Foxe. Accessed at https://www.biblestudytools.com/history/foxs-book-of-martyrs/an-account-of-the-persecutions-of-calabria.html.

30. John Foxe. Accessed at https://www.biblestudytools.com/history/foxs-book-of-martyrs/an-account-of-the-persecutions-of-calabria.html.

31. John Foxe. Accessed at https://www.biblestudytools.com/history/foxs-book-of-martyrs/an-account-of-the-persecutions-of-calabria.html.

32. John D. Hannah, *Invitation to Church History: World* (Grand Rapids, MI: Kregel Academic, 2018), 257.

33. A helpful discussion of each of these as well as Milton's biography and the sonnet "On the Late Massacre in Piedmont," which follows, can be found at the website for the Poetry Foundation: https://www.poetryfoundation.org/poets/john-milton.

34. Anonymous, *Chronicle* (ca. 1218), translated by James Harvey Robinson in *Readings in European History* (1905). Adapted, modernized, introduced, and prepared by Dan Graves. The first sentence was corrected for this publication ("am not" replacing "not not"). "Module 209: Waldo Sought a Truer Faith," Christian History Institute, https://christianhistoryinstitute.org/study/module/waldo-sought-a-truer-faith.

35. Jerry Pattengale, *Inexplicable: How Christianity Spread to the Ends of the Earth* (Tustin, CA: Trilogy, 2020), 55 (draft).

36. For a bulleted overview, see Mahanaim Cyber College, "Lecture 42: Albigensians," accessed January 26, 2022, http://en.mahanaim.org/NBoard/DB/text/Upload/130561946756_0.pdf.

37. Jerry Pattengale, ed., *A History of World Civilizations from a Christian Perspective* (unpublished manuscript), 419.

38. Nils Visser, "A Church of Wolves," *Medieval Warfare* 3, no. 4 (2013): 26–33.

39. John McManners, ed., *The Oxford Illustrated History of Christianity* (Oxford: Oxford University Press, 1990), 214.

40. Joseph Stevenson, trans., *The History of William of Newburgh* in *The Church Historians of England*, vol 4, part 2 (London: Seeleys, 1856), chap. 13.

41. John Foxe, *Foxe's Book of Martyrs*. Accessed at https://www.biblestudytools.com/history/foxs-book-of-martyrs/persecutions-of-the-albigenses.html.

42. See Don S. Armentrout and Robert Boak Slocum, eds., "Ecclesia," *An Episcopal Dictionary of the Church, A User Friendly Reference for Episcopalians* (New York, NY: Church Publishing Incorporated). Accessed at https://episcopalchurch.org/library/glossary/ecclesia.

43. Thieleman J. van Braght, *Martyrs Mirror*, trans. Joseph F. Sohm (1660), "Author's Invocation," Christian Classics Ethereal Library, https://ccel.org/ccel/vanbraght/mirror/mirror.ii.iv.html.

44. John Foxe, accessed at https://www.biblestudytools.com/history/foxs-book-of-martyrs/an-account-of-the-persecutions-in-venice.html.

CHAPTER 7: THE CHRISTIAN CRUSADES—A NEW TYPE OF MARTYR

1. Bernard of Clairvaux, quoted at Stephen Miller, "The Crusades: A Gallery of Martial Monks and Holy Kings," *Christianity Today*, originally published in "The Crusades," *Christian History*, no. 40 (1993), https://www.christianitytoday.com/history/issues/issue-40/crusades-gallery-of-martial-monks-holy-kings.html.

2. John Foxe and The Voice of the Martyrs, *Foxe: Voices of the Martyrs* (Bartlesville, OK: VOM Books, 2007, revised 2013), 18. It is of interest for our current project that the three recent books representing *The Acts and Monuments* in accessible abridged form skirt the Crusades. The above book commits only one-and-a-half pages to them. The otherwise wonderful books by Hendrickson Christian Classics (2003) and Kregel (2016) do not cover the Crusades other than those against the Waldenses and the Albigenses.

3. Muhammad ibn-Abdullah, quoted in Harold Kasimow and Alan Race, eds., *Pope Francis and Interreligious Dialogue: Religious Thinkers Engage with Recent Papal Initiatives* (Cham, Switzerland: Springer International, 2018), 150.

4. Nabeel A. Qureshi, *No God but One: Allah or Jesus? A Former Muslim Investigates the Evidence for Islam and Christianity* (Grand Rapids, MI: Zondervan, 2016), 130.

5. August C. Krey, *The First Crusade: The Accounts of Eyewitnesses and Participants* (Princeton: 1921), quoted in "Medieval Sourcebook, Urban II (1088–1099): Speech at Council of Clermont, 1095, Five Versions of the Speech," Fordham University website, accessed January 4, 2022, https://sourcebooks.fordham.edu/source/urban2-5vers.asp. For Baldric's volume see Steven Biddlecombe, ed., *The Historia Ierosolimitana of Baldric of Bourgueil* (Woodbridge, Suffolk: Boydell and Brewer, 2014).

6. Aristakes (recorded by Sibṭ ibn al-Jawzi), cited by Andrew Wilson in "The Seljuk Turks," Iran: The World's First Superpower, accessed January 4, 2022, http://www.the-persians.co.uk/seljuqs1.htm. Also quoted in John Julius Norwich, *Byzantium: The Apogee* (New York: Viking, 1991), 342–43.

7. The Mongols sacked Baghdad in 1258, and the Abassid Caliphate moved its capital to Cairo.

8. There remains considerable discussion on what constitutes a martyr during a crusade. See, for instance, Caroline Smith, "Martyrdom and Crusading in the Thirteenth Century: Remembering the Dead of Louis IX's Crusades," *Al-Masāq Islam and the Medieval Mediterranean* 15, no. 2 (September 2003), 189–196, https://doi.org/10.1080/0950311032000117485.

9. John D. Hannah, *Invitation to Church History: World* (Grand Rapids, MI: Kregel Publications, 2018), 218.

10. Robert G. Clouse, Richard V. Pierard, and Edwin M. Yamauchi, *Two Kingdoms: The Church and Culture through the Ages* (Chicago: Moody, 1993), 137.

11. The Mosque-Cathedral of Córdoba may have been a pagan temple to the Roman god Janus before it was a church.

12. Bernard of Clairvaux, quoted at Michael Gervers, "The Fighting Monks," *Christianity Today*, originally published in "The Crusades," *Christian History*, no. 40 (1993), https://www .christianitytoday.com/history/issues/issue-40/fighting-monks.html.

13. Jerry Pattengale, *Inexplicable: How Christianity Spread to the Ends of the Earth* (Tustin, CA: Trilogy, 2019), 68. There were various papal uses of indulgences and ways permitted to earn them, but these are primarily the ones pertaining to the Crusades.

14. Quoted in Pattengale, *Inexplicable*, 130. Bernard cites Romans 13:4 as his proof text.

15. Jerry Pattengale, *Is the Bible at Fault?: How the Bible Has Been Misused to Justify Evil, Suffering, and Bizarre Behavior* (Franklin, TN: Worthy, 2018), 159–176.

16. Kate Connolly, "Pope Says Sorry for Crusaders' Rampage in 1204," *The Telegraph*, June 30, 2004, https://www.telegraph.co.uk/news/worldnews/europe/italy/1465857/Pope-says-sorry-for -crusaders-rampage-in-1204.html.

17. Adelle Banks, "Campus Crusade for Christ Changes Name to 'Cru'; Keeps Evangelical Mission," *Washington Post*, July 20, 2011, https://www.washingtonpost.com/local/campus -crusade-for-christ-changes-name-to-cru-keeps-evangelical-mission/2011/07/20/gIQA54PMQI _story.html?utm_term=.97922663e812. See also David C. Mahan and C. Donald Smedley, "Parachurch Organizations: University Ministry and the Evangelical Mind," in *The State of the Evangelical Mind: Reflections on the Past, Prospects for the Future*, ed. Todd C. Ream, Jerry Pattengale, and Christopher J. Devers (Downers Grove, IL: IVP Academic, 2018), 55–99. During the American attempts to protect the citizens of Iraq and Afghanistan from Muslim terrorists in the twenty-first century, groups such as the Arab independence movement and Pan-Islamism movement curiously criticized these as modern "crusades."

18. For another theory on the impetus for this crusade based on Eastern sources placing it more squarely in Constantinople, see Peter Frankopan, *The First Crusade: The Call from the East* (Cambridge, MA: Belknap, 2012). He also concludes that the Eastern leaders never recovered prominence after the sack of Jerusalem and the shift of power, perceived or real, to Rome.

19. Fulcher de Chartres, *Chronicles of the First Crusade*, trans. M. E. McGinty (Philadelphia: University of Pennsylvania Press, 1941), 15–17.

20. Diarmaid MacCulloch, *Christianity: The First Three Thousand Years* (New York: Viking Penguin, 2010), 384.

21. Charles Warren Hollister et al., *Medieval Europe: A Short Sourcebook*, 2nd ed. (New York: McGraw-Hill), 189.

22. Medieval Sourcebook, "Urban II (1088–1099): Speech at Council of Clermont, 1095, Five Versions of the Speech," Internet History Sourcebooks Project, Fordham University, accessed January 5, 2022,accessed February 2, 2022, https://sourcebooks.fordham.edu/source/urban2 -5vers.asp.

23. J. Arthur McFall, "First Crusade: People's Crusade," Historynet, originally published in *Military History*, February 1998, https://www.historynet.com/first-crusade-peoples-crusade .htm.

24. John George Edgar, *The Crusades and the Crusaders* (Boston: Ticknor and Fields, 1860), 32.

25. Andrew Knighton, "Twelve Battles That Defined the Crusades," War History Online, February 11, 2016, https://www.warhistoryonline.com/medieval/12-battles-definedcrusades.html.

26. Louis Bréhier, "Peter the Hermit," *Catholic Encyclopedia*, vol. 11 (New York: Robert Appleton, 1911), http://www.newadvent.org/cathen/11775b.htm.

27. Hollister, *Medieval Europe*, 189.
28. Jerry Pattengale, background text for "Part 2: Heroines and Heroes," in the TV series *Inexplicable: How Christianity Spread to the Ends of the Earth* (TBN, 2020 State of Faith Project, 2020).
29. Qureshi, *No God but One*, 131.
30. Much of the Crusades section is adapted from Jerry Pattengale, ed., *A History of World Civilizations from a Christian Perspective* (unpublished manuscript).
31. Hollister et al., *Medieval Europe*, 129.
32. Bernard of Clairvaux, quoted in Pattengale, *Inexplicable*, 130. Bernard cites Romans 13:4 as his proof text.
33. Francesco Gabrieli, *Arab Historians of the Crusades*, trans. E. J. Costello (New York: University of California Press, 1989), 138.
34. Adapted from John Carey, ed., *Eyewitness to History* (Cambridge, MA: Harvard University Press, 1988), 36–37. Some of the Ottoman and later sources use "Mussulman" while referring to a Muslim.
35. Pattengale, *Is the Bible at Fault?*, 159–176.
36. James Brundage, *The Crusades: A Documentary Survey* (Milwaukee, WI: Marquette University Press, 1962), 213.
37. Steven Runcimen, "The Children's Crusade," *Christianity Today*, originally published in *Christian History* (1993), https://www.christianitytoday.com/history/issues/issue-40/childrens -crusade.html. The article is a summary from the magazine editors from Steven Runcimen, *A History of the Crusades*, 3 vols. (Cambridge, England: University Press, 1950–1954).
38. Thomas F. Madden, *The New Concise History of the Crusades*, rev. ed. (Lanham, MD: Rowman and Littlefield, 2005), 181.
39. Baibars, modernized in Qureshi, *No God but One*, 129. Following Qureshi, I further modified a few words to help update the translation.
40. John Foxe, accessed at https://www.biblestudytools.com/history/foxs-book-of-martyrs /persecutions-from-the-early-part-of-the-eighth-to-near-the-conclusion-of-the-tenth -century.html.

CHAPTER 8: THE PERSECUTIONS IN BOHEMIA

1. Martin Luther, quoted at "John Huss: Pre-Reformation Preacher," *Christianity Today*, accessed February 4, 2022, https://www.christianitytoday.com/history/people/martyrs/john-huss.html.
2. See Murray L. Wagner, *Petr Chelčický: A Radical Separatist in Hussite Bohemia* (Scottdale, PA: Herald Press, 1983).
3. "Ludmila (859–920)," *Women in World History: A Biographical Encyclopedia*, Encyclopedia.com, updated January 24, 2022, https://www.encyclopedia.com/women/encyclopedias-almanacs -transcripts-and-maps/ludmila-859-920.
4. "Ludmila (859–920)," Encyclopedia.com.
5. Rupert Christiansen, "The Story behind the Carol: Good King Wenceslas," *Telegraph*, December 14, 2007, https://www.telegraph.co.uk/culture/music/3674124/The-story-behind -the-carol-Good-King-Wenceslas.html.
6. Tom Manoff, "Wenceslas: A Goodhearted King and His Popular Carol," *All Things Considered*, NPR, December 22, 2011), https://www.npr.org/2011/12/22/144082845/wenceslas-a -goodhearted-king-and-his-popular-carol.
7. Elesha Coffman, "Jan Hus: Did You Know?," *Christianity Today*, originally published in "Jan Hus: Incendiary Preacher of Prague," *Christian History*, no. 68 (2000), https://www .christianitytoday.com/history/issues/issue-68/jan-hus-did-you-know.html.
8. Herbert B. Workman and R. Martin Pope, ed., *The Letters of Jon Hus* (London: Hodder and Stoughton, 1904), 90, https://oll.libertyfund.org/titles/huss-the-letters-of-john-hus.

9. Workman and Pope, eds., *The Letters of Jon Hus*, 202.

10. Thomas A. Fudge, "To Build a Fire," Christian History Institute, originally published in "Jan Hus: Incendiary Preacher of Prague," *Christian History*, no. 68 (2000), https://www .christianitytoday.com/history/issues/issue-68/to-build-fire.html.

11. "Today in History: Jan Hus Burned at the Stake 600 Years Ago," *People's World*, July 6, 2015, https://www.peoplesworld.org/article/today-in-history-jan-hus-burned-at-the-stake-600-years -ago/.

12. "John Huss: Pre-Reformation Reformer," *Christianity Today*, accessed July 20, 2022, https://www.christianitytoday.com/history/people/martyrs/john-huss.html.

13. This is from the Forbush edition of *Foxe's Book of Martyrs* (pages 188–89), and paragraph breaks and some minor wording changes have been made for the convenience of the modern audience.

14. Forbush, ed., *Foxe's Book of Martyrs*, 190.

15. "Today in History: Jan Hus," *People's World*.

16. Forbush, ed., *Foxe's Book of Martyrs*, 191.

17. Forbush, ed., *Foxe's Book of Martyrs*, 191.

18. Forbush, ed., *Foxe's Book of Martyrs*, 191–92.

19. "The Moravians and Their Hymns," Christian History Institute, originally published in *Christian History*, no. 1 (1982), https://christianhistoryinstitute.org/magazine/article/moravians -and-hymns.

20. "Count Zinzendorf, 1700–1760," STEM Publishing, accessed January 10, 2022, https://www .stempublishing.com/hymns/biographies/zinzendorf.html.

21. *Liturgy and Hymns of the Moravian Church or Unitas Fratrum* (London: Moravian Publication Office, 1903), https://archive.org/stream/liturgyandhymns00unknuoft/liturgyandhymns 00unknuoft_djvu.txt. Also see the revised edition, 1908, at https://openlibrary.org/books /OL7066720M/Liturgy_and_hymns_of_the_Moravian_Church_or_Unitas_Fratrum.

22. Frieda Looser, "The Wanderer," *Christianity Today*, originally published in "Jan Hus: Incendiary Preacher of Prague," *Christian History*, no. 68 (2000), https://www.christianitytoday .com/history/issues/issue-68/wanderer.html.

23. Renee Neu Watkins, "The Death of Jerome of Prague: Divergent Views," *Speculum* 42, no. 1 (January 1967): 104–29, https://doi.org/10.2307/2856103.

24. John Foxe, *Acts and Monuments* (New York: Robert Carter, 1855), 318.

25. John Foxe. Accessed at https://www.biblestudytools.com/history/foxs-book-of-martyrs /persecution-of-zisca.html.

26. William Byron Forbush, ed., *Foxe's Book of Martyrs* (Peabody, MA: Hendrickson, 2004), 183–84.

27. Forbush, ed., *Foxe's Book of Martyrs*, 186.

28. Forbush, ed., *Foxe's Book of Martyrs*, 187.

29. Forbush, ed., *Foxe's Book of Martyrs*, 188.

30. Forbush, ed., *Foxe's Book of Martyrs*, 188–89.

31. Forbush, ed., *Foxe's Book of Martyrs*, 189.

32. Forbush, ed., *Foxe's Book of Martyrs*, 189.

33. Forbush, ed., *Foxe's Book of Martyrs*, 190.

34. Forbush, ed., *Foxe's Book of Martyrs*, 190–91.

35. John Foxe, *Foxe's Book of Martyrs*, ed. Paul L. Maier and R. C. Linnenkugel, rev. ed. (Grand Rapids, MI: Kregel, 2016), 179–80.

36. Forbush, ed., *Foxe's Book of Martyrs*, 191–98. Emphasis added.

37. Hus, *The Letters of John Huss*, Herbert Brook Workman, ed., Robert Martin Pope, trans. (1904), https://oll.libertyfund.org/title/huss-the-letters-of-john-huss#lf1328 _head_033.

CHAPTER 9: THE PERSECUTION OF EARLY EUROPEAN REFORMERS

1. Though St. Jerome is credited with the Vulgate translation, it's not clear who finished the New Testament. And although the "official" Bible of the Catholic Church warrants a complex answer, the Vulgate carried that distinction for a time, and also became the basis for various translations for other languages (instead of the original Hebrew and Greek texts). For example, Wycliffe used it for his English translation. Likewise, in 1230 it was the version for the Parisian Bible (or Paris Bibles) that served as the standard text for college students during the rise of the universities. It was also the basis of the Confraternity Bible, produced in the mid-twentieth century for a fluid English reading. Eventually, the Catholic Church published a Bible translated from the Hebrew and Greek texts, the New American Bible, in 1970 (in response to Pope Pius XII's 1943 encyclical *Divino afflante Spiritu*).

2. Jerry Pattengale, *Is the Bible at Fault?: How the Bible Has Been Misused to Justify Evil, Suffering, and Bizarre Behavior* (Franklin, TN: Worthy, 2018).

3. Stephen J. Nichols, *The Reformation: How a Monk and a Mallet Changed the World* (Wheaton, IL: Crossway Books, 2007), 17.

4. See the works of Andrew Atherstone (Wycliffe Hall, Oxford University) for an engaging and responsible history of various evangelical groups, especially those linked to English heritage: e.g., Andrew Atherstone and David Ceri Jones, eds., *The Routledge Research Companion to the History of Evangelicalism* (New York: Routledge, 2018) and Andrew Atherstone and John Maiden, eds., *Evangelicalism and the Church of England in the Twentieth Century: Reform, Resistance and Renewal* (Woodbridge, Suffolk, UK: Boydell Press, 2014).

5. John Foxe, accessed at https://www.biblestudytools.com/history/foxs-book-of-martyrs/an -account-of-the-persecutions-in-the-valleys-of-piedmont-in-the-seventeenth-century.html.

6. Jerry Pattengale, *Inexplicable: How Christianity Spread to the Ends of the Earth* (Tustin, CA: Trilogy, 2020), 87. Also, for a tally of the more than 2,200 languages under translation into a vernacular Bible, see "Why Bible Translation?" Wycliffe Bible Translators, September 2021, https://www.wycliffe.org/about/why.

7. John Wycliffe, "On the Pastoral Office," trans. Ford Lewis Battles in *Advocates of Reform from Wyclif to Erasmus*, ed. Matthew Spinka, Library of Christian Classics, vol. 14 (Philadelphia: Westminster Press, 1953), 49–51. The Middle English version of this quote is in *Wyclif: Select English Writings*, ed. Herbert E. Winn (London: Oxford University Press, 1929).

8. "From the Archives: Wycliffe Causes Controversy over Eucharist," *Christianity Today*, originally published in "John Wycliffe: Bible Translator," *Christian History*, no. 3 (1983); https://www .christianitytoday.com/history/issues/issue-3/from-archives-wycliffe-causes-controversy-over -eucharist.html. Wycliffe was attacking the Catholic teaching of "transubstantiation."

9. William Wordsworth, "Wicliffe," *The Complete Poetic Works of William Wordsworth*, ed. Henry Reed (1848).

10. Thomas Fuller, *The Church History of Britain* (1837). For a lay-directed video on this, see "John Wycliffe : Worldwide Witness," Lineage Journey, episode 16, May 3, 2017, video, 3:06 minutes. Accessed at https://www.youtube.com/watch?v=0nSxt4tBhTM.

11. Dan Graves, "William Sawtrey, 1st Lollard Martyr," Christianity.com, May 3, 2010, https://www.christianity.com/church/church-history/timeline/1201-1500/william-sawtrey-1st -lollard-martyr-11629873.html.

12. Khen Lim, "The First Lollard to Burn," Lux Mundi , February 26, 2017, https://hosannaefcluxmundi.blogspot.com/2017/02/on-day-february-26-1401.html.

13. Salvatore Luzio, "Degradation," *Catholic Encyclopedia*, vol. 4 (New York: Robert Appleton Company, 1908), www.newadvent.org/cathen/04677c.htm. Vestments included the amice (hood), alb (long white robe), cincture (girdle), maniple (yard-long band on left arm), stole (strip, often embroidered silk), chasuble (worn over the rest), surplice (tunic with large sleeves), and cope (semicircular, worn on the chest).

14. Joseph Milner, *The History of the Church of Christ*, vol. 4, ed. Isaac Milner (London: T. Cadell, 1824), 168.

15. John Foxe and George Townsend, *The Acts and Monuments of John Foxe: With a Life of the Martyrologist, and Vindication of the Work*, vol. 3 (London: Seeley, Burnside, and Seeley, 1844), 239.

16. Foxe and Townsend, *Acts and Monuments*, 239–40.

17. *Foxe's Book of Martyrs*, ed. Forbush, 192.

18. "John Wycliffe: A Gallery of Wycliffe's Defenders, Friends and Foes," Church History, *Christianity Today* (1983); accessed at https://www.christianitytoday.com/history/issues/issue -3/john-wycliffe-gallery-of-wycliffes-defenders-friends-and.html.

19. Alan Kreider, "Protest and Renewal: Reformers before the Reformation," Christian History Institute, originally published in "Heritage of Freedom: Dissenters, Reformers, and Pioneers," *Christian History*, no. 9 (1986), https://www.christianitytoday.com/history/issues/issue-9 /protest-and-renewal-reformers-before-reformation.html .

20. "1417: Catherine Saube, Retroactive Anabaptist?," October 2, 2017 on ExecutedToday.com, originally appearing in Thieleman J. van Braght, *Martyrs Mirror* (Grand Rapids, MI: Christian Classics Ethereal Library), 647, http://www.executedtoday.com/tag/catherine -saube/.

21. Van Braght, "1417: Catherine Saube," http://www.executedtoday.com/tag/catherine-saube/.

22. *Foxe's Book of Martyrs*, "An Account of the Persecutions in Great Britain and Ireland, Prior to the Reign of Queen Mary," https://www.biblestudytools.com/history/foxs-book-of-martyrs/an -account-of-the-persecutions-in-great-britain-and-ireland-prior-to-the-reign-of-queen-mary-i .html.

23. *Foxe's Book of Martyrs*, "Persecutions in Great Britain and Ireland."

24. James J. Marino, "William Shakespeare's *Sir John Oldcastle*," *Renaissance Drama*, New Series, 30 (1999–2001): 93–114, https://www.jstor.org/stable/41917357.

25. Giorgio Vasari, *Artists of the Renaissance: A Selection from Lives of the Artists*, trans. George Bull (New York: Viking, 1979), 152.

26. David M. Reis, quoted at Kat Eschner, "A Fanatical Monk Inspired 15th-Century Italians to Burn Their Clothes, Makeup and Art," *Smithsonian*, February 7, 2017, https://www .smithsonianmag.com/smart-news/when-fanatical-monk-took-over-florence-and-burned-bunch -vanities-180962005/.

27. Jerry Pattengale, ed., *A History of World Civilizations from a Christian Perspective* (unpublished manuscript), 437–39.

28. Conciliarists at the Council of Constance were for the constitutional versus absolute rule discussion, whereas earlier reformers, like Marsiglio of Padua (d. ca. 1342), called for the total rejection of the papal monarchy. See Francis Oakley, *The Conciliarist Tradition: Constitutionalism in the Catholic Church, 1300–1870* (Oxford, UK: Oxford University Press, 2004). Also see Norman Tanner's review of *The Concilliarist Tradition* in the *Journal of Theological Studies* 56, no. 1 (April 2005): 252–54.

29. This allowed scholars to compare Church doctrine, often based on Latin translations, to the older Greek version—the original language of the New Testament.

30. Niccolò Machiavelli, *Machiavelli: The Chief Works and Others*, trans. Allan Gilbert, vol. 1 (Durham, NC: Duke University Press, 1965), 330–31.

31. Martin Luther, *Christian Liberty*, trans. W. A. Lambert (Philadelphia: Muhlenberg, 1943), 5–6.

32. Alan Kreider, "God's Left Wing: The Radical Reformers," *Christianity Today*, originally published in "Heritage of Freedom: Dissenters, Reformers, and Pioneers," *Christian History*, no. 9 (1986), https://www.christianitytoday.com/history/issues/issue-9/gods-left-wing-radical -reformers.html.

33. Heinold Fast, "Reformation durch Provokation: Predigtstörungen in den ersten Jahren der Reformation in der Schweiz," in *Umstrittenes Täufertum 1525–1975: Neue Forschungen*, ed. Hans-Jürgen Goertz (Göttingen: Vandenhoeck und Ruprecht, 1975), 87.
34. The Mennonite Conference of Eastern Canada named a new prep school after him in Waterloo, Ontario, Canada, in 1963—the Conrad Grebel University College, affiliated with the University of Waterloo. Its mission statement: "The mission of Conrad Grebel University College is to seek wisdom, nurture faith, and pursue justice and peace in service to church and society."
35. William R. Estep, *The Anabaptist Story: An Introduction to Sixteenth-Century Anabaptism*, rev. ed. (Grand Rapids, MI: Eerdmans, 1996), 74.
36. Estep, *Anabaptist Story*, 103. This is the recorded testimony of the eyewitness "Stephen Sprügel," dean of the philosophical faculty at the University of Vienna."
37. Leonard Gross, "Showing Them How to Die; Showing Them How to Live," Christian History Institute, originally published in "Radical Reformation: The Anabaptists," *Christian History*, no. 5 (1985), https://christianhistoryinstitute.org/magazine/article/showing-them-how-to-die-showing-them-how-to-live.
38. Gross, "Showing Them How to Die."
39. See Ruth A. Tucker, *Parade of Faith: A Biographical History of the Christian Church* (Grand Rapids, MI: Zondervan, 2011), chap. 13.
40. William M. Blackburn, *Ulrich Zwingli, the Patriotic Reformer: A History* (Philadelphia: Presbyterian Board of Publication, 1868), 257.
41. Blackburn, *Ulrich Zwingli*, 299.
42. Blackburn, *Ulrich Zwingli*, 299–300.
43. Blackburn, *Ulrich Zwingli*, 300.
44. Heinrich Bullinger, "Archives: Zwingli's Death on the Battlefield of Kappel in 1531," Christian History Institute, originally published in "Zwingli: Father of the Swiss Reformation," *Church History*, no. 4 (1984), https://christianhistoryinstitute.org/magazine/article/zwinglis-death-on-battlefield.
45. Michael Molinos, *The Life and Times of Michael Molinos*, in *The Spiritual Guide* (Beaumont, TX: SeedSowers, 1982), 116; Fox, *Book of Martyrs*, 130.
46. Molinos, *Life and Times*, *Spiritual Guide*, 13.
47. Molinos, *Life and Times*, *Spiritual Guide*, 117.
48. Molinos, *Life and Times*, *Spiritual Guide*, 125.
49. John Biggelow, "Bull of Innocent XI. Against Michel De Molinos," appendix C, in *Molinos the Quietest* (New York: Charles Scribner's Sons, 1882), 125.
50. Molinos, *Life and Times*, *Spiritual Guide*, 118.

CHAPTER 10: MARTYRS OF SIXTEENTH-CENTURY ENGLAND

1. See Peter Marshall, *1517: Martin Luther and the Invention of the Reformation* (New York: Oxford University Press, 2017).
2. Robert G. Clouse, Richard V. Pierard, and Edwin M. Yamauchi, *Two Kingdoms: The Church and Culture through the Ages* (Chicago: Moody, 1993), 257–58.
3. Alec Ryrie, "*Prologue*: When Did the English Reformation Happen? A Historiographical Curiosity and Its Interpretative Consequences," *Études Épistémè* 32 (2017), https://journals.openedition.org/episteme/1845.
4. Joan Acocella, "How Martin Luther Changed the World," *New Yorker*, October 23, 2017, https://www.newyorker.com/magazine/2017/10/30/how-martin-luther-changed-the-world.
5. Acocella, "How Martin Luther Changed the World."
6. "The Reformation," History.com, last updated September 9, 2019, https://www.history.com/topics/reformation/reformation.

7. H. G. Koenigsberger, George L. Mosse, and G. Q. Bowler, *Europe in the Sixteenth Century*, 2nd ed. (New York: Longman, 1989), 207.

8. John Foxe. Accessed at https://www.exclassics.com/foxe/foxe179.htm.

9. John Foxe. Accessed at https://www.exclassics.com/foxe/foxe179.htm.

10. Ancient, Medieval, and Early Modern Manuscripts, "The Execution of Sir Thomas More," *Medieval Manuscripts Blog*, British Library, July 6, 2016, https://blogs.bl.uk /digitisedmanuscripts/2016/07/the-execution-of-sir-thomas-more.html.

11. "1538: John Lambert, 'None but Christ,'" ExecutedToday.com, November 22, 2008, https://www.executedtoday.com/2008/11/22/1538-john-lambert-none-but-christ/.

12. John Foxe. Accessed at https://www.exclassics.com/foxe/foxe209.htm.

13. John Foxe. Accessed at https://www.exclassics.com/foxe/foxe209.htm.

14. John Foxe. Accessed at https://www.exclassics.com/foxe/foxe294.htm.

15. John Foxe. Accessed at https://www.exclassics.com/foxe/foxe294.htm.

16. John Foxe, *Acts and Monuments*, Forbush translation; accessed at https://www.biblestudytools .com/history/foxs-book-of-martyrs/rev-john-bradford-and-john-leaf-an-apprentice.html.

17. John Foxe. Accessed at https://www.exclassics.com/foxe/foxe298.htm.

18. John Foxe. Accessed at https://www.exclassics.com/foxe/foxe302.htm.

19. John Foxe. Accessed at https://www.exclassics.com/foxe/foxe302.htm. "Auricular confession," as defined in the *Catholic Dictionary*, is "The obligation by divine law of confessing one's grave sins, committed after baptism, to a qualified priest. It is called auricular confession because normally the manifestation of sins is done by word of mouth and heard by the priest before he gives absolution. (Etym. Latin auricula, the external ear.)" John A. Hardon, *Catholic Dictionary*, rev. ed. (New York: Image Books, 2013), s.v. "auricular confession." See "Auricular Confession," Catholic Culture, accessed February 12, 2022, https://www.catholicculture.org/culture/library /dictionary/index.cfm?id=32029.

20. John Foxe. Accessed at https://www.exclassics.com/foxe/foxe302.htm.

21. John Foxe. Accessed at https://www.exclassics.com/foxe/foxe302.htm.

22. John Foxe. Accessed at https://www.exclassics.com/foxe/foxe302.htm.

23. John Foxe. Accessed at https://www.biblestudytools.com/history/foxs-book-of-martyrs/dirick -carver-and-john-launder.html.

24. John Foxe. Accessed at https://www.exclassics.com/foxe/foxe303.htm.

25. John Foxe. Accessed at https://www.exclassics.com/foxe/foxe433.htm.

26. John Foxe. Accessed at https://www.exclassics.com/foxe/foxe294.htm.

27. Robert Bolt, *A Man for All Seasons: A Play in Two Acts* (New York: Vintage Books: 1960, 1990), 132.

28. Latimer and Ridley were burned at the stake on October 16, 1555, per *Foxe's Book of Martyrs* (1583 edition). This reflects the statement in Polycarp's martyrdom (AD 160) as recorded in Eusebius.

29. An engaging summary of the martyrdom of Ridley and Latimer is found in "A Tale of Two Martyrs: The Burning of Reformers Nicholas Ridley and Hugh Latimer," *Christianity Today*, originally published in "Thomas Cranmer and the English Reformation," *Christian History*, no. 48 (1995), https://www.christianitytoday.com/history/issues/issue-48/tale-of-two-martyrs.html.

30. Richard Cavendish, "Latimer and Ridley Burned at the Stake: The Oxford Martyrs Were Killed on October 16th, 1555," *History Today* 55, no. 10 (October 2005), https://www.historytoday .com/archive/latimer-and-ridley-burned-stake.

31. Melanchthon was one of the key leaders of the Protestant Reformation, and a prominent systematic theologian and educator (d. 1560). This work of his was one of three key releases on rhetoric (and reforming the whole educational approach); see William P. Weaver, "Melanchthon's Rhetorics and the Order of Learning: A Case Study in Library Database Research," *Reformation* 22, no. 2 (July 2017): 120–46, https://doi.org/10.1080/13574175 .2017.1387969.

32. A. Christian Pilgrim, *The Forbidden Book: William Tyndale and the First English Bible* (Shippensburg, PA: Lollard House, 1992), 53–54; see also the extended discussion of Bilney and Latimer on pages 51–58. This source is recommended, given the publishing house's link to the subject's heritage.

33. See "Lollards Pit—A Grim Tale of Execution!," *Norwich Tales, Myths, & More!* (blog), March 10, 2019, for a conversational reflection on the subject, replete with images. Today the Lollard Pit Public House (pub) has a plaque marking its macabre past—though debate remains on the pit's actual location. See https://norfolktalesmyths.com/2019/03/10/lollards-pit-a-grim-tale-of-persecution/. The resource section is helpful.

34. Clara H. Stuart, "Hugh Latimer: Apostle to the English," *Christianity Today* 24, no. 18 (October 24, 1980), https://www.christianitytoday.com/ct/1980/october-24/hugh-latimer-apostle-to-english.html.

35. Koenigsberger, Mosse, and Bowler, *Europe in the Sixteenth Century*, 292, 294.

36. "Thomas Cranmer: Genius behind Anglicism," *Christianity Today*, accessed February 12, 2022, https://www.christianitytoday.com/history/people/martyrs/thomas-cranmer.html.

37. "Thomas Cranmer," *Christianity Today*.

38. Robin Vose, "Introduction to Inquisition: Familiars and Officials," Hesburgh Libraries of Notre Dame, Department of Rare Books and Special Collections, University of Notre Dame, 2010, https://inquisition.library.nd.edu/genre-familiars-and-officials-introduction.

39. Cecil Roth, *The Spanish Inquisition* (New York: W. W. Norton, 1964), 123.

40. John Foxe, *Foxe's Book of Martyrs* (Gutenberg Online Project, Book 5): https://www.gutenberg.org/files/22400/22400-h/22400-h.htm#Page_76.

41. Thomas Brown confronted the bishop over his charges in January 1555, and called him a "bloodsucker."

42. John Foxe. Accessed at https://www.biblestudytools.com/history/foxs-book-of-martyrs/the-rev-george-marsh.html.

43. Megan L. Hickerson, "Agnes Prest (d. 1558)," in *A Biographical Encyclopedia of Early Modern Englishwomen: Exemplary Lives and Memorable Acts, 1500–1650*, ed. Carole Levin, Anna Riehl Bertolet, and Jo Eldridge Carney (New York: Routledge, 2017), 381.

44. These are available through the records of the borough chamberlains (household managers of the nobles or monarchs). Most of the county records offices in England have extensive records, along with churches and other institutions. However, this is certainly not without exception, such as in Chichester.

45. Megan L. Hickerson, "Agnes Potten and Joan Trunchfield (d. 1556)," in *A Biographical Encyclopedia of Early Modern Englishwomen*.

46. John Foxe. Accessed at https://www.exclassics.com/foxe/foxe333.htm.

47. *Foxe's Book of Martyrs*, ed. Marie Gentert King (Old Tappan, NJ: Revell, 1968), 330.

48. John Foxe. Accessed at https://www.exclassics.com/foxe/foxe368.htm.

49. John Foxe. Accessed at https://www.exclassics.com/foxe/foxe368.htm.

50. Carole Levin, "Women in *The Book of Martyrs* as Models of Behavior in Tudor England," *International Journal of Women's Studies* 4, no.2 (March/April 1981), 196–207, https://digitalcommons.unl.edu/cgi/viewcontent.cgi?referer=https://www.google.com/&httpsredir=1&article=1100&context=historyfacpub.

51. John Foxe. Accessed at https://www.exclassics.com/foxe/foxe353.htm.

52. John Foxe. Accessed at https://www.exclassics.com/foxe/foxe372.htm.

53. David Chazan, "A Century of Harry's Bar in Paris," BBC News, November 25, 2011, https://www.bbc.com/news/world-europe-15887142.

54. Lauran Mackay, "How Many Executions Was Henry VIII Responsible For?" History Extra, December 28, 2014, https://www.historyextra.com/period/tudor/how-many-executions-was-henry-viii-responsible-for/. The historical fiction television series *The Tudors* (2007–2010), created and written by Michael Hirst, accents the bizarre, scandalous, and gory character

of Henry VIII's reign. One description states: "All the splendor and scandal of England's 16th-century royal court comes to life in this series that follows notorious Tudor monarch Henry VIII," Netflix, accessed at https://usa.newonnetflix.info/info/70136129.

55. Richard Serjeantson, "Thomas More's Magnificent Utopia," Gresham College, lecture at Museum of London, November 22, 2016, celebrating the five-hundredth anniversary of Thomas More's *Utopia*, transcript and video, 46:39, https://www.gresham.ac.uk/lectures-and -events/thomas-mores-magnificent-utopia.

56. "The Book of Common Prayer," Prayer Book Society website, accessed February 4, 2022, https://www.pbs.org.uk/about/.

57. Peter Toon, "Second Sunday in Advent," *Common Book of Prayer*, The Prayer Book Society, accessed at https://www.pbs.org.uk/the-bcp/second-sunday-in-advent.

58. *The Acts and Monuments of John Foxe*, vol. VII (London: Seeley, Burnside, and Seeley, 1847), 383–84.

SECTION THREE: THE COLONIZATION OF PEOPLES THROUGH THE COLD WAR (AD 1991)

1. Larry Peterson, "The First Martyr of the Philippines, Lorenzo Ruiz," Aleteia, February 5, 2017, https://aleteia.org/2017/02/05/the-first-martyr-of-the-philippines-lorenzo-ruiz/.

2. Herbert Thurston, "Confraternity of the Holy Rosary," *Catholic Encyclopedia*, vol. 13 (New York: Robert Appleton, 1912), http://www.newadvent.org/cathen/13188b.htm.

3. Peterson, "First Martyr."

4. "St. Lorenzo Ruiz," Catholic Online, accessed April 9, 2022, https://www.catholic.org/saints /saint.php?saint_id=231.

CHAPTER 11: THE COSTS OF COLONIALISM IN THE AMERICAS

1. Timothy Dalrymple, "Justice Too Long Delayed," editorial, *Christianity Today*, June 10, 2020, https://www.christianitytoday.com/ct/2020/june-web-only/justice-too-long-delayed.html.

2. Justo González, theologian and author, speaks of this in *Inexplicable: How Christianity Spread to the Ends of the Earth*, part 3, "Glory Gold and God" (TBN, 2020), https://watch.tbn.org /inexplicable-how-christianity-spread-to-the-ends-of-the-earth/videos/inexplicable-part3.

3. See Paul E. Sigmund, "Religious Human Rights in Latin America," *Emory International Law Review* 10, no. 1 (Spring 1996): 173–82.

4. Valentina Pop, "George Floyd Protests Prompt Europe to Reckon with Racist Legacies of Colonial Past," *Wall Street Journal*, June 6, 2020, https://www.wsj.com/articles/george-floyd -protests-prompt-europe-to-reckon-with-racist-legacies-of-colonial-past-11591441201; John Campbell and Jack McCaslin, "George Floyd's Murder Revives Anti-Colonialism in Western Europe," *Africa in Transition* (blog), Council on Foreign Relations, June 16, 2020, https://www .cfr.org/blog/george-floyds-murder-revives-anti-colonialism-western-europe.

5. *Annual Report of the Wesleyan-Methodist Missionary Society, Year Ending December 1830*, cited in J. M. R. Owens, "Christianity and the Maoris to 1840," *New Zealand Journal of History* 14, no. 1 (April 1968): 18, http://www.nzjh.auckland.ac.nz/docs/1968/NZJH_02_1_03.pdf.

6. Francis Borgia Steck, "The Three Battalions in the Spiritual Conquest of Mexico," *Records of the American Catholic Historical Society of Philadelphia* 66, no. 1 (March 1955): 3–18, http://www.jstor.org/stable/44210361.

7. Paula Algeria, *La Educación en México antes y después de la Conquista* (Mexico, 1936), 76, 78, cited in Steck, "Three Battalions," 3.

8. The *Florentine Codex* by Spanish friar Bernardino de Sahagún is a sixteenth-century ethnic study giving the rationale behind colonization and reflecting the biases of that age. See also Camilla Townsend, "Burying the White Gods: New Perspectives on the Conquest of Mexico," *American Historical Review* 108, no. 3 (June 2003): 659–87.

9. Townsend, "Burying the White Gods."

10. Ondina E. González and Justo L. González, *Christianity in Latin America: A History* (New York: Cambridge University Press, 2008), 3.

11. See Suzanne Schwarz, "Reconstructing the Life Histories of Liberated Africans: Sierra Leone in the Early Nineteenth Century," *History in Africa* 39 (2012): 175–207, https://www.jstor.org/stable/23471003. The personal tragedies of the actual Middle Passage were harsh enough, and often continued into freedom. The ramifications of the slave trade and Christian responses can be found in many regions throughout the world—including places like Freetown (far from perfect, as many freed slaves, or "recaptives," felt they were "unwilling migrants subject to various forms of coerced labour in a system that was untried and untested." However, abolitionists who helped end slavery tried to assist freed slaves with lives thereafter. Granville Sharp (son of an archdeacon of Northumberland) was one of the leaders in this abolitionist movement, and though not a martyr, endured criticism and lack of some burial rights because of his role in the Nonconformist group—the British and Foreign Bible Society.

12. "Renaissance," History.com, last updated November 15, 2021, https://www.history.com/topics/renaissance/renaissance.

13. "Enlightenment," History.com, last updated August 27, 2021, https://www.history.com/topics/british-history/enlightenment.

14. "Enlightenment."

15. Lawrence S. Cunningham, "Martyrs Named and Nameless," *America*, October 2, 2006, https://www.americamagazine.org/issue/585/article/martyrs-named-and-nameless.

16. La Croix International, "Pope Canonizes First-Ever Latin American Martyrs, Calls Special Synod for the Amazon Region," *Catholic Digest*, October 16, 2017, http://www.catholicdigest.com/news/from-la-croix-international/pope-canonizes-first-ever-latin-american-martyrs-calls-special-synod-for-the-amazon-region/.

17. Jerry Pattengale, *Inexplicable: How Christianity Spread to the Ends of the Earth* (Tustin, CA: Trilogy, 2020), 110.

18. Pattengale, *Inexplicable*, 111.

19. Ramón Hernández, "The Internationalization of Francisco de Vitoria and Domingo de Soto," trans. Jay J. Aragonés, *Fordham International Law Journal* 15, no. 4 (1991): 1045–47, https://ir.lawnet.fordham.edu/cgi/viewcontent.cgi?referer=https://en.wikipedia.org/&httpsredir=1&article=1325&context=ilj.

20. Victor M. Salas Jr., "Francisco de Vitoria on the *Ius Gentium* and the American *Indios*," *Ave Maria Law Review* 10, no. 2 (2012): 331–41, https://lawreview.avemarialaw.edu/wp-content/uploads/2019/06/AMLR.v.10i2.salas_.pdf. The treatment of indigenous peoples is not an easy path to follow, whether looking at the papacy or local leaders. For example, Pope Paul III declared the papal bull in 1537 (*Sublimis Deus*) confirming the indigenous populations (targeting California and New Mexico, where a third of the populations were decimated) "their souls were as immortal as those of Europeans." Various other papal actions could be cited, like Pope Gregory XVI's 1839 bull condemning slavery and the slave trade (*In Supremo Apostolatus*), and efforts to combat racism with ordination and appointment of native clergy.

21. Edwin Markham, ed., *The Real America in Romance: An Authentic History of America from the Discovery to the Present Day*, vol. 13, *The Eagle's Wings: The Age of Expansion 1868–1910* (New York: William H. Wise, 1914), 388.

22. Bartolome de las Casas, *A Brief Account of the Destruction of the Indies* (translation of *Brevísima relación de la destrucción de las Indias*, Seville, 1552; R. Hewson, 1689; Project Gutenberg, 2007), "Of the Island Hispaniola," http://www.gutenberg.org/cache/epub/20321/pg20321-images.html.

23. John Maust, "Columbus and Christianity in the Americas: A Gallery of Champions for the Oppressed," Christian History Institute, originally published in "Columbus & Christianity,"

no. 35, *Christian History* (1992), https://christianhistoryinstitute.org/magazine/article
/columbus-and-christianity-gallery-of-champions-for-the-oppressed. Las Casas regretted one
major decision he could not retract—his recommendation of using African slaves instead of the
Latin peoples. He made this trying to save the lives of those in the Americas he had come to
love, and later would exhaust himself trying to help all slaves.

24. John Richard Slattery, *The Life of St. Peter Claver, S.J.: The Apostle of the Negroes* (Philadelphia:
H. L. Kilner, 1893), 67. This fundraising book reveals the author's distorted views. Like Alonso
Salvador and the prevailing European view during Claver's time, he was advocating European
paternalism and the notion that it is better to be a slave in South America than free and going
to hell in Africa as a pagan.

25. The UNESCO project reports among its five basic facts about Cartagena, Colombia: "Between
1595 and 1640, the Portuguese brought to Cartagena about 125,000 enslaved Africans." See
"The Slavery Route in Cartagena de Indias," Donde Cartagena, https://donde.co/cartagena
/articles/slavery-route-cartagena-de-indias-27287. This site is especially helpful as it gives the
details of historic sites associated with the slave route. See "The Slave Route" (A–Q).

26. Pattengale, *Inexplicable*, 115–16.

27. See Enrique Dussel, *A History of the Church in Latin America: Colonialism to Liberation
(1492–1979)*, trans. Alan Neely (Grand Rapids, MI: Eerdmans, 1981), 45–53.

28. See Gary Smith, "The History of the Catholic Church in Latin America and Liberation
Theology," unit 7 in "Society and Literature in Latin America" (curriculum unit 82.05.07),
vol. 5, 1982, Yale–New Haven Teachers Institute, https://teachersinstitute.yale.edu/curriculum
/units/1982/5/82.05.07.x.html. Also see Rollie Edward Poppino, *Brazil: The Land and People*
(New York: Oxford University Press, 1968), 81.

29. Anthony Huonder, "Antonio Ruiz de Montoya," *Catholic Encyclopedia*, vol. 13 (New York:
Robert Appleton, 1912), http://www.newadvent.org/cathen/13223c.htm.

30. *Encyclopaedia Britannica*, s.v. "Grito de Dolores," updated September 24, 2018, https://www
.britannica.com/event/Grito-de-Dolores.

31. Independence Day is actually September 16, though commonly (and erroneously) associated
with Cinco de Mayo.

32. Ana Gonzalez-Barrera, "'Mestizo' and 'Mulatto': Mixed-Race Identities among U.S. Hispanics,"
Pew Research Center, July 10, 2015, https://www.pewresearch.org/fact-tank/2015/07/10
/mestizo-and-mulatto-mixed-race-identities-unique-to-hispanics/.

33. *Encyclopaedia Britannica*, s.v. "Miguel Hidalgo y Costilla: Mexican Leader" last updated July
26, 2020, https://www.britannica.com/biography/Miguel-Hidalgo-y-Costilla.

34. *Encyclopaedia Britannica*, s.v. "Independence of Mexico," last updated April 8, 2022,
https://www.britannica.com/place/Mexico/Independence.

35. See Michael J. Gonzales, *The Mexican Revolution, 1910–1940* (Albuquerque, NM: University
of New Mexico Press, 2002).

36. Óscar Romero, *Voice of the Voiceless: The Four Pastoral Letters and Other Statements*, trans.
Michael J. Walsh, anniv. ed. (Maryknoll, NY: Orbis Books, 2000), 198.

37. The following site plays a recording of the event and displays photographs (warning:
includes graphic images): "Mons. Romero Últimas palabras Previo a su muertel (Audio
Original)," Sociedad Politica Social, May 22, 2015, video, 2:00, https://www.youtube.com
/watch?v=tC62Grvn2vM. His canonization ceremonies: "Canonisation of Oscar Romero,"
Caritas Internationalis, October 11, 2018, video, 3:18, https://www.youtube.com/watch?v
=EGROjsTwsaA; EWTN Live, "Holy Mass with Canonizations," Catholic News Agency,
Facebook live, October 14, 2018, video, 2:57:46, https://www.facebook.com
/CatholicNewsAgency/videos/mass-of-canonization-of-st-paul-vi-and-st-oscar-romero
/703369746701759/.

38. Jon Lee Anderson, "Archbishop Óscar Romero Becomes a Saint, But His Death Still Haunts

El Salvador," *New Yorker*, October 22, 2018, https://www.newyorker.com/news/daily-comment/archbishop-oscar-romero-becomes-a-saint-but-his-death-still-haunts-el-salvador.

39. González and González, *Christianity in Latin America*, 4.

40. Pattengale, *Inexplicable*, 118.

41. Junno Arocho Esteves, "Colombian Martyrs: Witnesses to the Point of Death," *National Catholic Reporter*, July 21, 2017, https://www.ncronline.org/news/vatican/colombian-martyrs-witnesses-point-death.

42. Esteves, "Colombian Martyrs."

43. Susan Abad and Nicholas Casey, "Pope Sees Two Slain Clerics as Martyrs for Peace in Colombia," *New York Times*, September 8, 2017, https://www.nytimes.com/2017/09/08/world/americas/colombia-pope-francis-farc-roman-catholic-church.html.

44. The original title is anything but short: *A short story of the rise, reign, and ruin of the Antinomians, Familists, and libertines that infected the churches of New-England and how they were confuted by the assembly of ministers there as also of the magistrates proceedings in court against them : together with God's strange remarkable judgements from heaven upon some of the chief fomenters of these opinions : and the lamentable death of Mrs. Hutchison : very fit for these times, here being the same errors amongst us, and acted by the same spirit : published at the instant request of sundry, by one that was an eye and ear-witness of the carriage of matters there* (London, 1644; 1692). For access to the full text, see Text Creation Partnership, accessed April 12, 2022, https://quod.lib.umich.edu/e/eebo/A65392.0001.001?view=toc. Winthrop actually spoke for the court during her trial that led to her banishment, and eventual death.

45. Edwin S. Gaustad, "Quest for Pure Christianity," Christian History Institute, originally published in "The American Puritans," no. 41, *Christian History* (1994), https://christianhistoryinstitute.org/magazine/article/quest-for-pure-christianity.

46. Jerry Pattengale and Christy K. Robinson talk about this in *Inexplicable: How Christianity Spread to the Ends of the Earth*, part 4, "Mavericks in the New World" (TBN, 2020), https://watch.tbn.org/inexplicable-how-christianity-spread-to-the-ends-of-the-earth.

47. Eve LaPlante, *American Jezebel: The Uncommon Life of Anne Hutchinson, the Woman Who Defied the Puritans* (San Francisco: HarperCollins, 2004), 237.

48. Mark A. Noll, *A History of Christianity in the United States and Canada* (Grand Rapids, MI: Eerdmans, 1992), 62.

49. John Foxe, *Foxe's Book of Martyrs*, ed. William Byron Forbush.

50. The names appear in various places, including "Lives of the Canadian Martyrs," Canadian Martyrs Catholic Church, Ottawa, Ontario, accessed April 12, 2022, https://canadianmartyrs.org/resources/canadian-martyrs/.

51. Eventually the Spanish would give up on efforts to claim and settle the eastern part of North America, though succeeded in establishing North America's oldest permanent settlement— St. Augustine, Florida.

52. Pattengale, *Inexplicable*, 159. Also see William J. Bennett, *America: The Last Best Hope*, rev. ed. (Nelson Books, 2019), 147–48.

53. Their martyrdom site (that of the village) is commemorated with a shrine in Auriesville, New York. In Canada their feast day is celebrated on September 26, and in the United States on October 19.

54. Pattengale, *Inexplicable*, 160–61.

55. "St. Isaac Jogues: The Martyr," excerpt from Pat Davis, "Our Saints, Our Story" (unpublished manuscript), St. Isaac Jogues Parish, accessed April 12, 2022, http://www.sij-parish.com/st_isaac_jogues_the_martyr.htm.

56. "St. Isaac Jogues."

57. *Encyclopaedia Britannica*, s.v. "St. Jean de Brébeuf," last updated March 21, 2022, https://www.britannica.com/biography/Saint-Jean-de-Brebeuf.

58. See Timothy G. Pearson, "Becoming Holy in Early Canada: Performance and the Making of Holy Persons in Society and Culture" (PhD thesis, McGill University, 2008), https://escholarship.mcgill.ca/concern/theses/fb494c06d?locale=en.

CHAPTER 12: THE NINETEENTH CENTURY: MARTYRS IN AN AGE OF ALLEGED PROGRESS

1. China Inland Mission, *China's Millions*, 1900, North American edition (Toronto: 1900), https://archive.org/details/millions1900chin/mode/2up.
2. "David Livingstone, 1813–1873," Gospel Fellowship Association Missions, November 11, 2005, https://gfamissions.org/david-livingstone/.
3. Robert G. Clouse, Richard V. Pierard, and Edwin M. Yamauchi, *Two Kingdoms: The Church and Culture through the Ages* (Chicago: Moody, 1993), 465. The entire chapter "The Church in an Industrial Age" is an excellent read and summary of this era, especially its treatment of the effect of the Industrial Revolution on the Church.
4. Charles Dickens, *A Tale of Two Cities* (London, 1859), chap. 1, Charles Dickens online, accessed April 16, 2022, http://www.dickens-online.info/a-tale-of-two-cities.html.
5. "Maximilien Robespierre: On the Principles of Political Morality, February 1794," at Modern History Sourcebook, Internet History Sourcebooks Project, Fordham University, 1997, https://sourcebooks.fordham.edu/mod/1794robespierre.asp.
6. Walter G. Moss, *An Age of Progress? Clashing Twentieth-Century Global Forces* (London: Anthem Press, 2008); Raphaël Franck and Oded Galor, "Flowers of Evil? Industrialization and Long Run Development," *Journal of Monetary Economics* 117 (January 2021): 108–28, https://www.sciencedirect.com/science/article/abs/pii/S0304393219302144?via%3Dihub.
7. H. De Marsan, "The Age of Progress" (New York, 1860), Social History for Every Classroom, accessed April 16, 2022, https://shec.ashp.cuny.edu/items/show/838.
8. C. Saunders, *Religious and Political Persecution of the Late Rev. John Smith, Missionary at Demerara* (London: J. Fairburn, 1824).
9. The antislavery lectures of those influenced by the late James Edward Oglethorpe, like Thomas Fowell Buxton, convinced him of this approach.
10. Anthony Sillery, *John Mackenzie of Bechuanaland, 1835–1899: A Study in Humanitarian Imperialism* (Cape Town: A. A. Balkema, 1971), 185.
11. Andrea Palpant Dilley, "The Surprising Discovery about Those Colonialist, Proselytizing Missionaries," *Christianity Today*, January 8, 2014, https://www.christianitytoday.com/ct/2014/january-february/world-missionaries-made.html.
12. Kenneth O. Hall, "Humanitarianism and Racial Subordination: John Mackenzie and the Transformation of Tswana Society," *International Journal of African Historical Studies* 8, no. 1 (1975): 100–103.
13. John Mackenzie, *Austral Africa; Losing It or Ruling It: Being Incidents and Experiences in Bechuanaland, Cape Colony, and England*, vol. 2 (London: Sampson Low, Marston, Searle and Rivington, 1887), 426.
14. Mackenzie, *Austral Africa*, 425–26.
15. "About VOM," Voice of the Martyrs website, accessed April 16, 2022, https://www.persecution.com/about.
16. John Foxe and Voice of the Martyrs, *Foxe: Voices of the Martyrs*, rev. ed. (Bartlesville, OK: VOM Books, 2013), 184.
17. Ronald A. Wells, *History through the Eyes of Faith: Western Civilization and the Kingdom of God* (San Francisco: HarperSanFrancisco, 1989), 154–55.
18. Wells, *History*, 172–74.
19. Wells, *History*, 172.
20. Wells, *History*, 172, italics in the original.

21. *The Missionary Smith: Substance of the Debate in the House of Commons on Tuesday the 1st and on Friday the 11th of June, 1824* (London: Hatchard, Seeley, Westley, and Arch, 1824), 210.

22. Charles M. Sheldon, *In His Steps: "What Would Jesus Do?"* (Chicago: Advance, 1898), 183.

23. Elizabeth Rundle Charles, *Three Martyrs of the Nineteenth Century: Studies from the Lives of Livingstone, Gordon, and Patteson* (London: SPCK, 1885), https://books.google.com/books?id= lswHAAAAQAAJ&printsec=frontcover#v=onepage&q&f=false.

24. Ted Olsen, "One African Nation under God," *Christianity Today*, February 4, 2002, https://www.christianitytoday.com/ct/2002/february4/3.36.html.

25. Olsen, "One African Nation under God."

26. Ruth A. Tucker, *From Jerusalem to Irian Jaya: A Biographical History of Christian Missions*, 2nd ed. (Grand Rapids, MI: Zondervan, 2004), 155–56.

27. Mark Galli, "The Paradox of David Livingstone: From the Editor—Livingstone—the Great Non-missionary," *Christianity Today*, originally published in "David Livingstone: Missionary-Explorer in Africa," *Christian History*, no. 56 (1997), https://www.christianitytoday.com /history/issues/issue-56/paradox-of-david-livingstone-from-editor--livingstone.html.

28. "David Livingstone: Missionary-Explorer of Africa," *Christianity Today*, originally published in "David Livingstone: Missionary-Explorer in Africa," *Christian History*, no. 56 (1997), https://www.christianitytoday.com/history/people/missionaries/david-livingstone.html.

29. David Livingstone, quoted at Ted Olsen, "The Other Livingstone," *Christianity Today*, originally published in "David Livingstone: Missionary-Explorer in Africa," *Christian History*, no. 56 (1997), https://www.christianitytoday.com/history/issues/issue-56/other-livingstone .html.

30. "David Livingstone: Missionary-Explorer of Africa."

31. George Albert Shepperson, "David Livingston: Scottish Explorer and Missionary," in *Encyclopaedia Britannica*, last updated March 15, 2022, https://www.britannica.com/biography /David-Livingstone.

32. Constitution of Zambia, 2016, amend. II, preamble, Constitution Amendment Act 2016, National Assembly of Zambia, January 5, 2016, https://www.parliament.gov.zm/node/4834.

33. Olsen, "One African Nation under God."

34. "David Livingstone," Experience Victoria Falls website, accessed April 27, 2022, https://www .experiencevictoriafalls.com/DavidLivingstone.php.

35. Henry Morton Stanley has quite the biography as well, and his contributions to African history are many and diverse. See Ted Olsen, "Post-Postcolonial Biography: Stanley in Africa," review of *Stanley: The Impossible Life of Africa's Greatest Explorer*, by Tim Jeal, Books and Culture Archives, *Christianity Today*, January/February 2008, https://www.booksandculture.com/articles/2008 /janfeb/13.12.html.

36. "David Livingstone: Missionary-Explorer of Africa."

37. "David Livingstone," commemoration, Westminster Abbey, accessed April 18, 2022, https://www.westminster-abbey.org/abbey-commemorations/commemorations/david -livingstone.

38. Charles, *Three Martyrs*, 284.

39. Stephanie Laffer, "Gordon's Ghosts: British Major-General Charles George Gordon and His Legacies, 1885–1960," (PhD diss., Florida State University, 2010; 33, https://diginole.lib.fsu .edu/islandora/object/fsu:181640.

40. Gordon to M. A. Gordon, October 6, 1878, in *Letters of General C. G. Gordon to His Sister M. A. Gordon* (London: Macmillan, 1888), 182–83.

41. Laffer, "Gordon's Ghosts," 71–72.

42. Charles, *Three Martyrs*, 285.

43. Charles, *Three Martyrs*, 285.

44. Laffer, "Gordon's Ghosts," 36.

45. See David Hilliard, "The Making of an Anglican Martyr: Bishop John Coleridge Patteson of Melanesia," *Studies in Church History* 30 (1993): 333–45, https://www.cambridge.org/core /journals/studies-in-church-history/article/abs/making-of-an-anglican-martyr-bishop-john -coleridge-patteson-of-melanesia/3A03EF52C4A227EE2A427200ECA2F0C2.

46. Jesse Page, *Bishop Patteson: The Martyr of Melanesia* (London: S. W. Partridge , 1890s; Pioneer, 2017, Kindle); David Hilliard, "Patteson, John Coleridge," in *Dictionary of New Zealand Biography* (1990), Te Ara: the Encyclopedia of New Zealand, accessed April 19, 2022, https://teara.govt.nz/en/biographies/1p10/patteson-john-coleridge.

47. C. H. Brooke, "The Death of Bishop Patteson," in *Mission Life: An Illustrated Magazine of Home and Foreign Church Work*, ed. John Halcombe, vol. 3, part 1 (London: 1872; Project Canterbury, 2006, trans. Terry Brown), 1–23, http://anglicanhistory.org/oceania/brooke _patteson1872.html.

48. Charles, *Three Martyrs*, 306–7.

49. Charles, *Three Martyrs*, 311.

50. Charles, *Three Martyrs*, 319.

51. "Théophane Vénard," Vietnamese Martyrs Website, accessed April 19, 2022, https://sites .google.com/site/vietnamesemartyrs/VietnameseMartyrs/theophane-venard.

52. Foxe and The Voice of the Martyrs, *Foxe: Voices of the Martyrs*, 195.

53. "Théophane Vénard." A mandarin is an official in the Chinese Empire.

54. Foxe and The Voice of the Martyrs, *Foxe: Voices of the Martyrs*, 196.

55. A. N. Arun Kumar, Geeta Joshi, and H. Y. Mohan Ram, "Sandalwood: History, Uses, Present Status and the Future," *Current Science* 103, no. 12 (December 25, 2012): 1408–16. African blackwood is considered the most expensive.

56. See James Douglas Gordon, *The Last Martyrs of Eromanga [Erromango]: Being a Memoir of the Rev. George N. Gordon, and Ellen Catherine Powell, His Wife* (Halifax, Novia Scotia: Macnab and Shaffer, 1863), 191; https://archive.org/details/thelastmartyrsof00gorduoft/page/192 /mode/2up?q=kill; A. K. Langridge, *Won by Blood: The Story of Erromanga, the Martyr Isle* (London: James Clarke, 1922), 76–77, https://archive.org/stream/wonbybloodstoryo 00lang#page/76/mode/2up/search/language.

57. Ebenezer Prout, *The Martyr Missionary of Eromanga: The Life of John Williams* (Philadelphia, 1844; CreateSpace Independent 2016, ed. Lucy Booker Roper), chap. 1, Kindle.

58. Steven Gertz, "Bringing Peace to Paradise," *Christianity Today*, originally published in "Christianity in India: A Faith of Many Colors," *Christian History*, no. 87 (2005), https://www .christianitytoday.com/history/issues/issue-87/bringing-peace-to-paradise.html.

59. Gertz, "Bringing Peace."

60. Gertz, "Bringing Peace."

61. Briony Leyland, "Island Holds Reconciliation over Cannibalism," BBC News, December 7, 2009, http://news.bbc.co.uk/2/hi/uk_news/england/hampshire/8398126.stm.

62. George N. Gordon and J. D. G. [James Douglas Gordon, his brother], *The Last Martyrs of Eromanga: Being a Memoir of the Reverend George N. Gordon and Ellen Catherine Powell, His Wife* (Halifax, Novia Scotia: Macnab and Shaffer, 1863), 191.

63. Gordon and Gordon, *Last Martyrs of Eromanga*, 194.

64. Stevenson to Colvin, December 1890, *Vailima Letters: Being Correspondence Addressed by Robert Louis Stevenson to Sidney Colvin, November 1890–October 1894*, vol. 1 (Chicago: Stone and Kimball, 1895), 81–82.

65. Cuthbert Lennox, *James Chalmers of New Guinea: Missionary, Pioneer, Martyr* (London: Andrew Melrose, 1902), 191–92.

66. "O Arise All You Sons," at "PNG Flag and National Anthem," Embassy of Papua New Guinea to the Americas, Washington, DC, accessed April 19, 2022, http://www.pngembassy.org/flag .html.

67. Nak-chun Paek, *The History of Protestant Missions in Korea, 1832–1910*, rev. ed. (Pyeng Yang, Korea: Union Christian College Press, 1929; Seoul, Korea: Yonsei University Press, 1971), 49. See also "R. J. Thomas' Deadly Mission in Korea," Christianity.com, May 3, 2010, https://www.christianity.com/church/church-history/timeline/1801-1900/r-j-thomas-deadly -mission-in-korea-11630539.html.

68. Paek, *History of Protestant Missions in Korea*, 49.

69. Franklin D. Rausch and Haeseong Park, "Christianity in Korea," *Education about Asia* 25, no. 1 (Spring 2020), https://www.asianstudies.org/publications/eaa/archives/christianity-in -korea/.

70. Jai-Keun Choi, *The Origin of the Roman Catholic Church in Korea: An Examination of Popular and Governmental Responses to Catholic Missions in the Late Chosŏn Dynasty* (Cheltenham, PA: Hermit Kingdom Press, 2006), 207.

71. Kirsteen Kim and Hoon Ko, "Who Brought the Gospel to Korea? Koreans Did," *Christianity Today*, February 9, 2018, https://www.christianitytoday.com/history/2018/february/korean -christianity.html; Clouse, Pierard, and Yamauchi, *Two Kingdoms*, 212; Daniel M. Davies, "The Impact of Christianity upon Korea, 1884–1910: Six Key American and Korean Figures," *Journal of Church and State* 36, no. 4 (Fall 1994): 795–820, https://www.jstor.org/stable /23919420. For a litany of helpful sources on this general overview of Christianity in Korea, see Davies, "Impact," 795n.

72. Jerry Pattengale, *Inexplicable: How Christianity Spread to the Ends of the Earth* (Tustin, CA: Trilogy, 2020), 193.

73. Pattengale, *Inexplicable*, 195.

74. Choi, *Origin of the Roman Catholic Church in Korea*, 191.

75. Choi, *Origin of the Roman Catholic Church in Korea*, 203.

76. Choi, *Origin of the Roman Catholic Church in Korea*, 203.

77. Choi, *Origin of the Roman Catholic Church in Korea*, 205–6.

78. Choi, *Origin of the Roman Catholic Church in Korea*, 208.

79. Clouse, Pierard, and Yamauchi, *Two Kingdoms*, 493.

80. Clouse, Pierard, and Yamauchi, *Two Kingdoms*, 502.

81. Nat Brandt, *Massacre in Shansi* (Syracuse, NY: Syracuse University Press, 1994), xiii.

82. China Inland Mission, *China's Millions*, 1900 ed., 111.

83. China Inland Mission, *China's Millions*, 111.

84. China Inland Mission, *China's Millions*, 111.

85. A. Henry Savage Landor, *China and the Allies*, vol. 1 (New York: Scribner's, 1901), 265–67.

86. J. Hudson Taylor, ed., *China's Millions*, 1890 ed. (London: Morgan and Scott, 1890), 141.

87. Pattengale, *Inexplicable*, 184.

88. Landor, *China and the Allies*, 272.

89. Hudson Taylor to Amelia [his sister], 1860, in Howard Taylor and Geraldine Taylor, *Hudson Taylor in Early Years: The Growth of a Soul* (New York: Hodder and Stoughton, 1912), 503.

90. James Martin, "The Story of the Ugandan Martyrs," *America*, June 3, 2011, https://www .americamagazine.org/content/all-things/story-ugandan-martyrs.

91. Owen S. Seda, "Medieval Morality and Liturgical Drama in Colonial Rhodesia: Early Christian Martyrs Dramatized," in *African Theatre 9: Histories 1850–1950*, ed. Yvette Hutchison and Jane Plastow (Rochester, NY: James Currey, 2010), 38–52. See also Peter Canham, review of *Mashonaland Martyr: Bernard Mizeki and the Pioneer Church*, by Jean Farrant, *African Affairs* 67, no. 266 (1968): 80–81, https://www.jstor.org/stable/720495.

92. Frederick Quinn, "Mizeki, Bernard (A)," Dictionary of African Christian Biography, originally published in Frederick Quinn, *African Saints: Saints, Martyrs, and Holy People from the Continent of Africa* (New York: Crossroads, 2002), https://dacb.org/stories/zimbabwe/mizeki -bernard/.

93. Terence Ranger, "Taking Hold of the Land: Holy Places and Pilgrimages in Twentieth-Century Zimbabwe," *Past and Present*, no. 117 (November 1987): 187–88, https://www.jstor.org/stable /650791.

94. Ranger, "Taking Hold," 188.

95. Serenhedd James, *The Cowley Fathers: A History of the English Congregation of the Society of St. John the Evangelist* (London: Canterbury Press Norwich, 2019).

96. See the vivid images at Michael Winn, "Blessed Martyrs of Pratulin," Royal Doors, January 23, 2017, https://royaldoors.net/blessed-martyrs-pratulin/.

97. Pope John Paul II, "Apostolic Journey to Poland," Homily of His Holiness John Paul II, Eucharistic Celebration, Siedlce, Poland, June 10, 1999 (Rome: Libreria Editrice Vaticana, 1999), https://w2.vatican.va/content/john-paul-ii/en/homilies/1999/documents/hf_jp-ii_hom _19990610_siedlce.html.

98. Mr. Bland, in Taylor, *China's Millions* (1890), 127.

99. John Foxe, *Foxe's Book of Martyrs* (Frankfurt, Germany: Verlag, 2020), 181.

CHAPTER 13: MILLIONS OF MARTYRS IN THE TWENTIETH CENTURY

1. For an extended passage from Timothy Keller on "The Healing of God," see *The Reason for God: Belief in an Age of Skepticism* (New York: Dutton, 2008), 94–99. There are various renditions of this quote, likely composites from his numerous speeches and prolific nature. A common web quote is, "Christ's miracles were not the suspension of the natural order but the restoration of the natural order. They were a reminder of what once was prior to the fall and a preview of what will eventually be a universal reality once again—a world of peace and justice, without death, disease, or conflict."

2. Alan Kreider, "God's Left Wing: The Radical Reformers," Christian History Institute, originally published in *Christian History*, no. 9 (1984), https://christianhistoryinstitute.org/magazine /article/gods-left-wing-radical-reformers.

3. Hudson Taylor to Mr. Berger, July 3, in Dr. and Mrs. Howard, *Hudson Taylor and the China Inland Mission: The Growth of a Work of God*, vol. 2 (London, 1918), "The Darkest Hour 1868–1869," art. 36–37.

4. Dan Wooding, "Modern Persecution," Christianity.com, May 3, 2010, https://www .christianity.com/church/church-history/timeline/1901-2000/modern-persecution-11630665 .html.

5. Justin D. Long, cited in Dan Wooding, "Modern Persecution."

6. Todd M. Johnson and Gina A. Zurlo, "Christian Martyrdom as a Pervasive Phenomenon," *Society* 51, no. 6 (December 2014), 679–85. Abstract and key findings of this article at Gordon -Conwell Theological Seminary, accessed April 24, 2022, https://www.gordonconwell.edu/wp -content/uploads/sites/13/2019/04/2Countingmartyrsmethodology.pdf.

7. Johnson and Zurlo, "Christian Martyrdom."

8. Eric Metaxas, *Bonhoeffer: Pastor, Martyr, Prophet, Spy*, rev. ed. (Nashville: Nelson Books, 2020), 470.

9. David Killingray, "'To Suffer Grief in All Kinds of Trials': Persecution and Martyrdom in the African Church in the Twentieth Century," *Studies in Church History* 30 (1993): 465–82, https://doi.org/10.1017/S0424208400011888.

10. James M. Nelson, *Psychology, Religion, and Spirituality* (New York: Springer, 2009), 427; Todd M. Johnson, "Christian Martyrdom: A Global Demographic Assessment," November 2012, Notre Dame, 4, https://mcgrath.nd.edu/assets/84231/.

11. David Neff, "Our Extended, Persecuted Family," editorial, *Christianity Today*, April 29, 1996, https://www.christianitytoday.com/ct/1996/april29/6t5014.html.

12. The debate has become more intense in 2020 about the plight of religious freedom, accented by closed churches during the pandemic while liquor stores and other businesses remained

open. However, the ongoing threats are the institutional, allegedly lodged in the majority of public universities, a number of federal courts, social media filters, etc. Interpreting the real for the perceived threats is for you as a reader, and a moving target. But what the stories in this book show is that massive Christian movements, at times the dominant religions in their countries or regions, were ruthlessly obliterated. Some of the signs of these historic transitions are alarming many American observers. See the *Alliance Defending Freedom Blog*, https://www.adflegal.org/blog/must-read. Also, see articles and books like Mary Everstadt, *It's Dangerous to Believe: Religious Freedom and Its Enemies* (New York: Harper, 2016); Mary Eberstadt, "Regular Christians Are No Longer Welcome in American Culture," *Time*, June 29, 2016, https://time.com/4385755/faith-in-america/; "These Are 3 of the Greatest Threats to Religious Freedom in America Today," CBN News, January 16, 2018, https://www1.cbn.com/cbnnews/us/2018/january/trump-proclaims-january-16-religious-freedom-day.

13. Wooding, "Modern Persecutions."
14. Paul Marshall, with Lela Gilbert, *Their Blood Cries Out: The Untold Story of Persecution against Christians in the Modern World* (Dallas: Word Publishing, 1997), 49.
15. Azmi Özcan, *Pan-Islamism: Indian Muslims, the Ottomans and Britain (1877–1924)*, The Ottoman Empire and Its Heritage, vol. 12 (Leiden, Netherlands: Brill, 1997).
16. Necati Alkan, "Süleyman Nazif's 'Open Letter to Jesus': An Anti-Christian Polemic in the Early Turkish Republic," *Middle Eastern Studies* 44, no. 6 (November 2008): 851–65, https://www.jstor.org/stable/40262625.
17. Open Doors, *World Watch List 2020* (Santa Ana, CA: Open Doors USA), 48.
18. Ramazan Kılınç, "Christians Have Lived in Turkey for Two Millennia—But Their Future Is Uncertain," The Conversation, November 21, 2019, https://theconversation.com/christians-have-lived-in-turkey-for-two-millennia-but-their-future-is-uncertain-127296.
19. Giles Milton, *Paradise Lost: Smyrna 1922: The Destruction of Islam's City of Tolerance* (London: Sceptre, 2008), 268–69.
20. Sarantos Kargakos, "The Slaying of Metropolitan Chrysostomos," unknown trans., *Oikonomikos Tachydromos*, October 8, 1992, Constantinople (website), http://fstav.0fees.net/chrisostomos.html?i=1.
21. Kargakos, "Slaying."
22. Marjorie Housepian Dobkin, *Smyrna 1922: The Destruction of a City* (New York: Newmark Press, 1998).
23. Lou Ureneck, *Smyrna, September 1922: The American Mission to Rescue Victims of the 20th Century's First Genocide* (New York: Ecco, 2016; hardcover published as *The Great Fire*, Ecco, 2015).
24. Esther Pohl Lovejoy, *Certain Samaritans* (New York: Macmillan, 1933), 141.
25. *The Encyclical Epistle of the Church at Smyrna concerning the Martyrdom of the Holy Polycarp*, Ante-Nicene Fathers, vol. 1 (1885), chap. 12, https://ccel.org/ccel/polycarp/martyrdom_of_polycarp/anf01.iv.iv.xii.html.
26. Irenaeus, *Against Heresies*, Ante-Nicene Fathers, vol. 1 (1885), bk. 3, chap. 3, no. 4, https://www.ccel.org/ccel/schaff/anf01.ix.iv.iv.html.
27. John Chapman, "Tertullian," *Catholic Encyclopedia*, vol. 14 (New York: Robert Appleton, 1912), accessed April 24, 2022.
28. I. C. Wakerley, "The 'Delicate Murder' of the Grand Duke Sergei of Russia (1905)," *Theoria: A Journal of Social and Political Theory*, no. 47 (October 1976): 3–4, https://www.jstor.org/stable/41801605.
29. Nadieszda Kizenko, "Feminized Patriarchy? Orthodoxy and Gender in Post-Soviet Russia," *Signs* 38, no. 3 (Spring 2013): 613, 616, https://www.journals.uchicago.edu/doi/abs/10.1086/668516. Also see Gary Marker, *Imperial Saint: The Cult of St. Catherine and the Dawn of Female Rule in Russia* (DeKalb, IL: Northern Illinois University Press, 2007).

30. "Grand Duchess Elizabeth," commemoration, Westminster Abbey, accessed April 25, 2022, https://www.westminster-abbey.org/abbey-commemorations/commemorations/grand-duchess -elizabeth.

31. "Grand Duchess Elizabeth."

32. Madipoane Masenya, "Masemola, Manche (B)," Dictionary of African Christian Biography, 2017, https://dacb.org/stories/southafrica/masemola-manche2/.

33. "Manche Masemola," commemoration, Westminster Abbey, accessed April 25, 2022, https://www.westminster-abbey.org/abbey-commemorations/commemorations/manche -masemola.

34. Frederick Quinn, "Maseloma, Manche (A)," *Dictionary of African Christian Biography*, originally published in Frederick Quinn, *African Saints: Saints, Martyrs, and Holy People from the Continent of Africa* (New York: Crossroads, 2002), https://dacb.org/stories/southafrica /masemola-manche/.

35. Mandy Goedhals, "Colonialism, Culture, Christianity and the Struggle for Selfhood: Manche Masemola of Sekhukhuneland, c.1913–1928," *Alternation* 7, no. 2 (2000): 99–112, https://journals.co.za/doi/pdf/10.10520/AJA10231757_224. Also see Madipoane Masenya, "Manche Masemola, (B)" *Dictionary of African Christian Biography*, 2017, https://dacb .org/stories/southafrica/masemola-manche2/.

36. Masenya, "Manche Masemola, (B)," note 1. See section "On Missionaries and Missions"; Masenya gives a helpful and candid assessment of and challenge to missionaries from the West entering non-Western cultures.

37. See Mandy Goedhals, "Imperialism, Mission and Conversion: Manche Masemola of Sekhukhuneland" in Andrew Chandler, ed., *The Terrible Alternative: Christian Martyrdom in the Twentieth Century* (London: Cassell, 1998), 30–45.

38. Greg Smith-Young, "Manche Masemola: A Living Stone," July 7, 2019, Elora United Church, https://elorauc.org/wp-content/uploads/2019/07/2019-07-07-Manche-Masemola.pdf. This is cited as an account written by Archdeacon John Tsebe, who performed her baptism.

39. Goedhals, "Colonialism."

40. Andrew Chandler, ed., *The Terrible Alternative: Christian Martyrdom in the Twentieth Century* (London: Cassell, 1998). This book covers the ten martyrs depicted above Westminster Abbey's Great West Door.

41. "Modern Martyrs," About the Abbey, History, Westminster Abbey, accessed April 25, 2022, https://www.westminster-abbey.org/about-the-abbey/history/modern-martyrs.

42. See Lee S. Huizenga, *John and Betty Stam: Martyrs* (Grand Rapids, MI: Zondervan, 1935).

43. John Stam to China Inland Mission officials, December 6, 1934, in Mrs. Howard Taylor, *The Triumph of John and Betty Stam* (Chicago: Moody, 1935), 130.

44. Mrs. Howard Taylor, *The Triumph of John and Betty Stam* (Chicago: Moody, 1935), 132.

45. "Betty and John Stam Martyred," Christianity.com, accessed April 25, 2022, https://www .christianity.com/church/church-history/timeline/1901-2000/betty-and-john-stam -martyred-11630759.html.

46. See Kathleen White, *John and Betty Stam*, Women and Men of Faith (Minneapolis, MN: Bethany, 1989).

47. Like most polymaths, Pavel Florensky was an innovative and provocative thinker. He was a deeply mystical theologian with a number of unconventional, though not unorthodox views. Among other things, he espoused a form of asexual same-sex spiritual union that would have its closest biblical parallel in the covenantal friendship of David and Jonathan in the books 1 and 2 Samuel. The formal term for this kind of relationship is *adelphopoiesis*, which is simply the Greek for "brother-making." And, like many Russian Orthodox thinkers from his era, Florensky was a proponent of so-called "onomatodoxy," also known as "Name Worshiping." Christians in this tradition have given elevated status to the name of God, to the point of suggesting, "The Name

of God is God himself." Outside of Russia this view has been very uncommon, though it too has some limited biblical precedent in the Deuteronomic "Name Theology" of the Pentateuch. Perhaps most controversially, Florensky also had an enduring interest in sophiology, which tended to identify God's essence with divine wisdom and refer to this under the name of Sophia, which is simply the Greek for "wisdom." The nuance in this viewpoint is highly contested and too involved to engage in a volume like this. However, whatever we think of these views, Florensky would die for his faith, and his commitment to core doctrines and Christ incarnate appear not to have been compromised or eclipsed by these beliefs.

48. Aleksandr I. Solzhenitsyn, *The Gulag Archipelago 1918–1956: An Experiment in Literary Investigation III–IV*, trans. Thomas P. Whitney (New York: Harper & Row, 1975), 670–71.

49. Loren Graham and Jean-Michel Kantor, *Naming Infinity: The True Story of Religious Mysticism and Mathematical Creativity* (Cambridge, MA: Belknap Press of Harvard University Press, 2009), 125–26.

50. "Saint Maximilian Kolbe," CatholicSaints.Info, accessed April 25, 2022, https://catholicsaints .info/saint-maximilian-kolbe/.

51. "Saint Maximilian Kolbe."

52. "Do Not Get with the Times," *Catholic Voice*, Catholic Archdiocese of Canberra and Goulburn, August 14, 2020, https://www.catholicvoice.org.au/do-not-get-with-the-times/.

53. For a discussion of the ecumenical nature of these martyrdoms, see Lawrence S. Cunningham, "Saints and Martyrs: Some Contemporary Considerations," *Theological Studies* 60, no. 3 (1999): 534–37, http://cdn.theologicalstudies.net/60/60.3/60.3.7.pdf.

54. Bishop Strong, quoted at Dan Graves, "Martyrs Remembered in Papua," Christianity.com, May 3, 2010, https://www.christianity.com/church/church-history/timeline/1901-2000 /martyrs-remembered-in-papua-11630773.html.

55. There are numerous memorials for martyrs along the coasts of the island countries, with many dating between 1878 and 1935—including both Pacific Islanders and foreign missionaries. A real impetus for the thread of Christian teachers (and martyrs) came through the work of Rev. George Brown, secretary of the Wesleyan Methodist Missionary Society of Australasia (1887–1908); see David Wetherell, "From Fiji to Papua: The Work of the 'Vakavuvuli,'" *Journal of Pacific History* 13, no. 3 (1978): 153–72, https://www.jstor.org/stable/25168334. Also, see Diana Dewar, *All for Christ: Some Twentieth Century Martyrs* (Oxford: Oxford University Press, 1980).

56. Graves, "Martyrs Remembered."

57. Judith M. Heimann, *The Airmen and the Headhunters: A True Story of Lost Soldiers, Heroic Tribesmen, and the Unlikeliest Rescue of World War II* (Orlando: Harcourt, 2007), 268.

58. Willfinger to Makahanap, September 24, 1942, quoted at "Ministry Trip to Kampung Baru," *The Forney Flyer* (blog), August 25, 2010, http://theforneyflyer.blogspot.com/2010/08/ministry -trip-to-kampung-baru.html.

59. Quoted in Dick Staub Sr., "A Noise of Many Voices," *Alliance Life*, September 2009, https://legacy.cmalliance.org/alife/a-noise-of-many-voices/.

60. J. M. C., "Christ Is God," *King's Business*, July 1930 (Bible Institute of Los Angeles), 331, https://online.flippingbook.com/view/199433/4/.

61. John Foxe and The Voice of the Martyrs, *Foxe: Voices of the Martyrs*, rev. ed. (Bartlesville, OK: VOM Books, 2013), 237.

62. For a detailed yet readable account, see Heimann, *The Airmen and the Headhunters*.

63. George Eliot, *Middlemarch* (Berlin, 1872–1873), bk. 8, ch. 87. Also see "A Hidden Life Review," review of *A Hidden Life*, directed by Terrence Malick, Culture Whisper, January 17, 2020, https://www.culturewhisper.com/r/cinema/a_hidden_life_review_malick_cannes/13954.

64. Tina Gayle, "Anschluss: The German Annexation of Austria Explained," History Hit, August 13, 2018, https://www.historyhit.com/anschluss-the-german-annexation-of-austria-explained/.

65. "Solitary, but Not Alone," *Denver Catholic*, March 28, 2016, https://denvercatholic.org/franz
-jagerstatter-solitary-but-not-alone/.

66. *Franz Jägerstätter: Letters and Writings from Prison*, ed. Erna Putz, trans. Robert A. Krieg
(Maryknoll, NY: Orbis Books, 2009), 187.

67. *Jägerstätter*, 182.

68. *Jägerstätter*, 175.

69. *Jägerstätter*, 190.

70. Pope Pius XI, quoted in *Jägerstätter*, 190n.

71. "Solitary, but Not Alone."

72. *Jägerstätter*, 243.

73. *Jägerstätter*, 245.

74. Metaxas, *Bonhoeffer*, 234–36, 246–53.

75. This is the version at the United States Holocaust Memorial Museum in Washington, DC.
See "Martin Niemöller: 'First They Came for the Socialists . . . ,'" United States Holocaust
Memorial Museum, Holocaust Encyclopedia, last updated March 30, 2012,
https://encyclopedia.ushmm.org/content/en/article/martin-niemoeller-first-they
-came-for-the-socialists.

76. "Dietrich Bonhoeffer: German Theologian and Resister," *Christianity Today*, originally
published in *Christian History*, "Dietrich Bonhoeffer: Theologian in Nazi Germany," no. 32
(1991), https://www.christianitytoday.com/history/people/martyrs/dietrich-bonhoeffer.html.

77. Dietrich Bonhoeffer, *Barcelona, Berlin, New York: 1928–1931*, Dietrich Bonhoeffer Works, ed.
Clifford J. Green, trans. Douglas W. Stott, vol. 10 (Minneapolis: Fortress, 2009), 317.

78. Bonhoeffer to Reinhold Niebuhr [1939], quoted in Eberhard Bethge, *Dietrich Bonhoeffer:
Theologian, Christian, Man for His Times: A Biography*, rev. ed. (Minneapolis: Fortress, 2000), 655.

79. See Mark Galli and Ted Olsen, *131 Christians Everyone Should Know* (Nashville: Broadman and
Holman, 2000), 378–80.

80. Bonhoeffer to Bishop Ammundsen, August 8, [1934], quoted in Eric Metaxas, *Bonhoeffer:
Pastor, Martyr, Prophet, Spy* (Nashville: Thomas Nelsen, 2010), 236.

81. S. Payne Best, *The Venlo Incident* (London: Hutchinson, 1950). This book's title represents the
disastrous capture of British spies and others at a café in Venlo near the border, and gives one
of the best insider accounts of the Nazi camp operations. See "The Venlo Kidnapping," *Times*,
February 19, 1948.

82. S. Payne Best, *The Venlo Incident: A True Story of Double-Dealing, Captivity, and a Murderous
Nazi Plot* (London: Frontline Books, 2009; London: Hutchinson, 1950), 200.

83. H. Fischer-Hüllstrung, quoted in Metaxas, *Bonhoeffer*, 532.

84. Bonhoeffer, quoted in Metaxas, *Bonhoeffer*, 531.

85. Dietrich Bonhoeffer, quoted at "Dietrich Bonhoeffer: German Theologian and Resister,"
Christianity Today, originally published in *Christian History*, "Dietrich Bonhoeffer: Theologian
in Nazi Germany," no. 32 (1991), https://www.christianitytoday.com/history/people/martyrs
/dietrich-bonhoeffer.html. The church where he preached was razed by the German bombing
in 1944; a new church was erected in 1958 and named the Dietrich-Bonhoeffer-Kirche.

86. "Blessed Maurice Tornay," CatholicSaints.Info, May 5, 2020, https://catholicsaints.info/blessed
-maurice-tornay/.

87. Kateri Tekakwitha Parish, "Bl. Maurice Tornay," Catholic Online, accessed April 26, 2022,
https://www.catholic.org/saints/saint.php?saint_id=7530.

88. See Janet Benge and Geoff Benge, "A Dangerous Task," in *Rachel Saint: A Star in the Jungle*
(Seattle: YWAM Publishing, 2004), chap. 1.

89. "Go Ye and Preach the Gospel: Five Do and Die," *Life*, January 30, 1956. For full images of the
pages, see https://issuu.com/mafuk/docs/life_mag_-_jan_1956_-_five_do_and_d/1?ff&e
=4462917/61317978.

90. Jim Elliot, *The Journals of Jim Elliot*, ed. Elisabeth Elliot (Grand Rapids, MI: Revell, 1978), 174.

91. The key reason for her separation from the mission organization (Summer Institute of Linguistics—now SIL International) was its decision to terminate her work there, mainly because an official anthropological review had revealed the near destruction of the indigenous culture. Opinions likely differ now and then on that issue, but the huge change that appeared extremely positive was that the introduction of Christian mores had radically reduced acts of violence among the Huaorani. She remains to this day a missionary hero associated with her originally sending unit, Wycliffe Bible Translators. See James A. Yost, "Twenty Years of Contact: The Mechanisms of Change in Huao ("Auca") Culture," in Norman E. Whitten Jr., ed., *Cultural Transformations and Ethnicity in Modern Ecuador* (Urbana, IL: University of Illinois Press, 1981).

92. Tyndale House remains a nonprofit publishing house, perhaps the largest publisher among those committed to Christian resources. The profits from its book sales go to ministries in line with its stated Christian mission.

93. Elisabeth Elliot, "Through Gates of Splendor," *Christianity Today*, June 10, 1957, https://www.christianitytoday.com/ct/1957/june-10/through-gates-of-splendor.html.

94. Edith G. Cherry, "We Rest on Thee," Timeless Truths, 1895, https://library.timelesstruths.org/music/We_Rest_on_Thee/.

95. "Esther John," commemoration, Westminster Abbey, accessed April 27, 2022, https://www.westminster-abbey.org/abbey-commemorations/commemorations/esther-john.

96. Vivienne Stacey, quoted at C. H., "Discipling Those Who Pay a Great Price for Faith: Esther John 1929–1960," blog, When Women Speak, April 4, 2016, https://whenwomenspeak.net/blog/disciplining-those-who-pay-a-great-price-for-faith-esther-john-1929-1960/.

97. Stacey, at C. H. "Discipling."

98. See the book by his widow, Lois Carlson Bridges, *Monganga Paul: The Congo Ministry and Martyrdom of Paul Carlson, M.D.* (Chicago, IL: Covenant Publications, 2004; New York: Harper & Row, 1966).

99. "Congo Ransom: A Good Man's Life," *Life*, December 4, 1964, 35.

100. "Congo Ransom," 35.

101. His home church was Rolling Hills Covenant Church, according to James Daane and J. D. Douglas, "Dr. Paul Carlson: A Life at Stake," *Christianity Today*, December 4, 1964, https://www.christianitytoday.com/ct/1964/december-4/church-and-state-dr-paul-carlson-life-at-stake.html.

102. "Congo Ransom," 42B.

103. C. Richard Hofstetter, "Political Disengagement and the Death of Martin Luther King," *Public Opinion Quarterly* 33, no. 2 (Summer 1969): 174, https://www.jstor.org/stable/2747758.

104. David J. Garrow, interview by Carol Costello, *CNN Daybreak*, CNN, transcript, August 28, 2003, http://www.cnn.com/TRANSCRIPTS/0308/28/lad.18.html.

105. Edward Gilbreath, "Catching Up with a Dream," *Christianity Today*, March 2, 1998, https://www.christianitytoday.com/ct/1998/march2/evangelicals-race-martin-luther-king-jr-30-years.html.

106. Brantley W. Gasaway, "'Glimmers of Hope': Progressive Evangelicals and Racism, 1965–2000," in *Christians and the Color Line: Race and Religion after Divided by Faith*, ed. J. Russell Hawkins and Phillip Luke Sinitiere (Oxford: Oxford University Press, 2014), 88.

107. Although he changed his son's name after his trip, the birth certificate was not officially changed until Dr. Martin Luther King Jr. was 28 years old (July 23, 1957).

108. Russel Moldovan, "Martin Luther King, Jr." *Christianity Today*, originally published in "Ten Influential Christians of the 20th Century," *Christian History*, no. 65 (2000), https://www.christianitytoday.com/history/issues/issue-65/martin-luther-king-jr.html.

109. Andy Rau, "Bible References in Martin Luther King, Jr.'s 'I Have a Dream' Speech," *BibleGateway Blog*, August 28, 2011, https://www.biblegateway.com/blog/2011/08/bible -references-in-the-i-have-a-dream-speech/.

110. Martin Luther King Jr., "I've Been to the Mountaintop" (speech given in support of striking sanitation workers, Mason Temple, Memphis, April 3, 1968), AFSCME, https://www.afscme .org/about/history/mlk/mountaintop.

111. "James Earl Ray," Biography, last updated May 3, 2021, https://www.biography.com/crime -figure/james-earl-ray.

112. Tom Jackman, "Who Killed Martin Luther King Jr.? His Family Believes James Earl Ray Was Framed," *Washington Post*, March 30, 2018, https://www.washingtonpost.com/news/retropolis /wp/2018/03/30/who-killed-martin-luther-king-jr-his-family-believes-james-earl-ray-was -framed/.

113. Joseph Tse-Hei Lee, "Watchman Nee and the Little Flock Movement in Maoist China," *Church History* 74, no. 1 (March 2005): 72, https://www.jstor.org/stable/4146313.

114. Witness Lee [Li Changshou], *Watchman Nee: A Seer of the Divine Revelation in the Present Age* (Anaheim: Living Stream Ministry, 1991).

115. Francis P. Jones, ed., *Documents of the Three-Self Movement: Source Materials for the Study of the Protestant Church in Communist China* (New York: National Council of the Churches of Christ in the USA, 1963).

116. "The Testimony of You Qi Wu—Watchman Nee's Friend and Cellmate," posted on YouTube March 7, 2022, https://www.youtube.com/watch?v=1HrnYKxwudY.

117. Joseph Tse-Hei Lee, "Watchman Nee."

118. "Watchman Nee's Life and Ministry," Watchman Nee (website), accessed April 26, 2022, https://www.watchmannee.org/life-ministry.html.

119. Watchman Nee, *The Normal Christian Life* (Carol Stream, IL: Tyndale, 1977), 2.

120. Wang Zhiming, quoted at Roberts Liardon, *God's Generals: Martyrs* (New Kensington, PA: Whitaker House, 2016), 296.

121. Liao Yiwu, *God Is Red: The Secret Story of How Christianity Survived and Flourished in Communist China*, trans. Wenguang Huang (New York: HarperOne, 2011), 107–112.

122. Excerpt from Liao Yiwu's interview in *God Is Red*, cited at Nigel Tomes, "Wang Zhiming: Chinese Christian Martyr, 1973," Church in Toronto, January 8, 2012, http://churchintoronto .blogspot.com/2012/01/wang-zhiming-chinese-christian-martyr.html.

123. Yiwu, *God Is Red*, excerpt at Tomes, "Wang Zhiming."

124. "Wang Zhiming," commemoration, Westminster Abbey, accessed April 27, 2022, https://www .westminster-abbey.org/abbey-commemorations/commemorations/wang-zhiming.

125. Yiwu, *God Is Red*, excerpt at Tomes, "Wang Zhiming."

126. "Wang Zhiming," Westminster Abbey.

127. "Wang Zhiming," Westminster Abbey.

128. These numbers vary greatly in different accounts. Yunnan seemed to be one of the most concentrated areas of Protestants at the time of the 1949 Communist takeover.

129. Mark A. Noll, quoted at Mary Wimberley, "Martyrdom's Place in History Told at Beeson Service," Samford University, April 4, 2012, https://www.samford.edu/news/2012/Martyrdoms -Place-in-History-Told-at-Beeson-Service. Considerable attention to modern martyrs is found in the August 2018 services at Beeson Divinity School addressing the theme "the Noble Army of Martyrs"; see Andrew Russell, "Beeson Divinity School to Focus on Martyrdom in Community Worship during Fall 2018," Samford University, August 23, 2018, https://www .samford.edu/news/2018/08/Beeson-Divinity-School-to-Focus-on-Martyrdom-in-Community -Worship-During-Fall-2018.

130. Carol Natukunda, "Archbishop Janani Luwum's Final Moments Alive," New Vision, accessed April 26, 2022, https://www.newvision.co.ug/news/1320841/archbishop-janani-luwums-final -moments-alive.

131. "Church of Uganda Stages 500km Pilgrimage to Commemorate Archbishop Janani Luwum," Anglican Communion News Service, February 18, 2020, https://www.anglicannews.org/news/2020/02/church-of-uganda-stages-500km-pilgrimage-to-commemorate-archbishop-janani-luwum.aspx.

132. Dana L. Robert, "The Influence of American Missionary Women on the World Back Home," *Religion and American Culture: A Journal of Interpretation* 12, no. 1 (Winter 2002): 64, https://www.jstor.org/stable/10.1525/rac.2002.12.1.59.

133. *Andrew Gerow Hodges Chapel: Beeson Divinity School, Samford University* (Birmingham, AL: Samford University, August 8, 2019), https://issuu.com/samford_university/docs/beeson_divinity_hodges_chapel_guide.

134. John Foxe, *Foxe's Book of Martyrs*, updated and abridged (Uhrichsville, OH: Barbour, 2001), 9.

SECTION FOUR: MARTYRS OF RECENT HISTORY

1. The names in this account have been changed to protect those involved, and family relationships may or may not be the same. The story is taken from those directly connected to the martyr, and the details are accurate. The names chosen are of Coptic friends of the authors not involved with this story.

CHAPTER 14: FROM THE SOVIETS IN EUROPE AND A CALIPHATE IN THE MIDDLE EAST

1. Anthony O'Mahony, "Archbishop Paulos Faraj Rahho," *Guardian*, March 31, 2008, https://www.theguardian.com/world/2008/apr/01/catholicism.religion.

2. "Pope's Quotes: Blood of Martyrs," National Catholic Reporter, September 26, 2016, https://www.ncronline.org/blogs/francis-chronicles/popes-quotes-blood-martyrs.

3. Eleanor R and olph, "Billy Graham Stirs Moscow's Religious Spirit," *Washington Post*, October 26, 1992, https://www.washingtonpost.com/archive/politics/1992/10/26/billy-graham-stirs-moscows-religious-spirit/0b243ce9-ff40-4a38-a6f1-3bbecde20ee2/.

4. "A Revival in Moscow: Billy Graham's Legacy in Eurasia," Mission Eurasia, March 13, 2018, https://missioneurasia.ca/articles/a-revival-in-moscow-billy-grahams-legacy-in-eurasia/.

5. Pew Research Center, *Religious Belief and National Belonging in Central and Eastern Europe*, May 10, 2017, https://www.pewforum.org/2017/05/10/religious-belief-and-national-belonging-in-central-and-eastern-europe/.

6. Justin Jalil, "Renowned Soviet Refusenik Vladimir Slepak Dies at 87," *Times of Israel*, April 25, 2015, https://www.timesofisrael.com/renowned-soviet-refusenik-vladimir-slepak-dies-at-87/.

7. "Jews in Former Soviet Union: Refusniks," Jewish Virtual Library, accessed September 2, 2020, https://www.jewishvirtuallibrary.org/refusniks; "Remember the Refuseniks?" *New York Times*, December 14, 1990, https://www.nytimes.com/1990/12/14/opinion/remember-the-refuseniks.html; Renee Ghert-Zand, "Once Heroes of US Jewry, Soviet Refuseniks Are Largely Forgotten. Not for Long," *Times of Israel*, December 22, 2019, https://www.timesofisrael.com/once-heroes-of-us-jewry-soviet-refuseniks-are-largely-forgotten-not-for-long/.

8. Sergei Bessmertny, "Alexander Men," Alexander Men (website), accessed September 2, 2020, http://www.alexandrmen.ru/english/index.html.

9. Wallace Daniel, "Aleksandr Men, Intellectual Freedom and the Russian Orthodox Church," *Kirchliche Zeitgeschichte* 24, no. 1 (2011): 92–119.

10. Jerry Ryan, "Struck Down, Orthodox Priest Alexander Men Also Struck a Chord," *National Catholic Reporter*, September 27, 2014, https://www.ncronline.org/news/people/struck-down-orthodox-priest-alexander-men-also-struck-chord.

11. Ryan, "Struck Down."

12. Ryan, "Struck Down."

13. Ryan, "Struck Down."

14. Ryan, "Struck Down."

15. Bessmertny, "Alexander Men."

16. See Galatians 5:13. Also see "Alexander Men: A Modern Martyr, Free in the Faith, Open to the World," Alexander Men (website), accessed March 18, 2022, http://www.alexandermen .com/Alexander_Men:_A_Modern_Martyr,_Free_in_the_Faith,_Open_to_the_World.

17. Grace Davie, *Religion in Britain Since 1945: Believing without Belonging* (Oxford: Institute of Contemporary British History, 1994).

18. Samuel Gregg, "The Passion of Father Jacques Hamel," *Catholic World Report*, August 17, 2018, https://www.catholicworldreport.com/2018/08/17/the-passion-of-father-jacques-hamel/.

19. Nicholas Zinos, "Father Jacques Hamel, Europe's First 21st-Century Martyr," *America*, July 26, 2018, https://www.americamagazine.org/faith/2018/07/26/father-jacques-hamel-europes-first -21st-century-martyr.

20. Gregg, "Passion of Father Jacques Hamel."

21. Zinos, "Father Jacques Hamel."

22. Gregg, "Passion of Father Jacques Hamel."

23. Gregg, "Passion of Father Jacques Hamel."

24. Zinos, "Father Jacques Hamel."

25. Gregg, "Passion of Father Jacques Hamel."

26. Zinos, "Father Jacques Hamel."

27. Gregg, "Passion of Father Jacques Hamel."

28. Zinos, "Father Jacques Hamel."

29. Zinos, "Father Jacques Hamel."

30. Gregg, "Passion of Father Jacques Hamel."

31. Zinos, "Father Jacques Hamel."

32. "Mother Teresa," North Macedonia Timeless, accessed March 18, 2022, https://macedonia -timeless.com/eng/about/about/did-you-know/mother-teresa/.

33. Krishna Pokharel and Philip Wen, "India Bars Foreign Donations to Christian Group Founded by Mother Teresa," *Wall Street Journal*, December 27, 2021, https://www.wsj.com/articles/india -bars-foreign-donations-to-christian-group-founded-by-mother-teresa-11640642739.

34. "Slain Missionary, Dr. Martha Myers, 'Gave Her All to People Who Were Suffering,'" Samford University, accessed March 18, 2022, https://www.samford.edu/news/2003/Slain-Missionary -Dr-Martha-Myers-Gave-Her-All-to-People-who-Were-Suffering.

35. Ivan Oransky, "Martha C. Myers," obituary, *Lancet* 361, no. 9363 (March 29, 2003): 1139, https://www.thelancet.com/journals/lancet/article/PIIS0140-6736(03)12857-7/fulltext.

36. "Slain Missionary, Dr. Martha Myers."

37. "Slain Missionary, Dr. Martha Myers."

38. Oransky, "Martha C. Myers."

39. Robert D. McFadden, "Victims Shared Affection for Yemenis, Families Say," *New York Times*, December 31, 2002, https://www.nytimes.com/2002/12/31/us/threats-and-responses-the-dead -victims-shared-affection-for-yemenis-families-say.html.

40. Sondra Washington, "Early On, Martha Myers' Selflessness Was Evident, Family Members Recount," Baptist Press, January 13, 2003, https://www.baptistpress.com/resource-library /news/early-on-martha-myers-selflessness-was-evident-family-members-recount/.

41. Erin Curry, "Martha Myers: A Life Dedicated to Caring for the Yemeni People," Baptist Press, December 31, 2002, http://m.bpnews.net/14945/martha-myers-a-life-dedicated-to-caring-for -the-yemeni-people.

42. Washington, "Early On."

43. Washington, "Early On."

44. Washington, "Early On."

45. Washington, "Early On."

46. Curry, "Martha Myers."

47. Washington, "Early On."

48. Oransky, "Martha C. Myers."

49. Washington, "Early On."

50. Jayson Casper, "Why We Opened a Christian University in Iraq amid ISIS' Genocide," *Christianity Today*, May 7, 2020, https://www.christianitytoday.com/news/2020/may/iraq -christians-erbil-chaldean-university-isis-rasche.html.

51. Teresa Adamo, "Karen Watson: A Life Given, Not Taken," *Bakersfield Californian*, February 10, 2006, https://www.bakersfield.com/archives/karen-watson-a-life-given-not-taken/article _bb492f0b-41bf-582b-9bee-f902a2ae7063.html.

52. Steve Rubenstein, "Beloved Missionary Killed in Drive-By Shooting in Iraq," SFGATE, March 17, 2004, https://www.sfgate.com/bayarea/article/BAKERSFIELD-Beloved-missionary-killed -in-2808206.php.

53. Erich Bridges, "Karen Watson, 10 Years On," *WorldView Conversation* (blog), March 11, 2014, http://worldviewconversation.blogspot.com/2014/03/karen-watson-10-years-on.html.

54. Rubenstein, "Beloved Missionary Killed."

55. International Mission Board (IMB), "Karen Watson: His Glory, Our Reward," Facebook, August 2, 2017, video, 5:46, https://www.facebook.com/imb.sbc/videos/10155560991309715/.

56. Bridges, "Karen Watson."

57. Bridges, "Karen Watson."

58. Bridges, "Karen Watson."

59. Bridges, "Karen Watson."

60. Rubenstein, "Beloved Missionary Killed."

61. Erin Curry, "'Keep Sending Missionaries,' Karen Watson Wrote in Letter," Baptist Press, March 24, 2004, https://www.baptistpress.com/resource-library/news/keep-sending-missionaries-karen -watson-wrote-in-letter/.

62. Bridges, "Karen Watson."

63. Bridges, "Karen Watson."

64. Tom Hoopes, "Father Ragheed Ganni, Hero Priest of Iraq," *Ex Corde*, Benedictine College, July 8, 2018, https://excorde.org/2018/father-ragheed-ganni-hero-priest-of-iraq.

65. Hoopes, "Father Ragheed Ganni."

66. Hoopes, "Father Ragheed Ganni."

67. Hoopes, "Father Ragheed Ganni."

68. Inés San Martin, "Martyrdom Causes of 5 Iraqis to Be Presented to Vatican in Early September," *Crux*, August 27, 2019, https://cruxnow.com/vatican/2019/08/martyrdom-causes -of-5-iraqis-to-be-presented-to-vatican-in-early-september/.

69. San Martin, "Martyrdom Causes of 5 Iraqis."

70. San Martin, "Martyrdom Causes of 5 Iraqis."

71. Pontifical University of St. Thomas Aquinas, "Servant of God: Fr. Ragheed Aziz Ganni," *Angelicum*, July 2020, 8–9, https://issuu.com/angelicum/docs/angelicummagsp2020_final _2020_without_donor_list_a/s/10965903.

72. James Gordon Meek, "Who Was Kayla Mueller, American ISIS Hostage?" ABC News, August 24, 2016, https://abcnews.go.com/International/kayla-mueller-american-isis-hostage /story?id=41545404.

73. Meek, "Who Was Kayla Mueller?"

74. Scott O'Neill, "Kayla Mueller Remembered," Presbyterian Church (USA), February 20, 2015, https://www.pcusa.org/news/2015/2/20/kayla-mueller-remembered/.

75. Meek, "Who Was Kayla Mueller?"

76. Meek, "Who Was Kayla Mueller?"

77. Paul Wood, "US Hostage Kayla Mueller 'Killed by IS,' Say Ex-Slaves," BBC News, September 10, 2015, https://www.bbc.com/news/world-middle-east-34205911.

78. Zack Beauchamp, "Read the Extraordinary Letter ISIS Hostage Kayla Mueller Sent Her Family before Her Death," Vox, February 10, 2015, https://www.vox.com/2015/2/10/8012881/kayla-mueller-letter.

79. Cassandra Vinograd, "American ISIS Hostage Kayla Mueller Is Dead, Family Says," NBC News, February 10, 2015, https://www.nbcnews.com/storyline/isis-uncovered/american-isis-hostage-kayla-mueller-dead-family-says-n303591.

80. Adam Goldman and Rukmini Callimachi, "ISIS Leader al-Baghdadi May Have Had U.S. Hostage Executed, Witness Says," New York Times, November 12, 2019, https://www.nytimes.com/2019/11/12/us/politics/kayla-mueller-baghdadi.html.

81. Vassilios S. Kyratzopoulos, "The Violations of the Treaty of Lausanne by the Turkish Republic 1923 to 1999," September 2007, https://www.academia.edu/6487178/The_violations_of_the_Treaty_of_Lausanne.

82. "Statement on Murder, Fire and Robbery at Shrine of St. Therapon of Patriarchate," Orthodox Observer News, (1998 news archives), Greek Orthodox Archdiocese of America, https://www.goarch.org/-/statement-on-murder-fire-and-robbery-at-shrine-of-st-therapon-of-patriarchate.

83. "Murder, Fire and Robbery at Shrine of St. Therapon."

84. Stephen Kinzer, "For Greeks in Turkey, Distrust Turns to Fear," New York Times, January 23, 1998, https://www.nytimes.com/1998/01/23/world/for-greeks-in-turkey-distrust-turns-to-fear.html.

85. Zenit News Agency, "Bishop Asked Prayers for Mideast before His Murder," ZENIT, September 23, 2010, https://web.archive.org/web/20120914165316/http:/www.zenit.org/article-30468?l=english.

86. Zenit, "Bishop Asked Prayers for Mideast."

87. Zenit, "Bishop Asked Prayers for Mideast."

88. Ramazan Kılınç, "Christians Have Lived in Turkey for Two Millennia—but Their Future Is Uncertain," The Conversation, November 21, 2019, https://theconversation.com/christians-have-lived-in-turkey-for-two-millennia-but-their-future-is-uncertain-127296.

89. Sandro Magister, "Blessed Are the Meek: The Life and Martyrdom of a Priest on Mission in Turkey," Catholic Culture, February 7, 2006, https://www.catholicculture.org/culture/library/view.cfm?recnum=6783.

90. John L. Allen Jr., "Struggling to Understand a Bishop's Murder in Turkey," National Catholic Reporter, June 11, 2010, https://www.ncronline.org/blogs/all-things-catholic/struggling-understand-bishops-murder-turkey.

91. Allen, "Struggling to Understand."

92. Allen, "Struggling to Understand."

93. Allen, "Struggling to Understand."

94. Michael J. Miller, "Delayed Justice for Bishop Luigi Padovese," Catholic World Report, February 6, 2013, https://www.catholicworldreport.com/2013/02/06/delayed-justice-for-bishop-luigi-padovese/.

95. CNN Politics, "Catholic Bishop Stabbed to Death in Southern Turkey," CNN Wire (blog), June 3, 2010, https://news.blogs.cnn.com/2010/06/03/catholic-bishop-stabbed-to-death-in-southern-turkey/.

96. Zenit, "Bishop Asked Prayers for Mideast."

97. Mindy Belz, They Say We Are Infidels: On the Run from ISIS with Persecuted Christians in the Middle East (Carol Stream, IL: Tyndale Momentum, 2016), 149.

98. "Love for Our Muslim Brothers and for Iraq in Mgr Rahho's Will," English News and Articles, Ankawa.com, April 20, 2008, https://www.ankawa.com/english/?p=1062.

99. Belz, They Say We Are Infidels, 148.

100. Anthony O'Mahony, "Archbishop Paulos Faraj Rahho," Guardian, March 31, 2008, https://www.theguardian.com/world/2008/apr/01/catholicism.religion.

101. Hannah Brockhaus, "This Priest and Three Companions Were Killed for the Faith in Iraq," *Catholic News Agency*, June 9, 2017, https://www.catholicnewsagency.com/news/this-priest -and-three-companions-were-murdered-for-the-faith-in-iraq-25347.
102. Belz, *They Say We Are Infidels*, 148.
103. Ross Colvin et al., "Iraqi Archbishop Found Dead, Al Qaeda Blamed," Reuters, March 13, 2008, https://www.reuters.com/article/us-iraq-archbishop-killing/iraqi-archbishop-found-dead -al-qaeda-blamed-idUSRAT00361720080313.
104. Belz, *They Say We Are Infidels*, 149.
105. Belz, *They Say We Are Infidels*, 149.
106. "Iraqi Christians Do Not Fully Embrace Verdict in Archbishop's Murder," Voice of America, October 27, 2009, https://www.voanews.com/a/a-13-2008-05-19-voa65-66648092/557502 .html.
107. "Iraqi Christians Do Not Fully Embrace Verdict."
108. Belz, *They Say We Are Infidels*, 153.
109. "Love for Our Muslim Brothers and for Iraq."
110. Belz, *They Say We Are Infidels*, 149.
111. John Pontifex, "Archbishop Paulos Faraj Rahho: Chaldean Archbishop of Mosul," obituary, *Independent*, March 15, 2008, https://www.independent.co.uk/news/obituaries/archbishop -paulos-faraj-rahho-chaldean-archbishop-of-mosul-796287.html.
112. "Love for Our Muslim Brothers and for Iraq."
113. "10 Reasons Why Filipinos Want to Work in Saudi Arabia," *Saudi Arabia OFW* (blog), accessed March 26, 2022, https://saudiarabiaofw.com/reasons-to-work-in-saudi-arabia/.
114. Weber, "Faith of Donnie Lama."
115. Weber, "Faith of Donnie Lama."
116. Barbara G. Baker, Compass Direct, "Two Filipino Christians Beheaded" (Ramon A. Williams, Religious Media Agency), Churchlink, July 16, 1997, https://www.churchlink.com.au /churchlink/worldscope/globalnews/filipino.html.
117. Weber, "Faith of Donnie Lama."
118. Pooya Stone, "Crimes against Christians in Iran: Remembering Bishop Haik Hovsepian Mehr," Iran Focus, January 19, 2020, https://www.iranfocus.com/en/terrorism/34218-crimes-against -christians-in-iran-remembering-bishop-haik-hovsepian-mehr/.
119. John Foxe and Voice of the Martyrs, *Foxe: Voices of the Martyrs: AD 33–Today* (Washington, DC: Salem Books, 2019), 291.
120. "The Persecution of Christians in Iran," Mission for Establishment of Human Rights in Iran, accessed March 26, 2022, https://mehr.org/persecution_of_christians.htm.
121. Foxe and Voice of the Martyrs, *Foxe: Voices of the Martyrs: AD 33–Today*, 292.
122. Foxe and Voice of the Martyrs, *Foxe: Voices of the Martyrs: AD 33–Today*, 292.
123. Foxe and Voice of the Martyrs, *Foxe: Voices of the Martyrs: AD 33–Today*, 293.
124. Foxe and Voice of the Martyrs, *Foxe: Voices of the Martyrs: AD 33–Today*, 292.
125. Barbara G. Baker, "Turkey: Malatya Murderers' 39-Year Prison Sentences Upheld," World Watch Monitor, July 25, 2017, https://www.worldwatchmonitor.org/2017/07/turkey-malatya -murderers-39-year-prison-sentences-upheld/.
126. Samuel Smith, "Jesus Told Widow of Tortured Missionary to Forgive Muslims Who Killed Him (Interview)," *Christian Post*, May 16, 2017, https://www.christianpost.com/news/jesus -told-widow-tortured-missionary-forgive-muslims-who-killed-him.html.
127. "Bloodbath in Turkey: Widow Forgives Murderers," Katholische Nachrichten (Catholic News Service), April 23, 2007, http://kath.net/news/16566.
128. Smith, "Jesus Told Widow of Tortured Missionary to Forgive."
129. Baker, "Malatya Murderers' 39-Year Prison Sentences Upheld."
130. Philip Rizq, "The Murder of Rami Ayyad," MidEastWeb Opinion Forum, originally published

at Philip Rizq, *Palestine Chronicle*, October 11, 2007, http://mideastweb.org/Rami_Ayyad_Murder.htm.

131. Rizq, "Murder of Rami Ayyad."

132. Nidal al-Mughrabi, "Prominent Palestinian Christian Killed in Gaza," Reuters, October 7, 2007, https://uk.reuters.com/article/uk-palestinians-christian/prominent-palestinian-christian-killed-in-gaza-idUKL0759985720071007.

133. Aaron Klein, "Christian Bookstore Owner Was Tortured before His Death," *New York Sun*, October 11, 2007, https://www.nysun.com/foreign/christian-bookstore-owner-was-tortured-before-his/64354/.

134. Klein, "Christian Bookstore Owner Was Tortured."

135. Catrin Ormestad, "'I Know How to Make You a Muslim,'" *Haaretz*, November 1, 2007, https://www.haaretz.com/1.4993232.

136. Ormestad, "'I Know How to Make You a Muslim.'"

137. Klein, "Christian Bookstore Owner Was Tortured."

138. Deann Alford, "Christian Bookstore Manager Martyred in Gaza City," *Christianity Today*, October 8, 2007, https://www.christianitytoday.com/news/2007/october/141-12.0.html.

139. Jeremy Weber, "'My Heart Is in Gaza,'" *Christianity Today*, March 10, 2008, https://www.christianitytoday.com/ct/2008/april/3.14.html.

140. Weber, "'My Heart Is in Gaza.'"

141. "Fr. Andrea Santoro: Witness of Faith in Turkey," EUK Mamie, April 12, 2018, https://www.eukmamie.org/en/rss-english/670-the-wake-p-project/9193-fr-andrea-santoro-witness-of-faith-in-turkey.

142. "Europe/Italy—Fr. Andrea Santoro: Man, Believer, a Pastor and a Witness of the Gospel," Agenzia Fides, November 28, 2016, http://fides.org/en/news/61264-EUROPE_ITALY_Fr_Andrea_Santoro_man_believer_a_pastor_and_a_witness_of_the_Gospel.

143. Mariagrazia Zambon, "A Volunteer in Turkey Remembers Fr. Andrea Santoro," AsiaNews, February 6, 2006, https://www.asianews.it/news-en/A-volunteer-in-Turkey-remembers-Fr-Andrea-Santoro-5317.html.

144. Zambon, "A Volunteer in Turkey Remembers Fr. Andrea Santoro."

145. Zambon, "A Volunteer in Turkey Remembers Fr. Andrea Santoro."

146. Peter McGraw and Joel Warner, "The Danish Cartoon Crisis of 2005 and 2006: 10 Things You Didn't Know about the Original Muhammad Controversy," *HuffPost*, September 25, 2012, https://www.huffpost.com/entry/muhammad-cartoons_b_1907545?guccounter=1; Stacy Meichtry, "Pope Eulogizes Priest Gunned Down in Turkey during Cartoon Controversy," Religion News Service, April 14, 2006, https://religionnews.com/2006/04/14/rns-daily-digest558/.

147. "1990: Pastor Hossein Soodmand, Apostate," ExecutedToday.com, December 3, 2008, https://www.executedtoday.com/2008/12/03/1990-pastor-hossein-soodmand-apostate/.

148. "Iran Bulldozes Grave of Pastor Executed for Apostasy," Article18, January 9, 2020, https://articleeighteen.com/news/5297/.

149. "UN Humanitarian Office Puts Yemen War Dead at 233,000, Mostly from 'Indirect Causes,'" UN News, United Nations, December 1, 2020, https://news.un.org/en/story/2020/12/1078972.

150. John Burger, "Eyewitness Report Details Brutality against Yemen Missionaries of Charity," Aleteia, March 17, 2016, https://aleteia.org/2016/03/17/eyewitness-report-details-brutality-against-yemen-missionaries-of-charity/.

151. Cindy Wooden, "Pope: Missionaries of Charity Killed in Yemen Are 'Martyrs of Charity,'" *Long Island Catholic*, 2016, https://licatholic.org/pope-missionaries-of-charity-killed-in-yemen-are-martyrs-of-charity/.

152. Burger, "Eyewitness Report Details Brutality."

153. Burger, "Eyewitness Report Details Brutality."

154. Burger, "Eyewitness Report Details Brutality."

155. Burger, "Eyewitness Report Details Brutality."

156. Saji Thomas, "Slain Missionaries of Charity Nun Revered as Martyr in Eastern India," Global Sisters Report, *National Catholic Reporter*, November 29, 2016, https://www.globalsistersreport.org/news/ministry/slain-missionaries-charity-nun-revered-martyr-eastern-india-43586.

157. Lilian Muendo, "Sister Marguerite, Rwandan Sister Killed in Yemen, Was a Surrogate Mother for Her Family," Global Sisters Report, *National Catholic Reporter*, June 3, 2016, https://www.globalsistersreport.org/news/ministry/sister-marguerite-rwandan-sister-killed -yemen-was-surrogate-mother-her-family-40151.

158. Lilian Muendo, "Sister Reginette, Rwandan Sister Killed in Yemen, Cared for People Since She Was a Teenager," Global Sisters Report, *National Catholic Reporter*, June 3, 2016, https://www .globalsistersreport.org/news/ministry/sister-reginette-rwandan-sister-killed-yemen-cared -people-she-was-teenager-40156.

159. Sister Rio to Sister Adriana, account of events by Sister Sally, fax, Missionaries of Charity, March 4, 2016, https://wp.aleteia.org/wp-content/uploads/sites/2/2016/03 /yemenmartyrsmissionariesofcharity3-4-16-21.pdf.

160. Rhoda Gayle, "Final Words of a Missionary Pastor to Wife, 'I'm Going Out to Evangelize,'" God TV, December 2, 2019, https://godtv.com/missionary-pastor-killed-turkey/.

161. Gayle, "Final Words."

162. Barbara G. Baker, "Korean Murdered in Southeast Turkey 'for Mobile Phone,'" World Watch Monitor, November 29, 2019, https://www.worldwatchmonitor.org/2019/11/korean-murdered -in-southeast-turkey-for-mobile-phone/.

163. Donna Rachel Edmunds, "Christian Evangelist Murdered in Southeast Turkey," *Jerusalem Post*, November 22, 2019, https://www.jpost.com/christian-news/christian-evangelist-murdered-in -southeast-turkey-608669.

164. Baker, "Korean Murdered."

165. Edmunds, "Christian Evangelist Murdered."

166. "Fear among Christians as South Korean Evangelical Pastor Murdered in Diyarbakir," AsiaNews, November 22, 2019, http://www.asianews.it/news-en/Fear-among-Christians-as -South-Korean-evangelical-pastor-murdered-in-Diyarbakir--48613.html.

167. Baker, "Korean Murdered."

168. "Frans van der Lugt: A Dutch Priest in Homs," BBC News, April 26, 2014, https://www.bbc .com/news/magazine-27155474.

169. "Frans van der Lugt."

170. "Frans van der Lugt."

171. "Frans van der Lugt."

172. Frans van der Lugt, "Dutch Priest Writes from the Ruins of Homs, Syria," trans. Aid to the Church in Need, *Long Island Catholic*, September 26, 2013, https://licatholic.org/priest-writes -letter-from-the-ruins-of-homs-syria/.

173. Van der Lugt, "From the Ruins of Homs, Syria."

174. Van der Lugt, "From the Ruins of Homs, Syria."

175. "Frans van der Lugt: A Dutch Priest in Homs."

176. "A Voice Crying in the Wilderness," *Economist*, February 10, 2014, https://www.economist .com/erasmus/2014/02/10/a-voice-crying-in-the-wilderness.

177. "Syria: Dutch Priest Fr. Van der Lugt Shot Dead in Homs," BBC News, April 7, 2014, https://www.bbc.com/news/world-middle-east-26927068.

178. "Frans van der Lugt: A Dutch Priest in Homs."

179. Tony Homsy, "A Man of Peace: Fr. Frans van der Lugt, SJ," The Jesuit Post, April 8, 2014, https://thejesuitpost.org/2014/04/11881/.

180. Homsy, "A Man of Peace."

181. Van der Lugt, "From the Ruins of Homs, Syria."

182. John Foxe, *Foxe's Book of Martyrs*, vol. 1 (Philadelphia: Woodward, 1830), 472.

CHAPTER 15: FROM ATHEISTS AND RELIGIOUS ZEALOTS IN ASIA

1. David Joannes, "Death of Pastor Samuel Lamb and His Impact on My Life," David Joannes (website), August 9, 2013, https://davidjoannes.com/death-of-pastor-samuel-lamb-and-his -impact-on-my-life/.

2. "Ministry History: Bishop M. A. Thomas," Hopegivers International, accessed March 28, 2022, https://www.hopegivers.org/ministry-history.

3. Catholic News Service, "Cardinal Zen Says He's Prepared for Arrest under Hong Kong Security Law," *National Catholic Reporter*, July 1, 2020, https://www.ncronline.org/news/world/cardinal -zen-says-hes-prepared-arrest-under-hong-kong-security-law.

4. Anderson Court Reporting, "Christianity in China: A Force for Change?" (transcript of panel discussion, Brookings Institution, Washington, DC, June 3, 2014), https://www.brookings .edu/wp-content/uploads/2014/05/Corrected-Transcript-Christianity-in-China.pdf.

5. "40 Christians Killed in Revenge Riot in an Indonesian Village," *New York Times*, January 26, 1999, https://www.nytimes.com/1999/01/26/world/40-christians-killed-in-revenge-riot-in-an -indonesian-village.html.

6. Tsukasa Hadano, "China's Christians Keep the Faith, Rattling the Country's Leaders," Nikkei Asian Review, September 10, 2019, https://asia.nikkei.com/Politics/China-s-Christians-keep -the-faith-rattling-the-country-s-leaders; Jamil Anderlini, "The Rise of Christianity in China," *Financial Times*, November 7, 2014, https://www.ft.com/content/a6d2a690-6545-11e4 -91b1-00144feabdc0.

7. CB Condez, "Chinese Special Task Force Rules in Favor of Henan Church over Disputed Land," *Christian Times*, April 30, 2016, https://christiantimes.com/article/chinese-special-task -force-rules-in-favor-of-henan-church-over-disputed-land/55004.htm.

8. Perry Chiaramonte, "Martyr Killed by Bulldozer Becomes Symbol of Growing Persecution of Christians in China," Fox News, January 12, 2017, https://www.foxnews.com/world/martyr -killed-by-bulldozer-becomes-symbol-of-growing-persecution-of-christians-in-china.

9. Chiaramonte, "Martyr Killed by Bulldozer."

10. "After Burying Woman Alive, Authorities in China Return Land to Her Church," AsiaNews, May 3, 2016, http://www.asianews.it/news-en/After-burying-woman-alive,-authorities-in -China-return-land-to-her-church-37393.html.

11. Qiao Nong and Brynne Lawrence, "Church Leader's Wife Dead after Buried Alive during Church Demolition," trans. Carolyn Song, ChinaAid, April 18, 2016, https://www.chinaaid .org/2016/04/church-leaders-wife-dead-after-buried.html.

12. Nong and Lawrence, "Church Leader's Wife Dead."

13. Nong and Lawrence, "Church Leader's Wife Dead."

14. Nong and Lawrence, "Church Leader's Wife Dead."

15. "After Burying Woman Alive, Authorities in China Return Land."

16. Chiaramonte, "Martyr Killed by Bulldozer."

17. Saji Thomas, "Q & A with Sr. Selmy Paul," Global Sisters Report, *National Catholic Reporter*, June 11, 2015, https://www.globalsistersreport.org/ministry/q-sr-selmy-paul-26716.

18. Nirmala Carvalho, "Murdered Nun Beatified in India; Sister Rani Maria a Martyr for Social Justice," Crux, November 4, 2017, https://cruxnow.com/global-church/2017/11/murdered -nun-beatified-india-sister-rani-maria-martyr-social-justice/.

19. Carvalho, "Murdered Nun Beatified."

20. Carvalho, "Murdered Nun Beatified."

21. Carvalho, "Murdered Nun Beatified."

22. Carvalho, "Murdered Nun Beatified."
23. Carvalho, "Murdered Nun Beatified."
24. NPR Staff and Wires, "10 Killed in Attack on Medical Team in Afghanistan," NPR, August 7, 2010, https://www.npr.org/templates/story/story.php?storyId=129045982.
25. Mark Memmott, "U.S. Eye Doctor Devoted Life to Afghans," The Two-Way, NPR, August 8, 2010, https://www.npr.org/sections/thetwo-way/2010/08/08/129062704/.
26. NPR Staff and Wires, "10 Killed in Attack."
27. "President Obama Names Presidential Medal of Freedom Recipients," press release, White House, November 17, 2010, https://obamawhitehouse.archives.gov/the-press-office/2010/11/17/president-obama-names-presidential-medal-freedom-recipients.
28. Wendy Lee, "Martyr's Widow: Be 'the Aroma of Christ,'" Baptist Press, October 21, 2010, https://www.baptistpress.com/resource-library/news/martyrs-widow-be-the-aroma-of-christ/.
29. Lee, "Martyr's Widow."
30. Paul Estabrooks, "The Cross—Tahir's Martyrdom," Standing Strong through the Storm—July 19, Crosswalk.com, https://www.crosswalk.com/devotionals/standing-strong-through-the-storm/standing-strong-through-the-storm-july-19.html.
31. Estabrooks, "The Cross—Tahir's Martyrdom."
32. Qaiser Felix, "Without Evidence Police Arrest Christian on Blasphemy Charges," AsiaNews, May 29, 2006, http://www.asianews.it/news-en/Without-evidence-police-arrest-Christian-on-blasphemy-charges-6298.html.
33. Felix, "Without Evidence Police Arrest Christian."
34. "Inquiry Demanded into Death of Jailed Muslim Who Became Christian," Union of Catholic Asian News, updated August 3, 1992, https://www.ucanews.com/story-archive/?post_name=/1992/08/04/inquiry-demanded-into-death-of-jailed-muslim-who-became-christian&post_id=41690.
35. *Victims of Religious Persecution around the World: Hearing before the Subcommittee on International Operations and Human Rights of the Committee on International Relations, House of Representatives*, 105th Cong., 2nd session (1998), 56.
36. "Inquiry Demanded into Death."
37. Estabrooks, "The Cross—Tahir's Martyrdom."
38. Estabrooks, "The Cross—Tahir's Martyrdom."
39. "About Gracia," Gracia Burnham Ministries, accessed March 29, 2022, https://graciaburnham.org/gracia/.
40. Gracia Burnham with Dean Merrill, *In the Presence of My Enemies* (Carol Stream, IL: Tyndale, 2004), 20.
41. Amy C. Rippel, "Missionaries' Plight Is Dire," *Orlando Sentinel*, January 21, 2002, https://www.orlandosentinel.com/news/os-xpm-2002-01-22-0201220192-story.html.
42. *Sentinel* staff and wire services, "American Hostage Dies in Philippines," *Chicago Tribune*, June 7, 2002, https://www.chicagotribune.com/sns-philippines-story.html.
43. *Sentinel* staff and wire services, "American Hostage Dies."
44. Burnham, *In the Presence of My Enemies*, 339.
45. "Burning Shame: The Killing of Graham Staines and His Sons by Bajrang Dal Activist," Hindutva Watch, originally published in Ruben Banerjee, *India Today*, February 8, 1999, https://hindutvawatch.org/burning-shame/.
46. Ms. Joceline, review of *Burnt Alive: The Staines and the God They Loved*, by Vishal Mangalwadi et al., *Golden Hands of Grace* (blog), December 19, 2012, http://goldenhandsofgrace.blogspot.com/2012/12/book-review-6-burnt-alive-staines-and.html.
47. Trevor Persaud, "Shahbaz Bhatti, Pakistan's Most Prominent Christian, Assassinated (Updated)," *Christianity Today*, March 2, 2011, https://www.christianitytoday.com/ct/2011/marchweb-only/shahbazbhatti.html.

48. "Pakistan Murder: Shahbaz Bhatti's 'Goodbye' Call," BBC News, March 3, 2011, https://www.bbc.com/news/world-south-asia-12639925.

49. "Pakistan Minorities Minister Shahbaz Bhatti Shot Dead," BBC News, March 2, 2011, https://www.bbc.com/news/world-south-asia-12617562.

50. Huma Imtiaz, "What in God's Name Is This?" *Open*, December 8, 2010, https://openthemagazine.com/features/world/what-in-gods-name-is-this/.

51. Declan Walsh, "Shahbaz Bhatti: Another Voice against Pakistan's Extremists Dies," *Guardian*, March 2, 2011, https://www.theguardian.com/world/2011/mar/02/shahbaz-bhatti-shot-dead.

52. "Punjab Governor Salman Taseer Assassinated in Islamabad," BBC News, January 4, 2011, https://www.bbc.com/news/world-south-asia-12111831.

53. Persaud, "Shahbaz Bhatti."

54. Persaud, "Shahbaz Bhatti."

55. Declan Walsh, "Pakistan Minister Shahbaz Bhatti Shot Dead in Islamabad," *Guardian*, March 2, 2011, https://www.theguardian.com/world/2011/mar/02/pakistan-minister-shot-dead-islamabad.

56. Walsh, "Pakistan Minister Shahbaz Bhatti Shot Dead."

57. Persaud, "Shahbaz Bhatti."

58. Persaud, "Shahbaz Bhatti."

59. "Sulawesi Christian Priest Killed," BBC News, October 16, 2006, http://news.bbc.co.uk/2/hi/asia-pacific/6054152.stm.

60. Benteng Reges, "Protestant Pastor Killed," AsiaNews, October 16, 2006, http://www.asianews.it/news-en/Protestant-pastor-killed-7483.html.

61. "Sulawesi Christian Priest Killed."

62. Reuters, "Asia: Indonesia: Christian Pastor Shot to Death," *New York Times*, October 17, 2006, https://www.nytimes.com/2006/10/17/world/world-briefing-asia-indonesia-christian-pastor-shot-to-death.html.

63. Patung, "Rev. Irianto Kongkoli," *Indonesia Matters* (blog), October 18, 2006, https://www.indonesiamatters.com/769/rev-irianto-kongkoli/.

64. Sugam Pokharel, Euan McKirdy, and Tara John, "Bombs Tear through Sri Lankan Churches and Hotels, Killing 250 People," CNN, updated April 25, 2019, https://www.cnn.com/2019/04/21/asia/sri-lanka-explosions/index.html.

65. Naaman Zhou et al., "Authorities Warned on 4 April of Potential Attacks, Sri Lankan Minister Says—as It Happened," *Guardian*, updated April 22, 2019, https://www.theguardian.com/world/live/2019/apr/21/sri-lanka-explosions-dozens-killed-and-hundreds-injured-in-church-and-hotel-blasts?page=with%3Ablock-5cbc29e58f08c89bd906580d.

66. Agence France-Presse, "US Official Chelsea Decaminada Wounded in Sri Lankan Easter Bombings Has Died, Bringing Death Toll to 258," *South China Morning Post*, May 9, 2019, https://www.scmp.com/news/asia/south-asia/article/3009471/us-official-chelsea-decaminada-wounded-sri-lankan-easter; "Sri Lanka Attacks: Easter Sunday Bombings Marked One Year On," BBC News April 21, 2020, https://www.bbc.com/news/world-asia-52357200.

67. "What We Know about the Sri Lanka Bombers," France 24, April 28, 2019, https://www.france24.com/en/20190428-what-we-know-about-sri-lanka-bombers.

68. "Violence, Discrimination against Christians Escalate in Sri Lanka," *Morning Star News*, October 19, 2018, https://morningstarnews.org/2018/10/violence-discrimination-against-christians-escalate-in-sri-lanka/.

69. "'What We Heard, We Didn't Like': NYPD Counterterror Chief Analyzes Sri Lanka Attacks," CBS New York, April 22, 2019, https://newyork.cbslocal.com/2019/04/22/john-miller-sri-lanka-terror-attacks/.

70. "Statement from Secretary of Commerce Wilbur Ross on the Passing of Chelsea Decaminada," Just The Real News, May 6, 2019, https://www.justtherealnews.com/exec-depts/statement-from-secretary-of-commerce-wilbur-ross-on-the-passing-of-chelsea-decaminada/.

71. Timothy Dolan, "Martyred for Her Faith in Sri Lanka," *Catholic New York*, May 22, 2019, https://www.cny.org/stories/martyred-for-her-faith-in-sri-lanka,19198.

72. Dolan, "Martyred for Her Faith."

73. "Sri Lanka Attacks: Who Are the Victims?" BBC News, April 26, 2019, https://www.bbc.com/news/world-asia-48002169.

74. "Former Attorney General Pays Tribute to Fr Rufus and Fr Des," Columban Missionaries, August 23, 2019, https://columbans.ie/former-attorney-general-pays-tribute-to-fr-rufus-and-fr-des/.

75. Frank Khan and Sarah Murphy, "Massive Hunt for Killers of Heroic Priest," Independent.ie, August 29, 2001, https://www.independent.ie/irish-news/massive-hunt-for-killers-of-heroic-priest-26078582.html.

76. "Irish Columban Pioneers," Columban Missionaries, accessed March 30, 2022, https://columbans.ie/about-us/irish-columban-pioneers/; "Columban Martyrs," Columban Missionaries, accessed March 30, 2022, https://columbans.ie/about-us/columban-martyrs/.

77. Miriam Donohoe, "Letter from Pope Read at Funeral Service for Irish Missionary Priest," *Irish Times*, September 3, 2001, https://www.irishtimes.com/news/letter-from-pope-read-at-funeral-service-for-irish-missionary-priest-1.325480.

78. Jean Harrington, *Murder in the Missions* (Blackrock, Cork, Ireland: Mercier Press, 2019), chap. 8.

79. "Theology of Risk," Theology of Risk, accessed March 30, 2022, https://theologyofrisk.com/.

80. Santasparrot, "Church of the Week: IAM," *theirsmineandours* (blog), December 7, 2014, https://theirsmineandours.wordpress.com/2014/12/07/church-of-the-week-iam/.

81. Anna E. Hampton, "How Has Persecution and Martyrdom of Christians Changed—2000–2020," *Better Than Gold Faith* (blog), February 12, 2019, https://better-than-gold-faith.blogspot.com/2019/02/how-has-persecution-and-martyrdom-of.html (site moved February 14, 2022, to theologyofrisk.com).

82. Avni Dervishi, "Tighten the Security of Aid Workers," April 8, 2015, Swedish Development Forum (FUF), https://fuf.se/en/magasin/skarp-sakerheten-for-bistandsarbetare/.

83. Rod Nordland, "Gunmen Kill Medical Aid Workers in Afghanistan," *New York Times*, August 7, 2010, https://www.nytimes.com/2010/08/08/world/asia/08afghan.html#:~:text=The%20gunmen%20marched%20them%20into,Aqa%20Noor%20Kentoz%2C%20said%20Saturday. Accounts vary slightly on details; see also Jason Motlagh, "Will Aid Workers' Killings End Civilian Surge?," *Time*, August 9, 2010, http://content.time.com/time/world/article/0,8599,2009399,00.html.

84. Liz Robbins, "Ten Aid Workers Killed by Taliban in Afghanistan," *Deseret News*, August 7, 2010, https://www.deseret.com/2010/8/7/20132871/10-aid-workers-killed-by-taliban-in-afghanistan.

85. Joshua Partlow, "The Taliban Kills 10 Medical Aid Workers in Northern Afghanistan," *Washington Post*, August 8, 2010, https://www.washingtonpost.com/wp-dyn/content/article/2010/08/07/AR2010080700822.html.

86. "A Look at the 10 Aid Workers Killed in Afghanistan," CNN, August 9, 2010, http://www.cnn.com/2010/WORLD/asiapcf/08/09/afghanistan.victims.list/index.html.

87. Reverend Charles Beckett in *The Global Impact Bible*, sr. ed. Jerry A. Pattengale (Franklin, TN: Worthy Publishing, 2017), 1649. Cheryl's testimony accompanies 1 John 3:16.

88. Jon Boone, "Pakistan Church Bomb: Christians Mourn 85 Killed in Peshawar Suicide Attack," *Guardian*, September 25, 2013, https://www.theguardian.com/world/2013/sep/23/pakistan-church-bombings-christian-minority.

89. "Pakistan Blasts: Burials amid Anger after Peshawar Church Attack," BBC News, September 23, 2013, https://www.bbc.com/news/world-asia-24201240.

90. Ismail Khan and Salman Masood, "Scores Are Killed by Suicide Bomb Attack at Historic Church in Pakistan," *New York Times*, September 22, 2013, https://www.nytimes.com/2013/09/23/world/asia/pakistan-church-bombing.html.

91. Boone, "Pakistan Church Bomb."
92. Titus Presler, "Peshawar All Saints' Update: Bomb Casualty Toll; Funds Appeal; Other Bombings," *Titus on Mission* (blog), September 30, 2013, https://titusonmission.wordpress .com/2013/09/30/peshawar-all-saints-update-bomb-casualty-toll-funds-appeal-other -bombings/.
93. Boone, "Pakistan Church Bomb."
94. Farhan Bokhari, "At Least 78 Killed in Pakistan Church Bombing," CBS News, September 22, 2013, https://www.cbsnews.com/news/at-least-78-killed-in-pakistan-church-bombing/.
95. Bokhari, "At Least 78 Killed."
96. Boone, "Pakistan Church Bomb."
97. "Pakistani Christians Mourn Deaths," photographs, Reuters, September 23, 2013, https://www.reuters.com/news/picture/pakistani-christians-mourn-deaths-idUSRTX13X89.
98. Thomas Patrick Hughes, "All Saints' Memorial Church, in the City of Peshawar, Afghanistan," March 26, 1885, Project Canterbury (2007), http://anglicanhistory.org/india/pk/hughes _peshawar1885.html.
99. Mohsin Raza, "Pakistani Christians Mourn Deaths," photograph, Reuters, September 23, 2013, https://www.reuters.com/news/picture/pakistani-christians-mourn-deaths -idUSRTX13X89. See the last photo in the series of fifteen pictures.
100. Mathew Schmalz, "Remembering Bishop John Joseph of Pakistan," Crux, May 6, 2015, https://cruxnow.com/church/2015/05/remembering-bishop-john-joseph-of-pakistan/.
101. "Thousands in Pakistan Mourn Bishop Who Shot Self," *Chicago Tribune*, May 8, 1998, https://www.chicagotribune.com/news/ct-xpm-1998-05-08-9805080141-story.html.
102. Linda S. Walbridge, *The Christians of Pakistan: The Passion of Bishop John Joseph* (New York: Routledge, 2003), 4.
103. "Thousands in Pakistan Mourn Bishop."
104. Walbridge, *Christians of Pakistan*, 94.
105. Walbridge, *Christians of Pakistan*, 170–71; quoted from John Joseph, *A Peaceful Struggle: A Collection of Bishop John Joseph's Writings against Black Laws and Discrimination*, ed. Khalid Rashid Asi (Faisalabad, Pakistan: National Commission for Justice and Peace, 1999).
106. Walbridge, *Christians of Pakistan*, 172; quoted from Joseph, *Peaceful Struggle*.
107. "Thousands in Pakistan Mourn Bishop."
108. Associated Press, "Pakistani Catholic Cleric Buried; Muslims Burn Christian Homes," *New York Times*, May 11, 1998, https://www.nytimes.com/1998/05/11/world/pakistani-catholic-cleric -buried-muslims-burn-christian-homes.html.
109. "Thousands in Pakistan Mourn Bishop."
110. "Faisalabad Remembers Bishop John Joseph, 'Martyr' of the Blasphemy Law," AsiaNews, May 10, 2012, https://www.asianews.it/news-en/Faisalabad-remembers-Bishop-John-Joseph,-martyr -of-the-blasphemy-law-24713.html.
111. "Faisalabad Remembers Bishop John Joseph."
112. Nasir Saeed, "Bishop John Joseph: A Life That Inspires beyond Death," *Christian Today*, May 10, 2012, https://www.christiantoday.com/article/bishop.john.joseph.a.life.that.inspires .beyond.death/29845.htm.
113. Saeed, "Bishop John Joseph."
114. Mehr Tarar, "The Story of Shama and Shahzad," *Express Tribune*, November 13, 2014, https://tribune.pk/story/790651/the-story-of-shama-and-shahzad.
115. "Christians in Pakistan Are 'Poorest of the Poor,'" Exaudi, November 23, 2021, https://www .exaudi.org/christians-in-pakistan-are-poorest-of-the-poor-2/.
116. Asad Hashim, "Pakistani Christian Couple Killed by Mob," Al Jazeera, November 2, 2014, https://www.aljazeera.com/news/2014/11/5/pakistani-christian-couple-killed-by-mob.
117. Hashim, "Pakistani Christian Couple Killed."

118. Catholic News Agency, "In Pakistan, 13 Sentenced Over Lynching of Christian Couple," *Crux*, December 1, 2016, https://cruxnow.com/cna/2016/12/pakistan-13-sentenced-lynching -christian-couple.

119. Hashim, "Pakistani Christian Couple Killed."

120. Caleb Parke, "Chinese Pastor Shared Christian Faith with 1,000 North Koreans before Execution, Defector Claims," Fox News, September 5, 2019, https://www.foxnews.com/faith -values/christian-china-north-korea-bible-persecuted-church.

121. Joshua Stanton, "Who Killed Pastor Han Chung-Ryeol?" *Free Korea* (blog), May 3, 2016, https://freekorea.us/2016/05/who-killed-pastor-han-chung-ryeol/.

122. Stanton, "Who Killed Pastor Han Chung-Ryeol?"

123. Stanton, "Who Killed Pastor Han Chung-Ryeol?"

124. Parke, "Chinese Pastor Shared Christian Faith."

125. Stanton, "Who Killed Pastor Han Chung-Ryeol?"

126. Voice of the Martyrs—USA, "Sang-chul: North Korea," Facebook, October 25, 2019, video, 6:59, https://www.facebook.com/vomusa/videos/2498617990458471/.

127. Voice of the Martyrs—USA, "Sang-chul: North Korea."

128. John Foxe, *Foxe's Book of Martyrs* (London: Knight and Son, 1854), 51.

CHAPTER 16: FROM CRIMINALS IN NORTH AND SOUTH AMERICA

1. "Joshua Saúñe," *Beeson Podcast*, episode 420, Beeson Divinity School, November 27, 2018, transcript, https://www.beesondivinity.com/podcast/2018/transcripts/beeson-podcast -episode420-saune-sermon.txt.

2. Valerie Richardson, "Kamala Harris, Mazie Hirono Target Brian Buescher Knights of Columbus Membership," AP News, December 30, 2018, https://apnews.com/003d11bf795de 6bcfbb5a6ada435944a.

3. Robert P. Jones, "Racism among White Christians Is Higher Than among the Nonreligious. That's No Coincidence." Think, NBC News, July 27, 2020), https://www.nbcnews.com/think /opinion/racism-among-white-christians-higher-among-nonreligious-s-no-coincidence -ncna1235045.

4. "North Carolina Teacher Separates Students Who Believe in God—Mocks Their Faith," Beginning and End, November 24, 2019, https://beginningandend.com/north-carolina-teacher -separates-students-who-believe-in-god-mocks-their-faith/.

5. Sarah Pulliam Bailey, "School Shooters Targeting Christians Is Not a New Claim," *Washington Post*, October 2, 2015, https://www.washingtonpost.com/news/acts-of-faith/wp/2015/10/02 /school-shooters-targeting-christians-is-not-a-new-claim/.

6. "Persecution Watch Prayer Conference Call for the Persecuted—Colombia," *Voice of the Persecuted* (blog), June 4, 2020, https://voiceofthepersecuted.wordpress.com/2020/06/04 /persecution-watch-prayer-conference-call-for-the-persecuted-colombia/.

7. "Expanded Story of Sister Dorothy Stang," Sisters of Notre Dame de Namur, accessed April 1, 2022, https://www.sndohio.org/sister-dorothy/expanded-story.

8. Lise Alves and Catholic News Service, "Brazil Remembers Sr. Dorothy Stang; Landless Defenders Still Threatened," Global Sisters Report, February 12, 2020, https://www .globalsistersreport.org/news/environment/brazil-remembers-sister-dorothy-stang-landless -defenders-still-threatened.

9. John Dear, "Sr. Dorothy Stang, Martyr of the Amazon," *National Catholic Reporter*, October 2, 2007, https://www.ncronline.org/blogs/road-peace/sr-dorothy-stang-martyr-amazon.

10. Alves and Catholic News Service, "Brazil Remembers Sr. Dorothy Stang."

11. Dear, "Sr. Dorothy Stang."

12. Dear, "Sr. Dorothy Stang."

13. Roseanne Murphy, "Planting Sr. Dot," Global Catholic Climate Movement, Laudato Si' Movement, May 30, 2019, https://catholicclimatemovement.global/planting-sr-dot/.

14. Dear, "Sr. Dorothy Stang."
15. Dear, "Sr. Dorothy Stang."
16. Dear, "Sr. Dorothy Stang."
17. Heather J. Johnson, "Rainforest," Resource Library, National Geographic, last updated May 11, 2015, https://www.nationalgeographic.org/encyclopedia/rain-forest/.
18. *They Killed Sister Dorothy*, directed by Daniel Junge (Just Media, 2008); see also *They Killed Sister Dorothy*, DVD press kit (New York: First Run Features), https://www.firstrunfeatures.com/presskits/dvd_presskits/sistedorothy_pk.pdf.
19. *Angel of the Amazon*, directed by Nancy Rhodes (Encompass New Opera Theater, 2011); see "*Angel of the Amazon*: A New American Opera about Sister Dorothy Stang by Evan Mack," Angel of the Amazon (website), accessed April 1, 2022, http://angeloftheamazon.com/.
20. Dear, "Sr. Dorothy Stang."
21. Chayenne Polimédio, "The Rise of the Brazilian Evangelicals," *Atlantic*, January 24, 2018, https://www.theatlantic.com/international/archive/2018/01/the-evangelical-takeover-of -brazilian-politics/551423/; Eduardo Campos Lima, "As Evangelicals Gain, Catholics on Verge of Losing Majority in Brazil," *National Catholic Reporter*, February 5, 2020, https://www .ncronline.org/news/parish/evangelicals-gain-catholics-verge-losing-majority-brazil.
22. Campos Lima, "As Evangelicals Gain."
23. C. Shepard, "Rachel Joy Scott," A Columbine Site, accessed April 1, 2022, http://www .acolumbinesite.com/victim/rachel.php.
24. "Columbine Shooting," History.com, last updated March 4, 2021, https://www.history .com/topics/1990s/columbine-high-school-shootings.
25. Shepard, "Rachel Joy Scott."
26. Sheba R. Wheeler, "Columbine Shooting Victim: Rachel Scott," *Denver Post*, April 23, 1999, https://www.denverpost.com/1999/04/23/columbine-shooting-victims-rachel-scott/.
27. Gabrielle Frank, "Survivor Stories: Craig Scott Reflects on the Columbine Shooting Nearly 20 Years Later," NBC New York, October 23, 2018, https://www.nbcnewyork.com/news/national -international/craig-scott-reflects-on-the-columbine-shooting-nearly-20-years-later/2086872/.
28. Darrell Scott, with Steve Rabey, *Rachel Smiles: The Spiritual Legacy of Columbine Martyr Rachel Scott* (Nashville: Thomas Nelson, 2002), 15.
29. Beth Nimmo and Darrell Scott, with Steve Rabey, *Rachel's Tears: The Spiritual Journey of Columbine Martyr Rachel Scott* (Nashville: Thomas Nelson, 2000), back cover.
30. *El Chapo*, season 1, episode 4, directed by Ernesto Contreras and Manuel Cravioto (2017); "'El Chapo' Fell into the Government and Amado's Trap: What Happened in Chapter 4 of the Series," Univision, June 14, 2017, https://www.univision.com/series/el-chapo/el-chapo-fell-into -the-government-and-amados-trap-what-happened-in-chapter-4-of-the-series.
31. "Rev Juan Jesús Posadas Ocampo," Find a Grave, accessed April 1, 2022, https://www .findagrave.com/memorial/19459480/juan_jes_s-posadas_ocampo.
32. *An End to Impunity: Investigating the 1993 Killing of Mexican Archbishop Juan Jesus Posadas Ocampo: Hearing before the Subcommittee on Africa, Global Human Rights and International Operations of the Committee on International Relations, House of Representatives*, H.R. Rep. No. 109-168, 109th Cong., 2nd session (2006), Homeland Security Digital Library, https://www .hsdl.org/?abstract&did=743365.
33. *An End to Impunity*; "Mexicans Remember Cardinal's Death," UPI, May 24, 1994, https://www.upi.com/Archives/1994/05/24/Mexicans-remember-cardinals-death/28667 69752000/.
34. Stephen Woodman, "Renegade Priest Still Speaking 'Language of the Poor,'" *The Mexican Labyrinth* (blog), July 31, 2014, https://themexicanlabyrinth.com/2014/07/31/renegade-priest -still-speaking-language-of-the-poor-2/.
35. *An End to Impunity*, 9.

36. *An End to Impunity*, 13.

37. *An End to Impunity*, 2.

38. Gabriel Le Bras, quoted in Héctor Gómez Peralta, "The Role of the Catholic Church in Mexico's Political Development," *Politics and Religion Journal* 6, no. 1 (2012): 17, http://politicsandreligionjournal.com/index.php/prj/issue/view/15.

39. "Carlos Slim Helu and Family," Profile, *Forbes*, accessed April 2, 2022, https://www.forbes .com/profile/carlos-slim-helu/; Megha Bahree, "Carlos Slim Disses Gates' and Buffett's Pledges to Give Away Their Billions," *Forbes*, October 29, 2010, https://www.forbes.com/sites /meghabahree/2010/10/29/carlos-slim-disses-gates-and-buffetts-pledges-to-give-away-their -billions/?sh=3be85fb74f13.

40. Amy Chua, *World on Fire: How Exporting Free Market Democracy Breeds Ethnic Hatred and Global Instability* (New York: Anchor Books, 2004), 62.

41. "Biography," Carlos Slim Helú (website), accessed April 2, 2022, https://carlosslim .com/biografia_ing.html.

42. Dan Wooding , "A True Warrior for God—the Powerful Story of Joshua Saune from Peru," *Favorite Stories* (blog), Berean Publishers, accessed April 2, 2022, http://www.bereanpublishers .com/berean/Favorite_Stories/a_true_warrior_for_god.htm.

43. Joyce Vollmer Brown, "Romulo Saune," in *Courageous Christians: Devotional Stories for Family Reading* (Chicago: Moody, 2000).

44. Wooding, "True Warrior for God."

45. "Joshua Saúñe," *Beeson Podcast*, episode 420, Beeson Divinity School, November 27, 2018, transcript, https://www.beesondivinity.com/podcast/2018/transcripts/beeson-podcast -episode420-saune-sermon.txt.

46. "Joshua Saúñe," *Beeson Podcast*.

47. "Rómulo Saúñe: Brave Pastor in the Peruvian Andes," Trailblazer Books, accessed April 2, 2022, http://www.trailblazerbooks.com/books/blinded/Blinded-bio.html.

48. Wooding, "True Warrior for God."

49. Wooding, "True Warrior for God"; "Joshua Saúñe," *Beeson Podcast*.

50. "Joshua Saúñe," *Beeson Podcast*.

51. Paul Estabrooks, "The Real Enemy," Standing Strong through the Storm (daily devotional, September 13), Bible Gateway, accessed April 2, 2022, https://www.biblegateway .com/devotionals/standing-strong-through-the-storm/2046/09/13.

52. "Serving in Peru: Donna Saúñe," Commission to Every Nation, accessed April 2, 2022, https://cten.org/missionary/donnasaune/.

53. "Rómulo Saúñe: Brave Pastor in the Peruvian Andes."

54. "Joshua Saúñe," *Beeson Podcast*.

55. John Sandeman, "Bibles for 98 Percent of the World Is in Sight," Eternity News, July 6, 2017, https://www.eternitynews.com.au/good-news/bibles-for-98-per-cent-of-the-world-is-in-sight/.

56. John Sandeman, "A Bible in Every Language Is Within Our Grasp," Eternity News, April 13, 2017, https://www.eternitynews.com.au/world/a-bible-in-every-language-is-within-our-grasp/.

57. Nicola Menzie, "Wycliffe's Colombia Bible Translation Project to Get Financial Boost from Expolit '13," *Christian Post*, April 10, 2013, https://www.christianpost.com/news/wycliffes -colombia-bible-translation-project-to-get-financial-boost-from-expolit-13.html.

58. Misty Bernall, *She Said Yes: The Unlikely Martyrdom of Cassie Bernall* (New York: Pocket Books, 2000), 99.

59. C. Shepard, "Cassie Renee Bernall," A Combine Site, accessed April 2, 2022, http://www .acolumbinesite.com/victim/cassie.php.

60. Bernall, *She Said Yes*, ix.

61. Lucy McCalmont, "Baseball Game May Have Saved Chris Singleton from Charleston Shooting," *HuffPost*, August 4, 2015, https://www.huffpost.com/entry/chris-singleton -charleston-espn_n_55c1183de4b0e716be076edb.

62. "Sharonda Coleman-Singleton Obituary," Legacy.com, accessed April 2, 2022, http://www.legacy.com/ns/sharonda-coleman-singleton-obituary/175109980.
63. Samuel Momodu, "The Charleston Church Massacre (2015)," BlackPast, September 30, 2017, https://www.blackpast.org/african-american-history/charleston-church-massacre-2015/.
64. McCalmont, "Baseball Game."
65. CSU Media, "CSU Dedicates Singleton Baseball Complex," Charleston Southern University, February 6, 2018, https://www.charlestonsouthern.edu/csu-dedicates-singleton-baseball-complex/.
66. Greg Garrison, "America's Church Shootings: At Least 91 Killed since 1999," AL.com, November 6, 2017, https://www.al.com/living/2017/11/post_346.html.
67. John Foxe, *Foxe's Book of Martyrs*, ed. Forbush (Philadelphia: John Winston, 1926), 167.

CHAPTER 17: FROM A NEW JIHAD IN AFRICA

1. Morgan Lee, "Five Years Ago, ISIS Executed 21 Christians on a Beach in Libya," *Quick to Listen*, podcast, 47:00, *Christianity Today*, February 19, 2020, https://www.christianitytoday.com/ct/2020/february-web-only/isis-martyrs-coptic-christians-five-year-anniversary.html.
2. "Status of Global Christianity, 2022, in the Context of 1900–2050," Center for the Study of Global Christianity, Gordon-Conwell Theological Seminary, 2022, https://www.gordonconwell.edu/center-for-global-christianity/resources/status-of-global-christianity/.
3. Wes Granberg-Michaelson, "Think Christianity Is Dying? No, Christianity Is Shifting Dramatically," *Washington Post*, May 20, 2015, https://www.washingtonpost.com/news/acts-of-faith/wp/2015/05/20/think-christianity-is-dying-no-christianity-is-shifting-dramatically/.
4. Jason Margolis, "The Redeemed Church of God Preaches the Gospel in the US," BBC News, February 12, 2014, https://www.bbc.com/news/magazine-25988151.
5. Duane Alexander Miller and Patrick Johnstone, "Believers in Christ from a Muslim Background: A Global Census," *Interdisciplinary Journal of Research on Religion* 11 (2015): article 10, https://www.academia.edu/16338087/Believers_in_Christ_from_a_Muslim_Background_A_Global_Census.
6. Miller and Johnstone, "Believers in Christ."
7. Miller and Johnstone, "Believers in Christ."
8. Todd M. Johnson, "Christian Martyrdom: Who? Why? How?" Gordon-Conwell Theological Seminary, accessed April 3, 2022, https://www.gordonconwell.edu/blog/christian-martyrdom-who-why-how/; "Persecution of Christians in 2016," Center for the Study of Global Christianity, https://us11.campaign-archive.com/?u=060e80f6eebfc8804f8049bad&id=c0d75f13c6&e=88b938d3be.
9. Peter Walker, "900,000 Christians Were 'Martyred' over Last Decade, Says Christian Research," *Independent*, January 13, 2017, https://www.independent.co.uk/news/christians-killed-martyred-900-000-last-decade-africa-boko-haram-al-shabaab-study-global-christianity-vatican-a7526226.html.
10. Mark Dike DeLancey, Rebecca Neh Mbuh, and Mark W. DeLancey, *Historical Dictionary of the Republic of Cameroon*, 5th ed. (Lanham, MD: Rowman and Littlefield, 2019).
11. "Driver, Cook Arrested in Murder of Archbishop," AP News, September 4, 1991, https://apnews.com/article/34a529467ba72507c86d572723755254.
12. Tatah H. Mbuy, "Assessing the Impact of Tribalism and Regionalism on the Development of Cameroon," in *Regional Balance and National Integration in Cameroon: Lessons Learned and the Uncertain Future*, ed. Paul Nchoji Nkwi and Francis B. Nyamnjoh (Bamenda, Cameroon: Langaa Research and Publishing, 2011), 186.
13. Yves Plumey, *Mission Tchad-Cameroun: L'annonce de l'évangile au Nord-Cameroun et au Mayo Kabbi, 1846–1986* (Editions Oblates: 1990), 472, quoted at Shanil Jayawardena Omi, "September 3: Yves-Joseph-Marie Plumey (1913–1991), Archbishop of Garoua," *OMI200*

(blog), September 3, 2016, https://omi200.wordpress.com/2016/09/03/september-3-yves
-joseph-marie-plumey-1913-1991-archbishop-of-garoua/.

14. Hippolyte Marboua, "French-Spanish Nun Killed in Central African Republic," ABC News,
    May 22, 2019, https://abcnews.go.com/International/wireStory/french-spanish-nun-killed
    -central-african-republic-63196302.

15. Reuters, "Gunmen Kill at Least 24 at Church in Burkina Faso," *New York Times*, February 17,
    2020, https://www.nytimes.com/2020/02/17/world/africa/burkina-faso-church-attack.html.

16. Simon Marks, "'We Looked to Escape Death': Violence Uproots Nearly 500,000 in Burkina
    Faso," *New York Times*, October 15, 2019, https://www.nytimes.com/2019/10/15/world/africa
    /burkina-faso-violence.html.

17. "Autopsy Raises Questions about Circumstances of African Bishop's Death," Catholic News
    Agency, June 7, 2017, https://www.catholicnewsagency.com/news/autopsy-raises-questions
    -about-circumstances-of-african-bishops-death-42709.

18. Pamela Bidjocka, "Bishop Jean-Marie Benoît Bala: One Year into Eternity," Cameroon Radio
    Television, May 31, 2018, https://www.crtv.cm/2018/05/bishop-jean-marie-benoit-bala-one
    -year-into-eternity/.

19. Ngala Killian Chimtom, "Cleric Alleges Cameroon Bishop Killed for Resisting Gay Priests,"
    Crux, August 5, 2017, https://cruxnow.com/global-church/2017/08/cleric-alleges-cameroon
    -bishop-killed-resisting-gay-priests/.

20. Edward Pentin, "Cameroonian Bishops Confirm: Bishop Balla Was Murdered," *National
    Catholic Register*, June 14, 2017, https://www.ncregister.com/blog/edward-pentin/cameroonian
    -bishops-confirm-bishop-balla-was-murdered.

21. "Autopsy Raises Questions"; Catholic News Service, "Cameroon's Bishops Confirm Bishop
    Jean-Marie Benoit Balla Was Murdered," *Catholic Herald*, June 15, 2017, https://catholicherald
    .co.uk/cameroons-bishops-confirm-bishop-jean-marie-benoit-balla-was-murdered/.

22. Chimtom, "Cleric Alleges Cameroon Bishop Killed."

23. "Bishop Bala Was Not Murdered: Cameroon Government Report," Catholic Culture, July 6,
    2017, https://www.catholicculture.org/news/headlines/index.cfm?storyid=32040.

24. Luca Attanasio, "Cameroon, the Death of Bishop Balla Still Surrounded by Mystery," La
    Stampa, August 24, 2017, https://www.lastampa.it/vatican-insider/en/2017/08/24/news
    /cameroon-the-death-of-bishop-balla-still-surrounded-by-mystery-1.34440681.

25. Chimtom, "Cleric Alleges Cameroon Bishop Killed."

26. Pentin, "Cameroonian Bishops Confirm: Bishop Balla Was Murdered."

27. Bidjocka, "Bishop Jean-Marie Benoît Bala."

28. Chimtom, "Cleric Alleges Cameroon Bishop Killed."

29. Attanasio, "Cameroon, the Death of Bishop Balla."

30. Chimtom, "Cleric Alleges Cameroon Bishop Killed."

31. Emeka Umeagbalasi, "Nigeria Is a Killing Field of Defenseless Christians," Genocide Watch,
    August 13, 2020, https://www.genocidewatch.com/single-post/2020/04/13/Nigeria-Is-A
    -Killing-Field-Of-Defenseless-Christians.

32. Umeagbalasi, "Nigeria Is a Killing Field"; Patrick Tyrrell, "The Horrific Killing of Christians in
    Nigeria," The Heritage Foundation, December 2, 2020, https://www.heritage.org/africa
    /commentary/the-horrific-killing-christians-nigeria.

33. *Fourth Population and Housing Census, Rwanda, 2012, Thematic Report: Socio-cultural
    Characteristics of the Population* (National Institute of Statistics of Rwanda, Ministry of Finance
    and Economic Planning, January 2012). See National Institute of Statistics of Rwanda,
    accessed April 3, 2022, http://www.statistics.gov.rw/datasource/42.

34. "World Watch List," Open Doors USA, accessed April 3, 2022, https://www.opendoorsusa
    .org/christian-persecution/world-watch-list/.

35. "Nigeria," Open Doors USA, accessed April 3, 2022, https://www.opendoorsusa.org/christian
    -persecution/world-watch-list/nigeria/.

36. "Trails of Death . . . Cries of Woe in Plateau," Sun News Online, September 16, 2017, https://www.sunnewsonline.com/trails-of-deathcries-of-woe-in-plateau/.

37. Mark Woods, "Nigerian Fulani Attack on Christian Village Leaves 20 Dead—9 of Them Children," *Christian Today*, September 12, 2017, https://www.christiantoday.com/article /nigerian-fulani-attack-on-christian-village-leaves-20-dead-9-of-them-children/113555.htm.

38. Jardine Malado, "Fulani Herdsmen Kill 20 Nigerians in Attack on Christian Village," *Christian Times*, September 13, 2017, https://www.christiantimes.com/article/fulani-herdsmen-kill-20 -nigerians-in-attack-on-christian-village/72844.htm.

39. "Trails of Death . . . Cries of Woe in Plateau," *Sun News Nigeria*, September 16, 2017, https://www.sunnewsonline.com/trails-of-deathcries-of-woe-in-plateau/.

40. PM News, "Fulani Herdsmen Kill 19, Injure 5 in Jos Village Attack," Sahara Reporters, September 9, 2017, http://saharareporters.com/2017/09/09/fulani-herdsmen-kill-19-injure-5 -jos-village-attack.

41. Felix Onuah, Buhari Bello, and Alexis Akwagyiram, "Nigeria's Buhari Urges Calm after Herdsmen Kill 19 in Central Plateau State," Reuters, September 9, 2017, https://www.reuters .com/article/us-nigeria-violence/nigerias-buhari-urges-calm-after-herdsmen-kill-19-in-central -plateau-state-idUSKCN1BK0CN.

42. "Nigeria's Christians Condemn Killings in Plateau, Urge Government to Intervene," World Watch Monitor, October 18, 2017, https://www.worldwatchmonitor.org/2017/10/northern -christians-condemn-killings-plateau-urge-nigeria-government-intervene/.

43. "Nigeria's Christians Condemn Killings."

44. "Christians Killed in Nigerian Attack," BWA News, Baptist World Alliance, October 23, 2017, https://web.archive.org/web/20171023235244/https://www.bwanet.org/news/news -releases/651-christians-killed-in-nigerian-attack.

45. Isaac Shobayo, "How Soldiers Aided Fulani to Massacre My People—Sunday Abdu, President, Irigwe Development Association," *Nigerian Tribune*, October 21, 2017, https://tribuneonlineng .com/soldiers-aided-fulani-massacre-people-sunday-abdu-president-irigwe-development -association/.

46. Yusuf, "A Day to Mourn Ourselves by Lasisi Olagunju," *Osun Defender*, May 28, 2018, http://www.osundefender.com/day-mourn-lasisi-olagunju/.

47. "Four Christians Killed, Head of High School and Family Shot in North-Central Nigeria," *Voice of the Persecuted* (blog), May 13, 2020, https://voiceofthepersecuted.wordpress.com/2020 /05/13/four-christians-killed-head-of-high-school-and-family-shot-in-north-central-nigeria/.

48. Yusuf, "A Day to Mourn Ourselves."

49. "Fulani Herdsmen in Nigeria Kill More Than 60 Christians in Five Weeks, Sources Say," *Voice of the Persecuted* (blog), April 7, 2020, https://voiceofthepersecuted.wordpress.com/2020/04 /07/fulani-herdsmen-in-nigeria-kill-more-than-60-christians-in-five-weeks-sources-say/.

50. "Nigeria: Herdsmen Ambush Christian Couple with Machetes in Plateau State," *Voice of the Persecuted* (blog), May 9, 2020, https://voiceofthepersecuted.wordpress.com/2020/05/09 /nigeria-herdsmen-ambush-christian-couple-with-machetes-in-plateau-state/.

51. Samuel Crowther, letter, September 3, 1841, quoted at Richard J. Mammana, "Samuel Ajayi Crowther," The Living Church, January 3, 2017, https://livingchurch.org/2017/01/03/samuel -ajayi-crowther/.

52. Crowther, letter.

53. John L. Allen Jr., "Faith, Hope and Heroes," *National Catholic Reporter*, February 23, 2001, http://www.natcath.org/NCR_Online/archives2/2001a/022301/022301a.htm.

54. Allen, "Faith, Hope and Heroes"; Namakula E. Mayanja, "The Quest for Peace Leadership: Remembering Archbishop Munzihirwa: Pambazuka News," Pambazuka News, November 2, 2015, https://www.pambazuka.org/human-security/quest-peace-leadership-remembering -archbishop-munzihirwa.

55. Allen, "Faith, Hope and Heroes."

56. Mayanja, "The Quest for Peace Leadership."

57. Richard Boudreaux, "Pope Honors 20th Century Christian Martyrs," *Los Angeles Times*, May 8, 2000, https://www.latimes.com/archives/la-xpm-2000-may-08-mn-27833-story.html.

58. Allen, "Faith, Hope and Heroes."

59. Allen, "Faith, Hope and Heroes."

60. Andrew Lawler, "Church Unearthed in Ethiopia Rewrites the History of Christianity in Africa," *Smithsonian*, December 10, 2019, https://www.smithsonianmag.com/history/church-unearthed-ethiopia-rewrites-history-christianity-africa-180973740/.

61. Lawler, "Church Unearthed in Ethiopia"; see also Acts 8:26-39.

62. Lawler, "Church Unearthed in Ethiopia."

63. "'There Will Be More Martyrs,' a Warning Four Years On from Christian Beheadings on Libya Beach," Premier Christian News, February 15, 2019, https://premierchristian.news/en/news/article/there-will-be-more-martyrs-a-warning-four-years-on-from-christian-beheadings-on-libya-beach.

64. "What Much of the Media Ignored in the Execution of 21 Coptic Christians," Aleteia, February 17, 2017, https://aleteia.org/2017/02/17/what-much-of-the-media-ignored-in-the-execution-of-21-coptic-christians/.

65. Morgan Lee, "Five Years Ago, ISIS Executed 21 Christians on a Libyan Beach," February 19, 2015, *Quick to Listen*, podcast, 47:00, *Christianity Today*, February 19, 2020, https://www.christianitytoday.com/ct/2020/february-web-only/isis-martyrs-coptic-christians-five-year-anniversary.html.

66. "'There Will Be More Martyrs.'"

67. Archbishop Angaelos (@BishopAngaelos), "Video Released by IS Beheading," Twitter, February 15, 2015, 2:56 p.m., https://twitter.com/bishopangaelos/status/567064820378517504.

68. "Five Years Ago, ISIS Executed 21 Christians."

69. "Five Years Ago, ISIS Executed 21 Christians."

70. "'There Will Be More Martyrs.'"

71. "Five Years Ago, ISIS Executed 21 Christians."

72. "Five Years Ago, ISIS Executed 21 Christians."

73. Martin Mosebach, *The 21: A Journey into the Land of Coptic Martyrs*, trans. Alta L. Price (Walden, NY: Plough Publishing, 2019), back cover.

74. Martin Mosebach, quoted at Claudia McDonnell, "Blood of the Martyrs," *Catholic New York*, February 27, 2019, https://www.cny.org/stories/blood-of-the-martyrs,18692.

75. "Five Years Ago, ISIS Executed 21 Christians."

76. Mostafa Salem, "Tears and Joy as Egyptian Christians Killed in Libya Laid to Rest," Reuters, May 15, 2018, https://www.reuters.com/article/us-libya-egypt/tears-and-joy-as-egyptian-christians-killed-in-libya-laid-to-rest-idUSKCN1IG2JU.

77. McDonnell, "Blood of the Martyrs."

78. McDonnell, "Blood of the Martyrs."

79. Ivan Oransky, "Annalena Tonelli," Lancet 362, no. 9399 (2003): 1943, https://www.thelancet.com/journals/lancet/article/PIIS0140-6736(03)14990-2/fulltext.

80. Rachel Pieh Jones, *Stronger Than Death: How Annalena Tonelli Defied Terror and Tuberculosis in the Horn of Africa* (Walden, NY: Plough Publishing, 2019), 17–18.

81. Jones, *Stronger*, 22–23.

82. Jones, *Stronger*, 24.

83. Oransky, "Annalena Tonelli."

84. Oransky, "Annalena Tonelli."

85. Oransky, "Annalena Tonelli."

86. Jones, *Stronger*, 17.

87. Kitty McKinsey and Laura Boldrini, "Mourners Remember Dr. Tonelli, Pledge to Continue Her Work," UNHCR, October 14, 2003, https://www.unhcr.org/en-us/news/latest/2003 /10/3f8c01827/mourners-remember-dr-tonelli-pledge-continue-work.html.

88. "10 Famous Martyrs and Why They Died (Updated 2020)," The Persecuted, July 13, 2020, https://thepersecuted.org/10-famous-martyrs-and-why-they-died/.

89. Tom Krattenmaker, endorsement for *Stronger Than Death*, by Rachel Pieh Jones.

90. Mariam Mohamed, endorsement for *Stronger Than Death*, by Rachel Pieh Jones.

91. John L. Allen Jr., "Bishop Pierre Claverie of Algeria: Patron for the Dialogue of Cultures," *All Things Catholic* (blog), *National Catholic Reporter*, October 26, 2007, https://www.ncronline .org/blogs/all-things-catholic/bishop-pierre-claverie-algeria-patron-dialogue-cultures.

92. Allen, "Bishop Pierre Claverie."

93. Jean-Jacques Pérennès, *A Life Poured Out: Pierre Claverie of Algeria*, trans. Phyllis Jestice and Matthew Sherry (Maryknoll, NY: Orbis Books, 2007).

94. Pierre Claverie, "Humanity in the Plural," *Nouveaux Cahiers du Sud*, January 1996.

95. Jean-Jacques Pérennès, "The Legacy of Pierre Claverie," *International Bulletin of Missionary Research* 31, no. 3 (July 2007).

96. Allen, "Bishop Pierre Claverie."

97. Allen, "Bishop Pierre Claverie."

98. Phillip C. Naylor, "Bishop Pierre Claverie and the Risks of Religious Reconciliation," *Catholic Historical Review*, 96, no. 4 (October 2010): 720–42.

99. Allen, "Bishop Pierre Claverie."

100. Allen, "Bishop Pierre Claverie."

101. Dr. Aylward Shorter, "Claverie, Pierre," Dictionary of African Christian Biography, 2003, https://dacb.org/stories/algeria/claverie-pierre/.

102. Allen, "Bishop Pierre Claverie."

103. Shorter, "Claverie, Pierre"; Allen, "Bishop Pierre Claverie."

104. Pérennès, "Legacy of Pierre Claverie."

105. Allen, "Bishop Pierre Claverie."

106. Naylor, "Bishop Pierre Claverie."

107. Kate Shellnutt and the Associated Press, "Sunday Church Attack Kills 14 in Burkina Faso," *Christianity Today*, December 2, 2019, https://www.christianitytoday.com/news/2019 /december/burkina-faso-church-attack-hantoukoura.html.

108. Agence France-Presse, "Unidentified Gunmen Attack Burkina Faso Church, Killing 14," The Defense Post, December 2, 2019, https://www.thedefensepost.com/2019/12/02/burkina-faso -hantoukoura-church-attack/.

109. Shellnutt and AP, "Sunday Church Attack."

110. Shellnutt and AP, "Sunday Church Attack."

111. Shellnutt and AP, "Sunday Church Attack."

112. Shellnutt and AP, "Sunday Church Attack."

113. Shellnutt and AP, "Sunday Church Attack."

114. Shellnutt and AP, "Sunday Church Attack."

115. Rose Achiego, "'I Choose to Love': Italian Sister Killed in Somalia on Final Stop before Sainthood," Global Sisters Report, May 21, 2018, https://www.globalsistersreport.org/news /ministry/i-choose-love-italian-sister-killed-somalia-final-stop-sainthood-53846.

116. "Sr. Leonella Sgorbati," Consolata Missionary Sisters, accessed April 5, 2022, http://consolatasisters.org/sr-leonella-sgorbati/.

117. Achiego, "'I Choose to Love.'"

118. Achiego, "'I Choose to Love.'"

119. Inés San Martin, "Nun Killed in Backlash over Regensburg Declared a Martyr," Crux, November 9, 2017, https://cruxnow.com/vatican/2017/11/09/nun-killed-backlash-regensburg -declared-martyr.

120. Roman Catholic Mission Somalia (RCMS), "Padre Pietro Turati: Franciscan Martyr in Somalia," *Roman Catholic Mission Somalia* (blog), February 6, 2016, http://rcmsomalia .blogspot.com/2016/02/padre-pietro-turati-franciscan-martyr.html.

121. RCMS, "Padre Pietro Turati."

122. RCMS, "Padre Pietro Turati."

123. RCMS, "Padre Pietro Turati"; "The Franciscan Martyr Father Pietro Turati," Vocazioni.net—Il portale della pastorale vocazionale, accessed September 6, 2020, http://www.vocazioni.net /index.php?option=com_content.

124. "Franciscan Martyr Father Pietro Turati," Vocazioni.net.

125. African Rights, "Facing Genocide: The Nuba of Sudan," OCHA, ReliefWeb, July 7, 1997, https://reliefweb.int/report/sudan/facing-genocide-nuba-sudan.

126. "A Death in the Family," Persecution Project, January 6, 2015, https://www.persecutionproject .org/news/general/a-death-in-the-family.

127. Enough Team, "Video: George Clooney behind Front Lines in Sudan's Nuba Mountains," The Enough Project, March 14, 2012, https://enoughproject.org/blog/video-george-clooney-behind -front-lines-sudan-nuba-mountains.

128. Samuel Totten, "The World's Unexplained Silence over Human Tragedy in the Nuba Mountains of Sudan," The Conversation, May 20, 2015, https://theconversation.com/the -worlds-unexplained-silence-over-human-tragedy-in-the-nuba-mountains-of-sudan-41987.

129. "Episode 4, Segment 3: Clooney Gets Bombed," *ASPIREist*, April 25, 2016, video, 5:54, https://www.youtube.com/watch?v=am0fp8VJtU0.

130. VOM USA, "Christian Singer Tragically Killed in the Nuba Mountains," Voice of the Martyrs Canada, February 26, 2015, https://www.vomcanada.com/su-2015-02-26.htm.

131. "A Death in the Family."

132. Rebecca Hamilton, "Inside Colin Powell's Decision to Declare Genocide in Darfur," *Atlantic*, August 17, 2011, https://www.theatlantic.com/international/archive/2011/08/inside-colin -powells-decision-to-declare-genocide-in-darfur/243560/.

133. ICC Investigation, Situation in Darfur, Sudan, ICC-02/05 (International Criminal Court, 2005), https://www.icc-cpi.int/darfur.

134. "Darfur Genocide," World Without Genocide, updated January 2021, http://worldwithoutgenocide.org/genocides-and-conflicts/darfur-genocide.

135. Eric Reeves, "Children within Darfur's Holocaust," *Sudan Tribune*, December 23, 2005, https://sudantribune.com/article13771/.

136. Lauren Lewis, "10 Facts about the Darfur Genocide," The Borgen Project, January 21, 2016, https://borgenproject.org/darfur-genocide/.

137. Eric Reeves, "Don't Forget Darfur," editorial, *New York Times*, February 11, 2016, https://www .nytimes.com/2016/02/12/opinion/dont-forget-darfur.html; *Sudan Humanitarian Bulletin*, United Nations Office for the Coordination of Humanitarian Affairs, no. 4 (January 18–24, 2016), ReliefWeb, https://reliefweb.int/sites/reliefweb.int/files/resources/OCHA_Sudan _Weekly_Humanitarian_Bulletin_Issue_04_%2818_-_24_January_2016%29.pdf.

138. Mark Tran, "Mapping the Darfur Conflict," *News blog*, *Guardian*, April 11, 2007, https://www .theguardian.com/news/blog/2007/apr/11/darfur1.

139. "Sudan and Darfur," Crisis Briefing, Jewish World Watch, accessed April 5, 2022, https://www .jww.org/sudan-and-darfur/.

140. "UN Officials Urge Support as Darfur Attempts to 'Turn the Page' from Conflict to Peace," UN News, United Nations, September 28, 2018, https://news.un.org/en/story/2018/09 /1021472.

141. "The 50 Countries Where It's Most Dangerous to Follow Jesus in 2021," *Christianity Today*, January 13, 2021, https://www.christianitytoday.com/news/2021/january/christian -persecution-2021-countries-open-doors-watch-list.html.

142. "50 Countries."

143. Sam Olukoya, "Islamic Extremists Kill Nigerian Pastor, Attack His Hometown," Federal News Network, February 28, 2020, https://federalnewsnetwork.com/world-news/2020/02/islamic-extremists-kill-nigerian-pastor-attack-his-hometown/.

144. "Nigerian Brethren District Leader and Ecumenical Leader Lawan Andimi Has Been Executed by Boko Haram," News, Church of the Brethren, January 21, 2020, https://www.brethren.org/news/2020/nigerian-brethren-district-leader-and-ecumenical-leader-lawan-andimi-has-been-executed-by-boko-haram/.

145. Jayson Casper, "Boko Haram Executes Pastor Who Turned Hostage Video into Testimony," Christianity Today, January 21, 2020, https://www.christianitytoday.com/news/2020/january/nigeria-boko-haram-kidnapped-pastor-hostage-video-testimony.html.

146. Casper, "Boko Haram."

147. Casper, "Boko Haram."

148. "ISWAP Child Terrorist Executes Christian Student," CSW, January 23, 2020, https://www.csw.org.uk/2020/01/23/press/4533/article.htm.

149. Ahmad Salkida (@A_Salkida), "To break some news can traumatize. I'm battling with one of such. Reverend Andimi, abducted by #BokoHaram was executed yesterday," Twitter, January 21, 2020, 2:02 a.m., https://twitter.com/A_Salkida/status/1219530749587677184.

150. Casper, "Boko Haram."

151. Casper, "Boko Haram."

152. Casper, "Boko Haram."

153. "Nigerian Brethren District Leader."

154. Muhammadu Buhari (@MBuhari), "The terrorist killing of Lawan Andimi, chairman of the Christian Association of Nigeria (CAN) in Michika, Adamawa State is cruel," Twitter, January 21, 2020, 2:17 p.m., https://twitter.com/mbuhari/status/1219715653038485504.

155. Muhammadu Buhari (@MBuhari), "I am greatly saddened," Twitter, January 21, 2020, 2:21 p.m., https://twitter.com/MBuhari/status/1219716567463796736.

156. Casper, "Boko Haram."

157. Casper, "Boko Haram."

158. "Egypt's Mohammed Morsi: A Turbulent Presidency Cut Short," BBC News, June 17, 2019, https://www.bbc.com/news/world-middle-east-18371427.

159. Raymond Ibrahim, "Muslim Brotherhood Slaughter Christian Woman," Christian Post, March 31, 2014, https://www.christianpost.com/news/muslim-brotherhood-slaughter-christian-woman.html.

160. Patrick Goodenough, "Egyptian Islamists Murder Young Christian, after Dragging Her from Car," CNSNews, April 1, 2014, https://www.cnsnews.com/news/article/patrick-goodenough/egyptian-islamists-murder-young-christian-after-dragging-her-car.

161. Goodenough, "Egyptian Islamists."

162. Todd Daniels, "Killed Because of the Cross: The Death of an Egyptian Christian," April 4, 2014, International Christian Concern, https://www.persecution.org/2014/04/04/killed-because-of-the-cross-the-death-of-an-egyptian-christian/.

163. Art Jahnke, "Machozi's Calling," Bostonia, Fall 2016, Boston University, https://www.bu.edu/bostonia/fall16/vincent-machozi-congo-machozis-calling/.

164. Paul Nantulya, "A Medley of Armed Groups Play on Congo's Crisis," OCHA, ReliefWeb, September 25, 2017, https://reliefweb.int/report/democratic-republic-congo/medley-armed-groups-play-congo-s-crisis.

165. "IRC Study Shows Congo's Neglected Crisis Leaves 5.4 Million Dead," OCHA, ReliefWeb, January 22, 2008, https://reliefweb.int/report/democratic-republic-congo/irc-study-shows-congos-neglected-crisis-leaves-54-million-dead.

166. "Tourisme," Beni Lubero Online, March 7, 2014, https://benilubero.com/category/culture/tourisme/.

167. Jahnke, "Machozi's Calling."
168. Jahnke, "Machozi's Calling."
169. Jahnke, "Machozi's Calling."
170. "Fr. Vincent F. Machozi, A.A. (1965–2016)," The Assumptionists, Augustinians of the Assumption-US, accessed April 6, 2022, https://www.assumption.us/about-us/portraits/224-fr-vincent-f-machozi-aa-1965-2016.
171. "Acquittals in the Death of Fr. Machozi Dismay Local Residents," Vatican News, September 12, 2018, https://www.vaticannews.va/en/africa/news/2018-09/acquittals-in-the-death-of-fr-machozi-dismay-local-residents.html.
172. John Foxe, *Foxe's Book of Martyrs*, ed. John Cumming (London: George Virtue, 1851), 890.

About the Authors

JOHNNIE MOORE is a popular speaker and acclaimed human rights and religious freedom activist known for his consequential work at the intersection of faith and foreign policy, especially in the Middle East. He is president of JDA Worldwide and president of the Congress of Christian Leaders. Rev. Moore's many awards and honors include the Simon Wiesenthal Center's prestigious Medal of Valor. He was twice appointed to the US Commission on International Religious Freedom, and in 2020 was named one of America's ten most influential religious leaders.

JERRY PATTENGALE is inaugural University Professor at Indiana Wesleyan University and holds distinguished posts at Sagamore Institute, Gordon-Conwell Theological Seminary, Waverley Abbey College (UK), Excelsia College (AU), and Tyndale House–Cambridge (UK). He was a founding scholar of the Museum of the Bible (Washington, DC).